Putin

The second edition of this extremely well-received political biography of Vladimir Putin builds on the strengths of the previous edition to provide the most detailed and nuanced account of the man, his politics and his profound influence on Russian politics, foreign policy and society.

New to this edition:

- Analysis of Putin's second term as President.
- More biographical information in the light of recent research.
- Detailed discussion of changes to the policy process and the elites around Putin.
- Developments in state–society relations including the conflicts with oligarchs such as Khodorkovsky.
- Review of changes affecting the party system and electoral legislation, including the development of federalism in Russia.
- Details on economic performance under Putin, including more discussion of the energy sector and pipeline politics.
- Russia's relationship with Nato after the 'big-bang' enlargement, EU–Russian relations after enlargement and Russia's relations with other post-Soviet states.
- The conclusion brings us up to date with debates over the question of democracy in Russia today, and the nature of Putin's leadership and his place in the world.

Putin: Russia's choice is essential reading for all scholars and students of Russian politics.

Richard Sakwa is Professor of Politics at the University of Kent, UK.

Putin

Russia's choice
Second edition

Richard Sakwa

Routledge
Taylor & Francis Group

LONDON AND NEW YORK

First edition published 2004
Second edition, 2008
by Routledge
2 Park Square, Milton Park, Abingdon, Oxon OX14 4RN

Simultaneously published in the USA and Canada
by Routledge
270 Madison Avenue, New York, NY 10016

Routledge is an imprint of the Taylor & Francis Group, an informa business

Typeset in Times by
Taylor & Francis Books
Printed and bound in Great Britain by
Antony Rowe Ltd, Chippenham, Wiltshire

British Library Cataloguing in Publication Data
A catalogue record for this book is available from the British Library

Library of Congress Cataloging in Publication Data
Sakwa, Richard.
   Putin: Russia's choice / Richard Sakwa. – 2nd ed.
     p. cm.
   Includes bibliographical references and index.
   1. Russia (Federation) – Politics and government – 1991 – 2. Putin,
   Vladimir Vladimirovich, 1952–I. Title.
   DK510.763.S247 2007
947.086092–dc22 [B]   2007008402

ISBN 978-0-415-40765-6 (hbk)
ISBN 978-0-415-40766-3 (pbk)
ISBN 978-0-203-93193-6 (ebk)

Contents

List of tables   vii
Preface to the second edition   viii
Acknowledgements   xii

1   The path to power   1
    The unlikely making of a leader 2
    Operation successor 17

2   Ideas and choices   37
    Who is Mister Putin? 37
    Normality, normalcy and normalisation 42
    Russia at the turn of the millennium 52
    Planning for the future 56
    The 'state of the nation' speeches 59

3   Putin's path   70
    Building the Putin bloc 71
    Putin and the people 83
    Leadership and style 90
    National democracy and Russia's 'third way' 95

4   Parties, elections and the succession   101
    Development of the party system 101
    Elections and electoral legislation 109
    Parliamentary realignment 123
    Putin, parties and government 127
    The Putin succession 129

5   Regime, state and society   135
    State and regime 136
    The 'liquidation of the oligarchs as a class' 143
    Freedom of speech and the media 150
    Judicial reform and human rights 155

6   Bureaucracy, incorporation and opposition   162
    Bureaucracy and corruption 162
    Civil society and para-constitutional representation 167
    Regime and opposition 175

7   Putin's 'new federalism'   186
    Segmented regionalism 186
    Features of the 'new federalism' 192
    State reconstitution and federalism 209

8   Reforging the nation   214
    National images and state symbols 214
    Social aspects of national identity 223
    Chechnya: tombstone or crucible of Russian power? 227

9   Russian capitalism   240
    Entering the market 240
    Models of capitalism – state corporatism? 249
    State, economy and society 259

10 Putin's new realism in foreign policy   267
    Towards a new realism 268
    Features of the new realism 274
    The new realism in practice 279

11 Conclusion: the power of contradiction   299
    Public politics 300
    Beyond transition 306
    The power of contradiction 310

    Appendix: Russia at the turn of the millennium   317
    Notes   329
    Select bibliography   370
    Index   376

Tables

1.1	State Duma election 19 December 1999	25
1.2	Presidential election 26 March 2000	32
4.1	State Duma election 7 December 2003	111
4.2	Presidential election 14 March 2004	116
9.1	Economic indicators 1996–2006	244
9.2	Russia's 'oligarchs'	252

Preface to the second edition

The coming to power of Vladimir Putin at the beginning of the new millennium signalled the onset of yet another period of rapid change. This was not the first time that a new century marked a turning point in Russian development. In 1703 Peter the Great began building St Petersburg and thus signalled the aspiration to modernise the country 'from above' along Western lines. His attempt, as Lenin put it, 'to chase out barbarism by barbaric means' by establishing the city on the Neva, established a pattern of accelerated modernisation that has been repeated periodically ever since. While modernisation from above provides a mechanism to kick-start development, it tends to foster bureaucratic authoritarianism and inhibit the growth of inclusive government and popular accountability. Putin is a native son of Peter's city, and Russia's first emperor is in many ways a model to him. As under Peter, a distinctive pattern of modernisation without modernity has once again emerged. A type of superficial Westernisation in form is created without the critical spirit, pluralism and political diversity that distinguishes Western modernity at its best.

In the early nineteenth century Alexander I brought Russia to the front ranks of the European powers, defeating Napoleon's Grand Army in 1812 and then, following the Congress of Vienna in 1815, made it part of the Holy Alliance of conservative powers. Various plans for constitutional reform, and debates over how best to Europeanise the country, ended in the defeat of the Decembrist uprising in 1825. The choice thereafter, with exceptions, was to try to modernise within the framework of autocratic government, a combination that collapsed early in the twentieth century. Russia at that time struggled to define its developmental path, torn between various populist, Slavophile and nationalist ideas on the one hand, and Western theories of modernisation on the other. Conservative, liberal and radical movements vied for dominance, with the most radical tendency of all, the Bolsheviks, in the end gaining ascendancy. Vladimir Lenin's choice in October 1917 was in favour of a non-market and anti-liberal socialist path of modernisation that later, under Joseph Stalin, represented a peculiar mix of Western technical modernisation, again 'from above', while rejecting the Western spirit of modernity.

In 1985 Mikhail Gorbachev, the last general secretary of the Communist Party of the Soviet Union (CPSU), tried to reform the Soviet system. His programme of *perestroika* (restructuring) sought to overcome the gap between form and content, but in the event precipitated the collapse of the Soviet system in its entirety, accompanied by the disintegration of the state in 1991. The imperial project was over, in both its Russian and Soviet guises, and a smaller Russian Federation emerged to find its way in the world. President Boris Yeltsin's reforms in the 1990s once again sought to turn Russia on to a new path by forceful means. A brief constitutional inter-regnum ended in 1993 with the forcible dissolution of the old parliament and the adoption of a new constitution in December of that year, the one that still operates today. Yeltsin's leadership was imbued with a certain spirit of 'Bolshevism of the market' when the dash for capitalist democracy was accompanied by the emergence of powerful oligarchic business groups and mass poverty. The country experienced the greatest economic collapse in peacetime of any country in history, with the national economy nearly halving in less than a decade. State capacity was diminished, governance chaotic, and criminality and corruption rampant. The 1990s have now gained almost mythical status in contemporary Russia as a period of disaster and collapse, even though the rudiments of a market economy were established and the foundations of a democratic polity created.

It was this legacy of hybrid modernisation with which Putin was forced to come to terms. Putin considered the communist attempt to modernise the country by revolutionary means as doomed to failure, although he accepted that the Soviet regime between 1917 and 1991 had brought the country some benefits. His view of Yeltsin's reforms appeared to be the opposite; as probably fated to succeed, but at a heavy price. Putin's government sought to come to terms with the various developmental choices made in the past. He was faced with a number of stark choices, while at the same time aware that each carried penalties. The choice now was not so much over the direction in which the country should move, since a broad consensus had finally emerged that Russia should become a capitalist democracy inte-grated with the West. There was less agreement, however, over the methods to be adopted in pursuit of these goals. Russia sought to find a new path that would break the vicious circles of past developmental choices. Russia's elites were now faced with finding a way for Russia to achieve mainstream modernity while maintaining its distinctive identity.

Yeltsin resigned on 31 December 1999, and the challenge facing Putin as he took up office as acting president was to overcome not only the legacy of the decade of rapid liberalisation that had followed the fall of communism, but to find a way of combining Russia's distinctive character with what appeared to have become universal norms of democracy and international integration. The dilemma facing Russia was the classic one facing late developers everywhere: is there only one main highway of development – what we can call the *evolutionary* view (predominant in Anglo-Saxon theories

of modernisation and comparative democratisation); or is the world populated by unique and relatively incommensurate civilisations, with their own
genetic patterns and distinctive societies – which we can term the *morphological* view (favoured not only by leaders resistant to Westernisation, but
also by some sub-national cultural communities)?

Nowhere has the tension between evolutionary and morphological approaches been sharper than in Russia. Today this takes the form not only in the
replay of old debates, such as the nineteenth-century Westerniser/Slavophile
controversy, but in endless permutations of purported contradictory civilisational choices: Atlanticism versus Eurasianism; liberalism versus neo-Sovietism;
and pluralistic, individualistic and autonomous civil society versus a state-
centred, corporatist if not collectivist social ethos. Putin's Russia was also faced
with practical choices: how could freedom be reconciled with the need to re-
establish effective governance; and how could the poor and outcast be protected as the economy shifted towards the market and international economic
integration? How could powerful executive authority, once again advancing
an agenda of modernisation from above, be reconciled with the development
of democracy, pluralism, federalism and civil society from below?

The country was far from being a blank slate on which Putin could write
at will, but at the same time his choices had the potential to determine the
pattern for decades to come. It is these choices and the dilemmas that lay
behind them that we shall explore in this book. We shall do so within five
interwoven strands of analysis. The first focuses on Putin's personal and
intellectual development, including a brief discussion of his childhood and
career. Putin's world view derived from an unusual biography and a distinctive ideology. Second, we examine Putin as leader, including the shifts in
elite structures that accompanied his presidency, and the question of continuity and change from the Yeltsin era. The interplay between individual
choices and structural constraints shapes and constrains all leaders. Putin's
leadership was characterised by the attempt to establish a power base while
maintaining a quasi-mystical relationship with the public. Third, the book
examines developments in institutional structures, including changes in party
laws, electoral politics, regional and federal relationships, and relations between
state and society. Fourth, we shall examine various policy arenas, notably
economic and foreign policy, as well as problems in the development of
national identity. Finally, the book ponders the nature of Russian politics
under Putin, and attempts a broader theorisation.

Putin inherited from Yeltsin a country that had had been an independent
and sovereign state for less than a decade and which had undergone the
trauma of rapid market development. He was also heir to a society that had
been ruled by a one-party communist system for over seven decades, and
which for most of that time had been locked in conflict with the capitalist
world. He was also the legatee of a political culture in which political authority
tended to be concentrated, state administration inordinately bureaucratised
and the development of a pluralistic civil society inhibited. The book examines

the thinking and dilemmas behind Putin's choices, and looks at how they worked in practice as he sought to reshape the Russian political system and national identity. In every area there were fundamental choices to be made and, as with leadership in general, the constraints were real but the decisional factor had the potential to achieve transformation.

The book is published at a time when the siren warnings of the development of a new Cold War sound ever more insistently. Putin's Russia stands accused of democratic backsliding and the reversal of the achievements of *perestroika*. Buoyed by the energy windfall, Russia is charged with asserting itself on the international stage and threatening regional and global energy security. To my mind this new Cold War would be a most peculiar and unnecessary one. As the reader of this book will soon see, there are undoubtedly elements of a *failed democratisation* process in Putin's Russia, and the details of this will shortly be examined; but at the same time there is much evidence to support the view that there remains much potential for *democratic evolutionism*. The story of democracy in Russia is far from over. Putin may not go down in history as the world's greatest democrat, but neither is he its murderer. His leadership witnessed sustained economic growth and pluralistic social development, while his political system, flawed though it may have been, retained the potential for renewed democratic advance.

Putin's leadership responded to the challenges that it perceived, and while the answers that it provided may not always be the ones that we like, at least they were rational responses to genuine problems, and made sense to the generation that had to live through yet another Russian transformation. In broad terms, we can now see that these were at best interim solutions, and Putin's leadership was yet another transitional one, in the sense that the model of governance that he devised was unsustainable in the long term. There were no easy answers to fundamental questions concerning method and policy, and as a result Putin's choices were characterised by a combination of strategic purpose and tactical flexibility. The legacy of the past certainly acted as one of the most important constraints on his administration, but at the same time powerful ideas for innovation and change were present. A balanced analysis of the various contradictions, ambiguities and dilemmas of Putin's leadership is possible, although when writing this book it sometimes felt as if any attempt at dispassionate analysis condemned one to the forlorn status of 'fellow traveller'. If by the end the assiduous reader will have gained a clearer idea of the nature of the choices facing Russia, an understanding of some of the achievements and failures of Putin's leadership, and a sense of the factors that determined his choices, then this book will have achieved its purpose. Putin's presidency represents an important chapter in the book of Russian democracy, but the work is still far from complete.

Richard Sakwa
Canterbury, Kent, UK
January 2007

Acknowledgements

The debts incurred in rewriting this book have become even more numerous than when I prepared the first edition in the first years of the new millennium. Many scholars have shared their time and expertise with me. I am especially grateful to Mikhail Afanas'ev, Vladimir Amelin, Yitzhak Brudny, Philip Boobbyer, Artour Demtchouk, Alexander Doroshchenko, Gilles Favarel-Garrigue, Vladimir Gel'man, Elena Hore, Yurii Igritskii, Mikhail Il'in, David Johnson, Svyatoslav Kaspe, Vladimir Kolosov, Anatolii Kulik, Bobo Lo, Alexander Markarov, Sergei Markov, Andrei Medushevskii, Lena Meleshkina, Andrei Melville, Valentin Mikhailov, Alexei Mukhin, Oleg Mramornov, Georges Nivat, James Nixey, Oksana Oracheva, Vladimir Pastukhov, Nikolai Petrov, Yurii Pivovarov, Thomas Remington, Neil Robinson, Cameron Ross, Viktor Rudenko, Andrei Ryabov, Jutta Scherrer, Elena Shestopal, Louis Skyner, Valeri Solovei, Elizabeth Teague, Vera Tolz-Zilitinkevich and Stephen White. I am most grateful to Philip Hanson for his invaluable advice and help with Chapter 9 'Russian capitalism'. The encouragement of Academician Alexander Chubaryan in Moscow has helped lift my spirits at crucial moments. Collaboration with the Institute of Law and Public Policy in Moscow, under the directorship of Olga Sidorovich, has been particularly fruitful, and I thank all there who have helped in the development of this work. The workshops of the Eurasian Political Studies Network, directed by Vitaly Merkushev and generously supported by HESP-OSI, Budapest, have provided a stimulating forum for discussion and learning with young scholars from post-Soviet Eurasia and Western Europe. The faults, of course, remain my own. Craig Fowlie and Natalja Mortensen at Routledge have remained supportive and helpful throughout. I am most grateful for the secretarial and other assistance of Alison Chapman, Ann Hadaway, Jean Hudson and Nicola Huxtable in the Department of Politics and International Relations at the University of Kent. It is my great pleasure to thank the Nuffield Foundation (Grant no. SGS/00730/G) for their assistance in the preparation of the first edition of this work; and the support of INTAS grant No. 04-79-7284 'Eurasian Political Studies Network: developing comparative studies of regime transformations in multicultural societies and the state and nation building process in the post-soviet region' in the preparation of this second edition.

1   The path to power

The state whose prospective rulers come to their duties with least enthusiasm is bound to have the best and most tranquil government, and the state whose rulers are eager to rule the worst.

Plato[1]

Putin's rise to power reflected one of the most unusual political biographies in recent years. Brought up in a communal apartment in Leningrad (from 1991 once again St Petersburg) and an enthusiastic participant in the rough and tumble of childhood play in the city's streets, only slowly did his leadership qualities emerge. Attracted to work in the Soviet Union's secret service, then known as the Committee for State Security (KGB), he went on to win a place to study law at Leningrad State University (1970–5), followed by a career in the KGB (1975–90), the last five years of which he served in the German Democratic Republic (GDR), the communist half of Germany until the fall of the Berlin wall in 1989. Entering public service the following year, he became a staffer of the former law professor, Anatoly Sobchak. Putin rose swiftly to become Sobchak's right arm when he became mayor of the city (1991–6). Sobchak's failure to win a second term in 1996 left Putin unemployed until he was offered a job in the Kremlin. Once in Moscow Putin's rise was meteoric: from an official in the presidential administration, up through minister of the service in which he had once worked, now renamed the Federal Security Service (FSB), and then as prime minister from 9 August 1999. On 31 December 1999, by some reckonings the last day of the century and of the millennium, president Boris Yeltsin unexpectedly resigned and Putin took over as acting president until elections on 26 March 2000 confirmed him as president for a four-year term. In March 2004 Putin was elected to a second term. How did Putin manage to achieve such an astonishing rise to become president of the world's largest country? In this chapter we shall examine his background and the decisive moments that led to the presidency, and in the next we shall discuss the situation that he faced and the ideas that shaped his politics. By the end of these two chapters we shall be able to answer the question that greeted his emergence as the leader of Russia: 'who is Mister Putin'?

The unlikely making of a leader

Vladimir Putin was a late child, born into a family of workers on 7 October 1952 in the centre of Leningrad, two tram stops from the central avenue, Nevsky Prospect, and not far from the Griboedov canal.[2] By the time he became president he had spent half his life living in a communal apartment, where several families shared basic facilities. In Putin's case, the house at No. 12 Baskov Lane had been built in 1859 as high-quality rented apartments. After the revolution each apartment was occupied by several families. The Putins moved there in 1944, into space at the disposition of the factory where his father worked.[3] By the time he was born Putin's parents were already in their forties, and as a late and only surviving child he was considered a 'gift for all their earlier sufferings and deprivations'.[4]

Putin's roots

Putin's paternal grandfather, Spiridon Ivanovich Putin, had been a cook employed for a time at Lenin's country house (Gorki), and following his death in January 1924 worked for Lenin's wife, Nadezhda Krupskaya. Later on several occasions he cooked for Stalin when the latter visited one of his Moscow region dachas (country houses). Spiridon later worked at the country house of the Moscow City Committee of the CPSU in Ilinsky, where the young Vladimir visited him. He died in 1965 aged 86.[5] Putin's father, Vladimir Spiridonovich, was born on 23 February 1911 and spent his childhood in the village of Pominovo in Tver *guberniya* (region), while his mother, Maria Ivanovna, was born in the same year (17 October) and lived in the neighbouring village of Zareche, both in the Turginovsky district about 60 kilometres from the regional capital of Tver. Although coming from different villages, the two met in adolescence and thereafter proved inseparable and were married at the age of 17 in 1928.[6] Their first son Oleg died before reaching his first birthday. Displaced by collectivisation, in 1932 the couple moved to Leningrad. Putin's mother worked in a factory while his father was drafted to serve in the submarine fleet. Just before the onset of the Great Fatherland War the Putins received an apartment in the Stary Peterhof district of Leningrad, where their second son, Viktor, was born. He died of diphtheria in the first year of the blockade (1942) and was buried in a communal grave. Maria's mother was killed by a stray bullet fired by the German occupiers of Tver region on 13 October 1941, her father died in 1947, while her older brothers disappeared without trace at the front.

Just before Leningrad was surrounded by the Germans in early 1942 Maria had the chance to leave, but she decided to stay since her husband was one of the city's defenders. He was assigned at first to a demolition battalion of the NKVD (interior ministry), and then fought in the so-called Neva pocket (*Nevskii pyatochok*), a redoubt on the left bank not far from Lake Ladoga that the Germans were never able to capture despite repeated assaults, a type of mini-Stalingrad. In the winter of 1942 Vladimir Spir-idonovich was severely wounded by a grenade in this area, and his wife nursed him back to health although he walked with a limp to the end of his life. On recovering he was employed by the Yegorov engineering plant, at the time making shells. As the blockade stretched towards the notorious nine hundred days, Maria Ivanovna was so debilitated that she could barely move and only her husband's soldier's rations saved her life. By the time the blockade ended in 1944 only 560,000 of the city's three million inhabitants remained: over 1.5 million had died of hunger and illness, 200,000 from bombs and shells, and 560,000 had been evacuated. Among the few who survived the whole siege were Vladimir and Maria.

By the time Vladimir Vladimirovich was born in 1952 his parents had endured much. His birth symbolised the end of the sufferings of the past and the privations of the war. They were a close-knit although strict family, and their mutual devotion is commented on by all biographers. His father worked as a toolmaker in the Yegorov plant, now making railway carriages and, from 1968, metro wagons. He was a model communist, genuinely believing in its ideals while trying to put them into practice in his own life.[7] In 1947 he became the secretary of the Party cell in his workshop, and in 1948 at the age of 37 took up evening classes and later joined the factory's Party committee. By contrast, Maria was a devoted believer, and although there were no icons in the flat she regularly slipped off to church, which in those days of official atheism and persecution suggested a person with deep-felt beliefs. She ensured that the baby Vladimir was christened into the Orthodox faith, although this was done in secret,[8] and she regularly took him to services.[9] His father knew of his wife's churchgoing but turned a blind eye, although a devoted communist.[10] Maternity leave was only two months, and to allow extra time to spend with her son Putin's mother worked in a succession of low-skill jobs: a concierge, a receptionist at a baker's and finally a lab assistant. In preschool years Putin and his mother spent most of the summer in their home village. Later Putin recounts that on the eve of an official visit to Israel his mother gave him his baptismal cross to have it blessed: 'I did as she said and then put the cross around my neck. I have never taken it off since'.[11]

Childhood and youth

On 1 September 1960 Putin started at School No. 193 on Baskov Lane, just opposite his house. Before the revolution the school had been a women's *gymnasium*, where Krupskaya had once studied. His form teacher was Tamara Chizhova, whose devotion to the class has been much commented upon.[12] The memoirs of his later teacher of German, Vera Gurevich, reveal that the young Putin was an energetic and strong-willed boy. Putin started learning German in after-school classes in April 1964, and according to Gurevich he had an aptitude for foreign languages. When she started teaching form 5A in September 1964 Putin was one of only a handful in the class of over 45 pupils who was not yet a member of the Pioneers (the Communist pupils' organisation), largely because of his rowdy behaviour. Gurevich, who became a family friend, recalls that out of school hours Putin would disappear for hours to play in the courtyard, called by Blotsky his 'window on the world',[13] mostly with older boys.[14] Courtyard life played an important part in shaping Putin's character. Putin was never particularly interested in music and soon gave up classes.

In the academic year from September 1965, sixth grade, his schoolwork markedly improved, with Putin taking a particular interest in history and literature. In this year he started taking sport seriously, first sambo and then judo. After an unsuccessful experiment with boxing, when his nose was broken, Putin joined the 'Trud' sports club in the autumn of 1965. There he met his trainer, Anatoly Rakhlin, who was profoundly to influence Putin's development. As Putin noted, 'Judo is not just a sport, you know. It's a philosophy. It's respect for your elders and for your opponent. It's not for weaklings'.[15] In 1973 Putin became a master at sambo, and in 1975 in judo, becoming in 1976 the city champion.[16] Putin travelled throughout the country as part of his team. Sport for Putin was a way out: 'If I hadn't taken up sport, who knows what would have happened. It was sport that took me off the street'.[17] One of his classmates recalls him as 'Soft and modest, even shy, but with a character of steel'.[18]

In sixth grade, too, Putin entered the Pioneers, and indeed came to head the class group as his peers soon looked to him for guidance.[19] Putin's rapid assumption of leadership of his Pioneer group, it may be noted, was an early indication of the speed with which his career would advance in the post-Soviet era. In those days one could not join the Komsomol (the Communist Youth League) without having been a Pioneer; and without membership the door would be closed to most good higher educational institutions and professions. At the beginning of eighth grade Putin entered the Komsomol organisation in a ceremony at the district Party committee. These were highly ideological organisations, but by this time political commitment was typically worn lightly and had largely become a matter of form. In the summer of 1968, after eighth grade, pupils were faced with a choice of where to continue their studies for the final two years before entering university. Putin, rather surprisingly, chose to enter a chemistry secondary school (No. 281). Blotsky notes that Putin took the decision on his own: 'It was already a feature of his character: Volodya would announce a decision, but would never explain the reasons for his choice'.[20] He continued with his German studies here. His class teacher, Mina Moiseevna Yuditskaya, who later emigrated to Israel, notes that although a passable scientist Putin was much more inclined to the humanities and in particular Russian history.[21] Having completed ninth and tenth grade, Putin left secondary school in 1970.

The Putin family shared their fifth-floor flat with two families, including an elderly Jewish couple and their grown-up daughter. The sink and gas cooker were in the corridor, without hot water or a bathroom, and of course there was no lift. Putin was long to remember the stairwell with a metal banister, where the boys hunted rats. At the end of seventh grade in 1967 the old couple in the communal flat finally received an apartment of their own and their room was turned into a kitchen, which became the scene of endless gatherings of Putin's friends.[22] Putin's parents bought a small country house in Kingisepp district of Leniningrad *oblast*, the spot where Putin's father had fought in the early part of the war, so as to be able to take the young Vladimir out of the city in the summers. This proved too far from the city so in 1969 it was sold and a closer dacha in Tosno was bought. At this house Putin would gather with his friends to play the guitar, sing songs and listen to recordings of Bulat Okudzhava, Vladimir Vysotsky and other popular chansonniers of the time, while in winter it was used as a base for skiing.[23] All would toil round the house, with Putin particularly enjoying chopping wood and fetching water in a churn fixed on a sledge. Later a banya (wooden bathhouse) was built and all enjoyed taking a steam bath. The young Putin was infamous for concocting cock-and-bull stories while remaining poker faced and laughing up his sleeve.[24] It was these realities of daily life of the late Soviet period that stamped Putin's character. As Putin put it in his book of interviews, 'I was a pure and utterly successful product of Soviet patriotic education'.[25]

The Brezhnev era (1964–82) was characterised by gradual improvements in standards of living, although by the late 1970s there were growing shortages and ever-lengthening queues, a period later described by Gorbachev as the 'period of stagnation'. The Brezhnev years represented a period of 'normality' the like of which the Soviet system had never known, with relative harmony at home while achieving superpower parity in 1975, although degenerating into the 'second Cold War' from 1979. Conditions for Putin's parents improved in 1977 when they left the communal flat in Baskov Lane and moved into a two-room apartment on Stachek Prospect. The smaller room was taken by Vladimir, and thus at the age of 25 for the first time he gained a small corner that could be called his own. By then he had been working with the KGB for two years, but there was no question of him getting a flat of his own. As Blotsky notes, 'In all of his years of service in intelligence, Vladimir Putin did not receive a single square metre of his own accommodation'.[26]

It was now safe enough to make anti-Soviet jokes (Putin appears to have been a master at telling *anekdoty*, and indeed all accounts suggest a strongly developed sense of humour),[27] and to read dog-eared copies of banned literature circulating in *samizdat*.[28] Putin by all accounts at an early age had a strong political awareness, enjoying political discussions in which 'he defended Russians and Russia'.[29] As long as people did not engage in unofficial political activity and make political demands of the regime, life in this period of relative non-market prosperity could be good. Life focused less on work and earnings than on social relationships and 'getting' (*dostat'*), rather than buying. His mother in 1972 was given a 30-kopeck lottery ticket as change in a buffet, and won a car – a Zaporozhets-966, mocked today but a magnificent trophy at the time. Instead of selling it she gave it to her son, and the young Vladimir became the family chauffeur. This decade and a half of calm from the late 1960s to the early 1980s stands in marked contrast to the following 15 years of upheaval that covered Gorbachev's launching of *perestroika* in 1985, the collapse of communism and the disintegration of the USSR in 1991, and Yeltsin's erratic shift to the market and democracy in the 1990s. Not surprisingly, opinion polls to this day reveal a strong bond of nostalgia for the golden years of Brezhnevite stability.

Facets of personal biography shape political preferences, and Putin's generational character is as a person of the 1970s (a *semidesyatnik*), a type that stands in sharp contrast to the previous generation, the people of the 1960s (known as the *shestdesyatniki*). The latter were shaped by Nikita Khrushchev's denunciation of Stalin in his 'secret speech' of February 1956 at the Twentieth Party Congress, and were inspired by a belief in the Soviet system's potential to reform into a more democratic form of socialism. The invasion of Czechoslovakia by the USSR and its allies in August 1968 stamped out attempts to create 'socialism with a human face', and put an end to popular belief in the humanisation of socialism. Nevertheless, it was this idea that motivated Gorbachev and to which he remained remarkably loyal despite all the vicissitudes of *perestroika*. Yeltsin repudiated reform communism in the late 1980s when he adopted the programme of the anti-systemic 'democratic' movement that called for market democracy of the Western type. As a *semidesyatnik* Putin had no ideological sympathy with reform communism, and in effect this generation was already post-communist even as the system lived out its last days. He strongly identified with the country but not with the system, reflecting the gradual 'reinvention' of Russia out of the declining Soviet carapace.[30]

Putin was influenced by the spy thrillers popular at the time, notably the book published in 1965 that later became a well-known film, *Shchit i mech* (*Sword and Shield*) (the KGB under Lenin was known as the 'sword and shield' of the revolution), about the daring doings of a Soviet secret agent, and the later television serial *Semnadsat' mgnovenii vesny* (*Seventeen Moments of Spring*), about the Soviet spy Stirlitz working in the foreign ministry at the heart of the Nazi regime. As Putin noted of his fascination with the spy-thriller genre, 'What amazed me most of all was how one man's effort could achieve what whole armies could not'.[31] Although both films were deeply patriotic, neither was particularly ideological: the struggle was to defend the Soviet motherland against its various enemies, not to defend the communist regime against its ideological opponents. This relatively non-ideological patriotism shaped Putin's personality and later took him into a career with the KGB. As he noted, 'For better or for worse, I was never a dissident'.[32]

'Moscow is silent'

Putin was at first interested in studying at the civil aviation academy, but in the end decided that he would try to enter the law faculty of Leningrad State University (LGU). The reason for this choice of academic path is interesting. Putin recounts how when in ninth grade (aged 16) in 1968 he turned up at the reception office of the Leningrad KGB at No. 4 Liteinyi Prospect (known as the 'Big House'). He was told, first, that they did not take volunteers (*initsiativniki*); and second, that they took only those with military service or university graduates. Asking what he should study, the KGB officer apparently told him that a law degree would be most appropriate.[33] It was at this time that the new (appointed in May 1967) head of the KGB, Yury Andropov, tried to modernise the repressive apparatus by attracting more intellectual and creative graduates into the profession.[34] The KGB was modernising just at the time when the modernisation of communism itself was crushed in Czechoslovakia. It was a rather romantic representation of the work of the security organs that led Putin to the KGB. Even his parents had no idea about the visit.[35]

Putin acted on the advice and sought to study at LGU. Competition was fierce, with some 40 applicants for every place, and Putin had none of the advantages other more privileged families enjoyed. Nevertheless, through sheer determination in 1970 at the age of 17 he managed to win entry. Putin thus became the fourth Russian leader (after Alexander Kerensky, Lenin and Gorbachev) to be a lawyer by training, and he was the only one of the three to have studied in the law faculty at LGU to finish full-time legal studies: Kerensky had begun studying history and philology before transferring to law, and Lenin had been an external candidate. Putin studied hard and engaged in few extracurricular activities except sport, and in the book of interviews stressed that 'I wasn't a Komsomol functionary'.[36] He continued with his sporting life and in the summers earned money as a building worker. His interest in civil law led him to take the course taught by Sobchak, already a leading lecturer in the department.[37] He wrote his final year diploma dissertation on the topic 'Principles of Successful Nations in the International Sphere',[38] an issue that would be rather close to his heart later. While at university, in March 1973, a tragedy occurred when Putin's close friend Vladimir Cheremushkin, whom Putin had encouraged to take up the sport, broke his neck in a sambo competition and later died.

It was at university that Putin at the last moment broke off his first engagement, for unknown reasons, when all the arrangements had been made, the rings bought and the suits hired: 'The cancellation was one of the most difficult decisions of my life ... But I decided that it was better to suffer then than to have both of us suffer after'.[39] This was about four years before his actual marriage. Putin's wife, Lyudmila Shkrebnëva, was born in Kaliningrad on 6 January 1958, and after a number of jobs became a flight attendant on the local airline. They met in March 1980 when she visited Leningrad with a friend and went to a show by Arkady Raikin at the Lensovet theatre. Later in 1980 she moved to Leningrad and registered to study in the philology faculty of LGU, gaining access through the workers' faculty (*rabfak*), a programme in the last year of its existence that allowed those with a working class background to enter higher education. She majored in Spanish language and literature while learning French as a subsidiary, and lived in a normal student hostel. They married after a three-and-a-half year courtship on 28 July 1983, when Vladimir was already 30 and working with the First Department (*Pervoe glavnoe upravlenie*, PGU, intelligence) of the KGB. They went to live with Putin's parents on Stachek Prospect. Lyudmila graduated in 1986, writing her diploma dissertation on 'The Participle in Contemporary Spanish'.[40] She later learned German well enough to become a teacher of that language in the early 1990s. On 28 October 1993 she had a near fatal motor car accident and was saved only by the timely intervention of the surgeon Yury Shevchenko, who under Putin became minister of health. Like her husband, Lyudmila is strongly religious, although like many 'first ladies', a role that she has never found particularly congenial, she is occasionally attracted to astrology. The role of 'first lady' is not something that particularly attracted her. The Putins' two daughters, Maria (b. 28 April 1985) and Katerina (b. 31 August 1986), were named after their grandmothers. They enrolled in Moscow's German school attached to the embassy, studying not only German and Russian but also English.[41] From September 1999 they studied at home. Both play the piano and violin, and are reputed to ski even better than their father. Once president, Putin was careful to protect their privacy.

In his fourth year at university the KGB made contact with him to discuss his 'career assignment', and he was invited 'to work in the agencies'. Putin readily agreed, having 'dreamed of this moment since I was a schoolboy'. On being asked whether he thought of the great terror of 1937 at this time, Putin responded: 'To be honest, I didn't think about it at all. Not one bit ... My notion of the KGB came from romantic spy stories'.[42] Work in 'the organs' at the time was considered a prestigious occupation and the selection was tough. He joined the KGB in the summer of 1975, trained for a year in the closed 401st KGB school in Leningrad, and then briefly worked in the Second Department (counter-intelligence) before being transferred to the far more prestigious and elite First Department,[43] monitoring foreigners and consular officials in Leningrad. As a KGB operative he also had to join the Communist Party. To his family and friends his cover was that he was a police officer with the CID. At the same time he continued his German language studies, something only allowed for officers 'with a future'.

The head of his section noted Putin's 'analytical turn of mind', and recommended him to the prestigious Red Banner (Krasnozammenyi) Institute in Balashikh in Moscow *oblast*. Named after Andropov in March

1984 following his death, it is now the Foreign Intelligence Academy but was then disguised as a research institute of the Ministry of Defence. Only those with strong language skills were accepted, and entrance involved a gruelling selection process. Putin was successful, and started there in September 1984, leaving his pregnant wife in Leningrad. The year-long training was tough at the Institute, including tests for physical stamina and mental endurance. Students were given a code name that began with the same letter as their real name, but could not be too close: Putin became Platov, and not Putilovsky or Putilin.[44]

Putin graduated in July 1985 and was posted to the KGB office in Dresden. He arrived in August, just at the time that Gorbachev's *perestroika* of the USSR began to take off. Thus at the age of 32 Putin came to an East Germany that was still what Putin himself called a 'harshly totalitarian country, similar to the Soviet Union, only 30 years earlier'.[45] The Stasi (the GDR secret police) ran a vast surveillance network, holding six million files on a population which was not much more than double that. Putin was no super-spy, as the former head of the Stasi, Marcus Wolf, has confirmed, although he was three times promoted during his stay in the country.[46] The KGB offices in Dresden were at No. 4 Angelikastrasse, just opposite the Stasi headquarters. The head of the city Stasi was Horst Bem, one of the hardest of the hardliners, who committed suicide after the fall of communism. Putin's job there was 'political intelligence' and to recruit agents to be trained in 'wireless communications', probably to gain access to Western technology and to monitor visitors to the giant 'Robotron' computer factory in the city that supplied the whole socialist camp. Numerous myths have grown up around Putin's work in East Germany, but Putin insists that his work was political rather than technical intelligence gathering.[47] He is alleged to have had a network of agents across the world,[48] but this is probably far-fetched. Contrary to much assertion, there is no evidence that he ran a Soviet–German friendship house in Leipzig (there was such an institution in Berlin), but he did visit Bonn frequently. In his leisure time Putin took up fishing so enthusiastically that 'even Germans were amazed at his pedantry' on the subject.[49] He also took up beer, although Putin was never one to drink to excess, and gained significantly in weight. He forged some close friendships with Germans at this time,[50] which he has maintained.

With the unfolding of Gorbachev's reforms the hard-line regime led by Erich Honecker became ever more isolated. On a visit to East Germany in 1989, paradoxically to celebrate the 40th anniversary of the founding of the state on 7 October 1949, Gorbachev warned that 'life punishes those who come late'. Putin may well have been involved in the Soviet plan (operation '*luch*') to replace GDR hardliners with reformers of the Gorbachev ilk.[51] Mass marches turned into protests, and on the night of 7–8 November 1989 the Berlin wall was breached. Back in Dresden the KGB was burning files on agents and operations so furiously that, as Putin put it, 'the furnace burst'.[52] Shortly afterwards, on the evening of 6 December, the KGB office was besieged by an angry crowd.[53] East Germany at the time hosted the 380,000-strong Western Group of Forces (WGF), and Putin called on the local Soviet army barracks for help but was told: 'We cannot do anything without orders from Moscow. And Moscow is silent'. It was at this point that Putin realised 'that the country no longer existed. That it had disappeared'.[54] Putin notes that 'intellectually I understood that a position built on walls and dividers cannot last'.[55] Later he argued that he was astonished that 'such a lifeless state form could still exist in Europe at that time'.[56] However, like many of his contemporaries, including the last communist head of Dresden, Hans Modrow, who after the fall of the wall went on to become premier and tried to establish in East Germany what Gorbachev called a 'humane, democratic socialism', the most bitter disappointment was that no alternative took shape and the Soviet Union made a hasty exit: 'They just dropped everything and went away'.[57] A rather chastened Putin returned from Germany, faced by serious choices about changing his life path.[58]

Second career: city functionary

In early February 1990 Putin returned to St Petersburg and turned down the offer to work at the headquarters of the Foreign Intelligence Service (SVR) at Yasenovo in Moscow, largely because no apartment was forthcoming. At that time accommodation was more important than career for the flood of service personnel returning from Eastern Europe and other Soviet outposts.[59] Instead he planned to study international law at LGU, hoping to write a doctoral dissertation and move into a new sphere of work, although as a friend told him, 'There's no such thing as a former intelligence agent'.[60] At LGU in March Putin was appointed head of the foreign section, *Inotdel*, and thus became assistant rector for international affairs while remaining in the 'active reserves' of the KGB. Putin maintained contacts with friends from the law faculty, and in this way entered the office of Sobchak, the 'democratic' chair of the Leningrad City Soviet from May 1990. The democratic movement in Leningrad was shocked at Sobchak's choice of Putin as his assistant, although Putin had made no secret of the fact that he was a career KGB officer. When questioned about this Sobchak liked to answer: 'Putin is no KGB operative but my former student'.[61] As for Putin, he entered second city politics, according to one of his friends, out of 'the romanticism of that period'.[62]

Russian presidential elections were held on 12 June 1991, when Yeltsin became the country's first president. The first mayoral elections were held on the same day, and Sobchak was elected. He took Putin with him as an adviser, and a fortnight later appointed him head of the newly formed city committee for foreign economic relations with responsibility for attracting foreign investment. Despite attempts to resign from the KGB earlier, when the letter apparently went astray, Putin finally resigned from the KGB with the rank of lieutenant-colonel on 20 August 1991, the second day of the attempted coup launched against Gorbachev's reform communism by conservatives. Putin's choice was unequivocal: 'As soon as the coup began, I immediately decided which side I was on',[63] although he notes just how hard the choice was since he had spent the best part of his life with 'the organs'.[64] During the coup Putin negotiated with the Leningrad KGB that they would maintain their neutrality, and as a reward Sobchak subsequently appointed him one of three mayoral deputies. With the dissolution of the old order Putin's membership of the CPSU simply lapsed. As with a whole generation, he did not leave the Party; the Party left him.

Revealing strong administrative talents and loyalty, Putin soon became known as Sobchak's 'grey cardinal', and from March 1994 to May 1996 he was first deputy mayor overseeing the law-enforcement agencies and the media. Sobchak refused to sign any document unless previously signatured by Putin. At the time when Putin was active in the city, St Petersburg became known as the crime capital of Russia. Before going on to head the national privatisation programme in 1992, Anatoly Chubais in 1990–1 was also a deputy to the chair of the Leningrad City Soviet, and it was at this time that he got to know Putin. Chubais's national privatisation programme allowed a small number of people to become extraordinarily rich, and gave birth to the 'oligarchs' (a term popularised by Boris Nemtsov in 1997), with whom Putin later engaged in battle. Although concerned with inward investment, no serious evidence of corruption has been found against Putin, although numerous charges have been made against him for his work during this period.[65] In particular, the scandal associated with the issuing of licences (with very high commission charges) to firms as part of a programme in 1992 to sell natural resources abroad to buy food is often mentioned.[66] The planned redevelopment of the area around the Moscow station to build a business, shopping and hotel centre is also cited. As a bureaucrat Putin was known to take short cuts to achieve a desired result, and gained the reputation of being a tough negotiator and a 'strong, effective and pragmatic leader'.[67]

Putin stood loyally by Sobchak even as the latter proved an extremely divisive figure and routinely ended up in conflict with the St Petersburg city council. Contrary to his boss, all the evidence suggests that Putin enjoyed a very good relationship with the city legislature. For the last year and a half of his term in office Sobchak was under investigation, among other things, for allegedly buying an apartment with city funds. Putin at this time was a member of prime minister Viktor Chernomyrdin's Our Home is Russia (*Nash Dom – Rossiya*, NDR) party, and in late 1995 led its unsuccessful parliamentary election campaign in the city, for which he was blamed by Chernomyrdin.[68] Despite this, in April 1996 (together with Alexei Kudrin) he was placed in charge of Sobchak's re-election campaign. The vote had been brought forward from 16 June to 19 May to shorten the odds for the incumbent, but even this did not help. Sobchak was successfully challenged by his other deputy, Vladimir Yakovlev, in a very dirty campaign, with numerous charges addressed towards Putin personally. Putin was no master of electoral 'black PR' (as the sophisticated 'election technologies' are called in Russia), and it was clear that he felt deeply uncomfortable in his role as election manager. In a television programme at this time Putin called Yakovlev 'a Judas', an epithet that he did not retract later.[69] Sobchak was later forced into exile in the face of corruption charges. Putin on 7 November 1997 organised a covert operation that smuggled him by medical plane to Finland and thence on to France.[70] There is clearly a contradiction between Putin's loyalty to his mentor and what could be considered a cavalier approach to the law. Sobchak could only return once Putin was acting president, only to die of a heart attack soon after. Putin's genuine anguish at the funeral of his teacher, sponsor and friend on 24 February 2000 was there for all to see.[71]

Third career: state official

Following Sobchak's defeat Putin made yet another decisive choice: he resigned from the city administration, refusing a job offer from Yakovlev.[72] He remained committed to Sobchak, even though this placed him in a career limbo. His trait of loyalty would serve him well in the next few years. Putin was now at a loose end, and moved out to his dacha, which he had been building for some years, only to have it burn to the ground six weeks later in August 1996. In the rubble only his Orthodox cross survived, a story that was later recounted by Putin's confessor Father Tikhon as a sign to Putin that in this world only spiritual values survive.[73] At that time, however, more practical matters faced him. Putin once again contemplated an academic career, entering the St Petersburg Mining Institute to complete his 218-page Candidate (*Kandidat*) dissertation on the exciting topic of 'The Strategic Planning of Regional Resources during the Formation of a Market Economy'.[74] The thesis examined strategic planning and the exploitation of the raw material base of St Petersburg and the Leningrad region as market relations developed. The basic idea was that irrespective of ownership the state has the duty to manage natural resource development, and thus the theme that was to preoccupy Putin as president – how the state can make best use of its natural resources – was already uppermost in his thoughts.[75] Putin successfully defended the thesis in June 1997, and became a Candidate of Economic Sciences (between an MPhil and a PhD).[76] In a follow-up article published two years later in the Institute's journal he developed the theme of the dissertation, arguing that the state should have the final voice in energy and natural resource policy. The chosen instrument to achieve this was not direct state management but vertically integrated financial–industrial groups.[77] This would be a managed market, to act as the counterpart of what later became known as 'managed democracy' (more on this in Chapter 2). In later years 'strategic planning' was to be one of the buzzwords of Putin's presidency, when he set up an institute by that name to advise him, and his conclusion that the country would be best served by establishing vertically integrated companies encompassing whole industries that could compete in world markets was applied. Active state intervention in the management of natural resources became the hallmark of his leadership.

This period of difficulty in fact proved to be an opportunity for advancement along an entirely different line. Nikolai Yegorov, the head of the presidential administration, planned to give Putin a job in the Kremlin, but as part of the purge of hardliners following Yeltsin's re-election in June–July 1996, Yegorov was dismissed and replaced by Chubais, who promptly suppressed the post. In the event, with the support of another St Petersburger, Kudrin (then head of the Kremlin's Main Control Directorate, GKU), Chubais offered Putin the job of head of public relations. Before he could take up this post, in June 1996 Pavel Borodin, in charge of the Kremlin's property service, brought Putin into the presidential administration, at first as head of the general affairs department and then as his deputy. Borodin was later to face corruption charges associated with the magnificent restoration of the Kremlin halls, notably the one named after St Andrew, by the Swiss company Mabatex. Putin for eight months was responsible for managing the vast portfolio of properties abroad (in 1995 there were 715 sites with an income of $10 million per annum), and defending the Kremlin's ownership against other claimants, notably the Ministry of Foreign Affairs.

Thereafter Putin's career went into overdrive through a series of lucky breaks; although this 'luck' was determined as much by character as by chance. On 26 March 1997 he was appointed a deputy head of the presidential administration and head of the Main Control Directorate, probably on the recommendation of its former head, Kudrin, who became a deputy finance minister. The GKU was the successor of the old Party Control Committee, headed for years under Brezhnev by Arvid Pelshe, whose office in Old Square Putin now inherited. His job here was to conduct audits of state agencies, and to help him Putin set up a powerful analytical office, gathering a vast amount of information on misconduct by state officials in government offices and the regions.[78] In his inspection of the state arms agency, 'Rosvooruzheniya', he found considerable evidence of malpractice, especially in delivery of weapons to Armenia, something that caused a major international scandal. It was at this time that Putin repeatedly stated that the Ministry of Defence could not reform itself.[79] Just over a year later, on 25 May 1998, he was appointed first deputy chief of staff responsible for relations with the regions. It was while working here that he got to know many regional leaders, and learnt that 'the *vertikal*, the vertical chain of government, had been destroyed and that it had to be restored'.[80] From 15 July he headed the presidential commission drafting treaties on the division of responsibilities between the centre and the regions.[81] It was experience gained at this time that prompted Putin to make the reform of regional relations the first priority of his presidency, notably by imposing a 'power vertical' as the backbone of his 'new federalism'.

Putin's administrative skills and loyalty did not go unnoticed, and on 25 July 1998 he was appointed head of the FSB, a job that he took up most reluctantly: 'I can't say that I was overjoyed. I didn't want to step into the same river twice'.[82] Once again Putin was subject to the endless vetting, the secrets and the closed life. Putin insisted that he returned to head the KGB 'not as a colonel [of the reserves] but as a civilian', coming from a responsible post in the presidential administration, and was thus a civilian leader of the security services.[83] A similar point could be made about Andropov, whose career prior to taking over the KGB had primarily been as a Party worker. On 29 March of the following year he was given the additional post of secretary to the Security Council, to replace Nikolai Bordyuzha who had been dismissed on 19 March, and thus became one of the most powerful men in Russia. At this time the Security Council became ever more dominated by FSB officials, perhaps as a counterweight to prime minister Eevgeny Primakov's advancement of his former colleagues in the SVR to government posts. Primakov had enjoyed a long career in international public policy, dealing in particular with Arab countries, before taking over as head of the Foreign Intelligence Service in 1991. He served as foreign minister between January 1996 and September 1998 before becoming prime minister following the partial default of August 1998.

As head of the FSB Putin proved a tough administrator, launching the eighth reorganisation of the agency in as many years, abolishing two key departments (economic counter-intelligence and defence of strategic sites) and firing about 40 lieutenant-generals and major-generals and about a third of its central staff (reducing it from 6,000 to 4,000). The personnel reductions were criticised for having been done mechanically, letting go those approaching or beyond pensionable age, and thus the most experienced, but these were precisely the ones with the strongest attachment to the old Soviet order. He reoriented the service away from its traditional obsession with domestic subversion towards the fight against corruption, organised crime, computer security and work in the regions. Putin also impressed his colleagues by declaring that coercive measures alone could not bring about the much desired order to society, and endorsed the development of civil society and pluralism.[84] Putin's long association with Sobchak won him no friends in the Lubyanka, since Sobchak had headed the parliamentary committee investigating the 'Tbilisi events' of April 1989 and the role of the military and security services in the deaths. To compensate, Putin brought in some of his friends from the security services in St Petersburg: above all Victor Cherkesov, with whom he had trained (head of the security services in the city and region, whose career in the KGB had begun by persecuting dissidents); and Sergei Ivanov, brought in from the SVR. Another of his close friends, Nikolai Patrushev, took Putin's place as head of the GKU and then replaced him at the head of the FSB. Patrushev was a fellow St Petersburger; they had studied law together, and the two had joined the KGB at the same time in 1975. It is clear that the FSB did not welcome Putin to its bosom as one of 'its own', and thus later commentary about Putin being little more than a tool of the security services is wide of the mark.[85]

In all of Putin's postings one detail remained consistent: the wages of his staff were always paid on time.[86] This may not seem such a big deal to Western readers, but in Russian circumstances, during the chaotic transition to capitalism, it was no mean achievement.[87] By the time that he was appointed prime minister in August 1999 Putin had already gained wide experience: he had travelled extensively across the country as a member of his sports team; he had completed a full-time higher education degree from one of the country's best universities; he had worked for a decade as a security official; he had lived abroad for five years; he had become the second figure in the politics of Russia's second city; he had successfully defended what was effectively a doctoral dissertation; and as a senior member of the presidential administration in Moscow he was already familiar with the problems of the regions, the workings of the government, the presidential apparatus and the security services. He was certainly far from the 'nobody' that some suggested on his appointment to the premiership. He had seen life in many aspects, and had grappled with genuine problems of management and modernisation. Putin's chequered biography no doubt later shaped his policies as president.[88] The various layers of his personal and professional experience built on each other; it was not in Putin's character to reject the past to move to the future.[89]

Character

Putin was the first Russian leader since Lenin to speak foreign languages, having a good command of both German and, later, English. He was the third leader to have completed a law degree, following in the footsteps of Kerensky and Gorbachev (Lenin had never finished his course). Apart from his close links with Germany, something that he maintained as president, before becoming president Putin had also twice visited America as Sobchak's assistant. The many times winner of the sambo championships of St Petersburg, a black belt in judo, and with a long record of effective work in the intelligence services, Putin is clearly a man of considerable self-discipline.[90] Even with a full-time job he was able to complete work on his Candidate dissertation. He also showed considerable flexibility and ability to adapt to changing circumstances. This pragmatism, however, was always constrained and operated within a severe code of what he considered correct behaviour. According to Mukhin, Putin's character is disposed towards the negotiated solution of conflicts, but in crisis situations he is prone to take forceful measures. He has a systematic approach to analysing problems, logical while at the same time cautious, combined with an intellectual and non-emotional way of dealing with issues. Hence his phrase (used about those guilty of the bombings in 1999, see below) about 'soaking the bandits in the John' (*banditov i v sortire zamochim*) is not part of his typical vocabulary, and he apparently apologised several times for using such semi-criminal (*blatnoi*) language.[91]

The memoirs of Strobe Talbott, deputy secretary of state between 1993 and 2000, mention Putin's role in the Kosovo crisis of 1999. Although not the key figure, Putin impressed the American 'by his ability to convey self-control and confidence in a low-key, soft-spoken manner'. According to Talbott at a meeting on 11 June 1999, when Russia's relations with the West were extremely tense, Putin 'radiated executive competence, an ability to get things done without fuss or friction', listening 'with an attentiveness that seemed at least as calculating as it was courteous'.[92] Putin had done his homework, and not only knew much about Talbott, but let him know that he knew, by referring for example to the Russian poets that Talbott had studied at Yale and Oxford. The effect on Talbott was unnerving but impressive. Substantively, Putin claimed that it had been his idea to propose Chernomyrdin to Yeltsin as Russia's envoy to former Yugoslavia, and thus helped broker a ceasefire.[93] As head of the FSB and secretary to the Security Council, Putin helped coordinate Russia's policy in this area, although we do not know his views on the dash on 11–12 June of 200 Russian troops from Bosnia to Pristina airport. We do know, however, that Putin sought to avoid an escalation of the conflict, despite the rising crescendo of threats issued by, among others, colonel-general Leonid Ivashov, head of the defence ministry's main directorate for international military co-operation. Talbott describes Putin's response to his concerns:

> Putin adopted the bedside manner of an experienced physician with a hypochondriac for a patient. Nothing on the Russian side had changed, he said soothingly. 'Who, by the way, is this Ivashov?' he asked. He made it sound not like a rhetorical question but a genuine expression of puzzlement about the identity of the three-star general who had been the Defense Ministry's principal representative on the Chernomyrdin delegation for the past six weeks and who had been constantly in the newspapers and on television, primarily denouncing Chernomyrdin and the agreement. Whoever Ivashov was, Putin continued, the statement that I found so alarming should be taken as an 'emotional outburst', not as a reflection of Russian policy or intention. There would be, he promised, 'one hundred percent cooperation and coordination' between our militaries while our differences were being worked out. 'Nothing improper' would happen . . . [94]

Putin's stance of apparently being surprised by information that was by then common knowledge was a trope that he was to repeat as president, notably when informed, while on a visit to Spain, about the arrest of the oligarch Vladimir Gusinsky. It was a type of distancing technique that was to serve him well personally, but was not a pose that would be expected from a president. In the case described by Talbott something 'improper' did happen: Russian troops seized Slatina airport at Pristina and war was probably only averted because the British general, Mike Jackson, refused to obey the orders of the senior American general, Wesley Clark. How much Putin knew of the background to the Russian action we do not know.[95]

The many biographies that have been published in Russia highlight a wealth of other personal details. For example, Bortsov notes that Putin's star sign is Libra (the scales), the only mechanical astrological representation and, we may add, a symbol that suggests balance and justice. Similarly, in the Chinese calendar Putin is a dragon, the most-favoured in Chinese cosmology and the only mythical creature in that particular bestiary.[96] Putin's characteristic rhetorical turn of phrase has been much analysed, typically answering a question with a question.[97] Talanov characterises Putin as an introvert, while at the same time being of the 'critic' type who tries to avoid allowing psychological conflicts to reach an emotional peak, whereas the 'artist' type tries precisely to bring crises to an emotional climax.[98] Avramchenko, one of the multitude of authors who wrote detailed plans on how Putin could save Russia, characterises him as 'moderate and cautious', while at the same time warning that Putin's insistence on an exclusively evolutionary approach and ban on radical changes would prevent the country moving 'off the path of destruction onto the path of accelerated development'.[99]

Many note Putin's sense of humour. When visiting Maritime *krai* as prime minister in the autumn of 1999, the governor Yevgeny Nazdratenko heaped lavish compliments on him, to which Putin replied: 'Yevgeny Ivanovich, you praised me so much that I began to think that I must have died'.[100] Putin's background as part of the 'St Petersburg mafia' provided him later with a pool, although relatively small, of clients and also with an orientation to the world that is Western-oriented and responsive to the needs of the country. It was this man who was now called upon to provide leadership in the post-Yeltsin era.[101]

Operation successor

For Schumpeter, the role of the people in a democracy 'is to produce a government', and it is in this light that he provides his classic definition: 'the democratic method is that institutional arrangement for arriving at political decisions in which individuals acquire the power to decide by means of a competitive struggle for the people's vote'.[102] The distorted nature of the competition for the people's vote in the 1999–2000 elections, however, has led many commentators to suggest that it was less than democratic. As Schumpeter went on to stress, the people not only vote to elect a government; they must also have the ability to evict it.[103] It is this absence of rotation in the transition from Yeltsin to Putin that casts a shadow over the whole process. Nevertheless, the succession was by no means as easy as it may appear in hindsight,[104] and Putin's character and choices played a large part in ensuring its success.

Putin's premiership

The fifth premier in two years, and the third in turn from the security services, Vladimir Putin was soon transformed from professional bureaucrat into a relatively independent political figure. On appointing Putin as prime minister on 9 August 1999 Yeltsin had declared him his successor. Experience suggested that this was a precarious position. Already at various points Yeltsin had considered Sergei Shakhrai, Vladimir Shumeiko, Oleg Soskovets, Alexander Lebed, Boris Nemtsov, Sergei Kirienko, Nikolai Bordyuzha, Sergei Stepashin and Nikolai Aksenenko as potential successors, and all had been found wanting and discarded. Yeltsin had been thinking about the succession since 1991, even when in the pink of health, but with greater urgency after his re-election in 1996 and multiple heart bypass operations that autumn. He set his administration one main task: 'the succession of power through the election of 2000'. They had four years to make sure that in 2000 the new president would be 'a person who would continue democratic reforms in the country, who would not turn back to the totalitarian system, and who would ensure Russia's movement forward, to a civilized community'.[105] The sacking on 23 March 1998 of his long-standing prime minister, Chernomyrdin, as someone in whose hands the country could not be entrusted, was part of the succession operation.[106]

The procession of prime ministers that followed – Kirienko (March–August 1998), Primakov (September 1998 to May 1999) and Stepashin (May–August 1999) – was in part determined by the logic of the succession. As for Bordyuzha, he had served 20 years in the KGB and latterly had been head of the Federal Border Service when on 14 September 1998 he was appointed secretary of the Security Council, and four months later on 7 December he became head of the presidential administration, an extraordinary concentration of power. Bordyuzha has been described as 'Putin No. 1', in the sense of the rapid rise of a relatively unknown security official, but the general consensus is that Bordyuzha lacked leadership qualities and proved not up to the task.[107] The economist Alexander Voloshin replaced him as head of the presidential administration on 19 March 1999, and Putin a few days later as chair of the Security Council. Stepashin's appointment was quite explicitly a stopgap while preparing the way for Putin.[108]

Yeltsin had first noticed Putin in 1997 when he headed the GKU and then when he was first deputy to the presidential chief of staff, Valentin Yumashev, with responsibility for work with the regions. 'Putin's reports', Yeltsin notes, 'were a model of clarity', and he was impressed by the businesslike way that Putin dealt with matters: 'Putin tried to remove any sort of personal element from our contact. And precisely because of that, I wanted to talk to him more'.[109] Yeltsin was also impressed by Putin's 'lightning reactions', responding calmly to Yeltsin's interjections. So when Yeltsin in the summer of 1998 was looking for a new director of the security services, his choice fell on Putin. Not only had he worked for many years in the security agencies, 'the more I knew Putin, the more convinced I was that he combined both an enormous dedication to democracy and market reforms and an unwavering patriotism'.[110] Yeltsin also appreciated Putin's sense of decency: when he dismissed officials at the FSB he always ensured that they had a 'soft landing', a new job or a generous pension (a trait that Putin continued as president). Yeltsin notes that Putin 'did not allow himself to be manipulated in political games. Even I was amazed by his solid moral code ... for Putin, the single criterion was the morality of a given action or the decency of a given person. He would not do anything that conflicted with his understanding of honor. He was always ready to part with his high post if his sense of integrity would require it'.[111] This was certainly the case when Putin gave up his job in the mayoral administration on Sobchak's defeat in 1996.

On 5 August 1999 Yeltsin summoned Putin and informed him of his decision to appoint him prime minister, and already then intimated that this was just a step on the way to 'the very highest post'. Putin was aware that this would mean harsh political struggles, especially in the forthcoming parliamentary elections. According to Yeltsin, Putin asserted that 'I don't like election campaigns ... I really don't. I don't know how to run them, and I don't like them'.[112] With the bitter experience of unsuc-cessfully running NDR's parliamentary campaign in 1995 and Sobchak's 1996 re-election campaign, Putin's comments were hardly surprising, and this attitude was to endure into the March 2000 presidential elections. The conversation ended with Putin agreeing: 'I will work wherever you assign me', reportedly said with military terseness. In introducing Putin to the country on 9 August, Yeltsin spoke of Putin as a 'prime minister with a future',[113] and talked of him as someone 'who can consolidate society, based on the widest possible political spectrum, and ensure the continuation of reforms in Russia'.[114]

Nomination as Yeltsin's successor for others had been the kiss of death. As Gennady Seleznev, speaker of the State Duma (lower house of parlia-ment) put it, 'If Yeltsin declares someone his successor, it means putting a cross on his political future. This has already happened many times'.[115] Putin himself considered the appointment temporary: 'I thought, "Well, I'll work for a year, and that's fine. If I can help save Russia from collapse, then I'll have something to be proud of". It was a stage in my life. And then I'll move onto the next thing'.[116] Putin's self-control was evident at this time; his father had died on 2 August (his mother had died of cancer in 1998), with the funeral taking place three days later. On 16 August the Duma ratified Putin's appointment by 233 votes for, 84 against and with 17 abstentions.[117]

Putin was appointed as a Yeltsin loyalist, and it appeared at first that he would enjoy little more freedom than his predecessors under Yeltsin's overbearing leadership. Like all of Yeltsin's prime ministers, Putin was not given independence to form his own cabinet and instead had ministers foisted on him by the presidential administration. Above all, Aksenenko, as a first deputy prime minister, openly pursued his own interests and those of the presidential 'family', the colloquial term for the combination of favoured oligarchs, insider politicians, political advisors, and some of Yeltsin's blood family members, above all his daughter Tatyana Dyachenko. On several occasions, as in the displacement of the head of the state's monopoly pipeline company Transneft, it appeared that Putin was ignored entirely. The influence of the family's oligarch allies remained strong, notably the most notorious of them all, Boris Berezovsky, and his ally, Roman Abramovich, known as the treasurer to Yeltsin's family. The energy minister Viktor Kalyuzhny and the interior minister Vladimir Rushailo, appointed to this post on 21 May 1999, were part of this group. We shall have much more to say later about the 'family'. At the same time, the last Yeltsin years were notable for their increased reliance on personnel with a military-security background,[118] a trend that was reinforced under Putin. Huskey goes so far as to describe developments under Yeltsin as the 'militarization of the presidency': 'Yeltsin was turning for administrative support to a group schooled in loyalty and discipline'.[119]

Putin certainly fits that description. However, he soon transcended the limitations of his post. On any scale, his metamorphosis was remarkable, and Putin soon emerged as the leading candidate in the presidential election. His support rose from 2 per cent in August, 15 per cent by the end of September, 25 per cent in late October and an astonishing 40 per cent in late November.[120] At least four factors help explain Putin's meteoric rise. The first is that the Kremlin put its entire weight behind him. His potential presidential rivals, above all Yury Luzhkov, the mayor of Moscow, and Primakov, were subjected to vitriolic attacks, above all in the various press and television outlets dominated by the Kremlin and its allies, notably the Public Russian Television (ORT) channel part owned by Berezovsky. The Primakov myth that he could become a wise elder statesman restoring the best of the Brezhnev years while ensuring economic and diplomatic success was systematically dismantled, and instead he was portrayed as a sick old man who symbolised the failures of the Soviet system. Although Putin undoubtedly enjoyed overt and behind the scenes official support, it was also during his premiership that the independent NTV station, founded by another of the dominant oligarchs, Vladimir Gusinsky, subjected Putin to an extraordinary barrage of personal attacks. With the stakes so high, in late 1999 the pre-presidential campaign on all sides was vicious.

Second, the renewed war in Chechnya turned out at first to be genuinely popular, unlike the first conflict in 1994–6. By the terms of the Khasavyurt Accord of 31 August 1996, signed by Alexander Lebedev for Russia and the guerrilla leader Aslan Maskhadov, the republic gained effective independence while a decision on its final status was delayed for five years. Russian troops were withdrawn and in February 1997, with Moscow's blessing, Maskhadov was elected president. However, in the face of growing lawlessness, Russia from early 1999 began to prepare for renewed conflict.[121] The turning point, according to Stepashin,[122] was the abduction on 5 March 1999 of Russia's deputy interior minister, major-general Gennady Shpigun, who had been dragged off a plane by Chechen insurgents at Grozny airport (his body was found in June 2000). It was clear that Maskhadov was losing control of the situation in the republic. As head of the Security Council and of the FSB, Putin responded by meeting with Yeltsin on 19 May 1999 and drafting the tough decree 'On Additional Measures to Fight Terrorism in Russia's North Caucasus'.[123]

The second war in the event was provoked by the infiltration by Chechen forces (some 1,500 insurgents led by the Chechen field commanders Shamil Basaev and the Saudi-born Habib Abd al-Rahman, known as Khattab) on 2 August 1999 into the Botlikh and Tsumadin districts in neighbouring Dagestan, and a few weeks later (5 September) a second invasion by a larger force into the Novolaksk district to the north of the first incursion. Memories of the savagery of Salman Raduaev's raid on the hospital in Kizlyar in January 1996 helped turn Dagestani popular opinion against this new Chechen attack. Moscow sent considerable forces to defeat the invasion and to destroy the fundamentalist salafite enclaves in Dagestan. In response, according to the official version, the insurgent forces (assumed typically to be Chechens, but also involving Dagestanis) decided to take the battle to Moscow and Russia. On 31 August one person was killed and 45 injured when a bomb damaged the underground Manezh shopping complex. Apartment blocks were bombed in Buinaksk, Dagestan, on 4 September killing 62 and wounding 174; on Guryanov Street in Moscow on 9 September killing 94 and injuring over 200; on Kashirskoe Highway in Moscow on 13 September killing 124; and a truck bomb tore the façade off an apartment block in Volgodonsk on 15 September, killing 19 and wounding 342. A primed bomb ready to destroy yet another apartment block was found in Ryazan on the night of 22–23 September, and although the FSB claimed that this had been a test exercise with a 'dummy' bomb, the incident still requires full explanation.[124] These terrible events created a climate of fear and, to a degree, retribution against Chechens, although the involvement of Chechens in these atrocities remains uncertain.[125] The pressure was on for some sort of response, and Putin's resolute statements and decisive actions, including the willingness to take personal responsibility, won him considerable popularity. Failure to act at this time would have conclusively discredited the Russian government.

On 1 October Russian forces moved into Chechnya. Military intervention was initially envisaged as a limited operation, but after the relatively easy occupation of the northern lowlands, troops crossed the Terek river in late

October and thus entered the heartlands of Chechnya (Ichkeria). Putin was the first leader for well over a decade to give full support to the military, and thus began to expunge memories of the 'Tbilisi syndrome', where politicians failed to take responsibility for military actions which they had ordered. While the defence minister Igor Sergeev was not enthusiastic about renewed war in Chechnya, a group of 'Chechen generals', led by the chief of the General Staff Anatoly Kvashnin and including Konstantin Pulikovsky, Gennady Troshev, Viktor Kazantsev and Vladimir Shamanov, were thirsting to take revenge for defeat in the first war.[126] Far greater troop concentrations were committed than in the first war, with over 100,000 (compared to 30,000–40,000) sent in to seize the major cities in the second stage of the operation, with the attack on Grozny beginning on 25 December and ending on 8 February 2000.[127]

Two years before the 11 September 2001 destruction of the World Trade Center in New York and the attack on the Pentagon, the war was presented as a 'war against terrorism', laying the foundations for the post-September alliance of Russia and the West. Putin later argued that he was willing to lay his career on the line at this time, but had decided 'that my mission, my historical mission – and this will sound lofty but it's true – consisted of resolving the situation in the North Caucasus'.[128] Putin's image as an 'iron chancellor' was created and sustained by his uncompromising approach to the Chechen problem. His use of street language in the press conference on 8 September, where as mentioned earlier he used the underworld jargon of 'soaking the bandits in the John', appeared at first as if it would be a public relations disaster, but in the event it only reinforced Putin's image as a man of the people. Far more importantly, at that press conference Putin insisted: 'Russia is defending itself. We have been attacked. And therefore we must throw off all our syndromes, including the guilt syndrome'.[129] Yeltsin gave Putin a free hand: 'I wanted people to start getting used to Putin and to perceive him as the head of state'.[130] Yeltsin explains Putin's surge in popularity in this way: 'Putin got rid of Russia's fear. And Russia repaid him with profound gratitude'.[131]

The third factor is that, unlike his predecessors, Putin soon enjoyed unprecedented power over policy making, and not only over Chechen issues. He could take credit for the raft of good economic news that began at this time and continued into his presidency: economic growth, rising living standards and resolute attempts to deal with wage arrears. Although formally liable to dismissal by Yeltsin at any time, Putin in the last months of 1999 acted with extraordinary confidence and independence. He was even allowed oversight over the power ministries, a presidential prerogative, something that no prime minister had ever been allowed before.[132] Putin was able to transform the prime-ministerial office into a quasi-presidential post, eclipsing Yeltsin personally. In the past whenever any politician threatened to outshine him, Yeltsin immediately cut his potential rival down to size. On this occasion the Kremlin clearly colluded and allowed Putin to dominate the political scene. With Yeltsin's declining health and vigour, the trend with the last few prime ministers had been in this direction anyway. All had seen their popularity ratings soar on appointment, and the office of prime minister (as in other semi-presidential systems such as France) is the natural springboard for the presidency.

Fourth, Putin appeared able to restore Russia's national dignity, adopting neither an obsequiously subservient nor an impotently assertive attitude towards the West. Putin tried to find a measured understanding of Russia's real needs and capacity. As a newspaper article put it, 'Putin must restore what Yeltsin destroyed: pride to feel part of a great power. Russians want respect, not sympathy'.[133] It soon became clear to both domestic and foreign observers that Putin represented a new breed of Russian politician, honest and intelligent and untainted by any demonstrable corruption. Putin clearly cared about Russia more than his personal interests. As noted by Sergei Kovalev, the human rights campaigner and liberal deputy, Putin represented 'an alternative both to a Communist restoration and the incompetence of "the democrats"'.[134] He quickly came to epitomise Russia, its sufferings and its aspirations and thus he was to become 'the president of hope'.

The 19 December 1999 parliamentary elections and the succession

On the eve of the election Nikolai Petrov wrote: 'The political era associated with the name of B. Yeltsin is entering history. The regime proved unable to reproduce itself, and the change of leader will entail the change of the entire political system, based on the personal power of that leader'.[135] There are at least three elements involved here: regime (that is, the political order created by Yeltsin), systemic reproduction and leadership succession. In the event, the system was able to reproduce itself, at least politically, by ensuring that the change of leader did not entail a change of regime.

Beneath the endless political crises, sackings, resignations and dramatic *démarches* in Russian politics from 1995, when Yeltsin's health had begun sharply to deteriorate, there lay a more profound struggle for the succession. By the time of his visit to Uzbekistan in October 1998 it was clear that the Yeltsin era was over. Yeltsin was only able to stand with president Islam Karimov's support. Klyamkin and Shevtsova note that the 1999 election represented 'an unprecedented campaign' in which the Duma elections became part of a struggle for far greater stakes.[136] They note that in most transition countries two electoral cycles are usually considered sufficient to judge whether democracy is consolidated, whereas in Russia this was the third, and if anything it only raised yet more questions about the nature of the emerging democratic order.[137] Throughout the 1990s elections had been conducted as plebiscites on the nature of the system rather than as a choice between governments; and when the choice is between regimes, people are effectively deprived of the choice between administrations. The threat from the Communist Party of the Russian Federation (CPRF) was now played up for all it was worth, and probably much more. Too often, notably in the 1996 presidential election, people voted through gritted teeth for Yeltsin as the 'lesser evil'. Earlier that year Yeltsin's bodyguard and influential advisor, Alexander Korzhakov, had asked why risk everything for the sake of democracy, and had advocated cancelling the presidential elections.[138] Yeltsin now finessed the problem by ensuring that the favoured candidate won.

This was by no means going to be a walkover, especially since a credible opposition had now emerged to supplant the communist opposition. In August 1999 an alliance had been forged between Luzhkov's Fatherland (*Otechestvo*) movement, established in December 1998 allegedly to campaign against the influence of the oligarchs, and the All Russia (*Vsya Rossiya*) bloc, set up in April 1999 by a group of powerful regional leaders including president Mintimir Shaimiev of Tatarstan and Putin's old sparring partner, Vladimir Yakovlev, the governor of St Petersburg. At the head of the new Fatherland – All Russia (OVR) bloc stood Primakov, who made no secret of his presidential ambitions. Stepashin's dismissal in early August had in part been provoked by his failure to prevent this challenge to the Kremlin emerging. In response, in September 1999 Berezovsky masterminded the creation of the Unity (*Edinstvo*) electoral bloc (also known as Medved, Bear), drawing initially on 39 regional leaders. A powerful bandwagon was set in motion on to which more and more regional and other leaders jumped, fearing for their positions if they ended up on the losing side after the electoral battles. Putin himself declared on 24 November that he would support Unity 'as a private citizen and friend of Sergei Shoigu',[139] the charismatic minister for Emergency Situations who had been placed at the head of the new party. Putin sought to present himself as a symbol of confidence and stability, promising to maintain Russia's system of power and property while radically renovating the state system and developing political and legal reform. Putin committed himself to constitutional continuity, although he argued that some institutional innovation could take place without necessarily changing the constitution itself. The campaign, as noted, was marked by the brutal denigration of the Kremlin's opponents, above all Luzhkov and Primakov. The partisan use of the media suggests that the election, while relatively free, was far from fair. Together with the emergence of the Unity bloc, the election was significant for the emergence of a new liberal bloc, the Union of Right Forces (*Soyuz pravykh sil*, SPS), bringing together nine small liberal parties and associations led collectively by Nemtsov, Gaidar, Irina Khakamada and the former prime minister Kirienko. The SPS attached itself to Putin's coat-tails, supporting the war in Chechnya, and the Kremlin reciprocated by indicating support for them.

The result (see Table 1.1) proved to be a vote of confidence in Putin and provided a launch pad for the presidential campaign.[140] Although the communists emerged with a plurality of seats, the pro-Putin government bloc led by Unity enjoyed a comfortable majority. However, its lack of genuine regional depth was reflected in the low number of single-member

Table 1.1 State Duma election 19 December 1999

Election association or bloc	Party list vote (%)	Party list seats	Single-member districts	Total
CPRF	24.3	67	47	114 (25.9%)
Unity	23.3	64	9	73 (16.6%)
OVR	13.3	37	29	66 (15.0%)
SPS	8.5	24	5	29 (6.6%)
LDPR	6.1	17	0	17 (3.9%)
Yabloko	5.9	16	4	22 (4.5%)
Others and against all (3.3%)	18.7	–	26	24
Independents	–	–	105 (23.8%)	105
TOTAL	100	225	225	450

Sources: *Vestnik Tsentral'noi izbiratel'noi komissii Rossiiskoi Federatsii*, No. 1 (91), 2000, p. 231; *Nezavisimaya gazeta*, 30 December 1999, p. 1; The results can also be found at the Central Electoral Commission's website www.fci.ru/gd99/.

Notes:
Out of some 108 million Russian electors, over 60 million voted, a turnout rate of 61.7%, comfortably exceeding the minimum 25% requirement. An additional 1.2% of the electorate cast invalid votes.

constituencies that it contested (13 per cent), winning only nine. Unity was unlike the earlier 'parties of power', namely Russia's Choice in the early 1990s, led by Yegor Gaidar (the architect of the first phase of Yeltsin's reforms), and then Our Home is Russia (NDR), because it had been established not as a governing party but as an instrument of electoral competition. Paradoxically, it went on to form the basis of a loyal bloc of deputies in the Third Duma (2000–3), and thus did effectively become the governing party. As Igor Shabdurasulov, who had managed Unity's election campaign on behalf of the Kremlin put it, 'The new State Duma will be of a principally different character. A peaceful revolution has taken place in Russia'.[141]

Yeltsin's resignation and the succession

The success of the hastily assembled pro-Kremlin electoral association Unity opened the way for the unexpected *dénouement* of the succession operation – Yeltsin's resignation on 31 December 1999. The process was carefully planned since, as Yeltsin admitted, 'there was no precedent for a voluntary resignation by Russia's head of state', and he clearly enjoyed taking everyone (including his closest associates) by surprise.[142] He had first intimated his plan to Putin two weeks earlier, on 14 December at his Gorki-9 residence. On being told that Yeltsin planned to make him acting president, Putin's immediate reaction was to say 'I'm not ready for that decision, Boris Nikolayevich'. Putin's hesitation, according to Yeltsin, was not a sign of weakness but 'the doubts of a strong person'.[143] Yeltsin insisted that 'The new century must begin with a new political era, the era of Putin', and the latter finally agreed.[144] They met again, this time in the Kremlin, on 29 December to arrange the details of the transfer of power, including the transfer of the nuclear suitcase. Yeltsin noted that Putin appeared 'a different man. I suppose he seemed more decisive', and notes how pleased he was with the way that the conversation went: 'I really liked Putin. I liked how he reacted, how he corrected several points in the plan – everything was clear and precise ... Strictly by the law, accurately, and dryly, we were implementing the article of the Russian constitution concerning the transfer of power'.[145] Putin would be acting president until pre-term elections were held within the mandated three months.

In his speech on 31 December, first broadcast at noon Moscow time and repeated hourly thereafter, Yeltsin spoke of his desire to have established the precedent of the 'civilised voluntary transfer of power' after the presidential elections set for June 2000; but 'Nevertheless, I have taken another decision. I am resigning'. There was now no danger of Russia returning to the past, and thus, Yeltsin argued, 'I have achieved the main task of my life' and he did not want to impede the smooth transition to a new generation of politicians. There was 'No reason to hang on to power when the country had a strong person worthy of becoming president'. He also asked for forgiveness: 'Not all our dreams came to fulfilment ... we thought we could jump from the grey, stagnatory totalitarian past to a light, rich and civilised future in one leap. I believed that myself ... But it took more than one jump'. He stressed that he was not resigning for health reasons. After the speech the nuclear suitcase was passed to Putin and, as a last gesture on leaving the Kremlin, he gave Putin the pen with which he had signed so many decrees and laws and said 'Take care of Russia'.[146]

Yeltsin's resignation broke the Soviet tradition of leaving office feet first, but it still remains a mystery. On the surface, the version presented by Yeltsin does make sense. The Duma elections had created a solid pro-government bloc in parliament and strengthened the position of the Kremlin's designated successor, Putin, while weakening all main competitors. Yeltsin had achieved his goal of creating a political conjuncture that allowed him to leave the political scene without fear for himself or for his political achievements. It was also clear that Yeltsin had been rapidly losing his physical powers, and thus his explicit statement that he was not resigning on health grounds reflected only his pride. There remain suggestions, however, that Yeltsin's resignation was not entirely his personal choice. Was he pushed by powerful figures in the Kremlin, seeking to capitalise on Putin's popularity and alarmed by Yeltsin's physical and mental deterioration? Equally alarming was the continuation of the investigation into various corruption charges swirling around the Yeltsin family, above all those associated with the Mabatex construction company that had spent some half a billion dollars on the refurbishment of the Kremlin halls. Borodin, in charge of the Kremlin property management department, allegedly siphoned some of the money into his pockets and that of Yeltsin's blood family. Did the 'men in grey suits' suggest to Yeltsin that it would be in the best interests of his family and himself to resign and accept the generous terms of the settlement or face a very uncertain future? Putin's first move, indeed, as acting president on 31 December was to sign a decree granting Yeltsin and future Russian presidents immunity from criminal prosecution, arrest, search or interrogation. The former president was entitled to 75 per cent of his monthly salary, state protection for himself and his family, and access to VIP lounges in Russia's airports, railway stations, ports and airports.[147]

While the interests of the country may have been served by Yeltsin's premature exit, democracy was not best served by the timing. As Yeltsin himself admitted in his resignation speech, his premature exit meant that Russia would not see one democratically elected leader transfer power to another in direct accordance with the stipulations laid down in the constitution. Instead, there was an attempt to pre-empt the choice of the voters by transferring power to a regime nominee for whom the most benign political environment had been established. Fearing that Putin's popularity would begin to wane if the elections were held at the stipulated time in June, they moved the elections forward to March. For the philosopher and writer Alexander Zinoviev, the whole business was little more than a 'political coup', insisting that 'there was no reason for Yeltsin to leave his presidential post just a few months before official elections'.[148] In a sad reminder of the way that life imitates art, the words of the popular anecdote come to mind: question, 'What is democracy in Russia?'; answer, 'Yeltsin's right to nominate his successor'. Even this is perhaps not the worst outcome. As the journalist Yulia Latynina put it:

> The system of succession that will guarantee the Kremlin's victory is a very positive development. For, in circumstances where the authorities and their opposition are equally corrupt, a corrupt regime based on succession is preferable to a revolutionary corrupt regime, whose ascension to the throne is accompanied by the hollow grunting of pigs rushing to the trough – and who, amid the cries of 'bribe-takers to jail', make the same pie all over again.[149]

According to Kovalev, the Kremlin simply selected Putin to become Russia's leader and then manipulated the political process to ensure that the voters formally elected him: 'Putin is the creation of a closed and non-transparent political system. The procedure of the elections simply rubber-stamped a decision that had already been taken by behind-the-scenes plotters. That is all'.[150] The war in Chechnya was used to rally society around the designated heir, although this was a high-risk strategy since there was the obvious danger that this could rebound against the Kremlin 'selectorate' itself. The first Chechen war had turned out to be deeply unpopular, and there was great danger for Putin in yoking his political fortunes to the renewal of war, however great the provocation.[151] In fact, Putin's victory represented far more than the manipulations of the Kremlin or the temporary advantage accruing from the pursuit of what was perceived to be a tragically necessary war. For good or ill, it reflected the nature and desires of the Russian people:[152] in looking at Putin, they saw themselves.

The 26 March 2000 presidential election

There still had to be an election, however, to legitimate the choice. The physical contrast between Putin and Yeltsin could hardly be stronger: one in the prime of life, physically in top shape, logical and calculating; while the other had a towering presence but was in physical decline, more spontaneous and intuitive. The choice had been made for a change of generations in a context in which all strong characters who could overshadow Yeltsin personally had been marginalised. This meant that by the time that the succession became an urgent issue, there were few politicians of significant stature who were credible candidates for the presidency. The question, moreover, is not just one of personalities but also concerns the nature of the system. Although Yeltsin throughout his leadership remained remarkably consistent in his broad strategic goals, the day-to-day management of affairs was erratic and shaped by Byzantine struggles between court politicians. These two factors – the lack of credible alternatives in the reform camp and the tactical irresponsibility of the Yeltsinite elite – facilitated Putin's path to power. From the first days of his appointment as prime minister it was clear that a leader had emerged who was ready, if not willing, to take responsibility for the fate of the country. Putin was far more than 'A political myth created by specialists in PR'.[153] Medvedev quotes Georgy Plekhanov's well-known thesis about the role of personality in history: when social needs and national interests cannot be met without the emergence of a hero, someone who sees further than others and acts as the crystallisation of the needs of the epoch, then such a hero usually appears.[154] In Putin's case, the need was 'to put an end to the time of troubles (*smuty*) and the transitional period, which had already lasted ten years'.[155]

   While in 1996 the contest polarised around Yeltsin and his veteran opponent Gennady Zyuganov, the head of the main opposition party, the CPRF, and represented a plebiscite on the continuation of reforms, by the time of the 2000 presidential elections such a primitive (even though politically highly effective) bipolarity was a thing of the past. The law on presidential elections, signed by Yeltsin before he resigned, stipulated that candidates had to collect 500,000 signatures (one million in normal circumstances), a requirement that thinned the field somewhat. Candidates also had to provide detailed financial information about themselves, their spouses and children. Eleven candidates cleared the hurdles to enter the race, but if none won more than 50 per cent of the vote in the first round then a second run-off election between the two top candidates would be held three weeks later. Given Putin's strong support right across the political spectrum, it was clear that a high turnout would benefit him. The worst scenario as far as he was concerned was that complacency over the certainty of victory would keep voters at home and for turnout to fall below 50 per cent (in which case the election would have been declared invalid and a rerun held four months later). The rather passionless campaign threatened precisely this outcome.

Putin's campaign was managed by the deputy head of the presidential administration (on leave), Dmitry Medvedev, who had been Putin's assistant throughout the Sobchak years. Other members of the presidential staff also helped: Alexander Abramov took responsibility for relations with the regions; Vladislav Surkov dealt with relations with parliament; and amongst the many from Yeltsin's old team was Igor Shabdurasulov. Numerous political consulting firms were hired, notably Gleb Pavlovsky's Foundation for Effective Politics.

A number of prominent politicians pulled out of the race even before it had begun. Notable in this respect was Primakov, the veteran Soviet-era politician who as prime minister had reinvented himself as a politician free from the corruption swirling round the presidency, and thus had emerged as a popular alternative. Equally Luzhkov, the charismatic mayor of Moscow, decided that it would not be wise to challenge the power of the Kremlin. This left a rather diminished field. No Russian election would be complete without Vladimir Zhirinovsky, the head of the misnamed Liberal Democratic Party of Russia (LDPR), and although initially disqualified by the Central Electoral Commission (CEC) he was later reinstated by the Supreme Court. Putin's main rival, however, was Zyuganov, although it was clear that some of the communist vote was drifting to Putin. Even the candidate Aman Tuleev, governor of the Kemerovo region, who had stood down in the 1996 election in favour of Zyuganov, stated that in these elections he would throw his support behind Putin in the second round as a man of 'higher qualities' than Zyuganov, particularly in areas such 'as professionalism, statehood, power and personality'.[156] Another serious candidate was Grigory Yavlinsky at the head of the liberal party Yabloko. This group had crossed the 5 per cent representation threshold in the December 1999 parliamentary elections but with a decreased vote, and now Yavlinsky's image of permanent opposition and increasingly mystical abstraction did him little good in the campaign.

Most of the other contenders were 'vanity' candidates in one way or another. The former prosecutor general Yury Skuratov, who had been dismissed by Yeltsin (although only after three refusals by the upper house of parliament, the Federation Council) for pursuing corruption investigations with perhaps too much vigour in 1999, sought to draw attention to corruption and the injustice of the case against him. The patriotic film director Stanislav Govorukhin sought to rally the people to the idea of a great Russia. Samara governor Konstantin Titov represented the liberal part of the Russian political spectrum. Despite talk the previous year that the regions were storming the Kremlin through various electoral blocs, Titov ended up the only serious regional leader to withstand the fire of the parliamentary election with his reputation intact. He remained, however tenuously, the only real candidate for the role of leader of the regions.[157] He was, however, unable even to gain the undivided support of his own party, with a number of groups within the SPS alliance declaring in favour of Putin.[158] Other candidates were the Chechen businessman Umar Dzhabrailov (the part owner of the Slavyanskaya Radisson Hotel implicated in the controversy surrounding the murder of the American businessman Paul Tatum, and later owner of the giant Rossiya hotel), Alexei Podberezkin at the head of the Spiritual Heritage organisation and former Zyuganov guru, and Ella Pamfilova, former minister for social affairs and head of the Movement for Civil Dignity. The former deputy head of the presidential administration, Yevgeny Savostyanov, pulled out at the last minute.

The election was perhaps most notable for who did not stand. We have noted that Primakov, who had appeared unstoppable a mere six months earlier, had seen his fortunes sink rapidly, while Luzhkov by the summer of 1999 had intimated that he would step out of the presidential contest. Lebed, once the great hope of authoritarian reformers, had decamped to Krasnoyarsk *krai* where, as governor from 1998, he faced a host of problems that ruled him out as a serious presidential contender. His death in a helicopter crash on 28 April 2002 means that we shall never know whether he would have been able to become a De Gaulle, a marginalised leader returning in triumph to the centre of political power. A possible future challenger to Putin had gone. As the Putin bandwagon gathered speed Luzhkov provided one of the most important endorsements for the new leader. On 15 March 2000 Luzhkov gave Fatherland's official blessing to Putin's campaign. Although Fatherland set a number of conditions, above all the preservation of democratic freedoms, an end to the political and economic ascendancy of the oligarchs, strengthening the state, and commitment to improving conditions in the social sphere, science and culture, these were not 'conditions' in any real sense since the endorsement preceded agreement on their acceptance and were thus designed to save face. Thus, one of the most important potential competitors for the presidency succumbed to the Putin effect.

The most difficult thing for most candidates was that Putin's own programme, in so far as he had one, encompassed almost every conceivable shade of opinion and thus allowed no space for a coherent alternative. As Luzhkov put it following the congress of Unity in late February, Putin's address on that occasion contained 'quotes, nearly intact', from Fatherland's documents.[159] Putin, moreover, enjoyed the advantages of incumbency of not only one post but two, as acting president and prime minister, and thus he was far from an ordinary candidate. These 'asymmetries' in the campaign were much remarked upon and led to fears that Putin harboured dictatorial ambitions. In addition, Putin appeared reluctant to provide details about his programme. Meeting with students on 8 February 2000 he stated that he would not hurry to publicise his election platform, lest it 'comes under attack'. He noted that 'As soon as you make it public, they will start gnawing at it and tearing it to pieces'.[160] This was certainly an interesting approach to campaigning in a democratic election.

His *Open Letter by Vladimir Putin to the Russian Voters*, published on 25 February 2000, was the closest Putin came to an election manifesto. He noted 'Our first and most important problem is the weakening of will. The loss of state will and persistence in completing things that have been started. Vacillation, dithering, the habit of putting off the hardest tasks for later'.[161] The letter contained important general principles about the need to improve the economy and people's living conditions, but was short on specific policies. The Centre for Strategic Studies, the think tank headed by Putin's colleague from St Petersburg, German Gref, that Putin had asked to produce a long-term programme for Russian development, had not yet been able to produce a detailed programme. Above all, with such a towering pre-eminence enjoyed by Putin and the weakness of all the other candidates, there was a danger of over-confidence and deafness to the views of others. The problem is not unique to Russia but can take particularly morbid forms here since the checks and balances against the abuse of power are so weak.

One factor in Putin's victory should be stressed: Putin's abilities as an image-maker. In Chapter 2 we shall discuss his *Russia at the Turn of the Millennium*, published in the last days of 1999 outlining his views on the Soviet past and his hopes for the Russian future. This was joined in early 2000 by the publication in book form of a series of interviews conducted over several days by the journalist Natalya Gevorkyan and her colleagues in one of Putin's state dachas.[162] They showed Putin's human side and offered an appealing updating of the log cabin to White House motif, although in this case it was from communal apartment to the Kremlin. The dynamic sense of rapid upward social mobility achieved through one's own efforts, aided admittedly by a great deal of luck and, latterly, official sponsorship, struck a chord in Russia's long-suffering population. The book showed Putin as a man surrounded by a loving family, with his wife Lyudmila and two daughters, and all the trials and tribulations attending the collapse of the Soviet empire when serving as a KGB officer in Dresden. Clearly, passages had been deleted or amended by the Kremlin minders, and Putin's image was carefully moulded. Putin was one of the new breed of politicians of that time, such as Bill Clinton in America and Tony Blair in Britain, for whom news management often acted as the substitute for policy, and for whom outcomes are shrouded in a dense fog of spin and show. Popularity for these 'post-modern' politicians is nurtured and tended like a delicate plant, with focus groups, private polling, 'triangulation' and the manipulation of information.

While the overall result (see Table 1.2) may have been a foregone conclusion there were at least three interesting subordinate outcomes. The first was

Table 1.2 Presidential election 26 March 2000

Candidate	Votes	Percentage (%)
1. Vladimir Putin	39,740,434	52.94
2. Gennady Zyuganov	21,928,471	29.21
3. Grigory Yavlinsky	4,351,452	5.80
4. Aman Tuleev	2,217,361	2.95
5. Vladimir Zhirinovsky	2,026,513	2.70
6. Konstantin Titov	1,107,269	1.47
7. Ella Pamfilova	758,966	1.01
8. Stanislav Govorukhin	328,723	0.44
9. Yury Skuratov	319,263	0.42
10. Alexei Pokberezkin	98,175	0.13
11. Umar Dzhabrailov	78,498	0.10
Against all	1,414,648	1.88

Sources: *Vestnik Tsentral'noi izbiratel'noi kommissii Rossiiskoi Federatsii*, No. 13 (103), 2000, pp. 63–5; *Rossiiskaya gazeta*, 7 April 2000, p. 3; The full results are in *Vestnik Tsentral'noi izbiratel'noi kommissii Rossiiskoi Federatsii*, No. 16 (106), 2000.

Notes:
The percentages are calculated from the total vote. Turnout: 75,181,071 (68.74 %); registered voters: 109,372,046; total valid ballots: 75,070,776.

the size of Putin's majority, and above all whether he would be able to win on the first round. Most polls suggested that this would be possible, and in the event was achieved, although with only a small margin above 50 per cent. An outright win endowed Putin's presidency with the sort of legitimacy that Yeltsin had enjoyed following his first-round victory in June 1991, but the small margin somewhat tempered the triumph. The second aspect was the degree to which this was a 'clean' election. There have been allegations that in some regions, for example Saratov,[163] votes were transferred from other candidates to Putin, while in Dagestan over half a million votes may have been added to Putin's total,[164] while in many places the bank of 'against all' votes may have been raided to Putin's advantage.[165] An oddity that has never been adequately explained is how the total electorate was able to rise in three months from 108.072 million eligible to vote in the Duma elections of December 1999 to the 109,372,046 announced for the presidential elections, and this at a time of sharp population decline and with no baby bulge recorded 18 years earlier (December 1981 to March 1982).[166]

The third interesting question about the outcome was whether the main challengers, Zyuganov and Yavlinsky, would be able to hold on to their electorates and leadership. Total failure would have undermined Zyuganov's claim to leadership of the left. Already Tuleev, during the campaign, as we have seen, was openly contemptuous of Zyuganov's leadership. In the event, Zyuganov's strong showing (29.2 per cent), improving on his party's performance (24.3 per cent) in the December 1999 Duma elections, reinforced his leadership of the communist opposition. However, his vote did not match the 32 per cent he received in the first round of the 1996 elections, let alone the 40 per cent he won in the run-off, and thus suggested a secular decline in the communist vote that condemned him forever to second place. Only two-thirds of the electorate that had voted for the CPRF in December 1999 cast their votes for Zyuganov in March, while a fifth voted for Putin. In particular, he lost ground in traditional communist strongholds. In the second round in 1996 Zyuganov came first in 32 of Russia's 89 regions, whereas in 2000 Putin came first in all but five regions. In Kemerovo Tuleev won handsomely, leaving Zyuganov victor in only four (the republics of Adygeia, Chechnya, Altai and Bryansk *oblast*). As for Yavlinsky, his leadership of the liberals had been challenged by Titov, calling on him to withdraw from the race, while Stepashin, although a member of Yabloko, openly declared his support for Putin. Despite fighting his best electoral campaign by far, Yavlinsky emerged with a reduced vote in comparison with 1996 (5.8 per cent as opposed to 7.3 per cent) and found his position as the putative leader of the democratic camp much weakened. Coming third in his home region of Samara, trailing behind Putin and Zyuganov with only 20 per cent of the regional vote, Titov resigned as governor soon after the election, but was then 'persuaded' by a mass upsurge of popular support to stand again in rescheduled gubernatorial elections.

It is clear that Putin did have a solid political base. Surveys during the Duma election revealed that the majority of SPS voters supported Putin for president; 'supporters of the right saw Putin as their natural ally', and thus the SPS leadership's alliance with Putin was more than a political calculation but reflected the aspirations of SPS voters themselves.[167] The SPS leaders, moreover (and in particular Chubais), saw in Putin a powerful ally who could strengthen their position. The SPS strategy of support for Putin, including his controversial policy in Chechnya, reflected the dilemma of the liberals throughout the era of post-communism in Russia: lacking a hegemonic social and electoral base of their own, they sought to use the presidency as an instrument to pursue their goals. Although not as prominent as in 1996, Chubais provided critical support for Putin's presidential bid.

Although Putin emerged in the first round with the level of support that Yeltsin had achieved in the second round in 1996 (53.8 per cent), they were drawing on somewhat different constituencies. Putin was able to win greater support from rural areas that had formerly been the bedrock of the communist vote, but he fared worse in the city of Moscow, winning only 46 per cent of the vote compared to Yeltsin's first round 61 per cent and second round 74 per cent in 1996.[168] In his hometown of St Petersburg, however, Putin romped to victory with 62.4 per cent of the vote. While the dichotomy between a 'red belt' (a swathe of regions in central and south Russia that had traditionally voted for the communists) and the rest had been maintained in 1996, by 2000 it had eroded to the extent that Putin could win in the traditional heartland red belt region of Krasnodar *krai*. If in the 1996 election 60 per cent of the military vote in the first round went to Alexander Lebed, and in the second round half went to Zyuganov, in 2000 about 70 per cent went to Putin.[169] He also gained the support of Russian citizens with the right to vote abroad. In Ukraine there were 36,000 registered Russian voters, a large proportion of them in the Crimea. Of the 20,631 people voting here, 17,820 (86.3 per cent) voted for Putin and only 1,321 (6.3 per cent) for Zyuganov, and in districts where only Black Sea Fleet personnel were registered, Putin's vote was slightly higher at 88.8 per cent, compared to only 4.9 per cent for Zyuganov.[170] The relative uniformity of Putin's support across Russia reflected the success of his strategy of appealing to all classes, social forces and ends of the political spectrum. It is clear that Putin's constituency was a broad one.

Surprisingly enough, in the context of the Chechen war, is the extent to which Putin drew support from the liberal wing of the electorate: the young, educated and economically successful.[171] Putin's electoral and political base was broad, and certainly did not depend on the fate of the war in Chechnya alone. While the war was certainly used by Putin and his campaign managers to demonstrate his qualities as a resolute and committed leader, Putin garnered far more support than that generated by the war alone. As Henry E. Hale put it, 'Russians clearly want a strong leader, capable of bringing order to their tragically unpredictable lives'.[172] Russians certainly wanted a strong and not corrupt leader, but they also wanted a democratic one.[173] Polls on the question of whether people preferred 'order', even if it necessitated some infringements on democracy, had been conducted since 1992, and some 70–80 per cent consistently considered order the priority.[174] When the question was posed differently, however, a strong majority also favoured the retention of democratic freedoms.[175] In this context, the idea of a 'strong state' has to be treated with caution: the only effective way forwards was for it to be both ordered *and* democratic.

At least some of Putin's popularity was derived from the post that he occupied rather than from the policies that he pursued. It also built on Yeltsin's support base, a remarkably consistent and stable electorate committed to Yeltsin's programme of market reform and liberal internationalism, if perhaps committed with rather less enthusiasm to Yeltsin personally. Yeltsin's winning coalition remained remarkably consistent over the years. In the June 1991 presidential election he received 45.5 million votes, in the April 1993 referendum his policies were endorsed by 36.5 million, and in the second round of the 1996 presidential elections he received 40.2 million votes. As Brudny puts it, 'a solid and stable majority of Russian voters rejected communist and virulent nationalist appeals to end the economic and political reforms enacted during Yeltsin's era despite economic dislocation, an increase in crime, and the blatant corruption which accompanied them'.[176]

Putin had refused to publish a detailed programme during the campaign, and held himself above the fray, acting as if he was not a candidate himself. In his press conference on election night (the first of the entire campaign) Putin declared that he considered campaigning an 'absolutely dishonest business', because 'you always have to promise more than your rivals, in order to appear more successful. And I couldn't imagine myself promising something, knowing that the promises could not be kept'. He insisted that he had kept himself aloof because 'it freed me from the necessity of misleading enormous masses of people', and he took pride in not reducing his candidacy to the level of that of his opponents.[177] Thus the whole electoral process was dismissed as somehow not worthy of an honest leader; probably correct, but rather naïve in a democratic polity. Putin did, however, praise the opposition politicians who, in his opinion, took a constructive position regarding his policy in Chechnya, or who supported him in the elections. He singled out in particular Zyuganov, Luzhkov and Primakov – the three people who had been credible competitors for the post of president. This was quintessential Putin, and reflects the code of honour in judo where the hand of friendship is extended to the defeated rival.

Others were rather less impressed. The Yabloko deputy, Sergei Mitrokhin, took a sceptical approach to the elections: 'One way or another, we will not be having elections in March but a plebiscite on an already designated successor'.[178] Yeltsin as we have seen had already suggested as much in his resignation speech. The reasons for Putin's victory, however, derived not simply from manipulation and the creation of the most benign environment possible for anointment through the ballot box. He represented the widespread yearning for stability in a society traumatised by disintegration and decline. In that context, Putin's 'anti-political' approach to the election, in which he waged a 'non-campaign', made sense.[179] A greater danger, however, lurked behind this approach, and that was the repudiation of politics itself as the mode of adjudication between interests and concerns in society. An anti-political approach can easily slip into populism, where the single will of society is represented by the charismatic leader without the necessity of mediating political institutions. Depoliticisation also allows administrative rationality to subvert the clash of views and political pluralism. This was certainly dangerous in conditions where Russia's 1993 constitution rendered the president virtually an 'elected tsar'.[180]

Conclusion

By any standards Putin's meteoric rise was astonishing. He seemed to be the living embodiment of the way that education acts as an escalator of social mobility. At the same time, his career in the KGB reflected both the crisis and opportunities in the late Soviet system. This was a time of growing disenchantment with the idea of communism, the decay of public administration as time-servers ruled the roost at home, and abroad the image of the Soviet Union was damaged by foreign adventures that culminated with the invasion of Afghanistan in December 1979. For an ambitious person like Putin, a career in the KGB, an organisation that enjoyed the reputation of being one of the few untarnished bodies remaining, offered a way out. The degree to which Putin took into account the horrors that the KGB's predecessor

2 Ideas and choices

We are a rich country of poor people. And this is an intolerable situation.

Vladimir Putin[1]

We noted in the Introduction that choices made in the first years of the century have proved decisive. The pattern, however, was modified with the launching of Gorbachev's *perestroika* at the end of the last century. *Perestroika* was accompanied by an intense debate over choices, including such fundamental questions as the balance to be drawn between the plan and the market, liberal pluralism and socialist values, and Party direction and democracy, and this was reflected in numerous works of the time.[2] At the same time, a powerful current argued precisely that Russia had no choice except to rejoin the West on the basis of shared democratic and market values.[3] The tension between evolutionary and morphological approaches was evident. The emergence of Russia as an independent state in December 1991 only exacerbated the debate between those who accepted this relative lack of choice and the nationalists, leftists and even some liberals (various brands of liberal statists and liberal patriots) who insisted that Russia must find its own path. Yeltsin's choice in the 1990s for Russia to take the path of liberal democracy, neo-liberal capitalism and international integration was contested. It was against this background of a country divided over its form of social organisation and its role in the world that Putin came to power. The early twenty-first century, like so many times before, was for Russia yet another liminal period, a time when many options seemed open and in which the country's leadership was well aware of the epochal choices facing them. In this chapter we shall examine the ideas and debates that attended Putin's coming to power, beginning with some divergent views of what Putin represented and a brief discussion of the nature of the system that he inherited.

Who is Mister Putin?

This was a question raised by Trudy Rubin of the *Philadelphia Enquirer* at the Davos economic forum in late January 2000,[4] and it was taken up with gusto by the media. There are at least three elements to the question. The first is denigratory – *who* is this nobody who dares to take on the office of president? A nobody, his detractors were quick to stress, who rose no higher than lieutenant-colonel in the security services, and who clearly had a shady past. For some of the intelligentsia, particularly from Moscow, there was an element of class hostility accompanied by typical metropolitan superiority: how could this boy from the tenements of St Petersburg presume to lead the country? The second is quizzical and methodological – *how* can we ascertain what Putin will do since his background is varied, and the KGB part far from open to scrutiny? He had now come to power as the nominee of a discredited president, too dependent on a small coterie of insider officials and oligarchs, and had not set out his views in a programmatic speech. The third is practical – *what* would Putin do now that he had been catapulted into power? To what extent would he be constrained by the peculiar circumstances that had conspired to take him to the presidency, or would he be able to pursue policies of his own? Although a flood of speeches and materials about his life soon appeared, there remained something hidden in his character and his leadership intentions. It was for this reason that the question posed at the head of this section sounded so insistently.[5]

Views about what Putin represented differed sharply. For Zinoviev, Putin coming to power represented 'the first serious attempt of Russia to resist americanization and globalization, which comes from the country's internal needs'. Zinoviev projected on to Putin his own hopes, but he recognised, like so many of his countrymen, that Putin had unusual characteristics: 'I have a feeling that neither the West nor the predecessor of Putin who made the appointment realized the potential of that man', and he warned that if the matter had been delayed the West could well have tried to prevent Putin from taking the office.[6] For Zinoviev the key tasks facing Putin were:

> Strengthen the basic results of the anti-communist coup of the Gorbachev–Yeltsin period, complete the formation of a post-Soviet social organism, overcome the glaring defects of the Yeltsin regime, normalise the living conditions of the Russian population in the framework of the new social organism, and normalise the position of post-Soviet Russia in the global community.[7]

Alexander Solzhenitsyn adopted a cautious view, distinguishing between Putin's platform and his personality. According to him, 'Putin's platform comes from Yeltsin and his entourage, the corrupt bureaucrats, the financial magnates. They are united by one great fear: that people will take from them everything they have stolen, that their crimes will be investigated and that they will be sent to jail'. Solzhenitsyn excoriated Putin's first official act as interim president that granted Yeltsin and his family immunity from prosecution. As for Putin's personality, Solzhenitsyn argued that 'He is in many ways a puzzle. We don't know how he will act as president. He stands at a crossroads. Either he can give in to his sponsors and lead the country inevitably to its ruin – and him with it – or he can break with clan loyalty and pursue his own policies'.[8] Either Putin would strike out on his own and repudiate Yeltsin and his legacy, or he would be swallowed up by the corruption and self-seeking greed of the Yeltsinite clan. In the event, Putin did neither. He did not openly repudiate the grouping that had brought him to power, but neither did he become their instrument. Instead, he navigated a difficult path in which his own policies gradually took shape within the framework of the system he inherited.

The dual nature of Putin's personality and leadership was much commented upon. An editorial in *The Guardian* noted that: 'Our pre-election question, "who is Vladimir Putin?", may now be confidently answered. It transpires that he is two quite different people wrapped into one'.[9] One face, allegedly, would engage with the West to create a business-friendly democracy committed to open markets, while the second face was turned inwards and revealed an uglier aspect, seeking to impose discipline and order by authoritarian means. There are elements of truth in this portrait, but the division is not so much a contrast between domestic and foreign policy but runs through all of Putin's policies simultaneously. This contrast was not just a facet of Putin's personality but reflected the nature of the system that he inherited. The order that Putin tried to install was not antithetical to democracy but sought to preserve the autonomy of the regime while calling for respect for law and observance of the constitution.

The highly concentrated nature of Russian politics meant that much depended on Putin's personal choices. To characterise these we can identify two elements in his political identity that coexisted uncomfortably. The first was his *neo-Soviet* facet, his nurturing in the late Soviet years when he imbibed the values, with all their contradictions, of the period, and then his 15 years of service in the Soviet intelligence agency. This neo-Sovietism is at odds with his *post-Soviet* identity, marking an unequivocal break not only with communist ideology (there appears to have been not much of that even in his neo-Soviet characteristics), but also in attitudes towards power, property and Russia's status in the world. Putin, like the philosopher Nikolai Berdyaev, considered the October 1917 revolution as the only way of preserving the country 'in those circumstances', although he condemned the Bolsheviks for becoming excessively ideologised and rabid centralisers.[10] Putin's post-Sovietism recognises not only that the Soviet Union was a failed utopian experiment (this is accepted even within the framework of his neo-Sovietism), but also accepts that this failure was rooted not only in the inadequacies of communist ideology but also in Russia's typically exaggerated views of its abilities, capacities and importance.

Putin's neo-Soviet face sought to restore dignity to the past and tended towards administrative methods rather than fully endorsing political pluralism and the clash of views. This was balanced by Putin's post-Soviet stance, imbibed as a student in the 1970s and probably reinforced by his years in Germany where he saw the old system collapse, then reinforced by his career as Sobchak's deputy in St Petersburg. Putin helped turn the city towards capitalism when he promoted international economic integration. His background as a denizen of this city also disposed him to a Western orientation. These two faces allowed Putin within the space of a few weeks to inaugurate a plaque in the Lubyanka honouring Andropov, the head of the KGB from 1967–82, and then to place flowers at the grave of Andrei Sakharov, one of the most outstanding liberal dissidents and victim of Andropov's 'second Cold War' of 1979–82. Mommsen reflects the contradictions in her evocatively titled article 'The Sphinx in the Kremlin',[11] and like Russia's state symbol, the two-headed eagle that looks both East and West, Putin looks both backwards and forwards.

The dualism characteristic of Putin's thinking is reflected in the idea of 'the dictatorship of law' (see also Chapter 5), a concept that he used during his election campaign in February 2000:

> In a non-law-governed (i.e. weak) state the individual is defenceless and not free. *The stronger the state, the freer the individual*. In a democracy, your and my rights are limited only by the same rights enjoyed by other people. It is on recognising this simple truth that the law is based, the law that is to be followed by all – from people in authority to the simple citizen. But democracy is the dictatorship of law – not of those placed in an official position to defend that law.[12]

The contradiction between rule *by* law and the rule *of* law can also be seen as authoritarianism versus liberalism, or statism versus pluralism. In structural terms, there was a conflict between attempts to *rationalise* the system without fundamentally changing the traditional pattern of personalised, dominant and often arbitrary leadership, or to *reorder* governance to make it genuinely more inclusive, law based and democratic. The dichotomy was one between attempts to *reconcentrate* state power, on the one hand, and the struggle to *reconstitute* it on the basis of the rule of law and the writ of the constitution, on the other.

Putin's reform project and leadership was indeed torn between these tendencies (which we shall explore later), but ultimately such an approach suggests a misleading polarity, as would any attempt to suggest a stark contrast between his authoritarian and patriotic instincts and his democratic and Westernising ideas. Later we shall see how these facets in his political identity sometimes clashed, but we shall argue that ultimately a new synthesis emerged that transcended these rather stereotypical stances. Mister Putin was more than just a product of his past and circumstances but was a dynamic political actor able to respond to new challenges and to learn from experience.

He was also a powerful, and in some senses, a charismatic leader. He emerged, as Elena Shestopal puts it, as 'not a living person but some sort of sacred figure, a symbol, a myth'. She notes that Putin is 'an interesting political type. He genuinely believes in European ideals, and is oriented towards European models of culture, politics and democracy. But at the same time he is a very Russian type'.[13] In a Kremlin-sponsored work Aleksei Chadaev examined Putin's ideological doctrine, arguing that his public policy had three main elements: democracy, as a way of developing the free individual; sovereignty, to develop a free nation; and material well-being, the attempt to improve social and economic welfare as the basis of the two other principles.[14] The book reflected Surkov's view that 'For democratic society to withstand disintegration and maintain solidarity and functionality, texts are absolutely necessary, texts which rule and unite people. A holy scripture of democracy is needed, if you like'.[15] For Chadaev, this 'scripture' in Russia's case came down to sovereignty, democracy and quality of life. Alexander Tsipko argued that 'In Putin, Russia has not only a rational, responsible, effective, competent, and certainly intelligent and sensible manager to run the company known as Russia; it also has a national leader with a true commitment, heart and soul, to the progress of national history'.[16] For his opponents, it was precisely Putin's attempts to run Russia as some sort of corporation that undermined political pluralism, entrepreneurialism and social activism.

This was reflected in Putin's academic works of the late 1990s. As we have seen, Putin defended his doctoral (*Kandidat*) dissertation in June 1997 at the St Petersburg Mining Institute. In 1998 he wrote an article, published the following year, summarising and extending his views on Russia's economic development. He argued that Russia would have to grow at twice the rate of the West to reduce 'Russia's lag behind the developed countries in terms of GDP per capita'. The basis for such growth would be the 'extraction, processing and exploitation of mineral raw material resources' above all oil and gas, of which Russia had abundant resources. To achieve this Russia would have to create vertically integrated financial–industrial corporations 'capable of competing on equal terms with Western multinational corporations'. The Soviet legacy meant that it was unlikely that Russia would be able to create competitive companies without state support. The state would also be required to defend the 'interests of society as a whole' and to act as the arbiter between competing economic interests and to obstruct the 'monopolistic behaviour' that would otherwise predominate and 'inhibits innovation'. Left to themselves, according to Putin, private businesses would not innovate.[17] This view runs contrary to much classical microeconomic theory, but provides some theoretical basis for the later assault against the Yukos oil company.[18] Market mechanisms would be used, but they would be constrained by strategic guidance by the state. As Putin put it, 'The state must regulate the extractive complex using purely market methods, and in this regard the state must assist the development of processing industries based on the extractive complex'.[19]

While state dominance of the energy sector may have some rationale, especially in circumstances of high demand and the commensurate high prices, this model was hardly likely to be effective in the manufacturing and service sectors. The article reflected a distrust of private enterprise, but at the same time Putin was unequivocal about the need for free market capitalism to develop in Russia. As in the political sphere, this was a model for modernisation from above. Putin's political personality was as full of contradictions as his policies, but ultimately there was a common thread to his actions – the attempt to modernise Russia, but to do that in a Russian way. The priority was sovereignty and security, with Russia moving as a stately caravan ignoring the views of 'ill-wishers' or those who 'bark'.[20] We can describe his programme as one of national democracy, where the democratic imperative is tempered by the government's perception of national developmental and security concerns. Putin's ideology can be labelled a type of strategic eclecticism, applying liberal principles in the economy, statism in domestic policy, and great power nationalism (*derzhavnost'*) in foreign policy. We shall have more to say about Putin's version of national democracy later.

Normality, normalcy and normalisation

Normality is always relative, and when we use the term the intention is not to suggest that somewhere (other than in the realm of theology) there is some perfectly normal state. Our measure of normality is derived from Russia's own traditional sense (expressed most forcibly by Peter the Great) that its development has in some ways been 'deviant' from a standard set in Western Europe, and in recent times more broadly in 'the West'. We are also well aware that the standard of normality set in the West is deeply problematic; after all, Emile Durkheim was convinced that the West European pattern of development over the last half millennium has been deeply morbid, if not pathological. At the same time, the development of a set of liberal rights, democratic methods, the rule of law and the individual right to economic self-affirmation (including property rights), as codified in the European Convention on Human Rights and subsequent protocols, defines a normality that, while failing to achieve medieval or Marxist visions of the unity of the social, political and religious life, do offer a viable model of civilisation. It is to this 'normal' civilisation that Russia under Putin aspired. As Maly puts it, 'For the majority of Russians today "normality" is defined on a scale borrowed from the West'.[21] As Voltaire noted, however, 'It is dangerous to be right on a subject on which the established authorities are wrong'; and thus there is the paradoxical danger that in the contemporary world the measure of normality is set by a hegemonic system that a priori excludes the possibility of diversity and contestation, the possibility of not being 'normal'. The attempt to combine Russian specificity and universal norms, evolutionary and morphological approaches, in a distinctive 'Russian way' under Putin, characterised in the later years of his leadership as 'sovereign democracy', was labelled once again as deviant, and his administration was vilified by Western analysts and much of the media in yet another outbreak of the deep-seated Russophobia that has characterised the West since the early nineteenth century.

The return to normality

Reform under Putin moved away from systemic transformation towards system management. Politics finally became 'normal', in the sense that larger constitutional questions over the shape of the polity gave way to governmental management of mundane policy questions. The period of constitutional politics, predicted by Dahrendorf to last 'at least six months',[22] in Russia effectively lasted about a decade but now gave way to the hard work of 'normal politics'.[23] The question of regime type, at least for the time being, has been resolved and the basic choices between institutions of government have been decided. Schumpeter argued that a successful transition occurs when 'abnormality is no longer the central feature of political life; that is, when actors have settled on and obey a set of more or less explicit rules'.[24] For the authors of a landmark study of democratisation, 'normality, in other words, becomes a major characteristic of political life when those active in politics come to expect each other to play according to the rules – and the ensemble of these rules is what we mean by a regime'.[25] Russia under Putin finally had a chance to move away, as Kaspe puts it, from its 'permanent condition of being "post" something or other'.[26] A transition is over when the initial period of uncertainty associated with regime change comes to an end, and in Russia we appear to have reached this point.

Andrei Shleifer and Daniel Treisman have provided an international political economy comparative context for contemporary Russian normality. Contrary to earlier arguments asserting that the Russian economy was value subtracting and in many respects 'virtual',[27] they argue that Russia's economic and political development is typical of a normal middle-income country, not a gangster or criminal state, and thus akin to Brazil or Mexico, and not Colombia.[28] Putin's politics cannot be understood divorced from the context of his times. A number of narratives combine, and to a degree compete, in his understanding of the world. Four of these are central.

1 The catastrophic 1990s – but we have to live with its consequences

The first provides the basis for Putin's return to normality, the fear that Russia in the 1990s came close to sacrificing the state to criminal and oligarchical interests. Russian democracy in the 1990s is associated with decline, chaos and the emergence of a type of 'warlordism', with over-mighty subjects challenging the prerogatives of the state. The association of democratic freedom with national decline, chaos and a diminished world status undermined the popular legitimacy of democracy itself. As Putin stressed in his interview of 31 January 2006, while the 1990s had given the country freedom, it had also been characterised by 'defeatism'. This myth, with myth here defined as the stories a country tells itself to make sense of its own past and place in the world, is a powerful one that grips the imagination of the country as a whole, and in this Putin reflects a common view. When asked by Spanish reporters on 7 February 2006 whether strengthening the state and the vertical of power would open the door to corruption, Putin retorted that this depended on how you defined state strengthening, and that a weak state was also a fertile terrain for corruption:

> And what is state weakening? It is the inability of the state to control the implementation of the laws that are adopted, and the inability to adopt needed laws in a legitimate way. Look at the situation of the mid-1990s – oligarchical groups substitute themselves for the state, take control over parliament, promote laws that are bad for society but needed for specific financial–industrial groups, and then influence their implementation through their representatives in governmental structures . . . Thus when we speak of strengthening the state, I do not mean the strengthening of the repressive apparatus. I mean the ability of the state to adopt laws required by society and the people and the ability of the state to implement these laws.[29]

Although condemning the 1990s, Putin did not take the next logical step and dismiss democracy as damaging for Russia, although this is an argument put forward by part of Russia's intellectual elite.[30] In practice Putin built on the achievements of the 1990s, although at the same time advancing a remedial view of what his government had to do to overcome the problems created by the Soviet and early post-Soviet eras.

The refusal to reopen the question of the legality of the privatisations of the 1990s was at first interpreted as a token of Putin's pusillanimity in the face of the entrenched interests of the 'family', the combination as we have seen of powerful business people, politicians, members of the presidential administration and blood members of Yeltsin's entourage. When a reversal did take place, as in the Yukos affair, it was not so much to remedy an earlier injustice but an attempt to build a state-dominated energy sector by redistributing the spoils of the earlier era. In broader terms, Putin's administration refused to engage in another social revolution. Putin accepted that Yeltsin's 'revolution from above' laid the foundations of a market economy and established the basis of a bourgeois social class in which democracy could be rooted. Putin also accepted that a wholesale review of the corruption accompanying the earlier privatisations would be socially divisive and disruptive. Only clearly provable criminal cases, he insisted, would be investigated. Putin thus exposed himself to the charge of prosecuting those who made their fortunes in the era of wild capitalism, the so-called oligarchs, in a selective and politically biased way.

2 *The West is ours, too*

Putin remained throughout a 'Westerniser'. His condemnation of communism in the *Millennium Manifesto* of 1999 was clear: 'The main thing is that Soviet power did not make the country prosperous, the society dynamic, or the people free. We spent seven decades heading away from the main road of civilisation towards a dead end' (see Appendix, p. 324). In his Federal Assembly address of 2005 he was unequivocal: 'We are a major European nation, we have always been an integral part of Europe and share all its values and the ideals of freedom and democracy. But we will carry out this process ourselves, taking into account all our specific characteristics, and do not intend to report to anyone on the progress we make'. Thus Putin's remedial view of Russian politics was committed to overcoming not only the 'abnormal' pattern of earlier Soviet and Yeltsinite development, but also a reassertion of new forms of Russian peculiarity – the evolutionary view was tempered by a characteristic morphological insistence on separateness. What Putin was not able, or even willing, to do was to sponsor a creative reformulation of the narrative of national success that would incorporate not only the process of democracy but its spirit as well.

3 *Legitimism, para-constitutionalism and the relegitimation of state power*

The shift from systemic transformation to system management is reflected in the concept of legitimism, Putin's belief in the existing order of things and refusal to change the constitution. This was highlighted in his very first policy statements, although repeated rather less frequently thereafter. Instead, institutional development, as we shall see with the establishment of the seven federal districts, the State Council and the Public Chamber, has assumed para-constitutional forms. Although the system of federalism, as outlined in the constitution, was modified by the establishment of the districts, the change was portrayed as affecting the organisation of executive power, and thus not requiring constitutional amendment. Another case of para-constitutional change is the adoption of the law on the merging of subjects of the federation and the incorporation of new subjects. While the constitutional order in all democratic societies evolves as a result of legislative activity and changes in political practices, there comes a point when quantitative changes, to use Marxist terminology, require a qualitative readjustment of constitutional doctrine. Changes to presidential terms or making the government and prime minister directly responsible to a parliamentary majority would probably fall into this category.

Emerging from the above is Putin's relegitimisation of state power. We have noted his view of the 1990s as a period of collapse and state weakness, and he now not only reasserted the state's prerogatives, especially in relations with regional leaders and big business, but he also sought to imbue the state with the mystique of power and as the bearer of the nation's destiny. In economics, as we shall see, a type of state corporatist capitalism emerged, while the 'étatist temptation' began to stifle social initiatives and party life, accompanied by the glorification of the security services.[31] The veneration of the state as the bearer of some mystical idea of national essence has a long tradition in Russia, but in a country where democratic institutions remain weak, the shift in the view of the state as an instrument to an end undermined its development as an independent arbiter between social interests and the adjudicator of rules.

4 Putin as an anti-revolutionary – towards bourgeois normality

Putin repeatedly repudiated revolution as an effective form of achieving positive political change. Putin's leadership is 'anti-revolutionary' in its explicit renunciation of revolution and extraordinary politics, and thus can be classified as the delayed fulfilment of the promise of 1989, the anti-revolution that puts an end to the whole cycle of emancipatory revolutionism inaugurated by the universalistic radicalism of the Enlightenment.[32] The fall of communism entailed the rejection not only of a specific revolutionary ideology, but of the revolutionary method (with its violence, polarisation and destructiveness) in its entirety. This was the promise of 1989 in Eastern Europe, and it was also reflected in Russia. Already Yeltsin had argued that 'Russia was tired of revolutions. It was tired of the very word, which implies either rebellion or a social cataclysm by an unseen force and means destruction and famine', and thus the country was opposed to the idea of 'class warfare' or 'social struggle' as part of what he called his 'radical reforms'.[33] By eschewing a revolutionary transformation, both Yeltsin and Putin were to make peace with the existing social order, and thus to bring Russia's long cycle of revolution to an end.[34]

On numerous occasions Putin returned to the point and it acts as a *leitmotif* of his thinking. There may well have been an element of self-preservation involved here, because as a former agent of the previous regime's security agency he was potentially culpable, but his arguments are much more profound than this. In his *Millennium Manifesto* he noted that the communist revolutionary model of development not only had not delivered the goods, but could not have done so. In his annual address on 3 April 2001 he sought to break the vicious cycle of revolution and counter-revolution, reform and counter-reform:

> We are not afraid of change and must not avoid it. However change, whether in politics or administration, must be justified by the situation. No doubt public apprehensions and fears do not appear out of nowhere. They emerge from the long-established logic that revolution is usually followed by counter-revolution, reforms by counter-reforms and then by the search for those guilty of revolutionary excesses and by punishment, all the more so since Russia's historical experience abounds

in such cases. As I see the matter, it is high time to say firmly that this cycle has ended. Enough is enough! There will be no more revolution or counter-revolution.[35]

He then insisted that 'Russia and its people require firm and economically viable state stability and we should long ago have learnt to live according to this normal human logic'. In his question and answer session with the Russian people in December 2001 Putin once again returned to the theme: 'As one of my acquaintances said, "Russia in the past century over-fulfilled its plan for revolutions". I hope that in the twenty-first century there will be no revolutions, that things will only be positive'.[36] In an interview shown on Russian television (RTR) on 7 October 2002, his fiftieth birthday, Putin said: 'I would like to remind you that I am a lawyer and I think that one's actions should be based on law, and not revolutionary expediency'.[37] On 7 February 2006 in an interview with Spanish media he once again returned to the anti-revolutionary theme, noting that both Spain and Russia in the twentieth century had suffered 'fratricidal civil wars', and thus both countries 'know how painfully this affects the fate of a people, or the fate of concrete individuals, families'.[38]

The repudiation of war and revolution as a method represents an epistemological break of enormous proportions between Gorbachev and Putin, and reflects the gulf that separates their respective generations. If Gorbachev in power reflected the preoccupations of the *shestdesyatniki*, the children of the Twentieth Party Congress, the thaw, Khrushchev's de-Stalinisation and its associated aspirations for reform communism, then Putin, as we have noted, is a *semidesyatnik*, a product of the 1970s and Brezhnev's stagnation. Under Brezhnev a 'bourgeois' mentality took root in Soviet life, focused not so much on ownership and accumulation but on domestic and individual concerns, and this emphasis on family matters permeated Putin's thinking.

Return to 'normalcy': the end of extraordinary politics

The 'return to normalcy' was a slogan popular in the United States after the First World War and reflected the desire for peace of a nation tired of military exertions. The idea has also been applied to the period of recuperation in the USSR following victory in the Fatherland War.[39] In the Russian context today the politics of normalcy reflect a country that endured over a century of revolutionary, military and secret police depredations. The attempt to link up with the past, to restore the torn fabric of society, to draw on intellectual traditions and cultural values of yesteryear, all reflect this post-traumatic pursuit of a usable past as the grounding of the present. Putin's pragmatic approach is rooted in the explicit attempt to base Russia's politics of the twenty-first century in the repudiation of 'revolutionary' and 'shock-therapy' politics of the twentieth. He is in effect saying to the Russian people: 'The period of emergency is over. Carry on with normal lives'. Putin's identification with the politics of normalcy was one of the most potent sources of his enduring popularity.

In the twentieth century Russia endured two experiments with modernisation from above: the Soviet attempt to achieve accelerated development through the planned economy; and the neo-liberal reversion to free markets in the 1990s. While very different in character, for those at the receiving end both were traumatic. Putin tried to move Russian politics away from these 'extraordinary' times towards a routine politics that could incorporate change but was constrained by concerns for systemic stability.

Following *perestroika* and the end of what some have called the seventy-four-year period of emergency between 1917 and 1991, however, there could be no simple return to 'normalcy'. The foreign minister Andrei Kozyrev, for example, argued that there could be no 'returning to a normal economy' because Russia had never known anything other than the totalitarian distribution of resources.[40] The Russian government under Yeltsin sought to take advantage of what Leszek Balcerowicz, the finance minister and architect of Poland's economic 'shock therapy' from 1989, explicitly termed 'extraordinary politics', the moment following the fall of communism when society expects radical changes.[41] In Poland this period of high legitimacy for fundamental reform lasted some three years, whereas in Russia it barely survived a few months. The neo-liberal reforms launched by Gaidar's radical government in the first days of 1992 soon ran into bitter opposition and by mid-year had been severely modified. The extraordinariness of the Soviet period had been perpetuated in new forms by the post-communist leadership.

Although extraordinary politics of the Balcerowicz sort soon came to an end, politics in the Yeltsin years were anything but 'normal'. Following the breakdown of the first set of post-communist Russian political institutions in September–October 1993, when Yeltsin forcibly dispersed the legislature in the Russian White House, a new constitution was adopted in December 1993 that lay at the basis of the system inherited by Putin.[42] For many, however, the consolidation that took place after 1993 has not been that of the independent institutions of democracy but of an excessively powerful presidency. In the economy a distinctive hybrid system emerged that appeared to borrow the pathologies of both the planned and market systems. Despite Yeltsin's rhetorical, and in many ways genuine, commitment to market reform, the 1990s were characterised by the emergence of a hybrid economic system. In politics, sharp polarisation between 'democrats' and an eclectic communist-nationalist anti-Western group meant that elections were less about changing governments than referenda on the very nature of the system that was to be built. Politics remained axiological, in the sense that ideological issues remained in the forefront of a polarised political community.

Yeltsin's presidency remained a 'regime of transition', devoted to the systemic transformation of the society and the marginalisation of opponents. Although the aim of Yeltsin's reforms was the creation of a capitalist democracy, his methods were divisive and on occasions flouted basic democratic norms and appeared to be an inverted form of the authoritarian order that he sought to overcome. This characteristic is highlighted, for example, by Reddaway and Glinski, who subtitle their analysis of the Yeltsin years 'market Bolshevism against democracy'.[43] They stress the continuation of extraordinary measures that flouted legality and which allowed the government to position itself above the laws that it imposed on the rest of society. Despite Putin's repudiation of the ideology of extraordinary politics and condemnation of the 1990s, his governmental practices perpetuated some of its characteristics.

There are many other features of Putin's politics of normalcy that could be identified, but there is one that is perhaps the most important and the source of all the others: Putin's attempt to reconcile the various phases of Russian history, especially over the last century. Tret'yakov talks in terms of 'the attempt to restore the links of time disrupted by Yeltsin',[44] but the problem is far more far-reaching than that. In his New Year message to the Russian people on 31 December 2000 Putin noted that it had been 'a year of cheerful and tragic events' but above all had seen the emergence of 'distinct elements of stability'.[45] At a Kremlin reception a day earlier he noted that the adoption of the anthem (Chapter 8) represented 'an important indication that we have finally managed to bridge the disparity between past and present'. He added that 'one cannot be in permanent contradiction with one's own history and the destiny of one's own country'.[46] Putin sought to put an end to this 'permanent contradiction', one that some see as having been imposed on Russia at the dawn of the modern era by Peter the Great's attempts to impose modernity by unmodern means. Since then, it could be argued, Russia had been living in a type of 'permanent transition' (with transition here defined as the attempt to impose models of modernisation devised elsewhere). This long transition, Putin suggests, has now come to an end.[47] Putin has repudiated the idea of Russia as an alternative type of modernity, and to myths of unrealised alternatives in Russia's history.[48] As far as Putin is concerned, the revolution is over and it is time for Russia to start living in the present. This means a very different appreciation of historical time and developmental paths.

Normalisation: between stability and order

Putin's politics of normality and a 'return to normalcy', however, are accompanied by disturbing overtones of 'normalisation', the term used to describe the pacification of Czechoslovakia following the Soviet invasion in 1968. Putin wanted normality, but the methods employed gave rise to elements of normalisation. The concepts of 'managed' and 'guided' democracy are openly proclaimed by some of Putin's advisors as preferable to the unpredictability and disintegrative trends so evident in the 1990s. Numerous terms have been devised to describe the state of affairs in countries like

Russia where the formal institutions of democracy are vitiated by informal practices. O'Donnell's concept of 'delegative democracy',[49] Zakaria's notion of 'illiberal democracy'[50] and Diamond's idea of 'electoral democracy'[51] are among the best known. This post-communist normalisation is very different from that imposed on Czechoslovakia by Gustav Husak in the wake of the Soviet invasion, yet in certain respects the attempt to subvert the free operation of politics and the accompanying dialectic of coercion, consent and consumerism, the three 'c's of late communism, find some echoes today.

Normalisation emerges out of the social nature of Russia's 'revolution from above'. In one of the most detailed analyses of Russia's fifteen-year revolution that began in 1985, Gordon Hahn argues that the result was not democracy but an illiberal system. Instead of being a 'revolution from below' (although he notes that there had been elements of popular mobilisation), Russia had endured a 'bureaucrat-led revolution from above':

> Russia's revolution from above involved the mass cooptation and incorporation of the former Soviet party-state's institutions and apparatchiks into the new regime. These institutions and bureaucrats constrained the consolidation of democracy and the market by bringing their authoritarian political culture and statist economic culture into the new regime and state, producing to date an illiberal executive-dominated and kleptocratic and oligarchical political economy.[52]

The institutions of the state in Russia, according to Hahn, were taken over by a group of radicals led by Yeltsin, who then 'proceeded to carry out a creeping bureaucratic revolution against the central Soviet party-state machine',[53] and, it may be added, against Gorbachev's vision of a humane, socialist and reformed Soviet state. Although they are modernising, revolutions from above are liable to lead semi-authoritarian, or at best semi-democratic, systems. According to Hahn they 'produce a state with very little autonomy from the former ruling class and the most powerful economic interests left-over from the *ancien regime*, producing non-liberal, oligarchic "state capitalist" economies in which economic elites maintain close ties to government, rent-seek and foster corruption'.[54]

Elite continuity perpetuates systemic features of the old regime. The tension between stability and order was a feature of Brezhnev's rule that in the end gave way to stagnation. Stability can be defined as the short-term attempt to achieve political and social stabilisation without having resolved the underlying problems and contradictions besetting society. Thus Brezhnev refused to take the hard choices that threatened the regime's precarious political stability, and thus his stability gave way to stagnation. Stability politics are characterised by 'manual' intervention in the political process, where the administrative regime fears the spontaneous manifestation of social and political demands. Order in this context is something that arises when society, economy and political system are in some sort of equilibrium.

An ordered society is dominated by spontaneous processes, whereas in a system based on the politics of stability administrative measures tend to predominate. As Samuel Huntington noted, political order in changing societies sometimes requires the hard hand of the military or some other force that is not itself subordinate to democratic politics.[55] The attempt to insulate the regime from social forces promoted 'managed democracy'.

Putin's approach to this administrative paternalism was deeply ambivalent. On a number of occasions Putin explicitly sought to distance himself from this sort of tutelary politics. For example, in his question and answer session with the Russian people on 19 December 2002, in response to a query about how the excesses of the media could be curbed, he insisted that 'it is impossible to resolve this problem, to resolve it effectively *that is* [italics added], simply with some kind of tough administrative measures'. This was linked in his view to the fact that the old Soviet-style politics that treated the whole population as infants was no longer viable since society had matured: '... our whole society is becoming more adult'.[56] Rather than seeing politics as a cultural struggle to impose a single truth, Putin appeared to accept a more pluralistic vision of societal diversity. At the individual level Putin did nothing to repudiate the personal freedoms gained after the fall of communism. However, it proved difficult to give adequate political form and expression to this diversity. His regime frequently intervened in spheres that in a genuinely democratic society are left to the interchange of pluralistic forces to resolve, including meddling in electoral matters. There is thus an element of 'normalisation', the manual control typical of 'stability politics', in Putin's Russia.

To sum up this section, Putin's approach was characterised by the pursuit of a politics of normality but was torn by the contradictions between normality, normalcy and normalisation. The fundamental tension was between trying to achieve a genuinely *ordered* system, where democratic institutions work largely free of political constraints and are accountable to the people, and a system that tries to impose *stability* from above by managing political processes, and thus impeding the free operation of political institutions. The contradiction between order and stability is one that has deep roots in Russia. Too often a genuine political order (*Ordnungspolitik*) has been reduced to *poryadok*, the coercive imposition of stability. This was the case with Brezhnev's stagnation, a peculiar type of late Soviet politics of stability and normality that proved to be far from stable and a 'normality' that turned out to be unsustainable, hence clearly abnormal. Putin's politics were torn between the desire to create a self-sustaining system that did not require 'manual control', and the fear that such an autonomous system would spin out of control. It was not clear whether Russia's Thermidor, the post-revolutionary attempt to achieve 'normalcy', would find an adequate balance between normality (order) and normalisation (stability). The traumatic birth of Russian democracy, accompanied by a revolution from above, should not detract from the very real democratic gains achieved in a remarkably short period. After all, not only Russia bears the 'scars of transition'. France endured De Gaulle's *coup de main* in 1958, and as late as 1968 Ralf Dahrendorf had very real doubts whether democracy had sunk into German popular consciousness.[57] One of Putin's central goals was to transform the democratic capitalist project from a state of emergency into an everyday part of Russian normality. Democracy was to be 'naturalised', that is, to be made part of Russia's natural order of things. As he was to discover, however, depoliticisation was not the best way to achieve this goal.

Russia at the turn of the millennium

Before Russia can move forwards, it needs to digest the past. This was reflected in Putin's *Millennium Manifesto* to which we have referred before. Posted on the internet on 29 December 1999, the document laid out in systematic form the thinking that would underlie his presidency.[58] The document was prepared by members of Gref's Centre for Strategic Studies, but we know that Putin carefully went through the draft and added his own comments and corrections.[59] The document thus provides a genuine insight into his thinking. Two days later Yeltin announced to a surprised people that he was giving up office and transferring presidential responsibilities to the prime minister. Putin had already been informed about the planned changes, and thus knew that his message would act as a type of manifesto for his presidency.

The formal name of the missive was *Russia at the Turn of the Millennium* and was significant not only for its content but also for the form in which it was presented. By posting it on the government website before publication in the press, Putin appeared to be making a statement about technical innovation and signalling his acknowledgement of the importance of communication with the people. This was campaigning of a new sort, however, based not on the soapbox and the electoral stump, but as the elucidation of a personal revelation and its transmission to the people. This quasi-religious approach to news management would characterise Putin's later relationship with the media, and indeed his approach to politics in general. In this case it was not so much that the medium was the message, but that the message reflected the inter-relationship of the personal and the epochal.

Putin outlined not only the challenges facing Russia but also sought to characterise the nature of global transformations taking place at that time, above all the shift towards post-industrial patterns of development. Under communist rule in the twentieth century Russia had fallen far behind, Putin argued, and things had been made much worse by the drastic reforms of the 1990s when under Yeltsin the country had been wrenched from Soviet-type socio-economic development and thrown in at the deep end of capitalism. The neo-liberalism predominant in that decade repudiated any significant managerial role for the state; Russia had moved from one extreme to another. After the fall of the communist system in 1991 Russia moved from a state-dominated system to its opposite, accompanied by a reduction in its GDP of 42 per cent making the country's economy, as Putin pointed out, ten times smaller than that of the USA and five times smaller than China's.[60] The economy was characterised by low investment, labour productivity and wages, with a pitiful volume of foreign direct investment (FDI). Russia was paying the price for the distorted pattern of Soviet development, above all excessive attention to raw materials and defence industries and the neglect of information technologies and the service sector, but also for its own 'mistakes, miscalculations and lack of experience' in the transition itself.[61] However, Putin insisted, Russia had now 'embarked upon the highway that the whole of humanity is travelling'. In other words, Russia had shed the communist illusion that it had found a viable alternative modernity to that practised in the West. For Putin, there was no alternative to the market economy and democracy. Thus a whole epoch had come to an end in which Russia, like Germany earlier, had sought a distinctive *Sonderweg*. This represented a choice of fundamental significance. The essence of Putin's path was that there was no special path for Russia, as the ruins of 1945 had demonstrated for Germany, but only accommodation to the mainstream of global developments.

As for his understanding of the communist epoch in Russia, Putin argued that it 'would be a mistake not to recognise the unquestionable achievements of those times', but he insisted that 'it would be an even bigger mistake not to realise the outrageous price our country and its people had to pay for that social experiment'. In words that echoed in a remarkable way Solzhenitsyn's assertion that communism represented 'a mad dash down a blind alley', Putin went on to argue:

> What is more, it would be a mistake not to understand its historic futility. Communism and the power of the Soviets did not make Russia a prosperous country with a dynamically developing society and free people. Communism vividly demonstrated its inability to foster sound self-development, dooming our country to lagging steadily behind economically advanced countries. It was a blind alley, far away from the mainstream of world civilisation.[62]

This was the first lesson to learn from the past and reflected the authentic voice of a man of the 1970s. It was closely associated with a second lesson concerning the way that change should be achieved. One of the strongest motifs in Putin's thinking in this document and later is the repudiation of revolution as a mode of political action in favour of 'gradual, prudent methods':

> Russia has reached its limit for political and socio-economic upheavals, cataclysms, and radical reforms. Only fanatics or political forces which are absolutely apathetic and indifferent to Russia and its people can

make calls for a new revolution. Be it under communist, national-patriotic, or radical-liberal slogans, our country and our people will not with-stand a new radical break-up. The nation's patience and its ability to survive as well as its capacity to work constructively have reached the limit. Society will simply collapse economically, politically, psychologi-cally, and morally.[63]

Putin would return to this theme repeatedly, as we shall have occasion to note, which reflects his commitment to a politics of normality.

A third lesson emerged out the previous two: Russia should find its own path and reject 'experimenting with abstract models and schemes taken from foreign textbooks'. The reforms of the 1990s were thus placed in the same category as the communist experiment that they sought to overcome: both had been characterised, according to Putin, by 'The mechanical copying of other nations' experience ... '.[64] This assertion clearly modifies the earlier repudiation of special national paths. The power that lies in this apparent contradiction is derived from the attempt to move away from excessive borrowing of foreign models while at the same time trying to avoid falling into the opposite extreme of repudiating the value of international experience.

This search for a distinctive Putinite 'third way' characterised his leader-ship (see Chapter 3). We may also add that the attempt to transcend the contradictions that characterised Russia's history, notably between the internationalist utopianism that lay at the root of Marxism and the national messianism that the ideology turned into under Stalin, was the source of much of Putin's power. Elements of both remained in many post-communist Russian political movements, including to a large extent in Zyuganov's CPRF. Putin's policies were based on the idea of a grand transcendence of the conflicts that had both shaped and torn Russia in the modern era. We may note here yet another very particular one that emerges out of his biography. In 1721 Peter the Great had moved the capital from Moscow to his new creation, St Petersburg, and thus set in motion a centuries-long rivalry. Lenin had moved the capital back to Moscow in 1918, and thereafter the northern city, living under the name of Leningrad between 1924 and 1991, had been overshadowed. Putin conducted much of his diplomacy from St Petersburg, including the Group of Eight (G8) leading industrialised nations summit in July 2006, and ensured that it became the home of a number of interstate organisations, with the Constitutional Court due to move there in 2008. Putin was not able to overcome the rivalry between the two capitals, but he certainly ensured a more balanced appreciation of the political significance of both. The cele-bration in 2003 of the three hundredth anniversary of St Petersburg, by then a city with five million inhabitants (not very far short of Moscow's eight million), appeared a moment of reconciliation not only between the two cities but also between Petrine and Muscovite Russia.

A number of other themes emerge from the *Millennium* message that later characterised Putin's leadership. One of these is the attempt to forge a national consensus to avoid once again dividing the country over basic values and orientations, as it had been after 1917 and in the 1990s. Putin unequivocally supported the constitutional principle against 'the restoration of an official state ideology in any form' and insisted that 'there should be no forced civil accord in a democratic Russia', although he stressed the importance of achieving 'social accord on such basic issues as the aims, values, and orientations of development'.[65] These could be achieved on the basis of traditional Russian values. Here he listed a number: *patriotism*, which should be free of 'nationalist conceit' and instead serve as the inspiration for making the country 'better, richer, stronger and happier'; *the greatness of Russia*, and here Putin insisted that 'Russia was and will remain a great power'; *statism*, one of the most controversial of Putin's arguments (that we shall discuss later); and *social solidarity*, whereby 'the striving for corporate forms of activity have always prevailed over individualism. Paternalistic sentiments have deep roots in Russian society'.[66] Although Putin's programme represented the transcendence of historical contradictions, here we apparently find one in his own thinking: between the values of liberal individualism and statist collectivism. How this was resolved, if it was, we shall see later.

The restoration of the state lay at the centre of Putin's activity as president. In his *Manifesto* he insisted that

> Russia will not become a second edition of, say, the USA or Britain, where liberal values have deep historic traditions. Our state and its institutions and structures have always played an exceptionally important role in the life of the country and its people ... Russians are alarmed by the obvious weakening of state power. The public looks forward to a certain restoration of the guiding and regulating role of the state, proceeding from Russia's traditions as well as the current state of the country.[67]

This did not represent a repudiation of liberal values, as some commentators have argued, but instead suggested that these values had to be adapted to Russian conditions. In later sections of the article Putin placed a strong state at the centre of his programme, but insisted that this had nothing in common with the totalitarianism of the past: 'A strong state power in Russia is a democratic, law-based, workable federal state'.[68] This was to lie at the basis of economic and other policies. Putin did not seek to find a middle path between, on the one hand, capitulation to Western values and, on the other, totalitarianism, since his choice was unequivocally that of Western market democracy. The problem was not in the lack of definition of the end, but in the means.

From the above it is clear that it was not so much the changes pursued by Putin that were so radical, since in many respects they continued the work of his predecessor, but the way in which they were conducted. Putin set himself the task of repudiating the sharp turns and revolutionary breaks that characterised so much of Russian history. In their place, he sought to achieve a type of politics of normality. This indeed is one of the most paradoxical features of Putin's leadership: its very ordinariness represented a radical break with the past. The attempt to reconcile the past with a future-oriented strategy, however, meant that Putin's politics were imbued with a post-Soviet spirit while often taking on a neo-Soviet aspect. It was the very force of this contradiction that acted as the source of much of Putin's power.

Planning for the future

Putin came to power with his own ideas about how to deal with the problems facing the country. At the same time, he sought to harness academic expertise to devise appropriate strategies. To this end he established the Centre for Strategic Development, headed by Gref, in December 1999. It was set an ambitious task: to devise a strategy for Russia's development over the next 10–15 years. Members of its Advisory Board included the economists Yevgeny Yasin, Vladimir Mau and Andrei Illarionov (who had by the end of the 1990s become bitterly critical of Yeltsin's macroeconomic policy and later became one of Putin's key economic advisors, before in turn resigning).[69] In an interview Gref suggested that the strategy of the Centre was based on the idea of developing a 'special', if not third way, for Russia.[70] Soon after the presidential elections Gref noted that 'Putin's position is quite radical and we must think about how to resolve the tasks before us'.[71] The unknown Putin soon revealed himself to be a liberal reformer. The need to move from a relatively self-regulating political system to a more directed system was vividly reflected in Gref's proposals for the reform of the structure of the presidential administration:

> At present, the social and political situation in Russia can be characterized as selfregulating and selfgoverned. The new President of the Russian Federation, assuming he really wants to ensure order and stability in the country for the period of his rule, does not need a self-regulating political system. He needs a political structure (institution) within his administration, which will be able not only to forecast and engineer desirable political situations in Russia, but also to provide operational management of political and social processes in Russian Federation and in the countries of the near abroad.[72]

The core of this new and more directed system of what came to be known as 'managed democracy' was the presidency. Gref later became the minister for trade and economic development, a conscious effort to reproduce on a more modest scale the Japanese experience, where the famed MITI (Ministry of International Trade and Industry) acted as the powerhouse for Japan's rise from post-war destruction to the world's second economic power. In the event, the reports produced by Gref's centre played only a marginal role in detailed policy formation, with the initiative passing firmly to the government headed until February 2003 by Mikhail Kasyanov. Putin's attempt to broaden the debate over policy options and the use of think tanks indicated at least a recognition of the need to have a variety of sources of information and policy options.

Under Gorbachev and Yeltsin a vigorous public sphere had emerged, and Putin now sought to use the intellectual energy available. One of Russia's leading think tanks is the Council for Foreign and Defence Policy (CFDP). Established in the early 1990s to provide strategic guidance and recommendations to the presidency and headed by Sergei Karaganov, the CFDP brings together an illustrious cast of academics and former politicians. In anticipation of a change of leadership, from late 1998 the council commissioned a major study of the problems facing Russia, designed explicitly as a programme for the new president. The report was published in 2000, just in time to be used by the new leader, and dealt (in its own words) not only with Russia's eternal question of 'what is to be done?', but focused above all on 'how it is to be done'.[73] The CFDP, Karaganov insisted, was a civil society association, and the 300 or so citizens who participated in the various discussions that produced the report sought to help the state and society devise a strategic concept for the country's development. The report covered all aspects of Russian policy, and below we shall give no more than a brief indication of its main ideas. Putin clearly took its main lessons to heart and his policies addressed the concerns voiced in this report.

In his introduction Karaganov listed the ills besetting Russia as it entered the new millennium: the failure of the reforms begun in 1992, the weakness of the state, the gulf between state and society and between the regions and the centre, and the decline in Russia's foreign policy position. All this, he argued, required a drastic change in the country's model of development. The experts agreed that the country found itself in a dead end: 'if the ruling class does not find in itself the strength to lead society towards a change of power and model of development, then Russia was doomed to decay and destruction'.[74] Russia, he insisted, should stop 'struggling against the phantoms and shadows of the past',[75] and for this reason there would be no special study of 'the Russian idea', the endless metaphysical search for the meaning of Russia, and instead 'the ruling class, all of society, must engage in self-limitation' and understand the need to renounce grandiose and unsustainable ambitions and focus on the real problems facing the country.

This rather pessimistic tone was reflected in discussion of the state of democracy in Russia, with the general view being that Russia, at best, was an 'unripe (or immature) democracy', with the absence of some key elements of a more developed democracy and with far too many 'superfluous' features, many of them inherited from the late totalitarian period.[76] While, for example, the country in the early 1990s had been federalised, it was on the basis of Soviet pseudo-federal territorial divisions. Territorial decentralisation verged on the feudalisation of the country. In case after case, above all with the military, the creation of a new institution was accompanied by the survival of the old. Behind the façade of reformed institutions 'there lie hidden Soviet, if not Stalinist, administrative practices'.[77] Everywhere there were 'grey zones where the rule of law confronted the world of informal relations, where the law is silent'.[78] Authority was unconsolidated, and thus power was unable genuinely to become state power.[79] These problems in political development had provoked three major problems: the lack of sustained economic development and the rational use of resources; the failure to defend the country's position in the world; and the difficulty in convincing society that democracy 'to the greatest degree reflects the interests of each and everyone, and thus gaining public support for democratic transformations that would ensure their practical irreversibility in Russia'.[80]

As for foreign policy, the report was scathing about Russia's conduct in the 1990s:

> The main thing is that the country's political class does not understand and does not want to understand obvious truths. Russia did not lose the 'Cold War'. It emerged from it with honour. But because of mistaken policies, unsteadiness, the traditional expectation of miracles, the almost deliberate weakening of the state, the endless postponement of hard decisions, we lost the *post Cold War world* [italics in original], snatching defeat from the jaws of victory.[81]

Among its many prescriptions, the chapter insisted that the country should normalise its relationship with the G8.[82] This was at the top of Putin's agenda at the G8 meeting in Japan in July 2000, and in July 2002 at the G8 meeting in Kananskis in Canada Russia was accepted as a full member and invited to host the 2006 summit.

Corruption was identified as one of the main challenges facing the country, with the reform of public administration considered the antidote. Transparency International identifies Russia as one of the most corrupt in the world; in 1999 and 2000 ranking 82nd among 99, but in 2001 ranking 79th out of 91 and by 2002 rising to 71st out of 102 (see Chapter 6). Although there is plenty of venal corruption (bribe-taking and the like), there is also systematic corruption arising out of the interpenetration of private and public affairs, the 'merging (*srashchivanie*) of the state apparatus and private capital'.[83] Under Stalin a powerful network of criminal gangs emerged harnessed to the state, but in the post-Stalin years they became a virtual 'state within the state', gaining enormous economic power as a result of Gorbachev's reforms. Under Yeltsin there was a virtual fusion of economic and political matters as business and the state effectively became one.[84] The notorious example was Berezovsky, dubbed by Klebnikov the 'Russian Rockefeller'.[85] By the time Putin came to power, by some estimates up to 40 per cent of business was in the 'shadow economy', employing over eight million people.[86] Whole regions appeared to have fallen into the hands of organised criminal gangs, notoriously Primorsk (Maritime) *krai*, the port and its infrastructure in Astrakhan *oblast*, and the oil and gas industries in Tyumen *oblast*.[87] Karaganov's report recognised the high degree of segmentation in the country, requiring differentiated anti-corruption strategies at the departmental, sectoral and regional levels.[88]

As for the crucial question of constitutional reform, the report noted the 'dialectical unity' between two opposed ideas: 'the need to ensure the stability of the basic law; and the need to introduce amendments, changes dictated by life itself'.[89] The report rehearsed all the fundamental arguments for and against changing the constitution, but in the end plumped for some mild corrections:

> There are two conclusions: either do everything possible to ensure that the authorities fulfil to the letter constitutional norms and raise their political and legal culture, or to render the constitution less 'dependent', stricter, remove some of its most glaring faults. It is clear that to achieve cultural change could take decades. This is an argument to introduce certain changes to the constitution.[90]

The authors however did not recommend converting Russia from what was effectively a presidential republic into a parliamentary one, and indeed insisted that such calls were extremely dangerous: 'a parliamentary republic is a one-wheel cycle, a presidential republic is a bicycle, while a presidential-parliamentary one is a tricycle, the most stable'.[91]

The 'state of the nation' speeches

The *Millennium Manifesto* and the *Strategy for Russia* documents provide two fundamental starting points for analysis of the challenges facing Putin's leadership as he assumed office. In this section we shall use his annual address to the Federal Assembly (the two houses of parliament – the Federation Council and the State Duma – taken together), which reflect changing priorities and concerns. Putin's annual address acted as a moment to take stock of priorities and served as programmatic documents, as well as of course justifying policies to the public. In examining them we should be aware that they were not exactly manifestos, yet they do reflect the evolution of Putin's thinking. Putin considered these speeches important documents, sending them back for rewriting until he was satisfied that they captured the tone and content that reflected his preferences.[92]

8 July 2000

In his first address on 8 July 2000 Putin focused on his favourite theme, the need to 'strengthen the state' and to establish 'a single vertical line of executive power' while pursuing liberal economic reforms. He dismissed 'speculation about dictatorship and authoritarianism' and stressed that his purpose was to create an 'effective and a democratic state ... capable of protecting civic, political and economic freedoms'. He condemned the 'unreasonable level of taxation' and conceded that the state had contributed to the development of corruption, capital flight and the shadow economy because the rules were vague and ill-defined. Russia was continuing to lose ground economically, despite some economic growth, and was in danger of becoming a third world state. More than that, the Russian nation was threatened with extinction if policies did not change. Although the rudiments of a democratic state had been built, 'quite often the distance separating laws from real life is too great' he insisted. So far only the outlines of civil society had developed and now 'patient work is required to make society the government's equal partner'. Russia had been unable, Putin insisted, 'to combine patriotic responsibility with what [Peter] Stolypin [prime minister between 1906 and his assassination in 1911] described as civil freedoms'. Putin sought to restructure political space by sponsoring the development of political parties as 'a permanent link between the people and the authorities'.[93] Specific tasks included tax reform, a law on parties, the legislative framework for a market economy, realistic social policy and administrative reform. The speech outlined a strategy for the reform of Russia that he proceeded to implement.

3 April 2001

This was one of Putin's most radical addresses. He began by looking back on the fulfilment of his earlier plans to reorganise federal relations, insisting that 'the period of the erosion of statehood is behind us'. He now talked about the development of judicial reform and the improvement of the quality of legislation. Along with the shadow economy, he argued, 'a kind of shadow justice had emerged' for those who had lost faith in the official system. The status of judges needed to be improved. In the economy capital flight was continuing (some $20 billion a year) and the country was 'still living predominantly in a "rent-based" rather than a productive economy'. An 'equilibrium' point had been achieved in the economy based on inactivity, provoked not only because of 'resistance to reform on the part of the bureaucracy', but the system itself was based on receiving what Putin called 'status' rent (bribes and compensation). Urgent administrative reform should focus on scaling back the bureaucracy. The number of federal and regional civil servants, he noted, had increased from 882,000 to over a million. Putin once again reiterated his belief that 'a state's efficiency is determined not so much by the amount of property it controls as by the efficacy of political, legal and administrative mechanisms for observing public interests in the country'. This is a point that Mikhail Khodorkovsky would have been interested to hear following the effective expropriation of his Yukos oil company in 2003. On foreign policy Putin failed to mention the USA and instead prioritised relations with the EU. He stressed the importance of economic factors in foreign policy.[94] Thus the relationship between the centre and the regions, legal reform, economic restructuring and administrative reform were the focus.

18 April 2002

His speech this year came in the wake of the 11 September 2001 events, and he took full credit for having made possible the creation of a 'durable anti-terrorist coalition'. Russia was 'building constructive, normal relations with all states in the world'. Judicial reform had moved forward, with most of the necessary acts and laws adopted, but the whole system needed to be made more humane. The focus of the speech, however, was on economic matters. Putin's insistence on the need to improve people's standards of living reflected his frustration that so little had been done in this sphere, although he did stress some of the government's achievements. He noted that in 2001 economic growth had continued, real incomes had risen by 6 per cent and unemployment fallen by 700,000. This meant a return just about to the level of 1998, before the financial crash in August of that year had nearly halved people's real incomes. There was still a long way to go before they reached the 1990 level, in communism's last days and before the disintegration of the USSR. Putin expressed dissatisfaction with the government's forecast of an economic growth rate of between 3.5 and 4.6 per cent, although this figure was probably a realistic one and he did not put forward any new ideas about how higher targets could be achieved.

This part of the speech reflected Putin's traditional face, where planning served the function of exhortation and encouragement. However, elsewhere in his speech the post-Soviet face was much in evidence, especially in his stress on the need to limit the state's role in the economy and his excoriation of government bureaucracy, warning that 'the habits of the command system persist' and urged serious administrative reform. This was balanced by his call for reform of the natural monopolies, the need to support science, and for the state to manage its property more effectively. Russia's integration into the global economy remained at the heart of Putin's economic agenda. Overall, there remained many grey areas in Putin's strategy for economic development and in his view of the proper role of the state.[95] Thus the struggle against terrorism joined familiar themes of administrative and legal reform, while the concrete tasks were set for the reform of the housing and utilities markets, the modernisation of the armed forces and the improvement of the management of state property.

16 May 2003

Putin's address in 2003 was postponed because of the war in Iraq and, it appears, because of his refusal to accept the complacency in some of the earlier drafts. As head of the executive the president had to take responsibility for the actions (or inaction) of the government. Earlier speeches had stressed the stabilisation of the system and the introduction of order, together with specific concrete measures (the payment of wages, the indexation of pensions, encouragement of small businesses and the like), in contrast to Yeltsin's abstractions like building the market and democracy. After ten years and more of upheaval, society wanted 'no more revolution, but calm and considered movement forward'.[96] In his speech Putin condemned complacency and warned of the dangers of stagnation. He warned that despite certain achievements the economic fundamentals were still 'very weak', with the country burdened by uncompetitive industries, excessive reliance on temporarily favourable international economic circumstances, administrative inefficiency and a declining population. He categorised the economic achievements as 'very, very modest', and set a ten-year target of doubling GDP. As long as the economy was not improved, Russia would not be able to become a rich and powerful country again. He warned that terrorism 'threatens the peace and security of our citizens', and insisted that the Russian army should be professional and well-equipped to defend the country. He praised those Chechens who voted in the March 2003 referendum in favour of remaining an 'inseparable part' of the Russian Federation, and insisted that the people of Chechnya should be given the chance to lead 'normal, human lives'. He warned against parliamentary populism in the forthcoming Duma elections, while welcoming them as a new stage in the development of the country's multiparty system. Most significantly, he looked forward to a 'professional and efficient government relying on the parliamentary majority' being formed after the elections.[97] Thus Russia was to be transformed into a great power, hence the need to double GDP, reduce poverty and, as in previous years, modernise the military.

26 May 2004

Putin's address now revealed a gulf between words and deeds, suggesting that instead of a dialogue between the leader and the people the discussion was beginning to assume the form of a monologue. The section on the economy no longer emphasised structural reforms but instead made the case for moving towards the market in the social sphere. The speech called for the development of the mortgage market, the reform of health care (compulsory and voluntary medical insurance), and the reform of education. There would be continuing reform of the raw materials export sector, while on army reform the president limited himself to generalities. As for the political system, Putin insisted that 'we must make a critical assessment of the state of our democracy'. He once again pledged himself to maintaining a liberal political course 'without turning back, but it was clear that Putin would reserve for himself the right to act as arbiter over the level of democratic rights that he thought appropriate for Russia. He condemned those who 'deliberately interpret the strengthening of statehood as authoritarianism', suggesting that they sought to weaken Russia. His condemnation of the lack of transparency in party budgets and party corruption appeared to apply only to opposition groupings. His comments about non-governmental organisations that are 'fed by an alien hand' harked back to the Soviet era.[98] The speech was imbued with a rather paternalistic and bureaucratic approach to the problem of managing society, rather than reflecting a confident and pluralistic democratic community of equal citizens. Russia's position in the world was to be strengthened, and the familiar litany of tasks was asserted: the doubling of GDP, poverty alleviation, dealing with the housing shortage, the modernisation of health care and, as always, military reform.

25 April 2005

Putin's sixth address to the Federal Assembly reflected a rather chastened mood. The speech came in the wake of the damage done to Russia's image and investment climate by the Yukos trial; the trauma of the Beslan school siege of 1–3 September 2004 (see Chapter 3); the raft of measures announced on 13 September, in the aftermath of the Beslan massacre, including the appointment of governors, which were seen to represent a retreat from democracy; the setback in the Ukrainian presidential election of autumn 2004 when Putin backed the loser, Victor Yanukovich, who in the event tried to steal the election from his rival, Victor Yushchenko, who then rose to power on the back of the 'Orange revolution'; and the widespread protests in early 2005 against the monetisation of social benefits. There was a general perception that Russia under Putin was backsliding into chaos and authoritarianism.

Putin used the occasion to stress three main tasks: the strengthening of legality, human rights and the political system to avoid a gulf opening up between the authorities and the people; the consolidation of the federation; and the liberalisation of the economic sphere. He insisted that the strengthening of democracy was the top priority for Russia: 'The main political-ideological task is the development of Russia as a free, democratic country'. Political freedom, he insisted, 'is not just necessary but economically beneficial'. He took issue with the political culture approach, which suggested that the Russian people were somehow not suited to democratic government, the rule of law and the basic values of civil society: 'I would like to bring those who think like that back to political reality ... Without liberty and democracy there can be no order, no stability and no sustainable economic policies'. Responding to Western criticism, however, Putin stressed that the 'special feature' of Russia's democracy was that it would be pursued in its own way and not at the price of law and order or social stability: 'Russia ... will decide for itself the pace, terms and conditions of moving towards democracy'. All this would be done in a legal way, warning that

'Any unlawful methods of struggle ... for ethnic, religious and other interests contradict the principles of democracy. The state will react (to such attempts) with legal, but tough, means'. This was in effect the manifesto of 'sovereign democracy'.

Putin described the break-up of the Soviet Union in 1991 as 'the biggest geopolitical catastrophe' of the twentieth century and a 'tragedy for the Russian people', and warned that the 'epidemic of collapse' was threatening Russia itself. He stressed, however, that the Soviet Union was a thing of the past, and the coherence of the Russian Federation today depended not on retreating from democracy but on strengthening democratic institutions and principles throughout society. He emphasised the gravity of the terrorist threat to Russia: 'Over the past few years a great deal has been done in the struggle with terrorism, but the threat remains serious, and we continue to receive heavy blows'. In the economic sphere he dropped all mention of the pledge given two years earlier to double GDP in ten years. Instead, he stressed Russia's need for greater foreign investment but noted the obstructions, some of which he insisted were required by national security. He called for greater clarity in delineating areas where the state had legitimate interests and areas open for foreign investment: 'It is time to identify the spheres of the economy where the interests of strengthening Russian sovereignty and security dictate the necessity of special control on the part of national and state capital'. He reiterated his call for the statute of limitations on the review of the controversial privatisations of the 1990s to be reduced from ten to three years, and for the introduction of a new flat rate 13 per cent tax on undeclared capital in order to encourage the return of 'capital flight' resources and to bring some of the black economy out of the shadows. He warned against the power of the corrupt bureaucracy, noting that 'The political and corporate bureaucracies behave no better than the government bureaucracy. I must warn them that ceding power to a corrupt bureaucracy is not part of our plans'. At the same time, he made no serious mention of the controversial topic of social reform, whose implementation earlier in the year had provoked the largest protests of his presidency.[99]

10 May 2006

It was widely anticipated that Putin's seventh address to the Federal Assembly would focus on foreign policy, in an environment where echoes of the Cold War sounded ever more insistently, above all by the USA vice-president Dick Cheney. In the event, the focus was firmly on domestic matters, and America's behaviour passed over in contemptuous silence. With Russia hosting the G8 summit in St Petersburg in July, Putin clearly did not wish to trespass on the agenda of that meeting. He did allow himself to note that 'Not everyone in the world has been able to move on from the stereotypes of bloc thinking and prejudices, which are a carry-over from the epoch of global confrontation, although there have been fundamental changes in the world'. He obliquely warned against the use of force in Iran: 'Methods of force rarely give the desired result and often their consequences are even more terrible than the original threat'; and remarked that 'The wolf knows whom to eat ... and is not about to listen to anyone', a reference to America's overbearing manner. It is also clear that Putin was dissatisfied with early drafts of the speech, and all the evidence suggests that he took an active part in their drafting, confirming our view that these speeches are more than mere acts of public rhetoric but reflected the deepest concerns of the administration.

With the economy continuing to grow for the seventh successive year and buoyant energy revenues – Russia earned $113 billion in oil revenues in 2005 and another $30 billion from natural gas exports – the speech projected a powerful image of a Russia that was independent and with an effective military ready to defend its vision of itself. 'We should always be ready to repel a potential external aggressor and international terrorism attacks, and should be able to respond to any attempt to exert foreign policy pressure on Russia', he said. He emphasised the role of strategic nuclear forces in this effort and announced that the nuclear triad would be substantially strengthened in the next five years, including the commissioning of two strategic nuclear submarines in 2006: 'Our army should have every opportunity to react appropriately to current threats, Putin said. 'The Army should include armed forces able to simultaneously fight in global, regional and if necessary several local conflicts'. Russia's defence spending, Putin insisted, should be comparable to that of other nuclear powers, although in 2005 some $20 billion was allocated to defence spending, against the Pentagon budget of $447 billion. Housing and other welfare issues for service personnel were also to be addressed. Support for the military, however, he warned, should be balanced by his enduring theme: domestic modernisation. 'We must not repeat the mistakes of the Soviet Union and of the Cold War. We must not sacrifice the interests of socio-economic development to develop our military complex. That is a dead end ... Our military and foreign policy doctrines should answer the most topical question: How can we fight not just against terror but against nuclear, biological and chemical weapons of mass destruction?'

The second main theme, to which much of the speech was devoted, concerned demographic issues and the need to support families to raise the birth rate. The 9 October 2002 census registered the country's population as 145.2 million, down from 148.6 in 1991, but with a natural decrease of 700,000 every year this had fallen to 142.5 in 2006, inadequately offset by the 100,000-odd who migrated each year from former Soviet states. Putin announced a special programme for the 2007 budget that would make 1,500 roubles (€40) monthly payouts to families for their first baby and double that sum for a second child, and announced that the government should give women at least 250,000 roubles (€6,755) as financial assistance following the birth of a second child. He was aware, though, that financial inducements on their own would not stem the fall: 'The problem of low birth rates cannot be resolved without a change in the attitude of our society towards the issue of family and family values,' he said. The problem of demographic decline had long exercised Putin, but never before had he devoted so much attention to the attempt to stem the falling fertility rate. Pensions would also be increased (up from the average of 2,764 roubles – €75 – per month) by another 20 per cent in 2007, a nice bonus in time for the 2007–8 electoral cycle.

Both themes reflected the concerns of Russian citizens and thus were 'nationalistic' to the extent that Russia's national needs were prioritised. Questions to do with the development of the 'nation' took priority over the development of the 'state'. Other issues addressed included making the rouble fully convertible by 1 July 2006, six months ahead of the target set in the 2003 address to parliament. He also outlined the administration's industrial policy designed to 'encourage investment in production infrastructure and innovation, while preserving financial stability', including the focus on the development of high-tech industries and a knowledge economy, and ordered the government to accelerate work to create aircraft and shipbuilding holdings in a bid to improve their competitiveness. Putin confirmed his commitment to Russia joining the World Trade Organisation (WTO), but warned that 'negotiations on Russia's membership in the WTO should not become a subject of bargaining over issues that have nothing to do with the activities of this organisation'. He reiterated his commitment to democracy: 'I am convinced that no important goal can be achieved in a country without ensuring human rights and freedoms, effective state organisation, democracy and civil society'. His broad position was outlined as follows:

> In recent years we have been working consistently to even out the disproportions that have arisen in the structure of the state and the social sphere. At the same time, as we plan the further development of our state and political system we should of course take account of the current condition of our society. In this connection, I shall note a major feature of our domestic life – the lack of public faith in some state institutions and in big business. It's clear why this is so. The great hopes of millions of people were bound up in the reforms of the early 1990s. But neither the authorities nor business justified those hopes. More than that, some members of those two constituencies, disregarding the law and common decency, embarked on a personal enrichment that was unprecedented in the history of our country – at the expense of the majority of citizens. As we work on the great national programme, which is designed to ensure the primary benefits for the masses, we have trodden on some toes.[100]

Neither the business class nor the bureaucracy could be trusted, in Putin's view, but that left only the political regime as the repository of people's aspirations, a rather convenient formulation that justified the executive's dominance over all other sources of social power in the country.

26 April 2007

Putin's final address focused on domestic issues, but the frustration he felt at the failure of the international community to accept Russia as a 'normal' country was palpable. On domestic issues the tone was positive, with less sense of threats to the country's existence than in some previous speeches. He noted Russia's achievement in becoming one of the top ten economies in the world, accompanied by a halving in the number of poor. He defended electoral changes on the grounds that the shift to a fully proportional system would foster the development of political parties (see Chapter 4), and that the central appointment of governors (see Chapter 7) would reduce the power of local clans. He noted that Russia's rise had provoked a negative reaction:

> To be frank, our policy of stable and gradual development is not to everyone's taste. There are those who, making skilful use of pseudo-democratic rhetoric, would like to return us to the recent past: some in order to once again plunder the nation's resources with impunity and rob the people and the state; and others in order to deprive our country of its economic and political independence. There has been an increasing influx of money from abroad being used to intervene directly in our internal affairs. Looking back at the more distant past, we recall the talk about the civilising role of colonial powers during the colonial era. Today, 'civilisation' has been replaced by democratisation, but the aim is the same – to ensure unilateral gains and one's own advantage, and to pursue one's own interests.

He spoke of the 'national projects' to develop health, education, agriculture, housing and infrastructure, of plans to invest in high technology to create a more competitive economy, a massive house-building drive (to be funded in part by the sale of Yukos oil company assets), an increase in power-generating capacity by two-thirds by 2020, including the construction of 20 new nuclear power stations, a new canal linking the Caspian and Black seas, and a rise in defence spending.

In the short section devoted to foreign policy, Putin announced a moratorium on Russia's implementation of the Conventional Forces in Europe (CFE) Treaty, first signed in 1990 between the 22 members of Nato and the now defunct Warsaw Pact and modified in 1999 to take into account the post-Cold War realities. However, only four countries – Russia, Belarus, Ukraine and Kazakhstan – had ratified the modified treaty, and 'Nato newcomers such as Slovakia [he meant Slovenia] and the Baltic republics', Putin noted, 'had not joined the CFE treaty altogether'. He rejected the link made by the Western powers between ratifying the treaty and Russia's Istanbul commitments stipulating the withdrawal of Russian forces from Georgia and Transdniestr. He also condemned Western plans to build elements of a missile defence system in Poland and the Czech Republic. It was clear that Putin felt aggrieved that Russia's unilateral concessions over the years had not been reciprocated by the West. The speech outlined a realistic appraisal of Russia's needs, but it also contained a strong element of hubris. It was not clear how sustainable Russia's economic revival would be if energy prices fell, and the weakness of public administration, accompanied by widespread corruption, was not addressed (although earlier speeches had tackled the issue). Russia was now in danger of over-estimating its strength, and of adopting policies that would isolate the country from its neighbours and the world.

He pointed out that this would be his last speech, and made the following point:

> I would like to note in this respect that each of my eight Addresses to the Federal Assembly has not only evaluated the situation in the country and its place in the world, but has also set priorities, including long-term priorities in the social sphere, in the economy, in foreign and domestic policy, and in defence and security. Though perhaps not complete, this constitutes in effect a fairly concrete and substantial conceptual programme for Russia's development. Its implementation requires constructive work from all sections of society and calls for immense effort and huge financial resources.

He noted that many had anticipated that his speech would 'concentrate mostly on summing up and evaluating what we have accomplished in our work together since 2000', but he insisted that 'it is not proper for us to evaluate our own work, and not time yet for me to set out my political testament'.[101] While Putin may have avoided an evaluation of his presidency, it is the task of this book to provide an interim assessment of the achievements and failings of his leadership.

Conclusion

All of the above suggests that politics have now become 'normal', in the sense that larger constitutional questions over the shape of the polity have now given way to governmental administration and the management of a functioning market economy based on private property and international economic integration. However, while a sense of normality undoubtedly returned to Russia after two decades of post-communist revolutionary upheaval, coming on top of the preceding century of revolutionary 'extraordinary' measures, there are also some disturbing overtones of 'normalisation'. Depoliticisation undermined the political pluralism essential for an effective democracy, and encouraged bureaucracy and corruption. There could be no simple 'return to normalcy' in Russia, since Russia's normality has always been accompanied by elements of the emergency and the improvised. Putin's aspiration was that at last Russia could enter a period akin to the normality enjoyed by the capitalist democracies of the West. We shall see in the following chapters the degree to which his hopes were fulfilled.

3 Putin's path

Forms of government are forged mainly in the fire of practice, not in the vacuum of theory. They respond to national character and national realities. . . . But when Soviet power has run its course, or when its personalities and spirit begin to change (for the ultimate outcome could be one or the other), let us not hover nervously over the people who come after, applying litmus papers daily to their political complexions to find out whether they answer to our concept of 'democratic'. Give them time; let them be Russians; let them work out their internal problems in their own manner. The ways by which peoples advance toward dignity and enlightenment in government are things that constitute the deepest and most intimate processes of national life. There is nothing less understandable to foreigners, nothing in which foreign interference can do less good.

George F. Kennan[1]

In Chapter 2 we explored some of the thinking about the problems facing Russia on Putin's accession and the choices facing him. Here we shall look more closely at Putin as a politician, examining the opportunities and risks that he confronted. He was constrained by the legacy of the past and the political and social order that he inherited, but as an active political agent he was able to shape agendas and build a political machine of his own. The development of Putin's power base reflected his broader political agenda. While Yeltsin's rule can be understood as a period of 'permanent revolution', Putin now assumed the role of consolidator, the Napoleon (not necessarily on horseback) to Yeltsin's Robespierre, the leader of a Thermidor in political relations. During the presidential campaign in 2000 Zyuganov had already called Putin a 'little Napoleon', and as Pavlovsky stressed, a Napoleon does not emerge out of nowhere, and not everyone could become a Napoleon.[2] Like Napoleon, Putin sought to rebuild the state and incorporate into the new order the progressive elements of the revolutionary epoch necessary for social development while discarding the excesses and the revolutionary froth. Putin adopted the key test of such a consolidating role, the so-called 'zero option': the prohibition on the redistribution of property and the legal persecution of those involved in the privatisation excesses of the past. Putin also favoured the larger zero option: the crimes and repression of the Soviet period were to be put to one side for the sake of social harmony. The Soviet and Yeltsin revolutionary periods now gave way to one of post-revolutionary consolidation.

Building the Putin bloc

Putin's career reflected the enormous changes that had taken place in Russian society since 1985. As Medvedev points out, Yeltsin could only challenge Gorbachev because he had belonged to the party elite for 20 years, whereas Putin was an outsider.[3] Adopted by the Yeltsin elite, he nevertheless remained an independent but isolated politician. Putin's refusal to launch wholesale investigations into the past can be interpreted as a pragmatic response to political weakness, but it also indicated a normative strategy of reconciliation and consensus building. Putin considered not only the Yeltsin chapter as closed but also the whole Soviet period that preceded it. Putin's choice, rare for Russia, was in favour of social and political reconciliation; but it was a choice constrained by the circumstances in which he came to power and by the realities of the country he was destined to rule. Yeltsin had achieved a political revolution but had built the new system on traditional social foundations. Much of the old elite remained in office since the system, to use Huntington's terms, had been transformed rather than replaced.[4] There was a permanent contradiction between Putin's policy preferences and the constraints imposed by the inherited structure of social and bureaucratic power.

Emerging as an unexpected president, Putin did not have a shadow government waiting to take over. The key problem facing him was the lack of a reliable team of his own and hence, according to Reddaway, he was forced to become a balancer of elite factions.[5] On several occasions Putin remarked, 'we have no personnel' ('*U nas net kadrov*'). According to Hahn, 'The logic of *nomenklatura*-led revolution from above predisposed the new regime to turn to *ancien regime* softliners in the hope of regaining the state's autonomy lost under *nomenklatura* capitalism'.[6] This dynamic had already come into play in the last few weeks of Kirienko's government in July 1998 in the attempt to appoint as economics minister Yury Maslyukov, a former member of Gorbachev's government and still a member of the CPRF, to what was meant to be a liberal government. The process had been marked much earlier, above all with the appointment of Primakov as foreign minister in January 1996, and then as prime minister in September 1998. It was during Primakov's premiership that the assault against the most prominent of the oligarchs, Berezovsky, was first launched through an investigation into alleged money laundering when he was at the head of Aeroflot, but in the event it was Primakov who was dismissed in May 1999.

The Putin elite was made up of a number of elements, whose balance changed over time. They included Yeltsinite officials (some of whom were associated with the 'family'); people from the military and security services, the *siloviki*; democratic statists; and a newer generation of reform-minded St Petersburg officials (many of whom had been associated with Putin personally).[7] These groups can be briefly characterised as follows.

The Yeltsinites – the 'family', oligarchs and Muscovites

One of the key tests of Putin's leadership was how he would relate to Yeltsin's elite: would Prince Hal turn against Falstaff? Many insisted that 'Putin is no more than a tool of oligarchical capital and at the same time the hope of those who wish to see the strengthening of *nomenklatura* capitalism'.[8] Andrei Ryabov, an analyst with the Carnegie Moscow Centre, argued that 'Yeltsin's style was feudal, but it worked. And now Putin is trying to completely change this relationship between the state and the elites, No one knows what the new relationship will look like'.[9] The Kremlin elites that had propelled Putin to power certainly tried to achieve the perpetuation of Yeltsin-style politics, 'Yeltsinism without Yeltsin', but Putin ultimately reforged the elite structure while not fundamentally repudiating the old system.

One of the major constraints on Putin in the early period was dependence on the oligarchs, the backbone of the old Yeltsin regime and the power base of the Muscovites. These elites were focused on the so-called 'family', the group of Kremlin insiders that included the head of the presidential administration, Voloshin, his deputy Surkov, the oligarchs Berezovsky and Roman Abramovich, Moscow banker Alexander Mamut, former Yeltsin presidential speech writer and former chief of staff Yumashev, Boris Yeltsin's daughter Tatyana Dyachenko, and Borodin, the former head of the Kremlin's 'property department' (for whom Putin had briefly worked), who became secretary of the Russia–Belarus Union in early 2000 on Putin's recommendation. Voloshin had once been Berezovsky's business partner and had then become presidential chief of staff under Yeltsin, a position that he continued to hold under Putin. Despite rumours about Voloshin's dismissal, he became the core of Putin's early team, in part because of his phenomenal stamina and ability to devour work.[10] In late 1999 and early 2000 it certainly appeared that Putin was constrained by the oligarchs, with Berezovsky and Abramovich taking advantage of the presidential election campaign to seize control of the bulk of Russia's extraordinarily profitable aluminium industry.[11] The oil and aluminium oligarch with close ties to the family, Abramovich, appeared untouchable, as did Mamut, although later Berezovsky's political influence was destroyed.

In numerous interviews it was Pavlovsky who invented the idea of a struggle between the *siloviki* (see below) and the 'family' as a way of explaining the difficulties and impediments in the way of implementing Putin's policies.[12] According to Petr Kozma, the family are a group of opportunists ready to turn their coats to remain in power.[13] That was the case, but the group, however amorphous, did place a constraint on personnel changes. The acting prime minister, Kasyanov, who had traditionally been close to the Yeltsin insiders, was confirmed as prime minister following Putin's formal inauguration as president in May 2000. It was Voloshin who allegedly countermanded Putin's attempts to appoint his St Petersburg colleague Dmitry Kozak as prosecutor general. Instead, the acting prosecutor general, Vladimir Ustinov, was confirmed in his post, and thus one avenue whereby the excesses of the Yeltsin years could have been exposed was closed off. As one commentator put it, with Ustinov's appointment 'any lingering doubts that Putin was an unwilling captive of the Family were dispelled'.[14] Ustinov acted as a powerful block on effective judicial reform and an enthusiastic supporter of the attack on Yukos. However, in certain appointments, Putin early on showed his teeth, notably in the dismissal of family member Viktor Kaluzhny as fuel and energy minister, replacing him by the little known Alexander Gavrin, suggesting at least an awareness of the need to show independence in forming the government. This independence gradually grew during Putin's leadership and, by the end, few suggested that Putin was not his own man. There was to be no Yeltsinism without Yeltsin.

Nevertheless, there was to be no radical break with the past. As Putin put it in his 24 June 2002 extended press conference, 'we are developing the country on the base that was established by the previous political leadership headed by the first president of Russia Boris Nikolaevich Yeltsin'. Pressed on his personal relations with Yeltsin, since the latter had been insisting on speedy union with Belarus, Putin answered 'He has his views on that question, and I have mine'.[15] Putin distanced himself from the 'family' faction, but remained constrained by its influence. Pavlovsky, after all, argued that Putin had been selected by the family 'not only according to the principle of loyalty, but [of] ... dependence'.[16] The precise nature of this 'dependence' was unclear: was there some sort of deal whereby Putin guaranteed no major personnel changes in the first year of his leadership? There are persistent rumours that Putin had promised Yeltsin not to conduct wholesale personnel or policy changes for a certain period of time, and there is some circumstantial evidence to support this. In his first significant government reshuffle, Putin dismissed the Yeltsin-era defence and interior ministers the day after he had served a year in office. Rumours abounded that the Yeltsinite elite held some sort of *kompromat* (compromising material) against him, to be held as insurance so that he did not trespass against their interests. This could help explain why Putin at times appeared so irresolute. As Yevgeniya Albats put it: 'Putin, weak and inconsistent as he has seemed up to now, is being torn apart by the two loyalties he inherited: first to the corporation, the brotherhood, the KGB which made him a man; second to "the family" which made him president'.[17] Perhaps the gravest danger that Putin faced in his early period of rule was that these two elements would come into conflict with each other.

Putin appeared suspicious of the 'old Muscovites', members of Yeltsin's 'family' and representatives of business in government. Throughout his leadership Putin had an uneasy relationship with the Moscow elite, and in particular the city's popular mayor, Luzhkov, whom he could not remove. Over time Putin asserted his authority, but always cautiously. In January 2002 he dismissed Nikolai Aksenenko as railways minister, followed by an investigation into his business affairs. Representatives of the core Yeltsinite elite were soon eclipsed, notably through Voloshin's resignation on 30 October 2003 in protest against Khodorkovsky's arrest five days earlier, and Kasyanov's dismissal as prime minister in February 2004. Kasyanov had apparently favoured the accelerated liberalisation of the economy and limits on state interference in economic matters.[18]

The siloviki

If the 'family' and their associated oligarchs was one constituency that constrained Putin's freedom of action, another was that exercised by what we may call the national security establishment. We noted in Chapter 1 that the late Yeltsin period saw increased reliance on security officials to staff the presidential administration, and Putin was one of that cohort. Neither Yeltsin nor Putin were interested in 'de-Sovietisation', and thus the whole vast nexus of connections, corporate culture and belief systems of the old era was perpetuated across the formal dividing line between 'communist' and 'post-communist' Russia. For critics of Russia's first two post-communist leaders, the line in effect disappeared. Putin certainly never repudiated his security background, and made a point of honouring its contribution, in particular on various anniversaries of the Cheka's foundation by Feliks Dzerzhinsky on 20 December 1917. For example, on 20 December 2003 at a ceremony in honour of the Day of Secret Service Workers, Putin argued that:

> For many generations of security professionals this day has become a symbol of courage, devotion to the cause and whole-hearted service to the motherland ... political views changed, but security of the fatherland, protection of its sovereign interests and, the main thing, the security of our citizens have always remained the principal objectives of your work. Yours is sophisticated and responsible work requiring supreme professional competence, personal integrity and courage.[19]

Former KGB workers are known as *chekisty*, and contemporary security officials in the FSB are proud to use this label. When considered together with other elements of the military and the security part of the state they are known as *siloviki* (force agency officials). This group was one of Putin's main sources of personnel, in particular those whom he had known during his years in Leningrad. Putin has been seen as heir to the Andropov tradition of attempting to modernise an ailing system by the firm hand from above, the model of authoritarian modernisation, although we argue that the parallel is of limited use.

Nevertheless, many have talked about the 'securitisation' of appointments, if not of the system as a whole. Putin certainly drew on the security establishment and his old roots in St Petersburg; and in many cases the two groups coincided. One estimate suggested that almost 40 per cent of top appointments in the early days came from the FSB,[20] and this trend was continued thereafter. According to Kryshtanovskaya and White, the proportion of those with a security, military or other law enforcement agencies in leadership positions rose from 4 per cent under Gorbachev to 11 per cent under Yeltsin, and then rose to 25 per cent by the end of Putin's first term as president, with the proportion even higher in the national government.[21] By early 2005 the *siloviki* made up just under a quarter of the top leadership, just over a third of the national government, and just under a fifth of each chamber of the Federal Assembly.[22]

A number of near contemporaries of Putin from his time as a KGB officer in Leningrad enjoyed close personal links with him and gained influence. The key figures were Putin's long-time associate with a record of 20 years in the intelligence service, Sergei Ivanov, Putin's replacement as head of the Security Council and appointed defence minister on 28 March 2001; Nikolai Patrushev, Putin's successor as head of the FSB; and Viktor Cherkesov, Putin's envoy (*polpred*) in north-west Russia. Ivanov rejected the argument that men from the security services had come to power, while at the same time denying that the Security Council was in any way becoming a shadow cabinet or a Politburo, insisting that it was and would remain a consultative body doing no more than preparing proposals for the president on strengthening national security.[23] Although the Security Council was given extraordinary powers to be applied during states of emergency, comparisons with the Politburo of old are rather far-fetched. Its influence has tended to rise and fall depending on the status of its secretary. When Ivanov was appointed defence minister, the Security Council once again sharply declined in significance.

The alleged pre-eminent role of the *siloviki* has been challenged by a number of studies. Rivera and Rivera demonstrate that while the number of *siloviki* in responsible government positions had indeed increased, this rise was not as big as Kryshtanovskaya and White had suggested – a threefold increase since 1998 rather than the reported sevenfold increase.[24] They conclude that claims about 'an emerging "militocracy" are real but overstated'.[25] Renz has questioned whether the growth in silovik numbers is a conscious strategy by Putin to enhance their influence, and she argues that there is no common 'military mindset' among them advocating relatively more authoritarian policies. In her view, they are far from dominant in the policy-making process.[26] Rivera and Rivera note that 'few analysts have expressed the expectation that a Kremlin dominated by *siloviki* will behave more aggressively in the international arena or observed any actual increase in the use of force by Moscow'.[27] Above all, they argue that this is balanced by the increased representation of business representatives in all spheres of

Russian public life, a nascent bourgeoisie that will in the long term perhaps have a far greater impact than the temporary assertion of silovik authority.

The influence of the *chekisty* is measured not only by their physical presence in the corridors of power, but also by their forceful self-belief that their destiny was to save Russia. In this version of the national narrative, Russia was beset by hostile external forces and their domestic allies to reduce the country to little more than a vassal of the West. Some of this was articulated by Putin's long-time associate Cherkesov, who in Soviet times had led the persecution of dissidents in Leningrad. Between 1992 and 1998 he headed the St Petersburg and Leningrad regional division of the FSB, and was appointed presidential representative to the North-West Federal District between 2000–3 before taking up the directorship of the newly formed Federal Anti-Narcotics Service (FSKN). In a well-publicised article in late 2004 he condemned those who attacked Russia's security services, calling it a war against 'chekism' comparable to the anti-communist campaign of the late 1980s. He insisted that they had a historic role to play:

> If I am correct, if chekists and our contemporary Russia are historically linked, then what an enormous responsibility such a link places on us ... History has placed the main burden of preserving Russian statehood on our shoulders.[28]

Cherkesov was far from alone in holding the view that the *siloviki* had been entrusted with the sacred duty of defending the motherland, and niceties like democracy should not get in the way of their task. Putin was at pains to distance himself from the latter view, but clearly the broad narrative of the *siloviki* as national saviours, with himself at their head, influenced his policies when it came to dealing with the oligarchs, notably in the Yukos affair. As a statist, however, Putin did not allow the *siloviki* to have it all their own way, however sympathetic he may have been to their views. They were, after all, just another corporation, and ultimately the only corporation Putin was interested in was the state.

The military and securitisation

The military was granted considerable latitude in the second Chechen war from September 1999 (Chapter 1). Putin, however, sought to limit the role of military hardliners in foreign policy. In February 2000 he effectively sidelined hawks like Leonid Ivashov, head of the Defence ministry's foreign affairs department, and General Anatoly Kvashnin, the chief of the General Staff, to allow a meeting with Lord George Robertson, the head of Nato. Soon after, in an interview with the BBC on 5 March 2000 Putin even went so far as to entertain the possibility that one day Russia might join Nato, albeit on 'equal terms' (see Chapter 10). Unlike Yeltsin earlier, rhetorical support for the military was translated into concrete policies and renewed efforts to achieve military reform. Although the status and coherence of the military as an institution rose considerably under Putin, it was not allowed to infringe on the prerogatives of the civilian leadership. Severe cuts in numbers were accompanied by continued moves away from a conscript to a fully professional service.

Although Russian law established a minimum of 3.5 per cent of GDP to be devoted to the military, under Putin spending stabilised at around 2.6 per cent, although in absolute terms there were significant increases in budgets to reflect the growing economy. In the first seven years of his leadership spending on the military increased fivefold. Defence expenditure in 2006 was 15 per cent of budgetary expenditure, down from the 24 per cent in 1994, but in absolute terms much higher. According to Putin, between 2000 and 2006 army financing increased by three and a half times, representing 2.6 per cent of GDP, which in absolute terms was $30 billion.[29] This was 25 times less than that spent by the USA and half that spent by China. The procurement programme was significantly improved, with the phased intro-duction of new ships, aircraft and armour. Training was improved and more units were combat ready. The aim was to create a more mobile, professional and technologically sophisticated army, with an increased emphasis on nuclear weapons to counter external strategic threats. Putin's state of the nation speech on 10 May 2006 was notable for its emphasis on military issues, warning of new and increasing threats from the arms race, America's plans to place conventional weapons on intercontinental ballistic missile (ICBM) boosters, and the swirling threat of terrorism, together with a hostile tone from the West as it lectured Russia on democracy.[30] Putin's response, however, was not a classic Cold War one, to increase military spending, but took the form of what Stephen Blank calls an 'asymmetric intellectual response'.[31] This confirmed the continued demilitarisation of Russian poli-tics, although in terms of personnel the presence of military and security officials continued to increase. This reflected less the militarisation of domestic politics than the civilianisation of the military. This was reflected in the appointment of Sergei Ivanov to head the defence ministry in 2001, the first civilian (although with a security background) to become defence minister since the Brezhnev period. The intense discussions over the content of a new security doctrine in 2006–7 reflected the struggle for the soul of Russian politics and its perception of the world.

The debate continues about whether security and military personnel in office mean the militarisation or 'securitisation' of politics in its entirety. For Bacon and his co-authors, Putin has confronted challenges, ranging from terrorism, media and religious freedom, immigration and economic globa-lisation, by endowing them with a 'security' dimension, but the prominence of a 'securitisation' discourse does not mean the triumph of the security apparatus. Putin's rule, in their view, is a far more complex phenomenon than simply the restoration of KGB rule.[32] The security component of the Putin bloc was itself far from homogeneous, and its support for Putin was at best conditional. An interview with Valentin Velichko, an ex-KGB general and head of the security service veterans' association Dignity and Honour, was revealing. He noted: 'Yes, we did help him [Putin] during a first stage, during the election campaign. But now, it's time to wait. Putin can go one way and continue working for the Family ... Or he can work for the state. Or he can work for himself. For the moment he hasn't shown anything yet'.[33] Velichko was an adherent of the Andropov approach to change, hoping for an evolutionary course like China's that developed a market economy while maintaining the authoritarian communist regime. There is no evidence that Putin shared such an approach. The Andropov way was not the Putin way.

Although they may not have been able to dominate the political agenda, Putin, did, however, allow a massive expansion in the security apparatus, broadly defined. In addition to the 1.2 million people in the armed forces, the interior ministry (MVD) had about another two million, the FSB (including now the Border Guard Service, which Putin brought back into the Lubyanka fold) and some allied services (including FAPSI, the communications intercept agency) up to half a million, and a number of other agencies, including Shoigu's emergencies ministry, the State Narcotics Service, and, if one includes private security agencies (ChOPs), together employed about another million personnel. As the opposition politician Vladimir Ryzhkov pointed out

> That makes a total of nearly 5 million people, mostly working-age men, employed in various kinds of military or militarized organizations – against a backdrop of Russia's disastrous demographic situation and shrinking labor forces. Maintaining the security and law enforcement agencies (*siloviki*), along with maintaining the bureaucracy, now accounts for the lion's share of federal budget spending.[34]

The development of this behemoth betokened not the onset of authoritarianism, but acted as a stultifying weight that depressed economic performance, encouraged immobility, and inhibited political pluralism and competitiveness. This group represented the core social basis of Putin's regime.

The 'Pitery'

There has long been a struggle between Moscow and St Petersburg for predominance in Russia, and Putin's arrival restored some of the second city's pre-eminence.[35] The St Petersburg newcomers (the 'Pitery') were divided into economic liberals (many of whom had worked with Putin in the city administration) and *chekisty* (from the first stage of his career). The key Pitery included the chief secretary of the presidential administration Igor Sechin, and the lawyer Dmitry Kozak, also a deputy head of the presidential administration (PA) and later presidential envoy to the Southern

Federal District. Another deputy head of the PA, responsible for personnel issues, is Victor Ivanov, who deserves special note since he was the KGB officer who recruited Putin into the agency in the mid-1970s and they have remained friends ever since. Sergei Mironov, previously the representative of the St Petersburg legislature, was elected on 5 December 2001 to head the Federation Council. Outside the Kremlin the Pitery included Sergei Pugachev, the head of Mezhprombank, who enjoyed close ties with Putin from their St Petersburg days. Pugachev provided financial support for the Pitery, while his association with the Orthodox Church earned him the moniker 'the Christian oligarch'. The Pitery provided many of the liberals in Putin's administration. Putin had worked with Dmitry Medvedev in St Petersburg as part of Sobchak's administration, and he became head of Putin's campaign team in 2000, and went on to become one of Putin's main advisors in the Kremlin. He replaced Voloshin as chief of staff in October 2003, and in the reshuffle of 14 November 2005 became first deputy prime minister and leading candidate to succeed Putin. The dismissal of Kasyanov in February 2004 was seen in part as the reassertion of the Pitery against 'Muscovites'.[36] Although the Pitery shared a common loyalty to Putin, they were divided on everything else, and thus cannot be considered a cohesive faction in Putin's administration.[37]

The economic liberals

Although Putin was to draw liberally on members of the old Soviet ruling class, above all its security apparatus, to staff his administration, they were typically kept far away from the management of the economy. Throughout Putin's presidency the core economic ministries remained in the hands of a group of economic liberals. Putin's old friend from St Petersburg, German Gref, remained at the Ministry of Economic Development and Trade, and Alexei Kudrin retained a firm hold on the finance ministry. We shall discuss the growing role of big business in Chapter 9, but here we can note that the commodities boom of the early 2000s generated a counterweight to the *siloviki*, the so-called *syroviki*, the energy and other raw materials giants.

The democratic statists

Putin's administration was characterised by functional segmentation, with each part of his ruling bloc focused in the main on their designated sphere, although on certain issues there was spectacular spillover (notably in the Yukos affair). The democratic statists concentrated on the management of public politics. Their leading representative is another deputy head of the presidential administration, Vladislav Surkov. He is the figure most closely associated with the practice of 'managed democracy', although the former presidential chief of staff, Voloshin, was the architect of this system. Surkov later advanced the notion of 'sovereign democracy'.[38] Some of the most active 'political technologists' were associated with this idea, notably Gleb Pavlovsky and Sergei Markov. For Markov there was no fundamental division between the liberals and the *siloviki*. As he put it, 'The *siloviki* are in charge of retaining the country's sovereignty and restoring the state's institutions, while liberals deal with economic reform and the functioning of the political system, what observers have described as managed democracy. This is a clear division of responsibility'.[39] This group had a distinctive idea of how democracy should work in Russian conditions, a view that denigrated the free flow of liberal pluralism.

Regional groupings

There were a number of 'factions' that remained outside the Putin 'bloc', notably Luzhkov's power base in Moscow, Yakovlev's team in St Petersburg (until he was replaced by Valentina Matvienko in 2003) and some other powerful regional power constellations, notably Mintimir Shaimiev in Tatarstan and Eduard Rossel in Sverdlovsk. Putin went out of his way to demonstrate his openness to enter into dialogue with regional elites, and despite his reassertion of central state power (Chapter 7), some of Yeltsin's readiness to accommodate regional leaders (but not any theoretical basis which could legitimate that power) was also practised by Putin. The merger of Unity with Luzhkov's Fatherland party in early 2002 to create United Russia (*Edinaya Rossiya*) represented the co-optation of the organised regional challenge to the Kremlin's power, but it did little to overcome the structural autonomy of parts of the Russian state. At the same time, federal power appeared exiguous in parts of the country. Russian state power weakly grasped the various North Caucasian republics, and at various points its fragility was revealed in spectacular attacks emanating from Chechnya. Putin's power base, as we have seen, remained St Petersburg, and on several occasions plans were mooted to move part of the federal government and central institutions to the city. There was much discussion of moving the Federation Council, but in the event only the Constitutional Court planned to move to the northern capital.

The middle class

One does not have to be a neo-Marxist to find the question of the class basis of Putin's regime an intriguing one. Three main candidates immediately present themselves: the security-military apparatus, the bureaucracy and the middle class. The first two are not properly constituted classes in any recognisable Marxist sense, while the third gained in sociological strength. According to Maleva, about 20 per cent of Russian families could be considered middle class.[40] On the basis of an examination of the electorate that supported Putin in 2004, a recent study has argued that Putin's base is rooted in 'a new middle class'. This is the real 'new class', not the bureaucratic office-holding class identified by Milovan Djilas as the real beneficiaries of Soviet-type systems.[41] This class has overcome and rejected the values of the socialist past but is unclear about the future. Putin, according to the author, reflects the characteristics of individuals imbued with the values of the professional espionage community. There is a thus a gulf between the aspirations and uncertainties of the new middle class, which at the minimum favour the creation of a law-based society and the development of a genuine project for national modernisation, and the silo-vik values represented by Putin.[42] Putin could offer a minimum level of security and state restoration, but the alliance between the new middle class and the security-bureaucratic apparatus was a temporary one, and if the latter fails to respond to aspirations for genuine democratic modernity in Russia, then a gulf will open up between the regime and society, presaging a new period of revolutionary upheaval.

Putin's bloc: factions not clans

Although there are discernible differences in the policy perspectives of the various factions surrounding Putin, it is important not to exaggerate the differences. It would be a mistake to envisage these differences of emphasis as stable clan-like formations. All factions shared a *gosudarstvennik* (statist) ideology, defending Russia's sovereignty and asserting its influence in the world. We use the term 'faction' rather than 'clan' advisedly. Thomas Graham in the mid-1990s suggested that clan-type structures had emerged as the shaping force of Russian politics,[43] but this was probably an exag-geration even then. The dominance of the 'family' in Yeltsin's last years was always unstable and represented little more than a fluid grouping based on immediate interests, although sharing in broad terms a commitment to a set of policy preferences (above all, keeping the communists and their allies out of power). Factions are far less substantive and enduring than clans.

The clan phenomenon is far less defined in Russia than in Ukraine and some other countries. Unlike in Ukraine, where clan-type structures repre-sent a combination of social, regional, economic and even ideological dif-ferences,[44] in Russia the political regime is more dominant, and interests less defined. The difference is an important factor determining divergent demo-cratisation trajectories in the two countries. In some Central Asian coun-tries clan structures (based on kinship ties and regional identities) and political administrations have to all intents and purposes merged, and this in turn gives rise to yet another type of political regime.[45] While in Ukraine there is a clear regional and sectoral basis to relatively stable groupings with a defined stance on public policy issues, the degree to which a stable 'clan' system has emerged can be questioned. Similarly, the attempt to apply a clan model to Kazakhstan politics has been questioned on the basis of the lack of empirically testable evidence.[46] The applicability of the model to Russia is even more problematical, since here things are far more situational, permeable and malleable. Executive authorities in the centre and the regions build up their own factions through personalised patterns of appointment, as seen most vividly in Putin's 'tail' from St Petersburg, and it would be far-fetched to call them a 'clan'.

There is an important difference between coalition building, which in Western democracies usually takes the form of a stable alliance based on the mutual self-interest of identifiable political forces, and consensus making, the attempt to draw people into a common project or around a common policy. The only time that coalition building had been attempted in post-communist Russia was in 1992, when Yeltsin sought to gain the support of party leaders for reform and in his struggle with parliament. The political system emerging out of the defeat of the old parliament in October 1993, and enshrined in the December 1993 constitution, focuses all fundamental political processes on the president. In the context of a weak party system and a hegemonic presidency, coalition building can at best be marginal. Instead, under Putin the presidency tried to rally individual political leaders, social and political groupings, and interests, as well as the public at large, to its cause. Putin's power was based not on a formal coalition of political groupings but on his ability to draw the factions under the wing of the hegemonic presidency. This worked as long as he remained a popular and effective leader, but, as the succession approached, the Putin bloc began to dissolve into its constituent factions.

In the short term, one of the immediate consequences of Putin's policy of consensus was his insistence that there would not be another grand redistribution of property. Instead, Putin drew a thick line under Yeltsin's own possible misdemeanours and those of the class that had profited from his rule. Putin's first official act as interim president had granted Yeltsin and his family immunity from prosecution. Putin's adoption of the 'zero option' represented a deliberate act of social reconciliation. It was motivated, we argued above, by practical considerations, but it also had a normative basis: putting an end to Russia's endless cycles of revolutions and counter-revolutions. This issue was particularly important in the context where some 60 per cent of the population, according to one poll, favoured the administrative confiscation of the wealth of the 'new Russians'.[47] Instead of the stark choice posited by many of either breaking with the Yeltsin family or remaining a dependent politician, Putin finessed the problem. He remained true to his commitments to Yeltsin and continued his policies, but the style of politics changed dramatically.

The Putin bloc remained a broad church, reflecting Putin's past, but its disparate nature was reflected in certain policy areas (above all the economy) by a loss of coherence. In general, although sharp policy disagreements swirled around Putin, it is only with great difficulty that these debates can be mapped directly on to factional struggles, such as Muscovites against Pitery, *chekisty* versus liberals. Putin did turn, as we shall see, against some of the more politically ambitious oligarchs, but worked happily with the rest. He did not become a captive of any particular grouping, such as the security establishment or the St Petersburg liberals, but allowed room for manoeuvre. As for popular support, it was clear that Putin nurtured the public as a farmer tends his stock, never pushing policies (such as reform of municipal services) so far or so fast as to threaten his popularity. Putin, however, was no populist, refusing to pander to the whims of public opinion and the often vengeful, xenophobic and angry moods to which the public is prey when whipped up by the 'birdseed' press (to use Ursula le Guin's term). Putin was certainly no Alexander Lukashenko, whose brand of populism in neighbouring Belarus was based on sensitivity to popular prejudices and a crude disdain for representative institutions, the courts and for all political institutions that could in any way limit the power of the presidency. More than that, in Russia the rudiments of a middle class had developed, and provided the bedrock for the politics of normality propounded by Putin.

Putin and the people

The entrenchment of the 'transitional winners' and their resistance to the reassertion of national state interests was an important constraint on Putin's power, but to overcome this obstacle Putin posed as the champion of the interests of 'transitional losers', the great mass of the people who had seen their living standards eroded, wages left unpaid, pensions falling into arrears and their savings lost. While Putin's policies have indeed been popular, Putin was far from populist himself. Neither was he simply the product of 'virtual politics', the beneficiary of the manipulation of political consciousness, processes and institutions by various powerful interests. These 'political technologies' are indeed highly developed in Russia, and a whole industry has developed bringing together academics, opinion polling experts and political aspirants, although it would be wide of the mark to argue that they have rendered the whole political process 'virtual'.[48] These technologies were particularly active in the 1999–2000 electoral cycle,[49] yet Putin's political charisma and programmatic identity cannot be reduced to this. Without a determined personality with a vision for Russia's future, no amount of manipulation would have ensured victory. In addition, Putin did largely deliver on his promise to pay wages and pensions on time, and this was no small achievement.

Popular views

It is clear that the country which Putin led suffered from a lack of confidence in the new order and public institutions. Some 80 per cent of the population appeared dissatisfied with democracy, a figure higher than the Commonwealth of Independent States (CIS) average (75 per cent) or that typical of the EU (50 per cent).[50] In spring 2001 just 2 per cent of the population thought that Russia was a democracy, while 21 per cent thought the country was moving in that direction and 27 per cent considered Russia more democratic than it had been in the Soviet era (although 17 per cent took the contrary view).[51] Questioned on the level of trust in institutions, churches came out top with 19 per cent evincing full and 28 per cent some trust. Second came the armed forces at 14 and 36 per cent, respectively, while near the bottom came the government at 7 and 24 per cent, parliament at 2 and 14 per cent, and political parties at a miserable 2 and 9 per cent, respectively.[52] Despite polls showing a clear popular distrust of the new democracy, when it came to elections participation has been remarkably high. The 54 per cent of eligible voters turning out in December 1993, 64 per cent in 1995, 62 per cent in 1999 and 55.7 per cent in 2003 suggest that scepticism is tempered by a certain commitment. In presidential elections turnout was even higher: in 1991, 75 per cent; in 1996 (first round), 70 per cent, and (second round), 69 per cent; in 2000, 69 per cent; and in 2004, 64.4 per cent. Public attitudes towards core values of democracy, tolerance, pluralism, the West and the like remain contested.

The central question on coming to power was whether Putin and his allies would challenge the Yeltsinite socio-political settlement, above all the bureaucratised neo-*nomenklatura* regime that had emerged in the 1990s that benefited from a country stuck half way between the plan and the market. To what extent did Putin have an independent political base? The answer to this question is crucial to understanding the room for manoeuvre that Putin had as president. As we saw in the previous section, the Putin consensual bloc was fragmented and lacked a single coherent programme. Pavlovsky raised the basic question: 'We are trying to determine now whose victory was the victory of Putin. On whom should he now rely?' He dismissed Unity as an adequate political base, and came up with the unexpected answer: 'The masses, which were not allowed to emerge on the political scene after 1991–3, have surged onto it today. And Putin is their leader'. He went on:

> One can argue in what sense he is the leader – the leader of the party of power or the leader of the opposition. I believe that those who chose Putin regard him as the leader of the opposition who seized power in Russia. For Putin's majority Putin is the leader of the party of opposition to the old regime.[53]

Putin's rise, in other words, can be seen as a distinctive variation on the theme of a revolt from below, reflecting revulsion against the corruption of the Yeltsin years while not rejecting the basic principles that Yeltsin's leadership had espoused. Putin's popularity was based at least in part on favourable comparisons with his predecessor, but also on a more positive projection of popular aspirations, hopes that were not totally devoid of rationality. In particular, the Putin bloc was anchored in the aspirations of the younger generation, who were more likely to support market reform, democracy and integration with the West than other age groups,[54] while at the same time imbued with patriotic sentiments and a sense of Russia's national self-worth.

Sooner or later there was a danger that the public would tire of the relentless projection of the Putin personality in the media. As the years passed it became clear that this would come later, if at all. According to poll results, Putin's popularity remained remarkably stable. After his first 100 days in office the Agency of Regional Political Studies (ARPI) revealed that some 54 per cent still evaluated him positively, giving rise already at this early stage to talk of a 'teflon president'.[55] One reason for Putin's popularity, of course, was that he was not Yeltsin. Between 1994 and 2001 the percentage of people holding Yeltsin personally responsible for the troubles of the 1990s nearly doubled from 18.1 to 34 per cent.[56] The basic feeling that Russia had become a happier place since Putin's accession remained. Two years into his leadership a growing number were positive about the system of government that he headed, although at 47 per cent this was still a minority. At that time 72 per cent rated the old Communist system positively, by far the highest positive ranking in any of the non-CIS post-communist countries.[57] The shaky foundations of the new order were reflected in the astonishing figure that half of Russians would approve of the closing down of parliament, and just over one-fifth thought that it could happen.[58] While trust in the political institutions of democracy was low throughout the region, in Russia it was lower still, with only 7 per cent trusting parliament and the same number parties.[59] Not surprisingly, both Yeltsin and Putin ran as independents.

Putin's approval rating throughout his leadership remained at a remarkably high and consistent level, with between 65 and 73 per cent with a positive attitude.[60] In contrast to Yeltsin's frequent absences 'working on documents', Putin did not have a single day off sick in the first three years of his presidency,[61] and few, if any, afterwards. Polls consistently found Putin's performance rated excellent by between 37 and 50 per cent of respondents, while another 36–48 per cent considered his performance satisfactory. On the third anniversary of his election in March 2003, 39 per cent found his performance excellent or good, another 46 per cent considered it satisfactory, and only 11 per cent thought that he worked badly.[62] A poll taken at the same time revealed that 38 per cent felt more positive about Putin than they had done on his election, 52 per cent the same and only 10 per cent worse. The reason for this was a strong sense (61 per cent) that Putin had managed to fulfil many of his plans during his presidency, while only 10 per cent felt that he had fulfilled none. As for his independence as a decision-maker, 61 per cent thought that he was influenced by other people while 37 per cent thought that he was his own man. A related question asked whether he was more independent now than three years earlier, and 66 per cent thought that he was more independent while 26 per cent thought that he was as independent as before. The response to the related question of whether Putin put his own popularity or the interests of the country first saw nearly 60 per cent agree with the latter proposition, while 28 per cent thought that he cared more for his popularity.[63]

A poll by the Levada Centre in December 2005 found that 75 per cent of respondents still approved of his work. The same poll revealed an extraordinary consistency over the years in popular views of Putin, although at that time positive views of him as an experienced politician and as a sympathetic person rose, while trust in his ability to ensure order and stability in the country decreased. The striking feature of the survey was that Putin on the whole reflected the policy preferences of the population, with just under half supporting the continuation of reforms but with a stronger state role and ensuring popular welfare, while only 10 per cent called for the continuation of reforms with a decreased role for the state, while another 11 per cent supported the swift and decisive implementation of reform. Only 22 per cent favoured a return to the Soviet system. The plurality of those surveyed (41 per cent) considered that Putin represented above all the interests of the security and armed services.[64] A detailed analysis of Putin's electorate of 2000 suggested that the majority continued to support him by inertia rather than by any strong commitment, although a strong core strongly identified with his policies and that of United Russia. The generational characteristics of his support base had changed, above all by becoming much younger.[65]

This was confirmed by studies conducted in 2005. Since Putin's election in 2000 the population had renewed itself by 7 per cent, and while Putin's aging supporters remained loyal to him largely out of inertia, his support base among young people (under 30) had grown, and reflected a positive commitment to his vision of Russia. The structure of Putin's support had changed, with 71 per cent of young people considering he was effectively fulfilling his duties. Some 40 per cent of his adepts were under 35, spread evenly among urban and rural constituencies and across the regions of Russia. Young people revealed greater loyalty to the authorities than older generations. These were the first post-Soviet generation, and turned out to be the most conservative social group while at the same time the most self-reliant and optimistic and also imbued with something new in Russia, an 'active, conscious patriotism'.[66] Support for Putin was not so much for the man himself as for continuity and a sense that there was no alternative to the system that he had created.[67] Nearly two-thirds supported United Russia, considering it the only 'genuine' party.[68] On average, the younger cohort evaluated the work of the government, State Duma and governors some 5 per cent higher than the rest of the population.[69]

How can we interpret Putin's long-term popularity? It is clear that the structure of his policies reflected not only elite preferences but had a mass base. But did then support for his policies suggest popular support for his relatively restrictive version of liberal statism, reflecting perhaps a political culture tolerant of anti-democratic practices? Stephen Whitefield examines the conundrum of Putin's popularity: if indeed Putin is responsible for the dismantlement of Russian democracy, then how can we explain his sustained popularity? Whitefield suggests a number of hypotheses to explain this phenomenon: Putin's popularity reflects the illiberal and undemocratic sentiments of Russians; Putin's leadership has changed the views of his supporters because of the illiberal outcomes, while his opponents take a more negative view; this leads to a bifurcated system of supports, for and against Putin. Whitefield suggests that a 'system performance' analysis is more convincing, in which Putin's popularity is based on perceived improved political and economic performance. His survey data discounts the growing illiberalism hypothesis, and the argument that Putin is supported by those with anti-democratic values is not upheld either. The data suggest that Russians on the whole do not hold the view that there has been significant democratic backsliding, while popular support for democratic norms and values has remained more or less constant. Opponents of democracy do not in the main support Putin, while those who seek the consolidation of government do not necessarily hold undemocratic views. In conclusion, Whitefield notes that 'Putin's popularity does not appear to rest on an "authoritarian" mass political culture'.[70]

Richard Rose and associates have argued that a president's popularity that is 'a mile wide' on election day can prove ephemeral, and examine the degree to which Putin's popularity may well have been an inch deep.[71] In the event Putin's popularity proved rather more enduring, but the approach does draw attention to the decidedly mixed approval ratings for his performance and that of his government on a number of policy issues. Approval of the work of his cabinet fell from 57 to 39 per cent in June 2000 alone, due apparently to the failure to end the war in Chechnya and fears that inflation was once again on the rise.[72] In December 2002 only 33 per cent thought that Kasyanov handled his job well, while 27 per cent thought not. The performance of his government was rated similarly, with only 24 per cent thinking it was doing a good job while 37 thought its performance bad.[73] In general, as noted, trust in political institutions in Russia scores poorly, highlighting the gulf between trust in the president and the political system over which he presided. Polls suggested a relatively low belief that Russia had become a democratic system.[74]

Putin's achievements in the sphere of foreign policy and democracy tended to gain more positive than negative ratings, but on issues such as whether Putin had been able to restore order to the country, limit corruption, improve the economy or resolve the Chechen crisis, then the negative ratings predominated.[75] For the majority of the population, trying to survive on small pensions and miserly wages, the big questions of macroeconomic policy, judicial reform and the like appeared very distant, especially since their interactions with the courts and other authoritative bodies tended to be dispiriting if not outright corrupt. Asked what they would ask Putin to do if presented with the opportunity, 47 per cent said 'raise living standards', 21 per cent 'establish an effective management system', 12 per cent 'stimulate economic development and employment', while only 2 per cent said 'end the Chechen war' and the same number focused on 'foreign policy'.[76]

The near mythical status of the 'Putin phenomenon' aroused much resentment, but it would not be fair to say that it was achieved by the deliberate suppression of alternatives.[77] Putin's popularity was sustained in part by the absence of anyone else who came even close to him in trust ratings. Although Putin's general approval rating remained astronomically high, this was not, as Elena Shestopal puts it, 'hypnotic blindness' but was tempered by an awareness, and indeed criticism, of his shortcomings and a recognition of his unattractive qualities.[78] Victory in the 2004 presidential election was assured not only because the regime controlled the central media but also because of the genuine lack of alternative candidates of stature.

Emergency situations

Putin's popularity was maintained despite the catastrophes that marked his presidency, although he did learn to manage these crises with greater skill. The sinking in the Barents Sea of the *Kursk* nuclear submarine on 12 August 2000 proved the greatest test to Putin's early leadership.[79] The craft had only entered service in 1995 and was considered the most modern and reliable in the submarine fleet. The explosion that tore the craft apart at 07.28 that morning killed 118 submariners and was caused by the leak of highly unstable hydrogen peroxide torpedo fuel. A first explosion then provoked a far more powerful blast in the nose of the submarine that sent it to the bottom. This was admitted only two years later by the government commission headed by Ilya Klebanov. Earlier various explanations had been advanced, including the idea that the Kursk had been struck by either an American or British submarine, or that a rocket from a nearby Russian battleship participating in the same military exercise may have been responsible. Putin's failure to break off his holiday on the Black Sea immediately drew much criticism, as did the extended delay before the offers of foreign help were accepted.[80] Worse than that, at a press conference when asked 'What happened to the *Kursk*?', he answered laconically and with a touch of heartlessness; 'It sank'. Putin later fulfilled his promise that the craft would be raised and the sailors given a proper burial.

By the time of the Dubrovka theatre siege of 23–25 October 2002 Putin was able to project an image of resolution and contrition. Over 800 people, watching the popular *Nord-Ost* musical, were taken hostage by 41 Chechen militants (19 of whom were women) headed by the young warlord Movsar Baraev. After three days of siege the security forces in the morning of 26 October forced entry using a gas to incapacitate the terrorists, all of whom were shot.[81] Official figures suggest that 129 hostages died, but Karina Moskalenko, the lawyer representing the victims, suggests that at least 174 perished, all but two from the effects of the gas, while the journalist Anna Politkovskaya estimated that the total was over 200. The carelessness of the emergency services caused many additional deaths, and only four days later were doctors informed that the gas was a fentanyl derivative. In his address to the people Putin stated:

> We succeeded in doing what seemed almost impossible – in saving the lives of hundreds of people. We showed that Russia cannot be forced to her knees. But now, first of all, I would like to address the relatives and friends of those who have perished. We could not save everyone. Forgive us.[82]

The fact that a large group of armed Chechens could capture a building in Moscow revealed the relative powerlessness of the state and the advanced decay of its institutions, and thus only reinforced Putin's exhortations to strengthen the state.

On 1 September 2004 militants directed by Shamil Basaev captured School No. 1 in Beslan in North Ossetia. The Beslan attack came after months of escalating atrocities. On 21 June some 200 militants, mostly from Chechnya, seized parts of Nazran, the capital of Ingushetia, and began murdering policemen. Some 100 law enforcement officials died, but equally shocking was the way that parts of the republic were seized with such ease. On 21 August fighters seized and held the centre of Grozny for three hours, with dozens of casualties. On 24 August there was a bomb blast in Kashirka street in Moscow, that same evening two planes were brought down by terrorist bombs with over 90 casualties, and on 31 August a bomb at the Riga metro station in Moscow killed 10 people and injured 30. The events in Beslan themselves have been characterised as Russia's 9/11, but much remains contested about the events. The local administration says 1,347 were taken hostage, whereas the prosecutor general, Vladimir Ustinov, stated that 329 of 1,156 hostages died. There is uncertainty also about the identity of the 32 terrorists, and even their number. One was a North Ossetian, there were a few Ingush, while six have been identified as Chechens. The chaos attending the final storming on Friday 3 September reflected the lack of overall coherence of the authority's response and ended in the deaths of 334 hostages including 186 schoolchildren. Several investigative commissions in the following years came up with conflicting accounts and this, as much as the tragedy itself, stoked anger in the region.[83]

The conflict spread out from Chechnya throughout the North Caucasus, with Dagestan becoming ever more unstable as militants killed policemen and attacked various civilian objects. As Vladimir Ryzhkov put it, the social contract between Putin and the people was no longer being fulfilled.[84] Following the Beslan events, Putin delivered dire warnings about the weakness of the state that had allowed this to happen. He followed up with a range of measures (which we shall discuss later) that together can be called a 'constitutional *coup détat'*, somewhat reminiscent of Charles de Gaulle's establishment of the Fifth Republic in 1958. Unlike France, however, it is not clear that Putin's measures substantively improved Russia's system of governance. The strengthening of the regime was certainly not the same as developing the infrastructural powers of a modern state.

Putin's resilient popularity could be taken as a sorry reflection of the condition of Russian politics, when so many of the population projected their hopes on one individual. As Avtandil Tsuladze put it, 'Putin appears to be the last hope of society for the preservation of stability'.[85] Putin can be seen as representative of the type that has a long pedigree in Russian history, the decisive leader who forges the nation's consolidation in a time of crisis. This usually took place at a time of a foreign threat, accompanied sometimes by internal disintegration. In Putin's case, the main threats were domestic. Putin's rise to power can be considered a type of 'revolt of the masses' against the venality and greed of the Yeltsin years. In this context it was perfectly logical for the reform of the federal system to be one of Putin's first priorities. It was an attempt, in the words of Andrei Ryabov, 'to bring more order and justice into society, since the arbitrariness of the regional barons is there for all to see'.[86] Equally, the struggle for 'social justice' meant for many an assault on the extra-democratic privileges of the oligarchs. Putin did not enjoy a stable power coalition, and some of the liberal economic reforms entailed harsh social consequences and for this reason Putin was most cautious in implementing them. This in turn meant that the reform impetus stalled, provoking the danger of yet another period of stagnation.

Leadership and style

Leadership is an essential, although often neglected, aspect of any democratic system. As Schumpeter argued, 'The classical theory [of democracy] did not do this ['give proper recognition of the vital fact of leadership'] but ... attributed to the electorate an altogether unrealistic degree of initiative which practically amounted to ignoring leadership. But collectives act almost exclusively by accepting leadership – this is the dominant mechanism of practically any collective action which is more than a reflex'.[87] Putin's presidency is a classic case where individual leadership can stamp its preferences on a period, although of course constrained by the conditions of that time. In addition to the important role of leadership in all democratic societies, there are factors particular to Russia. It is often argued that Russia has a cultural predisposition towards strong personalised leadership. In post-communist Russia this aspect of the country's political culture was boosted by the weakness of formal political institutions and the underdevelopment of societal representation, above all the relatively inchoate nature of the party system. In addition, the numerous crises affecting the country increased support for resolute leadership.

In terms of Weber's threefold delineation of modes of legitimation, traditional, legal-rational and charismatic, the latter has particular relevance. Roger Eatwell distinguishes between three types of charismatic leadership: coterie charisma, in which a leader inspires devotion among a relatively small inner core of followers; mass charisma, whereby the leader is able to generate broad popular sentiments; while the phenomenon of institutional charisma suggests that a charismatic bond may develop between institutions, such as a political party, or even the presidency as an abstract symbol of power, and its followers.[88] The charismatic bond, moreover, can be either affective or based on rational calculation.[89] Putin's charisma was distinctive but clearly of the mass type. He was a strong leader with a vision for the country's future that made him 'the president of hope'.

Archie Brown contrasts 'transformational' leaders, who change not just policy but the system as well, with 'transactional' ones, who may well achieve major policy changes but who remain within the bounds of the existing order.[90] He recognises that the characterisation of any particular leader depends on the categories of transformation that are chosen, and in our case this is particularly important. Putin repudiated the revolutionary approach to political change, and in the end he became a classic transactional leader. He worked within the parameters of the system inherited from Yeltsin, although he transformed the way that it operated. The pursuit of normalcy gave society a breathing space at the social level, but Putin's exclusive approach to political integration failed to overcome the gulf between leaders and the political community that is typical for Russia.

Putin's first period in power was marked by a flurry of activity, with attacks launched on a number of fronts simultaneously – against the regional barons, the oligarchs and the media. Important constitutional issues appeared to be resolved by bullying tactics and administrative means. Even with popular support, when faced with strong opposition Putin tended to conduct an orderly retreat. Putin backtracked, for example, when it became clear that the electorate would reject his favoured candidate (Matvienko) against the incumbent, Yakovlev, in the St. Petersburg gubernatorial elections in early 2000. In later years Putin was careful to prepare the ground before launching a policy; perhaps too cautious, hence the charges of the 'Gorbachevisation' of his leadership, taken to mean a style where rhetoric substitutes for action and crucial decisions are delayed.

Apparent policy reversals led the *Kommersant* weekly business magazine to editorialise about 'The weakness of the firm hand'.[91] The case could be made with equal conviction that Putin's leadership style reflected the firmness of the weak hand. It is clear that authoritarianism without the bedrock of institutional support can prove ephemeral. The potential social and institutional bases for authoritarianism in Russia included the security establishment and the military, together with some alienated intellectuals, but there is no evidence that Putin sought to forge such a coalition. The authoritarian populism practised by Lukashenko in neighbouring Belarus was not transferred to Russia. Putin did not seek to establish an alternative system to the representative democracy that had emerged in Russia in the 1990s; but, equally, his commitment to democratic values could only be proved by the flourishing of media freedom, the rule of law and ultimately the greatest challenge, the democratic rotation of the highest political office in the land in free elections. While the legitimacy of democracy in the 1990s was undermined by its association with economic failure, social hardship, criminality and waning prestige on the world scale, opinion polls still showed a strong core of support for basic democratic principles. Indeed, if the main criticism of government in the early period of Putin's leadership was that it was not strong enough, by the end of his first term the main charge was that the Russian state was not democratic enough. A sea change in the terms of discourse had taken place.

Putin's room for manoeuvre was limited by the existing socio-political and socio-economic structures. Did the pattern of property, privileges and power established under Yeltsin allow scope for radical political intervention and change? It soon became clear that an activist presidency could mobilise the population and state loyalists against the flaws of the Yeltsin regime in the name of Russia's honour and dignity. Putin found many to support such a reconstitution of the state and law and order. However, while Putin used the presidency as instrument for change, its power was constrained by Putin's lack of an organised mass political base. While United Russia was potentially such a movement, Putin feared becoming trapped by the emergence of this party as a genuine mass movement (Chapter 4).

Putin carefully managed his relationship with the press, and thus with the people. In addition to his annual address to the Federal Assembly, Putin typically held a major press conference every year, as well as an 'open-line' question and answer session with the population, and we shall have frequent occasion to quote from these. At his 18 July 2001 press conference, with some 500 domestic and foreign correspondents in attendance, Putin argued that his main achievement in office was the maintenance of 'stability and a certain consensus in society' that would allow the country's political and economic modernisation. He became angry when asked about the mopping-up operations (*zachistki*) in Chechnya, but was able to turn questioning about the status of the oligarch Berezovsky by asking 'Boris Berezovsky – who is that?' into humour. Berezovsky had accused Putin of harbouring authoritarian tendencies and planned to establish an opposition party (later called Liberal Russia). Putin called Berezovsky an 'irrepressible, indefatigable man', always 'appointing someone or overthrowing someone'.[92] In his similar press conference held a year later on 24 June 2002 Putin was more measured in his comments on Chechnya; clearly, he had learnt to control his emotions on this question. He was asked several questions about his relationship with Yeltsin, and as we have seen he was unwilling to criticise his predecessor but noted the difference of views on the

Belarusian question. In February 2007 Putin held his sixth set-piece press conference, which was likely to be his last one as president.

Certain familiar elements of a mini-cult of the personality began to emerge, with Putin's portrait obligatory in all offices of the presidential administration, in government departments and on the walls of the whole great army of officialdom. Whereas under Yeltsin portraits of Russian artists or historical leaders (usually Peter the Great) hung in the space vacated by Lenin, now Putin's features adorned the walls of the bureaucracy. Kemal Ataturk had had to work long and hard to become 'father of the nation', while Putin seemed to have adopted the pose *ex officio*. A spate of books on Ataturk reflected the comparison.[93] Putin's vigorous style gave rise to the accusation that he was guilty of a neo-authoritarian style of governing. He was even called by some a 'soft dictator'. His assertions about the need for a 'dictatorship of law' revealed perhaps more than he intended. The frontal assault on the old system of federal relations meant the developing constitutional order was less able to incorporate necessary correctives from the regional leaders themselves. The 1993 constitution had established a strong executive and, it has been argued, only formalised traditional Russian patterns of centralised and personalised governance.[94] Yeltsin's style of government had been highly personalised,[95] and this was accentuated by Putin's activist leadership style.

Putin's leadership was torn between traditional patrimonial and personalised facets, and the attempt to achieve more rational, impersonal and ordered administration. Some have stressed the origins of Putin's thinking in Andropov's plans to achieve an authoritarian modernisation of the country, and have argued that the increased role of security and military officials in Putin's new elite would give rise, to use Marc Raeff's phrase, to a 'well-ordered police state'. Such an approach misses the fundamental novelty of his leadership. Putin sought more than just a rationalisation of power for its own sake but a reordering of administration to achieve his definition of modernisation goals. Unless we adopt what would probably be the untenable position that all of Putin's speeches, declarations and exhortations were no more than a cloud of propaganda designed to put people off the track of his real ambitions, we have to take at more or less face value his understanding that governmental relations had to be placed on a more formal and institutional basis and operate according to the dictates of the constitution, and that this reordered administration should be used to achieve national developmental tasks. The contradictions accompanying the implementation of this programme are legion, but we need to be clear that this was the strategic direction in which Putin sought to take the country. In recognising this, as so often, the wisdom of the Russian people was greater than that of many professional pundits.

Was Putin weak or strong? Despite his great rhetorical vigour, Putin's position at times appeared weak and inconsistent, torn between the various factions, in particular the security apparatus and the 'family' that had made him.[96] It was clear that he came to power with the support of the 'family', but although he did not become their prisoner, he was constrained by the interests that it represented. At the same time, as a matter of principle Putin avoided alienating those whom he dismissed or did not trust. He invited Primakov and Luzhkov on trips abroad, and in general sought to ground his leadership in a broad consensual bloc. Relations within the bloc were personal and largely based on loyalty. Putin softened the edges of conflicts where possible. When dismissing someone from one post he offered them another in a system of sinecures and soft landings. This was the case with the governor of Primorsk *krai*, Nazdratenko, and it was also seen most spectacularly with General Gennady Troshev in late 2002. Having been dismissed from the command of the North Caucasus Military District when he refused to take up the command in Siberia, Troshev a few months later emerged as head of the Cossack affairs section of the presidential administration. Even Putin's long-standing *bête noire*, Vladimir Yakovlev, occupied a series of ministerial-level posts after losing the governorship of St Peterburg.

This was a pattern of behaviour that was in keeping with that exhibited earlier. Putin may well have been a product of the Soviet system at its most stable and most decayed, yet he emerged with a set of standards about personal and institutional behaviour that transcended the careerism and sycophancy that typically characterised the late Brezhnev years. An exemplary case of this is the incident recounted by the former prime minister, Primakov. On his dismissal from the premiership in May 1999 most of his former colleagues quickly sought to distance themselves from him, whereas Putin came over with the FSB Collegium to offer sympathy. As Primakov put it, this showed 'Putin to be a decent man'.[97] Despite his failed bid for the presidency, Primakov refrained from criticising Putin personally. He was appointed chair of the Russian Chamber of Commerce and Industry, a body that sought to encourage small and medium business, and as such Primakov was drawn into the Putinite establishment. Very few became permanent outcasts during Putin's presidency.

Putin's style of leadership was undoubtedly flawed, with an excessive emphasis on his own preferences and the enhancement of the already considerable powers of the presidency. However, it was clear that he was a conviction politician. Putin remained loyal to a core set of beliefs about the type of state and society he wished to see established. However, too often his convictions got the better of his political judgement, and instead of instilling order there was a danger that he would provoke chaos. To avoid this, Putin at times was forced to trim his convictions, leading to charges of inconsistency and weakness. Although it appeared that Putin would be tempted by grandiose visions of becoming 'the father of the people', in the event he proved to be a level-headed politician committed not to personal aggrandisement but to the development of the country. His purpose was transparent, although the methods employed were foggy and encouraged Kremlin-based factional struggles as opaque interests struggled for mastery of the policy agenda and, in due course, the succession. His speeches and declarations were not an elaborate screen to mask personal aggrandisement, the defence of favoured oligarchs or the remnants of the Yeltsin 'family', but a genuine attempt to modernise the country and to resolve the problems of the past, not by employing the methods of the past but by applying a forward-looking agenda of social, political and economic liberation for all. His aim, like that of his great hero Ludwig Erhard,[98] was capitalism with a human face, but the establishment of the Rhineland model of capitalism in Russia was to prove beyond his powers.

National democracy and Russia's 'third way'

The etymological root of the name 'Putin' derives from the word 'put', meaning path, and many commentators have enjoyed the play on words in talking of 'Putin's path' (*put' putina*). In this section we shall argue that Putin indeed sought to find a distinctive route for Russian development, but he refused to be limited by one single prescription as the best way to the future. As a Putin aide put it early in his presidency, 'There are a mass of pathways (*tropinok*), and the task is to keep moving in the right direction'.[99] At the same time, the stress in this book is that there were choices to be made, although these were not taken in a vacuum. Already in the early 1990s the main liberal organisation, building on the broad Democratic Russia coalition established in 1990, was Russia's Choice (*Vybor Rossii*), headed by the architect of Russia's neo-liberal economic reforms, Gaidar. By 1993 this body had transformed itself into the party Russia's Democratic Choice. The first name appeared to be a conscious decision to stress the alternatives facing Russia, while the second emphasised that with the fall of communism the only possible choice was democracy.

Between national and popular democracy: reinventing the centre

At the heart of the idea of national democracy, termed 'sovereign democracy' by democratic statists like Surkov, is the attempt to re-energise the centre ground of politics by emphasising national sovereignty and the autonomy of Russia's democratic tradition. It was clear by the late 1990s that the *perestroika* stream of democratic innovation had exhausted itself, with the final blow to this tradition being the failure of the traditional liberal parties (Yabloko and the Union of Right Forces, see Chapter 4) to cross the 5 per cent representation threshold to enter the Duma in December 2003. For many commentators this meant the end of Russian democracy in its entirety, but this was not the case. On the one hand, democracy was reinvented by the Putin regime 'from above', while, on the other hand, democracy 'from below' took the form of the development of a re-traditionalisation of social life. While civil society and associational life developed, much of this assumed 'uncivil' forms incompatible with the values of tolerance and pluralism. Putin's own enduring popularity was a form of this democracy from below that we shall call 'popular democracy', but this was counterbalanced by the regime-driven programme of national democracy. Caught between popular and national democracy, the liberal democracy of the *perestroika* era became increasingly marginal.

Although Putin was promoted as the representative of the Kremlin, he quickly distanced himself from the Yeltsin legacy. Putin's political and programmatic innovations, although broadly in keeping with the general thrust of Yeltsin's reforms, broke sharply with the methods employed and the style of rule. In his *Millennium Manifesto* Putin talked frankly about Russia's comparative economic backwardness, and condemned not only the faults of the Soviet system but challenged its status as a modernising regime. He stressed that an enormous effort would have to be undertaken to put Russia back in the front rank of developed powers, but insisted that Russia would have to do this in its own way. The precise nature of the increased role of the state in the economy remained unspecified, but the need for a new policy to develop key branches of the economy and to stamp out corruption was stressed. As for politics, the *Manifesto* stressed the traditional role of the state in Russian life but insisted that this was complementary to the development of democracy and human rights.

In the *Manifesto* and in later speeches Putin sought to move beyond traditional amorphous definitions of centrism towards a more radical future-oriented model. Putin in the 1999 Duma elections sought to present himself as a symbol of both confidence and stability, promising to maintain Russia's system of power and property while radically renovating the state system and promoting political and legal reform within the framework of the existing constitutional settlement. Putin committed himself to the maintenance of the existing constitution unchanged, although he allowed that the position of the government could be strengthened but that it should find support not just in parliament or in the form of the presidency but in 'the widest spectrum of forces ... in the country as a whole'.[100]

Victor Sheinis argued that victory in the December 1999 Duma elections went to the 'quasi-centre'.[101] The basic policy orientation of this quasi-centre, insofar as it has one, he argued, is right-wing economics and left-wing politics: economic liberalism accompanied by statist great power politics. Privatisation and other economic reforms would continue, but also the continued iron grip of the bureaucracy over the market. According to him, the 2000 presidential elections revealed 'the minimal movement towards a self-sustaining civil society' and 'the separation of the political class from the deep layers of society'. This gulf between the power system and society was something noted by many other commentators. This is why Sheinis' notion of a quasi-centre is so suggestive. It does not come from a historical convergence on the centre ground of policy, but from the opportunistic co-optation of political actors and ideas to ensure regime survival. Our argument is that under Putin a new type of centrism emerged, with a positive dynamic but also with some of the problems of centrist politics in general, and quasi-centrism in particular. In studying the development of centrist politics, therefore, we must evaluate the degree to which they represent a genuine dynamic politics of the centre or whether they are no more than the lowest common denominator typical of quasi-centrism, the politics of *trasformismo* that we shall discuss in Chapter 6.

The sharp polarisation that attended Yeltsin's rule gave way to an explicitly consensual and 'centrist' approach. Putin's centrism was not simply an avoidance of the extremes of left and right, of backward-looking traditionalists and nationalists or teleologically inspired Western-oriented modernisers. His centrism sought to generate a radical centrism of the type espoused by third-way thinkers like Giddens,[102] although Putin's third way is tailored to Russian circumstances.[103] At the heart of this programme was the attempt to increase the autonomy of the state from socio-economic and bureaucratic interests. For Kaspe the essence of Putin's centrism was that it was removed from the field of party politics, and elevated the presidency to a degree even above the political field.[104] This depoliticisation provided fertile ground for authoritarian consolidation; but increased governmental coherence and enhanced state capacity are the essential bases for any democracy. Political rights have to be accompanied by an adequate level of personal and social security for people to enjoy those rights. The contrast between democracy and order is to some degree a false one, since the one without the other is impoverished. However, the personification of political power and the attempt to legitimise the presidency by its association with supra-democratic values undermined accountability and responsibility.

Jowitt has argued that in the context of the strong 'Leninist legacies' in Eastern Europe, traditional attempts to strike a balance between economic development and democratic participation may not be effective. Liberal authoritarianism may well be a more 'desirable alternative' and a 'more practical response than the utopian wish for immediate mass democracy in Eastern Europe'.[105] It is precisely this tension between the authoritarian imposition of stability and democratic anarchism that Putin sought to finesse. Behind the talk of 'guided democracy' and 'manipulated democracy' (to use Sergei Markov's term) there lies the classical problem identified by Huntington in his classic work: how to maintain political order in changing societies.[106] Putin provided a new approach to the problem of institutionalising order between the old-fashioned establishment of a repressive stability system and the anarchy in social relations that characterised early post-communist Russia. Putin sought the internalisation of authority where power would move from being despotic and arbitrary to becoming infrastructural and legitimate,[107] but in the event he achieved less than this. His leadership did not achieve a shift from power to authority. He was unable to find a way between radical liberalism and conservative authoritarianism.

The politics of Russia's third way emerged out of traditional 'centrist' positions, but it was unable to achieve their development. Putinism reflects the political amorphousnous of the quasi-centre, but at the same time potentially transcends it. It is clear that support for Putin was based on the real appreciation of his policies, but at the same time this was accompanied by support for mythologised conceptions of what he was taken to represent: youth and vigour in contrast to Yeltsin's senescent debility; the impersonal pursuit of Russian national goals as opposed to selfish and irresponsible pursuit of enrichment and aggrandisement of personal power by Yeltsin and his acolytes; the continuation of economic reform accompanied by a crackdown on corruption, lawlessness and banditry; and good relations with the West based on genuine partnership rather than Russian kowtowing to Washington. Some of these representations turned out to be accurate but, perhaps more importantly, the extraordinary consistency of his popularity reflected the aspiration that Putin would offer not only a way out of the shortcomings of the Yeltsin years but also out of the dead ends of Russia's historical trajectory.

Liberal conservatism

Does Putin's centrism reflect a distinctive type of Russian third way or is it little more than a manipulated and opportunistic quasi-centre? A genuine third way, *à la* Giddens, is derived not simply from the repudiation of idealised notions of left and right, reflected in traditional class politics, but from attempts to create a genuinely radical politics of the centre. This is not a trivial political project, although much of the writing and commentary about the subject is indeed trite. The argument here can be reduced to the following: while the third way in the West is an attempt to come to terms with the apparent exhaustion of traditional social democracy and represents an attempt to renew it in the age of globalisation, Russia's third way, or genuine politics of the centre, is drawn from an older tradition, liberal conservatism. Writers like Peter Struve and Semyon Frank are drawn on to sustain the emerging consensus over a Russian third way based on support for the reconstitution of state authority and patriotism while continuing market reforms and international economic integration.

Although Von Mises always argued that there was no 'third way' or 'third system' between the Soviet and the American forms of social organisation, with the end of the Cold War and the ideological confrontation between East and West, the possibility of testing out a variety of paths is now more relevant than ever. We do not need to think in terms of only a 'third' way, of course, since there is no reason not to think in terms of a fourth, fifth and ever more ways. However, in our conception the notion of a third way is specific to the attempt to overcome the traditionally polarised nature of Western European and Russian politics: between socialism and capitalism, between market and non-market, between individualistic and collectivist approaches to social development; and between universalism and particularism. In that sense, a third way represents not an abstraction but a very specific response to Russia's self-identity and problems of development today. The tension between evolutionary and morphological approaches to civilisational development is perhaps the fundamental question of our epoch, and while the 'clash of civilisations' after 9/11 has focused on the perceived struggle between the Christian and Islamic worlds, Russia is still struggling to find its own way to reconciliation.

Alexander Yanov has identified a battle between two Russias. The first is the liberal one, inalienably part of Europe, what he calls 'Decembrist Russia'.[108] The second is one where geopolitical considerations rule supreme and trample the development of civil society, one based on the striving to achieve the restoration of territories like the Crimea and Sevastopol, confrontation with the West and autarchic economic policies. This is the Russia that Yanov dubs 'Slavophile'. Again, in this sphere as in others, Putin sought to overcome this sterile confrontation of tired stereotypes to forge a new forward-looking identity. Putin's third way, moreover, had little in common with those advocates of self-limiting *perestroika* who sought to find a third way between outright liberal democracy of the Western sort and the neo-Stalinist inertia of the Brezhnev era. Putin's ideology of normalisation fostered a post-revolutionary conservative consolidation that ultimately was unable to generate an indigenous long-term path of development, although it was able to provide a temporary stabilisation.

Putin's leadership was accompanied by a whole series of attempts to find new solutions to old problems. Twentieth-century Russia, for example, was torn between revolution and stagnation, a phenomenon that was repeated in miniature during Yeltsin's rule. Beginning with a revolutionary break in the first years of the 1990s, towards the end of Yeltsin's rule there were pronounced tendencies towards stagnation that once again came to the fore in Putin's second term. It was not clear that Putin was able to find a new way between revolution and stagnation that would allow the country to embark on a balanced and sustainable developmental path. Putin's third way was accompanied by the depoliticisation of the politics, the attempt to present tough policy choices as unchallenged common sense. Putin's third way was eclectic, borrowing ideas freely from all corners of the political spectrum, but in the end it was unable to sustain a credible, legitimate and authoritative narrative of its own.

Conclusion

Putin's presidency demonstrated the role that individual leadership plays in history. Putin's emergence was structured by the needs of the Yeltsinite succession; but his leadership was shaped by his personal preferences and character. He drew on disparate constituencies and sought to rule by consensus, but he was unable to generate a single coherent vision of his own leadership, other than the leadership itself. Putin's power was built on balancing the preferences of various factions, although none existed as a consolidated clan.

We argue that what may have looked like political indeterminacy in fact reflected a normative commitment to something akin to a distinctive Russian path. The third way approach can be seen as a way of avoiding hard choices and, by allowing the common sense of the period to become the prevailing ideology, the depoliticisation of the political process was enhanced. The essence of Putin's political programme was the attempt to construct a dynamic and future-oriented politics of the centre. By definition, such a programme is in danger of becoming amorphous to the point of meaninglessness; but it also had the potential to transcend traditional divisions and to lead the country on to a balanced developmental path conforming to native traditions while encouraging integration into the international community. Putin's centrism sought to do more than simply avoid the extremes of left and right but to generate a radical centrism tailored to Russian circumstances. Putin's commitment to the politics of normalcy was a way of healing the terrible divisions that had scarred Russian political life for over a century. Putin's market-oriented moderate centrism, combining a commitment to democracy with the appeal to strong leadership and 'sovereign democracy', may well have been an unstable syncretic mix, but it did at least offer an alternative to the failures of the past. The degree to which this promise was fulfilled we shall see in the following chapters.

4 Parties, elections and the succession

History proves all dictatorships, all authoritarian forms of government are transient. Only democratic systems are lasting.

Vladimir Putin[1]

In 1999–2000 the Kremlin had been able to beat off the challenge posed by various parties led by the likes of Luzhkov and Primakov, and in its place had created its own organisation, Unity, which not only countered the threat but also acted as the core of a pro-presidential bloc in the Third Duma (2000–3). Many observers at that time noted that civil and political society were weak, unable to constrain the actions of the political authorities or to ensure accountability. As a Russian study put it: 'Civil society remains in an embryonic condition and can only to a very limited degree define the domestic or foreign policies of the state ... there is a gulf between the views of the elite and the majority of the population on a number of questions'.[2] The gulf between the ruling elite and the broader political community became sharper as Putin's leadership progressed, although his bond with the people remained strong. Russian political identity was fragmented and political representation distorted, while Moscow's authority rang as a distant bell in large parts of the country. At the heart of Putin's state building project was the attempt to homogenise political space and to stamp the Kremlin's authority on political processes everywhere. How he tried to do this and to what extent he succeeded we shall examine below.

Development of the party system

Russia's party system developed in a peculiar way, with no shortage of parties but few enjoying extensive and consistent support.[3] Russia's political parties do not legitimise the authority of the government, while executive authorities at both the regional and federal levels tried to remain independent of parties. The nature of the 'parties' that have emerged in Russia is also distinctive. In broad terms, three types can be identified. The first can be described as *programme* parties, those with a clear platform adopted by some sort of process of inner-party democracy and pursued by the leadership and consistently presented to the public. The second in one way or another are *project* parties, created typically not long before the elections as part of an ulterior strategy of competing elite groups. A classic project party was Rodina in the 2003 election, designed to draw votes away from the Communist Party. The third type comprises various government-sponsored groupings to represent the system itself. This type can be described as *regime* parties, when they are sponsored by the ruling group, established to manipulate and shape political space and in some cases to act as what is called 'the party of power'. A 'party of power' can be defined as a political organisation created with the assistance of the executive to participate in elections and the legislative process.

Unity in the 1999 elections was a typical regime party. From 2003, however, the broader manifestation of Unity, United Russia (UR), now merged with Luzhkov's Fatherland, the regionally based All Russia, and some other parties, began to take on hybrid qualities as it sought to broaden its political base and enhance its popular legitimacy. As it became even more a hybrid *programme–regime* party it may just gain sufficient staying power to survive Putin's departure from office. The creation of Just Russia (JR, *Spravedlivaya Rossiya*) in October 2006 was designed to balance UR from a centre-left perspective, and thus moved straight into the programme–regime stage of development. The creation of JR restrained the development of UR into a dominant party.

Changes to the party system

To what degree has a consolidated party system emerged in Russia, or is the dominant characteristic still 'deconsolidation', the absence of effective interest-based and socially rooted organisations? In broad terms there has not been any significant shift from a party system based on 'ideology' (or values) to one based on interests, although some parties (notably the Union of Right Forces) have sought to root themselves in a definable constituency, in this case the 'winners' of the transition, the nascent middle class. The categories of 'winners' and 'losers', moreover, are not always clear-cut: a gain in one sphere, for example economic freedom, is compensated by a loss of access to privileges that were formerly free (for example, top quality university education). The development of a national party system up to 2004 was undermined by the ability of regional executives to control patronage and to influence electoral outcomes. The use of so-called 'administrative resources' by central and regional authorities, above all the manipulation of the 'virtual' world of the media and public relations, tended to set up a parallel sphere of politics that bypassed parties.

At various points there have been signs of an emerging pattern of partisan alignment, with a relatively consistent quarter of voters supporting the communists, about a quarter supporting a variety of liberal groupings, a large 'marsh' (*boloto*) in the centre, accompanied by a relatively high level of party recognition. This nascent stability was undermined by the 2003 elections, with sharp falls in the communist and liberal votes, compensated by the overwhelming victory of the centrist United Russia and the nationalist Rodina party. The system remains relatively fluid, characterised as a 'floating party system'.[4] Until Putin's reforms there were few institutional barriers to the entry of new parties, transforming Russia from a one-party state in the Soviet period to one with hundreds of parties. The proportional part of the December 1993 Duma election was contested by 13 associations, of which eight crossed the 5 per cent threshold; in 1995, 43 groups entered the fray, but only four entered parliament; in 1999, 26 party lists were registered and six parties crossed the 5 per cent threshold; while in 2003, despite Putin's attempts to narrow the field, 23 groups competed but only four won seats. There was not much continuity in parliamentary representation, either, with only 3 of the 8 elected in 1993 making it into the 1995 assembly, joined by three new parties in 1999, while of the four that made it into the 2003 Duma, two had enjoyed a continuous presence since 1993 (the CPRF and the LDPR), one since 1999 (United Russia), joined by the new party Rodina.

By July 2001 Russia had 199 officially registered parties and movements. Scott Mainwaring's observation that, despite the many challenges to them, parties 'have continued to be the main agents of representation and are virtually the only actors with access to elected positions in democratic politics',[5] is at best only partially true in the Russian case. Putin's reform of the party system precisely sought to consolidate this prerogative of parties, while reducing their number and turning them into genuinely national organisations. Whether he could also make them genuinely representative bodies with party elites responsive to the views of the membership and accountable to the social interests that they claimed to represent was another question. In numerous polls, parties came out as one of the least trusted institutions, and at the same time as one of the most corrupt.[6] A study showed that in 2000 only 0.7 per cent of respondents were members of a political party or organisation, while only 0.3 per cent were activists.[7] Total membership of all Russia's multitude of parties and organisations was no more than a million, about 1 per cent of the adult population. Thus party life was very much an elite affair.

Putin had enjoyed, as we have seen, an unspectacular career as a party member and official. In 1991 his membership of the Communist Party lapsed, and later he joined the emerging 'party of power', Russia's Choice, and then he moved on to the new party of power, Our Home is Russia (NDR). In May 1995 he was elected chair of the St Petersburg branch of NDR and entered the party's Political Council, a position of which he was relieved in June 1997.[8] Despite this, Putin has been a consistent advocate of enhancing the role of parties in Russian politics. In his Federal Assembly speech of 8 July 2000, Putin suggested that 'perhaps only public and political associations should have the right to nominate candidates to the post of head of state'. There had been periodic attempts in the 1990s to adopt a law on political parties, notably in July 1995 when the Duma got as far as adopting a law, but this had been vetoed by the Federation Council. Putin now returned to the issue to stimulate a party system with rather more impact on the political process, above all the selection of leaders. Berezovsky, however, argued that if such a plan was implemented, 'democracy will shrink in Russia'.[9]

One of the central changes of Putin's early period in office was reform of the normative framework governing party life. In December 2000 the presidential law on political parties, largely drafted by the Central Electoral Commission, was published, to receive its first parliamentary reading in February 2001. The bill was subject to over a thousand amendments, but the presidential version remained substantially intact.[10] The 11 July 2001 law on political parties supplanted the much-amended 1990 law on civic associations and sought to create a system consisting of fewer parties but with all of them becoming national in scale. The law stipulated that parties had to have a membership of no fewer than 10,000, with a minimum of 100 members in at least 45 regions, and 50 members in each of the remaining 44. This replaced the old minimum of 5,000 members to be registered as an 'electoral association'. The concept of 'national' comprised not only the idea of geographical reach but also how representative they were to be. Parties were not allowed to appeal to sectional interests, and those advancing religious, racial, ethnic and professional causes were forbidden. While not explicitly banned, regional parties were effectively ruled out by the membership rules, and thus pro-gubernatorial parties were expunged from the national political scene. Russian parties were thus prohibited from drawing on the power of the cleavages that have shaped Western party systems. Although it is possible to fight for broad social welfare issues, parties drawn from a single occupation are not allowed. Collective membership is banned. There are numerous rules on funding, including provision for state support for parties that receive 3 per cent of the proportional vote, win 12 single-mandate seats in parliamentary elections, or 3 per cent of the vote in presidential elections. Parties that failed to gather 2 per cent of the vote were to return the money for the free airtime on state radio and television stations that they had received during the campaign. Failure to pay will mean disqualification in the next election.

The law on parties was reinforced by a federal law of July 2002 that stipulated a mixed-member parliamentary electoral system in all of Russia's regions. The law, which came into effect on 15 July 2003, stated that regional parliaments were to be formed on the party principle, with half to be elected by proportional representation (PR). The cumulative effect was to undermine the 'regional fiefdoms' and to ensure that parties played a greater representative and political role across the country (see Chapter 7). In October 2004 the law on parties was modified to restrict further the scope for smaller parties. Parties from 1 January 2006 now needed a minimum membership of 50,000 and to have regional branches with no fewer than 500 members each in more than half of Russia's 89 regions where the population exceeded 500,000, and branches with no fewer than 250 people in the other regions. The financial rules became even more burdensome, including quarterly financial reports. To remain registered, parties had to demonstrate activism by participating in federal, regional or local elections at least once every five years.

The complex rules governing the registration process is managed by the new Federal Registration Service (FRS), created in 2005 by the Ministry of Justice. Even established parties had to go through the registration process, beginning with a congress to adopt the party's statutes, and the re-registration of regional branches to ensure that the party had branches in at least half the regions. The founding congress, with a minimum of 150 delegates from at least 45 regions, elects the party's leading bodies and adopts a programme. The party is then registered nationally, followed by the registration of its regional branches with local divisions of the justice ministry, and finally the central ministry validates the completion of the process. After registration, the ministry continues to monitor observance and has the right to suspend a party found to be contravening the rules. Suspension cannot take place during an election, and those parties that enter the Duma on party lists cannot be suspended within five years of their election. Parties have the right to appeal to the courts against suspension, and the final ruling on dissolving a party is taken by the Supreme Court. Parties not only have the right but *must* contest elections, and not only at the national level (parliamentary and presidential) but also at the regional (gubernatorial and legislative) and municipal levels. At the same time, parties are the *only* organisations allowed to contest elections. Civic associations may join an electoral bloc with parties, but cannot advance their own candidates.

The registration process following the adoption of the law and its 2004 amendments saw a restructuring of the party scene. Parties that failed to meet the new conditions lost the status of a political party and were either transformed into a social organisation or disbanded. The deadline to be reregistered was 1 January 2006. Many of the smaller parties disappeared from view, while others had a struggle to establish themselves in the new system. Plenty of anomalies were revealed. For example, Alexander Chuev's Christian Democratic Union was refused registration on the grounds that it was sectarian, although Christian Democracy is one of the dominant political trends in many Western European countries. Berezovsky's Liberal Russia was initially refused registration because of an alleged lack of precision in its regulations, and it later failed to survive. By October 2006 the Ministry of Justice had registered 35 parties, with some 20 organisations having fallen by the wayside. Some of the losers were surprising, and included Viktor Tyulkin's extremely active Russian Communist Worker's Party, as well as Mikhail Kasyanov's National Democratic Union, suggesting that registration according to the tough new rules was an effective way of eliminating some of the regime's irritants. In January 2007 the FRS announced that only 17 parties had been granted the right to take part in the December 2007 parliamentary elections, with the rest of the 35 having failed to comply with the rules on numerical membership or the number of regional branches. They could either become an NGO or dissolve themselves. The legislation had certainly not created a two-party system, but it had at least clarified what was a party and what was not, and which of them would be allowed to contest elections.

The 'party of power': United Russia and beyond

Putin's attempt to radicalise the centre enhanced the status of the traditional 'party of power', giving it the potential to become a classic ruling party. In the early 2000s this meant United Russia, combining the administrative resources of the state and an ideology of liberal patriotism, occupying the centre-right niche in the political spectrum. The initial base of United Russia (Unity) was regional officialdom, with the 39 founding governors (mostly not of the first rank) in autumn 1999 swelled by new cohorts once the success of the body became clear. In December 2001 the merger of Unity with Fatherland-All Russia and some other groups gave birth to United Russia, and by March 2006 the party had registered its one millionth member. In contrast, the CPRF, Russia's largest party for so many years, had a membership at that time of no more than 180,000. United Russia boasted of recruiting its second million by the parliamentary elections of December 2007, and had ambitions to achieve a Soviet-style membership of 10–15 million. This goal reflected a fundamental ambiguity in UR's strategy, since by definition a 'party' is part of something else, whereas the very name 'United Russia' appealed to some sort of transcendent unity of the Russian people, which in a multi-party system is a *contradictio in adjecto*.

It would be a misnomer to suggest that UR was the ruling party, since in Russia the parliamentary majority does not form the government. It was the party *of* power, but not a party *in* power. However, as we shall see below, UR dominated parliament and steam-rolled through the regime's legislative agenda. The party also had rather broader hegemonic ambitions, above all in the regions. In the 17 regional elections held in December 2005 and March 2006, the party finished first in the party list vote in all cases, winning, for example, 197 seats out of the 359 contested in the eight regional elections on 12 March 2006, or 55 per cent. The March regional elections were the first to use the common voting day, in this case for regional and local elections. Some 20 governors joined the party in 2004–5 alone, some of whom had been former communists and independents, and they brought with them key members of regional business, political and bureaucratic elites. The party enjoyed strong financial backing, an extensive regional network and, by the end of 2006, enjoyed a majority in 65 out of Russia's

88 regional legislatures and 65 governors were members. Nevertheless, the experience of regional elections suggested that the party would have difficulty gathering more than 40 per cent of the vote in national elections. The party dominated not so much through its own popularity but by the paucity of effective opposition.

United Russia's dominance meant that membership became essential not only for a political career but also for a bureaucratic one. The party of power was becoming the party of patronage as well. It appeared to be treading the well-worn path towards becoming a dominant regime-party, like the Party of the Institutionalised Revolution (PRI) in Mexico between 1929 and 2000, or even in Japan after 1955, and in Italy during the period of Christian Democratic predominance up to 1992. This applied, however, only as long as Putin's regime remained in power, and even he was ambivalent about allowing UR to become a hegemonic party. The experience of earlier 'parties of power' in the 1990s was not encouraging for the long-term viability of UR. Earlier incarnations, notably Democratic Choice (although less a 'party of power' and more a programme party since it had a clear ideology and an independent status) and Our Home is Russia, rapidly faded away once their sponsors lost political office. The case of Mikhail Prusak, the long-time independent-minded governor of Novgorod, is instructive in this respect, since after long resistance he finally joined UR 'for the sake of the region's inhabitants';[11] and it is not hard to see him leaving at the earliest opportunity. Fearing that UR would share the fate of earlier dominant parties once Putin stepped down in 2008, Surkov warned its party activists on 7 February 2006 that 'United Russia's task is not just to win in 2007 but to think how to achieve the party's dominance over the next 10–15 years'. Surkov warned the party that it would have to 'reduce its dependence on administrative resources' and would have to 'master the habits of ideological battle'.[12] The party would have to find new ways of ensuring that it remained meaningful for its membership, united on little else other than loyalty to Putin, and attractive to voters in the country. If the door to dominant regime party status was closed, then it would have to transform itself into a full-scale programme party.

For some in the Kremlin, an excessively strong UR was to be feared as much as a weak UR was for others, and this was one factor behind the creation of yet another regime party, this time intended to represent the centre-left part of the political spectrum. If Surkov was behind the development of UR, the new grouping was apparently sponsored by the *siloviki*. The formal merger of Rodina (Motherland) with the Party of Life and the Party of Pensioners took place at a congress on 28 October 2006 to create the new party Just Russia. The number of parties eligible to fight the 2007 elections was reduced to 17. The new party was headed by the speaker of the Federation Council and the former head of the minuscule Party of Life, Sergei Mironov, while Alexander Babakov, the former chairman of Rodina, became secretary of the new party's central council presidium. Mironov spoke of the party winning half a million members by the 2007 elections, although the experience of his leadership of the Party of Life did not inspire confidence that this could be achieved. Like Rodina in 2003, the aim was to wean away part of the membership and electorate from the Communists and Zhirinovsky's Liberal Democrats, and there was a project party facet to the new organisation. Just Russia declared its support for Putin, but stressed a rather more social democratic programme than UR, and thus tried to identify itself more as a 'party of the people' than a party of power. Whether there was such a left-wing constituency waiting to be mobilised would only become clear in elections, since much of the protest vote was probably more anti-bureaucracy rather than positively social democratic. United Russia now lost its position as the sole Kremlin party and the associated monopoly on 'administrative resources'. The creation of the new party could well create a more competitive parliament, perhaps dominated by two giant parties. Thus the elements of a classical two-party system were in place, although built from above. Whether they would be able to continue to be able to play a role in post-Putin society was an open question.

The Putinite attempt to create a party system national in scope and representing specific interests, values and programmes that could be put before the electorate may well be considered a rational response to political fragmentation and amorphous party development. Equally, the attempt to forge a national party system as an integrative force for the country as a whole makes a lot of sense, especially when faced with regional segmentation on a massive scale in the 1990s (see Chapter 7). However, there are a number of questionable features in the programme and the way that it was implemented. First, the elimination of regional parties divested the political scene of some of its diversity and colour. Although many regional parties were little more than vehicles for local executives, they did nevertheless act as a forum for local debate. A federal system without regional parties is quite unusual. Second, it is not clear what the optimal number of parties is for any particular country. The Italian elections of April 2006 saw no fewer than 174 parties and blocs taking part, with 35 parties represented in Silvio Berlusconi's coalition and 33 in Romano Prodi's. *Trasformismo* was alive and well in Italy, with an endless round of coalitions and reshuffles leading to sclerosis of the political system. Putin may well have been driven to avoid such a fate befalling Russia. However, constant changes to the legislation on parties – the 2001 law was substantively amended at least eight times – reinforced suspicions that the law was being shaped instrumentally. Third, the coherence of political parties as organisations may have been enhanced, but their role in the political system remained unclear. While Surkov endorsed the initiative by the Adygean branch of United Russia to nominate its candidate to become the next president of the republic, he insisted that it was too early for this experiment to be tried at the national level.[13] Fourth, the instrumental creation of project and regime parties could not but undermine trust in the party system as a whole. Independent political parties were squeezed out and replaced by pro-government creations. The attempt to manipulate political space, moreover, extended to the 'manual control' of electoral processes, to which we now turn.

Elections and electoral legislation

Russia's electoral system has been subject to constant tinkering since the onset of competitive elections. Following every election cycle the electoral legislation has been overhauled. Frequent changes to electoral rules have inhibited the routinisation of electoral conduct and voter expectations. The terms of political trade are in a state of constant flux, while the parties chasing the votes of the citizen have also changed considerably between electoral cycles, the characteristic feature of a floating party system.[14]

Electoral reform: phase one, 2000–3

A working group in the Central Electoral Commission (CEC) was established by presidential decree on 26 August 2000 to examine revisions to the electoral code, work that took into account planned changes to the law on parties. A new framework law on elections for parliament and the presidency was adopted on 12 June 2002, with specific laws for each, respectively, being signed into law by Putin in December 2002 and January 2003, and the whole package came into effect on 14 July 2003. Putin also signed into law the use of the automated vote counting system '*Vybory*'. Thus the normative framework for the parliamentary elections on 7 December 2003 and presidential elections on 14 March 2004 was in place, unusually, well before the elections themselves.

In keeping with the aim of raising the status of parties, only national parties now had the right to nominate candidates in federal and regional elections. The 2001 law still allowed the creation of political blocs, but these were now limited to three members, of which at least one had to be a political party. The amended party law of 2004 banned the creation of electoral blocs in their entirety, with the intention of forcing parties to merge to create more permanent viable electoral organisations. Individual citizens can still nominate themselves for office, but groups of voters are now deprived of this right, although in local elections non-political groups can still nominate candidates. Thus (starting with the 2007 parliamentary election) voter groups can no longer nominate candidates, and instead only candidates proposed by parties and individuals are allowed. The others have to collect two million signatures, with no more than 50,000 from any one region, a tough task for any party. There are much stricter rules requiring the full disclosure of a candidate's sources of financial support, a measure that will discourage independent candidates (those not belonging to a political party), while at the same time deterring candidates sponsored by criminal or other shady networks.

Parties entering parliament from 2003 enjoyed a number of new benefits. They are financed from the state budget according to the number of votes that they receive, and their candidates in later elections do not have to gather signatures or provide a deposit to participate. The law stipulated that at least three party-list groups had to enter the 2003 Duma (up from the minimum of two earlier). A new barrier of 7 per cent was put in place for the 2007 elections and, irrespective of the number of votes they obtain, a minimum of four parties have to enter parliament. Parties elected to the Duma must collect over 60 per cent of the vote between them. In regional elections, too, since December 2003 at least half of the seats in regional legislatures have to be elected through party lists, a move also intended to help structure public organisations.

Parties crossing the threshold to enter the Duma have the right to nominate their presidential candidate directly. Parties and blocs nominating a presidential candidate gain extra free newspaper space and airtime, in addition to that granted to all candidates. Half of this goes to candidates and half to the nominating parties, thus giving an advantage to party-nominated candidates. The aim clearly is to focus political competition on probably no more than five major parties. These parties are intended to act as a counterweight to regional executives if they are able to establish a powerful presence in regional legislatures, and at the national level they will counteract the influence of the oligarchs. One of them could sooner or later become the presidential party.

More broadly, the ability of electoral commissions and the courts to interfere in the electoral process by refusing to register or disqualifying candidates was restricted. In past elections, especially at the regional level, there had been some infamous cases when leading candidates had been removed from the ballot by the courts at the last moment. The most notorious was when the governor of Kursk *oblast*, Alexander Rutskoi, was struck off the list on the day before the election in October 2000. Now the causes that could provoke such actions have been pared down, and the right to cancel a candidate's registration for violating electoral legislation has been granted exclusively to the courts. This prerogative is itself limited and has to be done by a lower court at least five days before the election. In keeping with the general trend of trying to limit political arbitrariness at the regional level, the rules for forming electoral commissions changed. Regional and local government authorities no longer form the commissions, and instead higher level electoral commissions form the district, territorial and ward electoral commissions as well as nominating their chairs (in the past the commissions had elected their own chairs). Regional and local government administrations establish the respective regional and local commissions as in the past, but these commissions now have two members appointed by the higher commission and the chairs of these commissions are chosen on the recommendation of the higher commission. The aim was to reduce the influence of regional and local governments on electoral commissions. As in other spheres, centralisation was intended to promote rather than to undermine democracy, although the outcome tended to be more centralisation and less democracy.

The 7 December 2003 State Duma election

A total of 18 political parties and five blocs fought the election.[15] Turnout at 54.7 per cent represented a return to the relatively low level of December 1993 (54.8 per cent). The 'against all' category just missed reaching its own independent representation with 4.7 per cent of the vote (see Table 4.1), indicating voter protest against the choices on offer. The average 'against all' vote in single-mandate districts was 12.9 per cent, for which 7.7 million votes were cast, forcing a rerun in three where this category gained the most votes.[16] The greatest winner in the election undoubtedly was United Russia, taking 37.4 per cent of the PR vote and some 120 single-mandate seats, joined soon after by another 60 independents, giving them a two-thirds majority in the Duma with just over 300 seats.

Table 4.1 State Duma election 7 December 2003

Party	Votes (PR)	Turnout	Seats		
			From PR list	From SMD	Total
United Russia	22,779,279	37.57	120	103	223
CPRF	7,647,820	12.61	40	12	52
LDPR	6,943,885	11.45	36	0	36
Motherland (Rodina)	5,469,556	9.02	29	8	37
Representation threshold (5%)					
Yabloko	2,609,823	4.30	0	4	4
SPS	2,408,356	3.97	0	3	3
Agrarian Party (APR)	2,205,704	3.64	0	2	2
Other parties (16)	6,768,530	11.17	0	23	23
Against all	2,851,600	4.70	–	–	–
Independents		–	–	67	67
Total	59,684,768		225	222[a]	450

Sources: Central Electoral Commission *Vybory deputatov gosudarstvennoi dumy federal'nogo sobraniya Rossiiskoi Federatsii 2003: elektoral'naya statistika* (Moscow, Ves' Mir, 2004), pp. 29, 141, 192; www.izbirkom.ru/way/1269570/viboryrefer_obj. Accessed 13 January 2004.

Notes:
[a] In single-mandate districts in Ulyanovsk, Sverdlovsk and St Petersburg 'against all' gained most votes on 7 December. In repeat State Duma elections United Russia, LDPR and Rodina won one seat each.

Out of 108,906,250 million Russian electors, 60,712,300 votes were cast (55.75%), of which 59,297,970 valid votes were cast (54.73%), comfortably exceeding the minimum 25% requirement. An additional 948,409 (1.56%) cast invalid votes. Votes needed to cross the 5% barrier: 3,031,659. 42,838,865 votes (70.65%) were cast for the four groups exceeding the representation threshold.

United Russia scored significant successes where the regional head was part of UR's governing council, notably in Tatarstan, Mordovia, and Moscow city, where UR won 12 out of the 15 seats. United Russia tended to back candidates who were likely to win anyway.[17] The UR campaign was fought using the 'administrative resources' of regional leaders and privileged access to the media. Twenty-nine regional leaders even signed up as candidates on the UR list, even though they had no intention of taking up their seats, a practice that was later condemned in the Organisation for Security and Cooperation in Europe's report on the elections. In an interview on all main television channels on 27 November 2003, Putin noted 'Concerning United Russia, I can tell you that I am not a member of this party, but this is a political force that I have been able to rely on over these last four years and that has consistently supported me ... United Russia has shown itself capable of rising above a certain level of populism and not letting itself slip into populist mode, and has proven its ability to take responsible decisions and take on responsibility'.[18] He insisted that he had a right to make his speech at the UR congress on 20 September,[19] an event that Zyuganov and other opposition leaders had condemned as a cynical abuse of his position and a repudiation of his statement that he would remain above the fray.[20]

The UR manifesto adopted at its Third Congress on 20 September 2003 argued that the country faced a choice not only over membership of the next Duma, but about developmental paths, arguing that 'Citizens of Russia now have a real chance of choosing a successful future for themselves and the country'. Conceding that the party 'considers itself as a basis of support for the president', it argued that it was neither a party of the left nor of the right, but a 'realistic' one, asserting that the 'centrism' espoused by the party 'is not an ideology in the usual sense of the word', but was 'pragmatic, capable of resolving real problems for real people'. Its key principles were 'order and legality'. The document argued that the Russian state had found adequate reserves to overcome the crisis of the 1990s, and called for a government responsible to the parliamentary majority. The document insisted that the country was a 'self-sufficient civilisation', and that it should find a 'worthy' place in the international community, including speedy membership of the WTO as well as visa-free travel with the EU.[21] This programme in effect represented Putin's plans for his second term in office.

Liberal parties were effectively squeezed out of the Duma. The social democratic Yabloko won only 4.3 per cent of the vote, and thus failed to cross the 5 per cent representation threshold. The more neo-liberal SPS fared even worse, winning a mere 4 per cent. Together they won only seven constituency seats, down from the 49 in the previous Duma. In the Yeltsin era the liberal idea had been embodied by the president, and now the two parties proved unable to sustain it autonomously and to give it an effective institutional identity. In the early period SPS insisted that Putin was in effect pursuing their policies, symbolised by Sergei Kirienko's gift to Putin, when the latter was prime minister, of the large volume containing SPS's socio-economic programme. Nemtsov on numerous occasions had insisted 'Putin is fulfilling our programme'. The presence of Chubais, dubbed by one paper 'the chief crisis manager of Russian democracy',[22] represented an attempt to reinvigorate the SPS campaign and, despite his attempts to attract some of the patriotic vote by fishing in the murky waters of 'liberal imperialism',[23] the idea that Russia could build an economically 'liberal empire' on the ruins of the Soviet Union, was not a vote-winner. On 20 September Putin told foreign media that he would like to see both SPS and Yabloko part of the new Duma since they had been 'doing positive work'.[24] It appears that Putin resolved to leave SPS to its own devices, confident that with Chubais behind them they had the financial and organisational resources to cross the threshold. Yabloko was another matter, and Putin went out of his way to help them. Despite attempts in the last week by the Kremlin to boost support for Yabloko by giving it extensive television coverage, this was not enough to take it over the required threshold. This failure evidently came as something of a surprise to Putin himself, who had telephoned Yavlinsky late on election night to congratulate his party on entering the new Duma.

Following the election, SPS was torn between the view of those who considered that the party should have criticised the regime more consistently, while others argued that a principled liberal democratic position would have been enough. Yabloko comforted itself with the illusion that its failure derived from electoral fraud, and thus its leadership felt exonerated from facing the consequences of its refusal to ally with SPS. Yavlinsky engaged in speaking tours in the West in which he expounded on his favourite theme of the failure of the democratic transition in Russia, but failed to note his own part in that alleged failure.[25] His frenetic condemnation of Putin's government appeared a classic case of displacement activity, refusing to face up to his own failure. It was this attitude that was criticised by Khodorkovsky in a letter, significantly entitled 'The Crisis of Russian Liberalism' from prison on 29 March 2004.[26]

Rodina was established only four months earlier as a project party with the clear intention of stealing votes from the communists. It brought together the economist and former communist deputy Sergei Glaz'ev and Dmitry Rogozin, the founder of the Congress of Russian Communities (KRO) in the early 1990s. Rogozin had taken over as head of the international affairs committee of the Third Duma, and had acted as the presidential representative on the Kaliningrad issue in negotiations over the transit regime with the enlarging EU. Rogozin was a vigorous defender of the rights of 'Russians abroad', above all in the former Soviet states. Glaz'ev's main innovation in this campaign was a distinctive brand of anti-oligarch populism, and in particular the idea for a 'natural rent' tax on energy producers, something along the lines of New Labour's 'windfall tax' of 1997. The Kremlin's divide and rule policy was more effective than anticipated, and Rodina was able to steal away a significant part of the communist electorate, winning 9.1 per cent of the vote. Positioned as a party of the 'patriotic left', Rodina appealed to the two core elements in the communist position: its leftism and its nationalism. Rodina's programme was based on 'social justice and economic growth'.[27]

The CPRF fought a confused and passionless campaign. Conservative traditionalists flocked away from the CPRF to UR and Rodina, leaving the CPRF with a rump marginalised electorate. The CPRF vote collapsed, gaining less than half as many seats in parliament, 52 instead of 125, with only 12.7 per cent of the vote compared to 24.3 per cent in 1999. The authorities sought to link the communists to the oligarchs. The task was made easier by the contributions received from Khodorkovsky (with some Yukos executives on the CPRF list, notably former Yukos board chairman Sergei Muravlenko and Alexei Kandaurov, head of the analytical department of one of Yukos's divisions); by its ill-advised links with Berezovsky (in exile in London); and by campaign funds received from Viktor Vidmanov of Rosagropromstroi. Of the top 18 positions on the CPRF national list chosen at its Ninth Congress on 6 September, only seven were CPRF members. More than this, the communist subculture was undermined by a variety of Kremlin strategies, including launching Rodina, the Party of Pensioners, and splitting the party by supporting former Duma speaker Gennady Seleznev's breakaway movement. Under Putin the traditional 'red belt' of communist-governed regions disappeared, and these elections signalled that the CPRF, like its French counterpart a generation earlier, was gradually withering away.

The elections were attended by over 1,100 observers from over 48 states. The Organisation for Security and Cooperation in Europe (OSCE) considered the election to be 'free but not fair'. Their report condemned the elections for failing to meet international legal standards and accused the state-controlled media of bias towards pro-presidential parties, above all United Russia.[28] As a result, 'an unfair environment was created for other parties and candidates'. United Russia in particular was criticised for the way that its leaders used their ministerial offices to promote partisan aims. The conclusion was unequivocal: 'The main impression ... is of regression in the democratisation process in Russia'. The report praised the decision of the Constitutional Court on 30 October to lift the most restrictive provisions on campaign media (Article 48 of the law on elections), but the advantages of incumbency had been exaggerated by the inclusion of 29 federal subject heads on the UR list.[29] The inclusion of senior state officials, few of whom intended to take up their seats, was considered a 'direct and blatant deception of voters'.[30] The final report recommended, among other things, a review of the Law on Political Parties of July 2001 to remove provisions discriminating against the establishment of political parties by groups representing regional, local or minority interests (Section XV.B.11) and encouraged the authorities to move ahead speedily in plans to transform state broadcasting into an independent public service media to provide the public with impartial information during elections (Section XV.B.22). The extent of fraud is difficult to asses, but it had undoubtedly occurred, above all in some of the national republics, notably Bashkortostan, Tatarstan and Dagestan.[31] It is unlikely, however, to have significantly changed the overall preferences of voters. Yuri Levada, head of what was to become his independent survey company (Levada-Centre), suggested that the actual results achieved by SPS and Yabloko were not far off those predicted by his pollsters.[32]

Presidential election of 14 March 2004

Putin's enduring popularity was now confirmed in his re-election for a second term. His victory, however, was tarnished by a number of factors, including the withdrawal of some of the leading candidates and attempts to boycott the election. In the interval between the Duma elections and the presidential ballot in March 2004 a group of radical critics of Putin's administration created 'Committee 2008', headed by the chess grandmaster Gari Kasparov and including the journalists Yevgeny Kiselev (at the time editor of Khodorkovsky's *Moscow News*), Sergei Parkhomenko and Viktor Shenderovich. The idea, in Nemtsov's words, was to ensure that Russia's next president would be 'a person from the street, and not a successor appointed by Putin'.[33] By then Nemtsov had moved into complete opposition to Putin, arguing that the final two years of his first term had been squandered and had turned into 'stagnation and restoration'. A new system of governance had emerged which he characterised as Putinism: 'A one-party system, censorship, a puppet parliament, a tame judiciary, strong centralization of power and finances, and an exaggerated role for the secret services and the bureaucracy'.[34] The strategy now clearly was to establish a democratic alternative to Putin's regime. The general aim, in Shevtsova's words, was for 'society to return power to the control of society'.[35]

Committee 2008 and other liberals called for a boycott of the election,[36] since a turnout below 50 per cent would render them invalid. According to Yavlinsky, 'free, equal, and politically competitive elections are impossible' since the country lacked the three essential ingredients for a free election: independent courts, free mass media and sources of finance free from Kremlin influence.[37] Others suggested that the party in any case lacked the resources to collect the required two million signatures. Putin was infuriated by the idea of a boycott, arguing that its advocates were 'cowards' and that the idea was 'stupid and harmful' and proposed by 'losers'.[38] Divisions in the liberal camp, and within SPS itself, prevented them from agreeing on a common candidate for the presidency. At its conference in late January SPS refused to endorse Irina Khakamada's candidature. Despite Nemtsov's pleas in her favour, Chubais argued that he was unable to forgive her accusation that the regime had been behind the Dubrovka theatre siege in October 2002. Khakamada's presidential candidacy was supported by Khodorkovsky's former deputy, Leonid Nevzlin, but her exaggerated statements concerning the siege much weakened her appeal. The boycott idea only reinforced the divisions within the liberal camp, and deprived Khakamada, who resolutely and courageously fought the campaign to the end, of vital support. The liberals had been in equal disarray in 2000, when some had supported Putin and others the governor of Samara, Konstantin Titov.

The only other serious candidate was Glaz'ev, the former co-leader of Rodina with Rogozin, but the two had fallen out following the parliamentary elections. Buoyed by success in the Duma elections, Glaz'ev sought to present himself as an independent politician who would be a credible successor to Putin as president in 2008. As a study of Rodina puts it: 'Glaz'ev had turned from an ally to a rival', and thus Kremlin support dried up.[39] With the Kremlin's encouragement, Rogozin had become sole leader of Rodina and replaced Glaz'ev as head of its Duma fraction. Glaz'ev's former colleague refused to endorse his presidential ambitions and now supported Putin. Glaz'ev had been careful not to burn his bridges entirely with the CPRF, but the presidential race demonstrated that there could be no return for him to the Communist Party. Glaz'ev emerged much weakened as a result of the bruising campaign, despite his 4 per cent.[40] Zyuganov refused to participate in the elections and instead the communists were represented by the second rank figure Nikolai Kharitonov, who in the event did remarkably well, having been given significant media coverage in return for not pulling out of the race (see Table 4.2). The former speaker of the Duma, Ivan Rybkin, was backed by Berezovsky from London, but turned out to be a tragicomic figure. His withdrawal in mysterious circumstances, following a five-day disappearance in Kiev, gave rise to the term 'rybkinisation' of the opposition: incoherent, incompetent and insubstantial.

As in 2000, Putin fought a non-campaign, typical of his depoliticisation approach, although his strategy was extremely effective. By not engaging in debate with his opponents he reinforced their marginalisation and rendered their candidature and policy proposals irrelevant. Serious opposition had already been weakened by the withdrawal of experienced candidates such as

Table 4.2 Presidential election 14 March 2004

Candidate	Votes	Percentage (%)
1. Putin, Vladimir	49,565,238	71.31
2. Kharitonov, Nikolai (CPRF)	9,513,313	13.69
3. Glaz'ev, Sergei	2,850,063	4.10
4. Khakamada, Irina	2,671,313	3.84
5. Malyshkin, Oleg (LDPR)	1,405,315	2.02
6. Mironov, Sergei	524,324	0.75
Against all	2,396,219	3.45

Sources: Central Electoral Commission *Vybory prezidenta Rossiiskoi Federatsii 2004: elektoral'naya statistika*, (Moscow, Ves' Mir, 2004), p. 106; Central Electoral Commission: www.pr2004.cikrf.ru/index.html. Accessed 25 March 2004.

Notes:
Out of 107,727,274 million Russian electors, 69,292,875 (64.32%) took part, comfortably exceeding the minimum 50% requirement. 578,824 (0.53%) cast invalid votes.

Yavlinsky and Zyuganov, while Zhirinovsky appointed his bodyguard, the former boxer Oleg Malyshkin, to run in his place. Putin fought on his record, and also on a forward-looking programme of continued state and economic reform.[41] The slew of positive economic indicators undoubtedly helped, but Putin was careful not to ignore the very large proportion of the population still below the poverty line. He captured the social democratic electorate by promises to strengthen the social security system, the patriotic vote by declaring the need to strengthen the military, and the economic liberals by insisting on further modernisation of the economy. The dismissal of Kasyanov as prime minister *before* the election, and the appointment of the technocrat Mikhail Fradkov at the head of a slimmed down cabinet of just 17 ministers of an overwhelmingly liberal and modernising orientation, was a clear signal of Putin's intentions in his second term. It indicated that he was at last conclusively distancing himself from the remnants of Yeltsin's 'family'. In voting for Putin the electorate was supporting not only an individual but also the consolidation of a system and the development of a programme. It was, as Shevtsova notes, 'not so much an election as a vote of confidence in President Vladimir Putin'.[42]

Although Putin's victory was far from unexpected, the scale of his triumph should not be under-estimated and marked a significant improvement over the 53 per cent won in 2000 (see Table 4.2). In Tatartsan and elsewhere there were reliable reports of ballot box stuffing, while the extraordinarily high turnout in some regions undoubtedly suggests the enthusiastic use of 'administrative resources'.[43] However, the general conclusion that Putin gained the overwhelming endorsement of the Russian electorate cannot be gainsaid, winning in every single region.[44] He remained the symbol of national unity and of aspirations for a better life. In voting for him people had not simply been brainwashed by Kremlin propaganda or overwhelmed by 'administrative resources', but freely and rationally voted in support of Putin's measured, nationally oriented and mildly progressive form of leadership. Yavlinsky's assertions that the vote was a 'farce' is, as one journal article put it, 'an insult to the overwhelming majority of Russian voters who voted for Vladimir Putin, of their own free will and quite consciously'.[45] As far as Gleb Pavlovsky was concerned, the middle class gave their overwhelming support to Putin, and the growth in their numbers explains his improved performance. In his view 'the democracy of the urban middle class is a key political mechanism which must replace the former communist machine and the post-communist bureaucracy as a political player'.[46] No sooner was Putin re-elected for a second term than speculation began whether he would run for a third, although the 1993 constitution prohibits more than two successive terms.

Electoral reform: phase two, 2004–7

Following the Beslan events of 1–3 September 2004 the electoral system was transformed. Instead of the old system, where half the Duma's 450 members were elected in single-mandate districts (SMDs) and the other half from national party lists, Putin proposed that the whole assembly should be elected on the basis of proportional representation, thus abolishing representation from the 225 SMDs. The measure was introduced on the grounds that it would help unify the state and bring the people into the struggle against terrorism, although quite how it would do this is unclear. In his address to an enlarged meeting of the government, governors and officials on 13 September, Putin noted that 'National parties should become one of the mechanisms ensuring a real dialogue and co-operation between society and state in the war against terrorism'. In his view a purely proportional system of State Duma elections would achieve this. It would also help towards his long-term aim of reducing the number of small parties. It would also remove the bloc of independent deputies, elected from SMDs, who tended to be dependent on the governors. The great majority of the 67 'independent' deputies elected in 2003 joined United Russia. The mixed electoral system, and above all the SMDs, provided access to parliament for individuals and small parties and thus weakened the incentives for party consolidation.

The measure was not simply a response to the Beslan events, since it had been part of the proposals of the CEC for some time and had been presented in draft form as late as 31 August 2004. On that day Alexander Veshnyakov, the head of the CEC, had recommended numerous changes to Russia's electoral system, including not only a fully proportional system but also that elections should be held synchronously and that party lists should contain a minimum quota of 30 per cent women.[47] Even that was part of an endless debate about electoral reform. Already in 1995 Yeltsin had proposed that only a third of deputies should be elected from party lists, as part of his attempt to reduce communist representation. In 1997 he proposed that the Duma should be elected entirely from SMDs in two rounds, a motion defeated by the massed ranks of the CPRF, LDPR, NDR and Yabloko. In May 1999 Chernomyrdin suggested that the Duma should be dissolved and that the next Duma should be elected from SMDs alone. The decisive victory of UR in the December 2003 elections allowed precisely the opposite electoral system to be established.

The CEC plan was for all elections to be held on the same day, the third Sunday in March for executive authorities and the first Sunday in October for legislatures. The fixed date, in Veshnyakov's view, would damage only the incomes of PR consultants.[48] He insisted that the so-called independent deputies elected in SMDs were soon absorbed by party groupings; as of 31 August 2004 only 15 were registered with the CEC.[49] Veshnyakov insisted that 'in current conditions the proportional system is more democratic and is to a certain extent a guarantee of a multiparty system in Russia'.[50] He rejected as 'exotic' the OSCE recommendation following the December 2003 election that a special supervisory body should be established to monitor the media during elections. The powers and rights of election observers were to be extended, although election commissions were still not required to provide certified copies of the election result protocols, and thus the scope for falsification remained.[51] There were no plans to change the way that regional legislatures themselves would be elected, having only recently moved to a fifty-fifty system on the former model of the State Duma.

The president presented his version of the draft law to the Duma in December 2004, but deputies balked at a number of the provisions, and only after numerous amendments passed the second and third readings in May 2005. In particular, the Duma refused to accept that penalties should be imposed on parties whose top three national or leading regional candidates gave up their mandates. In response to OSCE criticisms of the 2003 election, Veshnyakov's original plan was that candidates who had no intention of taking up their seat would not only lose their mandate, but the party would lose the seat as well, but the idea was defeated. Deputies, above all from UR, clearly favoured the retention of some of the electoral tricks from the 2003 armoury. The new law would affect a whole raft of electoral legislation, some 13 laws in all, which were summed up in the new electoral law of 2005. If the first election law in 1994 had been 29 pages long, the 2005 law now ran to 325.

In the old PR system a party presented two lists, with 18 people on the federal list and a minimum of seven regional lists. The federal list was now reduced to three people, who would act as the face of the party, while there were to be a minimum of 100 regional lists, with a prioritised order of names. This would be a challenge for most of the smaller parties, and only UR, the CPRF and possibly JR were sure to do this. It was anticipated that about ten parties would contest the 2007 elections.[52] The ballot paper gives the name of the party and the names of the three federal candidates. The ballot in the regions would also have the name of the person representing the party in that region. Veshnyakov had hoped to prevent people elected in this way later withdrawing their mandates without punishment. The proposals reduced the permitted share of discarded signatures on nomination forms from the earlier 25 to 5 per cent, thus giving greater scope for lists to be rejected. The idea of a biannual common voting day was adopted.

The stipulation that parties must have at least 50,000 members in at least half of the country's regions was confirmed. The creation of party blocs is now prohibited, so each individual party has to clear the 7 per cent threshold to enter parliament. The argument against blocs was that they had been used as an underhand electoral strategy: once elected, at both the federal and regional levels, blocs had a tendency to dissolve, although the deputies elected in the name of that bloc retained their seats. Blocs had been created to attract the maximum number of voters, but did not then act as a cohesive entity in legislative assemblies. The consolidated political parties would now be forced to present voters with a defined political platform with national appeal. The higher representation threshold was designed to force consolidation, but according to the framers of the new law, this should be done well before the usual two to three months before the election. The premium would now be on the creation of durable parties, even though composed of various proto-parties in the first instance. The ambitions of leaders would now have to be curbed for the greater good – something that particularly affected the fragmented liberal part of the political spectrum. In the regional legislative elections on 8 October 2006, 14 political parties took part and ten gained seats, and it was these ten that would take part in the 2007 national parliamentary elections.

The 7 per cent barrier was complemented by a floating threshold to ensure that 60 per cent of the votes cast in any particular election would be represented; and that at least two parties entered the Duma. All those winning over 7 per cent would automatically enter the assembly, and the next largest parties would be allowed in until the 60 per cent threshold was reached. For those meeting these conditions, mandates would be distributed in the following way: the three on the federal lists, and then the people at the head of the regional lists in proportion to the votes cast in that region. There was thus a strong incentive for those on regional lists to work with the voters of that region. There would be tough competition not only between parties, but also within parties, above all in the selection process to ensure that attractive candidates were chosen, to ensure that they did well in specific regions. The new electoral system would weaken the predominance of UR, now deprived of the additional independent deputies. The Moscow Duma elections of December 2005 demonstrated the process at work. The 20 deputies elected by PR were shared between three parties, whereas United Russia took all 15 single-member seats.

Seats in the Duma are allocated on the basis of the size of a party's vote in each region. Large cities get fewer seats and smaller regions gain increased representation. In keeping with the constitutional principle that people can stand for election without restrictions, independent candidates will be able to fight elections, but they will have to pit themselves individually against parties. If they win more votes than the regional lists put forward by parties, they will be elected. This is unlikely and, even if they do win, it is not clear what they would be able to achieve on their own in a party-dominated parliament. Effectively, there will no longer be independent deputies but only deputies from specific party lists, and they will be responsible to that party for their work. If a deputy leaves the party from which they have been elected, perhaps to join a rival party or to become an independent, then that mandate is terminated.[53] A deputy loses their seat if they switch parties, but not if they are expelled from a party faction – in which case their mandate continues. If someone leaves voluntarily, then the party passes the seat to the next person on the list. The logic of the new 'imparative mandate' system was to allow winning parties to form the federal government and the executive bodies in Russia's regions, a fundamental change that Putin favoured but hesitated to implement. Despite inclining towards the idea in mid-2003, Putin thereafter resolutely opposed the creation of party-based government (see below). Other aspects included allowing only observers from parties participating in the elections to scrutinise the polls; thus the role of independent observers was eliminated. Once again there were attempts to restrict media coverage of elections and referendums. Media outlets would be liable to prosecution if they broadcast or printed false or erroneous reports during an election campaign.

The great majority of deputies would be wholly dependent on party structures at every stage of the process, from candidate selection through to Duma membership. On the positive side, the CEC argued that dependence on the administrative resources of regional leaders would diminish, and stressed that even in the old system independent candidates were forced to join a party faction in parliament, thus losing their independence. The new system was unlikely to see a reduction in the use of administrative resources. At the same time, a new law on referendums of 27 September 2002 prohibited them in the last year of a parliament or that of the president, while yet another law on referendums of 28 June 2004 severely limited the scope for independent initiatives in this sphere, reinforcing the ban on referendums on constitutional issues in the year before parliamentary elections and requiring two million signatures and an extensive initiative group (no fewer than 100 people in half the regions – 4,500 people, whose signatures had to be witnessed by a notary). Observers such as Georgy Satarov argued that the new system represented an 'electoral counter-revolution'.[54] Quite why this should be thought to be the case is unclear. The shift to a fully proportional system, introduced into the Ukrainian system as a result of the constitutional amendments adopted by the Verkhovna Rada at the time of the Orange revolution on 8 December 2004, was considered an advance for democracy. In Ukraine's parliamentary election of 26 March 2006 over 40 parties and blocs participated.

The tinkering with the electoral system did not stop there, and in 2006 the Duma adopted a UR-sponsored law that abolished the 'against all' option in elections. This was despite a decision of the Constitutional Court in November 2005 that not only recognised the legitimacy of the 'against all' category, but also recognised the right of electoral agitation in favour of this option. Since the introduction of this box on ballot papers in 1993 (to replace the old Soviet system of crossing out names), some 5 per cent of voters used this category in national elections to register their dissatisfaction, and in some regional elections the total has risen to about 15 per cent. As noted, in the 2003 election the 'against all' category nearly entered parliament as an independent group, while in three single-mandate districts the 'against all' vote was the largest and forced a re-rerun. The option encouraged turnout, but ensured that the protest vote was amorphous. The original idea in 1993 was to ensure that some of the protest vote was siphoned away from communists and others, and clearly by 2006 the regime felt confident enough to do away with this safety valve. The abolition of 'against all' was condemned by all opposition parties as further restricting the choices available to voters.

The abolition in November 2006 of minimum turnout thresholds, which had been 50 per cent in national elections, 25 per cent in regional and 20 per cent in municipal elections, further undermined the legitimacy of the electoral process. Veshnyakov argued that the move was 'premature', noting that there had been no problem with voter turnout in national elections, and that the step lacked popular legitimacy and was perceived to benefit only the authorities.[55] The change was accompanied by a range of restrictions being placed on canvassing, including a ban on criticising a rival candidate on television and in agitation materials, although the prohibition did not apply to printed publications or radio. Yet more reasons, including the ban on loosely defined 'extremism', were now available to the authorities to refuse to register or to remove a candidate. The June 2002 law against political extremism (see Chapter 5) was amended in 2006 to bar parties from contesting elections if one or more of their members were convicted of extremism. The cumulative effect of these changes, which came into force on 7 December 2006, would be a fall in turnout as citizens turned their backs on an ever-more manipulated electoral process.

Under Putin the Russian electoral system became ever more regulated, and the competitiveness of the whole process became ever narrower. If in the 1995 Duma elections 285 parties and movements were eligible to compete with a 5 per cent representation threshold, in 2003 movements were excluded and only parties that had met stringent registration requirements and had a membership of 10,000 could participate, reducing the number to 64. For the 2007 elections minimal membership was raised to 50,000; the threshold was raised to 7 per cent; single-mandate seats were abolished, thus inhibiting individuals nominating themselves as independents; electoral blocs were banned, preventing parties agglomerating into more powerful electoral blocs; the 'against all' option was no longer available; and the minimum turnout threshold had been abolished. The number of parties eligible to fight the 2007 elections shrank to 17. To cap it all, elections for regional executives had been abolished (see Chapter 7). As if this was not enough, the architects of 'managed democracy' attempted to micro-manage not just the system, but outcomes as well by banning candidates through the courts and the judicious use of 'administrative resources'. As Gel'man notes, 'Hyper-fragmentation and high competitiveness in Russia's electoral market were replaced by trends towards a monopoly of the ruling elite'.[56]

This was indeed the case, but as usual in Russia, not everything was absolutely predictable, especially as the period of uncertainty associated with the Putin transition approached. The mayoral elections in Samara on 8 October 2006, for example, where the incumbent from UR, Georgi Limansky, was defeated by an outsider candidate, Viktor Tarkhov, demonstrated that public politics was not entirely dead in the late Putin era and that competitive party politics, even in the new conditions, was possible. Tarkhov was supported by the Party of Life, one of the groupings that merged to become Just Russia, and suggested that the emergence of this new party, although just as much a regime party as UR had been, would ensure that Russian elections would not be entirely meaningless. Indeed, the free-for-all of the Samara elections was reminiscent of the 1990s, including the return of criminal elements into the electoral field.[57] However, at this time plans were advanced to abolish direct elections in regional capitals, which would put an end to this sort of lively political contestation.

Parliamentary realignment

The Russian polity tends towards 'superpresidentialism', with the corollary that the executive enjoys dominance over political life. Although Russia's presidency does have extensive powers, governing in partnership with the cabinet of ministers and the prime minister, it certainly does not rule alone. The legislature in Russia is far from marginal, and indeed, with Putin enjoying a working majority after December 1999, his reforms proceeded not by decree but through an enormous body of legislative activity. The degree to which the lower house (the State Duma) and the upper house (the Federation Council) of Russia's bicameral Federal Assembly can impose limits on presidential power and effectively hold it accountable, however, is another matter. The structure of the Duma, according to Ostrow, with its unlinked dual-channel design and poor co-ordination between the party and committee systems, reduces its ability to act as an effective check and balance on executive power.[58] Thomas Remington argues that the legislature has been able to act as effective partner to the executive, and thus the decree powers of the presidency have not been used to subvert the legislative process.[59] He notes that 'A sign of the end of the revolutionary era is the fact that the Kremlin is pursuing this policy agenda through legislation rather than by decree'.[60]

As in many other countries, parliament's standing in public opinion was rather low, based on a lack of public confidence in the competence and honesty of legislators. There was a widespread perception that many criminals had entered political life, and used the shield of parliamentary immunity to protect themselves against prosecution. Despite some infamous cases where this indeed had taken place, this was far from being a mass phenomenon.[61] One of the changes introduced by the new Criminal Procedural Code of July 2002 (see Chapter 6) was that parliamentary deputies lost their blanket immunity from criminal prosecution. A case can now be brought against a deputy without first having to obtain parliament's permission. Despite its poor image, the Duma since its first convocation in 1994 had produced an impressive body of legislation; during the Second Duma (1996–9), for example, over 500 bills were passed and signed into law by the president, and much of this (some 122 laws) was significant legislation of enduring importance.[62] The productivity of the Third Duma (2000–3) and the Fourth (2004–7) was if anything higher, providing the legislative basis for Putin's reforms.

Although the 1999 elections delivered a solid block of pro-presidential legislators, no party or group enjoyed an absolute majority (over half of the 450 seats), let alone a two-thirds constitutional majority. This had been the case in the first two Dumas as well, and this explains the non-majoritarian features of the Duma's internal organisation at that time. The Council of the Duma, which sets the legislative agenda, was comprised of all the party leaders with equal voting rights, irrespective of the size of the party group. Posts in the Duma's two-dozen odd committees were divided between the parties on a proportional basis, and the chairpersonships are highly prized. However, in the deal struck on 18 January 2000 between the Communists and Unity for the division of committee chairs and vice-speaker posts, the old principle of proportionality was abandoned, provoking a walk-out and protests by the other groups. Later the CPRF moved into opposition, in the first instance to the Kasyanov government rather than to the president himself, tabling a no-confidence motion in the government in March 2001. The CPRF argued that 'The lower house has turned into a branch of the government'.[63] On 4 April 2002 a reshuffle (probably Kremlin inspired) saw the Communists losing the leadership of seven of its committees, and their resignation from the others as they went into open opposition to the presidency. This in turn provoked a split in the CPRF as speaker Seleznev refused to resign his position and, following his expulsion from the CPRF on 25 May, he redoubled his efforts to develop his own party, Rebirth of Russia, on the basis of his 'Russia' movement. At the same time, both the Council and the committees are subject to votes on the floor of the house, and thus rank-and-file deputies are able residually to influence the legislative process.

The majoritarian nature of parliament intensified in the Fourth Duma. Following the 2003 election Yavlinsky argued that a 'one-party Duma' had been created. There was some truth in this. Instead of the traditional proportional sharing of committee chairmanships, however unfairly they may have been distributed earlier, a majoritarian 'winner takes all' system was now applied, with UR taking the leadership of all 29 committees. There had initially been plans to apply the quota principle, which would have allowed the other parties two or three chairs, but according to UR, the various statements by the opposition showed that they were not ready to assume an adequate level of responsibility. For the first time the head of a political association could also assume the chairmanship of a committee, reducing the number of leading posts in the assembly. United Russia took eight out of 11 seats on the Duma Council, the body that manages the Duma's agenda, and seven out of ten deputy speaker posts. The role of the deputy speakers in the legislative process increased, while that of the heads of party factions was diminished. From January 2004 the minimum number of members required to form an official Duma faction was raised from 35 to 55, further marginalising independent deputies.

The absence of a strong liberal bloc in the Fourth Duma represented a setback for Putin. The new Duma now lacked Yabloko and SPS, and was dominated by a huge 300-strong UR faction. There was a high turnover in Duma membership in the 2003 elections, with 54 per cent of those seeking re-election losing their seats. In effect a change of political generations took place. Those who had come to prominence in the late *perestroika* period and been active in the early years of the Russian parliament were swept away, and in their place a new class of 'parliamentarian-functionary' emerged. This was most notable in the case of UR. In addition to functionaries, a sizeable group of nationalists, by some accounts encompassing nearly 30 per cent of deputies, took their seats in the new assembly, many of them swept in on the Rodina groundswell.[64]

In institutional terms, power in the Duma increasingly focused on the party factions rather than the parliamentary committees. The introduction of the imperative mandate in 2006, whereby deputies are not allowed to leave the parties from whose lists they were elected, greatly strengthened the hand of faction leaders. The predominance of a small number of large groupings enhanced the power of the caucus leaders, and in particular that of the leadership of United Russia. Considered a pedestal party for the Putin administration, there is no doubt that the group acted as the 'transmission belt' of Kremlin concerns into the legislative process. At the same time, the diversity of views within UR meant that it acted as a sounding board for parliamentary and social concerns back to the presidency, and sometimes it even sought to introduce legislation that met with only equivocal support in the Kremlin.

The CPRF emerged as the main representation of the 'independent opposition', with very few allies on the liberal right to help them fulfil this role effectively. The Rodina faction, contrary to the expectations of its Kremlin sponsors, became the voice of the nationalist opposition. Although Rodina had a strong bloc in the Duma, albeit split between the 29 deputies in the People's Patriotic Union and 12 deputies in Sergei Baburin's People's Will fraction,[65] UR's dominance meant that Putin was not dependent on its votes to push through his legislative agenda. Rodina's leadership was divided, while its ideology remained an unstable combination of nationalist and social democratic themes. Rogozin turned out to be an uncomfortable ally of the Kremlin, who was far less willing than Glaz'ev to ally with the opposition in any shape or form. Rodina's derogatory racist advertising in the December 2005 Moscow Duma elections led to it being barred from the ballot. The party's aggressive nationalism turned out not to be not to the Kremlin's taste, and in March 2006 they engineered Rogozin's ousting and the election of the moderate Alexander Babakov as the party's head.[66] The latter in turn later became part of Just Russia.

With the solid bloc of UR and allied votes, combined with the fact that centrists now enjoyed the chairmanship of all significant committees and dominated the Duma's administrative apparatus, one could fairly say that Putin had tamed parliament, a dominance reinforced by changes to the Federation Council that will be discussed in Chapter 7. Ranged against this dominant coalition were the now depleted Communists, while Zhirinovsky's Liberal Democrats and Rodina remained nominally independent, together with the rump SPS and Yabloko. The Kremlin played an active part in managing its faction in the Duma, notably when the leadership of the UR group was changed in November 2002 when the ineffectual Alexander Bespalov was replaced by the interior minister Boris Gryzlov, who went on to lead the UR party as a whole.

With a working majority to support presidential policy, the legislative activity of the Duma in the early 2000s went into overdrive. Legislation in the early Putin presidency was largely initiated by the executive; some 72 per cent of all bills in the spring of 2000, for example.[67] In the session ending in July 2001 the emphasis was on reform of the federal system. Some 200 pieces of legislation had been voted upon, including a wide range of Kremlin-sponsored bills designed to reform Russia's political and economic system. These included revisions to the land and tax codes, and a number of 'debureacratisation' measures, including reducing the number of activities requiring licences from some 500 to 104, and the adoption of the law on parties. In the following year the emphasis was on reform of the judicial system and extending property rights, above all of land, with major laws passed: the Land Code, the Labour Code, the Criminal Procedure Code and the Administrative Code. All of this was in fulfilment of Putin's promise, at his first press conference as head of state, that his aim was Russia's 'modernisation'. The theme was taken up again a year later at a press conference on 18 July 2001 when he argued that this legislative activity marked a significant step towards 'the modernisation of the state's economy' and represented a 'substantial contribution toward the improvement of the country's political system'.[68] The presidential veto on legislation was now rarely used. The proportion of bills signed into law by the president increased from 61 per cent in the First Duma (1994–5), to 74 per cent in the Second (1996–99), and rose to 95 per cent in the Third (2000–3) and remained at that level in the Fourth.[69] As time passed, of course, there were fewer items of landmark legislation. Critical voices with some justice argued that much of this legislative activity lacked sufficient time to be improved by parliamentary debate, and indeed that the Duma had become little more than an extension of the Kremlin, a 'transmission belt' rubber-stamping its initiatives and thus confirming the views of those who argued that Russia had become a 'managed democracy'.

For Putin the Duma was now an effective ally to push through the reforms he wanted. Estimates in mid-2003 found that some 57 per cent of Putin's coalition in the Third Duma was made up of constituency deputies, and according to Hale and Orrtung they were 'the key to Putin's first-term legislative juggernaut'.[70] This was intensified in the Fourth Duma, and enhanced by the strong showing for UR. Although Putin now enjoyed a constitutional majority in the Duma, he refused to consider amending the constitution.[71] At the same time, there were limits to Putin's ability to get his way. As he noted in his 7 February 2006 Spanish interview, 'My influence on the Duma is naturally substantial but it is overly exaggerated because parliamentarians have their own opinion on some issues'. He used the example of the abolition of the death penalty, which he personally favoured but which would not find a parliamentary majority. 'I do not raise issues that would arouse a negative reaction or rejection', he stated, in a comment typical of his cautious style in routine politics.[72] In December 2006 only 27 deputies voted to ratify a protocol designed to streamline the workings of the European Court of Human Rights, despite Putin's strong endorsement of the measure. A fifth of all cases before the Court at that time came from Russia, indicating the lack of efficacy of the Russian court system. The status of parliament in popular opinion, never very high, was not improved, while the quality of the laws passed declined as the obedient majority pushed through the regime's agenda. Even worse, with its enormous majority United Russia shaped the rules of the political arena to suit its purposes.

Putin, parties and government

There is no reason to doubt Putin's oft-repeated commitment to strengthening the role of parties in political life, although he refused to join one himself. Legislation designed to consolidate Russia's party system was at the top of his political agenda on coming to power, with the adoption of a new law on political parties and the requirement that at least half of regional legislators were elected from party lists, and later changes to electoral legislation, above all the shift to a wholly proportional system for electing the national parliament, reinforced this policy. The next step would be the one taken early in the French Fifth Republic (despite De Gaulle's opposition) – the creation of a party-based government. In his state of the nation speech in May 2003 he noted: 'I believe it possible, taking into account the results of the forthcoming election to the State Duma, to form a professional and efficient government based on the parliamentary majority'.[73] The Kremlin administration had prepared a law to this effect, but at the last minute the plan was scotched.[74] A powerful group around Putin, bringing together *siloviki* and some liberals, feared that the passage of a constitutional amendment allowing a party or coalition of parties to form the government and nominate the prime minister would deliver the country into the hands of the oligarchs.[75] It was clear that the lobby managed to change Putin's mind on the question, and he did not return to the idea.

United Russia, not surprisingly, continued to favour the idea of a government formed out of the parliamentary majority. From 2002 there was much discussion, harking back to Primakov's premiership, of forming a government based on the dominant party and, as we have seen, the idea came up in Putin's May 2003 address. It was at this time that the Kremlin became concerned about Khodorkovsky's putative prime-ministerial ambitions, and it is quite possible that these fears prevented Putin taking this step. The idea of allowing the party with the majority in the Duma to nominate candidates for prime minister was once again aired in 2005. This was the step already taken in Ukraine in December 2004: the Verkhovna Rada majority, rather than the president, would appoint the prime minister and most cabinet ministers; and the president lost the right to dismiss the prosecutor general, which became the Rada's prerogative. The Russian constitution, however, is clear that the president appoints the premier (Articles 83(a) and 111(1)), although a new federal constitutional law stating that this appointment is made following the views of the Duma majority would probably suffice to make the change. Provisions stating that the prime minister cannot sit in parliament would also have to be changed.

United Russia looked as if it could become the core of a presidential catch-all party with Putin at its head. This is something that Yeltsin had always avoided doing on the grounds that he was 'president of all Russians', fearing that he would himself be constrained politically. Putin had a no less ambivalent relationship with the 'party of power' than Yeltsin, but in new ways. United Russia remained bound hand and foot to the governing regime and had failed, by the time of its first crucial test in the December 2003 parliamentary elections, to transform itself into a powerful independent, although pro-government, party. Putin's hesitancy over taking the decisive step towards creating a party-based government reflected strategic as well as tactical concerns. The political expression of Russian radical centrism remained the administrative regime and not the 'party of power', which was not allowed to become the party 'in power'. Putin relationship with UR remained ambivalent. In his press conference on 31 January 2006 Putin strongly refuted the idea of the government being formed by the parliamentary majority:

> As for a party-based government, everything is possible in the future, but I am against introducing such a practice in today's political environment in Russia. I am deeply convinced that in the post-Soviet area, while we have a developing economy, a statehood that is being consolidated and are finally determining the principles of federalism, we need strong presidential power ... so far, we have not yet developed stable national political parties. How under such conditions can we talk about a party-based government? It would be irresponsible.[76]

It was now clear that there would be no such change as long as Putin was president. Of course, there was nothing to stop UR nominating its own candidate for the presidency in 2008.

In the run-up to the 2007 election even the regime urged UR to find its independent ideological and organisational feet. Without Putin as president, the slogan 'We are the party of Putin' would be meaningless. In February 2006 Putin allowed himself to make some rather disparaging comments about the party, and in general his assessment of Russia's multi-party system was not positive:

Russian statehood is still in the development phase. It cannot be described as absolutely stable. We have no multi-party system in the European sense. There is one stable political party – the Communist Party of the Russian Federation. Another, still emerging, but already rather stable political force is United Russia. It is considered the ruling party, but it has not formed its ideology yet. Some dramatic ideological processes are still in progress inside.

United Russia had still to find its feet, to identify its priorities and to accept political leadership, including the readiness to make tough choices, if it wanted to lay claim to the centre-right political niche, Putin insisted. 'There must be a clear definition of what a centre-right ideology is all about in modern Russia'. He once again returned to the German example, mentioned in his press conference of 31 January 2006, where there had been protracted negotiations on forming the government following the inconclusive elections of September 2005. 'Germany was faced with the risk of a political stalemate', Putin said. 'It was the high level of political culture and the readiness of the former chancellor [Gerhard Schroeder] and his successor [Angela Merkel] to compromise that broke the deadlock'. If even a country with 'well-oiled political mechanisms of cooperation by the main political forces' could be afflicted by such a crisis, then what about Russia. In Putin's view, 'Deplorably, we still have nothing like that', and he warned that the next electoral cycle in 2007–8 would be 'a great test. I am prepared to say that thrice'.[77] Although UR fought hard to become the official presidential party, Putin refused to commit himself unequivocally and kept his options open. Putin, however, would no longer be president after 2008, and thus UR had to prepare for life without its benefactor.

The Putin succession

The greatest moment of weakness of any regime is the period of leadership transition. This universal rule applied with particular force in Russia as 2008 approached. The highest goal in the Russian political system is the presidency, but Putin was barred from seeking a third term by Article 81, Clause 3 of the constitution, which bans more than two consecutive terms in office for the same person. The system built in Russia since 2000 was focused overwhelmingly on Putin personally, although his leadership continued trends that had been taking shape already in the late Yeltsin years. Enjoying an extraordinarily high level of popular support that hardly wavered over the years, as the succession approached, ever more Russians wanted Putin to serve a third term.[78] A change of leadership would introduce a high degree of uncertainty, as Gorbachev's appointment in 1985 so vividly demonstrated. As Tret'yakov argued, succession since at least the time of Peter the Great entails a change of course. It was for this reason that he argued: 'In the current situation the interests of Russia as a nation and country, and also the development of democracy in the country, require the extension of Vladimir Putin in the highest post for one (I stress only for one) term'.[79] The Putin elite feared that their system did not have the internal strength to reproduce itself in the absence of the figure who had given the regime coherence and legitimacy for eight years. There was the natural fear that the successor would repudiate the Putin years, just as Putin condemned much of Yeltsin's legacy.[80]

Despite many calls to amend the constitution, and given his popularity and the extent of his support among the elite Putin could have done this, he resolutely opposed all plans to change the normative framework for his own convenience. Constitutions had been changed in Belarus and in Uzbekistan to allow Lukashenko and Karimov, respectively, to consolidate their authoritarian rule, and Putin feared to find himself in their company. Thus after 2008 Russia would find itself with a new president. Will the change represent just a change of leader, or a change of regime? The stakes could not be higher. As Sergei Markov notes, 'In Russia we lack traditions, political traditions of peaceful transfer of power from one leader to another'.[81] As with Yeltsin earlier, one paramount consideration was to ensure that Putin's successor did not launch any hostile actions against him or his associates. Other than that, Putin sought to ensure policy continuity, and to avoid the presidency falling into the hands of extremists of one stripe or another. Hence 'operation successor 2008' became one of the regime's main concerns from 2006 onwards.

The succession would effectively be decided in 2007, in the year before the election due in March 2008. Numerous imponderables entered the balance: whether Putin could maintain his popularity, the price of oil, the condition of the economy, the international situation, and much else. Even though Putin would undoubtedly try to ensure a smooth succession, there is no guarantee that his nominee would successfully come to power. However much 'administrative resource' was devoted to the issue, unless the presidential elections were blatantly rigged there always remained scope for an unexpected outcome. The first stage would be the parliamentary elections of December 2007 that would act as the 'primary' for the later contest. The post of prime minister had served Putin as the springboard for the presidency, and this would undoubtedly again be the case.

In the reshuffle of 14 November 2005 two of Putin's closest confidants were promoted. The defence minister Sergei Ivanov retained his ministerial portfolio but also became a deputy prime minister. The chief of staff of the presidential administration, Dmitry Medvedev, became first deputy prime minister, while remaining Gazprom chairman. At the same time, the governor of the energy-producing region of Tyumen, Sergei Sobyanin, became Putin's new chief of staff. Sobyanin had been elected governor of Tyumen region in January 2001, and he was a member of United Russia. The personnel changes helped consolidate an echelon of leaders who would be able to fill the gap when Putin's term in office came to an end. It also suggested a new dynamism to a presidency that appeared to have lost its way in the wake of the Yukos affair, protests over the monetisation of social benefits and the Orange revolution in Ukraine.

Medvedev was given the authority and resources to deliver on Putin's agenda announced on 5 September 2005 to achieve improvements in health, education, agriculture and housing. At his disposal was the Infrastructure Investment Fund, running at $2.44 billion in 2006, $2.55 billion in 2007 and $2.56 billion in 2008. The various 'national projects' announced by Putin in September 2005 sought to make a tangible difference to people's lives, and can thus be seen as part of the succession strategy and also represented Putin's attempt to create a permanent legacy of improved welfare. Medvedev took over as chair of the Council on National Projects (CNP), previously headed by Prime Minister Fradkov, and insisted that the aim was to avoid political intrigues and to 'making the life of the people considerably better'.[82] The establishment of the CNP was yet another example of Putin's para-constitutionalism, in this case establishing a parallel agency that duplicated the work of the government. In the event the Council was brought firmly under the aegis of the government, partly in response to widely expressed concerns about the unclear division of responsibilities. Putin sought to devise a mechanism to achieve quick improvements in standards of living and improved welfare services while avoiding inflation or the social protests that accompanied the monetisation of social benefits.

The 'national projects' portfolio, although fraught with danger if Medvedev failed to deliver, was a high profile post that would ensure extensive media coverage on issues that affected people's daily lives. At the same time, he would inevitably be pushing for greater social investment, bringing him possibly into conflict with the guardians of macroeconomic stability and the inflation reduction strategy, the finance minister Alexei Kudrin and the economics minister German Gref. As a Kremlin insider, Medvedev was familiar with all the factional concerns but appeared neutral in these conflicts, with no clear ideological position of his own. There was also an economic dimension to the appointment, since Medvedev remained chairman of the Gazprom board of directors. He strongly favoured the planned Pacific oil pipeline, following the Taishet–Skovorodino–Perevoznaya Bay route, and thus his enhanced authority was a factor in the decision to give priority to the Pacific rather than the Chinese route and to advance other economic projects in the Far East. Medvedev had long warned that the failure to develop Siberia and the Far East could tempt others to do and undermine Russia's territorial integrity. As could have been anticipated, the lack of substantial progress on the 'national projects' led to the search for scapegoats, with bureaucracy and regional leaders taking some of the blame.[83]

Ivanov's appointment was portrayed as an attempt to strengthen his reform of the hidebound defence ministry and to boost military reform. In other words, he was a defence minister with enhanced powers, rather than a deputy prime minister who also happened to be defence minister. Announcing the appointments on television, Putin stated that at a meeting a week earlier 'the participants expressed anxiety about the problems the defence ministry had been having in achieving its plans for future development ... these problems are connected with the lack of coordination between various ministries and departments'.[84] This suggested that Ivanov would have access to resources beyond that of the military industrial complex alone to enhance the potential of Russia's armed forces, while at the same time combating the tendency for the military to become even more commercialised. At the same time, Ivanov could provide crucial support for Medvedev's advancement, if that indeed would be the Kremlin's choice; or to act as a candidate in his own right if Medvedev faltered.

The changes appeared to weaken Fradkov's position as prime minister. Until the reshuffle, moreover, the liberal economist Alexander Zhukov was the only deputy prime minister. On 20 March 2006 Ivanov's position was further strengthened by his appointment at the head of a powerful new commission created to oversee state military procurement, a position that was not answerable to the prime minister. At the same time, Ivanov's deputy on the Defence Industry Commission, Vladimir Putilin, was given ministerial rank. Putilin had formerly been head of the defence and security department at the economic development and trade ministry. In his new role Ivanov took control of a budget of $25 billion, in addition to the $17 billion he oversaw as defence minister.[85] The change further overshadowed Fradkov, and appeared to give Ivanov the edge over Medvedev in the succession stakes. On 15 February 2007 Ivanov was promoted to first deputy prime minister.

The reorganisation brought the cabinet closer to the model of what it had been in the 1990s, with one first deputy prime minister and two deputy prime ministers, one with special responsibility for security and military-industrial issues, and the other responsible for economic and financial issues. The appointment of Sobyanin, one of the most important of Putin's appointments from the regions, suggested that the balance of Russia's federal relations could once again be tilted in favour of the regions. At the same time, as an outsider he was in a weak position to impose his authority on the presidential administration, and thus the influence of the deputy heads such as Igor Sechin and Vladislav Surkov became stronger.[86] Factional conflicts within the Kremlin intensified as the succession approached. The balance in the cabinet had also changed, with a rather stronger 'political' bloc that had been notable for its absence earlier.[87] More broadly, the reshuffle strengthened the moderates around Putin, who had been battling against a more militant group (the *siloviki*), led above all by Sechin, who had long been seeking to reduce Ivanov's influence. Clearly, Ivanov's enhanced profile brought him firmly into the field of contenders for the succession. Ivanov was deeply loyal to Putin personally, and while possibly not actively seeking the presidency, would no doubt put himself forward for the succession if asked by Putin. At the same time, Medvedev appeared a strong compromise candidate who would be acceptable to the liberals, the democratic statists and the *siloviki*.

The succession list was wide open, and all sorts of imponderables would intervene before the people could make their choice. The shortlist included Medvedev, Ivanov and Sobyanin. It also included representatives of the security factions such as Sechin, Patrushev and Georgy Poltavchenko. The chairmen of the two houses of parliament could not be excluded, Sergei Mironov and Boris Gryzlov. The list also included Kozak, the presidential envoy in the Southern Federal District, prime minister Fradkov, Vladimir Yakunin of Russian Railroads, and representatives of the regions, above all the governors Alexander Tkachev (Krasnodar), Alexander Khloponin (Krasnoyarsk), and Aman Tuleev (Kemerovo). Putin announced that he would name a preferred successor before his term ended, arguing that 'I have certain ideas about how to construct the situation in the country ... so as not to destabilise it, not to scare people and business. Everyone values the situation we have today – a calm, steady and stable situation'. He insisted that he would only recommend a successor, and that the final choice would lie with the people.[88]

As for Putin personally, he repeatedly stressed that he would leave office after two terms as stipulated by the constitution. Although greeted with scepticism at first, with all sorts of schemes advanced by commentators about how Putin could outwit the system to remain in power without formally breaching the letter of the constitution, as the 2008 changeover approached it became clear that Putin really did intend to stand down from the presidency, but he remained vague about what role he would fulfil thereafter. He issued numerous enigmatic comments about his post-presidential career. For example, in his televised question and answer session on 25 October 2006, his fifth since assuming office and in which some two million questions were sent in by the public, he reiterated that he would not try to run for another term, but that he would retain 'influence' over Russia after leaving office:

> But even after I no longer have my presidential powers, I think that, without trying to shape the constitution to fit my personal interests, I will be able to hold on to what is most important and most valuable for any politician, namely your trust. And building on this trust, we will be able to influence life in our country, to ensure that it follows a consistent path of development.[89]

If for some reason or another Putin reneged on his commitment to step down in 2008, then his further leadership would take place in crisis conditions and would be very different from his first two terms. It would mean a fundamental transformation of the nature of his power and of the state. This was something that Putin sought to avoid, but there were no doubt factions in his administration who wished for nothing less.

Conclusion

Putin's reforms transformed Russia's political space. The party system was restructured to ensure that there were fewer but stronger parties, but the effect was to provide the space for a dominant 'party of power' to emerge, United Russia. The establishment of a second leg to the system of state-sponsored parties, Just Russia, signalled that the regime feared the emergence of a dominant party system. Changes to the electoral system reinforced the legislation on parties, although the shift to a purely proportional electoral system would ensure the representation of at least three to four parties. United Russia emerged pre-eminent from the December 2003 election, and Putin was re-elected more by coronation than competition in March 2004. Parliament in the Putin years was dominated by UR and adopted the bulk of his legislation with little question, accompanied by a weakening of internal dynamism of the lower chamber as parties increasingly predominated over Duma committees. However, the spark of pluralism was not entirely extinguished in the Duma, but in the absence of a strong liberal presence the tone of debates and policies became increasingly nationalistic. A competitive party system on a national scale began to emerge, but parties are still not adequately embedded in the country's social structure, they do not effectively represent social interests, and above all they do not legitimate power or directly form governments. The spirit of managed democracy inhibited the development of a genuinely competitive political market place. It was not clear that Putin was quite ready for that – or indeed whether the country was.

5   Regime, state and society

When the state strengthens, the people become enfeebled.

Vasily Klyuchevsky[1]

Many adjectives have been used to qualify the political system that took shape under Putin's leadership. Most convey the sense of a democracy diminished in one way or another: 'managed democracy', 'controlled pluralism' and 'electoral democracy' are among the most common epithets to describe Putin's new order. The regime itself came to favour the concept of 'sovereign democracy', although Putin distanced himself from the term on the grounds that 'sovereignty' and 'democracy' operate at different conceptual levels.[2] So how best can we understand a hybrid system in which democracy has not been repudiated and remains the legitimating ideology, the formal letter of the constitution is observed, choices remain, votes can be cast in a relatively free, and even mostly fair, manner; but the options are constrained by an authority standing outside of the system that regulates the choices and which is not adequately accountable to the representative system? We have called this authority the administrative regime, focused on the political institutions of the presidency but rather broader than the president alone, standing between the impartial operation of the constitutional state and the exercise of popular sovereignty through the ballot box and representative institutions. In trying to get to grips with the nature of the regime we need to separate processes from outcomes. As for process, the regime under Putin sponsored changes to the party system, electoral legislation, parliamentary procedures and much more, all reflecting its Prussian-style management of democracy; but this febrile activity was less anti-democratic than para-democratic, not repudiating democracy but subverting its operation. As for outcomes, while there is undoubtedly evidence of administrative intervention in the electoral process, it would be an exaggeration to argue that results are entirely 'managed'. There is plenty in Russian politics that remains unexpected and surprising. It is too early to talk of Russia as a failed democratisation, and the potential for democratic evolution has not been extinguished.

State and regime

François Mitterand referred to the post of president, as created by De Gaulle in 1958, as a 'permanent coup d'état',[3] and shortly before his death he warned that French political institutions 'were dangerous before me and could become so after me'.[4] The presidency in France has been called a 'republican monarchy', and many felt that the situation was no less dangerous in Russia.[5] The presidency overshadowed all other political institutions to create what Klyamkin and Shevtsova call an 'elected monarchy'.[6] The paradox under Yeltsin, however, was the emergence of a strong presidency in a weak state, something that created a whole range of power asymmetries and distortions. This was not a problem unique to Russia. As Stephen Holmes has argued, the 'universal problem of post-communism is the crisis of governability produced by the diminution of state capacity after the collapse of communism'.[7] The creation of the presidency in the first place had been intended to compensate for the weakening power of the Communist Party, and now it filled the vacuum created by the ebbing of state authority and the weakness of civic initiative. As in the United States, the president was both head of state and head of government (although in Russia joined by a prime minister), and the fusion in one person of two separate symbolic and practical spheres undermined the constraints that the constitutional state could exert over the administrative regime.

Regime politics

At the heart of the regime system that emerged under Yeltsin was the oligarchy and its allies, which represented a fusion of financial and industrial capital with direct access to government. The traditional distinction between the market and the state was eroded, and lobbying interests enjoyed an extraordinarily close relationship with government. Russian politics became characterised by the salience not so much of the formal institutional structures of government and management but by informal relationships. Above all, given the weakness of the state, the emergence of what might be termed quasi-state actors became particularly important. For example, private banks and large energy companies (above all Gazprom and Unified Energy Systems – UES), acted as substitute sinews of the state, providing financial resources not available through general taxation and serving as indirect enforcers of federal policy, a feature that continued in new forms under Putin. A type of 'state' bourgeoisie emerged, dependent on access to the state, rather than a more independent entrepreneurial bourgeoisie.

Personalised leadership inhibited the development of institutions. The political regime was focused on Yeltsin and his family and operated largely independently from the formal rules of the political system, whose main structural features were outlined in the constitution. Behind the formal façade of democratic politics conducted at the level of the state, the regime considered itself largely free from genuine democratic accountability and popular oversight. These features, as Hahn stresses, were accentuated by the high degree of institutional and personal continuity between the Soviet and 'democratic' political systems. A Party-state ruled up to 1991, but under Yeltsin a regime-state emerged that perpetuated in new forms much of the arbitrariness of the old system. Both the regime and the constitutional state succumbed to clientelistic pressures exerted by powerful interests in society, some of whom (above all the so-called oligarchs) had been spawned by the regime itself. These constituted a fluid ruling group. We have suggested above that the 'family' represents one of the factions in the regime; the *siloviki*, democratic statists and various Pitery brought in by Putin also populate this fluid constellation.

The constitutional order enshrined in the December 1993 constitution is focused on the presidency. When the president is weak, so is the state. The effectiveness of the state is dependent on the strength of the presidency in general and on the character of the incumbent in particular. It is this entwining of institutional and personal factors in a weak constitutional order and underdeveloped civil society that gives rise to what we call regime politics. A regime here is defined as the network of governing institutions that is broader than the government and reflects formal and informal ways of governing and is usually accompanied by a particular ideology. The regime in Russia is focused on the presidency but is broader than the post of president itself. It can be seen as a dynamic set of relationships that include the president, the various factions in the presidential administration, the government (the prime minister and the various ministries), and the informal links with various powerful oligarchs, regional bosses and other favoured insiders.[8] While the presidency is at the head of the regime, the two remain separate and thus we can envisage a situation in which the presidency could be at odds with the administrative system which it nominally controlled. Indeed, we argue that Putin sought to use the administrative regime while trying to maintain his autonomy from it. To maintain elements of presidential autonomy Putin appealed to the revived constitutional state, a reinvigorated civil society and popular support.

The regime in Russia, where legitimacy is ultimately derived from the ballot box, is caught on the one hand between the legal order represented by the state (the formal constitutional institutions of administration and the rule of law), and on the other hand by the system of representative institutions (above all political parties) and accountability (primarily parliament). The regime acts as if it stands outside the political and normative principles that it has formally sworn to uphold, but at the same time is constrained by those principles. It is as much concerned with its own perpetuation as the rational administration of the country. For comparative purposes, we have noted that similar regimes relatively independent of the constitutional constraints of the rule of law and of popular accountability emerged in post-war Italy and Japan, and in general appear to be a growing phenomenon in the post-Cold War world.

Regime politics in post-communist Russia, therefore, is not like traditional authoritarianism, and the regime could not insulate itself from aspects of modern liberal democratic politics such as media criticism, parliamentary discussion and, above all, from the electoral cycle. The regime looked in two directions at once: forwards towards democracy, international integration and a less bureaucratised and genuinely market economy; while at the same time it inherited, and indeed perpetuated and reinforced many features of the past – bureaucratic arbitrariness in politics and the economy, a contemptuous attitude to the citizenry, anti-Westernism, pervasive patron–client relations, Byzantine court politics, widespread corruption and creeping patrimonialism in the economy as the state once again took strategic sectors, including a large part of the energy industry, back into its grip. Only when the regime is brought under the control of law and the constitution and within the ambit of political accountability can Russia be considered to have achieved democratic consolidation. This would be a revolution every bit as significant as the fall of communism itself in 1991 and would represent the 'redemocratisation' of democracy in Russia. It would subordinate the political process and regime actors to the legal constitutional system and render it more responsive to the needs of citizens. What Max Weber called sham constitutionalism, and which under Putin developed as para-constitutionalism, would give way to real constitutionalism where political institutions are subordinated to the rule of law and human and civil rights are defensible by law.

The 'dictatorship of law': pluralistic or compacted statism?

Putin's constitutional conservatism did not prevent considerable institutional and programmatic innovation. In his address of 8 July 2000, Putin argued that Russia must not remain a 'weak state', asserting that 'the only realistic choice for Russia is to be a strong country'. In his speech he stated: 'We have to recognise that the state itself was largely responsible for the growing strength of the unofficial, shadow economy, the spread of corruption and the flow of great quantities of money abroad ... An inefficient state is the main reason for our long and deep crisis'. Responding to criticisms that his attempts to remake the state could give rise to authoritarianism, he insisted: 'The battle between strong power and freedom is an old one, and at the moment this debate is giving rise to almost daily speculation on the themes of dictatorship and authoritarianism. But our position is clear. Only a strong and democratic state can defend the civil, political and economic freedoms of the population'. Putin emerged as something akin to a Jacobin or French republican state builder: seeking to ensure the universal and equal application of the constitution and the laws, accompanied by the homogenisation of political space and the establishment of a stable set of political institutions.

At the heart of Putin's statism was the universal applicability of law. Although the phrase 'dictatorship of law' became peculiarly Putin's own, it was a term first used by Gorbachev on 13 February 1991.[9] Putin first used the phrase in his speech to a conference of chairs of regional courts on 24 January 2000, and the idea was at the heart of his early programme of state reform. A week later Putin argued: 'The dictatorship of law is the only kind of dictatorship which we must obey', insisting that freedom without law and order 'inevitably degenerates into chaos and lawlessness'.[10] In his 8 July 2000 speech he argued that 'an era is beginning in Russia where the authorities are gaining the moral right to demand that established state norms should be observed' and that 'strict observance of laws must become a need for all people in Russia by their own choice'. In an interview soon after, he insisted that he sought to put an end to the situation in which Russians appeared to have become subjects of different regions rather than citizens of a single country.[11] This applied as much to economic as to civic life. Putin insisted that he was determined to put an end to the curtailment of economic freedoms in certain regions, where business was divided up between clan members and where the media and civil organisations were persecuted. Thus a secondary theme of Putin's statism was the restoration of coherence in central–regional relations. In his 8 July 2000 speech he stressed that 'competition for power' between the centre and regional powers has been 'destructive', and he argued that 'we have to admit that [Russia] is not yet a full-blown federal state'. Instead, Russia had 'created a decentralised state'.

While the presidency under Putin sought to carve out greater room for manoeuvre, Putin was hesitant to subordinate the regime entirely to the imperatives of the constitutional order or to the vagaries of the popular representative system (elections). Yeltsin earlier had feared that the untrammelled exercise of democracy could lead to the wrong result, the election of a communist government that would undo the work of building market democracy, threaten Russia's neighbours in pursuit of the dream of the reunification of the USSR and antagonise the country's Western partners. It was for this reason that factions in the regime had called for the 1996 presidential elections to be cancelled. The dilemma was not an unreal one, and reflected the regime's view that the Russian people had not yet quite matured enough to be trusted with democracy. Like the Turkish military and the army in some Latin American countries, the regime considered itself the guardian of the nation's true ideals. This was the ideology explicitly espoused by some of the regime's policy intellectuals such as Gleb Pavlovsky and Sergei Markov, and there was a certain logic to the view. However, we know that whenever the military acts against democracy as the 'saviour of the nation' the results are usually the opposite of those intended, and the regime's mimicry of the military stymied the development of a political order robust enough to defend itself against the enemies of democracy.

Thus when Putin undertook the task of rebuilding the state he was torn between a number of imperatives. The first and most obvious was his intention to clean up the regime's own act, to put an end to the most extravagant corruption and free access to political power by the oligarchs. This he managed to achieve, as we shall see, relatively quickly. The next task was to ensure the unimpeded and universal application of law throughout the whole country. While his federal reforms began to rein in the regional barons, the writ of law remained far from uniform. The third imperative, however, ran counter to the first two, namely ensuring that the predominance of the regime itself was not challenged. A fourth element was that within the regime Putin sought to broaden the autonomy of the presidency.

The resurgence of the state was thus torn between two forms, each of which gave rise to a distinctive type of statism. The first takes Putin's commitment to the maintenance of the principles of the existing constitution at face value, and accepts that the attempt to apply constitutional and other legal norms across Russia in a uniform and homogeneous way represented a genuine attempt not only to undermine the neo-medieval features of governance that had emerged under Yeltsin but also reflected a commitment to liberal universalism. This would include what Robert Dahl calls polyarchy in society, the institutionalised basis for a pluralistic politics.[12] From this perspective, we can describe the process as the *reconstitution* of the Russian state. Putin's statism represented an advance for democracy in the sense that the application of the law would be the same for all, including regional bosses, oligarchs and, presumably, the regime and presidency itself. This is very much a normative (that is, legal and constitutional) reconstitution of state power. The type of system that emerges out of this is a *pluralistic statism*, a democratic statism that defends the unimpeded flow of law and individual rights while respecting the pluralism of civil society and federal norms. Pluralistic statism takes as genuine Putin's commitments in his *Millennium Manifesto*, his various annual addresses to the Federal Assembly and many other statements arguing that a strong state should be rooted in a liberal economic order and a vibrant civil society.

However, the selective approach to the abuses of the Yeltsin era, the attack on segmented regionalism that threatened to undermine the development of federalism, and the apparent lack of understanding of the values of media freedom and human rights, suggested that Putin's reforms could become a general assault on the principles of federalism and democratic freedom. The dependence of the presidential regime on 'power structures', as part of an unstable alliance of the presidency, certain oligarchs and the power ministries, suggested that another, less benign, form of statism could emerge. We call this the *reconcentration* of the state to distinguish it from the reconstituted statism described above. State reconcentration gives rise to *compacted statism* in which the rhetoric of the defence of constitutional norms and the uniform application of law throughout the country threatens the development of a genuine federal separation of powers, media and informational freedoms, and which establishes a new type of hegemonic party system in which patronage and preference is disbursed by a neo-*nomenklatura* class of state officials. There were many indications that United Russia sought to become the core of a new patronage system of the type that in July 2000 was voted out of office in Mexico after 71 years.

From the very first days of his presidency Putin drew on constitutional resources to re-affirm the prerogatives of the state vis-à-vis segmented regional regimes. The struggle for the universal application of the rule of law, however, threatened to intensify at the federal level the lawlessness that characterised so much of regional government. Yeltsin's personalised regime represented a threat to the state, but its very diffuseness and encouragement of asymmetrical federalism allowed a profusion of media, regional and other freedoms to survive. Putin's new statism carried both a positive and a negative charge: the strengthening of the rule of law was clearly long overdue; but enhancing the powers of the regime and the presidency was not the same as strengthening the constitutional rule of law. While Putin stressed the strengthening of the state, too often it appeared that his interpretation of state strengthening was synonymous with the consolidation of the regime, and within the regime, the enhancement of the presidency. This was a strengthening that was based more on control and loyalty rather than trust. The weakening of the federal pillar of the separation of powers was not likely to enhance the defence of freedom as a whole. The key test would be whether the revived presidency would itself become subordinate to the new emphasis on the 'dictatorship of law', and thus encourage the development of a genuine ordered rule of law state, or whether it would attempt to stand aloof from the process and thus once again perpetuate the tradition of 'revolution from above', if only to put an end to the revolution, and thus reproduce typical patterns of authoritarian politics.

Putin's 'constitutional coup' of 13 September 2004

In the wake of the Beslan school siege of 1–3 September 2004, on 13 September Putin addressed an enlarged government meeting of some 150 people.[13] Putin announced a raft of measures intended to enhance the security of the country.[14] Putin spoke of the terrorists' attempt to achieve 'the disintegration of the country, the break-up of the state and the collapse of Russia'. For Putin, the very existence of the state was in question, and he insisted that 'We must improve the effectiveness of state bodies in resolving all the problems that lie before the country'. Of the seven measures announced that day, however, only one – the establishment of a special federal commission on the North Caucasus – was directly connected to dealing with the problems of which Beslan was a symptom. At least five of the other measures represented a sharp escalation in the strengthening of the 'presidential vertical': the appointment of governors; 100 per cent proportional representation in parliamentary elections; the establishment of a Public Chamber; the establishment of Khrushchevite voluntary patrols to maintain public order; and the creation of a 'crisis management system' to conduct the war against terror. The final measure, the re-establishment of a ministry responsible for issues of regional and ethnic policy, turned the wheel full circle to the early 1990s. The measures mentioned above were not so much anti-constitutional as para-constitutional. The events of September 2004 can be compared to 1958 in France and the launching of a 'constitutional coup'. Others have compared the events of September 2004 to the onset of Alexander III's reaction in the 1880s against his predecessor's period of 'great reforms'. Is this the moment, as Marxists say, when quantitative changes took the form of a qualitative alteration of the system?

The terrible events in Beslan have been seen by many as Russia's equivalent to the al-Qaeda attack on the World Trade Center and Pentagon on 9 September 2001. The debate over what 9/11 means continues to this day. For the Bush regime it was seen as the signal to launch a 'war on terror' in which human rights and the norms of international law could be suspended. Thus the concept of '9/11' consists of two aspects: the nature and meaning of the attack itself; and the response to the attack. For some commentators 9/11 represented an assault by militant Islam against all that was best in the West – tolerance, pluralism, human rights, democracy and the rule of law. Others interpreted the attack not as an assault against Western *values*, but as an attack against Western *policies*, above all in the Middle East. This twofold distinction applies equally to Russia: the immediate and underlying factors that provoked the Beslan attack; and the response of Putin's government. Here we shall focus on the second of these questions, and the first will be discussed in Chapters 7 and 8.

Beslan served as a catalyst to expose the underlying aspirations of the power system and accentuated the para-constitutional features of Russian politics. They do not directly contradict the constitution, but neither are they part of the letter of the existing constitution. At the same time, contrary to what Putin intended, they only fitfully strengthened the system of executive power or rendered the working of government more efficacious. Para-constitutionalism is intended to make government more efficient, but the result is to undermine the principles of constitutionality and ordered government. Para-constitutionalism is a strategy of the regime rather than one to develop the impartial and predictable workings of the constitutional state. By devising a series of measures that were intended as a response to a particular crisis, they were in danger of accentuating the scope and intensity of that crisis.

Beslan provided the opportunity for a number of measures to be implemented that had long been on the cards. It would be going too far to argue that this was a cynical exploitation of the tragedy, but it reflected the regime's sense of the dangers that the country faced, including fears for the integrity of the state. In his emotional address on 4 September Putin talked about the disintegration of the USSR and the failure of Russia to establish itself fully as a state ever since. Putin warned that the state had not proven effective in conditions of a changing world, warning that enemies were trying to seize a 'juicy morsel' from Russia. He argued that 'Russia is living under the conditions of a transitional economy and a political system that do not correspond to society's level of development'.[15] Putin talked in terms of international terrorism, but it is clear that fundamentally the violence in Beslan and elsewhere is a radical extension of the conflict in Chechnya. He stressed a generalised conspiracy by vague and unnamed forces, as in America after 9/11. The abstractness of the 'war against terror' allowed the Bush government to define its objectives at will, and to use this 'war' as justification for whatever measures it felt appropriate. The theme of the Russian state in danger was later developed by Surkov.[16] Putin returned to the topic in his Federal Assembly address of 25 April 2005, when he described the disintegration of the USSR as 'the greatest geopolitical catastrophe of the twentieth century'. This sense of the fragility of the Russian polity reinforced re-concentration, with its associated compacted statism, over pluralistic reconstitution.

The 'liquidation of the oligarchs as a class'

Under Yeltsin the institutions of a modern representative democratic state were introduced but at the same time they were emasculated. This contradiction was forcefully reflected in the development of the presidency itself; as an institution it became the centre of Russian political life, but as an organisation it was weakened by Yeltsin's personalistic style. The key test of Putin's leadership was whether there would be a genuine institutionalisation of the political process. One aspect of this was the differentiation of the state from the new business elites, the issue with which Putin began. As Thomas Graham notes, 'The trouble with this approach [the various attacks on the oligarchs] is that it is still unclear whether the Kremlin is taking true aim at the structural conditions that gave rise to the oligarchs in the first place'. These structural conditions, in his view, were 'the intertwining of power and property', something that stymied the development of both effective governance and efficient markets.[17] Only the clear separation of business from government would break the system that had given rise to oligarchic capitalism. For that an independent judiciary, a streamlined bureaucracy and more honest policing was required. Instead, while the collective political influence of the business magnates was broken, it was replaced by a type of state bureaucratic capitalism.

Struggle against the oligarchs

During the election campaign and in his address of 8 July 2000, Putin talked of the need to break the cosy relationship between big business and government. During the presidential campaign in early 2000, Putin had talked, in language reminiscent of Stalin's plan in 1929 to 'liquidate the kulaks as a class', of his aspiration to 'liquidate the oligarchs as a class', stressing the need to create a level playing field.[18] His central idea was that special interests, above all the oligarchs, should be kept 'equidistant' from the government.[19]

No longer were a select group of oligarchs to have privileged access to the corridors of power. They were no longer to exercise class power over the state, or indeed, to hold the state hostage whenever the regime needed financial or other support. Putin's discursive frame on this question is neatly summed up in his Spanish interview in early 2006:

> Back in the mid-1990s oligarchic groups substituted for government in Russia. They were elected to parliament and lobbied laws beneficial for specific financial and industrial groups instead of the society. They also ensured fulfilment of these laws through their representatives in high places. I do not think this meets the public interest.[20]

As with so many of Putin's other ideas, the broad analysis was undoubtedly correct and the policy implications probably right, but their application fell far short of aspirations. Selective attacks against certain oligarchs were not able to eliminate the regime's dependence on the business interests that had been spawned in the comprador phase of Russia's capitalist development, and the manner of the attack undermined the independence of the media and the judiciary.

Within months of his election, Putin launched a campaign against some of the beneficiaries of the free-for-all of the Yeltsin years. The first to feel the cold wind was Vladimir Gusinsky's Media-Most empire, which owned a number of periodicals but most significantly the independent television station NTV, which had been sharply critical of Putin. The Media-Most offices were raided on 11 May 2000, and on 13 June Gusinsky was arrested (while Putin was in Spain) and held in custody for four days (more on this below). Soon some of the country's biggest businesses came under the scrutiny of state agencies investigating alleged tax evasion and privatisation deals. The companies affected included Gazprom, Norilsk Nickel, Lukoil, and the biggest car manufacturer, Avtovaz. Norilsk Nickel had fallen into Vladimir Potanin's possession as a result of the notorious 'shares for loans' deals of 1995–6, and now the authorities called for the repayment of $140 million in compensation for his alleged underpayment when the plant had been privatised in an auction that he had helped organise. The inclusion of Avtovaz in the list suggested that the campaign was beginning to affect members of the 'family', the group of powerful politicians and oligarchs grouped around Yeltsin personally, since the mightiest of them all, Berezovsky, had gained his first million by milking the hugely loss-making motor company through his car dealership business, Logovaz. Berezovsky had moved on and his interests had diversified to include Aeroflot, the oil company Sibneft and the media (including a 49 per cent stake in the main TV station, ORT, the only one received throughout the CIS and the Baltic region).[21] As Berezovsky put it in June 2000, the way that business had been conducted in the last decade meant that no one 'could survive a serious government effort to find something to charge them with'.[22]

In July 2000 Putin criticised 'people who feel comfortable in conditions of disorder, catching fish in muddy waters and wanting to keep things as they are'. Yeltsin himself had occasionally talked in these terms, and Primakov had launched an investigation against some business leaders, notably Berezovsky and Alexander Smolensky, when he had been prime minister. In April 1999 Berezovsky had been charged with 'illegal business activity', but these charges were dropped in November (when Putin was already prime minister). The investigation into Berezovsky's activities, when Aeroflot's cash flow fell into his hands and was siphoned through various Swiss intermediaries, had been conducted by Yury Skuratov when he was prosecutor general, but Skuratov was dismissed from his post in Yeltsin's last year.[23] Berezovsky was notorious for running down the capitalisation of his companies. For example, Berezovsky had obtained Sibneft in 1995 at a deep discount, and although it produced 40 per cent as much oil as Surgutneftegaz, the market capitalisation of the latter (one of the best-managed oil majors in Russia) was eleven times higher. Berezovsky was the classic 'oligarch', combining financial, media and political power, more interested in politics than business.

Berezovsky's behaviour, as always, was marked by audacity and cunning. Having won a Duma seat in the December 1999 parliamentary elections in the single-member constituency of the North Caucasian Republic of Karachaevo-Cherkessia, Berezovsky gained immunity from prosecution – unless the Duma itself voted to strip him off that immunity. In a typically brazen move, he announced on 17 July 2000 that he planned to resign his Duma seat in protest at the 'authoritarian' trends in Putin's government,[24] saying that he did not want 'to take part in the destruction of Russia and the establishment of the authoritarian regime'.[25] He described the guarantee of immunity as worthless, which in his case it probably was since most deputies would have been only too glad to see him face the consequences of his asset-stripping and political adventurism.[26] His official letter of resignation was submitted on 19 July and highlighted three issues: the attempt to rein in regional leaders; the criminal cases opened against a number of businessmen; and the lack of attention devoted by Moscow to the problems in Karachaevo-Cherkessia. He called for an amnesty for all past economic crimes, denouncing the anti-corruption drive as 'an orchestrated campaign, directed at destroying major independent businesses',[27] and argued that 'Everyone who hasn't been asleep for the past 10 years has willingly or unwillingly broken the law'.[28]

Berezovsky moved into opposition, announcing the creation of a new party made up largely of regional governors, only a few months after he had created one for Putin (Unity).[29] Berezovsky argued that Russia needed 'a constructive opposition', or 'the process of centralisation will inevitably begin'.[30] Berezovsky brought together a group of like-minded deputies in the Duma to create a new faction, later to be known as Liberal Russia. This was intended to become the core of an anti-Putin coalition. Berezovsky still enjoyed control of ORT to exploit popular fears about Putin. In an interview on 27 June 2000 he argued: 'All the decrees, all the laws proposed by Putin are directed at again enslaving people. People were given a whiff of freedom, and now they are to be forced to their knees again'.[31] Similarly, on announcing his intention to resign from the Duma, he declared that he wanted to have no part in the 'destruction of Russia and the imposition of authoritarian rule'.[32] He condemned the Duma, calling it 'the Kremlin's legal department that obediently follows all orders and instructions'.[33] Berezovsky announced that he planned to merge all his interests into a single media holding company,[34] but soon afterwards he was forced to negotiate the sale of his stake in ORT.[35]

In November 2000 he went into 'exile' in London while continuing to sponsor the Liberal Russia party, until he was expelled from it on 9 October 2002 because of his overtures to the communists and nationalists. Russia's extradition request was refused in 2003 and he was granted political asylum, and he used Britain as a base to launch ever more strident calls for Putin's overthrow. He contributed at least $21 million to the Ukrainian opposition in support of the Orange revolution in late 2004 through his Civil Liberties Foundation. By January 2006 he was inciting anti-constitutional resistance: 'President Putin violates the constitution and any violent action on the opposition's part is justified today, and that includes taking power by force, which is exactly what I am working at'. For the past 18 months, he stated, 'we have been preparing to take power by force in Russia', with his favoured mode of regime change being an intra-elite coup since 'The majority and the mob never interested me'.[36]

The attack against certain oligarchs was interpreted as an attack against media freedom. Gusinsky joined Berezovsky in his condemnation of Putin's government. He asserted that the anti-oligarch campaign signalled the end of the democratic freedoms that Russia had enjoyed in the 1990s. As he put it, 'In Russia there used to be a police regime. It disappeared temporarily and now it is being rebuilt'.[37] Putin himself put a very different slant on events. In his interview with *Izvestiya* on 14 July 2000 he defended actions by the tax police and the federal prosecutor general's office against companies like Media-Most, Avtovaz, Lukoil and Potanin's Interros group. He insisted that 'the state has the right to expect entrepreneurs to observe the rules of the game', and he insisted that the state 'would act more vigorously toward the environment in which business operates. I am referring first and foremost to the tax sphere and the restoration of order in the economy'.[38] Putin insisted that all the oligarchs would be kept at equal arm's length from the government. By turning Berezovsky and Gusinsky into the Empson and Dudley of his regime, Putin sought to warn the rest that a new leader had arrived.

The assault against the oligarchs as a class was renewed in the run-up to the December 2003 parliamentary elections and the March 2004 presidential campaign. The target this time was Mikhail Khodorkovsky, at the head of the giant Yukos oil company. In early July 2003 the prosecutor general's office conducted a search of the company's Moscow headquarters and arrested the company's security chief Alexei Pichugin. On 2 July the head of the Menatep international financial association (Yukos's main shareholder) Platon Lebedev was arrested in connection with $280 million worth of share acquisitions in 1994, in the country's largest fertiliser company, Apatit. The charges against him were of large-scale fraud. Yukos's key shareholders Leonid Nevzlin and Khodorkovsky were questioned as witnesses in the Lebedev case. Months of pressure culminated in Khodorkovsky's arrest on 25 October in a dawn raid on his plane in Novosibirsk. He was kept in a pre-trial detention centre (Matrosskaya Tishina) in Moscow for many months, despite the appeals of an international group of defence lawyers to allow him out on bail. At the same time various threats were made against other oligarchs. A long-running case against Oleg Deripaska at the head of Russian Aluminium (Rusal), was resurrected, while the Kremlin made clear to Roman Abramovich, at the head of Sibneft, that his extravagant purchase of the Chelsea football club in London was frowned upon. The planned merger between Yukos and Sibneft to create one of the world's largest oil companies was suspended. Even the ultra-Kremlin loyalist Vladimir Potanin, at the head of Interros (the owner of Norilsk Nickel), was not immune to pressure when it became clear that Potanin was looking for ways to transfer some of his assets abroad.

The assault against Yukos signalled the Kremlin's determination to assert its authority over the business community. Numerous factors were involved in the case, ranging from Yukos's attempts to pursue an independent energy policy (favouring the building of a private pipeline to Daqing in North China rather than the Transneft-controlled route to the Far East and the Japanese market) to Khodorkovsky's eclectic support for numerous political parties, stretching from Yabloko to the Communists. Perhaps most controversial were Khodorkovsky's independent political ambitions, appearing to position himself for a possible leadership bid in 2008. More broadly, the 'social contract' between business and the Kremlin in 2000 was being redrafted. It was no longer enough for big business to stay out of politics: in the circumstances of a revived state, the economic sphere was to be controlled by the authorities and the oligarchs were to understand that their historic role as the creators of capitalism was over. A new model of political economy was to emerge in which the very notion of 'oligarch' was to become anachronistic.

The new rules of the game

The selective nature of the campaign provoked the suspicion that it was directed not so much against real crimes and corruption as against Putin's critics and opponents. While the attack was undoubtedly selective, it was far from arbitrary. Putin targeted those who had flaunted their closeness to power in the most provocative manner, allegedly abused their dominance of the media, or had egregiously exploited various tax minimisation schemes. Putin was setting the rules of the political game, and in attacking a few oligarchs he was disciplining the rest. There was an implicit threat: toe the line if you wish to keep the assets 'gained' in the 1990s.[39] By 2004 this was no longer enough, and commentators such as Lilia Shevtsova saw the renewed assault against the oligarchs as part of the revenge of the bureaucracy and so-called 'power structures' to establish a corporatist system. As far as she was concerned 'the oligarchy is a myth. Bureaucracy continues to be the dominant force within the Russian system of governance, as it has been through the ages'.[40]

Berezovsky had long warned against the danger from the left, epitomised above all by the Communists, but he found himself outflanked on the right, by a presidency in alliance with the security establishment. However, pervading the anti-oligarch campaign there hung the suspicion that one set of tycoons was using the law and the presidency against another. In particular, Roman Abramovich, who in early 2000 had participated in the creation of a holding that controlled most of Russia's aluminium production, was known to covet Norilsk Nickel and Gusinsky's NTV. Other oligarchs, notably Mikhail Fridman at the head of the Tyumen Oil Company (TNK), Oleg Deripaska and many more focused now on developing their businesses and kept out of politics. They willingly accepted the new rules of the game, including clearing major initiatives with the Kremlin, and thus went on to become key figures in the new era. While business was now taken out of politics, politics entered ever more decisively into business.

Twenty-one top figures of Russia's business elite met with the president on 28 July 2000 to lay down the ground rules of relations between the government and business. This was not the first meeting between the business elite and the Kremlin. In September 1997, in the wake of the Svyazinvest privatisation scandal, the top oligarchs had been invited to meet Yeltsin to lay down the rules of engagement. Not much had come out of that meeting, and the Kremlin now sought to ensure that the business leaders did not gain the impression that they were equal political interlocutors with the elected presidency. The aim of the July 2000 meeting was to establish the new rules of the game, in which the role of the state would be enhanced and respected. The attendees were an eclectic group, but equally notable were the absentees.[41] The agenda was established by Nemtsov, the leader of the Union of Right Forces Duma faction. He insisted that 'The business and power should not attack or blackmail each other, they should be partners working towards the economic recovery of Russia'.[42] The business leaders presented a three-point declaration to the government: first, for the Kremlin to declare a moratorium on any investigations into the legitimacy of privatisation over the past decade and not to initiate any redistribution of former state property; second, the business community must undertake to play by the rules, pay taxes and scrupulously obey the law; third, the government must rid itself of corrupt bureaucrats, while the business tycoons on their part must undertake not to use government institutions or bribe state officials to fight their competitors.[43] As many noted at the time, however, the link between power and property was hardly challenged by such an extra-constitutional 'pact', which in any case left out some of the key players.

The modification of Yeltsin-style politics was accompanied by fears that democracy would be swept away at the same time. Gusinsky argued that a 'police regime' was being established in Russia, and said that he feared for his life. He asserted that Putin had turned against him after Media-Most began criticising the war in Chechnya. He added that one of the reasons he had become a 'victim of persecution' is that Russians 'try to destroy' rich people, whom (he argued) they inherently envy and hate, and because he was a Jew.[44] Tretyakov provided a more subtle analysis of the situation. Several logical approaches, he noted, were in conflict here: while the Kremlin still saw the world in terms of the traditional nation state, the owners of NTV saw the world like any transnational corporation, above all one concerned with the media, as a single borderless sphere of economic activity.[45] At the same time, given the rather amorphous nature of most Russian parties, Gusinsky's media empire had become effectively the leader of the opposition to Putin, subjecting his actions and motivations to sharp criticism. When the interests of the state are seen as synonymous with those of the government, any criticism of the government can be seen as anti-state. As Tretyakov put it, Media-Most from the Kremlin's perspective was 'a radical opposition political party disguised as a media holding'.[46]

As long as Putin's anti-oligarch campaign was conducted by the presidency, the core of the old regime system of relations, there could be legitimate questions about its political selectivity. Instead of using the courts, he relied on strong-arm tactics led by the MVD, the FSB and the prosecutor general. Only when the anti-corruption campaign was conducted by a demonstrably free and independent judiciary would fears that it was designed to further political ends be allayed. There were signs of this in the enhanced role played by the Audit Chamber, an independent body authorised to monitor the use of federal budget funds and headed by the former prime minister and one-time head of the FSB, Sergei Stepashin. A law adopted in 2005 offered a partial amnesty for economic crimes committed during the privatisation of the 1990s, but the threat of tax investigations remained. The law allowed existing businesses to consolidate, but while the threat of criminal prosecution had receded, the threat from the state intensified.

On the eve of the Yukos case Putin noted:

> I don't really like the word 'oligarch' used to describe big business representatives in Russia. In the sense that we usually use this word, an oligarch is a person with stolen money, who continues to plunder the national wealth, using his special access to bodies of power and administration. I am doing everything to make sure this situation never repeats in Russia.[47]

He took up the theme in his address to the Federal Assembly on 10 May 2006 when he was unrepentant about having 'trodden on some toes'. He acknowledged that the phrase had been used by Franklin D. Roosevelt at the time of the great depression in 1934, but he vowed to continue on this path: 'And we will continue to tread on them. But these are the toes of comparatively few who seek to retain or gain position or riches or both by some short cut that is harmful to the greater good'.[48] In the event, Putin's new rules of the game opened the way for Russia's oligarchical (or comprador) capitalism to be transformed into a new system. The conglomerate-dominated Russian economy remained highly concentrated but its relations with government had changed. Putin met regularly with business leaders in round tables of the sort held in July 2000, but the days of oligarch dominance were over. Many companies saw improved corporate governance, greater transparency in financial process, greater economic competitiveness and an orientation towards profit rather than rent seeking. However, the state's whip hand in 2003 and the attack on Yukos represented the beginning of a new phase in which the administration sought to shape the economic sphere by sponsoring 'national champions', primarily in the energy sector, and to ensure that big business was 'socially responsible'. The security of property rights was undermined and as in Soviet days law was used instrumentally. The Yukos affair signalled a new model of political economy in which the line between the public and the private was no less blurred than in the 1990s, but now state capture gave way to business capture.[49]

Freedom of speech and the media

Putin's presidency was accompanied by persistent fears for media freedom. A warning issued by Putin's campaign headquarters on 4 March 2000 threatened 'an asymmetric response to acts of provocation' by the mass media, a rather more robust version of New Labour's rapid rebuttal unit in the 1997 British general election. The persecution of the Radio Liberty reporter Andrei Babitsky, the environmental reporter and retired navy captain Alexander Nikitin, the popular muckraking reporter Alexander Khinstein and others, all appeared to signal the end of the luxuriant but riotous profusion of press liberties that had emerged in the late 1980s and grown rankly under Yeltsin. Much of it, however, had become bent to the will of the oligarchs. The lack of a strong independent financial base and the weakness of the heavily monopolised advertising market meant that in the 1990s the state tutelage of the Soviet period was gradually exchanged for conglomerate dominance. Some independent radio stations and print publications did survive, but their existence was precarious.

Babitsky had been arrested in Chechnya on 16 January 2000 and then held incommunicado for a month before being exchanged for some Russian prisoners to the Chechen insurgents. On his release in Dagestan, he was accused of having false documents and was banned from leaving the country. In an extract from his book published in *Kommersant-daily* on 10 March 2000 (the later book text lost some of the toughness of the newspaper version) Putin was harsh about Babitsky ('observe the laws of your country if you are counting on those laws being observed with respect to you'), and former KGB agent Oleg Kalugin was described by Putin as a 'traitor'. However, when questioned about the propriety of appointing Pavel Borodin state secretary of the Russian–Belarusian Union before a full investigation of the allegations of his corruption while at the head of the Kremlin property division, Putin noted that 'there is a golden rule, a founding principle of any democratic system. It is called the presumption of innocence'.[50] As Yevgeny Kiselev noted during NTV's influential *Itogi* current affairs programme two days later, this smacked of double standards: Babitsky and Kalugin were branded traitors and enemies, while others enjoyed the presumption of innocence.

The information regime imposed on reportage of the second Chechen war adopted contemporary Western informational practices in times of warfare. Any non-official reporting of the war could be construed as 'anti-state activity'. Khinstein had written an article in *Moskovsky komsomolets* suggesting that the Kremlin had been involved in high treason. The response was not long in coming: being dragged out of bed and attempts made to section him in a psychiatric ward, claiming that he had incorrectly filled out his 1997 driving licence application by not fully declaring his mental health history. The raid by masked tax police on the offices of Gusinsky's NTV, the only national independent TV station, on 11 May 2000, followed on 13 June by his four-day incarceration, suggested a sustained assault against press freedom. A collective editorial of the democratic *Obshchaya gazeta* warned that Putin was building a 'dictatorship': 'It seems that the consolidation of ever more power in the hands of the president is not intended to implement some policy, since no policy unconnected with the consolidation of power itself has yet been announced, but has become an aim in itself'.[51]

It was unlikely that Gusinsky was any more corrupt than other oligarchs, but he was the head of an independent media company that was critical of Putin and the 'family'. NTV had been established in 1993, and during the first Chechen war from 1994 provided critical commentary on federal actions. In 1996 it had thrown in its lot with the regime as Yeltsin sought re-election, with the head of the station at the time, Igor Malashenko, arguing that Yeltsin represented the lesser evil compared to the threat of a communist comeback. In the late 1990s NTV was guilty of the worst accounting practices of the time, keeping a real and a fraudulent set of books, and ended up borrowing $1.2 billion from Gazprom. By the time of the 1999–2000 elections an air of hubris hung over the station. The personal attacks on Putin were quite vicious, although probably no less nasty than the attacks on Luzhkov and Primakov by Sergei Dorenko on the Berezovsky-dominated ORT. The sphere of mass media was certainly ripe for reform by the end of the 1990s.

In his first address to the Federal Assembly on 8 July 2000, Putin insisted that 'without truly free media Russian democracy will not survive, and we will not succeed in building a civil society'. In that speech he warned that many TV stations and newspapers promoted the political and commercial interests of their owners, arguing that some media engaged in 'mass disinformation' and were 'a means of struggling against the state'.[52] There could be few clearer examples where Putin's post-Sovietism – the acceptance of media pluralism and recognition that media freedom is the cornerstone of a democratic society – was at war with his neo-Soviet reactions, suggesting that the media in some way were guilty of 'anti-state' activities. The implications of this were made explicit in an interview shortly afterwards, where he questioned whether the Russian media were truly independent given the dominance of oligarchic interests: 'They fight more for maintaining their influence on the state than for freedom of speech and the press'. He added, however, that he considered the conflict between the media and the authorities 'artificial'. Putin insisted that the building of a strong and effective state must not lead to the violation of civil freedoms, and that Russia must not become a police state. Even here, though, there were echoes of his neo-Sovietism, reflected in his argument that democracy in post-Soviet Russia, imposed from above, had almost led to chaos.[53]

Already at this time some commentators (for example, Kiselev) argued that Putin was strengthening his personal power rather than the power of the state: 'What we understand by the state is not a bureaucratic machine headed by a former member of the power structures and security services, but a democratic Russia with its people'.[54] On 3 April 2001 a new management was installed at NTV and one of its first acts was to cancel the *Itogi* programme. Kiselev went on to become part of the consortium that took over TV6. The station then broadcast as TV Centre (TVS) under the supervision of a loyal board of directors headed by Primakov. The end of the old lively NTV was a great loss (especially the fine programmes of political analysis introduced by Svetlana Sorokina), but it should be noted that the crude attacks that it indulged in on leaders would never be countenanced in the West. Personal attacks in the Russian media reflect the coarsening of the Russian intelligentsia, whether affiliated to the regime or in opposition to it. Now a spirit of obsequiousness crept in that stifled the exuberance of earlier years.

Pressure on radio was also evident in the case of the Ekho Moskvy station, which had made a name for itself as fiercely independent. The old team was disbanded, and then a new group of independent journalists was allowed to take over, but ultimately it became part of the Gazprom-Media empire, although it remained strongly critical of the Kremlin. In 2001 Gazprom had taken over the newspaper *Segodnya*, formerly owned by Gusinsky's Media-Most group, and it was soon closed down. Gazprom-Media was established in the wake of this takeover and, in 2006, 86 per cent was still owned by Gazprom. The new-style NTV was not immune to political pressure either, and Gazprom-Media sacked the station's new manager, Boris Jordan, in January 2003 at the Kremlin's behest because of the way that the station had covered the Dubrovka theatre siege a few months earlier. Although Putin vetoed legislation adopted by the Duma in the wake of the October siege, which severely limited the reporting of terrorist actions and banned broadcasts of their statements, as 'too draconian', it was clear that he had strong views on the proper limits of media behaviour. Putin's strategy was to set out the parameters of acceptable journalistic behaviour, but then to allow a degree of freedom within these approved limits. As in his dealings with the oligarchs, the intention was to establish the rules of the game and use a few select cases to discipline the rest. This encouraged pre-emptive obedience and the imposition of self-censorship for fear of transgressing the bounds. The 'censorship control' of the Soviet era now gave way to 'ownership control', but even within this framework a degree of pluralism remained.

The Beslan events brought to the surface continuing tensions in Putin's attempts to ensure sympathetic coverage in the public sphere. The editor of *Izvestiya*, Raf Shakirov, was forced to resign in the immediate aftermath of the massacre, apparently for a wordless full-page picture on 3 September. The paper was published by Prof-Media, owned by Potanin, who was concerned not to upset the Kremlin and go the way of Khodorkovsky. In June 2005 Gazprom-Media bought *Izvestiya* from Potanin, followed by a noticeable decline in the quality of its news coverage. There are few who would argue that the development of the Gazprom-Media empire has been beneficial for media independence and investigative zeal. At the same time, nothing was done to prevent discussion (although usually in relatively small circulation newspapers) of controversial issues. The case of Alexander Ivanov, the son of the defence minister Sergei Ivanov, who hit and killed a pedestrian on a crossing, or the abuse of judicial procedures in the Khodorkovsky case, gained considerable coverage. The removal of Leonid Parfyenov from NTV's thoughtful 'Namedni' programme in 2004, however, signalled yet another nail in the coffin of lively independent broadcasting. The two newspapers formerly owned by Berezovsky also changed hands. In August 2005 *Nezavisimaya gazeta* was bought by Konstantin Remchukov, an assistant to German Gref.[55] *Kommersant*, owned by Berezovsky from 1999 to February 2006, also began to lose its once-famed objectivity. Berezovsky sold the paper to Badir Patarkatsishvili, an oligarch resident in Georgia who was *persona non grata* in Russia, and in August 2006 it was bought by the magnate Alisher Usmanov, the owner of a number of steelworks and also head of Gazprominvestholding, a fully owned subsidiary of Gazprom. The editor also changed at this time.

By 2006 Russia had 1,100 television channels (five major networks and three nationwide channels), 670 radio stations and 53,000 periodicals, half of which were financed by foreign capital. The internet became a major source of information, with 7 per cent of Russians logging on every day according to one survey.[56] Despite this profusion, surveys indicated that central television was the main source of information for 85 per cent of the population.[57] The main television channels – Channel One (formerly ORT), Russian Television, TV-Center and NTV – were firmly under Kremlin control, while Ren-TV was only slightly less obsequious in endlessly reporting on the activities of the authorities. From 2004 all panel discussions were pre-recorded, allowing provocative comments to be edited out. In its Press Freedom Index for 2006, Reporters Without Borders ranked Russia 147th out of the 168 countries it examined, lodged between Singapore and Tunisia.[58] The murder of the investigative journalist Anna Politkovskaya in Moscow on 7 October 2006 (Putin's birthday) brought the issue of media freedom to the fore. This murder was only one of a series that included the killing of the *Forbes* journalist Paul Klebnikov in July 2004. Since 2000, 13 Russian journalists had been murdered by paid assassins. There is no evidence that the Russian authorities were involved in these killings, but they did stand accused of not having investigated these murders with adequate vigour and of having tolerated the conditions that allowed these murders to happen.

Stung by what was perceived to be the relentless anti-Russia campaign in foreign media, the Kremlin unleashed a broad counter-attack. One aspect of this was the launch on 10 December 2005 of an international English-language TV channel called Russia Today to provide 'a Russian perspective on world events'. Hiring predominantly English presenters, the station's chief editor, Margarita Simonyan, defined its mission as 'the prompt provision of information about Russia to the general public abroad'. On Russian national domestic channels the old lively political discussion shows gave way to bland discussions or the imposition of the Kremlin's own spin doctors as political talk show hosts. The most egregiously cynical of these was the programme called 'Real Politics' hosted by Gleb Pavlovsky on NTV, reflecting the belief that politics in the post-Soviet world is little more than Machiavellian manipulation by elites of a shadow world governed by 'political technologies', in which puppet-masters play an Orwellian chess game devised by themselves.[59]

The scope for administrative intervention in media freedom remains strong in a situation where some 80 per cent of all printing presses and 90 per cent of TV and radio transmitters are state-owned. The state owns Russia Today TV, the All-Russia State Broadcasting Company (VGTRK), a controlling share of the 'First' Channel (formerly ORT), the RIA Novosti News Agency and, through Gazprom, the controlling share in Gazprom-Media holdings. Government subsidies for the regional media are no longer funnelled through regional government bodies but directly from the federal budget. Regional media remains highly politicised, typically acting as the mouthpiece of the governor but today less willing to criticise the central authorities. Only in some metropolitan areas, where independent sources of funding, including foreign, are available, are the principles of accuracy and unbiased reporting observed. Putin set his face against the abuse of media freedom by regional barons and oligarchs, but this did not mean that he tried to restore the genuine independence of the media. Putin repeatedly insisted that the building of a strong and effective state must not lead to the violation of civil freedoms, but media diversity was constrained not only by regime-sponsored ownership changes but also by the pressures of commercialisation. As in all the developed societies in the early twenty-first century, the media are driven ever more by ratings and subservience to corporate advertisers. Regime pressure and the lack of diverse sources of funding are the greatest threats to media freedom.

Judicial reform and human rights

Despite endless plans, the Russian judiciary until well into the post-communist era remained stamped by its provenance in the Soviet era, something that was reflected in the low level of judicial defence of citizens' rights and freedoms. As a law graduate Putin was acutely sensitive of the role that law plays in shaping social relations. Sharlet however argues that Putin's 'politics of law' was used as 'an instrument for re-engineering the distribution and flow of political power'.[60]

Reform of the legal system

The 1993 constitution established a unified national system of the administration of justice. The judicial system includes the procuracy, the *arbitrazh* courts (dealing with disputes between economic and other legally constituted organisations) and the normal criminal courts with the Supreme Court at its head. The Constitutional Court of 19 judges gives judgements interpreting the writ of the constitution in specific cases. The national judicial system acted as a barrier, however weak in some places, to the emergence of regional despotism. It was this obstacle to the medieval fragmentation of law that Putin sought to strengthen.

The overall scheme of judicial reform was masterminded by Dmitry Kozak, Putin's colleague from St Petersburg who had failed to become Procurator General in 2000, when faced by the hostility of the 'family'. The laws adopted in December 2001 were designed to improve guarantees for the human and civic rights of individuals and the economic rights of citizens. The intention was to move from the Soviet-style system, weighted in favour of judges and prosecutors and based on an inquisitorial ideology, towards a more adversarial system where the rights of the defendant and the courts were more evenly balanced. The measures included greatly increased funds for the judiciary, a new Criminal Procedure Code (UPK) that would transfer power from prosecutors to judges, and attempts to boost judicial responsibility by rendering judges more accountable. In all, by 2003, 11 major laws had transformed the judicial environment, with attempts to provide adequate funds to ensure the effective implementation of the reforms.

The introduction of the UPK on 1 July 2002 represented a landmark in law reform. The context was a court system marked by corruption (with Russians allegedly spending some $400 million a year in bribes to courts), the falsification of evidence and excessive brutality that at times became torture. The new Code was a core element of the reform of the legal system and represented a major overhaul of Russia's criminal justice system, intended to defend the individual from the arbitrariness of the state. The rights of defence lawyers were increased, periods on remand were cut, and the use of jury trials was extended. Under the new law it is the courts and not the prosecutors who sanction searches, arrest and detention for longer than 48 hours, a measure that was bitterly resisted by the procuracy. Thus habeas corpus laws were reinforced, while trials *in absentia* were abolished. The new Code grants detainees the right to a two-hour meeting with a lawyer before being questioned, and they can be remanded for only two days without an extension granted by a judge. The rules governing the use of evidence were also modified to make it easier to challenge the state's evidence and that of the police. The system of jury trials, which had for a number of years been limited to nine regions, was gradually extended to the rest of the country, with Chechnya in January 2007 the last planned to introduce them (in the event postponed for two years). The aim was to increase the acquittal rate, which had traditionally run at a less than half of 1 per cent whereas in Western Europe it is about 15 per cent and in the United States 25 per cent.

The new Code sought to reduce the number of people in pre-trial detention (about quarter of a million in 2002), who often faced years in limbo before being brought to trial. Lengthy gaol terms were imposed for relatively minor offences. With over a million people incarcerated, Russia's prison population was far higher *per capita* than all Western countries except the United States. At the same time, the government increased the number of judges from the 17,000 when Putin assumed the presidency to about 20,000 and raised their salaries fourfold. The aim was to ensure their independence and to increase their accountability by the adoption of new procedures for bringing miscreant judges to book. On the same day as the introduction of the new UPK, a new Administrative Violations Code came into effect. It imposed or increased fines for non-criminal offences such as traffic violations, bootlegging, prostitution, swearing in public or failing to carry a passport. At the same, a new law on the *advokatura* came into effect on 1 July 2001, while the powers of the arbitration courts (*treteiski*) were enhanced to provide a venue for the non-state resolution of commercial conflicts. New rules were adopted to ensure the enforcement of the decisions of the Constitutional Court.

Although the power of judges vis-à-vis prosecutors increased, the establishment of a 'qualifications commission', which hires and sacks judges, increased the dependency of judges on the executive. To bring the judicial reforms to the people, the Russian Association of Lawyers planned in 2007 to establish a national network of legal support centres, the equivalent of the British system of Citizen's Advice Bureaux, with Dmitry Medvedev one of the sponsors of the project.[61] At the same time, however, the Duma sought to limit the opportunities for lawyers to engage in entrepreneurial activities or any paid activity other than legal work. As Genri Reznik, the head of the Moscow Bar Association, noted, this would effectively render attorneys state employees and turn them into 'frightened, trembling rabbits'.[62]

Although there have been major changes in the legislative sphere, achievements in the field of enforcement have lagged behind. Even some of the normative achievements have come under attack. This is reflected in continuing controversy over the death penalty. The moratorium imposed by Yeltsin following Russia's accession to membership of the Council of Europe in February 1996 remained in place, but this had not been formalised in the UPK or by law because of opposition in the Duma and public opinion. Putin made known his personal view that the death penalty should be abolished by law, even though 80 per cent of the public supported its retention. Russia's murder rate (34 per 100,000 people), however, remained the second highest in the world, behind South Africa and triple that in the United States. It was for this reason that public opinion sought to visit the retribution of the death penalty on perpetrators of the most heinous crimes. There were loud calls for the death penalty to be imposed on Nurpashi Kulaev, convicted of participating in the Beslan atrocity, although in the event a life sentence was imposed in May 2006.

Although hard evidence is not easy to come by, it appears that the resurgent FSB was able to limit the pressure of organised crime on business. In cities such as Ekaterinburg and Tomsk, for example, the worst excesses of the 1990s protection rackets and the like were curbed, allowing small and medium businesses to develop. It may well be that organised crime, having taken over businesses, now became legitimate, but the old lawlessness had gone. At the same time, Putin attacked the system of *vory v zakone* (criminals in law), the criminal fraternity living according to a harsh set of rules separate from 'straight' society. Putin refused to accept these 'red zones', and now some of these criminals married, something forbidden to fraternity members, and entered mainstream society. Their influence on prison camps was also weakened.

Although there has been justified criticism directed against the Russian judicial system, much commentary has been exaggerated. The common image of Russian judges as incompetent and corrupt is very far from the mark. As Kathryn Hendley and Peter Murrell demonstrate in their study of the workings of the *arbitrazh* system, these courts were remarkably effective in disputes between businesses, although the implementation of decisions remained a problem.[63] In addition, when the state is a party to business disputes there have been concerns about the impartiality of judgements. The demand for justice has risen dramatically, with the number of people seeking to redress grievances through the courts rising from one million under Yeltsin to 6 million under Putin, with 70 per cent winning cases against government agencies. The court system increasingly fulfilled its role as contract enforcer and as an instrument for conflict resolution, leading to a decline in the use of violence as a way of achieving these aims.[64] The Kozak reforms mean that regional authorities are no longer able to interfere in judicial appointments and careers, and thus the judiciary has gained greater independence in the regions. As Popova notes, however, in issues that are of significance for the authorities in a situation where political competitiveness has declined, the independence of the courts is far from guaranteed. Russia is indeed, in her words, one of those 'Hybrid regimes that hover in-between full democracy and consolidated authoritarianism ... '.[65] Vladimir Pastukhov characterises the system as bi-legalism, with 'official' and 'unofficial' law competing with each other.[66]

In cases that were of concern to the authorities, the judicial system became prey to political interference. The Yukos case demonstrated the shortcomings in the Moscow judicial district, with judges who gave too many acquittals being sacked and with Soviet-style 'telephone law' making an unwelcome return. The planned move of the Constitutional Court to St Petersburg led to fears that it would become isolated from the political processes centred on Moscow. Putin noted in his 31 January 2006 press conference that the move would reduce the over-concentration of federal authorities in Moscow, and it was not uncommon in international practice, with the German constitutional court based not in Berlin but in Karlsruhe.[67] There were even rumours that Putin would return to his native St Petersburg as head of the Court.

The unexpected dismissal of Vladimir Ustinov as prosecutor general on 1 June 2006, and overwhelmingly approved by a surprised Federation Council on the following day, can be seen as part of Putin's continuing struggle to impose his authority. Ustinov's appointment in 1999 had originally been sponsored by the Yeltsinite 'family', and he had certainly not been Putin's first choice as prosecutor general in 2000, but as we have seen he had been unable to appoint his St Petersburg colleague, Kozak. Ustinov's appointment was approved by the Federation Council on 17 May 2000, and renewed for another five-year term in April 2005. Ustinov's removal was now associated with the renewed emphasis on the struggle against corruption, and was a delayed indication of Putin's consolidation of power. More than this, as the succession approached it appeared that the Sechin–Ustinov alliance was gaining adherents, including possibly the prime minister Fradkov, and even Moscow mayor Luzhkov.[68] The consolidation of this group would have deprived Putin of freedom of manoeuvre in the succession, and this is something that he would not allow. In the event, an extraordinary swap took place – the minister of justice Yury Chaika became prosecutor general; while Ustinov took on the newly vacated post of Minister of Justice. The procuracy remains a highly political office, even though formally the body does not have political functions. Under Chaika, the prosecutor's office took the lead in a number of high profile anti-corruption measures. Chaika insisted that his office would be more active in defending individual rights and established a department to monitor the observation of federal law to protect civil rights and liberties.[69]

Various webs of conspiracy sought to implicate the *siloviki*, or at least a 'rogue' faction, in the slow-motion murder of Alexander Litvinenko with polonium-210, apparently administered on 1 November 2006 and with death coming only on 23 November. Litvinenko was a former FSB officer who had been associated with Berezovsky, and thus with the old guard Yeltsinite faction, since 1994. He fled to London in November 2000 to join Berezovsky in campaigning against Putin's regime. Together they produced the film and then the book called *Blowing up Russia*, which, as we noted in Chapter 1, alleged that the FSB had been behind the bombings in September 1999. There had already been a long line of mysterious murders, including those of the State Duma deputies Sergei Yushenkov, who had been shot in April 2003, and Yury Shchekochikhin, who died of a mysterious illness with symptoms of poisoning in July 2003. Litvinenko's death from radiation poisoning, coming after the murder of the journalist Anna Politkovskaya on 7 October and the mysterious illness of the economist Yegor Gaidar on a visit to Ireland on 24 November, appeared to indicate a chain of events that were somehow linked. This certainly was Chubais's view, who argued that the 'chain of deaths of ... Politkovskaya, Litvinenko, and Gaidar would perfectly correspond to the interests and the vision of those people who are talking about a forceful, unconstitutional change of power in Russia as a possible option'.[70] The aim of the faction apparently was to force Putin to stay in power after 2008, by creating conditions in which it would be impossible for him to step down. The incident had deleterious foreign policy implications. The Russian foreign minister, Sergei Lavrov, conceded that 'It is of course damaging our relations'.[71] He referred to relations with Great Britain, but the damage was far wider. The Duma, moreover, had passed a law in July 2006 allowing the Russian authorities to eliminate their enemies worldwide, reminiscent of the Israeli government's remorseless hunt and killing of the perpetrators of the Munich Olympic massacre in 1974. Already Russian security forces had assassinated the former Chechen vice-president Zelimkhan Yandarbiev in Qatar in February 2004.

Human rights

As long as the war in Chechnya continued, Russia would stand indicted of violations of human rights. Russia was condemned by the Parliamentary Assembly of the Council of Europe (PACE), with its voting rights suspended for six months in the second half of 2000, while domestic bodies, like the Moscow Helsinki Group in its annual human rights reports, condemned the systematic use of torture and extra-judicial executions. Although the number of 'disappearances' had fallen, Memorial reported at least one hundred in 2006.

A number of landmark human rights cases caused considerable concern. Alexander Nikitin had faced charges of divulging state secrets in contributing to a report, based on openly available documentation, to the Norwegian environmental group Bellona on the environmental dangers posed by rusting nuclear submarines in the Barents Sea. Acquitted by a St Petersburg court in December 1999, his case was only finally closed in September 2000 by the refusal of the Supreme Court to reverse the acquittal. The military journalist

Grigorii Pasko was subjected to an equally long drawn-out series of trials and postponements over charges, first made in 1997, that he had committed state treason by disclosing information about the environmental dangers posed by the Pacific Fleet to the Sea of Okhotsk. The treason conviction on Pasko aroused particular controversy. On 25 June 2002 the Supreme Court's military section upheld the conviction and, although soon pardoned, Pasko refused to accept that he had been guilty of any crime. The case of Mikhail Trepashkin was particularly disturbing. A lawyer and former FSB colonel, he had tried to discover the truth about the apartment bombings of September 2000. Instead, in May 2004 he was sentenced to a four-year prison term for revealing state secrets and illegally carrying a pistol in his car. Released on parole in September 2005, he was re-incarcerated two weeks later after the state successfully appealed against the parole decision. The academic Igor Sutyagin was also charged with revealing state secrets, even though the materials he used were all in the public domain. The Krasnoyarsk physicist Valentin Danilov was sentenced to 14 years' imprisonment for allegedly passing secret information to China. These and other cases added to popular concerns about human rights. It was not clear whether these cases were the exception, with the security services lapsing back into old habits, or whether they were becoming part of the new rules of the game. As in other spheres, were a few exemplary cases intended to act as a warning to the rest?

The troubled passage of the law on alternative civilian service (ACS) can also be considered in the light of the human rights declared in the constitution. The law adopted in July 2002 came into effect on 1 January 2004 and was the harshest of all those proposed to the Duma and faithfully reflected the concerns of the military. Applicants for ACS have to prove to the conscription commission that military service is against their convictions. ACS will normally be served outside the applicant's region of residence. ACS in civilian bodies lasts 42 months (for those with higher education, 21 months), while in military bodies it lasts 36 and 18 months, respectively. The punitive nature of the ACS law led many liberal deputies in the Duma to amend the law to allow men to undertake ACS in their home regions.

The Presidential Human Rights Commissioner's annual reports under Vladimir Kartashkin had often been hard-hitting documents. In July 2002 he was replaced by another respected activist and Duma deputy, Ella Pamfilova. She had been a vociferous critic of the conduct of the 1994–6 Chechen war. On her appointment she insisted that her main aim was to help people 'defend their rights in a civilised manner and to protect them from the caprices of bureaucrats and other people'.[72] An amendment to the federal constitutional law on the Human Rights Commissioner in October 2006 enhanced their right to initiate parliamentary investigations into human rights abuses. Russia also had a human rights ombudsman, one of the three posts in the gift of the Duma (the other two are the heads of the State Bank and the Auditing Chamber). Oleg Mironov was chosen for a five-year term in May 1998, and lamented the fact that he had only been received once by Putin, soon after the latter's election.[73] His annual reports were particularly critical of judicial abuses of human rights, above all in Chechnya. His successor, Vladimir Lukin, was a former Yabloko MP, and no less an independent figure.

The reconstitution of the state became the central theme of Putin's programme. For the first time in 15 years, power in Russia was being consolidated. There were, however, profound ambiguities between state strengthening and liberalism, between the rationalisation of power and its reordering. We have argued that state strengthening has two faces: one sees state power being rationalised through reconcentration to emerge as a force in its own right and pursuing its own interests against those of the market, society and the individual; whereas the second face is a liberal one whereby the state is reordered through reconstitution to assume its proper role as the defender of individual liberties, property rights, and acts as regulator of market relations. The former would be a 'well-ordered police state', whereas the latter would be a pluralistic society. There is no more powerful defender of human rights than a strong liberal state; but equally, even a weak authoritarian one threatens the rule of law and civic rights.

Conclusion

Between civil society and the state a relatively autonomous power system emerged, a special type of regime, which was largely independent and unaccountable to the former and parasitic on the latter. The regime is located between the constitutionality of the state and accountability to the people. Putin's greatest achievement was to regularise the relationship between the regime and the state, but there remained a gulf between the regime and society. Civil society associations, above all trade unions and the media, were not adequately integrated in forming the social order while retaining their independence. There were fundamental tensions in Putin's state building strategy between a liberal and a more authoritarian approach. We characterise this contradiction as one between the reconstitution of the state, on the basis of law and the supremacy of the constitution, and reconcentration, where pluralism is undermined and social activity subordinated to the interests of the governing group. Putin's reforms sought to remake the state; but they also carried the danger of limiting the hard-won freedoms of Russia's untidy, unfinished but genuine democratic revolution of the 1990s. Putin may just be able to reconcile order and liberty, and thus complete the programme outlined by Peter Stolypin at the beginning of the century, but this time in a democratic form. What the autocracy and the communist regime failed to do may just be within the country's grasp today: to become a free, democratic and ordered state. Unfortunately, there are signs also of a new Leviathan being born.

6 Bureaucracy, incorporation and opposition

> I believe that one of the main purposes of the state is to create rules – universal rules – in the form of laws, instructions, and regulations. And second, to comply with these rules, and guarantee their compliance.
>
> Vladimir Putin[1]

In the first post-communist years the hypertrophy of Soviet power gave way to the atrophy of the Russian state. The ability of government to impose its will on society, to extract adequate resources and to sustain the symbols of legitimate power weakened. Putin's immediate and intense concern to revive the Russian state emerged directly from his own background as witness to the dissolution of the ideological structures that had sustained authority for so long and to the disintegration of the institutional sinews of government. The overriding theme of Putin's writings and speeches, as we have seen, was the need to restore the ability of the state to act as an independent political force, no longer at the mercy of oligarchs, regional bosses or foreign interests. In the previous chapter we noted that the restoration of state power tended towards centralised reconcentration rather than pluralistic reconstitution. An interventionist executive, even if its aims were benign, entailed the danger of recreating the traditional system of monocentric and bureaucratised power.

Bureaucracy and corruption

In the 1990s Russia became a dual state, with the institutions of the constitutional state undermined by the arbitrariness of the administrative regime. The system may have been arbitrary in some policy areas, above all in its personnel policy, but it was mostly not above the law. It certainly manipulated the electoral system to its advantage, but it did not suspend the electoral process or simply reduce it to a 'balloting charade'. It was clear that Putin believed that only an evolutionary approach to Russia's problems could transcend and heal the wounds of the past and move from regime to governance. With the basic institutions in place, Russia did not need any more revolutions. It did, however, require reform. Unfortunately, the institutional reorganisations of the Putin era failed to achieve the shift from power to governance. Bureaucratisation and corruption were the proxy causes of this failure, while depoliticisation only reinforced the insulation of the administrative regime and its legions of employees from genuine popular control and accountability.

The bureaucratic morass

The hybrid nature of the new order was nowhere more vividly manifest than in the contrast between the formal commitment to democracy and the free market, and the Soviet administrative colossus on which the new democratic order was precariously perched. In the post-communist era the state bureaucracy grew enormously and became one of the most rigid and reactionary forces in the country. In 1990 the whole Soviet administrative apparatus, including central, regional and local government and the ministries, numbered 662,700,[2] but by 2000 the bureaucracy in Russia alone numbered over a million *chinovniks*. If all administrative personnel at the federal and regional levels are included, the total rises to 1.2 million,[3] and, despite attempts at reform, this had risen to 1.5 million by 2006. In 2005 alone another 150,000 public servants were appointed. A relatively small proportion was federal, numbering, 35,600 in 2004 (up from 25,000 in 2000), whereas in the regions the bureaucracy swelled to 1,283,000 in 2004.[4] In Khabarovsk region, for example, 1,300 employees of the regional and municipal administrations were overshadowed by the 14,000 federal public servants whose salaries were paid by Moscow.[5] The recruitment mechanisms of many of these officials were far from competitive, being dominated by 'informal relations and personalised practices'.[6] The post-Yukos merging of public and private interests in the creation of massive state-dominated conglomerates, accompanied by political centralisation, enhanced the role of the bureaucracy. This great army may well have been the core of Putin's social basis of support but it also represented a major political challenge.[7] As Tretyakov put it, 'This leviathan (the state bureaucracy) must be subordinated to Goliath (the president)'.[8] Putin was well aware of the problem, and he increasingly echoed the sentiments of Nicholas I: 'Do you think I rule Russia? Thirty thousand officials rule Russia, that's who'.

This sense of powerlessness in the face of a bureaucratic morass became one of Putin's enduring themes. In his Federal Assembly address on 16 May 2003 Putin lambasted the bureaucracy, which had 'proved ill-prepared for working out and implementing the decisions appropriate to the country's present needs', although it knew how to 'accumulate administrative clout':

> The powers of our bureaucracy are still vast. But the number of powers it possesses does not match the quality of government. I have to stress that the source of this is nothing other than the superfluous functions of state government bodies. And yet, despite the huge numbers of

functionaries, the country has a severe dearth of personnel at every level and in all government structures. There is a dearth of modern managers, of efficient people.[9]

In his 2005 address he once again returned to the theme: 'Our officialdom still largely constitutes a closed, at times simply arrogant, caste that sees public service as a kind of business'.[10] In his interview with Spanish media on the eve of his visit on 7 February 2006 Putin argued that 'We should limit the power of bureaucrats, make them comply with laws, and provide for the transparency and openness of bureaucratic procedures'. This was tempered by concern for 'the rights of their family members', since 'They are people like us'. In the same interview he stressed the need for a stronger government, denying that this meant 'the reinforcement of repressive institutions' but 'the government's capacity for adopting and implementing laws needed by society'. This model of effective government was central to his discursive frame, accompanied by anti-oligarchical sentiments.[11] The intensification of the 'power vertical', however, could not but strengthen the power of the bureaucracy, and the lack of openness had the same result. By the time of his 10 May 2006 Federal Assembly address his frustration was palpable: 'Despite all the efforts we have made, we have still not managed to remove one of the greatest obstacles facing our development, that of corruption'.[12] Yet the growth of bureaucracy and corruption was inherent in the Putin administration's manner of governing, undermining the separation of powers and creating a wholly dependent institutional structure, while fostering state capitalism and monopolism in the economy and a bloated security apparatus.

Plans for administrative reform moved forwards only very slowly. They were designed to achieve the functional restructuring of state service by reducing the number of state agencies and the size of the bureaucracy.[13] The plan devised by Dmitry Kozak, at the time cabinet chief of staff, in early 2003 spoke of reducing the number of ministries from 24 to 15–17, while the economic development ministry, on the basis of Kozak's plan, divided the 5,000 functions performed by the state into three categories: setting regulations, applying regulations, and providing state services, with many to be abolished in their entirety.[14] Ministries were to be responsible for the strategic development of policy; agencies were to provide services to public and sector-specific economic activities; while services would be responsible for state oversight and monitoring of implementation. The overall aim was to decrease the number of bureaucrats, and to remove their pressure on economic development, above all small and medium businesses.

The Kozak reforms sought to remove bureaucratic barriers to business development, but in the event made little headway, especially with his redeployment to the North Caucasus in September 2004 following Beslan. The separation of regulatory and oversight functions ran into the sand. According to Alexander Obolonsky, a noted specialist in the field, this was the fifth administrative reform since the end of the USSR, each one trying to reshape the Russian bureaucracy to meet the needs of a market democracy. He noted that senior bureaucrats were able to increase their incomes on average fivefold in a range of illegal ways, and even drastic increases in state service salaries would do little to improve the workings of the bureaucracy. The only effective way of overcoming the entrenched Soviet mentality of officialdom, in his view, would be the organisation of recruitment on a competitive basis with examinations, an experiment tried by Sergei Kirienko when he was presidential envoy to the Volga Federal District.[15]

The problem of corruption

While Putin may have strengthened the state, in the sense of restoring its prerogatives in the constitutional sphere and over the regions, there remained a dangerous permeability in state–society relations, and the starkest form of this was corruption. This is not the place to have a lengthy discussion of the meaning of the term, but our working definition is that corruption takes place when the logic of one system (say the market) undermines the logic of another (for example, public service by officials).[16] In the late Soviet period certain parts of the state system, notably in education, health and highway patrols (GAI), had become thoroughly corrupted, with the sale of services and extensive bribe taking. Almost everything became marketised, including the state itself, with the disbursement of state assets at knock-down prices as only the most spectacular aspect.[17] The Yeltsin period was one of rampant corruption, despite several desultory attempts to halt the frenzy. Despite Putin's emphasis on good government, it is notable that he did not launch any sustained struggle against corruption. On the eve of the 2003–4 electoral cycle there was an opportunistic campaign against 'werewolves in epaulettes', targeted in particular against corruption in the militia, but following the elections little more was heard of this. Anti-corruption campaigns are notoriously tricky, and some even argue that they are counterproductive. This was clearly Putin's view. Instead he sought to improve the pay and conditions of state officials, judges and others particularly susceptible to bribery, and in this way hoped to remove one of the conditions that sustain corruption.

There is not much evidence to suggest that the strategy was working. According to Berlin-based Transparency International in its 2005 Corruption Perceptions Index (CPI), Russia was one of the most corrupt countries in Europe, and brought the country 30 spots down in its rankings to place it among Albania, Niger and Sierra Leone in 126th place.[18] This finding was confirmed by a survey published by the Indem Foundation in 2005, following an earlier survey in 2001.[19] The surprising finding was the extent of the growth in corruption in the business sphere, with the average size of each bribe growing on average sevenfold, with the gross income of officials growing at least fourfold. As the head of Indem, Georgi Satarov, put it, 'corruption is a manifestation of the inefficiency of government at all levels', and with Russia's great natural wealth at a time of buoyant prices, it was not surprising that the scale of corruption had increased. He noted that Russia had almost 100,000 dollar millionaires, and several dozen dollar billionaires.[20]

According to the Indem survey, Russians pay $3 billion in bribes a year, and the incidence of corruption of all sorts, including various kickbacks and deals cut with bureaucrats for protection, had risen from $33bn in 2001 to $316bn by the end of 2005.[21] With so many ways of making extra money, it is not surprising that government service became so popular. The willingness of Russians to offer bribes, however, had markedly decreased, from 75 to 53 per cent, except in matters relating to the military draft, where corruption had grown by 70 per cent. Corruption had increased in enlistment offices, education and in land acquisition agencies, with the level of corruption lowest in the pension, employment, housing maintenance and housing registration spheres.[22] In its 2006 report on corruption Indem argued that in 2005 39 million corrupt deals had been carried out, with the average business person having to pay a bribe on average twice a year. Seven per cent of a company's turnover on average was devoted to bribes to corrupt officials, with the so-called 'corruption tax' comprising 1.1 per cent of GDP. Only one bribe-taker out of 100,000 was imprisoned.[23] In February 2004 Satarov took the lead in establishing a Public Anti-Corruption Council (OSA), bringing together a number of NGOs in the field. OSA organized a network of offices across the country, collecting evidence of alleged corrupt behaviour by regional and local business people, politicians and officials. Only in April 2004, and possibly in response to Satarov's initiative, did the Duma establish its own Anti-Corruption Commission, headed by deputy Mikhail Grishankov.

As the 2007–8 succession approached the administration also stepped up its anti-corruption campaign.[24] If Chechnya had been the predominant theme in the 1999–2000 electoral cycle, and the struggle against the oligarchs in 2003–4, then the war against corruption became the centrepiece of the elite's struggle to remain in power in 2007–8. In his 10 May 2006 address Putin had called corruption 'one of the greatest obstacles facing our development', and this was followed by a wave of high-profile corruption cases that reached up into the higher echelons of power, and implicated a regional governor and the mayors of two regional capitals. However, the perception that the anti-corruption campaign was no more than a pre-election stunt undermined its legitimacy.[25] As part of the campaign, deputy prosecutor general Aleksandr Buksman announced that Russia's army of bureaucrats were raking in £125 billion annually, not far off the state's total annual revenues. He revealed that in the first eight months of 2006 alone police had discovered 28,000 cases of corruption, a third of which were connected with bribe taking.[26]

The situation in some other post-Soviet states had improved, with the perception of corruption decreasing in Estonia and Kazakhstan. The model of political economy developed under Putin fostered a new kind of permeability between the state and business, in particular in the state-dominated part of the economy. No other country in the world allows state or government members to be members of corporate boards, whereas in Russia a system of interlocking membership developed.[27] Putin insisted that this ensured that state interests were observed and was perfectly normal, especially since in his view the people involved did not get paid for this extra work.[28] Managerial transparency and business efficiency was not improved by the conflict of interests the cross-appointment of political and business appointments fostered. For many only a change of regime in 2008, with a clear separation between the interests of the Kremlin and the bureaucratic class, could provide an atmosphere conducive to a real struggle against corruption, accompanied by a more pluralistic political climate that would finally expose bureaucrats to public scrutiny.

Civil society and para-constitutional representation

This is not the place to discuss at length the meaning of civil society but simply to note that the core meaning, derived from Roman notions of society, is based on the idea of a partnership between individuals of equal legal status. From this, a 'civil society' is a legal and political order in which individuals interact with others, sometimes in groups, but retain their own identity and interests, as opposed to a system based on kinship, hierarchy, tradition, patronage or power. Political theorists like John Locke took this further to include the consent of the ruled, and in contemporary understanding the emphasis is on a network of civic associations outside of the control of the state, guaranteed by law, and with the ability to promote their programmes and pursue their interests.

The Civic Forum

Although in the late communist years a competitive model of state–society relations predominated, the early post-communist years reasserted the idea of a necessary partnership. However, in some regions state failure and corruption encouraged the idea that civil society should make up the shortfall and assume the burden of delivering welfare and other state services.[29] Nevertheless, the state still performs its traditional functions and delivers most welfare goods, although increasingly in partnership with third sector organisations. If civil society can be measured by the quantitative development of public and associational life, then Russia has all the hallmarks of having one.[30] The enormous development of the NGO sector reflects a strong current of civic activism, with some 400,000 registered in 2001, rising to over half a million in 2006. However, measured more qualitatively, above all in terms of the autonomy of social actors, their ability to intervene effectively in decision-making processes, to mobilise public opinion in a way that can change the approach of public authorities, the reach of the public sphere in all the far-flung regions of the country, and indeed in the ability of civil society to modify traditional notions of public order, to ensure the impartial application of law and to ameliorate its own pathologies, then civil society in Russia is found wanting.

The nascent democracy furthermore, according to commentators such as Shevtsova, was further undermined by the reassertion of state power and the regime's attempts to control social and political processes.[31] A number of terms have been devised to describe attempts by the state to manage civil society: GONGOs – governmentally organised non-governmental organisations; MANGOs – manipulated non-governmental organisations; and GRINGOs – governmentally regulated and initiated non-governmental organisations.[32] Fears in the NGO community that they would become one of these tame beasts fuelled heated debates in 2001 over whether to participate in the administration's plans to hold a Civic Forum, where the country's social and human rights organisations could engage in dialogue with the regime. Would participation threaten NGOs with co-optation, or would engagement in fact deepen government support for the development of civil society, above all in the regions? That, at its most simple, was the debate that raged in the months before the forum was actually held in November of that year. The involvement of Pavlovsky and Markov in organising the Civic Forum did not help matters, since they were identified as the proponents of 'managed democracy'. Markov, however, insisted that the president's demonstrative support for NGO development would strengthen the hand of civic and social associations in the regions.

The Forum's organising committee on 11 October stressed that 'Civil society in Russia exists and is developing', noting that according to some estimates about one million people worked in NGOs, and that the social, legal, medical, cultural, educational and other services offered by NGOs directly affected about 20 million people. The aim of the Forum was to provide 'serious discussion of paths of development for civil society in Russia and its relationship with state power'. It was for this reason that the event would be attended by representatives of all three branches of the state. The committee sought to allay fears that the Forum would turn into a 'parade of loyalty' to the government. The committee ended by declaring that 'Civil society is neither a vassal of power nor its opponent'.[33] The Civic Forum on 21–22 November 2001 sought to address the vexed question of relations between the state and civil society. In his speech on 21 November Putin argued:

> We have a good chance of combining the forces of the state with the energy of a democratic society. We should not get carried away, but we are making some progress already. The time is coming when being a Russian citizen will be prestigious. ... Civil society should have its own foundations, it should feed on the spirit of freedom. Only then will it become civil society. No, our civil society is not yet formed, but I do

not think that there is a country where civil society has been formed the way it should have been. This is a necessary and continuous process in democracies, and in Russia it is only beginning.[34]

The experience of some third world countries suggested that civil society should 'give up on the state', since the state was predatory and incompetent. Putin forcefully rebutted any such arguments, but at the same time insisted that civil society could not be created 'from above'. Instead, he called for a partnership of the state and civil society to seize the 'historical chance', otherwise both would find themselves on the 'margins (*zadvorkakh*) of civilisation'. This was a theme to which he returned in his annual address to parliament on 16 May 2003:

> We often talk about the greatness of Russia but a great Russia isn't just a great state. First and foremost, it is a modern, developed society, one that won't come about of its own accord. A fully fledged and developed civil society will only emerge in conditions where there is a drastic reduction in the functions of the state apparatus, where mistrust between various groups in society is surmounted and, most importantly of all, it will only be possible if there is national unity in assessing the strategic objectives the country faces. The creation of conditions such as these, without the active involvement of political parties, is impossible.[35]

The experience of the Civic Forum was to be remembered in the wake of the Beslan events.

The Public Chamber

According to Putin in his 13 September 2004 speech, a Public Chamber would act as a platform for broad dialogue, to allow civic initiatives to be discussed, state decisions to be analysed and draft laws to be scrutinised. It would act as a bridge between civil society and the state. The Public Chamber can be seen as the continuation of the Civic Forum by other, more formal, means, reflecting a rather corporatist view of public representation. The speech was followed by debate over the role and composition of the chamber. It was not clear whether it would only provide expert advice or whether it would be able to exercise accountability functions. Where it would fit into the governance system was equally unclear: would it be completely independent, or subordinate to the presidential apparatus? Who would make up this body and how would they be selected? Public opinion surveys suggested that there was strong support for the inclusion of youth, women's and veterans' organisations, trade unions and employers' associations, and those who represented the social and economic interests of the population.[36]

On 16 March 2005 the State Duma overwhelmingly adopted the law on the creation of the Public Chamber by 345 votes to 50; it was signed into law by Putin on 4 April; and it came into effect on 1 July.[37] The Chamber was established as a type of 'collective ombudsman',[38] although its powers are purely consultative. Its duties included the review of draft legislation and the work of parliament, and the monitoring of federal and regional administrations. It can offer non-binding recommendations to parliament and the government on domestic issues, comment on legislation, request investigations into possible breaches of the law and request information from state agencies. The Chamber has 126 members: one-third is selected by the president, intended to be authoritative individuals who would be neither politicians nor business people; the second group is nominated by the first from national civic associations; and once in office these two groups in turn choose the remaining third, representing regional non-governmental organisations. The body's funding and offices are allocated by the presidential administration.

Putin appointed the first tranche of 42 members in September 2005, including representatives of the major religious confessions, sports figures, academics, policy analysts, scientists and NGO representatives. In November the second group was selected by the first. The second group consisted of four types of member: the most numerous were various little-known voluntary assistants, including Yulia Gorodnicheva, a student of Tula State University and an activist of the Our Own (*Nashi*) movement, who had earlier been invited to meet with Putin. This category was reminiscent of the 'milkmaids' in the old Supreme Soviet, and indeed the system of quotas reinforced memories of the late unlamented Soviet parliamentarianism. The second group consisted of popular personalities, journalists and sportspeople, which included the popular singer Alla Pugacheva, the general director of Mosfilm Karen Shakhnazarov, the chess grand master Anatoly Karpov and the TV commentator Nikolai Svanidze. The third group included prominent lawyers: Gasan Merzoev and Genri Reznik; and the fourth group comprised business leaders, notably Vladimir Potanin, president of Interros, and Mikhail Fridman, chairman of the board at Alfa-Bank.[39] The third tranche came from regional activists, and were nominated by regional conferences that each sent 20 delegates to attend conferences at federal district level, although at each stage federal inspectors representing the president were active. Seven of the 42 came from the creative unions; trade unions and university administrators each had five seats; representatives of veterans' and women's groups had only three each, much lower that their numbers at the regional conferences; while the representatives of youth and human rights organisations were notable by their absence.[40] A total of 90 (71 per cent) chamber members were residents of Moscow and St Petersburg. The single largest group was the 17 (13.5%) business people, representing not so much civil society but economic society. The 16 academics made up the second largest group, while the third is 12 representatives of art and culture. The body included representatives of Russia's four 'traditional' religions.[41]

At its first plenary meeting on 22 January 2006 Putin warned the Chamber that it would face a struggle to impose its authority over state officials reluctant to accept supervision from the new body. The Chamber would advise on the distribution of state funding for public initiatives, with the state providing 500 million roubles ($18 million) to support NGOs in 2006, as well as supervise the 'huge' social spending, with $4.6 billion designated to be spent on the 'national projects' of health, education, agriculture and housing in 2006–7. The Chamber should also, Putin stressed, ensure that the news media are unbiased and independent.[42] The Chamber unanimously elected Yevgeny Velikhov, director of the Kurchatov nuclear research institute, as its secretary, with Sergei Katyrin, vice-president of the Russian Chamber of Commerce and Industry, as its deputy secretary. Seventeen commissions were formed, with 15 out of the 17 chairs being the Kremlin's nominees.[43] The Chamber formed a governing council comprising the secretary, his deputy and the chairs of the 17 commissions. The Chamber set up its own website and print publication, and at its first meeting adopted its statutes. The chamber has to hold at least two sessions a year and publish an annual report on civil society. Members of the Public Chamber were allocated to all the Duma's committees, which work in a closed regime, participating above all in the development of laws in their early stages.[44] This function clearly overlapped with the experts of the Duma's legislative committees. Among the immediate issues addressed by the Chamber was the new NGO law (see below) and efforts to confront racial hatred. At the founding meeting Leonid Roshal, the well-known pediatrician and respected independent voice, argued that the rushed adoption of the NGO law, without taking into account the opinion of the full chamber, had been a mistake. He warned that politicians who stoked ethnic hatred should be prosecuted since it could lead to Russia's disintegration, which is what 'many in the West want and may be financing'.[45]

Critics asserted that Putin had established yet another presidential vertical, with at most a handful of the Chamber's members clearly independent.[46] There was a well-founded fear that the chamber would exercise a monopoly in lobbying for civic initiatives.[47] For the economist Vitaly Naishul the Chamber was yet another attempt to create a feedback mechanism with the people, and he noted that Russia lacked a common national-political language: 'The reformers speak in one tongue, enterprise directors and bureaucrats (*chinovniki*) in another, while people in a tram or bath-house (*banya*) in a third. Today this situation has become critical'.[48] The new Chamber worked in co-operation with the state, a characteristic of Russian civil society, but on numerous occasions, as in the conflict over the adoption of the NGO law, the Andrei Sychev bullying case in the military and the development of the Butovo district in South Moscow, it demonstrated that it was not afraid to stand up to the authorities. The Chamber also had an uneasy relationship with the Duma. It is not clear whether Putin intended to create such a bothersome organ, but it is certainly perceived to be an instrument of presidential power designed to introduce a new channel of public accountability against overbearing officialdom and comfortable parliamentarians. This example of Putin's para-constitutionalism created an instrument for the presidency to use against the regime, thus enhancing Putin's autonomy.

The law envisaged that the creation of a central Chamber would be followed by the creation of similar bodies in the regions. Some had been in existence for a number of years, notably in Novgorod where a Social Chamber had been established in 1994 as part of what the regional authorities called a 'social partnership'.[49] A *guberniya* public assembly had been established in Yaroslavl a decade earlier, and one in Kaliningrad had been in existence already for five years. In Kemerovo a civic chamber, consisting of 78 social and 21 non-profit regional organisations, was established in 1994, and had discussed regional laws on environmental and demographic problems. Twenty-two regional chambers were listed on the Public Chamber's website in February 2006.[50] Most of these had been created spontaneously, but they were now brought within the ambit of the new structure, leading to fears that they would lose their independence or even be abolished in favour of the new structures. The new regional chambers were overwhelmingly created from above, and not by civil society organisations themselves. The status and powers of the new regional chambers moreover remained vague,[51] and there were numerous disputes whether representatives of political parties or religious organisations could be chosen. The new bodies were formed in various ways. In Novosibirsk, for example, the regional chamber consisted of 132 members divided into three parts, with 44 in each. The first was made up from the *raions* (districts), the second from civic associations selected by the regional assembly (not the governor), and the third chosen by the first two from 'the most authoritative and respected' people proposed by experts and professional associations. In Kemerovo a new law on the chamber was adopted on 22 February 2005, consisting of 45 members: 15 selected by the governor, 15 by the regional legislature and the remaining 15 by the first two. The old body was to be dissolved, although it did not give up without a fight.[52] In Chechnya a 25-person public chamber was created in October 2006, and at its first meeting the republic's human rights commissioner, Nukhazhiev Nudri, noted that pre-trial torture by security forces had become one of the region's major problems.

The politics of duplication in the Russian political system have often been noted. This was the case within the presidential administration under Yeltsin, in relations between the presidential administration and the government, with the formation in 2000 of the State Council, which duplicated much of the work of the Federation Council. Now work that should properly have been the preserve of the State Duma was transferred to this new body, a type of non-political parliament. The existence of the Public Chamber could not but diminish the role of parliament, which should act as the primary tribune for the expression of popular concerns. More than this, concerns were voiced by civil society organisations that the new chamber would seek to exercise some sort of tutelary role over them. Ludmila Alekseeva, the head of the Moscow Helsinki Group, argued that, having established a 'vertical of power' over administrative bodies, the regime now sought to do the same over civil society: 'There has been this idea to organize civil society, which has already developed in our country, according to this vertical of power. But this is a crazy idea. As soon as you organize civil society into this vertical of power, it stops being civil society. It becomes a pathetic appendage of the government. And it is destroyed'.[53] The system of surrogates is not provided for in the constitution, although it does not violate the letter of the constitution. Para-constitutional accretions to the constitution were designed to enhance efficacy but in practice undermined the development of a self-sustaining constitutional order and the emergence of a vibrant civic culture and civil society.

Non-governmental organisations (NGOs)

In the early period of Putin's leadership associational life flourished, although sources of funding and the legitimate scope of work were contested. An NGO was considered established as soon as it held a founding meeting, and there was no need to register. At the same time, while Russian funding for NGOs had been rising in the early 2000s, notably through the work of the Yukos-funded Open Russia Foundation, the attack on Khodorkovsky made Russian donors more cautious. The reliance on foreign support for civil society organisations had already been a notable feature in Russia, and a whole literature describes both its positive and perverse consequences.[54] With funding from abroad and only 92 NGOs formally registered, this was clearly a situation that Putin's administration, with its constant impulse to regulate, could not tolerate. The para-constitutionalism that was apparent in institutional development now extended to the attempts to transform NGOs into para-governmental organisations.

Matters came to a head with plans to adopt a new law to regulate NGOs in late 2005. The bill's sponsors, a cross-party group from all four Duma factions, had taken their cue from Putin's warnings, notably in his Federal Assembly address of May 2004, about NGOs 'fed by an alien hand'. Concerns had increased in the wake of the Ukrainian Orange revolution that NGOs were being supported from abroad to continue the wave of 'colour revolutions', seen already in Serbia with the overthrow of Slobodan Milošević in 2000, then in the 'rose' revolution in Georgia in November 2003, which brought Mikheil Saakashvili to power, and again in Kyrgyzstan in the 'tulip' revolution of February 2005, which saw the overthrow of president Askar Akaev. The fear that Western-sponsored civic activism would be used as a battering ram to achieve 'regime change' provoked Alexander Lukashenko to clamp down on the flickering remnants of independent NGO

activity in Belarus.[55] The American strategy of supporting civil society organisations to achieve regime change through people power was also applied
in Iran. Berezovsky, as we have seen, was calling for Putin's overthrow, by
illegal means if necessary. It was in this context that Putin issued warnings
that the unmonitored financing of political activity from abroad was
impermissible.

It is therefore not surprising that Putin supported the draft adopted on
23 November 2005.[56] The new law focused above all on ensuring the depoliticisation of NGOs, to be achieved through intense vetting during a complex registration procedure, and much tighter financial monitoring. Branches
of foreign NGOs were to register under the same rules as applied to Russian
bodies. The law provoked a storm of criticism from Russian human rights
organisations, foreign politicians and organisations, including the European
Parliament, which urged Russia to ensure that the law conformed to Council of Europe standards. The Public Chamber, at that point still only two-
thirds formed, appealed to the Duma to postpone discussion of the law until
the full Chamber had a chance to examine its provisions, and in general
clearly disapproved of the speed with which the law was being rushed
through. The most penetrating criticism of the law came from Ella Pamfilova, the head of the Presidential Council for Civil Society Institutions, and
Vladimir Lukin, Russia's human rights ombudsman. The general principle
of regulating NGO activity was not in question. In the United States, for
example, since 1938 there have been draconian laws restricting the activities
of foreign NGOs, formulated in the Foreign Agents Registration Act. The
point is that the law should be transparent and immune to arbitrary interpretation, and in turn should serve to make the activities of Russian NGOs
more transparent and accountable.

These protests had an effect, and the law adopted by the Duma on 23
December 2005 no longer required branches of foreign NGOs to reregister
as local bodies, but officials would still be allowed to ban them if they
threatened 'Russia's sovereignty, independence, territorial integrity, national
unity and originality, cultural heritage and national interests'. The law was
published on 17 January 2006 and came into effect on 10 April.[57] Russia's
NGOs had to register with the Federal Registration Service within six months
of the bill becoming law, but if they wished to continue to operate infor-
mally they did not need to register as legal entities. A court decision is
required before an individual can be prevented from establishing an NGO,
whereas earlier the authorities could deny registration if they simply sus-
pected the founder of extremism or money laundering. Organisations have
to provide detailed reports on the spending of foreign funds, even if the
money is used for philanthropic purposes. It was clear that the wording of
the law remained far too vague, leaving the authorities with almost unlim-
ited discretion in deciding whether to register an NGO or to close it down.
In March 2006 the prosecutor general's office froze Open Russia's account,
on the grounds that the new NGO law prohibits someone who has been

prosecuted (in this case Khodorkovsky) from being the founder and sponsor of a public organisation. Open Russia had been one of the most generous sources of funding for NGOs in Russia. At the same time, the complexity of bureaucratic requirements inhibited the formation of organisations in a field well known for the rapid turnover of groups. Access to foreign sources of support became more complicated. The new accountability measures, however, had a positive side effect in encouraging the professionalisation of NGO activity and the improvement in NGO governance. The new measures encouraged the payment of trained accountants to manage NGO funds, and fostered managerial and financial discipline.

Improvement in the management of NGOs, of course, depends on whether the law is applied on a non-discretionary basis, something that was far from guaranteed. The law stipulated that branches of foreign NGOs had to submit their documents by 18 October 2006. By the end of 2006, 189 foreign NGOs had been registered, with 12 more pending. This was not quite the mass cull suggested by the foreign media, but some well-known Western NGOs did have some difficulties, demonstrating that the power of the Russian bureaucracy was undiminished. The bureaucratic assault covered friend and foe alike, and thus now the Russian Orthodox Church was required to provide state agencies with the names of their worshippers and the contents of their sermons. This aspect of the NGO law revived the practices of the Soviet era, when all religious organisations were tightly controlled by the state.

In the sphere of politics, only GRINGOs and associated creatures would be allowed to operate. Puppet NGOs, like the Kremlin-sponsored Nashi (Our Own) youth movement, did little but discredit the regime. The development of the ideology of 'nashism' (our people) reflected a tribal approach to politics in which the concepts of 'us' and 'them' were accentuated (see below). The NGO law revealed the state's fears and insecurities, and in particular its 'Orange paranoia', and as such testified less to its strength than its weakness. It also suggested that Putin was listening rather too closely to his friends in the Lubyanka, and was thus losing his independence. This appeared confirmed by the allegations in January 2006 that four British diplomats in Moscow had been engaged in espionage, including the use of an electronic 'rock' to transmit information, and the payment of large sums in cash to NGOs. The association of spying with foreign support for NGOs was clearly an operation to discredit NGOs and to demonstrate to the Russian population the need for the law restricting the activities of NGOs. The liberal debacle of December 2003 meant that there were few alternative voices to act as a counterbalance. The NGO law, even if it conformed to international standards, further undermined already weak civic activism.

Regime and opposition

The weakening of a coherent opposition to the regime in parliament and beyond was a dual process. On the one hand, the administration exerted itself to shape and manage the political arena. For Vladimir Gel'man the problem of opposition was more than one of personalities but a result of the structural changes of the Putin years that had systematically reduced the opportunity structure for opposition forces. These changes included access to the mass media and to the rules governing party and parliamentary life, including the ban on the formation of electoral coalitions.[58] As the authors of the Trilateral Commission's report on Putin's Russia put it, 'A pattern has thus developed in which the concept of an independent and lawful loyal opposition is entirely alien. Political activity is either sanctioned by the Kremlin or treated (if it appears to threaten the Kremlin's interests) as a hostile and illegitimate force that has to be crushed'.[59] On the other hand, opposition forces failed to devise an optimal strategy or to provide a coherent and attractive alternative to the regime. On the 'supply' side attempts to forge a coherent opposition, such as Kasparov's 'Committee 2008', were redolent of the 'irreconcilable oppositionism' of the extremists of the early 1990s and indeed of Milyukov-style liberalism of the constitutional monarchy period in the 1900s, and were attractive to few. The failure of the two main liberal parties, Yabloko and SPS, to fight on a common platform in the 2003–4 elections led to the elimination of both as serious political players. Their continued failure to unite thereafter, although they worked together in some elections, led oppositionists such as Vladimir Ryzhkov to dismiss them as serious political players. Ryzhkov's own attempts to forge a moderate and coherent opposition fell victim to the inherent fissiparousness of the Russian democratic movement, and the administrative snares of the regime.

Trasformismo

Pavlovsky, one of the main ideologists of the administrative regime, insisted that it was not so much the authorities that represented the 'empire of façades', but society and its institutions, which he argued were 'dreadfully weak' at all levels, and thus there were no serious interlocutors in society with whom the authorities could interact. As far as he was concerned,

> The social milieu is fragmented. Democracy does not work without 'political publicity', which ensures contacts between members of society, between cultures varying territorially and ethnically, between the authorities and the common people. Social life has been divided and monopolised by small groups of people, engaged in their own actions – self-presentation, self-aggrandisement, show-politics ... Our parties have no political will to work with the masses.

The vacuum created by the waning of the communists was being filled by various extremist groups, skinhead-type organisations often working with the local police in various rackets: this, Pavlovsky insisted, was also a type of 'civil society'. Despite the existence of about half a million non-profit organisations in Russia, it was difficult to work with most, above all human rights activists, since they appeared too ready to condemn the authorities for undermining freedom rather than working with them: 'You need to create these liberties first':

> Crazed envy between organisations has been prominent in Russia. In the social sphere the authorities have been searching for anarchists, spies and rebels, even though ordinary citizens have settled down long ago and do not want to shake up the state. A dissident conspiratorial mindset exists among the human rights activists: supposedly, we know for sure – there is a group within the Kremlin where plans to eliminate rights and liberties are being developed. The only disputed point is whether this group is headed by Putin, or he is only condoning its actions. What kind of social partnership can be created in this atmosphere?[60]

Pavlovsky raises a number of important issues: the ambivalent nature of civil society; the degree to which democratic freedoms had become a popular value that could not be easily withdrawn; society itself was weak and unable to defend its own interests coherently and positively; the old dissident mindset, dating from the period when they were the only civil society, still considered the authorities as the enemy (hence the difficulty in establishing a partnership); society itself was prey to morbid pathologies that could only be dealt with through state action; and the reluctance of political parties to take responsibility for trying to shape social processes by building strong organisations rooted in civil society.

It is in this context that we can compare Putin's regime to that which took shape in late nineteenth-century Italy. There, too, a distinctive type of governance regime emerged in a society in which organised interests were simultaneously weak and divisive, where a hegemonic middle class was lacking and in which depoliticisation became endemic. Agostino Depretis, of Stradella, Piedmont, was leader of the 'historic left' that replaced the government of the 'historic right' in 1876, and he went on to serve sporadically as prime minister in 1876–8, 1878–9 and 1881–7. The differences between left and right by 1882, as Seton-Watson puts it, 'already small in 1876, were now rapidly vanishing. Right and Left were becoming conscious of what they had in common. The two in fact constituted a broad liberal party of the centre'. Depretis understood this situation and in the autumn of 1882 he dissolved parliament and in an electoral speech in Stradella on 8 October he outlined a new programme of reconciliation. Criticising those who continued to harp on divisions between left and right, he declared: 'We are a progressive government, and if anyone wishes to transform himself ... to accept my very moderate programme, can I reject him?'[61] The new political concept of *trasformismo* was born to describe the acceptance of support from any quarter, although it was soon turned into an abusive epithet by the left and the right. The word also came to be used as a synonym for corruption and stagnation, since Depretis's leadership degenerated into a pragmatism that turned into unprincipled expediency.

Putin's government tried to stand above the historic divisions of the modern era, and indeed, intentionally sought to reconcile the forces that had torn Russia apart in the twentieth century. In conditions where democracy is forced to create the conditions for its own existence, the democratic process was managed by a force standing outside democracy. The administrative regime was an active political player, fighting to get its candidates elected in regional and other elections. The state was both referee and player, shaping the terms of engagement as well being an active player in political struggles. The role of opposition parties was particularly difficult in the Putin era because of the polymorphous nature of his leadership. As Nemtsov noted 'Putin has amazing communicative qualities . . . When he is with me he is a rightist, but when with Zyuganov he is a leftist'.[62]

The systemic opposition

The main criticism directed against Putin by Zyuganov's Communists was not that his government subverted democracy but it did not deliver the desired social and economic goods. The CPRF found itself caught between moving further towards social democracy (a path advocated by Seleznev, the economist Sergei Glaz'ev and one of the CPRF's most important sponsors, Gennady Semigin), in which case it could find itself merging with the regime, or moving into extreme opposition. Surkov and other political managers did all they could to exacerbate divisions in the Communist movement, but they were pushing at an open door. The CPRF under Zyuganov kept to its ineffectual 'national communist' path and headed for the 'dustbin of history'.[63] The relative passivity and lack of intellectual sharpness in the CPRF's opposition to Putin meant that Zyuganov can be considered a co-architect of the Putinite stabilisation; and for this reason the ruling elite sought to maintain a strong left-wing but ineffectual presence in parliament. As Medvedev notes, 'Putin was able to do what Yeltsin could not: eliminate the "irreconcilable" opposition'.[64]

It was left to the 'democrats' to carry the banner of real opposition. Yavlinsky was convinced that Russian democracy under both Yeltsin and Putin was largely a sham, a view no doubt encouraged by the failure of the system to make him leader. He insisted that 'political time in Russia is flowing backward'; a 'guided democracy' had emerged' in which 'The bosses remain in power regardless of the will of the voters'.[65] Yavlinsky's Yabloko had been in permanent opposition to Yeltsin's regime, but at first he argued that Putin's administration should be given a chance to prove itself. Many of his ideas were in any case incorporated into the government's programme, although he retained his reservations. For example, he agreed that governors should be dismissed from their posts if they violated laws or the Russian constitution, but insisted that this should be only done on the basis of a court decision. As he argued, 'The actions that are being undertaken can make sense only if the independence of the judicial system and mass media is strengthened simultaneously'.[66] As he put it on another occasion, 'A repressive police state is no alternative to a semi-criminal oligarchy. Pinochet is not an alternative to Yeltsin'.[67] Yavlinsky was careful not to attack Putin personally, but his condemnation of the system intensified during Putin's tenure. He insisted that the power system sought to establish a controlled or managed democracy in which a democratic façade covered the Kremlin's ambition to create a single power centre. In this system the State Duma and other democratic institutions played a largely decorative role. As far as he was concerned, 'the parliament has been completely transformed into a puppet of the executive branch'.[68] He insisted that Yabloko's unification with SPS would be problematical since Yabloko prioritised individual rights and liberty and had a different relationship with the political authorities, and this was reflected in rather different electorates.

The SPS in the early period tried both to ride with the horses and run with the hounds, declaring itself part of the 'ruling opposition'.[69] At first supportive of Putin, Nemtsov's criticisms became increasingly harsh as he sought to establish SPS's independent political credentials. He argued that 'Putin has built a controlled democracy in Russia – with state-controlled TV, with Chechnya, and by extorting budget funds from the regions. He is turning the Federation Council into a "House of Lords" … Controlled democracy has its own internal logic. The screws can only be tightened … in the long run, the strategic choice of Russia is at stake: a choice between democracy and dictatorship'.[70] The SPS had long argued that Putin's programme was basically theirs, and were particularly keen to take credit for the Land Code, allowing the sale of land (a bitterly divisive issue in Russia), and for the judicial reforms. However, Nemtsov berated SPS for having failed to prevent the establishment of 'managed democracy':

> I mean the staking on bureaucratic capitalism: the president is depending exclusively on the bureaucratic and power elements and is giving the bureaucracy, which he himself came out of, carte blanche. I also mean Chechnya, where the force variant is being insisted upon exclusively with maniacal stubbornness. I also mean the 'cleansing' (*zachistka*) of the parliament, both the upper and the lower chambers. I mean the centralisation of both the budget and [state] power, the sharp violation of the balance of power in general.[71]

Nemtsov also criticised 'the practically complete monopolisation' of national television, and argued that Putin had inherited 'oligarchic capitalism', and all that he had done was to remove two of the most odious from the arena (Berezovsky and Gusinsky) but left the rest to rule the roost. Putin remained a slave to the 'family' and the *siloviki*, leading, in Nemtsov's view, to the construction of bureaucratic capitalism in Russia that squeezed small and medium businesses and impeded the creation of a strong middle class. By the time of the December 2003 elections Nemtsov had moved into resolute opposition to Putin, arguing that the final two years of his first term had been squandered and had turned into 'stagnation and restoration'. A new system of governance had emerged which he characterised as 'Putinism': 'A one-party system, censorship, a puppet parliament, a tame judiciary, strong centralisation of power and finances, and an exaggerated role for the secret services and the bureaucracy'.[72]

Ryzhkov, one of the few democrats not damaged by the 'liberal debacle' of December 2003, insisted that Yabloko and SPS had to be dissolved and a new united democratic body formed.[73] With the representation threshold set at 7 per cent, unity in the liberal camp was not only politically expedient but essential if they were to stand a chance of entering parliament in 2007. He tried, with little success, to create a united democratic grouping on the basis of the old Republican Party, established during the tail end of *perestroika* but hardly visible since. Irreconcilable opposition took the form of Committee 2008, established in early 2004, which later evolved into the All-Russian Civic Congress, and at its first meeting on 12 December 2004 Ludmila Alekseeva (head of the Moscow Helsinki Group), Gari Kasparov and Georgy Satarov, the head of the Indem Foundation, were elected as co-leaders. At the second Congress on 12 December 2005 the resolution on 'Civil society and the 2007–8 elections' warned that 'The deconstruction of democratic institutions in Russia is proceeding apace, together with the stifling of civil society and the establishment of an authoritarian regime. Instead of the separation of powers, power is becoming fused: the president and his entourage fully control parliament and the judicial system … Instead of the development of a multiparty system, a one-party system (*edinopartiinost'*) is being introduced'.[74] In their New Year greeting they insisted that 'The authorities are concerned with only two things: the oligarchy (not all bureaucrats have become oligarchs yet) and the succession of power (to allow the thieving to continue)'.[75] The group participated in the actions of the 'Other Russia' protests against the G8 summit in St Petersburg in July 2006 and other radical actions.

The weak development of opposition in Russia is due to far more than regime suffocation, let alone repression. There is no doubt that 'managed democracy' was a far from propitious environment for the development of independent social and political organisations. At the same time, Kagarlitsky identifies corruption as a factor undermining the development of an autonomous opposition. In a report published in early 2006 Kagarlitsky accused Yabloko of sacrificing its policy programme to gain the support from oligarchical benefactors, while the Union of Right Forces was accused of having an 'extremely high level' of corruption, while its activists were accused of making money by criminal means. Kagarlitsky argued that political corruption doomed 'all of the opposition's actions, right from the start. People in the opposition parties are pursuing their own personal and tactical objectives. The last straw for our group was the CPRF's decision to campaign against the housing and utilities reforms in alliance with an ultra-right organization, the Movement Against Illegal Immigration [DPNI]. This reveals a lack of political principles. That's why we say there is a need for a revolution within the opposition'.[76]

Non-systemic opposition and popular mobilisation

In the early 1990s Yeltsin took politics off the streets and gave it a structured form, more or less within the bounds of the constitution. Politics was now conducted within known limits, and the effervescence of popular mobilisation of the *perestroika* years and the period of 'dual power' between 1991 and October 1993 came to an end. Mass civic participation entered a period of hibernation. At the margins, mostly on the right, some groups continued to incite violence, and it was against this that Putin sponsored the law 'On Counteracting Extremist Activity', which was adopted by the Duma in June 2002. The bill covered religious, social and other organisations and the media. The definition of 'extremist activity' proved controversial. Article 1 of the law defined it as:

> the planning, organisation, preparation for or execution of actions aimed at the forcible change of the constitutional order or violation of the territorial integrity of the Russian Federation; the undermining of the security or the assumption of the governing powers of the Russian Federation; the creation of illegal armed formations; terrorist activity; the incitement of racial, ethnic or religious discord or social discord in connection with violence or calls for violence; humiliation of national dignity; the organisation of mass unrest, hooliganism or acts of vandalism motivated by ideological, political, racial, ethnic or religious hatred towards a particular social group; the propaganda of exclusivity, superiority or inferiority of citizens on account of their attitude towards religion, social status, race, nationality, religion, or language.[77]

This would appear to adopt an attitude of robust liberalism: rights can be exercised as long as they do not infringe the rights of others. However, the procedures associated with the implementation of the provisions of the law raised some disquiet. A whole organisation is liable to prosecution or banning if any of its sub-divisions is found guilty of extremism, as defined above. An initial warning is sent if any part of an organisation commits extremist activity (Art. 7). If a leading member of an organisation makes extremist statements without stating that these were their personal views, then the organisation has to denounce the statements or actions of the person (Art. 15). The 1997 law on religion was modified by the passage of this law, to replace the grounds for the banning of a religious organisation with the above definition of extremist activity; the grounds were thus expanded from actually carrying out actions to planning or making calls for this activity. The law on extremism, as noted, was amended in 2006 to apply more rigorously to elections.

Despite the law, racially motivated attacks continued, amid accusations that the police were reluctant to investigate racist crimes, often classifying them with the much milder offence of 'hooliganism'. In 2004, 256 racist or religious attacks were recorded in which 46 died; while in 2005 the number of attacks rose to 413, with 31 deaths; and in 2006 there were 520 attacks and 54 deaths.[78] There was disturbing evidence of the emergence of an ultra-nationalist fringe, including at least 50,000 violent skinheads and a variety of neo-Nazi groups. African and other foreign students became the subject of attack, while anti-semitism seeped into public discourse, in particular through the Rodina group of Duma deputies. On 4 November 2005 the Euro-Asian Alliance of Youth and Rogozin's Rodina organised an unprecedented march of some 3,000 nationalists (the 'Russia March', see Chapter 8), while 23 February 2006, formerly Red Army day but now used to honour the 'Defender of the Motherland', saw a wide spectrum of opposition group-ings, some with Nazi emblems, calling for the overthrow of the government. The Russian 'street' was beginning to speak, and in unpleasant tones, something that clearly alarmed the 'control freaks' in the Kremlin.

Rodina filled the gap left by the fragmentation in September 2000 of the far right Russian National Unity Party (RNE), led by the charismatic Alexander Barkashov.[79] Barkashov had been deputy to Dmitry Vasiliev in the notoriously anti-semitic *Pamyat'* organisation during *perestroika*, but split in 1990 to found RNE, and throughout the 1990s this organisation absorbed the energies of the wilder reaches of the far right.[80] As far as Rodina's leader, Rogozin, was concerned, 'Rodina is the instinct of self-preservation of the nation, the form for its self-affirmation and struggle'. The party was disqualified from participating in the December 2005 Moscow Duma elections because of a racist television advertisement, although Rogozin claimed that up to 30 per cent would have voted for his party.[81] Intolerance was on the rise, with one poll finding that 58 per cent of ethnic Russians supported the slogan 'Russia for the Russians', compared to 46 per cent in 1998. Nearly 60 per cent favoured the restriction of migration from the South Caucasus and Central Asia.[82] Putin took a strong stand against anti-semitism and xenophobia, calling the latter 'a serious and painful problem ... State policy is aimed at putting an end to outrages of this kind consistently and resolutely'.[83] Some critics, however, discerned the Kremlin's hand behind some of the ultranationalist statements, setting them up as a foil to highlight the administration's moderation in comparison, especially as the 2007–8 elections approached. This hypothesis is undermined by the Kremlin's clear hand in ensuring that Rogozin was displaced as leader of Rodina on 25 March 2006, and replaced by the rather more level-headed Alexander Babakov (who went on to become part of Just Russia). Putin himself bemoaned the rise in racist violence in the country, noting that 'extremist groups were becoming ever more aggressive, taking ever harsher forms', and warned that the MVD had failed to react adequately.[84]

The National Bolshevik Party led by Eduard Limonov was one of the most resolutely anti-Putin of all opposition groupings, espousing a type of leftist radical nationalism.[85] The nationalist threat was countered by the establishment of various regime-sponsored organisations, notably the Nashi (Our Own) organisation. Opponents called the ideology of this body 'nash-ism', which is not dissimilar in sound to 'fascism'.[86] Most radical national-ists fared badly in the polls, yet some of their ideas were incorporated into mainstream parties such as Rodina, the LDPR and the CPRF. For Surkov, Russia was faced with two great dangers: 'the party of oligarchic revenge', which even after the Yukos affair was still being touted as a threat, and what he called the 'isolationists'. He refused to describe them as 'patriots', even though they described themselves as such:

They are almost like Nazis, people who advance the petty thesis that the West is frightful, that the West is threatening us, that the Chinese are advancing, the Muslim world is coming our way, that Russia is for the Russians ... I think that if national isolationists come to power in our country we will get a worse copy of the Soviet ... bureaucratic state but void of Soviet greatness. With absolute inevitability that would become a ludicrous parody and lead the nation to demographic cata-strophe and political collapse ... It is very dangerous to provoke ethnic conflicts in our country. ... We know this from our recent past. We were once convinced that Kazakhs, Ukrainians and other comrades were a burden for Russia ... We all know where this led to. We lost half of the country, half of the population, half of the economy and so on. If now we believe again that certain people are to blame, we may lose the other half of the country and the other half of the economy. ... Russia must be for Russians, Tatars, Mordovians, Ossets, Jews, Chechens, for all our peoples and for the entire Russian nation.[87]

While Putin's administration had come to understand the danger of inter-nal racism, it was less sure how to respond to the phenomenon of exter-nally directed xenophobia. Numerous polls suggested that Russians had begun to see Poles, Georgians and Ukrainians as virulently anti-Russian, while the constant hectoring from the West, and in particular from the United States, about Russia's alleged misdemeanours in relations with its neighbours and further afield, combined with accusations of democratic backsliding, aroused growing popular resentment, a phenomenon that the government may not have fanned but certainly did little to combat. Embargos on Moldavian and Georgian wine and other goods, accompanied by the deportation of Georgian illegal immigrants in 2006, smacked of state-sponsored racism.

The early 2000s were characterised by a relatively low level of popular mobilisation. However, there was a consistent rumble of discontent, which at times burst out in more sustained acts of popular dissatisfaction. This was particularly the case in early 2005 in response to the law on the monetisation of social benefits. While the conditions for a 'colour revolution' were absent,[88] there was nevertheless a potential for mass non-formal engagement in political life. On 8 March 2006, for example, there were demonstrations in Perm against the conduct of mayoral elections and the disqualification of some candidates. Some weeks earlier there had been demonstrations protesting against the four-year jail sentence of the motorist Oleg Shcherbinsky, who had caused the death of the popular governor of Altai *krai*, Mikhail Evdokimov, when his motorcade travelling at over 100 mph had run into the hapless driver. The case was seen as one where privileged bureaucrats ran roughshod over the rights of the common man, as well a defence of the rights of normal motorists. A retrial was held and Shcherbinsky was acquitted. People power could prove a court wrong and could defeat the authorities in a battle for their perceived rights. Elsewhere there were disturbances provoked by ethnic conflicts. In 2005 alone there were 'ethnic riots' in a number of North Caucasian regions, notably in Krasnodar, Rostov and Astrakhan, when Cossacks and Kalmyks came into conflict with Armenians, Greeks and Chechens, and in 2006 ethnic clashes in Kondopoga (see Chapter 8) left two dead. There were numerous attacks against migrant workers, in particular Uzbeks and Tajiks. It was clear that xenophobic themes would figure prominently in the 2007–8 electoral cycle.

Putin's regime was primarily concerned with imposing stability on the country. The excesses of the 1990s were curbed, but while the regime may have been successful in its negative agenda of damping down unwanted activity, including keeping the worst aspects of nationalistic mobilisation at bay, a more positive agenda was missing. The suffocation of active citizenship was perhaps the greatest failure of Putin's presidency: independent funding was restricted, political activity channelled, open debate in the central media controlled and Muscovite recentralisation reasserted. While Putin gave the country stability and a sense of hope for the future, he failed to achieve a sense of popular ownership for his reforms. Putinite modernisation was very much a top-down process, with little independent popular engagement. Public politics became ever more a Moscow elite affair, and ever less public.

Conclusion

Democracy is as much about cultural attitudes to power and authority as it is about institutions. Russia clearly now has the whole gamut of democratic forms, but the spirit with which they operate is not yet imbued with those 'habits of the heart' that Tocqueville insisted were essential for the democratic operation of a polity. The problem lies not only in what some have argued to be flaws in Russian democracy's institutional design, with an overweening presidency, or the emergence of a relatively autonomous regime between the state and the people, but also with the characteristics of political society as a whole. Russia still lacked an opposition that could monitor authority and inform citizens, it remained difficult for voters to assign responsibility for policy outcomes, and the electoral process could only imperfectly vote incumbents out of office. As the Eurasia Party chairman, Alexander Dugin, put it, 'Our political system has been created in haste, constantly assimilating absolutely immature players ... Russian people believe, feel and judge according to other standards than those offered by political parties and political technologists'. As Dugin insisted, 'Mr Putin basically stands alone as a party. Contrary to United Russia, he epitomises a real political party, representing the historical interests of a social and national majority'.[89] To paraphrase Bertolt Brecht, lucky the nation to have such a one-person party; but sad that it needed one. The restructuring of political space under Putin moved in the direction of creating the instruments of popular representation and accountability, but the administration's fear that they would be used against them stifled the social initiative, enterprise and confidence required to create a vibrant democratic society.

7 Putin's 'new federalism'

The strengthening of central authority was at the heart of Putin's reform of federal–regional relations, and was something with which he had been concerned even before assuming the presidency. His policies, moreover, reflected ideas that had been aired with increasing vigour in the 1990s. The reassertion of the prerogatives of the state, as we have seen, could take either pluralist or compacted forms, and Putin's reforms tended towards reconcentration, but it was not clear that even the pluralistic elements could be contained within the framework of federalism. Renewed state activism threatened to lead to defederalisation, that is, the erosion of the separation of powers between the central authorities and the regions. The creation of seven federal districts, each headed by a presidential representative (*polpred*), to establish a presidential 'vertical' of power undermined the federal character of sub-national units. Regional autonomy, however, in the Yeltsin years had often taken undemocratic forms: instead of federalism a type of segmented regionalism emerged. Regional 'barons' had subverted the powers of the federal authorities, and in many cases had established authoritarian systems. Although regional leaders had adopted certain neofeudal traits, as a collective institution they nevertheless represented one of the most effective constitutional constraints on the powers of the Russian presidency and central state. Putin's partial dismantling of segmented regionalism in itself did not enhance federalism, and in any case was forced to accommodate the interests and relative autonomy of some of the most powerful regions. Federalism during his presidency was undermined from above and below.

Segmented regionalism

In the 1990s the old hyper-centralised Soviet system gave way to the fragmentation of political authority and contesting definitions of sovereignty.[1] Attempts to build federalism from the top-down were countered by the regions, which managed, *de facto* if not *de jure*, to ensure a significant bottom-up devolution of power.[2] Under Yeltsin a complex and unstable balance was drawn between the prerogatives of the centre and the powers enjoyed by the regions. The tension between central and regional claims concerned not only practical issues of governance and finances, but also focused on fundamental competing sovereignty claims. The evolving practice of 'asymmetrical federalism' affected the very definition of the state. A distinctive type of segmented regionalism emerged as Russia in effect fragmented along the lines of the 89 regions, with the federal authorities in effect becoming a ninetieth. It was forced to bargain, from a position of weakness, with what the 1993 constitution called the 'subjects of the federation'.[3] The way that national groups and regions had been incorporated into the Soviet order now cast a long shadow over the system that followed. The perpetuation, for example, of ethno-federalism is a vivid example of path dependency, whereby earlier decisions about institutional arrangements foreclosed later options. Attempts by constitutional drafters in the early 1990s to create a uniform system of territorial federalism were defeated by the entrenched interests of the sub-national units named after titular nationalities. The 1993 constitution affirmed that there would be 21 of these, as well as ten autonomous *okrugs* (districts), all of which except Chukotka are part of a larger region, and one autonomous *oblast* (Jewish). It was thereby implied that the other units, namely the six *krais*, 49 *oblasts* and two cities of federal significance (Moscow and St Petersburg), represented in some way 'Russia'. Despite attempts by nationalists to play on this, all of Russia's regions were ethnically mixed and there could be no easy separation into ethnic Russian and non-Russian.

Historical legacies

Segmental incorporation under Yeltsin now gave way to segmented regionalism. The federal authorities at the centre entered into asymmetrical bargaining relations with the subjects of the federation. One of these, Chechnya, claimed outright independence, while Tatarstan for a time became an autonomous enclave within Russia. Russia appeared to turn into a federation of mini-states, many of which were little dictatorships in which freedom and human rights were abused by regional leaders.[4] The Yeltsinite regional bargain basically suggested to the regions and republics that they had a free hand as long as they did not threaten secession.[5] As in the Ottoman and Habsburg empires, local privileges were granted in return for loyalty. The development of civil society was inhibited, since these were privileges granted not to individuals but to corporate groups and ruling elites. The free hand extended to the manipulation of elections allowed titular ethnic groups and authoritarian executives to consolidate their dominance. Until the abrogation of the results of the elections for the head of Karachaevo-Cherkessia in May 1999, no election result had been rescinded. The segmentation of federal relations undermined individual rights.[6]

In some instances segmentation drifted towards full-scale regional separatism.[7] In the years that followed Yeltsin's infamous declaration on 5 August

1990 on a visit to Kazan, for federation subjects to 'take as much sovereignty as you can swallow', republics expanded their *de facto* sovereignty by adopting laws creating a legal space increasingly distinct from that established by Moscow. Chechnya declared itself independent in November 1991, while Tatarstan, Bashkortostan, Khakassia and Yakutia increasingly disassociated themselves from federal Russia. The unifying role of the military was lost, and indeed the army became increasingly dependent on the regional authorities. The federal authorities were unable to guarantee basic civil rights in the regions, and even lost control over regional branches of its own state agencies. Depending on the size of the region, there were between 36 and 54 of these employing a total staff that rose from 380,000 in 2000 to approach a million by 2006. As Smirnyagin noted, 'This giant army of federal employees has long functioned as if no one was in charge'.[8] The local branches of the procuracy, the MVD (internal ministry) and other ministries fell into the hands of governors and local presidents. Only the KGB's successor, the Federal Security Service (FSB), withstood regional 'capture'.[9]

Segmented regionalism in Russia appealed to the language of federalism but in practice undermined the capacity of the state and the legal-normative prerogatives of the federal authorities. Sub-national autonomy is not the same as federalism, just as the reassertion of the prerogatives of the central authorities does not automatically signify defederalisation. As Burgess has stressed, federalism is all about the mutual recognition of legitimate spheres of responsibility at the national and sub-national levels.[10] At least three factors encouraged Russian federalism to develop in a rather more competitive zero-sum manner, where an advantage for the regions is seen as a loss for the regions, and vice versa. First, the Soviet legacy of ethno-federalism endowed Russia with two very different constituent elements: the republics based on a titular nationality (or group of nationalities in the case of Dagestan, Kabardino-Balkaria and others) based on a specific territory and regions based on territory alone. This provided a powerful impetus to the segmentation of regionalism along the lines of this division, as one group sought equality and the other to maintain its differential privileges. A second factor promoting segmentation was the weakness of autonomous rational bureaucratic administration, civic associations and pluralistic political cultures in the regions themselves, a factor stemming from both the tsarist and Soviet past. Russia's ambiguous legacy of state development, in which the government (or regime) tended to act as the substitute for legal-rational administrative governance on the one hand and the stifling of autonomous associational life in society itself on the other, led the regime to substitute for the state and society. Tolerance for societal and regional autonomy was limited.

The attempt to establish a federal system in which structural and cultural factors encouraged a competitive rather than a co-operative dynamic provoked segmentation rather than federalism. The recognition that the federal separation of powers means limitations on all sides was slow in coming. When the state and civil society were weak and modern administrative structures underdeveloped, the autonomy of regional leaders was exaggerated. They viewed themselves as quasi-sovereign actors, a tendency reinforced in the ethno-federal republics by the appeal to the national histories of the titular nationalities.

The practice of segmented regionalism

Post-communist Russian regionalism expressed specific bureaucratic and social interests that became increasingly deeply entrenched. Available political resources were deployed against the centre and other federal subjects to ensure freedom of action to attract investment (above all foreign), to enhance the dominant role of the titular ethnic group in the relevant republics and *okrugs*, and to ensure relative autonomy from popular accountability (by diminishing the authority of local legislatures, manipulating electoral contests and by establishing regional 'parties of power'). Although the regional institutions of the USSR created powerful patronage and political networks, their persistence was determined by specific regional coalitions able to exploit the new political and economic conditions.[11] The underdevelopment of political institutions and personalised patterns of leadership left regional elites unaccountable to local electorates and relatively immune from central supervision. Up to Putin's accession they were largely left to enjoy the gains that they had made in the early phase of anarchic democratisation and marketisation.

Regional segmentation took a number of forms. The most dramatic manifestation of federalism *à la carte* were the 42 power-sharing treaties signed between the leaders (not, it should be noted, by the subjects as a whole) of 46 regions (three- and four-sided treaties were signed with some multi-layered regions) and the federal authorities, beginning with the first signed with Tatarstan on 15 February 1994 and the last signed with Moscow city on 16 June 1998. When initially mooted in the early 1990s by Sergei Shakhrai, the adviser to Yeltsin on federal issues, the idea had been to have only three with the most intractable regions, Tatarstan, Chechnya and Kaliningrad, but the process cascaded into a veritable avalanche. The treaties formalised the emergence of asymmetrical federalism, where the rights of separate regions were negotiated on an *ad hoc* and often conjunctural basis. The terms of many of these treaties, especially various annexes and annual supplements, were not made public, and their net result was to accentuate the asymmetries in federal relations. The bilateral treaties allowed customised deals between the centre and the subjects, and to that degree Yeltsin had a case in arguing that they 'strengthened Russian statehood',[12] yet they could not but undermine basic principles of constitutional equality and political transparency. On 15 July 1998, Putin took over responsibility for the treaties from Shakhrai and signed no more. Instead he focused on preparing a new law on defining the powers of the regions and the centre (the Law on Regions), which was adopted after he had moved on to head the FSB.

At least 50 of the 89 local constitutions and charters contradicted the federal one, while a third of local legislation violated in one way or another federal legislation. The constitutions of Bashkortostan and Tatarstan and the regional charter of Tula *oblast* were exemplary cases of subjects claiming rights not allowed for in the national constitution, derogating from the principle of equality between subjects of the federation. Legal space was also fragmented. According to the Justice Ministry, an examination of 44,000 regional legal acts, including laws, gubernatorial orders and similar documents, found that nearly half did not conform to the constitution or federal legislation.[13] On 24 June 1999 the first serious attempt to redress the situation was the adoption of the long-awaited law 'On the Principles of Dividing Power between the Russian Federation Government and the Regions' (the 'Law on Regions' that Putin helped draft).[14] It stipulated that all new federal and regional laws had to be adopted in conformity with this law, and that all previously adopted legislation and treaties had to be brought into line within three years (by 29 July 2002). The law formalised the procedures for the adoption of power-sharing treaties, stressing above all that everything was to be done openly, thus forbidding secret clauses and sub-treaties.

The asymmetry in federal relations was reflected most strongly in budgetary matters. The principles underlying inter-regional transfers have been the subject of considerable controversy.[15] The complex allocation of tax revenues at the point of collection and from the federal budget became the defining indicator of Russia's failure to establish itself as a genuine federation. The whole notion of 'donor' or 'subsidised' region depends to a large degree on definition. By May 1999 there were only 13 donor regions,[16] but this did not mean that all the others were recipients: about a third received nothing from the centre. In addition, the various bilateral agreements allowed large differences in the amounts of tax revenue transferred to the centre. Tatarstan, for example, passed on only 50 per cent of its VAT revenues to the federal budget, while other regions transferred 75 per cent of what is the most effectively collected tax in Russia. The fundamental fact of fiscal dependency for most remained, although the degree to which the centre used the system of transfer payments for overtly political purposes has been contested.[17] Daniel Treisman argued that during Yeltsin's rule transfers were used as 'bribes' to encourage loyalty among the more fractious regions, rather than as 'rewards' for those who demonstrated loyalty.[18] Others have argued, however, that transfers to a large degree were not used politically but reflected relatively objective criteria of need rather than a mechanism of punishments and rewards.[19] Regions dependent on the centre for subsidies, whatever their political complexion, were forced to establish good relations with the Kremlin to ensure the continued flow of financial resources. Moscow's enduring control over the allocation and disbursement of funds to the regions is the main cement holding the federation together while at the same time undermining genuine regional autonomy.

The growing economic divergence between regions reinforced federal asymmetries. Some regions have access to world markets through the sale of energy, raw materials or basic finished industrial goods, giving them an independent resource in the federal bargaining game. For example, if Khanty-Mansiisk was an independent state, it would be the world's second largest oil producer. In this context, it is impossible to talk of 'the regions' as a single unified actor, since that would suggest unified and purposive collective action. Some regional executives were able to take immediate advantage of the opportunities opened up by the transition to a market economy, while others reliant on antiquated industrial plants suffered. Non-governmental actors, moreover, were an increasingly important element framing Russia's political and economic space. The large energy producers and primary materials exporters negotiated directly with subject-level leaderships, and at times indeed appeared to conduct their own foreign policies. Yukos's plans to build an independent pipeline to Murmansk threatened to undermine Transneft's monopoly in this field. The sectoral fragmentation of Russia, with powerful lobbies enjoying direct access to government at all levels, was reminiscent of the old Soviet economic ministries.[20]

Some regions sought to become international actors in their own right. Between 1991 and 1995 Russia's regions signed over 300 agreements on trade, and economic and humanitarian co-operation with foreign countries. While these agreements may have helped resolve some regional economic problems, they undermined Moscow's monopoly on foreign relations. While some regions inhibited problem solving, particularly those in the Far East that opposed the border agreement with China, others like Karelia, Pskov and Kaliningrad acted to stabilise their regional foreign relations. Over half of Russia's regions are borderlands, and need the support of the federal authorities in dealing with their neighbours. On the broader stage, Russia's domestic religious and ethnic balance is an important factor in foreign policy. During the Kosovo war of 1999, for example, president Shaimiev of Tatarstan threatened to send Tatar volunteers to support the Muslim Albanians if Russian nationalists assisted the Serbs, while at the beginning of the second Iraq war in 2003 Tatar volunteers gathered to defend Iraq from coalition forces. The Muslim Central Spiritual Board in Ufa at that time declared a jihad against coalition forces. Some 20 million people have some sort of Islamic background, and it is the country's fastest growing religion. The preferences of Russia's regional leaders thus became part of the complex tapestry of Russia's foreign relations. To co-ordinate regional and federal foreign policy, the Duma in January 1999 adopted a law stipulating that regional authorities liaise with the Foreign Ministry in negotiations with a foreign government.[21] A special department was established by the ministry dealing with regional matters, with branch offices in regions and republics that were particularly active in foreign affairs. The principle that only the federal government had the right to sign international treaties (*dogovory*) was jealously guarded, and upheld by numerous judgements of the

Constitutional Court.[22] The Kremlin also imposed its veto over direct regional participation in foreign financial markets, and thus all aspects of foreign economic engagement need central approval.

In the regions an extremely heterogeneous pattern of regime types emerged, ranging from the relatively democratic in Perm, Novgorod, Arkhangel, Samara and St Petersburg, to the outright authoritarian in Primorsk *krai* under Nazdratenko and Kalmykia under president Kirsan Ilyumzhinov. Peter Kirkow identified the emergence of a type of local corporatism in the regions (on evidence drawn largely from Primorsk *krai*), marked by 'the institutional entanglement of politics and economics'.[23] In other words, regional regimes emerged that paralleled the emergence of the regime at the centre. There was also diversity in types of state-political structure. Udmurtia was a parliamentary republic (until a referendum in early 2000), Samara was a fully fledged presidential republic, Dagestan was governed by a form of consociational democracy in which a state council tried to balance and represent the ethnic diversity of the republic, while Moscow city replicated the 'super-presidentialism' of the central government. This diversity in part reflected local traditions, the dynamic of elite relations, and the ethnic and social composition of a particular republic, and in turn affected policy outcomes. It is most unusual to have such a great variety of sub-national regime types and governmental structures in a democratic federation, and is reminiscent of the way that the diversity prevalent in the United States before the Civil War allowed many non-democratic systems to flourish. It certainly impeded Russia's development as a democracy. Segmented regionalism influenced state building, undermining the emergence of a unified national market, legal space and Russia's coherence as an international actor. It is against this segmentation of political, economic and juridical development that Putin set his face.

Features of the 'new federalism'

Instead of enjoying an ordered federal separation of powers, the country fell prey to spontaneous processes of segmented regionalism. The development of asymmetrical federalism may well have provided a framework for the flexible negotiation of individual tailor-made solutions to Russia's diverse ethnic and political composition,[24] but it failed to do this within the framework of universal norms of citizenship. Instead, segmented regionalism fragmented the country economically and juridically. By the end of Yeltsin's presidency Russia was not only a multinational state, but was also becoming a multi-state state, with numerous proto-state formations making sovereignty claims vis-à-vis Moscow.[25] Regional leaders decided if and when they would obey the constitution. While the constitution does not pursue a consistent model of federal relations, with a large and contested sphere consigned to the joint jurisdiction of regional and central authorities (Article 72), it was on the grounds of the restoration of constitutional authority that Putin fought segmented regionalism.

The conceptual framework of new federalism

This was the situation facing Putin on coming to office. The reorganisation of federal relations to reverse the leakage of sovereignty from the centre to Russia's sub-national units was at the top of his agenda. In the 2000 presidential election he won a decisive victory in the great majority of Russia's regions, and in 2004 he came top in every region, and this endowed his federal reforms with popular legitimacy. His experience working in the presidential administration in 1997–98 clearly influenced his thinking, but he also drew on a deep-seated sentiment that had been apparent since the early 1990s about the need for a 'strong centre'.[26] According to one study, 49 regions in the 1993 elections had favoured the centre reasserting itself against regional fragmentation.[27] Segmented regionalism had emerged as one of the greatest threats to the political integrity of the country, but the reassertion of the central state in the name of uniform administration and the unimpeded writ of law was uneasily squared with demands for a genuine devolution of authority to the regions. Was there a way of making the two processes – state reconstitution and federal decentralisation – not only compatible, but actually mutually supportive? Could Putin find a new balance in relations with the regions that would guarantee the sovereignty of the central state in the spheres that properly belonged to it, while providing for the devolution of sovereignty where appropriate?

We argue that the resurgence of the state under Putin was torn between two forms: compacted statism, using the rhetoric of the defence of constitutional norms and the uniform application of law throughout the country but threatening the development of a genuine federal separation of powers; while pluralistic statism defends the unimpeded flow of law and individual rights while respecting the diversity of civil society and federalist norms. In part this tension derives from the ambiguities in the 1993 constitution, which is capable of a permissive or a constrictive reading of federal relations. The permissive interpretation sustains *pluralistic* statism; while a more constrictive reading gives rise to *compacted* statism. It is compacted not so much because of any notional agreement between the parties, although, as we shall see, this element does play a part, but above all because through compaction, a concept rather broader than centralisation, the relative pluralism, media freedom and regional diversity that had emerged under Yeltsin were threatened. Unresolved tensions in the constitution and the readiness of the Constitutional Court to back his interpretation of its provisions concerning federalism means that our distinction between reconstitution and reconcentration is eroded. In federal affairs, it is precisely reconstitution that takes on the guise of reconcentration. As during the Soviet years, there was a danger that the system would become federal in form but unitary in content.

In his 8 July 2000 address Putin stressed that 'competition for power' between the centre and regional powers has been 'destructive', and he argued that 'we have to admit that [Russia] is not yet a full-blown federal state'. Instead, Russia had 'created a decentralised state'. Putin's response to segmented regionalism was, literally, to *reconstitute* the state; that is, to place the constitution at the centre of relations between the centre and the regions. The aim was to achieve constitutional federalism rather than the *ad hoc* asymmetrical federalism and segmented regionalism that had emerged under Yeltsin. At the heart of Putin's reform of federal relations was the attempt to ensure that the writ of the constitution ran unimpeded throughout the territory of Russia. In his book *First Person*, Putin stressed the importance of an independent judiciary together with greater federal control over the regions,[28] and now he began to implement this programme. In numerous speeches Putin stressed the need to

> guarantee all citizens equal rights and equal obligations. We want to ensure the undeviating observance of Russian laws throughout the territory of the country so that the rights of citizens are observed equally strictly in Moscow and in any other region ... We are striving to strengthen and consolidate the state as the guarantor of the rights and freedoms of citizens.[29]

As he put it in another interview at that time, 'the establishment of a single legal space' involved 'not only the equal application of federal laws in the localities, but also the strict correspondence of normative acts adopted there to the constitution'.[30] At the rhetorical level, therefore, the reassertion of federal law did not threaten the development of federalism but instead sought to ensure that Russia became a single legal space, with the principles of legality and individual rights enshrined in the constitution enforced throughout the country. The legal offensive against segmented regionalism sought to bring regional charters, republican constitutions and all other normative acts into conformity with the constitution and federal law. However, the struggle for the 'dictatorship of law' entailed a centralisation that could be construed as an attack on the devolved prerogatives of federal subjects.

Segmented regionalism gave rise to unequal and partial citizenship. In response, Putin proposed the universal application of laws and constitutional norms to promote the development of uniform citizenship. It is for this reason that Putin's initiatives were welcomed by regional democratic movements, hoping that the president would force regional leaders to live up to international standards of human rights and democratic accountability.[31] Putin's declarations in defence of constitutional principles encouraged oppositionists in some of Russia's regions to protest against the development of local authoritarian regimes. In a joint letter to Putin, various oppositional groupings in Tatarstan, including communists and some nationalists, expressed concern that 'Tatarstan's constitution, laws, and political leadership violate the Russian Constitution'. The letter argued that the powersharing treaty between Tatarstan and the federal government failed to address the contradictions between federal and republican laws, allowing the latter to violate the former. The growth in Shaimiev's personal power was condemned while the rights of the population were restricted. The letter also argued that the republican legislative branch had no authority at the local level since local legislators were controlled by mayors directly appointed by Shaimiev. Local judges, moreover, were dependent on republican and local authorities and could not independently evaluate citizen complaints that their rights were being violated. The text warned that the residents of Tatarstan no longer felt that they were residents of Russia. In conclusion, the groups called on Putin to appoint a presidential representative in the republic, something that Yeltsin had never done.[32] The letter was evidence of pressure 'from below' for the reconstitution of state authority to defend the norms of universal democratic citizenship throughout the Russian Federation. The strengthening of the independence of the judiciary, notably through the greater independence of judges and the introduction of jury trials, represented an important step on this road.

In his broadcast of 17 May 2000 Putin noted that 'a fifth of the normative acts adopted in the regions contradict the country's basic law, and the constitutions of the republics and the charters of the regions diverge from the Russian Constitution'. Regional governments had until October 2000 to bring regional laws into accordance with federal norms. Putin insisted that his measures 'fully fit into the framework of the existing constitution'. He noted that some had urged him to take even more radical action, including the direct appointment of governors. At the time he insisted that he believed in the continued election of regional heads since this had become 'part of our democratic constitutional order'; a view, as we shall see, that he was to change later. Putin insisted that the strengthening of the state was not to be interpreted simply as an authoritarian reorganisation of state capacity, above all its coercive resources, but was associated with a concept of individual security. As he put it in his concluding remarks in his broadcast of 17 May:

> Dear citizens, you know as well as I that the weakness of power affects above all millions of common people. The price of state disorder is personal insecurity, threats to property, housing and ultimately our future and that of our children. This is precisely why we need strong and responsible authorities ... That is why I was elected Russian president, and it is this policy that I intend to pursue firmly and consistently in the future, just as we are doing today.[33]

He was as good as his word, and no sooner was he confirmed in office than he set about reorganising the structure of Russia's federal system.

Features of the new federalism

Putin's response to regional segmentation was to appeal to the principle of 'the dictatorship of law', and in particular the unimpeded flow of constitutional and juridical authority throughout the Russian Federation. He insisted 'We must gather the state, and we will do this'.[34] The defence of centralisation to ensure the uniformity of law and legal standards throughout the federation ran perilously close to becoming defederalisation. We have noted earlier that this was in keeping with the Jacobin tradition of state building, and clearly French unitary centralism in a federal state provokes numerous contradictions. Sub-national sovereignty claims are rendered illegitimate, even though federalism as a principle is all about shared sovereignty. Fundamental issues were obscured by Putin's attempts to reconstitute the state, above all the meaning and form of state sovereignty. Was Russia to become a genuine federation, in which law would be defined in accordance with the normative spatial division of sovereignty; or would it take the form of *de facto* regionalism, where an effectively unitary state grants rights to devolved units, in which case a very different definition of sovereignty would operate? To what degree would the experience of the regions be taken into account in reconstituting a *federal* state? Below we list some of the key changes in federal relations under Putin.

1 Federal districts

The centrepiece of the new 'state-gathering' policy was Putin's decree of 13 May 2000 dividing Russia's 89 regions into seven larger administrative districts.[35] They were part of what came to be called the 'power vertical'. Putin's hero, Peter the Great, had divided the Russian empire into eight regions and established the new government institution of Governors General in 1708. Putin's innovation did not formally change the existing territorial–administrative divisions, but the establishment of an administrative layer between the federal centre and the regions reduced the significance of the latter. The new federal districts (FDs) are headed by presidential envoys (*polpredy*) appointed by the president, thus undermining the principle of regional democracy, and are directly subordinate to the president. The aim was to restore the 'executive vertical', but in effect a 'triangle' was established with the new FDs added to relations between the regions and Moscow. The *polpredy* organise the work of federal agencies in the regions, with particular attention to the law enforcement bodies, monitor the implementation of federal policy, provide the federal authorities with information on what is going on in the regions, and advise and make recommendations on federal appointments. They also work with the eight old inter-regional associations to devise social and economic policies, although the fact that the borders of the two entities do not coincide makes such a 'co-ordinating' role extremely difficult. The envoys have far greater powers than the old representatives,[36] 'monitoring the implementation' rather than facilitating the observance of federal laws, decrees and presidential instructions.[37] With the shift to appointed governors in 2005 the role of federal envoys became increasingly anachronistic.

2 The Federation Council

On 17 May Putin announced that he would submit a package of laws to the State Duma designed 'to strengthen and cement Russian statehood',[38] and reform of the upper house of Russia's bicameral parliament, the Federation Council (FC), was at the heart of this. The first convocation of the FC in 1993 had been formed by direct election in the regions, but a 1994 law made the heads of the regional executive and legislative branches directly members of the upper house. Now Putin suggested a return to a variant of the earlier system, to allow senior figures to 'concentrate on the specific problems facing their territories'.[39] The FC was to be composed of two permanent representatives from each region, one nominated by each region's executive branch and one by the legislature. The new 'senators' were to be delegates of the regional authorities rather than popular representatives. The law of 5 August 2000 conceded that a governor's appointment of a representative could be blocked by a two-thirds majority in the regional legislative assembly within two weeks. Dismissal was also to be approved by a two-thirds majority of the local legislature. Regional legislatures were able to nominate and recall their delegates according to their own procedures.[40] Agreement was also reached over a 'soft turnover' of Federation Council members, with governors leaving the Federation Council as their terms expired, or by 1 January 2002 at the latest. A large number of governors faced election in the autumn of 2000, and were not able to return to the upper chamber.

Important questions about the constitutional status of the new-style Federation Council remain. The upper chamber according to the 1993 constitution, has the right to declare a state of emergency, to authorise the use of the military abroad, to appoint and remove the prosecutor general, and many other important functions. With the new assembly made up of nominated figures, is it appropriate for these tasks to remain with the assembly; would it not be better for them to be fulfilled by the Duma? A constitutional amendment would be required to make the change, yet Putin refused to countenance formal constitutional change. The reform raised important institutional questions, above all the weakening of checks and balances, however rudimentary they may have been. This was reinforced by the shift to the appointment of governors in 2005 (see below). The term of a governor's representative in the FC is the same as that of the nominating governor, so if a governor's term ends prematurely, so does that of the representative. The abolition of gubernatorial elections clearly undermined the separation of powers at the federal level. This state of affairs was unsustainable, and hence there was much discussion during Putin's second term of returning to a directly elected upper chamber. This was an issue that Putin's successor would have to deal with as a matter of urgency.

3 The State Council

The creation by presidential decree on 1 September 2000 of a para-constitutional consultative body known as the State Council under the president further undermined the Federation Council. Since the body is consultative, its creation did not require amending the constitution. The State Council is made up of regional leaders, allowing them to retain direct access to the national leadership, and thus its creation appeared a sop to the regional leaders displaced from membership in the Federation Council. Its presidium consists of seven regional leaders serving for six months each, one from each federal district. It meets in plenary session once every three months to discuss two main topics, usually prepared by commissions headed by a presidium member. The State Council took on functions that were the prerogative of parliament, including discussing regional and federal reform, but its views lacked legislative force.

4 Dismissal and dissolution

A second bill in 2000 sought to provide a mechanism whereby the heads of regions could be removed and regional legislatures dissolved if they adopted laws that contradicted federal legislation. Although in principle the courts already enjoyed the power to dismiss governors, two court decisions were required stating that the governor had violated federal law. The law adopted by the Duma on 19 July 2000 allowed the president to dismiss regional leaders, including governors of *oblasts* and presidents of republics, for violating federal laws. A court ruling was required to confirm that an official had broken the law and a letter from the prosecutor general that a case had been opened against a regional leader. To dissolve a regional legislature, the president has to submit a bill to the State Duma.[41] Nazdratenko was the first victim of the new presidential powers (which came into effect on 1 February 2001), resigning from the post of governor of Primorsk *krai* on 5 February 2001 after nearly a decade of misrule. Although the full power of the new law was not applied against him, the threat (in the form of repeated inspections) apparently was enough for him to step down. On 4 April 2002 the Constitutional Court confirmed the president's right to fire governors and the State Duma's power to disband regional legislatures. The sacking power became moot once the system of appointing governors was introduced in 2004. Federal interference could take a number of other forms, including the dismissal of representatives to the Federation Council. On 14 May 2006 the head of the FC, Sergei Mironov, dismissed four members of the upper house (from the Nenets AO, the Yamal-Nenets AO, Khakassia and Primorsky *krai*), ostensibly as part of an intensified anti-corruption campaign. Following token resistance, the relevant regional assemblies ratified Mironov's action.

5 The end of the sovereignty of sub-national republics

In a decision adopted on 7 June 2000 the Constitutional Court declared unconstitutional the sovereignty declarations adopted by most of Russia's republics.[42] The ruling dealt specifically with the case of Gorno-Altai, but clearly had wider implications. In its judgement, the Court took a rather narrow state-centred view of sovereignty, arguing that 'the constitution of the Russian federation does not allow any kind of state sovereignty beyond the sovereignty of the Russian Federation', and went on to assert that 'the subjects of the Russian federation do not have sovereignty, which from the start belongs to the Russian Federation in general'.[43] The ruling against any devolution of sovereignty to the republics was justified on the grounds of equity: it would, they insisted, be unfair for such an imbalance to persist vis-à-vis the other subjects of the federation (reflecting a classic postulate of the French republican tradition). In a further ruling, the Constitutional Court supported the Putinite principle that only the federal government had the right to establish courts and determine criminal procedures, thus denying the regions the right to set up their own courts or to establish rules for their operation. The stick, bent so strongly towards the republics in the period of the 'parade of sovereignties' in 1990–1, was now pushed back the other way.

6 Legal conformity

The struggle to bring legislation into conformity with federal norms began with decrees issued on 11 May 2000 demanding that Bashkortostan, Ingushetia and Amur bring their regional laws in line with the Russian constitution and federal legislation.[44] On 16 May another decree was issued with respect to Smolensk *oblast*.[45] Bashkortostan turned out to be the most resistant to bringing its constitution into line with that of Russia, fearing that doing so would make Russia once again a unitary state. A federal law in 2003 obliged Russia's regions to ensure that all local laws that contradicted federal legislation had to be removed by mid-2005. The reassertion of federal law sought to bring regional charters, republican constitutions and all other normative acts into conformity with the constitution and federal law. However, there was widespread resistance to the harmonisation campaign, including the usual foot-dragging as well as more overt opposition.[46] Speaking at a meeting of the Council of Legislators (representing regional assemblies) on 16 March 2006, Putin argued that regional legislation could help improve the quality of national laws, but he emphasised that 'strengthening the unity of legal space is our most important national priority'. He noted that only ten regions had brought their laws fully into conformity with federal norms, and that in many of the regions that had failed to do so 'these infringements lead to restrictions on the rights and freedoms of citizens. This is absolutely inadmissible'.[47]

7 Independence of the judiciary

Already in early 2000 the Chair of the Supreme Court, Vyacheslav Lebedev, announced that henceforth all courts – from the top down to the regional and lower courts – were to be financed solely from the federal budget. The aim was to eliminate the courts' financial dependence on regional governments, something that obviously compromised their independence. At the same time, the salaries of judges were to be raised to improve their level of 'professionalism' and 'honesty'.[48] The federal authorities at this time won a court victory that allowed courts of general jurisdiction (with the Supreme Court at the apex of this system) to rule on the constitutionality or illegality of regional constitutions and laws.

8 The end of bilateral treaties (mostly)

The end of the bilateral treaty process had already been indicated at the end of Yeltsin's presidency, with no new treaties having been signed from June 1998. Existing treaties were not renewed or were repudiated by the regions themselves. The first to do so was Dmitry Ayatskov in Saratov in Summer 2001, and between 21 December 2001 and 20 May 2003 33 treaties were renounced. In his address on 18 April 2002 Putin noted that of the 42 regions that had such agreements, 28 had already been revoked.[49] A treaty with Yakutia was signed on 26 September 2002 modifying the 1995 treaty. That left only nine treaties with 12 of the staunchest regions, including some key republics. A law of 7 July 2003 ordered that unless all existing treaties were renewed in conformity with existing legislation within two years, they would lapse. Since none were able to do so, despite attempts by Yakutia, they all lapsed on 8 July 2005. This in itself did not ensure Putin control over the regions, and the abrogation of the treaty process did little to diminish the control exerted by regional potentates in Kalmykia or Bashkortostan.

Although the time of a 'treaty federation' had gone, there were two exceptions. The first was the renewed treaty with Tatarstan, ratified against considerable opposition by the Duma on 9 February 2007.[50] Shaimiev had earlier convinced Putin to abandon his plans for two-term limits on the incumbency of regional executives, and now he forced Putin to backtrack on this issue. After two years of work the new document, which took the form of a federal law and thus required parliamentary approval, made no mention of sovereignty or self-determination (unlike the Yeltsin-era treaty), but it did allow a special status for Tatarstani citizenship by the inclusion of a paper insert in federal passports, which also carried the republic's coat of arms, and allowed the republic to declare Tatar the official language. Candidates for the republican presidency have to know the Tatar language. There were tax exemptions on mineral resources, and the agreement stipulated the joint regulation of economic, environmental and other issues associated with the distinctive features of the republic. This in effect confirmed the republic's control over the local oil industry. With a new electoral cycle imminent, Moscow needed Shaimiev's ability to deliver votes. There were also concerns, as in Chechnya, to undermine Islamist and separatist movements in the republic – issues that had prompted the bilateral treaty process in the first place in 1994. However, the planned treaty with Tatarstan was rejected by the Federation Council on 21 February 2007 by 93 votes to 13, with 15 abstentions, and thus the whole process was derailed.

Long-drawn-out discussions with Chechnya tried to formalise its exceptional status in the Russian Federation with a bilateral treaty. Delays were provoked by Moscow's fears of granting excessive powers and privileges to the Chechenised leadership in the republic, above all in the economic and taxation spheres. The prime minister, Ramzan Kadyrov, was particularly keen to assert the republic's control over the oil industry. The *siloviki* in the Kremlin and their allies did not trust Kadyrov, and opposition to a power-sharing treaty with the republic was led by Igor Sechin in the presidential administration, Sergei Mironov in the FC and Viktor Ilyukhin, head of the Duma's security committee. One of Kadyrov's first acts when elevated to the presidency in March 2007 was to renounce the idea of a special treaty.

9 Fiscal federalism

The attempt to recreate a national market became one of the central planks of Putin's regional policy. The general weakening power of regions assisted the struggle against the 'virtual economy' (the network of barter and non-payments) that was very much regionally based. The federal government, moreover, began to revoke many of the tax concessions granted by his predecessor. On 26 July 2000 the second part of the new Tax Code was over-whelmingly approved by the Federation Council (128 to 13), even though it caused an immediate fall in regional tax revenue. The lion's share of tax and duties revenue went to the centre, including VAT receipts, income taxes, excise and customs duties, and natural resource taxes, while all that was left for the regions was transport tariffs, a portion of profit taxes, and property and gaming taxes. The new Tax Code was designed to be easier to understand, as well as to implement. Its main feature was the greater centralisation of collection and distribution of taxes. Income tax revenue at the close of Yeltsin's term was collected 50:50 between the federal government and the regions, but now was divided 70:30 in the federal government's favour. The reform provided for much greater redistribution of revenues between the regions than had hitherto existed. Not surprisingly, the poorer regions (the great majority) supported the bill, while the richer minority, led by Moscow mayor Luzhkov, argued against it. The government now intended to pursue an active regional policy: concentrating more resources and redistributing them as part of a conscious strategy of levelling some of the disparities between regions. The 2007 budget envisaged that a third of all spending would be distributed to the regions through the centre. The formula for this redistribution was far from clear, with half going out according to known criteria to support various programmes, whereas the other half was discretionary, and thus to a degree arbitrary. Tatarstan, Bashkortostan and the North Caucasus did well out of this system, together with St Petersburg and some Siberian regions. The whole system of inter-budgetary transfers, designed to avoid misappropriation, encouraged game playing, with regions under-playing their own performance to gain extra funds.

Very few of Russia's regions have achieved economic self-sufficiency, with a dozen of the most successful regions accounting for over 50 per cent of Russia's GDP. Rising electricity and fuel prices meant that even regions with large manufacturing plants lost revenue because of falling profit from tax revenues. The economic gap between regions was increasing despite growing transfers. In a report to the State Council, Krasnoyarsk governor Alexander Khloponin reported that 'the gap between regions in terms of per capita GDP, by which the figure for the richest regions was 64 times that for the poorest in 2000, approached a factor of 300 in 2005'. In 1999, federal transfers to regions represented 9 per cent of total federal spending; in 2001, 18 per cent; but already by 2005 it represented about a third of all spending.[51] The intractable problems in the North Caucasus, with a spreading insurgency in the region combined with grave social tensions and ethnic conflicts, prompted Kozak, the presidential envoy to the Southern Federal District, to suggest that the degree of federal devolution should be in inverse proportion to the level of subsidy that they received from the centre: 'The more money the centre provides, the less regional power'.[52] From January 2007 an external administrator in Moscow assumed some responsibility for the management of subsidised regions. This is 'federalism as you pay', and represents central intervention on a drastic scale, effectively undermining the federal division of powers. In 2007 a more coherent regional policy was implemented, designed to encourage successful regions while preventing the poor ones from sinking entirely, while those in the middle would get targeted developmental support. Regional performance is tracked by Rosstat, the national statistics agency.

10 Institutional uniformity

We have noted above the rich diversity in institutional forms that had developed in the 1990s. Russia had a rich variety of regional legislatures: some were bicameral while others were unicameral, some deputies were professional and paid, while others were volunteers, and electoral systems also varied. This was now reversed and a single model for all regions imposed. This meant, for example, that the bicameral assemblies in Adygeya, Dagestan and Kabardino-Balkaria were abolished, while in Dagestan consociational elements were dropped in favour of the standard model of an appointed governor nominated by Moscow. However, the single design was not imposed everywhere, with Chechnya being granted the exceptional right to create a bicameral assembly.

11 Regional governors: from election to appointment

As Russia emerged as an independent state in December 1991, Yeltsin postponed regional elections and for the next four years appointed governors.

However, this was always considered a temporary arrangement, and from 1996 they were all elected. Although enjoying an autonomous political legitimacy derived from popular election between 1996 and 2004, according to the constitution (Articles 5.3 and 77.2), governors are part of a single vertically integrated executive structure. In recognition of this, some regional governors themselves called for the abolition of direct elections and the formal re-subordination of regional executives to the federal authorities. Yeltsin's traditional style of managing the regions, where relative independence and selective privileges had been granted in return for support for the Kremlin at the federal level, now gave way to a period of federal activism.

The vagaries and uncertainties associated with elections encouraged some governors to contemplate giving up whatever legitimacy they may have gained through the electoral process and returning to the old system of appointment from the centre. The law allowing governors a maximum of two terms was signed on 19 October 1999, coming into effect on 19 October 2001, giving the governors a two-year grace period.[53] On 25 January 2001 the Duma adopted a generous amendment to the law, and counted the first term of the governor as the one starting after 19 October 1999, allowing 69 regional executives to run for a third term, and an additional 17 to serve a fourth. The Kremlin on the whole was successful in getting its favoured candidates elected in regional executive elections, with 11 out of the 15 going its way in 2002.[54] In Ingushetia, neighbouring the war-torn Chechen Republic, the Kremlin forced the resignation of president Ruslan Aushev, who had been extremely critical of Kremlin policies, and in his place engineered the 'election' of FSB general Murat Zyazikov following the disqualification on a minor technicality of the leading (and pro-Aushev) candidate Khamzad Gutseriev. A number of authoritarian presidents were re-elected for a third term.[55] Despite the extra powers granted to the presidential administration, it was notable that these were not used in the case of Nazdratenko, and instead a deal was struck that allowed him to resign and be rewarded a plum job in Moscow as head of the federal fisheries service (until he disgraced himself there, too, and was relieved of his post in February 2003, but then popped up as a deputy head of the Security Council in May 2003, in part to keep him out of the way and to prevent him returning to Primorsk *krai*).

In his 13 September 2004 speech Putin proposed that regional executives be elected by the legislative assemblies of the territories 'at the representation of the head of state', a procedure used for the appointment of prime ministers. The federal law of 11 December 2004 established the system whereby the president nominates a candidate for the post of governor no later than 35 days before the end of the incumbent governor's term, and there are opportunities for consultation between the president and the legislature before a candidate is nominated. Regional legislatures have two opportunities either to reject or approve a candidate, who must be over 30 years of age and is appointed for a five-year term. Over half of the relevant assembly must support the nominee for the candidate to become governor.

If a regional legislature twice fails to approve the presidential nominee, at the third attempt the president is entitled to appoint an acting regional head for up to six months and to dissolve the legislature by decree, with new elections to be held within 120 days of the decree entering into force. Dissolution, however, may only take place after a month-long cooling-off period for discussions between the president and legislators. Appointed governors are permitted to serve more than two consecutive terms, thus the interminable debates on two-term limits were rendered anachronistic at a stroke.

The appointment of governors undoubtedly reduced the autonomy of the regions, and raised the question whether the new system is compatible with any serious definition of federalism. On 21 December 2005 the Constitutional Court ruled that the new procedures were not a violation of 'the principle of the division of powers and federalism ... *in the current historical circumstances* [italics added]'.[56] This decision has been interpreted to indicate the spinelessness of the Constitutional Court vis-à-vis the authorities, and thus its inability to act as a bulwark against authoritarianism.[57] Popular opinion, moreover, favoured the continued elections of governors.[58] A bill adopted by the Duma in December 2005 allowed the majority party in regional assemblies to nominate a candidate, and this was praised later, as noted, by Surkov when implemented in Adygeya. In his televised press conference on 31 January 2006, Putin singled out the adoption of the law allowing victorious parties at the regional level to participate directly in the formation of the executive authorities as one of the major achievements of 2005, insisting that the new system was 'far from the appointment of executive heads from Moscow'. The new system, in his view, would allow the appointment of governors who were 'sensitive to regional problems, but who were also vitally aligned with national interests'.[59] The extent to which regional views would be decisive was unclear, since the central party leadership would have the final say in proposing the nominee.

Appointed governors became little more than ordinary bureaucrats dependent not on the wishes of the electorate but on the federal executive.[60] In some cases individuals were appointed who would never have won an election, but who were individuals of ability and integrity. This was the case with the appointment of Mukhu Aliev in Dagestan in February 2006. However, the weakening of the democratic basis for regional executives threatened the federal separation of powers and the status of the post. Ever fewer governors figured on the list of the most influential Russian politicians. The abolition of term limits allowed some long-standing governors further to extend their incumbency, as with Shaimiev's reappointment in March 2005. An egregious case was that of Murtaza Rakhimov of Bashkortostan, whose 16 years in power was extended by another five-year term in October 2006. With parliamentary and presidential elections coming up, Putin clearly wanted a trusted figure in charge of this important republic. Overall, in the first two years of operation of the new system no regional assembly rejected a nomination. The appointment of governors in certain respects made little difference to the dynamics of regional politics. In the Soviet era, after all, regional and republican bosses had been appointed, and that did not stop the 'parade of sovereignties' that ultimately led to the independence of the union republics.

12 Regional party and election systems

The weakness of party representation at the regional level under Yeltsin was striking. In 1998 only 635 (18 per cent) of the 3,481 elected deputies had been nominated by political parties, overwhelmingly from the CPRF.[61] Despite Putin's attempt to extend the reach of the national party system to regional politics, the trend in the early part of his leadership was if anything in the opposite direction. Fewer governors were elected who had explicitly declared their party affiliation, and ever more declared independents were elected to regional legislatures.[62] The influx of the representatives of big business into regional legislatures sharpened the struggle for the redistribution of resources.[63] The emergence of a dynamic presidency put all parties in the shade, and at the regional level party groups, however active, found it hard to have any effect on governor–business networks.[64] Regional assemblies had traditionally been dominated by executives and powerful business or other local elites, and Putin now sought to break up these local blocs that had together too often in his view conspired to undermine the writ of the constitution.

The 2001 law on parties abolished the right of regional parties to be registered as political parties, and thus to contest regional or national elections. We noted above the end of the legal sovereignty of regions, however defined, and this measure now undermined their political sovereignty. Regional elites could conduct politics only through participation in national parties, and, until the creation of Just Russia, this was primarily through the 'party of power', United Russia. This of course limited their freedom of manoeuvre, which was undoubtedly part of the intention. Putin sought to achieve the homogenisation of political space, which in positive terms can be seen as the creation of a single political community. Russian federalism, however, was stripped of yet another element of the diversity that is characteristic of federalism as a principle.

Amendments to the law on elections of July 2002 stipulated that regional executives had to be elected in at least two rounds, while from July 2003 elections to regional legislatures followed the national pattern of the time: half of their members are elected from party lists proposed by national parties; and the other half are elected from single-mandate districts. The introduction of party-list elections allowed central politicians to exert more influence over regional elections, an area where governors had hitherto predominated. When the legislation was passed, few of the fifty-odd parties registered at the national level had vibrant regional networks, and even the active ones were usually dominated by the local governor. This now changed as parties merged and consolidated their resources, although United Russia remained predominant in regional elections. Putin's reforms of the party system meant that they were now less a mechanism for intra-elite dialogue and were forced to become more active political players at the regional level. The 7 per cent national representation threshold was introduced into a large number of regional electoral systems, further consolidating the predominance of a handful of national parties. The changes were accompanied by the abolition in some places of minimum turnout requirements. Independent regional politicians had earlier been able to fight single-mandate seats in Duma elections, but they now had to fight their way on to national party lists, where they had to negotiate various gatekeepers. The ability of independents, well known in their regions, to enter the national legislature, was reduced. The holding of regional elections across the country twice a year (March and October) further diluted specifically regional issues and brought regional politics firmly into a single national political community.

13 Merging of regions

There has been a long discussion about merging Russia's 89 regions into a smaller number of larger units. India has only 25 federal subjects, Germany 16, Canada 10, although tiny Switzerland has 26. The aim was to create more manageable and economically viable units, but the effect would be to move from a national-territorial to a primarily territorial federal system. Russia has by far the largest disproportion between the population in the largest unit, Moscow, at 5.8 per cent of the federation, and the Evenk autonomous *okrug*, coming in at only 0.01 per cent, a ratio of 443, compared to India's 342.6 and Switzerland's 84.2, down to Austria's 5.6.[65] The creation of the seven federal districts appeared to be a para-constitutional halfway house on the way towards the creation of larger federal units. Towards the end of Putin's first term there was much discussion about creating 28 large *guberniyas* based simply on territory, with ethno-federalism to give way to national-cultural autonomy. It remained unclear whether these 28 super-regions would be part of a federal system of *zemli* (like the *Länder* in Germany), as discussed in various constitutional drafts in the early 1990s, or part of a unitary Russia, as before 1917. The attempt to 'de-ethnicise' Russian federalism, however, is fraught with danger and if mishandled has the potential to destroy the country.

In December 2001 a federal constitutional law was adopted that permitted regions to merge, laying out detailed procedures that were amended in November 2005 to allow governors, in consultation with the president, to initiate referendums. Under Putin regional unification was of two sorts. The first involved the merger of two ordinary regions, with the idea, for example, of unifying Pskov and Novgorod, and St Petersburg with its surrounding Leningrad region. None of these discussions came to anything. The second was the attempt to end the *matreshka* doll element of Russian regionalism by merging national autonomies in a compound region with the nominal outer layer of the doll. A number of compound regions were transformed, led by the merger of Perm region and the Komi-Permyak autonomous *okrug* to create Perm *krai* on 1 December 2005. Referendums approving merger also took place in 2005 in the Evenk and Taimyr autonomous *okrugs* in Krasnoyarsk region to create a unified Krasnoyarsk *krai* on 1 January 2007, and the Koryak autonomous *okrug* (AO) merged with Kamchatka *oblast*, which led to the creation of a new region on 1 January 2007.

Referendums on 16 April 2006 in the Ust-Orda Buryat AO and Irkutsk region approved their merger, although it had been quite a struggle for Putin to push this through. The Buryats in their small AO feared the loss of an independent identity, but in the event they became part of the Greater Irkutsk region that formally came into being on 1 January 2008. Plans continued to merge Chita region with the Aginsk Buryat autonomous *okrug* to create the Trans-Baikal *krai*. In Arkhangel region merger attempts were opposed by the oil-rich Nenets AO, fearing the loss of economic privileges if it merged with the poorer region. Plans to reconstitute the old Chechen-Ingush Republic were opposed by the Ingush, while the Adygeya Republic strongly resisted merging with Krasnodar *krai*. Local elites feared the loss of their status, since, with just 24 per cent of the population, ethnic Adygs held the majority of public offices, a situation that began to provoke a long-delayed reaction from Russians. A merger would shift powers of patronage out of Adygeya to the larger unit.[66] The planned referendum in October 2006 on the merger of the Altai *krai* with the Altai Republic was accompanied by major protest action by Altais, who feared losing their identity, and merger plans were shelved. This demonstrates the limits to Putin's alleged 'authoritarianism', and indeed highlights his gradualist approach to such issues. Although Putin's style is incremental and para-constitutional, at a certain point changes to Russia's territorial organisation may require a wholesale constitutional revision.

14 Local self-government and the delineation of powers and functions

Regional executives have long sought greater control over local self-government, including the power to fire mayors and dissolve legislatures in towns and cities on their territory. In his proposals on how to rebuild a new Russia, Solzhenitsyn argued that the only genuine way for Russia to be reborn was through the development of local self-government and the revival of the tsarist-era *zemstva*.[67] The actual number of sub-national governments in any one district of Russia ranged from two to four, and there was significant confusion over the budgetary and legitimate legal rights of the various levels. There was no precise correspondence between levels of government and levels of the intra-regional budgetary system.[68] We have noted that by 2006 the regions were allotted only one-third of revenues, but Russia's 11,500 municipalities in 2003 received only 14 per cent of the third, even though their budgetary commitments comprised 30 per cent of regional expenditures. Half of them did not even have budgets of their own.

In a follow-up measure to earlier reforms of federal relations, on 26 June 2001 Putin established a commission to examine federal relations as a whole, and the role of the treaties in particular, under the leadership of his close colleague Kozak. The commission sought to develop the legislative basis for the division of power between the federal, regional and local levels of government. The constitution's assignment of a number of responsibilities to joint jurisdiction had proved to be a recipe for confusion, and now the idea was to draw up a list of functions and designate them to specific levels. The role of the bilateral treaties would be reduced (when not abolished in their entirety) and subordinated to the constitution, federal law, presidential decrees and federal government directives. The aim was to establish a common set of rules for all regions and to provide them with equal rights. The 22-member commission included a number of governors (including Shaimiev) and sought to proceed, in a manner typical of Putin, by consensus. The commission sought to delineate what bodies were responsible for what at each of the three levels (national, regional and municipal) of governance. Resources and the division of taxes were central to the commission's work, as was the accountability of public bodies, with an attempt to clarify lines of financial and public accountability. To achieve this, local self-government had to be rationalised. In 2002 the country had 153,000 local self-government units (including sub-units within regions and municipalities), with 90,000 comprising fewer than 100 people and 24,000 with fewer than 1,000. The two-year legislative process came to an end with the adoption of a new law (law 133) on local self-government on 6 October 2003, with implementation to begin on 1 January 2006, with some provisions delayed until 2008.[69] A new standardised system able to fulfil its responsibilities and with adequate resources was to be introduced. There was now to be a uniform system, with 'settlements' (*poselniya*) at the lowest level, for the first time granting villages certain powers of self-rule. They in turn are grouped into some 24,000 'municipal formations', doubling the number of old municipalities, while large cities retained their existing powers to govern themselves. Each unit of local government would be divided into an executive (*uprava*) branch and legislative (*munitsipalitet*) branch, with most funding going to the former (typically 90:10). Unfunded mandates would no longer be allowed, raising fears that the reform would lead to sharp cuts in social programmes.[70] By mid-2006 about half of Russia's regions had implemented the provisions of the new system. In the event, the complexity of the new system, including the demarcation of the borders of the new local government districts, led to the postponement of the wholesale implementation of the new law until 2008. A key point of contention was the allocation of enterprises, the main source of revenues, between the regions and the municipalities.

Putin's new federalism thus entailed a range of institutional innovations, but above all a new philosophy of central–regional relations. The old segmented regionalism was undermined, although far from overcome, but the new federalism was very much a top-down process of political reform. We shall examine some of the ambiguities in the final section.

State reconstitution and defederalisation

Just as Putin sought to distance the oligarchs from the centre of political power, so, too, he sought to remove the regional barons from what could be seen as excessive influence over government policy. Putin put an end to Yeltsin's liberalism in this respect, and repudiated sub-national claims to 'sovereignty'. The difference between oligarchs and regional leaders, however, was that the latter were part of the system of the constitutional separation of powers in a federal system. Thus the 'distancing' of regions from federal power could not but assume defederalising traits. The transformation of the Federation Council from a club of governors and heads of regional legislatures to one of representatives markedly limited the access of regional leaders to central power. The creation of the para-constitutional State Council did bring regional leaders back into the policy process, but only with a consultative voice, and this served only to reinforce their real loss of power as a corporate group. New powers allowing the president to dismiss elected regional heads and legislative assemblies, followed by the shift to the appointment of governors, demonstrated that a new era in managing federal–regional relations had begun. Yeltsin's traditional style of managing the regions, where relative independence and selective privileges had been granted in return for support for the Kremlin, now gave way to a period of federal activism and attempts to reassert central authority and prerogatives.

Asked about the federal and local government reforms at his press conference on 31 January 2006, Putin defended the rebalancing of powers and authority:

> Very often – and also in the course of today's news conference – we looked at how the heads of the regions of Russia come to power. I would like to draw your attention to the fact that this is not merely the centralising of the authority in Moscow – although partially, of course, this is fair, because the president plays a larger part in bringing a figure of government to power together with a legislative assembly of a region. However, at the same time we are decentralising power in areas where we think that the issues are more effectively dealt with – or where issues may be more effectively dealt with – at a local level. This is not just pulling the rope in Moscow's direction but more a common-sense redistribution of authority for a more effective and sensible resolution of issues facing citizens of the Russian Federation. The most important thing is the provision of financial resources for the tasks that are given to the regional and local authorities. I hope the situation where any power delegated from the centre is accompanied by the allocation of the

appropriate funds will become an absolute rule, which never happened until now. This is precisely why we have driven the education system and the primary link of the health care system into a dead end. We transferred all powers to the municipalities but did not provide them with funds in the early 1990s. We should put an end to this situation.[71]

As far as Putin was concerned, a necessary rebalancing of powers had been achieved, but were his reforms compatible with the federal separation of powers? While too much ethno-federalism and regional segmentation had undermined the coherence of the state, too much centralism could have a similar result. As one scholar puts it:

While the constitution stresses the concentration of power in the presidency and central legislative supremacy, only the independent constitution making and the bilateral treaties create preconditions for a federal 'social contract'. Without forms of asymmetry, Russia's political system would be barely more than the substitution of former party centralism with presidentialism, while formally retaining the legacy of Soviet federalism.[72]

The idea of a presidential 'vertical of power' usurped the autonomous role of regional leaders and reduced them to little more than the executors of what Putin called 'federal functions', in effect, the decisions of Moscow. In a federation animated by the federal spirit, regions have a reserved area in which they have the constitutionally entrenched right to take autonomous decisions. The attempt in the 1990s to call this decision-making sphere 'sovereignty' provoked a backlash under Putin that drastically reduced the entire sphere of autonomy. A measure of the loss of power is that in the three years to the end of 2005 the State Duma debated only about 8 per cent of the proposals advanced by the regions, and of the 451 proposals made in 2004, only two were adopted.[73]

The manner in which Putin approached the regions is also noteworthy. Putin tried to avoid alienating the regional leaders, refusing to engage in populist forms of mobilisation and anti-elite rhetoric. In his television broadcast of 17 May 2000 Putin was at pains to stress that his recently announced package of draft laws was 'not directed against regional leaders'; on the contrary, he insisted that 'regional leaders are the most important support for the president and will act as such in the strengthening of our state'.[74] As he put it on a later occasion, the 'management reforms' (*upravlenchenskie reformy*), are 'not to limit the rights of the regions. Our historical experience proves that super-centralisation and the attempt to manage "all and everything" from Moscow is ineffective ... I am convinced that the real self-dependency (*samostoyatel'nost'*) of the regions is one of the most important achievements of the last decade'.[75] Putin went out of his way to demonstrate his openness to enter into dialogue with regional elites, conducting an active policy of meeting with regional leaders, although not of the back-slapping sort that Yeltsin enjoyed. He thus forestalled concerted opposition from the regions and republics.

Although Putin sought to avoid a direct confrontation with regional leaders, the creation of a presidential federal administration shifted power away from regional elites. As more and more federal agencies transferred their main regional offices to the seven new FD capitals, regional governors lost one of their main sources of local control. As one report put it, they were now reduced to 'ordinary medium-rank officials'.[76] The reassertion of central authority challenged the rights of the subjects of the federation. As the then president of Ingushetia, Ruslan Aushev, put it following the Duma's override vote on the president's power to remove regional executives accused of violating the law and to disband regional legislatures: 'What kind of federation is it if the president can remove the popularly elected head of a region or disband the regional legislature?' He insisted that the plan violated 'democracy and parliamentarianism'.[77] Nikolai Fedorov, president of Chuvashia, noted: 'we all aimed for and tried to build a state with the rule of law. But it turns out now that society – or at least the prevailing atmosphere – is such that the will of the emperor, the will of the president, is law'.[78] Fedorov thus acknowledged the high level of popular support for Putin's reforms, something that the regional elites were unable to ignore.

We have noted Putin's comment in his book *First Person* about Russia being 'created as a supercentralised state'.[79] Were these policies vis-à-vis the regions now a concrete manifestation of these traditions? The question can be considered within the framework of theories of sovereignty and their relationship to Russian practices. For the republics in Russia, sovereignty came to be equated with federal non-interference in their internal affairs and a degree of economic autonomy. Instead of developing a sustained legal framework for federalism, under Yeltsin a segmented regionalism emerged reflecting not so much the spatial separation of powers but the fragmentation of political authority. Sovereignty claims by regional leaders in the republics gained little support among the non-titular peoples, and even titular groups were divided. The fragmentation of citizenship was particularly resented. A survey in Komi revealed that 60 per cent of the ethnic Russians considered themselves primarily citizens of Russia rather than of the republic.[80] The legal offensive against segmented regionalism brought regional charters, republican constitutions and all other normative acts more into conformity with the constitution and federal law. The net effect of Putin's measures was to reduce the influence of regional leaders on federal policy, but in return their control over regional politics was confirmed. The move towards legal uniformity was blunted by concessions to the governors as the country entered the 2003–4 and 2007–8 electoral cycles. Overall, centre–regional conflicts became less politicised and in keeping with the general drift towards depoliticisation under Putin. The courts, above all the Constitutional Court, played a more active role in managing federal relations.

Regional authorities had long been condemned for transforming their territories into separate fiefdoms where they ruled like the boyars of old, apparently insulated from the writ of federal laws and the constitution, but it is unclear whether the reduction in their powers actually increased the democratic rights of citizens. Yulia Latynina argued that the changes did little more than substitute 'the arbitrary rule of the governors' with 'centralized arbitrary rule'.[81] Changes to the federal system were far more complex than that, and the cumulative effect of Putin's reforms created a new and more dynamic pattern to regional politics. As Chebankova notes:

> The rapid development of a national party system in the regions, the growing significance of regional assemblies and legislative elections, alongside the consolidation of regional elites, have demonstrated the potential to undermine the centre's ability to control the provinces.[82]

The vote for Putin in March 2000 had been, according to one observer, for 'the instilling of order in the country and for strong authority that could defend everyone from the highhandedness of bureaucrats and ensure the supremacy and dictatorship of law at all levels'.[83] However, regional authorities had acted as an important 'check and balance' against the overweening power of the centre, and now this federal element in the separation of powers was undermined. Putin's attempt to rein in the regions was not only about the reassertion of federal authority but also about defending the rights of citizens. Regional leaders were to obey the constitution and share power with the people. The country now was to live according to one constitution and one set of laws regardless of the region where one lived. However, the attempt to ensure legal homogeneity itself can be considered a simplification: in the USA each state has different laws, up to and including different approaches to the death penalty. Putin set his face against an asymmetrical model of state development, but federalism is all about legally guaranteed heterogeneity – within the limits of the constitution and the normative commitment to democracy. It is not clear whether Putin's reforms were able to reconcile the homogenising tradition of the modern democratic state with federalism.

Conclusion

What is Russian federalism for? Is it to provide a framework for the national development of ethnic minorities, to act as a bulwark against what Lenin called 'Great Russian chauvinism', to provide decentralised administration and tailored solutions for Russia's huge territory, or to act as a fourth pivot to guard against the possibility of the restoration of an authoritarian government in Moscow? We still do not have answers to these questions. What we do know is that segmented regionalism threatened the rights of minorities and of individuals. It was in response to this that the countervailing universalistic agenda represented by the national state was asserted. This reassertion took two forms: the establishment of a direct presidential supervisory mechanism (the 'power vertical'); and a broader strategy of developing robust political institutions, such as regional legislatures and competitive national political parties, that would make regional political elites more accountable to their own constituents as well as to the national political community. Although the success of his attempts to restore the 'vertical of power' remains contested, at the level of political theory Putin's 'new federalism' is rooted in the Jacobin republican state building tradition, where citizenship is considered individual, universal and homogeneous. As in other spheres, Putin sought to establish the rules of the political game, and then left the actors involved to play it – although the referee was sometimes not averse to picking up the ball and running! The assimilationist aspect of French (unitary) nation building threatened the accrued rights of ethno-federal formations, while the attack on 'asymmetry' reduced the diversity at the heart of federalism. The tension between the reassertion of the prerogatives of the centre and federalism's promise of shared sovereignty is still not resolved.

8 Reforging the nation

We have been trying to make our choice for a long time – whether to rely on the advice, help and credits of others, or to develop on the basis of our own traditions (*samobytnost'*) and our own strength. Many states in the world were faced with a similar choice. If Russia remains weak, we will indeed have to make this choice. This will be the choice made by a weak state, a weak choice.

Vladimir Putin[1]

The Russian Federation emerged as an independent state in 1991. The unthinkable had happened, and the once mighty world power, the USSR, had disintegrated with little warning into 15 independent states. In an imperial and then Soviet guise, Russia had been an empire for three centuries, and now it lost territories accumulated over centuries. The independence of the Baltic republics of Estonia, Latvia and Lithuania together with Moldova was one thing, since they had only been reincorporated during the Second World War, but the separation of the Slavic republics of Ukraine and Belarus was something else. A diminished Russia emerged, unclear about its own identity and fearful about its place in the world. Yeltsin unequivocally accepted the reality of a smaller country, and thus the Yugoslav scenario of endless wars to maintain a 'greater Russia' (such as those fought by Slobodan Milošević under the slogan of a 'greater Serbia') were avoided, but no consensus had been achieved by the end of the 1990s on Russia's proper size and character. National identity is about defined and defensible space; it is also about imbuing that space with a sense of common purpose and destiny. This was the challenge that faced Putin on assuming the presidency.

National images and state symbols

Charles Tilly and others have long argued that states make war, and wars make states,[2] but another no less important process from the nineteenth century onwards was the way that disparate peoples were forged into nations by states.[3] The failure of the Russian Empire to achieve this is one reason for the collapse in 1917,[4] and in a paradoxical way the Soviet state also failed ultimately in its nation-building efforts.[5] Where autocracy and communism had failed, could a democratic Russia now forge a nation-state out of its nearly two hundred nationalities, four main traditional religions and enormously diverse climatic conditions in the world's largest territorial agglomeration? As Ernest Renan put it, a nation is constituted by 'the possession in common of a rich legacy of memories' accompanied by 'present-day consent, the desire to live together'. For the past not to become the source of conflict, since every community 'has its own memories' with little in common, Renan argued that a nation is forged as much by what is forgotten as what is remembered, a point with particular relevance for the North Caucasus. At the same time, Renan insisted 'a nation's existence is ... a daily plebiscite'. In other words, the past can be both the basis of unity as well as division; and ultimately the peoples making up a nation must want to live together.[6] As Putin noted in his *Millennium Manifesto*,

> The fruitful and creative work, which our country needs so badly, is impossible in a split and internally disintegrated society, a society where the main social sections and political forces do not share basic values and fundamental ideological orientations. Twice in the outgoing century Russia has found itself in such a state: after October 1917 and in the 1990s.[7]

In previous chapters we have seen how Putin tried to create a political nation in which everyone would be equal as citizens, but the question remained about how this could become a cultural nation that would allow individuals to be different as people and peoples to be different as cultural communities, but all combined within a single political community. This is less about multiculturalism, since the peoples of Russia share fundamental aspects of a common educational system and even values, but *pluriculturalism*. Pluriculturalism is about differential ways of participating in a single civilisation. Would Putin become a great nation builder on the lines of Kemal Ataturk, who forged the modern Turkish state out of the detritus of the Ottoman empire after 1922, or would he fail, like so many before him, to find an adequate political form to express Russia's diversity and unity?

National values

The trauma of *perestroika* and Yeltsin's headlong rush to the market undermined popular respect for the country's institutions. As Kolosov and his colleagues put it, Russian citizens 'had an extremely pessimistic and negative attitude towards their own country and a lack of faith in its future'.[8] They note the identity crisis that struck the country. The bipolar world had collapsed and with it Russia's superpower status, while internally the state lost its commanding position in social life. It was as if Russia and the rest of the developed world lived in different historical time: in the West, globalisation and regional integration shaved off layers of sovereignty, whereas in Eurasia the borders between countries were hardening and the Westphalian state system was being recreated. For Kolosov the acute identity crisis could be defined as a period in which 'ethnic or other specific cultural regional or social groups create obstacles to the self-identification of the majority of citizens with the political-territorial community'.[9] It was this debilitating pessimism, sense of humiliation and identity crisis that Putin sought to overcome.

At the heart of Putin's attempts to make Russia a 'normal' country was the struggle to overcome the divisions of the past. Already in 1996 Yeltsin had urged his aides to find a 'national idea' around which the country could unite: 'There were various periods in the Russian history of the twentieth century – monarchy, totalitarianism, *perestroika* and, finally, the democratic path of development. Each stage had its own ideology. We do not have it'. He allowed one year for the new idea to emerge.[10] Although in his *Millennium* article Putin insisted that 'I am against the restoration of an official state ideology in Russia in any form',[11] on several occasions he returned to the question of what should constitute the core principles of a revived Russia. He insisted that the basis of social accord would be patriotism: 'Large-scale changes have taken place in an ideological vacuum. One ideology was lost and nothing new was suggested to replace it'. He insisted that 'Patriotism in the most positive sense of this word' would be at the core of the new ideology.[12] Soon after the 1999 Duma elections Putin went further in specifying the elements of this ideology: 'It is very difficult to strive for conceptual breakthroughs in the main areas of life if there are no basic values around which the nation can rally. Patriotism, our history and religion can and, of course, should become such basic values'.[13] In his *Millennium* article Putin identified Russia's 'traditional values' as 'patriotism', '*gosudarstvennichestvo*', (statehood) and 'social solidarity'. He defined patriotism as 'a feeling of pride in one's country, its history and accomplishments [and] the striving to make one's country better, richer, stronger and happier'. He insisted that 'When these sentiments are free from the tints of nationalist conceit and imperial ambitions, there is nothing reprehensible or bigoted about them'.[14]

Putin's nation building thus focused on four key elements. At its heart was an integrative patriotism that rejected the exclusivity associated with the concept of nationalism but instead encompassed pride in Russia's diversity, its history and its place in the world. This was to be buttressed by a strong political authority (statehood, *gosudarstvennost'*) that could maintain internal order, the integrity of the country and assert the country's interests abroad. Third, the pragmatic patriotism was to be supra-ethnic and statist, and it was on this basis that segmented regionalism was attacked, to create a homogeneous constitutional space in which the ethnocratic rights of titular elites were to be subsumed into a broader political community. As Fish puts it, recentralisation was part of Putin's agenda of 'separating ethnicity from identity'.[15] And finally, the new nation state was to be socially just. In Russia's straitened circumstances the latter was perhaps the most difficult to achieve. Putin's efforts to ensure that wages were paid on time, that the savings deposits that had been rendered worthless by the near hyper-inflation of the early 1990s were compensated (at least in part), that pensions were increased to at least the level of inflation, and that the costs of utility and other economic reforms did not bear down too hard on the poor all suggest that he took the idea of 'social solidarity' seriously. There was not much here about a rights-based liberalism, yet the lack of emphasis on pluralism and individual human and civic rights was balanced by Putin's emphasis on the rule of the law. His ideology, as we have noted before, was liberal conservatism.

One issue remained unresolved during Putin's leadership, and in many ways could not be resolved – coming to terms with the past. The stress on autonomy in foreign policy was accompanied by an integrative patriotism at home that feared opening old wounds, having learnt from the experience of Gorbachev's *perestroika* that too much *glasnost'* (openness) can lead to the disintegration of the state. Whether this was the correct lesson is a moot point, but it certainly encouraged a refusal to take moral and political responsibility for the past. As we shall see in our discussion of foreign policy, Russia's self-image is as one of the victors at the end of the Cold War. In the last years of *perestroika*, so the dominant narrative goes, Russia by its own efforts shook off the burden of the communist regime and the grasp of the imperial centre. Russia was not defeated, and therefore unlike Germany or Japan in the wake of the Second World War, it achieved an act of self-liberation. It was perhaps this that riled the Western powers and Russia's former Soviet neighbours – Russia refused to act the part of grateful supplicant but sought to take its rightful place in the world as just another normal great power and as a cultural centre.

While this narrative is a powerful one, it is challenged by others. Of all European post-communist states, only Russia faces the problem of coming to terms with an imperial past. For former Soviet republics such as Estonia and Latvia (and in a different way Georgia), Russia's failure to apologise for the crimes committed against them by the Soviet Union meant that Russia failed to accept responsibility for its own past. Ukrainian nationalists even hold Russia responsible for the famine of 1932–3, even though the Kuban and the Volga region were no less afflicted. Demands for apologies at the time of the sixtieth anniversary of the end of the war in May 2005 looked to many Russians as part of a concerted anti-Russian campaign. The Poles, seized by a mood of conservative populism, joined in, calling for another apology over the Katyn murders of Polish officers and reservists in 1940–1, instead of honouring the memory of the nearly million 'Soviet' soldiers who died in the liberation of the country from Nazi Germany. The Gorbachev administration had recognised Soviet guilt in 1989, and now Putin insisted that not all the sins of the USSR could be laid at Russia's door. When the victims of Stalinist repression become an instrument in the struggles of insecure nationalist elites, all are demeaned. Admittedly, there is no room in Putin's discourse for Stalin and his victims, and this silence, which was reflected in the closure of some official archives and the failure to provide official recognition of past crimes, was an unsustainable position. Putin as a matter of principle asserted that Russia was not responsible for the past, although he was willing to allow Russia to take credit for historical achievements. There was a stark contrast between Germany's acceptance of responsibility for the crimes of the Nazi regime and post-communist Russia's steadfast refusal to adopt a similar position, including payment of compensation for victims.

Both Yeltsin and Putin on occasion did honour the victims of Soviet crimes, notably on visits to Budapest and Prague, but were reluctant to do so in post-Soviet Eurasia. The cult of 'victimhood', it should be noted, is a controversial one. The geopolitical use of the memory of victims was at its sharpest in the resolution condemning communism adopted by the Parliamentary Assembly of the Council of Europe (PACE) on 25 January 2006 by a majority of 80 in favour, 70 against and the rest abstaining. The resolution condemned the totalitarian ideologies of communism and Nazism for mass crimes and the suppression of human rights, and urged post-communist governments and parties to promote the study of the historical record of communist regimes, and to ensure the appropriate socialisation of populations through school textbooks and days of memory.[16] No direct equation was made between the totalitarianisms of the left and right, but the equivalence drawn between Nazism and communism (not Stalinism) denigrated the whole 74 years of the USSR's existence as fundamentally illegitimate. Even at the height of the Cold War such a motion was never considered, and this capitulation to right-wing populism did little to foster reconciliation and the recovery of historical truth.

Putin's own narrative was typical of many Russians. He allowed de-Stalinisation to continue, above all through Alexander Yakovlev's Presidential Commission on Rehabilitation of the victims of Stalin's crimes, but he did little actively to encourage anything that could contribute to the profound de-Stalinisation of national consciousness. Russia's official position that the Soviet occupation of the Baltic republics in 1940 had been legitimate and legal enraged the local populations. Human rights organisations such as Memorial, created on 30 October 1988, continued to explore Stalin's crimes by seeking out mass graves, and by honouring the memory of the dead in various ways, yet its work was under constant threat. The FSB did not encourage investigation of the sins of its predecessor organs. Putin's selective de-Stalinisation was in evidence in the limited scholarly access allowed to the Kremlin's presidential archive (formerly the Politburo's archive). However, Nanci Adler is only partially correct in suggesting that 'It is much riskier and more destabilising for a regime to disinter skeletal memories that are embedded so closely to the foundations on which it still rests',[17] since the contemporary Russian state (unlike Gorbachev's Soviet Union) certainly does not fundamentally rest on Soviet foundations. The resistance to full-scale de-Stalinisation is not so much systemic as cultural and generational.

As we have seen, Putin had joined the KGB largely out of patriotic rather than communist ideals, and this patriotic thread now sought to ensure that what he considered the positive aspects of the Soviet experience, and indeed the positive work of the security agencies in defending the motherland, were honoured. Russia did indeed require a period of 'rigorous retrospection', as the Latvian president Vike-Freiberga put it,[18] but as far as Putin was concerned it was no one's business but Russia's to decide on the pace and timing of this. This is a fair position, but in combination with the resurgence of the *siloviki* and the slowing pulse of the public sphere, the neo-Brezhnevian denial of problems stifled the dynamic development of public life. The psychological atmosphere under Putin once again provoked fear, caution, and concern that there was little to protect the individual against the arbitrary actions of the state. Putin's refusal to allow the memory of the late Soviet period, which included the years of his youth, to be discredited in a perverse way allowed the spirit of those years to be revived.

Symbols and symbolism

A nation exists as much at the level of symbols and images as it does in material facts. The democratic government in 1917 was fatally weakened by its neglect of the symbolic side of state development, and its very designation as 'provisional' undermined loyalty. This was a mistake that Putin would not repeat, and he tried to do this by embedding the state in popular legitimacy, and transforming the people into a political and cultural nation.

A nation only exists when it shares a set of symbols and orientations towards its own history. In the 1990s Russia had remained bitterly divided in this respect, with the CPRF insisting that Soviet communism had reflected Russia's national greatness, while liberals pointed out the enormous costs in human lives and ultimately in relative economic backwardness. Now Putin sought to reconcile Russia's various pasts to overcome the divisions between 'reds' and 'whites', 'greens' and 'blacks'. This was most vividly in evidence in the adoption of the country's symbols and anthem.[19] In the 1990s Russia had muddled through with a number of temporary arrangements. The former tsarist state tricolour (white, blue and red), used by the provisional government in 1917, had become the flag of the democratic movement in the late Gorbachev years, and symbolised the defeat of the coup in August 1991. No law, however, had been formally adopted under Yeltsin making this the state flag because of opposition in the Duma. Similarly, the state emblem (the two-headed eagle) had been used, but no law had been adopted. With the fall of communism, a new anthem had been devised drawing on the work of Mikhail Glinka, but this wordless melody had never struck a popular response. The governments that ruled for the few months following the fall of tsarism in February 1917 had also not been able formally to adopt the symbols of the state, and this had been one of the defining aspects of its 'provisional' character. The nationalist opposition in the 1990s considered Yeltsin's government another set of *vre-menshchiki* (provisionals), destined to be swept away by the patriotic and nationalist-communist tide.

Putin ended the provisional quality of the post-communist regime. The 'new' national anthem adopted on 25 December 2000 was the old anthem composed in 1943 by Alexander Alexandrov, with new words written by the author of the original lyrics, Sergei Mikhalkov (the father of film director Nikita Mikhalkov).[20] On the same day, the two-headed tsarist eagle, stripped of the shields denoting Muscovy's victory over the former Russian principalities, but with the addition of two small crowns flanking a large one intended to symbolise the sovereignty of the Russian Federation and its republics, became the state emblem. On 8 December the tricolour was confirmed as the Russian flag. It thus appeared that all three periods of Russian twentieth-century history had been reconciled: the tsarist, Russia's brief experiment with democracy in 1917 and the Soviet. For many, however, the restoration of a version of the Soviet anthem reflected Putin's neo-Sovietism at its worst.[21] One of the harshest critics was Yeltsin, who implied that the change was symbolic of a broader rejection of post-communist reform. The charge was misjudged and could only be taken seriously if Putin had tried to restore the hammer and sickle.

There were other arenas of symbolic contestation. One of the most controversial was over what to do with Lenin's embalmed remains rotting away slowly in the shrine built on Stalin's orders on Red Square following Lenin's death in January 1924. Putin repeatedly stressed the need to maintain the stability of society and consensus, and he was well aware of just how explosive this issue could become for the country.[22] At his press conference on 18 July 2001 he stated that he opposed the removal of Lenin's body from the mausoleum because many Russians still 'associate the name of Lenin with their own lives'. The reburial of the leader of the Bolsheviks and founder of the Soviet state would send a signal to people that 'they had worshipped false values' and would threaten the existing political and social balance.[23] It need hardly be added that Putin was one of those who had grown up under Lenin's shadow, and an attack on the first Soviet leader would cast a shadow over his own life experience. In addition, up and down the land statues of Lenin still adorn the central squares of countless towns, and the main street is often still a Lenin Prospect. An attack on Lenin in Moscow would provoke bitter controversies everywhere else. At the time of his seventy-fifth birthday Yeltsin expressed astonishment that Lenin and Stalin still retained their popularity:

> Neither Lenin nor Stalin would be on my list of outstanding Russians of the last century, though some of our politicians still admire them. It's a puzzle for me. It is so easy to read the documents and learn how many millions of people died because of the barbarity and brutality of those politicians. But Stalin is still high in popularity ratings, and Lenin is lying in the Mausoleum in Red Square.[24]

Putin's policy acknowledged the sensitivities of the older generation, but by letting sleeping dogs lie the wounds of the past failed to heal, and no new narrative of reconciliation, recognition and atonement emerged.

The patriotic celebration of victory day (9 May) in the Great Fatherland War was as elaborate as ever, with a wide array of world leaders invited to Moscow to celebrate the sixtieth anniversary of the end of the war in 2005. Rather than celebrating a common victory, the event was used, as we have seen, by some countries as an opportunity to lecture Russia on its failings. The anniversary of the October revolution (7 November) since 1996 had been celebrated as a day of Concord and Reconciliation, but Yeltsin had hesitated to fill the event with concrete meaning (peace was notable by its absence, and it was never clear who or what was to be reconciled). In 2005 the holiday was shifted to 4 November to commemorate the defeat by a civil militia of the Poles occupying the Kremlin in 1612 during the 'time of troubles', and it was henceforth known as the Day of National Unity. The new holiday was designed to foster the patriotic spirit and thus to help heal the wounds of Russia's terrible twentieth century, but by giving the day an overtly nationalist flavour the authorities stored up trouble. In 2005 various hard-line nationalists, including the Movement Against Illegal Immigration (DPNI), banded together to stage a public rally called the Russian March demanding the expulsion of foreign nationals and the like. In 2006 the organisers planned an even larger Russian March, including the former Rodina leader Dmitry Rogozin, proclaiming slogans such as 'Kondopoga – a hero city'. What had begun as a drunken brawl between Slavs and people of Caucasian nationality in the industrial city of Kondopoga in Karelia on 1–2 September 2006 left two ethnic Russians dead. Revenge attacks turned into racist clashes by groups of angry Russian youths against all the peoples of the Caucasus. Alarmed, the Kremlin banned the march, arousing the condemnation of nationalists and liberals alike. Instead of providing a focus for national consensus, National Unity Day turned out to be divisive and accentuated ethnic divisions.

Putin's restoration of the Soviet anthem and tolerance for Lenin was taken by 'democrats' to symbolise his neo-Sovietism. These sentiments were reinforced by Putin's decision to restore the red flag as the symbol of the Russian army, and then in 2002 returning the red star as the emblem of Russia's armed forces. Many took this to be a sign of a continuing 'velvet restoration' of the old order in Russia. In the same year, the national day, 12 June, was no longer celebrated as Independence Day, since that was considered to stress rather too much the break-up of the Soviet Union, and instead it became Russia Day, emphasising, as Putin put it on 12 June 2006, that it was 'a day of tribute to Russian statehood, the country, and the historical choice' the people of Russia made in the early 1990s. 'It is owing to that choice that we can live and work in a democratic state and free society, a society where the main value is man and his free spirit'.[25] Putin was even less comfortable with the celebration of the defeat of the August 1991 *putsch*, and deeply ambivalent about Russia's emergence as an independent state in December of that year. These formative moments in Russia's state development had a strong negative element – the dissolution of the Soviet alternative in August, and the disintegration of the Soviet state in December – and hence celebration was coloured by regret. On the tenth anniversary of the August coup, for example, Putin travelled to the White Sea monastery of Solovetsky, used as a prison camp by the Bolsheviks, and thus he avoided having to take a stand one way or another on the significance of the event. The pattern was repeated in later years, and the fifteenth anniversary of the coup and Soviet disintegration passed almost unnoticed.

The celebration of the adoption of the constitution on 12 December 1993 could have been used as the symbolic founding of a new democratic Russia, but, under Putin from 2005, the day was removed from the list of national holidays. Russia's constitution is an almost classically liberal document, yet a mere three years later, in 1996, Yeltsin was already looking for a new 'national idea', suggesting that the constitution was somehow an inadequate document to encapsulate the aspirations of the people, and less than a decade after its adoption 12 December was no longer a national holiday. This undermined the legitimacy of the constitution and weakened its role as the moral as well as legal compass for society, and indeed eroded the liberal idea as a whole.

However, as always with Putin, this was balanced by post-Soviet sentiments. An example of this was his intervention in late 2002 in the long drawn-out saga of restoring the name of 'Stalingrad' to the city on the Volga that had been the site of one of the world's greatest battles from November 1942 to February 1943, with some two million dead, and which marked the turning point in the Second World War as the German advance was halted and then reversed. After Stalin's death, Khrushchev had renamed the city Volgograd, and many democrats after 1991 wished to see the pre-revolutionary name of Tsaritsyn restored (derived from a Tatar word and nothing to do with the tsar), just as Leningrad had become St Petersburg, Kalinin had gone back to Tver, Molotov to Perm and Kuibyshev to Samara, although Lenin's birthplace (officially) remained Ulyanovsk and not Simbirsk. Advocates of honouring the battle noted that there was a Stalingrad Square and a metro station by that name in Paris, but none in Russia. However, Putin insisted that Russia was not France, and that 'the return of the name of the city in our country at present would, I am simply convinced of this, generate some sort of suspicions that we are returning to the times of Stalinism'. He insisted that the final decision should lie with the regional legislative body, and whatever was decided at the local level should be ratified by the national parliament.[26] Putin's caution on this question was fully justified. On the sixtieth anniversary of the end of the battle in 2003 the plaque next to the eternal flame by the Kremlin wall was changed from Volgograd to Stalingrad, and it soon became a shrine not only to the memory of those who died there but also to the man whose name it bore.

Social aspects of national identity

The attempt to forge a new Russian consciousness took place at the symbolic level, but it was also rooted in deeper currents of social thought and belief.

Patriotism and images of the nation

Putin was clearly imbued with a deep Russian patriotism, but he had absolutely nothing in common with the various trends of Russian nationalist mysticism. The 1990s had spawned hundreds of nationalist movements and trends. One of the most thoughtful, for example, was the 'Spiritual Heritage' (*Dukhovnoe nasledie*) movement led by Alexei Podberezkin. He had formerly been an ally of the communist leader Zyuganov, and had acted as one of the theologians of the peculiar form of national-communism espoused by the CPRF under Zyuganov's leadership, but Podberezkin had separated from the Communists before the 1999 Duma elections. The split was itself an indication of the declining power of the CPRF to bridge the nationalist and communist movements. Podberezkin participated in the March 2000 presidential elections, espousing the idea of a specifically 'Russian way'. His programme sought to modernise the 'Russian idea' for the new period, but as so often with 'national ways', the work was permeated by a strange combination of metaphysical abstraction and ruthless national realism.[27] Podberezkin ended up tenth in a field of 11 (see Table 1.2).

Following the 1999 apartment bombings in Moscow and elsewhere, Yeltsin was careful not to identify any national group as responsible: 'This enemy does not have a conscience, shows no sorrow and is without honour. It has no face, nationality or belief. Let me stress – no nationality, no belief'.[28] Simonsen has argued that Putin was less nuanced and sought to incriminate the Chechens as a nation, allegedly demonising all Chechens as 'terrorists' and 'bandits'. He argues that in the earlier part of his presidency 'Putin was less sensitive to issues of ethnicity than his predecessor, meaning that his statism is not devoid of an ethnic element',[29] a feature that he dubbed 'ethnocentric patriotism'.[30] Putin's alleged willingness to allow racism against Caucasians to grow during the second Chechen war, and his identification of Russia and the Soviet Union primarily with ethnic Russians, as in his Victory Day speech on 9 May 2000: 'The people's pride and Russian [*Russkii*] patriotism are immortal. And therefore no force can triumph over Russian [*Russkii*] arms or defeat the army', appeared evidence of this.[31] However, on innumerable occasions Putin was at pains to ensure that policy was not 'ethnicised', and he sponsored the 2001 law and later amendments against political extremism. Putin sought to devise an idiom allowing Russian patriotism to encompass tolerance and pluriculturalism, a formula that was itself divisive.

Putin was in the line of the liberal statists (*gosudarstvenniki*), a tendency that had emerged early in the 1990s and whose most coherent exponent was Boris Fedorov, leader of the small liberal party Forward, Russia!. Fedorov was a resolute champion of an assertive Russian identity: 'I am personally not willing to abandon a single one of the notions "great Russia", "great power", "introducing order", and "patriotism"', he insisted.[32] The liberal statists were joined by the neo-Eurasianists in asserting Russia's interests, above all in the former Soviet Union. Sergei Stankevich, a political advisor to Yeltsin, was one of the first to try to combine a liberal Russia with the assertion of a great power foreign identity, taking a hard line against Ukraine concerning the Black Sea Fleet stationed in Sevastopol, and indeed suggesting that following a referendum Crimea, in which the majority of the population are ethnic Russians, could become an independent state and later reunite with Russia.[33] Vladimir Lukin, one of the founders of the liberal Yabloko party and in the mid-1990s ambassador to the USA before returning to Moscow and chairing the Duma's foreign affairs committee and then becoming human rights ombudsman, was another liberal for whom relations with Ukraine became crucial. He fought long and hard against the signing of a Russo–Ukrainian treaty that hardened the existing borders. The mayor of Moscow, Luzhkov, also expressed hard-line views about the status of Sevastopol, insisting that it was a Russian city.[34] The CPRF and a whole raft of nationalist groupings expressed similar sentiments, although in much harsher terms.

Although Putin inherited this strong liberal statist tradition, there are some crucial differences. First, Putin has no time for Eurasianism in any but the mildest form. As a Petersburger, Putin has been consistently a Westerniser and repudiated any idea of Russia as a balance holder between East and West, or as a separate civilisation distinct from that found in the West. As far as Putin is concerned, Russia is part of the West, and that is the end of the story. He recognises, of course, that Russia has vital interests in Asia, but these are strategic and economic rather than civilisational. Second, Putin unequivocally accepted the existing post-Soviet territorial settlement, and thus repudiated any hopes that the 'red-brown' nationalists had of Russia becoming a revisionist power seeking to challenge the territorial integrity of neighbouring states. This was seen at its starkest in Putin's relations with Ukraine, where Russian policy sought active engagement, but with at best mixed results. Putin resisted repeated calls for the incorporation of Abkhazia and South Ossetia, although warned that the situation would change if Kosovo's independence was recognised. Third, Putin was unequivocally liberal in his patriotism, accepting the market and rejecting demands for protectionism or any number of models of autarchic development. Fourth, Putin was well aware that in a multiethnic country such as Russia there was an overriding need to preserve interethnic peace and that 'manifestations of xenophobia and crime inspired by interethnic enmity' were 'absolutely inadmissible and the authorities should react to it resolutely'. Anything else could threaten the integrity of the state.[35] Putin was a civic nation builder in which the various ethnic nations – including the Russian, Tatar and others – would be able to pursue their own cultural identities as long as this did not come into conflict with the provisions of the constitution and the political nation that it represented. Putin, in short, espoused a new type of inclusive patriotism, in which pluriculturalism was balanced by an implicit assumption that ethnic Russians were the state building nation.

In the eyes of patriots, Yeltsin's acceptance of a smaller Russia was tarnished by his responsibility for the disintegration of the USSR. Putin was unsullied in this respect, and dealt with the issue in the spirit of sentimental realism. Putin insisted that 'He who does not regret the break-up of the Soviet Union has no heart; he who wants to revive it in its previous form has no head'.[36] Many in Russia, however, still based their platforms on reunification, if only of the Slavic part of the old Union. This was particularly the case with the leader of the Communists, Zyuganov. Gleb Pavovsky in 2000 argued that 'Zyuganov is the leader of an opposition that simply does not want to recognise Russia or live there', with his campaign focused on a non-existent USSR, whereas the majority of the voters 'have moved to a national Russia'.[37] Under Putin the 'what country are we living in?' question was resolved: the answer was Russia – no more and no less. Putin saw the former Soviet states as a reservoir from which Russia could draw people to satisfy its economic needs and to compensate for its demographic problems, with a low birth rate and high mortality rates, especially for men, but not as a sphere for geopolitical reintegration. As Putin noted, 'these are people with our mentality for whom Russian is practically a native language and who have practically the same cultural and, quite often, the same religious background'.[38] He gave no indication, however, of any desire to renew Russian imperial adventures in the region, although he was robust in defending what he perceived to be Russia's interests.

Organised religion and the state

The 2002 census identified 182 different peoples (nations) living on the territory of Russia. However, the census did not ask a specific question about religious affiliation, and thus we can only guess and use historical data to establish the numbers professing and practising allegiance to any particular faith. The legislation regulating the life of organised churches of September 1997 identified four 'historical' religions in Russia: Orthodoxy, Islam, Buddhism and Judaism. Dozens of others existed, some of which like various militant Protestant groups conducted active proselytising work, much to the alarm of the official Orthodox hierarchy. Others, notably the Roman Catholic Church, have long existed in Russia with a community numbering over half a million, but Rome and its acolytes are regarded with suspicion verging on paranoia by the leadership of the Russian Orthodox Church (ROC). The Pope's creation in February 2002 of four new dioceses in Russia enraged Patriarch Aleksii II, who responded by blocking John Paul II's visit. This hostility has deep historical roots, reaching back as far as the division in 395 of the Roman empire into a Western part based in Rome and an Eastern empire rooted in Constantinople (Istanbul today). The schism between the two faiths, Catholicism and Orthodoxy, was formalised in 1054, and since then very different traditions of religiosity, attitudes towards rationality and faith, have taken root. Orthodox suspicion towards Catholicism is perhaps best reflected in the views of Fedor Dostoevsky who, like the Slavophiles with whom he was associated, argued that Catholicism's acceptance of secular rationality had opened the way to the Reformation and the decline of spirituality in the West.[39]

Putin was comfortable dealing with centralised hierarchies, and its absence in Islam complicated relations with the state and Putin personally: 'The demonstrative friendship with one Moslem spiritual leader would automatically create not only a group of Islamic friends, but also a weighty opposition'.[40] Orthodoxy has a quite exceptional role to play in the development of Russian national identity and the very idea of Russianness. In the last years of the Soviet period and in the early post-communist years, Aleksii II and other clerics had been elected to the Soviet and Russian parliaments, but by 1993 they had withdrawn from active campaigning and clerics were forbidden from running for office. The church refused to endorse particular candidates or specific party platforms.[41] This withdrawal from partisan activity was one factor allowing the church to retain a high degree of trust as a social institution.[42] The ROC remains torn between modernisers and hard-line anti-Westernists. The dominance of the ROC today is reminiscent of that enjoyed by the Church of England, although the formal separation of church and state stipulated by the 1993 constitution precludes the ROC becoming the established church. Article 14.1 states that 'The Russian Federation is a secular state. No religion may be established as the state religion or a compulsory religion', while Article 14.2 insists that 'Religious associations are separated from the state and are equal before the law'. Although ROC has retreated from direct participation in political life, it seeks to present itself as the non-partisan keeper of the nation's spiritual values.

Although not the state religion, Orthodoxy was certainly for Putin the religion of the state. Putin's father had been an active communist, but he had tolerated his wife's religious belief. Putin imbibed his Orthodox faith from his mother and remains a committed believer, although he strove hard to avoid alienating the many other faiths in the country. In his public activities Putin stressed Russia's religious pluralism, but in his private life he attends Orthodox services and, according to his wife Lyudmila, 'He is a very good man who lives according to Christian principles'.[43] He has a 'spiritual father' (*dukhovnyi otets*), apparently the deputy head of the Sretensky Monastry (just round the corner from the Lubyanka) archimandrite Tikhon.[44] On a visit to the Vaalam monastery in Lake Ladoga in August 2001 Putin remarked that without Orthodoxy there would be no Russia. This certainly is Tikhon's belief. He is no liberal, insisting that it was a false choice to believe that the only alternatives facing Russia were 'the horrors of Isamic terrorism and the no less terrible power of those who seek to achieve total American hegemony'. Tikhon is a member of the editorial board of the journal *Russkii dom* (*Russian House*), which is associated with a television programme of that name, funded by the banker Sergei Pugachev.[45] Putin enjoyed a particularly close relationship with the Patriarch, and on numerous occasions sought his advice.[46] For many Russians the church is the source of values and traditions around which a post-communist national identity could be constructed. This was reflected in Putin's message of congratulations to Aleksii II on the tenth anniversary of his enthronement in 2000: 'The church is recovering its traditional mission as a key force in promoting social stability and moral unity around general priorities of justice, patriotism, good works, constructive labour and family values'.[47] The Orthodox Church, moreover, was also a symbol of the unity of the East Slavs, and thus reflected the larger identity of Rus' as the people of Eurasia divided by the borders that had sprung up since 1991. The church helped in part to fill the vacuum left by the demise of the Communist Party and its version of the ideology of Marxism–Leninism, and thus acted as a source of values around which much of the nation could unite. However, the quasi-official role played by the Orthodox Church and its close relationship with the state under Putin suggested to many that it could act as a new instrument of state ideological control.[48]

Chechnya: tombstone or crucible of Russian power?

The year 1991 was for the Soviet Union what Robert Jackson calls 'the Grotian moment', the reshuffling of the title to sovereignty.[49] Bartkus has theorised these liminal periods in the constitution of states as the 'opportune moment' when the weakening of central government (or foreign intervention) raises the prospects for success of a bid for independence.[50] In both the former USSR and Yugoslavia, however, the Grotian moment was limited to existing union republics, and, despite repeated wars, the new borders have been upheld. The 1993 Russian constitution does not recognise the right of secession for any of its units. The Chechen secession bid was an attempt to expand the Grotian consensus without a basis in just cause, something that distinguishes this case from that of Kosovo, whose putative secession is clearly grounded in the remedial right to put an end to the persistent violation of human rights.[51] International law and practice does not recognise the unilateral right to secession under whatever conditions and through any procedure, however democratic (like a referendum). International law also stresses that however just a war (*jus ad bellum*) it should be fought in a just way (*jus in bello*). Putin's war in Chechnya may well have been a just war, but too often it was fought unjustly.[52]

Putin's war

The Chechen case demonstrates just how high the costs of separatism and partition through wars of secession can be.[53] Although Chechen separatists see the contemporary conflict through the prism of a three-hundred-year struggle against Russia colonialism,[54] there is a considerable literature demonstrating that ethnic conflicts are seldom resolved by partitioning states.[55] The problem, of course, is one of definition. Is Russia (like France over Algeria) in the position of an imperial state that will sooner or later have to accept the loss of colonial possessions, once the unacceptably high cost of attempting to hold is understood? Or is Russia faced with a situation where its very national existence and democratic achievements are under threat by an armed insurgency and, like the Union forces in the American Civil War, cannot but fight the war to a victorious conclusion? Henry E. Hale argued that 'Chechnya is a localized issue focused around the perceived threat of terrorism, not a symptom of naked Russian aggression'.[56] Both wars were relatively insulated from the mainstream of Russian political life and exerted remarkably little influence on it.[57]

Rather than Chechnya, in Lieven's words, becoming the tombstone of Russian power,[58] for a time in late 1999 (as we saw in Chapter 1) Chechnya served as the crucible for the restoration of that power. As Trenin and Malashenko put it, 'Owing equally to the government's weakness and corruptibility, Russia failed to respond to the Chechen challenge, thus sending a clear message to neighbouring countries and beyond that a power vacuum existed inside Russia from the Caucasus to the Kremlin'.[59] In his *Millennium Manifesto* Putin insisted that Chechnya was 'where the future of Russia is being decided'. In a television statement on 23 January 2000 he noted: 'In my opinion, the active public support for our actions in the Caucasus is due not only to a sense of hurt national identity but also to a vague feeling ... that the state has become weak. And it ought to be strong'.[60] For Putin the war in Chechnya was about preventing the disintegration of Russia, and the associated horrors that would entail.[61] The second Chechen war provided Putin's springboard to the presidency; but of far greater significance was the sense that Russia, too, had interests, and someone was now willing to take responsibility for defending them.

The two Chechen invasions of Dagestan in August 1999 followed by the spate of apartment bombings, together with sustained hostage taking and the effective collapse of civil order in Chechnya, provided Russia with the *casus belli* for a renewed military intervention in September 1999. Fear that the Chechen zone of insecurity would move up the Volga and spread to other republics and result in the Yugoslavisation of Russia provoked the second war. An 'enclave of banditry', to use Putin's term, was established in Chechnya that threatened not only its immediate neighbours but also the trans-Caspian republics of Kyrgyzstan and Uzbekistan.[62] As far as Putin was concerned,

[T]he essence of the situation in the Caucasus and Chechnya was a continuation of the collapse of the USSR. It was clear that we had to put an end to it at some point ... My evaluation of the situation in

August [1999] when the bandits attacked Dagestan was that if we don't stop it immediately, Russia as a state in its current form would no longer exist. Then we were talking about stopping the dissolution of the country. I acted assuming it would cost me my political career. This was the minimum price that I was prepared to pay.[63]

The interviewer followed up with the following intriguing question: 'Does the fact that Lenin gave Finland independence many decades ago give you an allergic reaction? Is Chechnya's secession possible in principle'? To which Putin answered:

It is possible, but the issue is not secession. ... Chechnya will not stop with its own independence. It will be used as a staging ground for a further attack on Russia ... Why? In order to protect Chechen independence? Of course not. The purpose will be to grab more territory. They would overwhelm Dagestan. Then the whole Caucasus – Dagestan, Ingushetia, and then up along the Volga – Bashkortostan, Tatarstan, following this direction into the depths of the country ... When I started to compare the scale of the possible tragedy with what we have there now, I had no doubt that we should act as we are acting, maybe even more firmly.[64]

Putin thus viewed the Chechen issue in stark terms. The Khasavyurt Accord of 31 August 1996, as we saw in Chapter 1, granted Chechnya *de facto* independence following the war of 1994–6, and contained a 'postponed status' clause that delayed the final settlement of the republic's status for five years. The leader of the Chechen insurgents, Aslan Maskhadov, had been elected president for a five-year term on 27 January 1997, and even after his term formally expired in early 2002 he remained the leader of the Chechen national movement. The peace agreement between Russia and Chechnya of 12 May 1997, in which both sides forever renounced war, did little to allow stable government in the republic. Maskhadov's authority was challenged by militant field commanders, especially those who had assumed militant Islamic identities (like Shamil Basaev and Khattab, who had also fought in Afghanistan). Putin was particularly scathing about this period:

During the criminal regime's rule [1996–9], local people, their own fellow citizens, were being shot publicly in squares. Not to mention the atrocities committed against representatives of federal services, servicemen, and so on. It was a criminal regime that was elected when bandits and international terrorists held people at gunpoint. We know full well what followed. The next day they lost control of the republic. Totally different people emerged behind their backs, seeking and trying to use Chechen hands to achieve aims that had nothing to do with the interests of the Chechen people – the creation of the notorious caliphate that we have already talked about here. Those were the aims set by the Maskhadov regime. Otherwise, there would have been no attack on Dagestan.[65]

Hailed at the time as a welcome relief to war, the Khasavyurt Accord became associated with a betrayal of national interests and the establishment of a permanent zone of conflict.

Putin's thinking remained torn between two concerns: security and sovereignty. Even before the 11 September 2001 attacks, security (the defeat of terrorism) tended to predominate over sovereignty issues (the defence of the territorial integrity of the Russian Federation), but the latter concern was never far from the surface. Putin expressed Moscow's view at the January 2000 CIS summit in Moscow when he defended the territorial integrity of states, as opposed to the principle of national self-determination, in the resolution of problems in the Caucasus.[66] Such a stance suited both Georgia, with a challenge to its territorial integrity from Abkhazia and South Ossetia and Azerbaijan, in danger of losing control permanently over Nagorno-Karabakh. However, Moscow's closest strategic ally in the region was Armenia, a country that could not but be dismayed by such an inflexible stance as it sought to achieve the reunification of Nagorno-Karabakh with Armenia. The Russian notion advanced between 1996–9 of 'common-states' in the cases of Georgia-Abkhazia, Azerbaijan-Karabakh and Moldova-Transdniester was now shelved. Putin later that year told top military officials that 'Chechnya's formal status is not so important today. What is important is that this territory should never be used by anybody as a springboard to attack the Russian Federation', but it appears clear that Putin himself did not consider Chechen independence a realistic option.[67]

After 9/11 Putin was quick to point out the alleged connections between Osama bin Laden and the rebels in Chechnya, identifying radical Muslim fundamentalism as the core threat to the West. Putin declared that Russia and the United States now had a 'common foe' and agreed to assist the USA in the 'war on terror'. He added the reservation that the degree of co-operation 'will directly depend on the general level and quality of our relations with these countries and on mutual understanding in the sphere of fighting international terrorism', suggesting that co-operation was dependent on toning down criticism of the conduct of the Russian campaign in Chechnya.[68] After 11 September, Russia became part of the international 'coalition of the willing', and criticism of the way that Russia conducted the campaign in Chechnya became more muted. Putin had appointed his close ally Sergei Ivanov as Russia's first civilian defence minister, and he now gave the military considerable leeway in setting the agenda in the Caucasus, allowing them to avenge what they saw as the humiliating defeat represented by Khasavyurt.

Putin distinguished between the first war, which he linked to 'Russia's imperialist ambitions and attempts to rein in the territories it controls', and the second, which he characterised as an 'anti-terrorist operation'.[69] Others, however, like former presidential advisor Emil Pain, characterise Russia's entire policy as 'colonial wars'.[70] Protracted warfare in Chechnya degraded the quality of Russian political and social life, especially since there was a tendency to dehumanise the Chechen insurgents, the Chechens as a people and Russian servicemen. By the time Grozny was recaptured in February 2000, Russian losses were officially stated to be 1,458 servicemen killed and 4,495 wounded since the start of military operations in the North Caucasus on 2 August 1999,[71] a figure that had risen to 4,572 deaths and 15,549 wounded by June 2003.[72] In the first two years of war some 65,000 Russian soldiers had been turned into cripples, about the same number as in the ten years of the Soviet conflict in Afghanistan.[73] According to official sources, some 13,500 insurgents were killed in that time. Purely military losses between 1991 and January 2006 were 3,501 killed and 32 disappeared without trace.[74] Civilian losses remain a matter of controversy, but were certainly no fewer that 30,000–40,000, compounded by Maskhadov's decree that all those working to restore the civil infrastructure and civic administration were to be killed, a position that he later modified when he stated that the insurgents would 'no longer commit terrorist acts against civilians'.[75] Despite certain military successes, the lack of a clear Kremlin strategy in the second war led many to adopt the term 'victorious defeat' to describe the stalemate.[76] Another report noted wryly that 'Russia has won. The war continues'.[77]

A confidential report sent to the Kremlin in March 2003 by the pro-Moscow Chechen administration, headed since 12 June 2000 by Akhmad Kadyrov, admitted that at least 1,314 civilians had been murdered by the authorities in 2002.[78] The killing of Malika Umazheva, a courageous human rights activist and the former head of Alkhan Kala village, stands out for its blatant contempt of basic norms of human decency. She was abducted by federal forces on 29 November 2002 and was soon found dead. The only trial of a senior Russian officer in either of the Chechen wars was against Colonel Yury Budanov, accused of raping and murdering a Chechen girl, Elza Kungaeva, in 2000. Against all the evidence, he was acquitted on the grounds of diminished mental responsibility on 31 December 2002, but after a retrial was sentenced to ten years in prison on 27 July 2003. The case is comparable to that of Lieutenant William Calley, whose platoon on 16 March 1968 raped and murdered 400 Vietnamese civilians in My Lai. After a long cover-up, the case finally came to court, but his sentence of life imprisonment with hard labour was soon commuted to 20 then ten years, before being released by President Richard Nixon. All other parties to the massacre were acquitted, and most of the 300,000 letters sent to the White House concerning the case supported Calley. Public opinion in both Russia and America sought to license the atrocities by the heat of war.

There were attempts by the Russian government and the commanders in the field to humanise the war. On 27 March 2002, for example, the commander of Russian forces in Chechnya, Colonel General Vladimir Moltenskoi, issued order No. 80 that soldiers involved in operations, especially 'cleansing' ones (*zachistki*), should not wear masks and be able to be held responsible for their actions. All the evidence suggests that the order was ignored.[79] Even the deputy from Chechnya to the State Duma, retired MVD general Aslambek Aslakhanov, and Kadyrov had difficulty gaining entry to blockaded villages (for example, Mesker-Yurt). Once in, Aslakhanov faced 'a collective moan' about the beatings civilians had endured, and only quick action managed to retrieve young people from an ambulance provided by the military, which in all probability would have ended with their deaths so as to eliminate witnesses. In an interview Aslakhanov was asked:

> How is one to explain the extreme cruelty exhibited by the federal forces towards the Chechen civilians? [He responded] 'Not one of the leaders of the MVD, the FSB, or the Ministry of Justice has been held responsible for the conducting of cleansing operations in Starye and Novye Atagi, Kurchaloi, Tsatsan-Yurt, Assinskaya, Argun and Chiri-Yurt, where young people disappeared and they later found their mutilated bodies ... They are lying! They are lying to the president, lying to the State Duma, to the Council of Federation, to the government, and to their ministers. They are lying to the citizens of the Russian Federation, claiming that stabilisation is occurring. The result of so-called cleansing operations is that [Chechen] pupils in schools are now leaving for the forests in order to take revenge for their relatives who suffered during the special operations.[80]

Despite attempts to restore civilian administration led by Chechens, the heavy-handed *zachistki* alienated even pro-Moscow Chechens.[81]

Squaring the circle

Russia had a strong case to make about the necessity of the war, in effect dealing with an armed uprising that did not conform to any extant theory of secession and which, for good measure, invaded its neighbours.[82] Public opinion in Russia at first remained supportive of the campaign (rising to an astonishing 70 per cent by early March 2000), angered that the Chechen insurgents had taken over 1,500 individual hostages in their years of effective independence and now tried to take the 146-million strong population of Russia as a collective hostage in the court of world public opinion. Putin compared the threat as comparable to times when the very existence of the Russian state was under threat. The national unity engendered by what was perceived as a just war against nationalist expansionism, terrorism and aggressive fundamentalism, however, was both precarious and dangerous. By 2002 public opinion had shifted towards support for a negotiated settlement,[83] and by late 2005 support for Putin's policy in Chechnya had fallen to only 4 per cent, with 58 per cent of the view that despite official declarations to the contrary, the war was continuing. Only 21 per cent supported the continuation of military operations, while 69 per cent favoured peace negotiations.[84] The danger came from the boost the war gave to militant Russian nationalism and racist extremism.

While there may have been general acknowledgement in the early years that the Chechen problem required decisive action, the stubborn resistance of the insurgents, the continued evidence of military brutality and corruption, severe abuses of the human rights of Chechen civilians, all fed a growing revulsion. Despite the presence of some 80,000 troops in the republic even basic security could not be guaranteed. Bombs exploded and officials were killed in Dagestan, Russian military helicopters were downed, police stations bombed, the government headquarters in Grozny was attacked by bomb-laden lorries killing 72 officials on 27 December 2002, and the war was taken to Moscow with the Dubrovka siege in October 2002, and children taken hostage in Beslan in September 2004. The counter-terrorism operation may have been over in Chechnya, but terrorism continued. Moscow's policy of 'Chechenising' local administration added another layer of hostility and resentment, with tensions between local and federal political actors, and transformed the conflict into the bitterest form of all – civil war.

Although the military tried to gain control of the security agenda in the region, seeking not only operational but also strategic discretion, Putin ensured that presidential policy was not 'captured' by any particular group. In May 2002 the system of rotation of appointments in the interior ministry was reintroduced, designed to ensure that local police chiefs remained independent of regional bosses. The post of commander-in-chief of the ground forces, abolished in 1998, was now restored and the commanders of the military districts were to report to him, while he in turn answered directly to the defence minister rather than to General Staff.[85] The head of the North Caucasus Military District, General-Colonel Gennady Troshev, was one of the first victims of the policy intended to reassert civilian control over the military, and the powers of the defence ministry over the more conservative General Staff. Troshev had been born in Grozny and represented a rare breed of relatively effective professional and not corrupt soldiers.[86] He was also dedicated to Chechnya in his own way, and when ordered in December 2002 to take up a new appointment as part of the rotation of military-district commanders, he refused on the grounds that the Chechen people needed him – and the next day (18 December) he was fired. The incident confirmed that Russia's Chechnya policy was fragmented between numerous agencies and individuals, both in Moscow and in the republic itself, with military affairs alone handled by some five bodies.[87] The civilian bodies were no less fragmented. Troshev's dismissal, however, was a clear signal that the day of the independent general in Russia was over.

In early 2003 Putin declared that the 'counter-terrorist operation' was over, and in his press conference of 31 January 2006 he once again stated 'I think that it is possible to talk about the end of the counter-terrorist operation in Chechnya'.[88] Putin would have liked to declare victory and leave, but it was not so easy, especially since, as he recognised, the war had spread to large parts of the North Caucasus. The Russian presidential spokesman on the issue, Sergei Yastrzhembsky, argued in May 2001 that the conflict in Chechnya was likely to last for years, noting that there were some thirty low-intensity conflicts in the world, and Chechnya would probably join their number.[89] Few avenues were available for the political regulation of the conflict, and while Russia would not lose the war, it was unclear what a 'victory' would look like. The conflict continued to poison Russian politics and threatened to inhibit Russia's further development as a democracy. As Furman put it, Moscow's approach to both Chechnya and the Chechens left him unable to 'imagine a peaceful integration of Chechens into Russian society'. His conclusion was that Russian democracy was impossible without Chechen independence.[90]

With no acceptable political solution in sight, the conflict rumbled on throughout Putin's presidency, undermining his international stature, dividing society, brutalising domestic policy, and inflaming other conflicts in the Caucasus. There were desultory attempts to find a negotiated settlement, but as far as Moscow was concerned it was not clear with whom to negotiate. In July 2002, as the influence of the 'Arabs' in the Chechen secession struggle weakened, Maskhadov and Basaev reforged their alliance, while at the same time Kazbek Makhashev was named as Maskhadov's representative for discussions with Moscow.[91] Faced by a military leadership that considered the Khasavyurt agreement a betrayal and 'stab in the back', Putin's own room for manoeuvre was severely circumscribed. Although the war slipped far down the list of popular priorities, polls showed growing support for negotiations with the rebels, rising to 60 per cent in January 2003 while only 30 per cent favoured continued military operations.[92]

In his question and answer session with the Russian people on 19 December 2002 Putin insisted that 'a bad peace is always better than a good war',[93] but there appeared to be little movement in this direction. Putin refused to countenance the imposition of a state of emergency, which would have suspended even the semblance of political normality in the country. Primakov outlined a stage-by-stage approach to peace: a ceasefire followed by roundtable talks with all parties to find some acceptable solution.[94] The former speaker of the Russian Supreme Soviet, Ruslan Khasbulatov, an ethnic Chechen, tried to act as an 'honest broker', meeting with Maskhadov's representative Akhmed Zakaev in Istanbul. Their peace plan proposed that Chechnya would be granted a 'special status' whereby it would enjoy a high degree of domestic and foreign autonomy and would not be a subject of Russia, but would come under Russian legislation on a number of questions. Maskhadov approved of the plan, but it would require the support of international organisations like the OSCE to secure its implementation. In the meantime, the pro-Moscow administration headed by Kadyrov pushed ahead with its own plans for a new constitution for the republic. The search for a negotiated solution was imperilled (perhaps deliberately) by the Dubrovka events of October 2002. The Kremlin toughened its stance against negotiations, especially since Maskhadov had been slow publicly to condemn the action. There remains the suspicion that he condoned the attack as a way of bolstering his authority with the warlords, a strategy that had proved tragically futile (because it ultimately provoked the second war) in the inter-*bellum* period of 1996–9, and was no more successful now.

Chechenisation

Moscow instead pushed ahead with the constitutional option that would provide the basis, it was hoped, on which new legitimate authorities could be constructed. The draft was adopted on 11 December 2002 by a Congress of the Chechen Peoples in Gudermes, and on the following day Putin approved the holding of the referendum and the election law for the republic's new institutions, including the presidency, later in the year. The October 2002 census allegedly found a population of over a million in the republic, whereas the true figure was unlikely to be any more than half a million. These widely diverging figures hardly inspired confidence that the referendum would come up with an accurate reflection of popular feelings. In his October 2002 session Putin defended the Chechenisation option:

> To move away from the situation we have today, there is no question that we have to gradually hand over the reins of power completely to the Chechen people. It's not possible to do this without a legal basis, without a constitution. Without this, it would not be possible to elect legitimate bodies of power, a president, a parliament. If we don't do this, we will not be able to get away from what we have today. The process is difficult, but without these political processes, it is just not possible to put the situation in Chechnya on a legitimate footing, and subsequently bring the economic and social situation back to normal.[95]

The draft of the new constitution, proposed by the pro-Moscow administration, was released (in Russian) in January 2003, with the referendum on its adoption held in the republic on 23 March. The Russian authorities did everything to stimulate participation in the vote, with Putin on 16 March appealing on television for the population of Chechnya to participate, promising in the event of the document being adopted a special bilateral treaty that would grant Chechnya 'broad autonomy'. The constitution contained many concessions that Putin had repudiated in relations with other regions, also promising 'wide autonomy' and embracing once again the principle of a bilateral treaty. On 23 March voters were presented with three questions: to approve the new constitution; accept a draft law on the election of the president; and a draft law on the election of parliament. An extraordinary

89.48 per cent of the war-torn republic's adult population allegedly took part, with 95.97 per cent approving the constitution, 95.4 backing the presidential election law and 96.05 supporting the draft law on parliamentary elections. In his address to the nation in May, Putin praised the result:

> Today I especially thank the Chechen people, for their courage, for the fact that they did not allow themselves to be intimidated and do not allow themselves to be intimidated now, for their wisdom, ever-present in ordinary people who instinctively know what's right and wrong. People in Chechnya had a heartfelt awareness of their responsibility and human interest. Finally, the referendum there showed that the Chechen people legitimately regard themselves as an inseparable part of a unified Russian multinational people.[96]

The road was now open for the election of a new president on 5 October 2003. The election of Akhmad Kadyrov was a foregone conclusion since the main alternatives were not admitted to the ballot in one way or another. Kadyrov's assassination in a bomb blast on 9 May 2004 did not derail Putin's 'Chechenisation' plans, and in new elections on 29 August 2004 the former Chechen minister of the interior, Alu Alkhanov, was elected. Two days later militants captured School No. 1 in Beslan. Elections to the republic's parliament, held on 27 November 2005, were the final stage in Putin's plans to restore a semblance of normality to Chechnya. Managed by the local pro-Russian administration, the results were a surprise to no one. United Russia took nearly 70 per cent of the vote, while the Communists gained what in the circumstances was an impressive 12 per cent, with the liberals and Eurasians receiving about 10 per cent each. The right to vote of some 16,000 Russian soldiers stationed in the republic further distorted the result. As Putin put it in his 31 January 2006 press conference, the elections represented 'the completion of the process of creating the organs of state power in the Chechen Republic'.[97]

The Kremlin assisted and supported the rise of Ramzan Kadyrov to effective power in the republic, even though his rule was based on systematised violence and systematised corruption. Since his father's death in May 2004 Kadyrov junior had consolidated his hold on power in the republic through the use of a semi-independent 5,000-strong militia force, which terrorised his opponents and subordinated his allies. He seized control of financial flows in the republic, and exercised an extensive patronage network focused on the payment of tribute to himself, recouped by the imposition of charges on others. The Chechenisation policy appeared to legitimate the use of unlawful force by legitimate authorities. The number of killings and disappearances declined, but the atmosphere of fear and intimidation remained. The Chechen constitution stipulates a minimum age of 30 for the presidency, but with his thirtieth birthday on 5 October 2006 Kadyrov, by then prime minister, became a real contender for the highest office in the republic. There were clear tensions with Alkhanov, especially over the management of the oil industry and other economic assets, while Kadyrov also came into conflict with other pro-Russian commanders in the republic, notably the field commander Sulim Yamadaev. Russian security services, in particular the GRU (military intelligence), had major doubts about Kadyrov's suitability as leader of Chechnya and were notoriously hostile to the transfer of full authority to Chechens. It is for this reason that Moscow agreed to only a partial Chechenisation of affairs in the republic, with the appointment of Russians to key posts in the MVD and other government agencies. The MVD, headed by Rashid Nurgaliev, was granted chief responsibility for security in the North Caucasus, thus reducing interagency confusion. By 2008 conscripts were to be replaced in their entirety by contract service people. In the event, on 2 March 2007 Kadyrov was formally confirmed as president of the republic, and Alkhanov was deployed to work elsewhere.

Jihad or nationalism?

The insurgency was far from over. According to Basaev, a grand council of field commanders met in Chechnya in 2002 and approved the extension of the war to the rest of the North Caucasus.[98] There is no evidence that Maskhadov repudiated this strategy, even though on 14 January 2005 he tried to impose a unilateral ceasefire to give peace negotiations a chance, but this was probably far too little far too late.[99] In an interview at this time, Maskhadov argued that 'I'm deeply convinced that Putin is far from reality about what is really going on in Chechnya today', arguing that the security forces were feeding him false information, and suggested that everything could be resolved if he and Putin were to meet face-to-face: 'If we are able to open the eyes of our opponents, the Russian leaders, peace can be established'.[100] This was not to be, and Maskhadov was assassinated by Russian forces on 8 March 2005.

  Leadership of the insurgent forces passed to Abdul-Khalim Sadulaev. Whereas in his last months Maskhadov had sought to find a route towards negotiations, Sadulaev, the self-declared president of the Chechen republic of Ichkeria, had no interest in peace talks other than those that would lead to the recognition of Chechen independence. He broadened the war to encompass the whole of the North Caucasus, and on 2 May 2005 he divided the western 'front' into seven sectors (Ingushetia, North Ossetia, Kabardino-Balkaria, Stavropol *krai*, Karachaevo-Cherkessia, Adygeya and Krasnodar) and named commanders of those sectors. He also named new commanders of the eastern 'front' as a whole and of four of its sectors (Gudermes, Argun, Kurchaloi and Grozny).[101] Basaev, the butcher of Beslan, was now brought in as first deputy prime minister. Their aim was to establish an Islamic state in Chechnya and to achieve the 'decolonisation' of the whole North Caucasian region through a 'national liberation struggle'.

The nationalistic state-building rationale for the Chechen insurgency had given way to jihad. In May 2005 the 'North Caucasian front' was established to coordinate insurgent actions, and in November 2005 Sadulaev declared that there would be no peace negotiations with the Russians until 'the Caucasus is freed from the boot of the Russian occupiers'.[102] Thus Maskhadov's death provoked the further radicalisation of the militants and the extension of the insurgency. The original goal of building an independent Chechen state was now subsumed into a broader civilisational war against the corrupt West, with the Russian state, in their view, only its most boorish manifestation.[103] This was the view of the chief ideologist of the North Caucasian jihad, Movladi Udugov, propounded through his Kavkaz Centre website. The attack by over two hundred militants on Nalchik, the capital of Kabardino-Balkaria, on 13 October 2005 was a clear sign of the widening of 'jihad', as was the onset of a creeping civil war in Dagestan.

Federal forces continued to be withdrawn from Chechnya, falling from 80,000 in early 2005 to about 37,000 a year later, with plans for full withdrawal by 2007–8. More regiments with Chechen soldiers were formed, with the Vostok (east) and Zapad (west) battalions joined by the new Sever (north) and Yug (south) regiments in 2006. Interior ministry (MVD) forces, now largely Chechenised, took on more military responsibilities, although the authorities feared insurgent infiltration of the police forces. The authorities scored a number of successes against the militants. Sadulaev was killed on 17 June 2006, and on 9–10 July 2006, on the eve of the G8 summit in St Petersburg, terrorist number one, Shamil Basaev, was finally killed. Leadership of the insurgency passed to the veteran field commander Dokku Umarov, who proved to be an effective guerrilla leader, opening up two new fronts, 'Urals' and 'Volga Region', confirming Putin's fears about the spread of the insurgency. Umarov shifted the emphasis away from jihad back towards national liberation and the secular rhetoric of freedom.

Estimates of the strength of the insurgency vary, but most suggest that there were no more than 800 insurgents in the region, with perhaps no more than 200–300 fighters in Chechnya itself, dug into their mountain retreats.[104] Despite attempts by the authorities to suggest that the war was over, the situation remained far from normal in Chechnya and the region. A report from Dmitry Kozak, the presidential envoy to the Southern Federal District, in Summer 2005 examined the situation in the region as a whole, while a second analysed the deteriorating security situation in Dagestan. The material leaked to the press spoke of corruption, clan-based political and criminal structures, a rampant shadow economy and the widespread alienation of the population from ruling elites, threatening social stability and economic development. The result was the increasing radicalisation and Islamisation of society, at its sharpest in Dagestan where up to 7 per cent of the republic's 2.5 million population were assessed as being ready to take part in armed struggle. The role that Moscow's policies played in exacerbating the situation was not examined. The federal government sought to preserve stability by appointing leaders with whom it could work, and thus the system of appointed regional heads devised after Beslan with the North Caucasus in mind came into its own. The appointment of Mukhu Aliev to succeed the long-serving Magomedali Magomedov in February 2006 was a good example of Moscow's attempt to maintain continuity while trying to achieve renewal at the same time, contradictory goals that would be difficult to reconcile. At the same time, while military forces were being reduced in Chechnya, they were greatly increased in the North Caucasus as a whole, accompanied by frequent military exercises.

Is there a way of squaring the circle: of accommodating Chechen demands while maintaining the integrity of the Russian state? The problem of managing sub-national sovereignty claims remains unresolved, despite the enormous literature on the question. Do you 'appease', and if so, are you on the 'slippery slope' to independence; or can timely concessions, however lopsided these may render a federal system, avert more radical separatist demands?[105] The experience of the Russian Federation in the 1990s is that flexibility and asymmetry can help preserve the system, however untidy it may look to the constitutional lawyer. The problem of Chechnya ultimately, however, can only be resolved in Chechnya itself. Maskhadov's death closed one option, the transformation of guerrilla leader into statesman; but the aspirations of the Chechen people for a dignified and peaceful life based on historical justice, national affirmation, political pluralism and good governance, within the broader framework of some sort of association with Russia, is the only way that the country can find a way out of perpetual war.

Conclusion

Putin sought to restore faith in the symbolical level of governmental action, the belief that the government was acting in the national and popular interest and that this new, smaller, Russian state was a legitimate successor to the various regimes that had preceded it, and thus was worthy of respect, and indeed, of veneration. As far as Putin was concerned, Russia was not a rump USSR but a country with long traditions of its own. But this new entity had still to become a genuine political nation, sharing not only common rules as defined by the constitution but also enjoying a certain affective cohesion. For Putin the political and the emotional levels of nation building went together, and the fact that he represented a clear vision for both was one of the main sources of his enduring popularity. Putin was able to make Russians feel better about themselves. The process was highly contradictory, and with the continuation of the war in Chechnya and a spreading insurgency in the North Caucasus, elements of crisis remained.

9   Russian capitalism

> The trouble is that, from the point of view of its democratic stability and the ability of its political system to correct its own flaws, Russia is a borderline state. It is too rich for a Chinese or Korean-style modernization – and too poor to resist politicians' attempts to embark on that path.
>
> Konstantin Sonin[1]

Putin modified the close and unhealthy relationship between the state and the economy that had developed under Yeltsin. The privileges of various business and commercial structures had turned into a specific type of 'state within the state', with their own media empires, house politicians, television channels and security services. Hellman described developments under Yeltsin as 'partial reform equilibrium', with regional bosses and oligarchs taking advantage of an economy stuck midway between the plan and the market.[2] Although the degree to which a balance had been achieved is unclear, this 'equilibrium' was now upset by the emergence of an activist presidency. The principle of 'equidistance' between business interests and the state had been advanced in the struggle against certain oligarchs, but the result was a change in the nature of Russia's political economy. Putin inherited an economy that was barely emerging from the traumas of rapid marketisation and privatisation, and, while he built on the legacy, a remarkably benign economic environment allowed a new economic model to be applied.

Entering the market

In 1985 the Soviet Union had the world's third largest economy, but in GDP per capita terms it ranked only 43rd. The nadir came in 1998, seven years after the start of the reforms, by which time Russian GDP had fallen by 42 per cent, and some two-fifths of the population fell into poverty. By the time Putin came to the presidency, Russian economic power had slipped well out of the top dozen, and it took 135th place in per capita terms, rubbing shoulders with the likes of Costa Rica. Not only was a large proportion of the population impoverished by the shift to the market, but inequality had greatly risen. By March 2003 Russia could boast of 17 billionaires, most of whom had made their money in the energy sector,[3] while at that time the average monthly income was 3,868 roubles (about $110) with some 30 million people (22 per cent of the population) gaining less than the minimum living wage of just under 2,000 roubles. It was to take eight years of growth before Russian GDP recovered to the 1989 level.

From the Washington to the Moscow consensus

The political economy of Yeltsinism looked both forwards, towards effective liberalisation, the market system and integration into the global economy, and backwards, towards bureaucratic regulation, arbitrary state intervention and insider dealing. Central and regional leaderships exploited opportunities for asset stripping, rent seeking and other pathologies of a semi-marketised economy to maintain their grip on power. The so-called oligarchs had carved up the economy between themselves, and their influence penetrated into the corridors of power. These relations were far from stable and had a disruptive effect on the development of a national market, economic competitiveness and an effective political system. At some point this regionalised and oligopolistic system would have to give way to a more coherent, although not necessarily more liberal, order.

Between 1991 and 1997 the economy shrank each year and inflation was in triple digits, approaching hyper-inflationary levels in 1992. The economy returned to growth in 1997, but the economic crisis of 1998 showed how fragile the recovery had been. The government was unable to collect sufficient taxes to cover its expenditure as the budget deficit rose to about 8 per cent of GDP. Enormous subsidies were still paid to loss-making enterprises and the government had not been able adequately to cut its expenses, even though it collected (although arbitrarily and incompetently) some one-third of GDP in tax revenues, similar to the US level. The government, headed in the final period by the liberal Sergei Kirienko, resorted to issuing a mountain of government bonds (GKOs) at ever-increasing interest rates, until the whole pyramid collapsed in the partial default of 17 August 1998.[4] Numerous banks went under, severely weakening the economic power of the oligarchs, and many foreign financial concerns lost their speculative investments. The threefold devaluation of the rouble that followed allowed the economy to enter a period of recovery. Domestic producers could now compete with imports, and demonstrated that the IMF had earlier been wrong in arguing that the absence of domestic productive capacity would fuel inflation if the value of the rouble fell. In fact, there had been excess capacity, and this was now taken up to allow import substitution (especially in consumer goods and foodstuffs), with imports halving in the year after the crisis. It was clear, as Joseph Stiglitz (chief economist at the World Bank 1997–2000) and others have argued, that the IMF's strategy of artificially maintaining the value of the rouble up to 1998 through loans had not only been mistaken but had saddled Russia with unnecessary debt.[5]

The 1999–2000 elections marked a turning point in that for the first time in a decade there appeared to be a near-universal consensus in support of the development of capitalism, although some sought to add distinctively Russian features. A post-Washington consensus had emerged, what we may call the 'Moscow consensus'. The Washington consensus, the term coined by John Williamson to describe the neo-liberal policies adopted by a number of Latin American states in the mid-1980s, focused on fiscal and monetary discipline, currency convertibility, price and trade liberalisation and the privatisation of state enterprises. These policies were imposed to varying degrees by Russia, India and other countries that had adopted socialist-inclined developmental strategies. Economies were opened up to international influences and domestic monopolies broken up and privatised. In the post-communist countries this was accompanied by falls in economic activity. The Moscow consensus is in some ways reminiscent of the original aims of the IMF as devised by John Maynard Keynes in 1944: 'the promotion and maintenance of high levels of employment and real income and the development of the productive resources of all members as primary objectives of economic policy'.[6] The neo-liberal Washington consensus instead focused on budget cuts, privatisation, deflation, structural adjustment and the like.

The new consensus in Moscow sought to combine both the old and neo-liberal approaches, with continued engagement with international economic and financial organisations, regular debt repayments, the maintenance of macroeconomic stability by necessary fiscal measures, the end of threats to renationalise industry, and the gradual modification of protectionism. The old debate between 'shock-therapy' and 'soft-landing' gradualist approaches gave way to recognition that a necessary condition for economic development was a state strong enough to ensure the rule of law, property rights, transparency in economic transactions such as privatisation, the fostering of improved corporate governance, and the collection of adequate tax revenues to sustain normal functions.[7] More had to be done, as Stanley Fischer put it, to 'enforce the rule of the game for a market economy', including strengthening tax systems, fiscal transparency, government accounting, the legal system and corporate governance.[8] Economic success is most unlikely in conditions of state failure, but the dangers of an overbearing and intrusive state were equally recognised. The nostrums of the market fundamentalists of the earlier period were rejected in recognition of the fact that market failure is just as bad as state failure. Not everything can be left to Adam Smith's increasingly palsied 'invisible hand'; government has an important part to play in the economy.

Thus, even before Putin came to power, the radical rejectionists of market-oriented reform had been marginalised, while neo-liberal free marketers and state dismantlers had been discredited. The 1990s had been a harsh learning experience for the Russian political elite. The great majority understood that any attempt to achieve quick fixes outside the constraints of the emerging consensus would have unpredictable and probably dire consequences. State reconstitution in the sphere of the economy meant establishing institutions strong enough to prevent state capture by countering the power of the oligarchs. The key, as Hedlund puts it, 'is not the performance indicators as such, but the institutional arrangements that determine performance'.[9] The Moscow consensus focused on a more active social policy, a stronger state role in establishing a more friendly investment climate to achieve the recapitalisation of the economy, and a stronger role for the state in managing the economy. This was the programme that Putin was to pursue.

From bust to boom: economic performance under Putin

Putin took power at a time when the country was enjoying a mini boom. Although poverty was widespread, wage arrears endemic and the debt crisis permanent, the economy had returned to growth. The rudiments of a market system had been established, painfully and corruptly but nevertheless there.[10] Putin had not personally been involved at the national level in the grimy process of capitalist transformation, above all privatisation, and thus could enter office with relatively clean hands, although the shadow of corruption charges from his period in St Petersburg, when he was encouraging foreign investment, hung over him. For Putin the transition was over, although he did not deny that much remained to be changed.[11]

Putin's early years were accompanied by extraordinarily favourable economic circumstances, and Russia was a major beneficiary of the commodity price boom of the early twenty-first century. Above all, the price of oil remained high, bringing in enormous revenues and endowing Russia with a large trade surplus. The price of oil rose from its 1998 trough of $12 (in part the reason for Russia's crisis that year) to average $61 in 2006 (see Table 9.1). Every dollar rise in the price of oil provides the Russian exchequer with a $1 billion in extra revenue. By 2006 Russia's oil and gas industries accounted for 35 per cent of Russia's exports, but 55 per cent of export revenues, 40 per cent of gross fixed investment, and, through taxes, 52 per cent of all revenues to the state treasury, up from 25 per cent in 2003. In June 2006 for the first time Russia extracted more oil than Saudi Arabia.[12] By 2006 energy production represented 16–20 per cent of Russian GDP. Although energy exports played a critical role in Putin's mini 'economic miracle', this should not be exaggerated. As one commentator put it, 'It would be wrong ... to state that the growth in the Russian economy in the last seven years reflects nothing else than the boom in oil prices'.[13] A study by the Rand Corporation suggested that increased energy rents accounted for between one-third and two-fifths of economic growth between 1993 and 2005.[14] The substantial rise in real incomes fuelled a consumption boom that in turn generated economic growth.

The paradox of the 'natural resource curse' can be taken too far. Although undoubtedly energy revenues enhanced rent seeking and corruption, and indeed weakened political accountability, the sheer size of the Russian economy means that not all of this can be laid at the energy export door. Putin's prudent fiscal policies sought to keep the 'Dutch disease' at bay, when energy exports bring in large revenues that raise the value of the currency, pricing domestic goods out of export markets and sucking in imports. A 'stabilisation fund' was created on 1 January 2004 to collect export duties and extraction tax from the price of oil exceeding $27 a barrel (initially $20), and reached over $90 billion by the end of 2006, or 8.5 per cent of GDP. It was initially kept in a rouble-denominated account in the Central Bank but in 2006 was fully converted into foreign currencies and invested in AAA-rated government securities. The attempt to 'sterilise' this money and to set up a counter-cyclical fund was a prescription in all good macroeconomic textbooks, but the temptation to draw on the fund for current expenditure was enormous. A World Bank report in April 2006 recommended that Russia invested the energy windfall in stocks and bonds outside Russia, which would provide a source of income for decades ahead, even when the oil price had fallen, and this is what Russia did. As the report noted, 'Future textbooks on Russian history will likely evaluate the economic policies of the current government to a large extent on how effectively it manages the country's growing oil wealth'.[15] There were plans to divide the resources into a reserve fund to cushion the budget with liquid assets, and a future generations fund to be invested in blue-chip companies.

Putin continued Yeltsin's policy of macroeconomic stabilisation, above all of the national currency. Budgets were adopted on time and not only were balanced but showed increasing surpluses. Some successes were evident,

Table 9.1 Economic indicators 1996–2006

Year	GDP change (%)	Inflation (%)	Investment growth (%)	Average Urals Blend oil price (USD per barrel)
1996	−3.6	22	−22.5	20.4
1997	1.4	11	2.0	18.5
1998	−5.3	84	2.6	12.0
1999	6.4	36.5	1.0	17.3
2000	10.0	20.2	17.2	26.9
2001	5.1	18.6	7.5	23.1
2002	4.7	14.0	2.5	23.5
2003	7.3	12.0	12.0	27.3
2004	7.1	11.7	10.8	34.1
2005	6.4	10.9	10.5	50.0
2006	6.9	9.0	13.0	61.0

Sources: GDP growth 1999 and 2004: Troika Dialog, *Russia Economic Monthly*, January 2007 (Rosstat data; some revisions by Rosstat). GDP growth in 2006: the 6.9 is a preliminary figure, from MinEkon in RFE/RL *Newsline*, 29 December 2006. Inflation (for consumer prices, December–December): *OECD Economic Surveys: Russian Federation* (Paris, OECD, 2000), p. 34. Investment growth 1996–8: UN ECE, *Economic Survey of Europe*, No. 2, 2003, Appendix Table B3. With grateful acknowledgement to Phil Hanson.

above all reflected in the fall in inflation (Table 9.1). The thousandfold price rises that had characterised the early phase of Russian capitalism in the early 1990s now gave way to relative price stability, although the still rather high inflation eroded the cheap rouble advantage. The benefits of the currency devaluation of 1998 declined, especially since high energy prices led to an over-valued rouble. At the same time, indicators for investment growth improved, and in the early 2000s investment in fixed capital exceeded GDP growth, but at 19 per cent is still quite low relative to GDP and thus inadequately compensates for the shortfall of the 1990s. The introduction of a 13 per cent flat rate on personal incomes much improved tax collection rates, but while the tax on corporate profits was reduced from 35 to 24 per cent, the abolition of allowances on investment meant a rise in the effective tax rate from 17 to 24 per cent.[16] With economic reform incomplete, the investment capacity of the economy was limited, as was its ability to absorb investment. By late 2006 total accrued foreign investment exceeded $130 billion, with $35 billion in foreign ($10bn of which was FDI) and $10 billion in domestic investment having been attracted in that year alone. There had been a small net capital inflow in 2005, which in 2006 rose to an inflow of over $30 billion.[17] Although market capitalisation in 2005 almost doubled, with stock market capitalisation reaching 80 per cent of GDP by early 2007, labour productivity gains remained stubbornly low. The accelerated shift to the full convertibility of the rouble was one remedy, and on 1 July 2006 the long-awaited change took place, making it cheaper for foreign investors to buy Russian bonds and easier for Russians to invest abroad.

In late 1991 Russian foreign debt was $65.3 billion, but by 1997 had tripled to $110 billion. Debt repayment peaked in 2003, when the country was due to pay $17 billion, but early repayments reduced the total and the anticipated debt repayment shock did not happen. In 1998 debts came to 130 per cent of GDP, some 60 per cent when Putin came to power in 2000, and fell to 35 per cent in 2003 and to the extraordinarily low level of 18 per cent in 2006 – on average in the EU, debt represents 60 per cent of GDP. Windfall energy revenues were used to pay back creditors, which had the additional advantage of being non-inflationary. In 2006 the bulk of the Paris Club debt to creditor states was paid off, and the total foreign debt had fallen to $50 billion by 1 October 2006, saving billions in annual interest payments. Under Putin there was no default of the sort that had hit Russia in 1998, and the country's credit rating rose steadily. Although Putin insisted that the country could not afford to compensate savers in full for the loss of their savings during the inflation of 1989–92, the government did apply a rolling policy of repayments, with the ultimate aim of providing recompense in full. Acknowledgement of this problem and Putin's attempts to resolve it earned him considerable popular respect.

Gold and foreign exchange reserves rose from $12 billion in 2000 to $268 by late 2006, the third largest in the world after China ($875bn) and Japan ($852bn), with Taiwan ($257bn) relegated to fourth place.[18] The economy was growing, inflation was down, investment was up, the mortgage market was developing rapidly, and there were trade and budget surpluses. Indeed, the budget surplus was becoming a problem, rising from 4.3 per cent of GDP in 2004, to 7.4 in 2005, and nearly 9 per cent in 2006. Russian GDP since 1999 has grown 300 per cent in dollar terms, from $196 billion to $765.5 billion in 2005, and, with the high exchange rate, topped the $1 trillion mark in early 2007. However, as German Gref, the minister for economic development and trade, noted, the existing sources of growth, above all rapid development in the oil and gas sector, spare capacity and a relatively low rouble exchange rate, were exhausted and the only means to maintain high growth rates was to increase labour productivity and to diversify the economy.[19]

Although Putin encouraged the development of small and medium-sized enterprises (SMEs), and had simplified the registration procedures to encourage more start-ups, the weight of the bureaucracy and lack of developed financial services meant that the sector only grew slowly. In 2001 SMEs made up 90 per cent of all businesses in Russia, and by 2003 this had increased to 94 per cent. Over the same period their share of total employment rose from 45 to 47 per cent, and market share rose from 40 to 47 per cent.[20] SMEs in Russia account for less of total GDP than is typical for more developed transition economies. Russia had fewer than a million SMEs, whereas Poland had four times as many with only a quarter the population. However, Vladimir Kontorovich has argued that low population density across large parts of the country inhibits small business development, and that the density of small businesses around large conurbations like Moscow and St Petersburg follows Western patterns. Nevertheless, the weight of start-up registration formalities, payments for numerous licences and permits, the burden of arbitrary fire and health inspections, and the ever-present fear of the mafia stifled the development of this sphere. However, in many regions the SME is the predominant source of tax revenues, since large business were registered in the capitals or offshore. There is also a very large individual entrepreneur sector operating in grey markets that contribute much to regional economies, notably in the North Caucasus.

In June 2002 the United States officially declared that Russia was a market economy, in November the EU followed suit, while in October the country was removed from the blacklist of the Financial Action Task Force (FATF), a 29-nation agency established by the OECD in 1989 to fight against money laundering. Slow progress was made in reform of the energy, transport, banking and utility sectors. Attempts to break up Gazprom into separate production and distribution companies were stymied, while reform of the giant electricity company United Energy Systems (UES), headed by the architect of privatisation Anatoly Chubais, was only slowly implemented. The international business community was attracted by the economic and political stability achieved by Putin's administration, accompanied by the decline in inflation and the growth in gold and currency reserves. The privatisation process was now rather more ordered, although uncertainties surrounding the government's list of strategic enterprises in 2006 complicated matters. Federal reform had removed some of the obstacles to investing in the regions, with regional leaders no longer quite so prone to impose themselves as business partners.

Despite Russia's partial political estrangement from Europe, a capitalist Russia as far as economics was concerned is a European country, and this intangible factor, if the conditions are right, favours the extension of the European sphere of prosperity to Russia. The investment, moreover, was not just in the energy sector but included food, timber and other processing industries, communications, chemicals, defence and aviation industries as well as natural resources. At least $45–50 billion left the country each year between 1992–8, but, according to Central Bank data, this had fallen to $10 billion in 2002, but rose thereafter to stabilise at about 5 per cent; but with the introduction of capital convertibility in mid-2006 this was less narrowly defined 'capital flight' than various capital transactions. According to some estimates about 30 per cent of the money illegally expatriated in 1999–2001 returned, and to encourage the process the government considered the reduction of taxes from the usual 13 per cent to an 'amnesty rate' of 5 per cent. An unknown proportion of incoming funds had previously escaped, reflected in the high investment figures from Cyprus. Russia's investment climate under Putin, however, was far from reaching its full potential, with an unclear national investment strategy, concerns about the security of property rights, pervasive corruption by the burgeoning bureaucracy, and reels of red tape produced by inaccessible officials, especially by the customs service.

The number of Russians below the poverty line after the 1998 crash was as high as 64 million, but by early 2002 this had fallen to around 35 million. In 2006 alone the number of people living in poverty halved. For the majority of the population, however, life improved significantly. Eight years of strong economic growth, averaging 6.8 per cent, allowed substantive increases in real wages. Real incomes rose by 11.5 per cent in 2006 alone, while pensions went up by 5.3 per cent. The average monthly wage in late 2006 was 11,000 roubles, or $415 (just under $5,000 per annum), still relatively low but four times higher than when Putin came to power. Per capita GDP at purchasing power parity by late 2006 had risen to $9,902.[21] Wage arrears continued in some sectors as companies sought to become more competitive by diverting resources from their wage fund, but in general arrears continued to fall. Unemployment remained relatively low, and in 2006 out of Russia's total labour force of 74.4 million people (51% of the total population of 142.4 million), 5.6 million were unemployed, or 7.5 per cent. Even though average living standards had risen, official statistics on social stratification had not been released for a number of years.[22] In terms of income inequality Russia was in 97th place (out of 127), between Costa Rica and the Ivory Coast.[23] Putin's long-time economic advisor, Andrei Illarionov, insisted that income differentiation in Russia was not that extreme, with a decile ratio of 14:1

(the income of the top 10% compared to the income of the bottom 10%), whereas in many Latin American countries, notably Brazil, it was 50:1.[24] In 2005 the top 10 per cent accounted for 29.7 per cent of all household income, whereas the bottom 10 per cent shared only 2 per cent.[25] By March 2006 Russia boasted 32 domestic billionaires, together with two more who lived in the UK, Leonard Blavatnik and Roman Abramovich, the latter the highest ranking Russian in the world table, in eleventh place.[26] In 2006 the stock market rose by 65 per cent.

With relatively low housing and utility costs and thus high disposable incomes, these improved material conditions fuelled a consumer boom. Consumer credit developed from almost nothing in 2000 to $40 billion in early 2007, about 5 per cent of GDP, which while relatively low in comparative terms – in Western European it is about ten times higher – represented a huge change for Russia. A middle class comprising some 20 per cent of the population developed, although 70 per cent remained lower middle or working class, while 10 per cent enjoyed an elite life style. Vast new shopping malls were built on the outskirts of the big cities, and Russia leapt up to become the world's twelfth largest consumer market.[27] Although GDP per capita improved significantly, life expectancy stagnated at an average of 65 years, although for men by 2003 it was a shocking 58.8 years (for women 72).[28] The United Nations Development Programme Annual Human Development Index in late 2006 ranked Russia 65th out of 177, with poor scores on access to health and education, although Russia enjoys near 100 per cent literacy. By 2005, according to the World Bank's *World Development Index*, Russian GDP per capita had jumped up the league tables and was now in 54th place (out of 177), between Trinidad and Tobago and Brazil. Average income was in 56th place, between Bulgaria and Lebanon.

The governments of Kasyanov and Fradkov were dominated by economic liberals, and even though the presidential administration was largely staffed with people of a statist bent, in general Putin's administration followed orthodox liberal economic policies. However, the experience of the 1990s, together with earlier socialisation in the Soviet period, left their mark on Putin and a section of his administration. For them the ideology of leaving everything to the market was inadequate, and the call of old-fashioned state interventionism ultimately proved irresistible, although in a mild form. Calls by neo-liberals like Illarionov for a massive cutback in government spending from the 35 per cent of GDP inherited by Putin (which had risen to 36.8 per cent by January 2006) to around 12 per cent were rejected. At the same time, neo-socialists like Sergei Glaz'ev argued that Putin's policies represented little more than the 'planned genocide' of the Russian people, compared to Yeltsin's 'chaotic genocide', and he called for a revolutionary attack against the 'oligarchs', the bureaucracy and massive increases in social spending.[29] Instead, Putin stuck to orthodox economics, and spending on the 'national projects' and the like increased the public sector's share of GDP spending by about only 5 per cent. That was his post-Soviet side, but his neo-Soviet instincts were reflected in his exhortations, like a Communist Party general secretary in the old days, to raise growth rates, as in his 2002 Federal Assembly address, and in the following year he demanded a doubling of GDP within a decade. For GDP to double within a decade an annual average growth rate of at least 7.2 per cent is required. The *dirigiste* wing of his administration called for far more robust state intervention to dominate the 'commanding heights' of the economy, and in the event they succeeded in establishing a type of neo-New Economic Policy, comparable to the NEP of the 1920s where the socialist state dominated large industry in a sea of small-scale capitalist and peasant enterprises. The analogy is far from exact, yet it does suggest some of the flavour of the economic system that had been established by the end of Putin's leadership. Russian capitalism had arrived, but it was of a peculiar sort.

Models of capitalism – state corporatism?

Putin came to power committed to the liberal development of the Russian economy. He enacted a range of pro-business measures, including a cut in the tax rate on corporate profits from 35 to 24 per cent, a reduction in the compulsory repatriation of export earnings from 75 to 50 per cent and a cut the number of business activities requiring government licences from over 500 to 100. However, the system that emerged out of the conversion of the centralised Soviet economy and the wild privatisation of the 1990s was far from being a classical capitalist market system. The economy was dominated by powerful actors, with influential 'oligarchs' at their head.[30] In 1996 the oligarchs had played a crucial role in re-electing Yeltsin, and in 1997 Berezovsky bragged about the power of the '*semibankirshchina*' (rule of the seven banks) and their ownership of half of the Russian economy. A study in 2002 found that the eight largest conglomerates controlled 85 per cent of the shares in the country's top 64 firms.[31] Under Yeltsin the oligarchs became part of the power system, and although Putin tried to maintain 'equidistance' from them, he could not ignore them.[32] The classic question was posed: who rules Russia?[33]

State and market

Russia inherited a dual economy from Yeltsin: a privatised market-oriented sector, and a state-dominated one; whereas under Putin the two converged. Monopolies like Gazprom and UES, in which the state has a large stake, were often forced to act in non-market-oriented ways. In particular, they were unable to charge market rates for their products and were forced on occasion to act as the source of indirect subsidy for whole economic sectors and communities. With domestic prices fixed by the state, the energy companies sought to increase exports where they could charge market rates – but only after they had supplied the domestic market with government-set quotas. For most large energy producers, domestic sales are considered little more than a 'charitable contribution', since export prices were considerably higher.[34] At the same time, the 1,600 defence industry enterprises represented an enormous opportunity, since they remained research intensive and focused on exports (since there was little money for domestic procurement); in 2005 they exported a record $5.2 billion worth of arms. The defence industries were also a threat, since many required extensive modernisation and in some towns were the only industry. Under Putin, state-dominated oil companies, notable Rosneft, became the instrument through which the whole sector was cowed.

In the 1990s the term 'financial–industrial group' (FIG) had been used to describe two things: officially registered combines, usually based on traditional enterprises; and unregistered conglomerates of banks and enterprises. The former had been sponsored in particular by the deputy prime minister Oleg Soskovets as a model of state-sponsored economic development, but in that predatory and pathologically rent-seeking era they had not provided a coherent model for either economic development or rational state–economy relations, and the idea had fallen out of favour. Instead of state-directed integration, powerful economic players emerged out of the fire of Russia's headlong rush to the market. The sealed bid auctions of 1995 and the subsequent investment auctions signalled the rise of these groups. There is no single term used to describe them. Yakov Pappe, for example, uses the term 'industrial–business groups' (IBGs),[35] while Dynkin and Sokolov talk of 'integrated business groups' (also IBGs).[36] We shall use the term 'financial–industrial conglomerates' (FICs), used by Sergei Kolmakov and others,[37] as a way of stressing the concentration of capital that they represented while emphasising the ramshackle nature of many of these emergent corporations. By the late Putin era these FICs had consolidated ownership, often at the expense of minority shareholders, and emerged as modern corporations.

Dynkin and Sokolov note that as a result of historical circumstances there are only two forces capable of acting as agents of modernisation in Russia: the state and big business.[38] The state had played a large role in industrialisation in both the tsarist and Soviet periods, and in the 1990s the baton was passed to big business. Only FICs enjoyed trained and qualified staff, managerial skills, leading technologies and financial resources. In the absence of an effective banking system and capital markets, FICs drew on internal sources of finance or borrowing on bond markets. The top eight independent FICs in 2002 employed 1.76 per cent of Russia's workforce of 64.3 million, yet provided a quarter of the country's exports and a third of the country's tax revenues.[39] Each of these companies had a core enterprise (typically extractive or processing) around which a constellation of businesses turned, including a bank, insurance company, media holding, distribution networks and transport, with a range of support services including hospitals, security, recreation services and even agricultural enterprises. Lukoil's holdings even included the Tchaikovsky Symphony Orchestra. The

FICs thus mimicked the typically Soviet vertically integrated holding, since external supplies could never be guaranteed. Only AFK Sistema in Moscow (part of Luzhkov's fiefdom) was not based on raw materials but on 'post-modern' science and high-tech industries. At their head typically was an 'oligarch' (see Table 9.2), although after the Yukos case they kept a low political profile and should perhaps simply be called 'economic magnates'. These organisations had been formed as part of a process of adaptation to the uncertainty and hazards of the transition to the market, but now took on a stable character. Self-sufficiency is characteristic of enterprises in the early stages of extensive capitalist development, as with American companies in the early decades of the twentieth century (the Ford Motor Company for example had its own rail system and farms, carpentry workshops and newspaper), West European companies in the 1950s, Japanese *keiretsu* in the 1950s and 1960s, and the South Korean *chaebols* up to the present time. The Russian economy continues to be marked by enormous concentration, with the country's 23 largest firms estimated to account for just under a third of Russia's GDP.[40]

The underdevelopment of the banking system and financial mediation services (insurance companies, pension management, investment and venture capital agencies) made entry into the market particularly difficult for new companies and expansion hard for established businesses. Russian banks are notoriously under-capitalised, with only Sberbank entering the *Financial Times*' 2001 list of top 13 banks in Eastern Europe, compared to seven in Poland. Russian banks simply do not have adequate resources to finance business development, to fund new entrepreneurs or to provide the specialist skills for complex financial services for business and product development.[41] Before his assassination on 13 September 2006, Andrei Kozlov, first deputy chair of the Central Bank, had been working to close down questionable banks, shutting 90 out of 1,200, including 33 in the summer of 2006 alone. A more normal customer-oriented banking service only slowly began to emerge. In these conditions, only FICs could accumulate resources for development and investment not only in their own businesses but also through acquisitions, possibly in partnership with Western companies. Under-investment in the Russian economy in the 1990s would cast a long shadow over the potential for Russian economic development, a historic deficit that would require massive foreign direct investment. Although this was rising in the 2000s, it remained minuscule in comparison to what was required and to what competitors like China were receiving.

Foreign investment was deterred by a sad litany of minority shareholders losing their assets. A $480 million deal whereby BP bought 10 per cent of the shares in Potanin's Sidanko in November 1997 turned very sour when Mikhail Fridman's rival TNK took over one of Sidanko's main producing subsidiaries, while at the same time Sidanko was restructured, further reducing the value of the minority stake. After a long struggle, BP's assets were returned in 2001. BP retained a long-term commitment to Russia and

Table 9.2 Russia's 'oligarchs'

Name of 'oligarch'	Name of business	Main activities of the business
Abramov, Alexander	Evrazholding	Coal, steel
Abramovich, Roman	Former head of Sibneft, governor of Chukotka	Energy, politics
Alekperov, Vagit	Lukoil head, Imperial Bank	Energy, banking
Anisimov, Vasily	Metalloinvest	Finances, extractive industries
Aven, Petr	Alfa Group, head	Banking
Baturina, Elena	Inteko	Construction, mainly in Moscow
Berezovsky, Boris	AvtoVaz, Sibneft	Car dealership, energy (in exile in London)
Bogdanov, Vladimir	Surgutneftegaz	Energy
Chubais, Anatoly	United Energy Systems (RAO UES)	Electricity monopoly
Deripaska, Oleg	Russian Aluminium (Rusal), GAZ	Non-ferrous metals, automotive manufacturing
Fedun, Leonid	Lukoil	Energy
Frolov, Alexander	Evrazholding	Coal, steel
Fridman, Mikhail	Alfa-Group head, TNK-BP	Energy and metals
Gusinsky, Vladimir	Most-group	Media, banking (in exile in Israel)
Ivanishvili, Boris	Mikhailovsky mining	Extractive industries
Kerimov, Suleiman	Nafta-Moscow	Energy
Khan, German	Alfa-Group, TNK-BP	Banking, energy
Khodorkovsky, Mikhail	Yukos-Menatep head	Oil, banking, light industry (stripped off assets in 2003–4, currently in prison camp)
Kuzmichev, Alexei	Alfa-Group	Banking
Lebedev, Alexander	National Reserve Corporation	Banking, aviation
Lisin, Vladimir	Novolipetsk steel	Ferrous metals
Makhmudov, Iskander	UGMK (Urals Mining & Metals Company)	Extractive industries
Mamut, Alexander	MDM Bank, former head	Banking
Melnichenko, Andrei	MDM Group	Metals
Mikhelson, Leonid	Novatek	Gas
Mordashev, Alexei	Severstal	Ferrous metals
Nevzlin, Leonid	Yukos	Energy (in exile in Israel)
Popov, Sergei	MDM Group	Metals
Potanin, Vladimir	Interros, Norilsk Nickel, Sidanko	Metals, energy
Prokhorov, Mikhail	Norilsk Nickel	Metals
Rashnikov, Victor	Magnitogorsk metals	Ferrous metals
Rybolovlev, Dmitry	Urakkali	Fertiliser
Shvidler, Yevgeny	Sibneft	Energy
Tariko, Rustam	Russian Standard Bank, Standart Vodka	Finances, drinks

Name of 'oligarch'	Name of business	Main activities of the business
Tsvetkov, Nikolai	Uralsib	Oil, insurance
Usmanov, Alisher	Metalloinvest	Iron and steel
Vainstok, Semyon	Transneft head	State pipeline monopoly
Vekselberg, Viktor	TNK-BP, SUAL Holding	Energy, aluminium
Yevtushenkov, Vladimir	AFK Sistema head	Telecommunications, finance and services
Yorikh, Vladimir	Kuznets Coal, Mechel	Coal, steel
Zyuzin, Igor	Yuzhny Kuzbass, Mechel	Coal, steel

returned to the fray. The $6.75 billion deal struck in February 2003 between Lord Browne of BP Amoco and Fridman's TNK created Russia's third largest oil company, TNK-BP. If the global assets of the two companies are taken together then this was the world's largest, producing 2.57 million barrels per day and with the world's second largest reserves. BP had at last found a new source to replace its ageing fields in Alaska and the North Sea, while TNK, whose corporate governance had greatly improved, was given the seal of Western approval. A spate of mergers in 2003 saw Yukos and Sibneft try to create a company with a combined market capitalisation of $35 billion – from companies that had been privatised by Khodorkovsky and Berezovsky eight years earlier for merely $259 million. The new company would have had the world's largest reserves of oil and been fourth in production terms.[42] Although the government initially approved the merger,[43] plans to sell a large stake abroad and fears that the new company would be able to influence government policy led to the dismantlement of Yukos (Chapter 5), a process driven by Rosneft. The state used Gazprom to revise the 1994 production-sharing agreement in the Shell-led Sakhalin-2 oil and gas project. In December 2006 a deal was reached whereby Shell's stake fell from 55.5 to 27.5 per cent, while the stakes of Shell's Japanese partners Mitsui and Mitsubishi fell to 12.5 and 10 per cent, respectively, and Gazprom's rose to 51 per cent plus one share. In the energy sector the state became ever more prominent, although this was not renationalisation but 'deprivatisation'. In general, however, by 2006 privately owned companies represented 80 per cent of all enterprises, while the state's share fell to 4 per cent. Over the previous decade, employment in private enterprises rose by 41 per cent, while falling by 15 per cent in state enterprises.[44]

The challenge facing the post-communist world is very different from that facing developing countries. Instead of building the infrastructure of an industrial society, the aim is to shift to competitive market forms of operation and to achieve the most efficient use of resources. The Soviet era endowed Russia with large plants, and this element of 'path dependency' to a degree predetermined the concentrated structure of Russian business. Only the FICs, as the most dynamic and competitive elements of the economy, could withstand international competition. As outlined in Putin's

Candidate dissertation, the state sought to work in partnership with them to modernise the economy. The FICs were to act as the locomotives pulling the Russian economy towards modernity. They would have to adapt in response to changes in the world economy and probably needed to focus on core business interests and divest themselves of non-commercial activities. The FICs would also have to conform more to the accounting and other standards of corporate behaviour of the best corporations in the West. This would require the active partnership of the state to ensure property rights and contracts, a stable and equitable tax regime, a benign investment climate, the development of the banking system, less predatory bankruptcy laws and incentives for technological innovation. Other scenarios were also possible, notably destructive predatory rivalries and the break-up of these businesses. Putin certainly sought to realise the first scenario by safeguarding property rights (with some notable exceptions) and tried to create a secure climate for investment at home and abroad. As one businessman put it, 'Russian industry is now able to restructure: the age of stealing is over; the age of arrogance is over; the age of instability is over'.[45]

The FICs consolidated their dominance at home and then cast their horizons wider. Timber processing was highly concentrated with ten plants accounting for 85 per cent of output. The industry was ripe for the predatory attack of FICs, and the state stood by as the oligarchs (such as Deripaska's Siberian Aluminium) brought some of the major plants under its control. As Yulia Latynina noted, only within the framework of 'vertically integrated fiefdoms' would businessmen be protected from the attacks of other oligarchs.[46] This group increasingly set its gaze on global markets. For example, Lukoil planned to invest $27 billion abroad by 2017. Russia's largest steel company, Evraz, in which Roman Abramovich owned 41 per cent of stock, bought Oregon Steel Mills. Norilsk Nickel agreed to buy the nickel assets of another US company. Russia in 2006 bought a stake in EADS, the parent company of Airbus Industrie, but hopes that this would give them a seat on the board were blocked. At the same time a number of companies raised significant capital by launching initial public offerings (IPOs) in foreign money markets. Alexei Mordashov's Severstal raised nearly €1 billion for 10 per cent of his company in London in 2006. Severstal had already gone global, and had some 90,000 employees in Europe and North America. His bid earlier that year to take over Europe's largest steel group, Arcelor, failed, but it was anticipated that he would bid for other steel-making companies. In October 2006 Oleg Deripaska's Rusal merged with the smaller Sual and the Swiss-based Glencore to create the giant United Company Rusal, producing 16 per cent of the world's aluminium.[47]

The role of Gazprom and the oil majors in the globalisation of Russian companies is well-documented. In the CIS area, telecommunications giants such as Vimpelcom and MTS dominate the market. Some have argued that Russia has applied a form of 'soft power' to reassert its interests in post-Soviet Eurasia, the idea of 'liberal imperialism' as advanced by Anatoly

Chubais during the 2003 parliamentary elections.[48] However, the empirical evidence for this is thin.[49] Putin's strategy since the Yukos case was undoubtedly to build 'national champions' that could compete in international markets, but this encountered significant political resistance in the West, reinforcing Russia's existing concerns about the application of 'double standards'. The decision of the US State Department in August 2006 to impose sanctions against Rosoboronexport (established in 2000, and which by 2007 had gained a monopoly for state arms exports) and Sukhoi for allegedly violating the Iran Non-Proliferation Act of 2000 was a case in point, and threatened, for example, Sukhoi's participation in Boeing's Super-Jet 100 project (sanctions against Sukhoi were lifted in November 2006). The irony of sanctions being imposed on Russian companies before they were applied to Iran was clear.

Capitalism with a corporatist face

Oligarchic capitalism enjoyed its heyday in 1996, following Yeltsin's re-election as president with their help, up to the partial default of August 1998. The FICs at this time enjoyed direct access to political power, with some of the more notorious oligarchs either joining the government directly (such as Potanin in 1996–7) or enjoying access to the corridors of power, like Berezovsky. However, the appointment of Primakov as prime minister in September 1998 and the pre-electoral divisions within the elite at the end of the Yeltsin era placed them on the defensive. Some businesses supported the opposition that looked set to take power, led above all by Luzhkov and his Fatherland organisation, which in August 1999 joined forces with the more regionally based All-Russia association. The Yeltsin system was collapsing, and with it the 'family' regime system that connected the political and business worlds. While some companies (for example, Lukoil) adopted a cautious wait and see attitude, those most closely associated with the 'family', such as the Berezovsky empire Sibneft and Siberian Aluminium, as well as Chubais's electricity giant UES, had most to fear from the end of the regime and thus were the most active in devising a 'succession' strategy. The fierceness of the parliamentary electoral campaign (which was also a struggle of oligarchical groupings) from August to December 1999 reflected the high stakes involved. The FICs were by no means the puppet masters behind the political actors, yet their financial support of political associations and individuals was a fundamental element of the political process at this time.[50] Just as the Kremlin acted as a vast pseudo-party, so oligarchic corporations acted as party substitutes lower down the political hierarchy.

Big business had to a degree usurped the functions of the state, and indeed often rendered politicians little more than their clients, a feature that remains in certain regions, especially those based on extractive industries. This phase then gave way to that of oligarchic capitalism, based on some powerful personalities who tended to see their own businesses as little more than a source of cash flow and whose relationships with the state were neither institutionalised nor structured. The arrival of liberals like Nemtsov and Kirienko into the government in the spring of 1997 signalled an attempt to limit the oligarchs and to reform the anarcho-capitalist power system, a programme accelerated by the financial crisis of 1998. The outcome, according to Dynkin and Sokolov, was to reveal that 'the oligarchy was not so much a genuine political force as a phantom of mass consciousness'.[51] That may well be the case, but the combination of FICs and the state bureaucracy was certainly very real, and was intensified in new ways under Putin. An early example of this oligarchy–state alliance, within the framework of Putin's new rules of the game, was the involvement of Oleg Deripaska's Russian Aluminium company in the purchase and subsequent restructuring of the Gorky Automotive Works (GAZ). In a globalising world the power of states is reckoned to be eroding while that of transnational corporations is growing, but in Russia under Putin a distinctive system emerged where FICs provided the state with resources for its industrial policy, and in general acted as substitute sinews of the state. The interests of big business and the state did not always coincide, of course, and the development of the state and Russian capitalism were characterised by numerous political contradictions. The very idea of an industrial policy, where certain branches are prioritised for development, was criticised for belonging to an earlier industrial age, and while it may have worked for Japan and South Korea in the post-war period, it was inappropriate for a post-industrial world where it was almost impossible to identify the shape of the future economy and where human development was crucial.[52]

Whether the dominance of these groups is tantamount to corporatism has been the subject of considerable debate.[53] Corporatism refers to a situation where the state grants certain groups a monopoly on representation in return for loyalty and occasional rights over choosing their leaders, with the group concerned then exercising exclusionary rights over demand articulation. Putin sought to practise a policy of 'equidistance' from the oligarchs, with some of them (notably Berezovsky, Gusinsky and Khodorkovsky) largely removed from the Russian political arena by going into exile or gaol. Others, however, appeared to have become a new type of 'transmission belt' for Kremlin policies. They were allowed to enjoy what they had gained in the heady 1990s as long as they invested in the 'real' economy, such as motor manufacturing (as in the example of GAZ, above), or supported political movements and actions to the Kremlin's liking (Rosneft). Representatives of big business were also important in framing political strategies, particularly in the sphere of industrial policy. Arkady Volsky, the president of the Russian Union of Industrialists and Entrepreneurs (RUIE), was one of the great survivors in Russian politics, having reinvented himself several times since coming to prominence during Andropov's brief leadership from November 1982 to February 1984, and led the RUIE from 1991 to 2004, when Alexander Shokhin took over. The RUIE itself had evolved considerably.

From being a mouthpiece of the 'red directors', addicted to state subsidies and dependent on protectionism, the RUIE had become one of the most coherent and well-organised interest groups. On Putin's accession the ranks of the RUIE were swelled by the new tycoons, oligarchs and other entrepreneurs eager to come under the protection of its corporatist umbrella. Putin's corporatist instincts did not neglect the other side of the equation either, and he met regularly with Mikhail Shmakov, the leader of the federal trade union organisation, the Federation of Independent Trade Unions of Russia.[54]

Under Putin a new model of business–state relations began to emerge, characterised above all by greater formalisation. The role of business associations was greatly increased, particularly that of the RUIE for big business. Putin met regularly with them as he shifted towards the greater institutionalisation of governmental practices. Medium business was represented by Delovaya Rossiya, while small business was served by the Organisation of Entrepreneurs' Organisations of Russia (Ob'edinenie predprinimatel'skikh organizatsii Rossii, OPORA). The influence of the RF Chamber of Commerce (Torgovo-promyshlennoi palaty RF) greatly increased with Primakov's appointment as its head in 2001. The old informal relations now gave way to the creation of a new *system* of relations that allowed a certain depoliticisation of state–economy relations and reduced the level of conflicts within the business world itself. This did not however mean that the FICs had withdrawn from politics, and neither did it signal that the old model of oligarchy/bureaucracy had disappeared.

The Russian economy remained fundamentally bureaucratised. This is not just a question of the 10,000-odd state enterprises (*gosudarstvennykh unitarnykh predpriyatii*, GUPs, including those in the defence sector) that operated not entirely by the laws of the free market, but of the suffocating power of the economic bureaucracy, imbued with a Soviet spirit, that instinctively tried to stifle any non-state economic initiative in a sea of regulation. Under Putin the economic bureaucracy was now joined by various *siloviki* who sought to get their share in the endless churning of the national product by the state. Although over three-quarters of the Russian economy had been privatised, bureaucratic pressure in direct or indirect forms (including outright illegal ones) meant that the state still effectively managed at least three-quarters of economic life. It is for this reason that Illarionov insisted that economic growth could be increased only if state expenditure was sharply reduced. The heavily statised economy was not only the ideal breeding ground for corruption and stagnation, but the struggle of economic factions and interests also subverted democracy. By 2005 Illarionov was arguing that 'This year Russia has become a different country. It is no longer a democratic country. It is no longer a free country'.[55]

State-owned companies extended their hold by gaining control over private enterprises. Rather than outright nationalisation, this was instead deprivatisation. The takeover of Yukos's main production asset, Yuganskneftegaz, in December 2004 allowed Rosneft to emerge as a global major. In September

2005 Gazprom bought 73 per cent of one of the largest private oil companies, Sibneft, for $13.1 billion from the owner of Chelsea football club, Roman
Abramovich. The aim was to transform Gazprom and Rosneft into national
energy champions able to compete with such international giants as BP,
Exxon Mobil and Chevron. The idea of enhancing state control over 'strategic' assets spread into other spheres, notably engineering, manufacturing
and banking. The state effectively took over the country's largest heavy
engineering company, OMZ, and the helicopter company Kamov. In
December the state won control of Avtovaz, the country's largest motor
manufacturer, by appointing officials to dominate its board and through
Rosoboronexport's purchase of a controlling (62%) stake for $350 million.
In 2006 Rosoboronexport bought a two-thirds stake in Avisma, one of the
world's main producers of titanium. The company was headed by Sergei
Chemezov, a KGB operative who had served with Putin in East Germany in
the 1980s, and who was sometimes named as a possible successor, especially
after he joined the ruling council of UR in December 2006.

In 2005 the state was the most active player in the mergers and acquisitions market, using either state-owned companies or companies serving
state interests. The total value of mergers and acquisitions deals doubled in
comparison with 2004 to $56 billion, with the state's share in 2004 26 per
cent, and in 2005 31 per cent, or $17.4 billion. The major deals included
Gazprom's takeover of Sibneft, and deals conducted by Vneshtorgbank,
Rosneft, UES and Svyazinvest subsidiaries. The state bought into profitable
sectors. State-owned companies like Gazprom liberalised their share-trading,
and the Russian market opened up to competition, with Siemens for example being allowed to buy into Power Machines at the same time as UES
increased its stake. ConocoPhillips bought a stake in Lukoil for $2.7 billion.
The state regained control of a quarter of the oil market though Rosneft's
capture of Yuganskneftegaz and Gazprom's acquisition of Sibneft. At the
same time, the process of privatisation continued, with the sale of the state's
stake in Svyazinvest (estimated at $3.3 billion), and an IPO of Rosneft
shares.[56] There would also be much greater consolidation of the banking
sector, with the state bank absorbing competitors. The political significance
of all this activity was not clear, but with large reserves of petro-dollars the
state consolidated its hold over profitable sectors of the economy, while the
economic consequences were unlikely to be positive, since state-owned companies in Russia have not been noted for their efficiency. The liberal former
head of the presidential administration, Dmitry Medvedev, insisted that
state ownership and management had 'far from exhausted their potential'.[57]

A very different view was taken by Illarionov, who dubbed these developments 'quasi-nationalisation' and argued that they imposed a 'corporate'
model on Russia and distanced the authorities from the people, while
establishing an unequal playing field for business. While some businesses
were granted subsidies and supported, others, he argued, were landed with
huge back tax claims.[58] According to Illarionov, state interventionism

harmed the economy, already leading to falls in investment in the oil sector and falling rates of oil production. He noted that since Rosneft had taken over Yukos's main oil field, production and revenues had fallen while costs had risen.[59] On 27 December 2005 he resigned, arguing that his ability to influence policy had been considerably reduced. He insisted that the decision to resign had been his own, and that he had not been asked to leave. He noted that when he had been appointed economic advisor in April 2000 he had signed up to 'broaden the economic freedoms of Russian citizens', but instead 'there is no place for economic freedom in the new model; its main principle is selectivity and discrimination'.[60]

State, economy and society

Putin insisted on the 'equidistance' policy concerning business interests, but he was not interested in a mass revision of the anarchic privatisation exercise of the 1990s. He did seek to have some of the property, worth about $15–20 billion, stolen by Gazprom insiders, restored to the company. The struggle for control over the state-owned Slavneft in early 2002, however, showed that politics had not entirely left the sphere of business, but in certain respects this was perhaps the last of the old-style oligarchical struggles where ownership issues were resolved in behind-the-scenes struggles in the corridors of power.[61] Andrei Piontovsky notes that those who argue in favour of some sort of 'controlled democracy' to accompany economic development based on giant corporations, like the *chaebols*, were once again imposing on Russia an anachronistic model, one that would be inappropriate for a post-industrial society.[62] What remains indisputable is that big business remains a central player in the Russian political scene, sponsoring parties and acting directly to influence political outcomes. Putin's attempt to establish a rather more robust national party system can be interpreted as part of a strategy not only to open regional elite structures but also to establish a countervailing power to big business, once more institutionalised and with independent political resources.

Programmes and reality

Do Putin's policies in the economic sphere add up to much more than a shift towards 'a more pro-state, socially oriented model of mutant capitalism'?[63] Putin's economic programme emerged only gradually, suggesting great difficulties in combining what might appear at first sight to be its contradictory commitment to greater liberalisation and increased state oversight. Was the state to remain a central player *in* the economy, or would it restrict itself to ensuring a benign economic and regulatory framework *over* the economy? On a visit to Ivanovo on 7 March 2000 Putin called for greater economic freedom, arguing that 'The higher the degree of freedom of economic entities, the higher the development of the state'.[64] On many occasions Putin condemned the prevalence of bureaucracy and insisted that 'Administrative bodies should be transparent, clear and comprehensible … We should do everything to rid ourselves of superfluous bureaucracy in the economy'.[65]

The economic programme outlined by German Gref on 28 June 2000 was permeated by a liberal spirit and openness to the world economy. The aim was to establish the conditions for stable economic growth to restore Russia to the ranks of the world's major industrialised nations. How this could be achieved remained unclear. The plan firmly sought Russia's admission into the World Trade Organisation (WTO). The attempt to protect domestic producers by high import tariffs was recognised to be pernicious, encouraging smuggling, protecting inefficient domestic producers and inhibiting the technological modernisation of Russian industry. The tax system was to be overhauled, changing the basis of the division of tax revenues between the centre and the regions. As we saw in Chapter 7, budgetary revenues were now centralised, with a far higher proportion of VAT and other revenues going to the centre, a move supported by the majority of governors, who sought more generous subsidies, while of course opposed by donor regions. At the same time, ideas were advanced for reducing budget expenditures, mostly at the expense of regional budgets and social spending.[66] In the social sphere resources were to be more targeted on need, with benefits cut except to those families with incomes under the living minimum. For the others, private health care and education were to be introduced. Although Russia had seen many economic programmes since independence, all had been implemented half-heartedly and often pursued incompatible goals at the same time. The economic programme prepared by Gref was coherent and suggested integrated solutions to Russia's economic problems. However, the government under Kasyanov put forward its own plans, and although elements of Gref's plan were implemented, overall coherence was lost. Although the position of liberal pro-market economists in Putin's government was strong, they were not agreed among themselves about the optimal economic strategy.

Russia was the last of the major industrial countries to join the WTO. Russia applied in 1993, but it was only under Putin that serious negotiations started. The debate divided the Russian business community, but Putin was unambiguously of the view that only through membership could Russian industry be modernised. Certain sectors stood to lose, above all agriculture, light industry and manufacturing. WTO entry would make it harder for the government to take into account the specific needs of the regions, possibly leading to the closure of plants and greater unemployment. Membership would also force energy price rises for residential and industrial consumers. Cheap energy, reflecting Russia's abundant resources, was a way of compensating for low wages and standards of living, and thus membership could exacerbate social tensions. In the industrial sphere, cheap energy acted as a subsidy and allowed Russian goods to maintain a competitive edge. WTO membership would force manufacturing quality to rise if these goods were to find international markets, and even the domestic market would become more competitive as foreign goods gained greater access. Membership would affect certain sectors particularly hard, like the aluminium producers enjoying cheap electricity from the massive hydroelectric schemes in Irkutsk *oblast* (Bratsk). However, even within sectors there were divisions, as in the motor industry. Car manufacturing represents 9 per cent of national industrial output and employs 10 per cent of the working population. Some companies feared the influx of foreign competition, whereas others argued that Russia's bad roads and severe climatic conditions would allow the robust domestic product to keep its market share. The cheapness of the cars, above all Ladas produced by the giant Avtovaz works in Togliatti, would secure them a substantial market come what may. Oil and gas companies favoured WTO entry since it would open up Western markets for them, as it would for the timber industry, occupying fifth place in the country's GDP.

It was anticipated that WTO membership would force Russian business to become more transparent and prevent certain companies from enjoying an 'exclusive' relationship with the state – and as a result enjoying preferential tax breaks and other privileges that would be illegal under WTO rules and would render Russia liable to large fines. Putin pushed ahead with WTO membership against the advice of some of the oligarchs, illustrating the increasing autonomy that the state enjoyed during his presidency, but at the same time his ambitious entry date of 2003 proved unfeasible. The EU imposed tough conditions on Russian entry, including ratification of the Kyoto Protocol. By early 2006 Russia still had to complete negotiations with Australia, Colombia (the sticking point for these two was sugar) and the USA, with the latter demanding that Russia abolish customs duties on aircraft imports, grant access for foreign banks and insurers to operate in Russia directly, and strengthen intellectual property rights, notably to prevent copyright violations. The WTO itself was wracked by disputes over farm trade and pharmaceuticals, and the Doha Round, focusing on liberalisation in the service sector, ran into the sands. What appeared to be America's excessively politicised approach in the final stages of the negotiations, linking WTO membership with an ever more bizarre list of concerns ranging from Russian policy to Iran to the price of yogurt in Moscow, alienated Russian officials. Even Putin became irritated, noting at a meeting with entrepreneurs that the USA's demands were artificial. As he put it in his typically vivid style, Western markets 'are completely limited. They chatter about free trade but in fact everything is closed, and you can't worm your way in there'.[67] Putin's hopes of announcing membership at the G8 summit in July 2006 were disappointed. The shifting criteria prompted a growing backlash and the idea that membership could be postponed indefinitely. In the event, the final hurdles in negotiations with America were surmounted and an 800-page agreement was signed on 19 November 2006 that differed little from the agreement that had been ready to sign at the time of the G8 summit.[68] In Washington, as in Moscow and in Brussels earlier, politics appeared to trump economics.[69]

Real relations in the law and economy in the 1990s had developed in parallel with the formal development of institutions, the bi-legalism that we noted in Chapter 5. As Skyner puts the argument, 'Russian laws exist, but they do not regulate real relations of subjects of the law, one of the main reasons for this situation being that real relations between subjects of law in Russia are established in a dimension that is parallel to the one at which formal legal regulation is aimed'.[70] These are not so much Western-style 'grey zones' formed in parallel with state administration and in opposition to it, but are established within the state and sustained by its resources. The existence of these non-formal spheres is increasingly recognised, and that is perhaps one of the first steps towards overcoming them. In this context any administrative reform would entail a thoroughgoing cultural revolution that would require changes to the role and functioning of the state and its relationship with society. Societal demands, fuelled by contemporary needs of a market economy, for constitutionalism and secure property rights come into contradiction with the attempts of the state to preserve and reproduce its own expanded functions, based on traditional Soviet-type relations, in which property rights remain ill-defined and rhetorically subject to popular control. These contradictions help explain the many tensions in the development of Russia's market economy and require a socio-legal rather than institutional explanation.

Economy and environment

Nowhere was Putin's post-Sovietism stronger than in his attempt to create a benign business climate. Putin's pro-market instincts, however, appeared at times to reproduce some of the excesses of Western capitalism at its most environmentally hostile. Encouragement of rapid resource development appeared to be at the expense of ecological balance. Putin's post-Sovietism was imbued with a neo-Soviet approach that regarded nature as no more than the field for human exploitation, irrespective of the consequences. This was in evidence in one of Putin's first acts on coming to power: the abolition of the State Committee for Environmental Protection, dissolved on 17 May 2000. The environmental protection agency had been created as a ministry in 1991 under Gorbachev, but had been downgraded to a state committee in 1996 following Yeltsin's re-election. In his drive for administrative rationalisation, the job of environmental protection was transferred to the Ministry of Natural Resources, a move that many considered akin to placing the fox in charge of the hen-coop. The old Committee had been criticised for its intrusive (some argued exploitative, and indeed corrupt) interference in business, but its abolition represented a drastic reduction in the state's capacity for environmental regulation and monitoring. At the same time, the State Committee on Forestry was also eliminated. The appointment of Alexander Gavrin, who had close links with Lukoil, the country's biggest oil producer, as energy minister added further to the impression that business had captured government in this sphere.

The need for an environmental protection agency would appear to be indisputable. According to Viktor Danilov-Danilyan, who headed the committee when it was abolished, some 61 million Russians live in environmentally dangerous conditions. In 120 cities air pollution is five times higher than established standards. Every month about a million tons of oil spill out of pipelines and into Russia's ground soil and water. At least 30 per cent of Chechnya was an ecological disaster zone as a result of the 26 oil wells that burned for months during the second Chechen war.[71] Above all, the weakness of regulatory oversight over Russia's nuclear industry was notorious. None of Russia's 29 nuclear power plants has a full safety certificate, yet Russia planned to build another 23 nuclear power stations, as well as 40 advanced fast breeder reactors. While the Chernobyl nuclear catastrophe of 26 April 1986 is well known, the contamination by three disasters in 1946, 1957 and 1967 caused by the nuclear waste produced by the Mayak plant 50 miles north of Chelyabinsk, the centre of the Soviet nuclear weapons production system, was if anything worse than that caused by Chernobyl. The Soviet Northern Fleet based on the Kola peninsula, near the border with Norway, dumped submarine reactors, spent fuel and other nuclear waste into the sea.

It was in connection with this that Alexander Nikitin, the former naval captain mentioned in Chapter 5, produced a report for the Norwegian environmental group, Bellona. As a result he was arrested by the FSB in 1996, and Putin, at the head of the FSB in 1998–9, defended the action on the grounds that environmental groups provided a cover for foreign spies. Nikitin was cleared by the Supreme Court in April 2000, but the result could hardly be claimed as a resounding victory for freedom of speech. Indeed, the FSB refused to let the case die and, through the prosecutor's office, filed an appeal with the Supreme Court's Appeals Collegium. The Nikitin case appeared to be symptomatic of the way that environmentalists, human rights activists and others were treated under Putin. In addition, the government in 2001 forced through legislation allowing the importation of nuclear waste for reprocessing, although public opinion was solidly against. As part of the deal to get EU approval for Russia to join the WTO, the Duma ratified the Kyoto Protocol in October 2004, allowing it to come into force in February 2005.

The route of the East Siberian–Pacific Ocean (ESPO) pipeline, running from Taishet in Irkutsk *oblast* to Perevoznaya bay near Nakhodka in Primorsk *krai*, aroused particular controversy. The initial route suggested by the Transneft pipeline monopoly would have run less than 500 metres from Lake Baikal's northern shore. In a seismically unstable area, this raised widespread concern about an oil spill threatening the lake's unique biosphere.

In a meeting in Tomsk on 26 April 2006, after he heard presentations by experts, Putin insisted that the route should run at least 40 kilometres north, beyond the lake's watershed, so that, in case of any spill, the oil would run in the opposite direction. This added at least a billion dollars to the costs of construction, but the decision delighted environmentalists. Construction on the pipe began in April 2006, and in the event ran even further north on the far side of a mountain range. The Rosprirodnadzor agency, although subordinated to the natural resources ministry, under its deputy director, Oleg Mitvol, showed its teeth in a number of cases in 2006, notably on the alleged environmental damage caused by the Sakhalin-2 energy project, developed by a consortium headed, as we have seen, by Shell and in conflict with the Russian government over the terms of its production-sharing agreement (PSA). Critics argued that environmental abuses were used to wrest control of the project from foreign companies, and to give Gazprom a controlling share.[72] Mitvol, a businessman who had made his fortune in the 1990s before entering government service, was even willing to take on Gazprom, accusing it of serious environmental violations.

In all fields Putin's presidency adopted strongly pro-market policies. In agriculture the new Land Code adopted in 2001 allowed the private sale and purchase of commercial and residential land in cities and villages. Only about 2 per cent of the country's land area came under the provisions of this law, but it opened up the prospect for the development of a mortgage industry to provide the funds for investment. Later, the Land Code was amended to allow the sale of agricultural land. Some 22 per cent of the world's forests are in Russia, and the natural resources ministry, with the encouragement of the World Bank, sought to improve the investment climate for logging in Russia. Russia's natural resources were now ruthlessly exploited, regardless of sustainability or the environmental consequences.

If the environment was to suffer as a result of Russia's modernisation, so was labour. The new Labour Code adopted on 30 December 2001 restricted collective bargaining to the unions representing a majority of the workers in an enterprise. Employers had more scope to agree fixed-price labour contracts, and the hiring and firing of workers was made easier. The minimum wage was set at the subsistence level. The greatest criticism of the new Labour Code was directed against its regulations concerning the role of trade unions in labour relations. As in other countries, the drive for labour market flexibility eroded workers' rights. The corporatist note sounded here, too, with malleable trade unions being favoured over those which took a more militant approach to defending the interests of their members. It appeared that some of the worst aspects of predatory capitalism now came to replace oppressive communism. Some of the inconsistencies of the 2001 Labour Code were ironed out by amendments adopted in 2006. Putinite stability ensured that employers observed labour legislation more consistently, and labour rights became more secure. In general, the labour movement was one sphere in which the Putinite instinct to regulate, and thus to suffocate, did not operate. In conformity with international norms, trade unions in Russia do not have to register and there are no minimum membership requirements, although, to be legally licensed, a minimum membership of three is required. By 1 January 2005 Russia had no fewer than 57,515 trade unions!

Conclusion

A significant cultural shift was achieved during Putin's leadership. Endless talk about Russia's civilisational destiny now gave way to a pragmatic recognition that in the modern world, as Weimar Germany had earlier recognised, 'economics had become destiny'.[73] Putin enjoyed a benign economic environment, with high prices for oil and the benefits of the threefold devaluation of the rouble in August 1998 stimulating domestic production through import substitution. Putin built on this by ensuring greater political stability and transparency in government–business relations, new tax, labour and land codes, a new criminal code and attempts to debureaucratise the environment for small businesses. The new 'Moscow consensus' curbed the excesses of the oligarchic capitalism but there was no return to Soviet-style autarchy. Putin's model encouraged a controlled extension of market relations accompanied by elements of deprivatisation in the energy and some other strategic spheres. However, the failure to tackle the bureaucratisation of the economy and some heavy-handed state interventionism meant that there was no economic miracle, although there was sustained economic growth averaging over 6 per cent. The state's intervention was selective, however, being most prominent in the energy sector and in some strategic industries, as in the creation of the United Aviation Construction Corporation. Other sectors, characteristically in the metals sphere, were left to get on with it in the private sector. The Kremlin, for example, had no objection to the merger of Sual and Rusal to create a global aluminium major. Russia became part of what Goldman Sachs in 2003 had called the BRIC group of emerging economies – Brazil, Russia, India and China – although some questioned Russia's membership in such a group.

A new model of capitalism emerged during Putin's presidency. Putin sought to finesse the fundamental contradiction that faced Russia as it moved to the market: the giant and monopolistic *structure* of economic interests inherited from the Soviet Union, accompanied by the creation of exclusive and predatory holding companies in the 1990s; and the new type of economic *relations*, state-sponsored monopolies joined by bandit capitalism. The encouragement of concentration in financial–industrial conglomerates tried to take advantage of these giant concerns by turning them into capitalist multinationals. Putin's policies were pro-big business, but the development of small and medium enterprises was relatively neglected. At the same time Putin established a more structured relationship with the business community that could be seen as an attempt to create a 'managed market economy'.[74] Putin was unequivocally in favour of Russia's economic integration into the international economic system as the only way of pulling the country out of relative economic backwardness, but the strategy for domestic economic reform was hesitantly implemented. Sooner or later the state would take a less prominent role in the economy, and Russian business would then be able to assert its political muscle. Full-scale liberal capitalism would have arrived in Russia, but that day would come only after Putin left office. In this as in so many other spheres, Putin laid the foundations for his successors to build on.

10 Putin's new realism in foreign policy

> The only realistic choice for Russia is the choice to be a strong country, strong and confident in its strength, strong not in spite of the world community, not against other strong states, but together with them.
>
> Vladimir Putin[1]

There is an unusual consensus in the Russian political elite that the country is a 'great power', although there are disagreements over what a great power should look like in the post-Cold War era. America on its own today spends more than half of all the world's military allocations, a concentration of power that even Rome at its height could not emulate. In this context, Russia's claim to be a great power has an inherent revisionist dynamic. The country's mere existence as an independent source of influence, power and civilisational authority is perceived by some as a challenge to the status quo. Russia's identity is bound up with a view of itself as an autonomous power with a distinctive role to play in the Eurasian region and in the world at large. With enormous reserves of hydrocarbons and other natural resources, enjoying huge technological and cultural achievements, and with a history as an ally in the defeat of continental dictators, Russia considers itself different from other medium-ranking powers. Although in the 1990s it found itself trapped in poverty amidst a sea of plenty, its location at the Eastern end of the European sphere of prosperity suggested that sooner rather than later its fortunes would improve. The problem facing Putin was how to convert potential into reality. He was well aware of the great gulf between rhetoric and reality, and sought to tailor Russia's ambitions to feasibility while not losing sight of what made Russia different. Within the framework of what we call a 'new realism', Putin sought to craft a policy that asserted Russia's national interests while integrating into the world community. The shedding of exaggerated illusions about Russia's status in the world, however, did not mean that the rest of the world would be willing to accept Russia into the international community on its own terms. Putin's new realism was devised precisely at a time when much of the Western world was seized by what Sergei Karaganov calls 'democratic messianism'.[2] The 'new realism' emerging in Russia came into contradiction with the West's focus on the 'regime question', the quality of Russia's democracy.

Towards a new realism

For over two decades since Mikhail Gorbachev launched *perestroika* in 1985, Russia has been engaged in a grandiose modernisation process. An essential part of this has been the attempt to find a new relationship with the developed West, but a satisfactory balance between integration and autonomy has not yet been found.[3] The dual and contradictory position of Russia on the world stage on Putin's accession in 2000 has been characterised as follows.

> On the one hand, it has many of the attributes of a world power – in the club of nuclear powers, a permanent seat in the UN Security Council, participates (although not always on an equal footing) in summits of world leaders. On the other hand, its present economic capacities clearly do not correspond to its still surviving nominal military power and political influence. In many respects Russia has declined to the level of a less developed country.[4]

This is perhaps a too negative reading of Russia's economic position. Although when Putin came to power Russia's economy was not much larger than Holland's (about $600 billion), by the time he ended his second term its GDP exceeded the trillion mark. However, this pales in comparison with America's $13 trillion and the European Union's $12 trillion, while China in 2006 overtook the UK to become the world's fourth largest economy with a GDP of nearly $2 trillion. The request for the American defence budget in 2007 of $550 billion was not much less than the total Russian GDP in 2000 and exceeded all of its competitors combined, while defence spending in China at that time was some $75 billion, compared to Russia's $20 billion. On a relatively narrow economic base, Russia tries to maintain a space programme, advanced strategic rocket development, 1.1 million men in the armed services, an extended welfare system and a bureaucracy that is bigger than the Soviet Union's, while at the same time positioning itself for a leading role in world affairs. This mismatch between ambition and capacity imbued Russian foreign policy in the 1990s with a bombastic and ineffectual edge,[5] while Russian statesmen such as Yevgeny Primakov insisted that Russia would continue to play a major role in the international system because of its willingness to assume the responsibilities of a major actor.[6] There was clearly a gulf between the way that the outside world saw Russia and the pretensions of its elites and many of its citizens. This was an explosive situation, with an aggrieved Russia potentially becoming a disruptive force in the world community.

Ideological trends

Putin's overriding purpose from the very first days of his presidency, in keeping with his general programme of 'normalisation', was to regularise

Russian foreign policy. Russia was to be treated as neither supplicant nor potential disruptor, but as just one more 'normal' great power, although of course Putin defines 'normality' in his own way. On the basis of this, McFaul and Goldgeier have argued that post-communist Russian foreign policy does not follow the pattern anticipated by realist thinking. According to them Russia has become a 'joiner', and does not conform to the 'balancing' stance anticipated by classical realist theory.[7] For Ambrosio, a state can either try to balance the major power in the international system, or bandwagon with it: the choice depends on the structure of the environment and the country's political culture. In Russia's case he identifies three strands: the Atlanticists, favouring alignment with the United States and the West (the bandwagoners); the imperialists, who favour the reassertion of Russia's power in opposition to the West (the balancers); and the neo-Slavophiles, sharing the sentiments of the imperialists but who stress the development of the country's Slavic identity.[8] According to Zimmerman, the fundamental divide is indeed between Westernisers and Slavophiles, in a reprise of nineteenth-century debates, with the Slavophiles intent on counterbalancing American hegemony and finding an autonomous developmental path.[9]

A fourth strand should also be noted here, the Eurasianists, who insist that Russia remains the core of a distinctive civilisation based on the unique mix of peoples who have shared a common destiny for nearly a millennium. There are many strands of Eurasianism, including: a pragmatic Eurasianism that simply reflects the fact that Russia is both a European and an Asian power; neo-Eurasianism, with a more imperialist inflection that denigrates the East as a substantive element while playing up geopolitical factors; an inter-civilisational Eurasianism, focusing on Russia's multiethnic identity;[10] and a mystical Eurasianism that sharply distinguishes the mega-region as the spiritual counterpoint to Western degradation.[11] Putin if anything is a pragmatic Eurasianist, but even this is tempered by his unequivocal Europeanism and he has little truck with Eurasianism's characteristic anti-Westernism, however wary he may be of Western hegemonism. Elements of all four positions informed Russia's foreign policy under Putin, but a modified form of neo-Slavophilism is predominant, no longer so much concerned with the development of a Slavic identity but focused on Russia's autonomous development in partnership with the West but reasserting its great power status.

This could be the recipe for confusion, but under Putin this multi-faceted approach has allowed a sophisticated although essentially ambiguous policy to be pursued. Russia's policy has traditionally been firmly located in the realist tradition, but this is now tempered by awareness that integration with the West can only effectively take place when Russia puts its own house in order and is able to define its identity and place in the world. Democracy is certainly an element of that identity, but subordinate to other overriding goals such as state unity and national survival. Russia's realism is thus tempered by a continuing strand of idealism – that Russia is part of a European civilisational identity and should be accepted on its own terms as an equal member of the international community – while on a practical level there is no shortage of instrumental short-term politicking. These three models of foreign policy making – the realist, idealist and instrumental – are far from mutually exclusive. On the basis of all of this, Russia's foreign policy under Putin can be described as a 'new realism'. It is a realism concerned not so much with balancing as joining, while at the same time tempered by neo-Slavophile concerns about autonomy and uniqueness, and pragmatic Eurasianist notions of balance between East and West. As Tsygankov puts it, 'Russia's attitude is essentially accommodationist', and, in contrast to earlier policy, the country did not try to exploit the threat posed by unipolarity by forging a counter-alliance.[12] The focus of Russian policy was post-imperial state building. Like all post-imperial states, however, relations with former partners and subordinates are uneasy. The new realist pattern was already established during the presidency of Boris Yeltsin, but, as we shall see, Yeltsin's realism became coloured by a specific definition of pragmatism that retained much of the classical competitive approach to realism in foreign policy. It was only under Putin that engagement with the West moved onto a more stable and co-operative basis, although relations continued to be soured by the regime question – the nature of the political system emerging in Russia.[13]

Conceptual innovation

Under the stewardship of Primakov the concept of 'pragmatism' predominated. Primakov's so-called 'pragmatism' in foreign policy achieved few positive results, alienating Russia's friends and confirming the hostility of those traditionally suspicious of its intentions. Russian foreign policy in the late 1990s was built on fake history and mythopoeic representations of traditional alliances. Foreign policy in this period was imbued not so much with an 'essential ambiguity' as with a fatal dualism and appeared to operate at two levels: what Russia really wanted (foreign policy A) and what it was forced to do (foreign policy B). The tension led to incoherence and confusing signals. By the time he came to power Putin found himself in a position remarkably reminiscent to that facing Gorbachev when he became general secretary in 1985: associated with sullen allies and opposed by increasingly militant foes. Primakov's pragmatism was rooted in a highly traditional understanding of realism, underscored by a heavy dose of anti-Western Sovietism and by calls for 'multipolarity', a code word for balancing. Primakov's multipolarism sought to use the instruments of multilateralism to sustain and manage a competitive view of the world, a traditional realist approach. This is in contrast to policies that genuinely seek to build on the normative values embedded in multilateral organisations to transcend great power rivalries.

These views and contradictions were reflected in the three major documents adopted in Putin's first year as president. They were designed to clarify the risks and opportunities faced by Russia and identify ways of dealing with them. The significance of these documents should not be exaggerated, and in many ways they reflected the priories and preoccupations of the earlier period rather than setting a programme for Putin's leadership, but all demonstrated the tensions in Russia's view of the West. The first to be adopted was a new *National Security Concept*, to replace the 1997 version, which was signed into law on 10 January 2000.[14] The document reflected deep concerns about the external environment. The August 1998 economic meltdown that revealed Russia's vulnerability to speculative international financial markets, the use of Nato forces with an unclear UN mandate to bomb Serbia between March and June 1999, Nato's enlargement in March 1999 to encompass Poland, Hungary and the Czech Republic, strategic arms control tensions and renewed war in Chechnya, all provoked a rethinking of the international environment. The *Concept* expanded the list of external threats to Russia's security, noting in particular the weakening of the Organisation for Security and Co-operation in Europe (OSCE), the UN and the Commonwealth of Independent States (CIS). The document described the tension between a multipolar world, in which relations are based on international law and an acceptance of a significant role for Russia, and attempts by the USA and its allies to carve out a unipolar world outside of international law. Talk of 'partnership' with the West disappeared, and instead more emphasis was placed on more limited 'co-operation'.[15] To complement the above, a new *Military Doctrine* (replacing the 2 November 1993 version) was ratified by presidential decree on 21 April 2000. The 'no first use' of nuclear weapons postulate, already weakened in the 1993 doctrine, was given added detail, and as part of the reassessment of the risks facing the country the document called for the forward deployment of troops outside Russian territory.

The new *Foreign Policy Concept* of 28 June 2000, replacing Yeltsin's 23 April 1993 document that some have seen to be imbued with excessive idealism,[16] stressed that Russia's policy should be rational and realistic and designed to serve Russian economic and political interests.[17] The link between domestic and foreign policy was reinforced. The *Concept* asserted that the 'relationship with European states is a traditional priority of Russian foreign policy', although Russia's integration into Europe's political and economic space was no longer mentioned. As with all these documents, contradictory perceptions jostled cheek by jowl, with Russia defined as a great power in one paragraph and as fundamentally pragmatic in the next. The tone however was a realistic one, stressing the need to find a 'reasonable balance between its objectives and possibilities for attaining these objectives'. The document called for Russia to lead the development of a multipolar world, a policy explicitly designed to counter the threat of US global domination under the guise of 'humanitarian intervention' and 'limited sovereignty'. The emphasis in relations with the CIS shifted from multilateralism to bilateralism, a change that Putin adhered to throughout his leadership, while the need to protect Russian ethnic minorities in the former Soviet states was noted. Good relations with Europe, the USA and Asia were stressed, in that order, although the openly anti-American tone was noticeable. In the wake of Nato's intervention over Kosovo the tone was bitter; nevertheless the *Concept* stated that Russia was interested in constructive co-operation with Nato 'in the interests of maintaining security and stability in the continent and is open to constructive interaction'.[18] Commenting on the *Concept* on 25 April 2002 in a speech devoted to the two-hundredth anniversary of the Russian foreign ministry, the foreign minister, Igor Ivanov, stressed that 'Russia has consciously given up the global Messianic ideology that had been intrinsic to the former USSR and at the end of its existence had come into insurmountable contradiction with the national interests of the country'.[19] The *Concept* broadly set the parameters for policy, but as so often with these documents real life quickly passed it by.

A number of theories were applied to sustain Russia's exaggerated idea of its role in the world, notably various strains of neo-Eurasian thinking drawing on the ideas of the 1920s and 1930s. This was based on the belief that Russia's position imbued it with unique geopolitical advantages that effectively forced it to be a great power and to make a bid for world leadership. Time had moved on, however, and Dmitry Trenin argues that China's growing strength in the East and the instability of the Islamic South, means that Russia's only geopolitical future lies with the West, including accelerated integration with the EU and solid relations with the United States.[20] Trenin stresses that Russia's integration with the West has to take into account national peculiarities, and thus the liberal project of Westernisation had to adopt a patriotic form.[21] In the 1990s this Western-style modernisation had been destructive of Russia's self-identity, and now Putin sought to rehabilitate the project of integration, but in an autonomous form. The enthusiastic Atlanticism of the early 1990s has gone; and at the same time there is little trace of Eurasianism in his thinking, but much about Russia's position in Eurasia.[22] Putin has not gone so far as the new strain of critical geopolitics that questions the imperatives of space and geography, but his thinking is remarkably free of the traditionally static, monolithic and zero-sum representations of Russia's role in the world. In short, Putin sought to normalise the debate on Russian foreign policy, stripping it of neo-Eurasianism features rooted in nineteenth-century views of competitive advantage while acknowledging twenty-first-century realities.

From periphery to core

With the fall of communism the old East–West bipolar world has given way to a more concentric version that lies at the basis of the post-communist neo-imperial approach. A number of core states enjoy the 'democratic peace'[23] while the periphery remains a zone of conflict and economic hardship.[24] In the zone of peace the normative framework of international relations

developed since the Second World War applies, regulated by the core institutions of contemporary modernity, whereas in the periphery the West
asserts a renewed mandate to operate according to traditional great power
norms.[25] In practice, the notion of the 'West' here divided, with America
under president George W. Bush taking a more assertive approach, whereas
much of Europe remained committed to consensual international norms.
While Europe is forced to rely on diplomacy and other 'soft-power' instruments, America can apply the whole armoury of hard and soft tools. Indeed,
as Robert Kagan argues, Europe's weakness has forced it to emphasise
normative soft power as a way of undermining the legitimacy of American
full-spectrum hard-power predominance.[26] Although 'the West' is far from
homogeneous, with the EU struggling to ensure that the concept does not
become a synonym for America, there remains a dividing line somewhere in
Eurasia beyond which there is a non-West. The EU itself is not quite sure
where the line should be drawn, hence continuing debates over the eligibility
of Turkey and Ukraine as EU members. As far as Russia is concerned, fear
that it would be relegated to the periphery and treated as such provoked a
range of defensive reactions. These were particularly apparent over secessionist issues (Kosovo, Transdniester, Abkhazia and South Ossetia, not to
mention Chechnya) and in relations with the former Soviet republics. The
lands between Russia and the EU became a sphere of competing 'near
abroads', especially with the launch of the European Neighbourhood Policy
(ENP) in 2003. The collision was particularly vivid at the time of Ukraine's
'Orange revolution' in late 2004, when Putin ill-advisedly and demonstra-
tively supported the official candidate to replace president Leonid Kuchma,
Victor Yanukovich, against the outsider candidate, Viktor Yushchenko, who
in the event won the extraordinary third-round ballot.

Russia sought to move from the periphery to the core in international
politics. Neo-realists would argue that this is simply a function of Russia's
recognition of the actual distribution of power in the international system,
while liberal realists like John Ikenberry would go further and argue that
liberal values have a positive attraction, especially when the USA exercises
its hegemony in a consensual way.[27] From an international political economy perspective, growing policy convergence reflected the failure of state-
led semi-autarchic modernisation programmes and the changed opportunity
structure offered by economic globalisation.[28] In practice Russia's move from
outsider to a core member of the leading group of nations would prove
traumatic for all concerned, especially at the time of the partial default of
August 1998, yet ultimately the scale of the achievement should be recognised. Under Yeltsin the country appeared to enter a twilight zone of semi-
acceptance, but the strategic direction had been established, and it was on
this that Putin built.[29] In various and uneven ways the West tried to devise
strategies to make integration possible. Relations remained stable, although
on occasions bumpy, with bodies such as Nato and the EU, although
Russia joining either of them was ruled out in the conceivable future. In the

early 2000s, as Dov Lynch puts it, Russia still faced the same problems as in the 1990s, the attempt to gain 'an equal voice on major security developments in and around Europe without incurring the costs of membership, which is seen to impose restraints on Russia's domestic room for manoeuvre'.[30] Neither Nato nor the EU, moreover, were rushing to invite Russia to join. Structural impediments remained on all sides, including Russia's own problems, above all economic weakness, criminality, corruption and political divisions. There remains a fundamental contradiction in Russo–Western relations captured by the traditional terms used to describe nationality politics in the Soviet Union: while *sblizhenie* (coming together) is accepted by all, there remain fundamental reservations about *sliyanie* (merging).

The legacy of Cold War suspicion only slowly dissipated, and on the Russian side indeed was occasionally replenished by Russia's halting acceptance of the sovereignty of former Soviet states, heavy-handed peacekeeping operations in the breakaway Transdniestria territory in Moldova and in Abkhazia in Georgia, war in Chechnya, unsophisticated rhetorical support for the Serbian strongman, Slobodan Milošević until his overthrow in October 2000 and crude attempts by Primakov to play the Chinese 'card' against the West. These policies reflected a traditional concept of power, where the ultimate sanction was coercion and war. It appeared that although rhetorically Russia favoured good relations with the West, it would insist on remaining part of an alternative pole of world politics and advance a different ideology of international affairs. We shall argue below that this is a misinterpretation of Russian thinking, since Russia's broad aim was not to set itself up as an alternative but as the champion of the autonomy of sovereign states. Residual elements of alternativity were in tension with the striving for autonomy, especially when America set itself up as the champion of 'geopolitical pluralism' in the post-Soviet sphere over which Russia claimed a *droit de regard*. It is for this reason that so much of Russian foreign policy has a dual character, with Russia becoming both an insider and an outsider.[31]

In the post-Cold War era traditional 'hard power' approaches have to a degree been delegitimised by the normative values associated with 'soft power', where the emphasis shifts to 'the ability to set the political agenda in a way that shapes the preferences of others'.[32] Putin, like the EU, no doubt appreciated the value of soft power in proportion to the absence of effective instruments of hard power. Putin was deeply committed to a new realism that rejected much of the zero-sum logic of traditional views of international politics. However, while he sought to normalise both goals and practices, his 'new realism' ran into the sands and by the end of his presidency there was much talk of a renewed 'Cold War'.

Features of the new realism

Article 86 of Russia's 1993 constitution renders foreign policy a presidential prerogative, and hence in institutional terms the priorities of the incumbent are decisive, especially in policy areas that are of high priority. Putin clearly enjoyed acting as a world statesman, and maintained a tight grip on Russia's foreign policy priorities. He has been pragmatic, but he has decisively rejected the pragmatism of the weak of the earlier period. Putin's pragmatism lacks Primakov's double-edged characteristic and instead inhabits the real world of opportunities, risks and agency. Under Putin foreign policy completed its trajectory from the alleged idealism of the early 1990s, through a period of 'pragmatism' in the second half of the decade, towards a 'new realism'. Most of the elements were already visible under Primakov and even earlier, in particular his predecessor, Andrei Kozyrev, who had shaped Russia's foreign policies as it emerged as an independent state from 1990 until his resignation in January 1996. Kozyrev had long been criticised for his idealism (dubbed 'romanticism') and uncritical Westernism. In the 'new realism' there was a much sharper recognition of the limits of Russian power, accompanied by a recognition that more could be gained through partnership with the West than through competition. This did not mean giving up aspirations to global influence, which evoked some sharp criticism abroad, but on the whole Putin's foreign policy was cautious and avoided alienating potential friends in the West. He was not always able to maintain this balancing act.

The new realism has not given up the notion of Russia as a 'great power', but the definition of what it means to be a great power has changed as well as the way it should behave. The type of influence that Russia now sought was as part of a responsible community of nations, rather than as an outsider challenging that community. Russia would be a power acting as part of the status quo rather than as a putative revisionist power setting itself up as a competitor to the global hegemony. The style and priorities of policy were also to change. According to the foreign minister, Igor Ivanov, 'Russian foreign policy will be independent, predictable and transparent'.[33] Putin devoted considerable attention to Russia's image abroad, exhorting the diplomatic corps on numerous occasions, notably when addressing them at the foreign ministry building on 12 July 2002 and again on 12 July 2004, to improve Russia's international prestige. Particular attention was to be paid to the preservation of Russia's leadership role in the CIS.[34] The new realism is characterised by a number of key features.

1 The first is the *economisation* of Russian foreign policy. In many public statements Putin insisted that the country's foreign policy had to be subordinated to domestic economic interests.[35] In a keynote speech at the foreign ministry on 26 January 2001 Putin stressed that Russia's strategic aim was 'integration into the world community', and for this the priority task of Russian diplomacy was the promotion of Russia's economic interests abroad.[36] In a speech to the staff of the Ministry of Foreign Affairs (MFA) in September 2002 Putin insisted that advancing Russia's business interests was equal to traditional political reporting.[37] As we saw in Chapter 9, Putin did not waver in his commitment to see

Russia join the WTO, although numerous domestic constituencies were opposed, and indeed were sceptical about the benefits of Russia's membership of G8.[38] Similarly, despite domestic hostility, Putin steered Russia towards ratification of the Kyoto protocol, making possible the adoption of a watered-down version of its CO_2 emission-reduction targets.

2   On numerous occasions Putin stressed another key feature of his foreign policy, its *Europeanism*. Already in the early period of Russian independence Yeltsin's policy advisor Gennady Burbulis argued that none of the problems facing the country could be 'solved without learning from the European experience'.[39] In the book of interviews published in his first months in office Putin insisted that 'we are a part of Western European culture. In fact, we derive our worth precisely from this. Wherever our people might happen to live – in the Far East or in the South – we are Europeans'.[40] At his first EU–Russia summit in May 2000 Putin stressed his affinity with Europe, insisting that Russia 'was, is and will be a European country by its location, its culture, and its attitude toward economic integration'.[41] He repeated the idea in the 26 January 2001 speech, arguing that the 'European direction is traditionally the most important for us'. In the same vein, addressing the conference of Russia's ambassadors in July 2002 he argued that economic ties with the EU, especially in the energy sphere, remained the top priority. He did not ignore Russia's other concerns, including accession to the WTO, without which he insisted Russia could not realise its potential.[42] Thus Russia pursues a 'greater Europe' policy, in which it sees itself as part of a single bloc stretching from the Atlantic to the Pacific (the traditional pan-European ideal). However, this is a pan-Europeanism that meshes uneasily with the integrationist agendas of the institutions of 'official Europe' (above all the EU).

3   Some commentators have identified a third leg to Putin's policy, namely its *securitisation*.[43] For authors in the tradition of the Copenhagen school of international relations, security in the post-Cold War era is less about direct threats than about the perception of risk, with the concept of risk defined rather more strongly than general threats or problems.[44] Against the background of the second Chechen war and the terrorist attack on the USA in September 2001, Putin insisted that Russia's policy in Chechnya and co-operation with the 'coalition of the willing' were part of the same problem, namely, dealing with the global security threat. While sovereignty questions were not absent in Putin's approach to the Chechen war (the struggle to maintain the territorial integrity of Russia), the security motif became the predominant one. The West's reluctance to subsume the Chechen conflict into international security management left Russian diplomacy perplexed.

4   The shift from alternativity to *autonomy* can be seen as a fourth strand in thinking, and is reminiscent of classical Gaullism. The discourse of multipolar globalism under Primakov was based on the notion of Russia

as an alternative pole balancing that of the West, and indeed working as a competitive actor in the international system. A notable example of this was the attempt to establish a troika consisting of Russia, France and Germany at the meeting of the heads of government of the Council of Europe in October 1997. Elements of troika thinking have periodically resurfaced during Putin's presidency, notably on the eve of the second Iraq war, but Putin resolutely refused to be trapped into taking sides with one wing of the West against another. Although all denied any anti-American intent, it was clear that the troika approach was seen as a way of counterbalancing American power. Like France under De Gaulle, Putin insisted that Russia would be an autonomous actor, but not an alternative to, let alone in competition with, the West. As Igor Ivanov stressed, Russia would defend the idea of 'a democratic, multipolar system of international relations', but stressed that 'Russia is by no means looking for a pretext for rivalry'.[45]

5   A fifth aspect of Putin's foreign policy was its emphasis on *bilateralism*. Although Russia in the 2000s sought a qualitative improvement of its relationship with multilateral bodies such as the EU and Nato, and policy remained committed rhetorically to broader international multi-lateralism based, above all, on the United Nations, Putin clearly felt most comfortable with state-to-state relations, often based on personal ties. The world from Moscow's perspective remains one of sovereign states, although tempered by a constrained multilateralism. Multilateral bodies were supported to the degree that they amplified Moscow's view of the world, but were marginalised, as in Russia's increasingly difficult relations with the OSCE and even ultimately with the CIS, when they did not. The OSCE proved a thorn in Putin's side, insisting that Russia ful-filled its commitment given at the OSCE's Istanbul summit in November 1999 to withdraw its forces from Transdniestria and Georgia, criticising Russia's conduct of the Chechen war, and issuing a ringing denunciation of the December 2003 parliamentary elections. In turn, Putin and the Russian side insisted that 'Turning the OSCE into the supervisor only over the post-Soviet sphere, in our view, is completely wrong. It was not created for this'. He noted that there were plenty of other regional pro-blems for the OSCE to deal with.[46] As for the CIS, a host of smaller groupings undermined the organisation's work as a broad multilateral body. Following the 'rose revolution' in Georgia in November 2003 and the Orange revolution in Ukraine in late 2004, by 2005 there was serious talk about disbanding the organisation in its entirety, and there was a marked shift towards the 'economisation' of relations within the bloc. In particular, Russia sought to impose world market prices on energy exports to Ukraine and even its close ally Belarus. Faced with the strug-gle to maintain its position in Eurasia, Putin assiduously nurtured good relations with European leaders. As Igor Ivanov put it, 'One of the fun-damental tenets of Russia's European policy is the expansion of bilateral

relations with individual countries ... Over the past decade, Russia's relations with virtually all these countries have been taken to a qualitatively new level. We have become privileged partners in our co-operation efforts with such countries as Germany, Great Britain, France, Spain and others. We feel this is exceptionally valuable'.[47]

The concept of 'privileged partner', clearly, was used rather broadly, and in some respects relations with certain countries were especially privileged – notably in the case of Germany. As Putin noted at the Yekaterinburg summit with Germany of October 2003, he had met with Schroeder 20 times since 2000, arguing that 'such intensive contacts fully reflect the dynamics of Russo–German interaction'.[48] The notion of a 'strategic partnership' between the two countries has even been mentioned,[49] but as we know from previous experience with such rhetoric (notably Primakov's talk of a strategic partnership between Russia and China), reality does not always meet expectations. Bilateral relations offer the opportunity for the stronger partner to act as the advocate of the weaker. Thus Germany championed Russia's membership of the Paris Club of sovereign creditors, and both France and Germany at the beginning of Putin's second term, in particular after the Beslan events, sought to blunt the wave of criticism addressed against Russia.

6   It is this that gives rise to a sixth element of the new realism, namely its *constrained great powerism* (*derzhavnost'*). This is an approach that takes Russia's status as a major international power for granted, accepts Russia's need to join the West and to enter or develop robust relationships with its political, security and economic institutions, but at the same time has become rather more secure in its own worth and thus more controlled. This is conditioned by the shift from alternativity to autonomy mentioned above. This new confidence allowed Putin to view the American security presence in Central Asia and the South Caucasus after 9/11 with equanimity, and in general to view relations with the West rather more as a positive-sum game. The constrained element declined in Putin's second term, as Russian policy became more self-confident after several years of economic growth, windfall energy rents, fewer domestic challenges and what were perceived to be unfair Western criticisms of domestic developments.

7   A final element in the new realism is, quite simply, Putin's attempts to '*normalise*' relations with the West and the world. Russia under Putin was a status quo power, despite the disruption of world order represented by the rise of American power. On coming to office Putin sought to devise policies to overcome Russia's isolation and to establish good relations with the West in general and Europe in particular. Russia would do this by applying the principles of the new realism. One key aspect was the rejection of traditional Russian *Sonderweg* illusions. Putin repudiated the idea of a special path for Russia, arguing that for the first time in centuries Russia was not seeking any unique path of development. Putin sought to find the golden mean (no longer defined as a third way)

between what had been perceived as humiliating subservience to the West since the late 1980s and the bombastic assertion of great power status that predominated in the late 1990s. Russia's traditionally idealised view of the world now recognised a few hard realities: the economy could no longer maintain aspirations to superpower status; the EU was enlarging and its sphere of concerns was casting an ever deeper shadow in the East; Nato was here to stay and increasing numbers of Russia's neighbours wanted to join, including (perhaps most humiliatingly for 'pragmatists' of Primakov's ilk) Ukraine; and the CIS could not be used as an instrument for Russian aggrandisement but would have to be based on genuine partnerships or it would wither away.

These are the outlines of the new realism pursued by Putin. However, it appeared that most Western leaders, especially during his second term, were unconvinced. Russia's alleged authoritarian turn was condemned following the Beslan school siege in September 2004, when Putin announced a raft of measures including the appointment of governors and a purely proportional parliamentary electoral system, and was intensified after the Ukrainian débâcle. In response, Russian policy began to lose some of its new realist hue and reverted somewhat to traditional competitive realism.

The new realism in practice

Russian foreign policy in the Putin era was characterised by conformity to the realities of power relations in the international system while at the same time redefining what constitutes Russia's national interests. A type of constrained adaptation to the international system emerged in which the strategic direction was clear – integration without accession (although in the long-term accession is not excluded); but the pace and form of integration would remain at Russia's discretion. Constrained adaptation is the counterpart of constrained *derzhavnost'*, and complements the policy of autonomy without alternativity. Domestic reconstruction became the priority, but at the same time external ambitions in Eurasia and the world are not abandoned.

Relations with America

In Putin's early years there appeared to be a shift from an American-centred foreign policy towards a greater European orientation. In part this was a response to America focusing on its own elections, and the more critical approach adopted by the new president, George W. Bush, in contrast to president Bill Clinton's wager on Yeltsin.[50] However, at their meeting in Ljubljana, Slovenia, on 16 June 2001, Bush and Putin established a remarkable personal rapport. Although the Bush camp had earlier repudiated Clinton's politics of charm, Bush now outdid his predecessor: 'I looked into that man's eyes and saw that he is direct and trustworthy. We had a very good dialogue. And I saw his soul'.[51]

Russia's dramatic choice to join the 'coalition against terror' after the events of 11 September 2001, therefore, built on earlier developments. Nevertheless, Putin's personal role in that fateful decision was decisive, and rode against the advice of the military and the uncertainty of public opinion. Putin was the first to telephone Bush after the al-Qaeda attack, and he offered not only sympathy but stressed that Russia would stand full-square with the United States in the struggle against international terrorism. Putin gave concrete form to the new alliance in a television broadcast on 24 September in which he outlined five areas of co-operation. Russia would provide information at its disposal about terrorist bases and its secret services would co-operate with Western counterparts; Russia would open its airspace to planes carrying humanitarian provisions to areas where anti-terrorist operations were taking place; air bases in Central Asia would be made available to Western planes; Russia in case of necessity would participate in search and rescue operations; and Russia would support the internationally recognised government in Afghanistan with military and other supplies.[52] This policy of close co-operation was the logical conclusion of Putin's earlier approach.

Although there has been much commentary about the strength of popular anti-American feeling, a number of commentators after 9/11 noted, in the light of the outpouring of genuine popular sympathy for those who had suffered, that this had probably always been exaggerated.[53] At times of international tension, as during the Kosovo crisis in 1999, the number of Russian citizens who considered America a potential enemy peaked at 48 per cent; by 2001 this had fallen to 13 per cent.[54] For most citizens of St Petersburg, Russia's Western identity is not questioned and Putin, too, has no doubts about the matter. After 11 September he made a calculated decision (although this choice was in keeping with his intuition and Yeltsin's precedent) that Russia's security and broader interests lay in alliance with the West. At a stroke, Russian ambiguities and doubts about Russia's civilisational identity, whether it was part of the West or an alternative to it, found a framework in which to be resolved. However, Putin's courageous stance following 11 September did not mark a fundamental repudiation of long-standing Russian concerns or interests. Putin's choice in favour of normalising relations with the West had been taken long before; and afterwards, as seen by his stance during the second Iraq war, it was clear that good relations with the West did not mean becoming America's junior partner.

Following 9/11 the Kremlin co-operated with the US on a number of key issues: the Afghan war; the deployment of US forces in Central Asia and, later, in Georgia; arms control; and acceptance in December 2001 of America's unilateral abrogation of the 1972 Anti-Ballistic Missile (ABM) Treaty. Although no formal deal was struck in return for Russia's support for the allied intervention in Afghanistan in late 2001, Russia made no fuss about the placing of US troops in Central Asia, but expected USA–Russia trade restrictions to be lifted, in particular the repeal of the Jackson–Vanik amendment of 1974 that tied trade relations to Jewish emigration. Not only did the restrictions remain in place as a permanent threat to Russian access to the USA market, although suspended annually by presidential action, but in March 2006 Congress repealed the amendment for Ukraine while leaving it in place for Russia. As Konstantin Zatulin, director of the CIS Countries Institute put it, 'The Americans are cynically wielding this Cold War anachronism as a cudgel'.[55] Other possible benefits for Russia were also slow to materialise. In February 2002 Russian public opinion was incensed at what Putin called 'non-objective judges' at the Winter Olympic Games in Salt Lake City, and soon afterwards the bitter trade war over punitive American tariffs on Russian steel imports and Russia's reciprocal ban on 'Bush chicken legs' revealed how fragile (or perhaps just how 'normal') the relationship between the two countries was. It appeared that Russian policy had once again, as during Gorbachev's *perestroika*, entered a period of unilateral concessions. Nato enlargement to include the Baltic republics, the stationing of American troops in Central Asia and even in Georgia was considered by Putin as 'no tragedy', while Putin considered America's withdrawal from the ABM Treaty 'no threat to Russian security'. In March 2004 Nato enlarged to encompass seven new countries that had earlier been part of the Soviet bloc. Although 40 per cent of Nato's 26 member states are now former communist states, Russia's response was remarkably muted, and even included renewed talk about Russia's possible membership.

Russia's concessions aligned the country as part of the 'coalition against terrorism' but there appeared to be few material gains. Putin had joined the coalition as a matter of principle, so discussion of tangible benefits may be misplaced. Russia did gain two immediate advantages: a muting of Western criticism of its behaviour in Chechnya (and indeed, a partial reclassification of the war as a front in the international struggle against terrorism); and the overthrow of the hated Taliban regime in Afghanistan (which had long threatened Russia's ally Tajikistan) by the Russian-backed Northern Alliance forces. The signing of the Strategic Offensive Reduction Treaty during Bush's visit to Moscow on 24 May 2002 was another positive aspect, with each side pledged to reduce their stockpile to no more than 2,200 warheads by 31 December 2012. Although the treaty allowed warheads to be dismantled rather than destroyed and there was no verification procedure, the Duma ratified what became known as the Moscow Treaty on 14 May 2003.

The old Soviet and Primakovian politics of linkage in negotiations and symmetry in concessions gave way to a new understanding of diplomacy that some saw as a new version of Gorbachevian capitulationism. In his survey of 'The world after 11 September', Primakov insisted that not much had changed except America's improved geopolitical position in Central Asia and the Caucasus and the increased dangers of American unilateralism.[56]

This was a view shared by much of Russia's political elite including the foreign minister, Ivanov, who insisted on an appropriate role for the United Nations.[57] In this context Russia's stance during the Iraq crisis should not have come as a surprise. On numerous occasions Ivanov's successor as foreign minister, Sergei Lavrov, called for Russia's legitimate interests and concerns to be recognised by the West. In an interview in November 2005, for example, he argued:

> Understanding the lawfulness of our [Western] partners' interests, we expect that they would acknowledge the lawfulness of ours on the territories adjacent to our borders, and which 15 years ago constituted a single country along with Russia and which still have economic, cultural, social ties and sometimes strong family ties. Do not forget that some 25 million ethnic Russians live in the countries bordering Russia.[58]

Even though Putin's European and Western orientation came naturally to him, there was no evidence that he sought to resurrect Soviet-style attempts to drive a wedge between the American and European wings of the Western alliance, and in this respect he was genuinely post-Soviet. In part this may have been recognition that, despite tensions and conflict, the alliance was built on solid foundations of mutual interest, and that any attempt to exploit divisions would be counterproductive. This self-denying ordinance was particularly impressive as the USA under Bush entered a period of international activism. Paradoxically, the divisions within the West became most apparent just at the time when Russia renounced attempts to exploit them. For some, Europe is emerging from its dependence on America and will in the long term become a global geopolitical rival to America.[59] In the Iraq crisis Russia sought to act as mediator between Europe and America, a role Britain had traditionally tried to play. Russia, like France, insisted that any war against Iraq should be conducted under the aegis of the UN, and that the legitimate interests of Russia (and France) in the country should be respected in a post-Saddam Iraq. Russia found itself torn between the two faces of the West: the interventionist Anglo–American bloc and the Franco–German 'axis of peace'.[60] In populist terms, these could be dubbed the 'wild West' and the 'normative West'.

Putin's second term was marked by increasing tensions in Russo–American relations. Attention remained focused on traditional areas of co-operation, notably security and non-proliferation of weapons of mass destruction, although energy supplies became an increasingly important mutual concern. American–Russia bilateral trade in 2003 amounted to only $7.1 billion, making the USA Russia's seventh largest trade partner, while Russia ranked in 38th place among America's trade partners.[61] At the same time, in 2004 the USA allocated $880 million for various assistance programmes in Russia.[62] It was clear at their meeting in Bratislava on 24 February 2004 that both men had invested considerable personal and political capital in ensuring that their relationship remained cordial. Putin's blunt (some would say reckless) support for Bush's re-election in 2004 reflected just how precariously personal the relationship between the two countries had become.[63] James Richter notes that Bush and Putin shared a psychological profile focused on the order and discipline that was lacking in their youths, and emphasised individual choice rather than the management of problems in consensual and multilateral ways.[64] Putin clearly preferred Bush's realist approach based on national interests than what he feared would be the Democrats' focus on 'values' (the Wilsonian tradition), which it was assumed would be more critical of Russian domestic policy.[65] Following the Democratic capture of both houses of Congress in the November 2006 mid-term elections, the Russian 'stick' was used to beat the Republicans, although not as much as anticipated since attention was focused on the Iraq quagmire.

There were numerous points of tension in the relationship, notably Russia's supply of technology and materials for Iran's nuclear energy programme, as well as Russia's vigorous arms sale programme, including the supply of anti-aircraft missiles to Syria. The Russian contract to build the nuclear power plant in Bushehr, Iran, caused considerable acrimony, especially after the election of the militant Mahmoud Ahmadinejad in 2005, a veteran of the Iran–Iraq war and an ardent supporter of Iran's uranium enrichment programme. America's policy of isolating Iran, and indeed of support for Saddam Hussein's war on Iran in the 1980s, now bore its bitter fruit. American support for the various 'colour' revolutions in Georgia, Ukraine and Kyrgyzstan seemed to pose a threat to Russia itself, especially when American officials openly declared the strategy of using Iranian civil society to overthrow the legitimately elected Ahmadinejad government. It appeared that the USA was trying to build an arc of containment around Russia, stretching from the Baltic in the north to Central Asia. The authors of a recent report note, '[T]he gap between glowing rhetoric and thin substance has grown. This shallowness leaves USA–Russian ties bereft of constituencies wider than leaders and a few highly placed government officials and increasingly vulnerable to growing choruses of skeptics'.[66] The authors argue that the fashionable distinction drawn between 'interests' and 'values' in foreign policy was a false one, insisting that the way that a state defines its interests reflects its values: hence 'disagreements between Russia and the USA reflect differences in how we frame and define our interests'.[67] In Russia there was a renewed stress on self-sufficiency and sovereignty, while America asserted its global hegemony in ever more strident tones.

This was reflected in the Council on Foreign Relations Independent task force report of early 2006, which subjected Russian policy, and ultimately Russia itself, to sustained criticism, insisting that Russia was taking the 'wrong direction'.[68] As far as many Russians were concerned, 'What really upsets the United States is Russia's unique role in the global energy market'.[69] Washington's ability to influence Russian policy appeared limited, even though Bush's new *National Security Strategy* of 16 March 2006 noted that 'America is at war' and insisted that 'We seek to shape the world, not merely be shaped by it'. Russia, equally, like the rest of the world, had little leverage over Washington. Talk of a 'strategic alliance' between the two countries was redundant, especially since it appeared that there was no common vision or shared set of values. The speech of vice-president Dick Cheney at a conference of East European leaders in Vilnius on 4 May 2006 argued that 'opponents of reform are seeking to reverse the gains of the last decade, and warned Russia against its alleged abuse of the energy instrument: 'No legitimate interest is served when oil and gas become tools of intimidation or blackmail, either by supply manipulation or attempts to monopolize transportation'. He conceded that 'None of us believes that Russia is fated to become an enemy', but he insisted that 'Russia has a choice to make', the 'return to democratic reform'.[70] The content of the speech and its hectoring tone provoked a storm of protest in Russia, while the venue suggested that America was intent on forging an anti-Russian front in what were called in the interwar years the *Zwischenraumländer*, the lands in-between two power centres.

While the neo-conservatives in Washington stressed the imperial and global role that the promotion of democratic values should play, Moscow asserted the sovereign right of each country to define democracy as it saw fit, the ideology of 'sovereign democracy' that came to the fore after the Orange revolution. However, the two countries shared a minimalist view of international integration. As Nikolai Zlobin puts it, 'Bush needs the Kremlin only as an ally in the war against terrorism, which suits Putin perfectly'.[71] The democratic transitions in Georgia and Ukraine placed USA–Russian relations under strain and challenged Putin's definition of 'new realism', especially when it came to competition for influence over CIS states. Their relationship appeared based more on rhetoric that the reality of strategic co-operation, with competing goals in the former Soviet space. As Zlobin notes, in Bush's first term 'Washington managed to whittle down bilateral co-operation to its politico-military aspect only ... [while America] went to great lengths to prevent relations from deepening or becoming more strategic ... [and] in no way kept America from squeezing Moscow out of almost every sphere of international authority'.[72] Dmitri Trenin sums this up well:

> Western relations with Russia can no longer be described in terms of integration, as it is traditionally understood, that is, gradually drawing Russia into the Western institutional orbit. For that, there is neither particular demand on the part of Russia nor sufficient supply on the part of the United States or the EU. Nato and the EU, which were so successfully used with regard to the countries of Central and Eastern Europe, will have to remain idle in the case of Russia. The famous 'double integration elevator' cannot take Russia aboard because Western institutions simply do not have the capacity to do so.[73]

Putin's second term was overshadowed by fears of the emergence of a type of post-ideological Cold War, in which Russia's alleged democratic back-sliding (the regime question) was used to isolate Russia. The potential for a significant divergence between Russia and an America pursuing an intolerant and instrumental 'democratic messianism' was enormous. Russians increasingly came to perceive America's democratic imperialism as a threat.[74] As Anatol Lieven notes:

> Historians of the future will look back with amazement at U.S. foreign policy at the turn of the millennium, especially with regard to Russia. . . . at a moment when both the U.S. and Russia face the common enemy of Islamist terrorism – hard-liners within the Bush administration, and especially in the office of vice-president Dick Cheney, are arguing for a new tough line against Moscow along the lines of a scaled-down Cold War. . . . Some proposed U.S. policies toward Russia seem deliberately provocative. . . . why castigate Moscow for working with dictatorships when Washington has long done the same thing, routinely accommodating any dictatorship possessed of sufficient oil? Why lecture Russia on the need to adopt 'universal market practices' and then howl when it raises its prices for supplying energy to its neighbors to market levels? Why give huge amounts of U.S. aid to one Georgian leader after another just because they are anti-Russian, even after they become corrupt potentates? . . . And this kind of moral autism, alas, is seen in the attitudes of the American establishment toward many other countries. It reflects not only nationalist conformism but a chronic failure on the part of official and semiofficial U.S. analysts to do their first intellectual duty: to place themselves in the shoes of ordinary people in other countries and try to see the world through their eyes.[75]

In effect, Russia was being punished for its aspirations for autonomy and its attempts to find its own way to a viable modernity.

Dependence and inter-dependence with the European Union

The EU after the 1 May 2004 enlargement (Estonia, Latvia, Lithuania, Poland, Czech Republic, Slovakia, Hungary and Slovenia, together with Cyprus and Malta), the rejection of the constitution by France and Holland later that year, and the accession of Bulgaria and Romania on 1 January 2007, has focused more on absorbing its new members than on the management of external relations. The EU's conditionality vis-à-vis Russia, perceived to be selective and instrumental, always irked Russia, considering itself by right a European country and thus resentful of an organisation that claimed the prerogative to decide what was and what was not European. Russia deeply resented the EU's claim to be the arbiter of civilisational achievement, and with it the establishment of a binary division: either European or not – especially when Russia found itself excluded amid allegations of democratic backsliding.[76] According to Sergei Yastrzhembsky, the deterioration in Russo–EU relations had been provoked by the accession of the former communist countries, who had allegedly 'brought the spirit of primitive Russophobia' to the EU.[77] Under Putin's leadership, however, these concerns would not become predominant, despite concerns about 'Orange' technologies being applied to Russia. The EU failed effectively to allay Russia's sense of grievance over the Russian minorities in Estonia and Latvia, and indeed, sense of betrayal by the West, and his successor could well pursue policies more in the spirit of *ressentiment*.

Putin remained committed to close links with the EU, despite numerous points of tension and problems. The EU is Russia's main economic partner, with bilateral trade reaching €96.5 billion in 2004. This represents 50 per cent of Russian trade, although Russia made up only 3.3 per cent of EU-15 trade. Russia has 27 per cent of the world's gas reserves, mostly found in Siberia, and supplies a third of Western European gas needs and is the primary supplier to Turkey. With a developed network of supply pipelines to Europe, Russia supplies 50 per cent of all gas imports. Russia also supplies the EU-27 with one-third of its oil needs. With the decline of North Sea reserves, it is estimated that the EU will import 70 per cent of its energy needs by 2030. This stimulated the search for alternative sources of energy to avoid excessive dependence on Russia, and prompted fears that the existing dependence has blunted EU criticisms of perceived democratic failure in Russia. The brief interruption in gas supplies in the first days of 2006 as part of a pricing dispute with Ukraine was taken as a wake-up call to diversify supplies. At the same time, over 60 per cent of Russia's export revenues come from energy, and the bulk of that is exports to the EU, and Russia derives 40 per cent of its budget from the sale of natural resources to the EU. It is clear that Russia is as dependent on the EU as the EU is on Russia for its energy supplies. The establishment of an Energy Dialogue in October 2000 attempted to regulate this system of mutual dependency, dealing with issues like security of supply, energy efficiency, infrastructure (above all pipelines), investment and trade. However, the energy dialogue did not become an energy partnership, especially since Russia refused to ratify the transport protocol to the 1994 Energy Charter Treaty, which sought to regulate the energy market in Europe.

The Partnership and Cooperation Agreement (PCA) of 24 June 1994 came into force on 1 December 1997 and provided the framework for bilateral relations, including biannual EU–Russia summits. It devised common policies in the four fields of trade and economic co-operation; science and technology; political dialogue on issues of mutual concern, including democracy and human rights; and justice and home affairs issues, such as drug trafficking, money laundering and organised crime. The EU's Common Strategy on Russia of June 1999, valid for four years, sought to provide greater coherence in its relations with Russia, dealing with such areas as the consolidation of democracy, the integration of Russia into a common European economic and social space, stability and security in Europe and beyond, and coordinated approaches to common challenges such as environment and migration. The PCA was due to expire on 30 November 2007, but could be automatically extended unless either side gave notice of its termination. During the Finnish presidency in late 2006 it was agreed that the new Stability and Co-operation Pact would take the form of a Strategic Partnership Treaty between the EU and Russia, encompassing energy issues and a range of new instruments, to provide for a genuine strategic partnership.

The EU summits were used by Putin to reaffirm his belief that Russia was part of Europe. However, the 2004 enlargement brought the EU to the borders of Russia and raised new problems in its wake. There were major problems over access, the visa regime and other issues concerning the Kaliningrad exclave, separated from Russia by Lithuania and Belarus. In Helsinki in October 1999 Putin had suggested that Kaliningrad could become a 'pilot region' for EU–Russian relations, and in a sense it did. The conflict over the status of the region came to a head at the EU–Russia summit on 29 May 2002, when the EU sharply rejected all Russian proposals to deal with the problems arising from the imposition of the Schengen regime on the EU's new members. Later in the year (11 November) an agreement allowed the use of a facilitated transport document (FTD) system from 1 July 2003 for Russian citizens travelling between Kaliningrad and other parts of Russia.

The 31 May 2003 St Petersburg Russia–EU summit (the eleventh) adopted the four Common Spaces concept: economy, external security, justice and home affairs, and research and culture. The November 2003 Rome summit adopted the Common European Economic Space (CEES) concept, modelled initially on the European Economic Area, which included the EU-15 and Switzerland, Iceland and Norway, extending the four freedoms enshrined in the Single European Act of 1986 (freedom of movement in goods, capital, services and labour) to partner countries. While practical work on the four spaces continued, above all in the form of 'roadmaps' adopted at the May 2005 Moscow summit, EU–Russian relations in this as in other spheres appeared unable to move beyond the stage of 'dialogue' towards 'partnership'.

On 11 March 2003 the European Commission adopted the 'Wider Europe' Communication, outlining a new framework for relations over the next decade with Russia, the western newly independent states (Belarus, Ukraine, Moldova) and the southern Mediterranean including Israel and the Palestinian Authority.[78] Russia wished to have nothing to do with the programme when it later became the European Neighbourhood Policy (ENP). These countries do not have the immediate prospect of EU membership, but they now share a border with the EU. The aim of the ENP is to surround the EU with a ring of friendly states while encouraging them to adapt to European norms and standards. This would be achieved by opening up its markets to neighbours and facilitating the free movement of goods, services, people and capital within the region. At the same time, the ENP policy ruled out these countries becoming EU members in the near future. As Chris Patten noted, 'Over the past decade, the Union's most successful foreign policy instrument has undeniably been the promise of EU membership. This is not sustainable. For the coming decade, we need to find new ways to export the stability, security and prosperity we have created within the enlarged EU'.[79] The western Eurasian states, above all Ukraine, were disappointed about being lumped in with North Africa and the Middle East, whose membership of the EU has been ruled out by Brussels. The possibility of accession for west Eurasian states has not been excluded, but the ENP does not mention it. The countries feared that the EU's policy of 'deepened co-operation' instead of 'integration' would be applied to them for the long term as well.

Conflicts in the Balkans demonstrated that only Nato had the capacity to intervene decisively within a multilateral framework, whereas the EU had shown itself paralysed and divided. It was for this reason that in 1999 the EU sought to provide muscle to its diplomatic activity by building on what had earlier been called its Common Foreign and Security Policy (CFSP) to develop a European Security and Defence Policy (ESDP). On this basis a 60,000 strong joint combat force was established. Russia was thus faced with two overlapping security organisations in the West, one well-established and the other with growing ambitions in this sphere, neither of which was enthusiastic for Russia to join. As far as Moscow was concerned, the EU appeared to be taking on an ever-more tangible presence in its traditional areas of influence, and for many in Russia this was taking on a neo-imperial guise.

Russia's traditional *Realpolitik* approach to foreign policy found it difficult to grasp that the EU could speak with one voice on behalf of all of its members, and that its normative dynamic was more than an instrument of policy but a genuine commitment to a shared set of values. Russia's doubts on this count were exacerbated by the EU's apparent failure to address Russia's concerns over the status of Russian minorities in Estonia and Latvia. The introduction of the Schengen visa requirements placed restrictions on cross-border transit, especially across the border between Poland and Kaliningrad. It appeared that the West in the guise of the EU was intent on reinforcing Russia's traditional view of itself as an alternative, and competitive, geopolitical subject, and thus attempts by post-communist Russia to find a way of adapting to Western norms and to become part of the West while affirming its own identity, however contradictorily these goals were pursued, were rebuffed. As Yuri Lotman argued, the dualistic opposition between Russia and the West, played out in various guises such as the struggle between Orthodoxy and Catholicism, had long acted as the deep structure of Russian development, providing long-term continuity in Russian culture.[80] As Morozov puts it, 'the West has indeed played the role of constitutive outside for Russian political community, an absolute negation which allows the Russian Self to be constituted'.[81] Putin did not see the world in this way, but his successor may.

Nato and its enlargement

As far as Putin was concerned, Russia was *part* of the West, if not always *of* the West. For his critics, however, Putin's 'new realism' meant little more than the continuation of Russia's geopolitical shrinkage. This was particularly in evidence over Nato and its enlargement. From the first, Putin signalled an open mind on the question. On a visit to Britain in Spring 2000, asked by David Frost about Russia's membership of Nato Putin answered: 'Why not?' The answer was not so much a serious bid for membership, but a signal (as Putin put it in the same interview) that 'Russia is part of European culture and I can't imagine my country cut off from Europe or from what we often refer to as the "civilized world" ... seeing Nato as an enemy is destructive for Russia'.[82] At the Genoa G7 summit in July 2001 premier Silvio Berlusconi of Italy worked hard to promote his strategy of opening Nato to closer Russian engagement. Russian representatives, withdrawn at the time of the Kosovo crisis in 1999, returned to Nato headquarters, and in February 2001 Nato's information office in Moscow was reopened. Nato worked hard to ensure that enlargement would not be at the price of excluding Russia.

Putin's response to 11 September emphasised a strong relationship between Nato and Russia. Blair in particular sought to bring Russia into an enlarged security community, although stopping short of actually inviting it to join the organisation. The establishment in June 2002 of a reconstituted Nato–Russia Council built on the 1997 Russia–Nato Founding Act, but instead of the model being 19 Nato members relating to Russia singly, the new 'Nato at 20' elevated Russia symbolically to equal rank with all the others and thus represented yet another step in the transcendence of the Cold War. The issues to be dealt with by the new body included the struggle against terrorism, proliferation of weapons of mass destruction, management of regional crises and peacekeeping, anti-ballistic missile defence and search-and-rescue operations. Even though the Cold War had once again ended, Russia was still treated as a special case and the unwieldy character of the new body reduced its ability to deal effectively with complex issues.

Russia's elites were particularly exercised over enlargement. Nato's first expansion, bringing in Poland, Hungary and the Czech Republic in March 1999, coincided with Nato's bombing of Serbia during the Kosovo conflict between March and June 1999. Polls suggested that public opinion was also opposed to the organisation's extension to the East.[83] Although the war on terror after 11 September was not conducted within the aegis of Nato, it later took the lead in Afghanistan. Nato's enlargement paradoxically took place at a time when its role was undermined by the creation of *ad hoc* coalitions of the willing, as in the second Iraq war of 2003. Rather than the anticipated and rather limited expansion, the Nato summit in Prague on 21–22 November 2002 went for the 'big bang' approach and invited almost all the former communist states to join, with the exception of those in the

Balkans. The three Baltic republics (Estonia, Latvia and Lithuania) joined along with Slovakia, Slovenia, Romania and Bulgaria in April 2004. After 11 September Russian resistance to the inclusion of the three Baltic states weakened. Even Ukraine on 23 May 2002 announced that it would seek membership of Nato, although its leadership admitted that it would take at least eight to ten years for this to be achieved.[84] The door was left open for a further enlargement that would include at the minimum Croatia, and possibly Albania and Macedonia. It would be a long time before Serbia, Montenegro or Bosnia would be able to join. As for Ukraine's aspirations, Yushchenko vigorously renewed Ukraine's aspirations for Nato membership. Belarus was not even in the running because of president Alexander Lukashenko's authoritarianism.

Russia in Asia

For most of the late 1990s Russian diplomacy sought to forge an Indian–Chinese–Russian triangle as a counterbalance to the USA and Nato. The Indian link in this chain was always the weakest, but even the Chinese one was beset with contradictions. The success of China's 'four modernisations', launched by Deng Xiaoping in 1979, in contrast with Russia's travails in the 1990s, meant that the Chinese path of authoritarian modernisation (in which the Communist Party acted as the instrument of capitalist restoration) appeared attractive to many in Russia.[85] With both Russia and China emphasising the need for a 'multipolar' world and the 'territorial integrity' of states (that is, Chinese support for Russia's war in Chechnya and Russia's support for the 'one China' policy that claims Chinese sovereignty over Taiwan), there were plenty of points in common in the Russian and Chinese views of the world.[86] The Russo–Chinese link was built on a number of shared concerns: the struggle against 'unipolar' hegemonism; against 'humanitarian' interventionism (the principle of non-interference in internal affairs);[87] Islamic secessionism (Chechnya, Kosovo, Xinxiang); arms sales; opposition to Nato enlargement; developing economic links; and some mutual acceptance of Russia's hegemony as a guarantor of order in Eurasia. These common concerns, however, would not become a full-blown 'strategic partnership' if for no other reason that China throughout its history has avoided such 'entangling alliances'. Putin has avoided talking of a 'strategic partnership' with China, although he has stressed their common interests.

The shift from alternativity to autonomy had important practical outcomes. The end of the Cold War had been followed by the supremacy, indeed triumphalism, of 'the West', and Russian and Chinese calls for the restoration of a multipolar world reflected concern about the unbalanced world system that had emerged as a result of the disintegration of the USSR and the end of bipolarity and superpower balance. In the event, in the post-Cold War world the Eastern pole could find no satisfactory political form or ideological rationale. Under Putin, grand geopolitical schemes of world order, favoured by Primakov, moved down the list of Russian priorities. In particular the idea of a 'strategic partnership' with China was de-emphasised, although arms sales and the deepening of economic ties continued.[88] The concepts of 'East' and 'West' were rethought. There would be no distinctive third way between, on the one hand, the traditional Cold War confrontation between East and West, and on the other hand, the unabashed reduction of modernisation into Westernisation. Russia under Putin was resolutely not a revisionist power, and thus tried to avoid becoming the core of a balancing coalition.

The relationship with China focused on arms and energy. Following an agreement on military-technical co-operation in December 1992, China became one of Russia's main markets for arms sales, averaging US$1 billion annually in the 1990s, rising to US$2 billion in the 2000s. Co-operation deepened significantly following the war in Kosovo, with up to 2,000 Russian specialists working in Chinese laboratories on advanced weapons projects.[89] Arms sales to China basically kept Russian defence industries afloat in a time of hardship. However, there were points of tension in the relationship. Sections of the Russian military and political elite harboured concern over a potential military threat from China. With Russia supplying 95 per cent of all arms imported by China in the early 2000s,[90] the transfer of sensitive military technology and know-how to China alarmed many Russian strategists, fearing China's rise to great power status. Moscow was concerned that China was buying Russian military technology and know-how while avoiding the purchase of large ready-made stocks of military hardware. Already one of the world's most advanced fighter planes, the SU-27, was being assembled in China. Moscow's view that China sought to achieve technology transfer to develop its own defence production capabilities while lessening its dependence was correct. Gradually China entered the arms market in its own right.[91] While the two countries were hesitant about engaging in a strategic partnership, fears that the United States sought nuclear superiority over both China and Russia, as argued in a well-known article,[92] encouraged nuclear and ballistic missile co-operation. In the energy field, relations had soured because of Russia's decision to build the East Siberian–Pacific Ocean (ESPO) oil pipeline to the Pacific coast first, serving the rich Japanese and Korean markets, rather than to Daqing, as the Chinese had hoped. However, during his visit to China on 21–22 March 2006 a deal was signed for two pipeline projects that would supply China with 80 billion cubic meters of gas by 2011. With the EU increasingly wary of Russia as a supplier, especially following the January 2006 interruption of gas supplies across Ukraine and the January 2007 interruption in oil supplies across Belarus, Russia also began to look for ways of diversifying its markets.

Trade between Russia and China began from a low base, totalling only $6 billion in 1999, but rose rapidly in the Putin era and reached the $50 billion mark in 2006. Russia became one of the main destinations for Chinese overseas investment. However, there was a major imbalance in the structure of trade. Leaving aside arms sales, Russian exports were primarily oil and oil products and unprocessed timber, while China sent increasing volumes of machinery and manufactured items, including cars. Chinese economic power was particularly strong in Siberia and Russia's Far East, exacerbating Russian fears over the fate of the underpopulated, underdeveloped and isolated Eastern regions of the country, sharing a 4,300-kilometre border with China. The population of the Russian Far East is eight million and that of Siberia 25 million, and both are decreasing, whereas north-east China's population is approaching 300 million. The three provinces closest to Russia (Heilongjiang, Jilin and Liaoning) have a combined population of 80 million, provoking Russian concern about inflows of people from China. Estimates suggest that there are some two million illegal Chinese immigrants in Russia's eastern territories. In contrast to the rapid development of the Pacific region as a whole, the Russian Far East remains backward and underdeveloped.

The 'Shanghai Five' (Russia, China, Kazakhstan, Kyrgyzstan and Uzbekistan) was established in the mid-1990s as a confidence-building measure and to help resolve a number of outstanding issues, above all the demarcation of borders. The formal establishment of the Shanghai Co-operation Organisation (SCO) at a summit in Shanghai on 14–15 June 2001 as a regional multilateral mechanism for security and co-operation marked a qualitative step change in the intensity of relations. China has been intensifying its economic presence in the region, above all in the energy sphere, but now the SCO legitimated the Chinese presence in Central Asian politics. Its creation underscored the shift away from a 'strategic partnership' between Russia and China towards a more pragmatic relationship based on shared interests and concerns. Although the SCO insisted that it was not a military alliance, its founding charter enshrined the classical collective security principle that each member would assist another requesting help against attack by terrorists, separatists or extremists, and military exercises were conducted under its auspices.

The SCO was the antithesis of the liberal universalist principles proclaimed by the leading Western powers, and instead took a hard-headed realist approach to international politics based on interests rather than 'values'. The SCO established an anti-terrorism centre in Shanghai in January 2004, and Russia and China held their first ever joint military exercises in August 2005. By 2006 India, Iran, Mongolia and Pakistan had been granted, and Belarus had applied for, observer status, while America's application for observer status in 2005 was refused. There were plans at that time to give the observers full membership, and to rename and reform the organisation. China's developing economic ties in Central Asia, focusing on energy and pipelines but broadening out into manufacturing, trade and banking, were accompanied by its strategic goal to minimise Western influence in the region.[93] This was a concern shared by Russia, although China's own growing weight in the area could not but worry Moscow. The SCO helped manage potential Sino–Russia rivalry over Central Asian energy and economic resources, and co-ordinate security co-operation. Although a non-aligned body and not directed against a third party, the SCO's status and role was fundamentally ambiguous and signalled the emergence of a bloc with the potential to counter American hegemonic ambitions.

Russia and Japan were unable to sign the much-awaited bilateral treaty by the end of 2000, as promised by Yeltsin and the then Japanese prime minister Ryutaro Hashimoto at the 'no-neckties' summit in Krasnoyarsk in November 1997. The problem remained active into the Putin era. The fundamental obstacle to the improvement of bilateral ties remained: the conflict over the Kurile Islands, called by Japan the Northern Territories (Habomai Islands, Iturup (Etorofu), Kunashiri and Shikotan Islands), occupied by the USSR since 1945. For Japan the question was motivated primarily neither by economic nor security concerns but by the very principle of territorial integrity; similar feelings informed Russia's refusal to give up territory.

Russia's turn to the West and multi-layered relationship with the East reflected a more profound turning away from the South. The former USSR had posed as champion of the third world and, however ambivalently, it reflected aspirations for global social justice and a more equitable world order. The collapse of the Eastern pole of the bipolar world left the South without a powerful champion. From being the core of the East, Russia now became a rather isolated North. Under Putin, Russia turned decisively to the West while at the same time recasting its Eastern policy. This was no longer an Easternism provoked by failure to become Western, but an attempt to forge a realistic and mutually beneficial relationship. It also represented a move beyond the Eurasian 'bridge' metaphor of Russia linking East and West and an affirmation that Russia was a destination in itself. For Putin the Eurasianist notion of Russia between East and West was a bridge leading nowhere. Dmitry Trenin argued that China's growing strength in the East, and the instability of the Islamic South, meant that Russia's only geopolitical future lay with the West. This would mean accelerated integration with the EU and solid relations with the United States.[94] It was clear that Eurasianism had died, both intellectually and geopolitically. It was unable to sustain a coherent foreign policy.

Towards a new post-Soviet Eurasia

Surrounded by relatively weak states and with powerful security threats emanating from the South, Russia sought to reassert some sort of hegemony over the region. There were different ways in which this could be achieved, either coercively or co-operatively, and Russia appeared to pursue both simultaneously.[95] Popular opinion strongly favoured the reintegration of the post-Soviet space, although links with Belarus, Ukraine, Kazakhstan and Moldova came top of the list.[96] The great strategic problem facing Russia was the challenge of foreign policy diversification by its former brother Soviet states. It was apparent that the CIS had failed to become the great counter-European institution that some in Moscow had anticipated, but it was far less clear what would take its place.

The CIS never lived up to the aspirations of some of its founders. It proved unable to regulate disputes between its own members, covering not only conflicts over borders, support for insurgency in other member states, economic relations, and on occasion open war, between Armenia and Azerbaijan over the disputed territory of Nagorno-Karabakh. Fear of Russian domination from the very beginning prompted countries like Ukraine to impede the institutional and political development of the CIS, while all (with the exception of Belarus) actively diversified links away from Russia towards the West and regional powers. In security affairs, membership of Nato had become the open aspiration of countries such as Georgia, Ukraine and Azerbaijan. The establishment of an American security presence in Central Asia and the South Caucasus after 11 September was a vivid manifestation that old patterns and regional alliances had given way to a far more fluid global geopolitical situation.

Although Putin may have had a sentimental regard for the recreation of some sort of post-Soviet integrated space, his approach in practice was ruthlessly new realist. Unlike Primakov, he realised that the CIS would not be able to act as the focus for integration, but his vision of Russia as a 'normal' great power presumed a degree of Russian dominance in the region. This dominance, however, would have to be cost effective. For him, post-Soviet Eurasia was the immediate sphere for the pursuit of Russian interests and concerns, while recognising the inviolable sovereignty of the post-Soviet states. As we shall see, Putin is a legitimist, and this defined relations with Russia's neighbours. The adoption of a new citizenship law in July 2002 revealed the new unsentimental approach, with the CIS states seen as the source of labour while at the same time cutting off all those who had failed to claim Russian citizenship by then. The new law finally drew a line between who was and who was not a Russian citizen and thus was designed to play its part in reinforcing Russia's national identity. The term *sootechestvennik* (compatriot) was to be used henceforth strictly to describe Russian citizens living abroad, and not the great mass of ethnic Russians living in the former Soviet republics.[97] On a visit to Armenia in early 2005 Putin referred to the CIS in the past tense, and from the summer of 2005 Russia stressed that relations with post-Soviet Eurasia had to be placed on a strictly economic basis.

The most vivid evidence of the decline of the CIS was the creation in 1996 of the GUAM group of states (Georgia, Ukraine, Azerbaijan and Moldova), with Uzbekistan joining in April 1999 and leaving in 2004. The initial concern of the group was to ensure Russian compliance with force limitations within the framework of the OSCE's Treaty on Conventional

Forces in Europe. The long-term aim was to stay outside Russia's orbit and Russian-dominated bodies like the CIS Collective Security Treaty (CST) and the Eurasian Economic Community (EurAsEc).

Russo–Ukrainian relations at the best of times were not easy, with fears in the latter of 'Ukrainophobia' in Russia, characterised by numerous publications questioning Ukraine's legitimacy as a state, as a distinct people, and its pro-Western policies. From the other side, 'Russophobia', especially in western Ukraine, appeared to be the defining force of Ukrainian national identity. Russia was characterised as neo-imperial, and every manifestation of self-assertion was condemned as a recrudescence of the worst aspects of the past. It appeared too often that Ukraine was less Russia's 'constitutive other' than its 'destructive other', stimulating intolerance and militant revanchism accompanied by a low level of public discourse. All this came to the fore during Ukraine's Orange revolution in late 2004. Putin appears to have drawn a number of lessons from the experience. The first was not to go too far out on a limb in support of candidates in various elections, and thus Russia studiously avoided giving demonstrative support to Askar Akaev in his election campaign in Kyrgyzstan in February 2005. Another was his insistence on the 'economisation' of relations in the post-Soviet sphere. In his press conference of 31 January 2006 he noted that Russia was subsidising Ukraine to the tune of $3–5 billion a year, and got very little benefit in return. This was the background to the attempt to raise gas prices to world levels.

Putin maintained Yeltsin's policy of support for the various *de facto* states left behind in the detritus of the break-up of the USSR. One way or another Russia continued to support Abkhazia's struggle for autonomy from Georgia. Russia's support for the intransigent and corrupt regime headed by Igor Smirnov at the head of the breakaway Transdniester region of Moldova, however, was liable to cause Putin considerable embarrassment. Russia had agreed at the OSCE summit in November 1999 to withdraw its forces from the region by December 2002, and failure to do so undermined international trust in his leadership. Russia was reluctant to fulfil its pledge made at the OSCE summit in late 1999 to close down its Gudauta base in Georgia by July 2001 and to negotiate the closure of the Batumi and Akhalkalaki bases. By 2005, however, Russia began its withdrawal from the latter, although there was no sign of the removal of its 1,200 soldiers in Transdniestria, guarding the huge Soviet-era weapons dump. The problem of the *de facto* states in former Soviet territory is part of the broader problem of the point at which a secessionist movement can be recognised by the international community. With the beginning of 'final status' talks on Kosovo in 2006, the status of other conflicts became even more pressing. Putin in his 31 January 2006 press conference drew the connection:

> Principles have to be universal, otherwise they cannot inspire trust in the policy we are pursuing. And conversely, we will always be casting

doubt on the fairness of one decision or another. The same applies to Kosovo. If someone believes that Kosovo can be granted full state independence, then why should we refuse the same to the Abkhaz or the South Ossetians?[98]

His remarks were prompted by moves to grant Kosovo 'conditional independence' from Serbia, traditionally a Russian ally. Russia's official position was to support Serbia's territorial integrity. Putin's position was clear: if Kosovo was granted some sort of independence, then why should the same principle not apply to Abkhazia and South Ossetia? The principle of self-determination, however, was a two-edged sword, and if it was to become 'universal', then why should Chechnya also not be granted independence?

Putin sought to find effective institutions to formalise links with willing CIS partners. The Collective Security Treaty had been established in Tashkent in 1992 and represented one of the very few successful attempts to build a broad multilateral body within the framework of the CIS, with eight countries having joined by 1994.[99] But it also reflected the weakness of such bodies, and Azerbaijan, Georgia and Uzbekistan never took part in any Treaty activities and abandoned it altogether in 1999. On the very day in June 2002 that the new partnership council was established with Nato, Putin signed the papers that transformed the CST into a Collective Security Treaty Organisation (CSTO). The CSTO at that time united Armenia, Belarus, Russia, Kyrgyzstan, Kazakhstan and Tajikistan, while Uzbekistan 'rejoined' at the CSTO summit in Minsk on 23 June 2006. The Central Asian rather than Western focus remained, with Russia deploying aircraft to the Kant airbase near Bishkek in Kyrgyzstan. In May 2003 the CSTO was given ambitious security tasks, including a joint military command in Moscow, a rapid reaction force, a common air defence system and 'coordinated action' in foreign, security and defence policy.[100]

At the same time, Russia tried to reinvigorate economic links in the region. In October 2000 Belarus, Kazakhstan, Kyrgyzstan, Tajikistan and Russia signed a treaty strengthening their existing customs union, which was now renamed the Eurasian Economic Community (EAEC, or EvrAsEs). The aim was to establish a free trade and unified customs system, and to coordinate relations with the WTO. A number of institutions were to promote these goals, including an Integration Committee, an EAEC Parliamentary Assembly and an EAEC Arbitration Court. At the EAEC St Petersburg summit on 25 January 2006 Uzbekistan joined the organisation, underscoring the country's geopolitical shift towards Russia and the strengthening energy partnership between the two. The prospects of genuine economic integration within the framework of the EAEC are not bright. Russia also took the lead in establishing in September 2003 a Common Economic Space (CES), bringing together the more advanced economies of Russia, Ukraine, Belarus and Kazakhstan. It sought to create a free trade zone to facilitate the free movement of goods, services, capital and labour (on the model of the EU's Single European Act of 1986). It should be noted that bilateral trade between Russia and Ukraine reached $16 billion in 2004, an increase of 40 per cent over that attained in 2003, and made Ukraine Russia's third largest trade partner after Belarus and Germany. Despite close economic ties, Ukraine was ambivalent about the CES, fearing that it could jeopardise links with the EU. Russia, Belarus and Kazakhstan by mid-2006 were ready to sign the documents creating the CES, and hoped that in due course Ukraine would join.

One of the key principles of Putin's relations with CIS states was his emphasis on legitimism. In domestic affairs from the very first he stressed that he would not change the constitution and would abide by its stipulations, and in technical terms he has done just this, and this principle has also been applied to post-Soviet Eurasia. This led him to support authoritarian leaders, such as Islam Karimov in Uzbekistan and Alexander Lukashenko in Belarus, establishing a type of latter-day 'holy alliance' against colour revolutions. Following the killings in Andijan on 13 May 2005, Uzbekistan established closer links with Russia, in particular in the sphere of energy policy, and requested the removal of American bases from the country. Putin's legitimist approach is reinforced by his aversion to revolutionary changes of power.[101] Putin's legitimism is reinforced by issues of geostrategic advantage, but the principle was also applied in cases where Russia's national interests were less clear-cut. Putin's over-emphatic support for the succession of power from Leonid Kuchma to Victor Yanukovich in Ukraine in late 2004 ignored the fact that the final winner, Viktor Yushchenko, had forged strong economic and political ties with Russia when he had been finance minister. In relations with the former Soviet states, however, this has not made Putin a neo-Brezhnevian, and Russia's lack of intervention in support of Askar Akaev at the time of the tulip revolution in March 2005 makes it clear that no updated version of the Brezhnev doctrine is in the offing, despite the threat of pre-emptive strikes beyond Russia's borders made in the aftermath of Beslan.

Regional alliances however were not able to substitute for bilateral links, the most intense of which was with Belarus. There was strong and consistent public support for unification with Belarus, with 62 per cent in support in 1997 and 72 per cent in November 2000, while on average only 15 per cent were opposed.[102] Russia's link with 'Europe's last dictator',[103] Lukashenko, was understandable in purely *Realpolitik* terms but did little to enhance Russia's reputation as a democracy. Putin rejected Lukashenko's plan of 10 June 2002, insisting that unification should not be at the 'expense of Russia's economic interests'. He refused to countenance Lukashenko's demands that Belarus, whose economy was only 3 per cent of Russia's, would have 'rights of veto, sovereignty and territorial integrity' unless Russia had them too, and spoke against creating 'a supranational organ with undefined functions'.[104] Although integration issues dominated Belarusian politics throughout Lukashenko's presidency, support for unification among Belarusian citizens dropped significantly. If, in 1994, 45 per cent were in favour, by 2002 this had fallen to 16 per cent.[105] Even though the state tradition may have been weak, Belarusians were even less willing to give it up. Russia feared granting Belarus control over economic and monetary policy in the joint state, and was not too keen on paying for the privilege of integrating with Belarus. While the Belarusian economy was certainly dependent on Russia, above all in the sphere of energy, Lukashenko tried to ensure that it did not fall into the hands of Russian big business, and this was yet another reason for his resistance to privatisation and insistence on pursuing the 'Belarusian economic model'. At the CIS summit in Minsk on 28 November 2006 Putin reiterated Moscow's intention to move energy prices to a market basis without exception, and a deal signed in the last minutes of the year saw steep immediate rises in the price paid for Russian gas that by 2011 would bring Belarusian prices up to world levels. Lukashenko responded by imposing a surcharge on Russian oil transiting the country through the 'Druzhba' pipeline, provoking supply fears in Germany and other destinations. There would be no union between Russia and Belarus while Putin and Lukashenko were leaders, and even less likelihood of one afterwards.

Conclusion

Policy under Putin entered a period of new realism in which the view of Russia as an alternative pole to the West gave way to a struggle for Russian autonomy within the framework of a positive-sum view of the world. The West of course did not always reciprocate, and the potential for Russian policy to return to the competitive pragmatism typical of Primakov's stewardship did not disappear. Putin's reassertion of what he perceived to be Russia's proper place in the world threatened the existing balance of relationships and increasingly provoked zero-sum confrontations. The structural problem of inserting a new power into the international system on equal terms was unprecedented; and it is a problem that the world is again facing as China begins to assert itself on the international stage. Putin built his 'new realist' foreign policy on a rather tenuous and narrow institutional and social base, and it is far from certain that his policy of positive engagement with the West would be continued by his successors. Putin's aim was to transform Russia's potential into reality, and he believed that this could be done only in partnership with the West. However, if faced by the choice of either moving ever closer to the 'Western world' or cherishing the dream of restoring the country's status as a great power, it was not clear which way Russia would go.

11 Conclusion

The power of contradiction

Russia should be and will be a country with a developed civil society and stable democracy. Russia will guarantee full human rights, civil liberties and political freedom. Russia should be and will be a country with a competitive market economy, a country where property rights are reliably protected and where economic freedom makes it possible for people to work honestly and to earn without fear or restriction. Russia will be a strong country with modern, well-equipped and mobile armed forces, with an army ready to defend Russia and its allies and the national interests of the country and of its citizens. All this will and should create worthy living conditions for people and will make it possible to be an equal in the society of the most developed states. And people can not only be proud of such a country – they will multiply its wealth, will remember and respect our great history. This is our strategic goal.

Valdimir Putin[1]

In his work on political leadership Machiavelli applied the classic distinction between *fortuna*, or random luck, and *virtù*, success emanating from the intrinsic qualities of the person. Putin's meteoric rise to become president of Russia was certainly characterised by an awesome degree of luck, but without a strong touch of *virtù* this luck would have probably availed him nothing. Periods of war and dislocation often allow outsiders to come to power, but in Putin's case leadership succession took place in peacetime, although of course in far from settled circumstances. Putin's rise reflected the structural conditions of a society desperate to put an end to utopian experimentation and to overcome the bitter divisions that this had provoked. His own background, as a child of the 1970s, loyal to the old regime yet sceptical about it, deeply patriotic yet having internalised the pluriculturalism that the communist regime proclaimed (although did not always practice), and a natural European for whom the question of Russia's civilisational identity was resolved, meant that he reflected the aspirations of society for consolidation and closure. Above all, it was clear that for Putin power was not an end in itself, to achieve self-aggrandisement and to enjoy the trappings of pomp and ceremony, but to achieve goals to serve what he considered the country's needs. Below we shall sum up some of the themes explored in this book and provide the first steps towards a balanced assessment of Putin's presidency.

Public politics

We have argued that drawing a simple dichotomy between Putin's neo-Soviet and post-Soviet faces is inadequate, although not untrue. These two faces undoubtedly co-existed in uncomfortable tension, but the fundamental dynamic of Putin's leadership, and what prevented one becoming predominant over the other, was the attempt to devise an autochthonous path that would transcend the sterile divisions of the past. It does not really matter what this is called, and various labels have been applied including some notion of a Putinite third way as the basis for 'managed democracy' or 'sovereign democracy'. Putin doggedly asserted that Russia's future lies with Europe, the West and democratic capitalist modernity, while insisting at the same time that this did not mean that Russia had to repress its own identity or give up the pursuit of its national interests. He finally managed to convince the people that the promised land of democratic capitalist modernity was attainable and an improvement over communist pseudo-development even though, like the Israelites of old, many a Russian cast a wistful glance back to the comforts and security of Egyptian (read Soviet) captivity. A new mood of social optimism could be discerned. As 2007 arrived the Public Opinion Foundation reported that 67 per cent of respondents expected the new year to be favourable for them.[2] The benefits of the transition to normalcy were beginning to outweight the costs.[3]

State reconstitution or reconcentration

Putin believed in strong and effective central government. He also believed in strong leadership, especially his own. He was in favour of democracy, but the coherence of the state in his mind was even more important. He is a Jacobin state builder of the old school. We have seen that Putin's programme of state reassertion is capable of at least two broad and very different interpretations: reconstitution as a pluralistic law-based model; or reconcentration as a more authoritarian attempt to impose authority over recalcitrant social actors in which it is the regime that is consolidated rather than the constitutional state. In the first version the aim is to achieve the supremacy of the constitution and to ensure the development of polyarchy. However, the dangers of the very uncivil society that Putin inherited, where the major independent actors were the oligarchs, regional bosses and criminal elements, encouraged the state to concentrate power in itself to counterbalance these overweening social interests. It is the 'contradiction' between these models and approaches that dominated politics in the Putin era.

Putin's policies can be understood only in the context of the time, coming after Yeltsin's ten years at the helm when social and political relations had been degraded, although certain freedoms had become established. As the public relations expert and Kremlin election adviser Gleb Pavlovsky put it, 'Yeltsin did not build a state. He led a revolution for ten years ... '.[4] It was for Putin to consolidate the tenuous democratic freedoms that had emerged out of Yeltsin's permanent revolution. His task was to build an effective state, freed from the corruption, clientelism and dependency of the Yeltsin years. However, during the first two years of his rule Putin concentrated on building the presidential 'vertical', in the next two he focused on re-election, and his second term lacked focus. Putin reversed the disintegration of the state, but he was not able to build a state strong enough to prosecute corruption or to provide the framework for ordered democratic politics. In his early years Putin had been able to impose a sense of purpose and unity to the very concept of 'the state', but towards the end it appeared once again to be disintegrating into factional struggle. The Yeltsinite 'conglomerate state' began to reappear. From this perspective it could well be that Putin's historical 'mission' was no more than to consolidate and legalise the results of the social revolution that had taken place in the Gorbachev–Yeltsin years, but at the same time to strip them of the defects of the Yeltsin period.[5] Having done that, the Putin presidency lost its dynamism.

We have identified a darker neo-Soviet face to Putin's rule. The veteran human rights activist, Sergei Kovalev, argued that 'It was not accidental that KGB Lieutenant-Colonel Putin became president of Russia'.[6] Schooled in the worst traditions of the Soviet Union, it was argued that Putin's liberal veneer could not hide his authoritarian centralisation of power. Freedom of the press appeared an early victim, while the development of Russia as a unitary state, in practice, despite formal commitments to federalism, was reminiscent of the worst Soviet days. Once again a climate of fear pervaded social relations, with contacts with foreigners frowned upon and a number of people gaoled for 'anti-state' activities. The secret police intercepted email and telephone traffic, but proved unable to root out corruption. Putin, some argued, turned out to be little more than a more active version of Brezhnev. His rhetorical commitment to the 'dictatorship of law' perhaps revealed more than he intended, showing his lack of understanding of the need for an independent judiciary to regulate a genuinely free market.[7]

This is only one part of the story. Characterised by contradictory social processes, we argue that Putin did not abandon the attempt to achieve the necessary reconstitution of the state through largely democratic means. He remained committed to the 1993 constitutional settlement and sought to work through legal means to rebuild the state and social order. He was very much a constitutional legitimist, something that inevitably took on the aura of Holy Alliance conservatism. However, this was in tension with Putin as a representative of the type that has a long pedigree in Russian history, the decisive leader who forges the nation's consolidation in a time of crisis. This usually took place at a time of a foreign threat, accompanied sometimes by internal disintegration. In Putin's case, the main threats were domestic. In his reform of the federal system Putin sought to bring some order and justice into a society where the arbitrariness of the regional barons was plain for all to see. He pushed through over 200 major pieces of legislation that affected most aspects of government and society. In addition, the struggle for 'social justice' entailed an assault on the extra-democratic privileges of the oligarchs while trying to ensure basic standards of living for the population. The putative legitimacy of the emergency leader is reinforced by a second theme in Russian history, that of modernisation from above. Not trusting the people or autonomous civic activism, the leadership group takes upon itself responsibility for development. In both the late Soviet period and post-communist Russia, this depoliticisation gives rise to bureaucratisation and internal factional struggles. Thus another facet of Russia's reforming leaders is also apparent: early activism is ground down by the bureaucracy and energy dissipated in court intrigues. Putin's consensual approach could be seen as excessive caution that allowed the remaining oligarchs and the bureaucracy to blunt the reforming impulse. The revenge of the bureaucracy, as Gorbachev discovered, is a terrible thing. Rather than achieving the 'normality' prevalent in Western democracies, a deeper Russian 'normality' began to reassert itself.

The rules of the game

Yeltsin's goals and the policies pursued by Putin have much in common. Economic modernisation, the creation of a democratic state and international integration are all policies begun by Russia's first president. However, Putin's leadership style differed substantially from that of his predecessor. Revolutions are characterised by chaos, the weakening of the state and illegality, but there then follows a phase of post-revolutionary stabilisation. Putin's leadership represented such a period. Putin rejected revolution as a method and sought to build a law-governed state based on stable institutions and predictable rules. However, the concept of 'rules of the game' is not one derived from an ordered legal state but from the realm of what Tregubova calls 'bandit ethics', with the law used to punish those refusing to abide by the new rules.[8] On gaining popular legitimacy through the ballot box, Putin wasted no time in beginning to apply the new model of politics.

In regional affairs the aim was to overcome segmented regionalism to make the federal system more structured, impartial, coherent and efficient. Regional leaders, legislatures and local government were to abide by uniform rules. At the centre of this was a new relationship with regional governors and with the oligarchs. A flurry of initiatives changed the way that the central authorities related to other centres of power: seven federal districts were established; regional governors were removed from the Federation Council; and finance and law enforcement agencies were removed from regional subordination and 'refederalised'. The old segmentation decreased, with regional laws and republican constitutions beginning to converge with federal constitutional and legal norms, the state's own agencies in the regions brought back under central control, and some of the more egregious centrifugal tendencies checked. However, regional reforms have not been able to overcome institutional confusion, and in some cases instead of being resolved these contradictions have intensified. For example, the reform of the Federation Council raised in sharper form the idea that it should be formed through direct elections. There was clearly a breakdown of the principle of the separation of powers when the president appointed a governor (even with regional input and consent), then this governor delegated a representative to the upper chamber, a body designed to act as a check on the executive. A new type of 'circular flow of power' was established in which presidential power became self-perpetuating. New tensions have emerged, as between the presidential envoys and the government: the envoys have been urged to ensure federal control over ministerial branches in the regions but the representatives themselves do not sit in the cabinet. Relations with the presidential administration are not always smooth, while relations with the governors are structurally unstable.

The legal separation of powers in the spatial context, the fundamental principle of federalism, was trapped between segmented regionalism and the Putinite reassertion of state power. Putin's reforms are centralising insofar as they seek to fulfil the liberal republican ideal of equality of law across the whole territory, but in practice they have managed to reproduce new forms of segmentation, but at a higher level. Institutional fragmentation continues, and instead of a power 'vertical' being established, we have a power 'triangle', intensifying bureaucratic conflicts and complicating public administration. The interests of regime perpetuation have undermined state reconstitution. All federations are designed to constrain central political power, but not all do so with equal effect. In Russia, regional regimes acted as a check on the central authorities; a type of horizontal separation of powers emerged that to a degree compensated for the inadequacy of the vertical separation of powers in the constitutional order established in December 1993. Russian regionalism emerged as a more effective check, if not democratic balance, on executive authority than the relatively weak legislature and judiciary. Thus, although Putin may well have sought the democratic reconstitution of the state, the weakening of the regional 'fourth pivot' acting as a check on the central authorities undermined the democratic separation of powers. The reconstitution of the state, although a laudable aim in itself, in the regional context undermined the development of a democratic and federal pluralism.

Putin's economic policy sought to apply prudent fiscal policies, to make some amends to the population for earlier losses, to balance the budget, to repay foreign debts, to build up reserves, and in general to avoid succumbing to economic populism. A new model of political economy came to the fore. While there was never any question of repudiating the basic principles of market capitalism, the liberal model that dominated the Anglo–American world in the late twentieth century was modified. Just as Japan had never adopted the *laissez-faire* capitalism of the Atlantic West, so Russia (like China) devised its own mixed system of state capitalism and free markets. This was most apparent in the energy market, where Putin refused to rely on the free market and sought instead to achieve bilateral ties with Western markets and a state regulated system at home. Putin regarded the liberal access principles to pipelines, reserves and markets embodied in the Energy Charter Treaty of 1994 with horror, and refused to sign up to its principles. Of course, the *fortuna* of high energy prices helped Putin's government to maintain stability, but this stability was double-edged and encouraged complacency. One of the architects of Russia's transition to the market in the early 1990s, Egor Gaidar, warned that the country was repeating the mistakes of the USSR, with excessive reliance on high energy prices and the absence of a long-term strategic modernisation of the economy. He pointed out the weakness of imperial governmental systems, and implied that any attempt by post-communist Russia to reprise this path would threaten the very existence of the country.[9]

Some of the most odious oligarchs were exiled; the liberalisation of the economy continued and new incentives for development put in place; and in foreign policy Russia unequivocally turned to the West, but on terms that it considered 'normal'. The oligarchs were evicted from the corridors of powers, and the policy of 'equidistance' meant that the relationship was now structured through such bodies as the RUIE. As long as the oligarchs did not flaunt their power and wealth, they were allowed to get on with their business – which was now to be business and not politics. Even the insider oligarchs understood that new patterns of behaviour were required. Many adapted to the new circumstances and transformed themselves from 'oligarchs' into business people. This, however, did not save oligarchs with political ambitions, such as Khodorkovsky. At the same time, the regime increasingly insulated itself from organised social pressure and pluralistic democratic institutions.

Putin sought to redefine the terms of Russia's relations with the rest of the world within the framework of what we have called a 'new realism'. Dealings with the West were now to be practical and goal oriented, and no longer filtered through visions of geopolitical competition or the chatter of 'the clash of civilisations'. Putin's own personality, as a target-oriented pragmatist, was now applied to the conduct of foreign policy. Russian foreign policy became 'normal' to the extent that the logic of primordial struggle for pre-eminence (xenophobia) was abandoned together with its accompanying opposite extreme, the slavish copying of Western models (xenomania). Instead, as demonstrated over Chechnya and some other issues, Russia under Putin pursued what it perceived to be its own interests. The same applies to the question of democratisation. Putin's strategic choice towards the Western model of universalism would be achieved largely by Russia's own efforts; the decade of Western 'aid' in the 1990s was at best marginally helpful in ensuring a continued commitment to marketisation, but harmful in distorting economic policy formation. Putin's presidency put an end to idle speculation about 'who lost Russia?'. Russia's destiny would be forged in Russia, and nowhere else. Pursuing a morphological approach, Putin sought to craft a model of normality that combined Westernisation with something broader, taking into account Russia's particular history, traditions and place in the world. It is only by combining the universal and the particular that a country can find what is normal for itself.

Putin's attempts to modernise Russia's political institutions was driven by domestic imperatives rather than by external pressures. The development of a distinctive regime system, in which democratic legitimation was accompanied by the relative independence of the power system from popular control, and the emergence of oligarchical capitalism and bureaucratic neo-patrimonialism, were products of Russian circumstances, although of course shaped by interactions with the global economy and political society. Putin's presidency represented the attempt to establish a set of rules that could sustain and guide the revival of the state, in both its domestic and foreign aspects. These rules could be summarised as follows: regional leaders as a group were not to make claims on national power; business leaders were to keep out of state management and co-ordinate their actions with the regime; and foreign powers could no longer expect to discipline and punish Russia. While there were authoritarian elements to his leadership, perhaps more important is the fact that it was authoritative. We have suggested above that Putin represented a 'revolt of the masses' against the venality and greed of the Yeltsin years. This revolt gained not only popular but also widespread elite support. It allowed the institutions of the Russian state, born in the trauma of the dissolution of communism in August 1991, the disintegration of the USSR in December of that year, and the birth of the new constitutional order in the bloodshed of October 1993, to gain a deeper legitimacy that had been so signally lacking in the Yeltsin years. Although a majority had voted for the new constitution on 12 December 1993, the vote had always been tainted by accusations of fraud and was certainly stained by the polarised circumstances in which it was adopted. Putin now sought to ground the constitutional order in a set of political practices that would give it a new lease of legitimacy. Putin inherited an unstable political order, but gradually imbued it with a greater sense of permanence. The 'provisionality' of post-communist Russian governance did not entirely disappear, and could not do so until the structural gulf between regime, state and society had been transcended, but the ground rules of the new order at home and abroad were now more firmly established.

Post-communist Russia developed as three orders superimposed upon each other. The first was the traditional statist one (Napoleonic or Andropovist) in which the emphasis is placed on the power vertical. In this model, whenever a potential autonomous centre of power, official or civil, emerges, the Kremlin moves to co-opt or suppress. The second is the system based on patronage and patrimonial relationships, in which horizontal networks create clusters that become remarkably impervious to the impartial operation of law and political power. The strongest of these developed in economic society, where the fusion of bureaucracy and oligarchical networks even began to shape political space, enjoying far greater financial and media resources than political parties. These informal relationships were particularly strong in the regions. The third political order is that of liberal democracy, based on normative principles of universal citizenship, the electoral constitution of power and legal and political accountability. To a degree Putin used the first and the third to counter the powers of the second. There remain disagreements, however, over how to evaluate the balance between these two. Many critical voices suggest that the first order greatly overshadows the third to establish a self-perpetuating ruling corporation, a type of elective monarchy that has not destroyed the patronage order but rendered it subordinate to the bureaucratic-authoritarian regime. We have drawn the comparison with Italian *trasformismo* of the 1880s where expedience ruled the practice of government and support was solicited from all quarters. The basis of government was enlarged to include those among the opposition ready to 'transform' themselves into supporters of the government. In Russia critics argue that the lack of independent democratic institutions and the presidency's attempts to bring all political processes under its control sapped the energies of the fledgling democracy that had emerged under Yeltsin. Putin insisted that the condition for the development of vigorous political and civil associations was the reassertion of an ordered state system.

Beyond transition

The notion of a post-communist *transition* was abandoned in favour of a more systematic attempt to transform the country into a democratic market system. The ideology of transition gave way to one of consolidation. Although the changes launched by Yeltsin were continued, and in many respects deepened, the way that change was managed changed dramatically. The changes were no longer couched in revolutionary terms, although the outcome in the long term was no less revolutionary than Yeltsin's. Putin's rejection of the revolutionary method was accompanied by the development of a politics of normality in which procedure and institutions began to take priority over revolutionary expediency and personalised leadership. The intention now was to 'live in the present' by putting an end to revolutionary leaps of faith into the future. This 'present', moreover, was to be defined within a politics of the possible, a pragmatic acceptance of the 'normality' of the West and belief in the depoliticised superiority of the regime.

Democratisation and universal citizenship

Putin inherited a country that had the full gamut of democratic institutions, but it was not a fully fledged or 'consolidated' democracy. One of the reasons for this, quite apart from Yeltsin's personal eccentricities, was that the state itself lacked a firm institutional base. Linz and Stepan have stressed that 'Democracy is a form of governance of a modern state', and therefore 'without a state, no modern democracy is possible'.[10] Was Putin able to transform Russia's imperfect democracy into something better? By putting a conclusive end to the border question (unless negotiated and agreed with all parties), he at least ensured that the vessel in which a putative democracy could develop was assured. The *boundary* question was effectively resolved, although at some point Belarus or some other region could possibly join. He also insisted that the fledgling political institutions created in the 1990s and formalised by the 1993 constitution should be given a chance to work, and thus he consolidated the *polity*, the formal institutions of the state. Putin established a new set of rules in relations between state and society, oligarchs and government, regions and the centre. Finally, his policies, above all regional and judicial reforms, were designed to ensure that the question of *regime type* was closed: as far as he was concerned, Russia would be a democracy or it would be nothing, but the problem of the quality of democracy was not addressed. Thus Putin explicitly insisted that the period of transition was over. As a discursive trope, of course, this meant that certain issues and problems, whether they had indeed been resolved or not, were removed from the agenda. It would be for Putin's successor to face the challenge of democratising democracy in Russia.

Putin's reassertion of central authority in defence of the writ of the con-stitution represented the defence of a particular vision of democracy. Although there were undoubtedly elements of reconcentration at work (the 'normalisation' factor that accompanied the striving for normality), the overall thrust of Putin's reforms was an attempt, literally, to *reconstitute* the state, to place the constitution at the centre of regional relations. For some this was no more than a new form of Russia's traditional tendency towards centralisation; but the case could be made with equal plausibility that it offered an opportunity to move away from asymmetrical federalism and asymmetrical power relations in general towards a more balanced form. Asymmetrical federalism not only granted differential rights to regional leaderships, but effectively established different gradations of democratic citizenship to those living in different parts of the country. Asymmetrical power relations meant that the citizen had little recourse against the rich and powerful through the courts, or against wilful bureaucrats in day-to-day dealings with the state administration. The attempt to achieve a uni-versal and homogeneous type of citizenship lay at the heart of Putin's attempt to reconstitute the state. Citizenship was now to be equal across the whole country and rather less 'lumpy'. No longer was the exercise of citi-zenship to vary between republics and regions, and indeed between classes.

That at least was the idea, but soon Putin was forced to recognise that the enormous asymmetries in power and wealth across the country could not so easily be reduced, and even he was forced to engage in bargaining and compromises that left the country far short of the universal model that he had initially announced. Putin announced the new rules of the game, with an end to the bilateral treaties with the regions and with the oligarchs kept at an equal distance from power, but the regime was both a player and the referee. The regime's own interests in survival came into contradiction with the ideals that it proclaimed.

State consolidation acted as both the facilitator of democratisation and its gravedigger. Putin's centralisation of state power was designed to equalise the rights of citizens across Russia, no longer impeded by various neo-feudal localistic, patrimonial or ethnocratic regimes. In this sense, Putin was more of an equaliser than a centraliser, reducing heterogeneity in the name of universal citizenship. However, the basis of this equalisation was less full civil and democratic rights than equality in subordination. The regime's micro-management of political processes left little scope for the political autonomy of society or for effective independent and competitive pluralism in party politics. Pluralism was no means abolished, but it remained latent rather than fulfilled in vigorous public politics. To this extent, Putin's administration remained transitional and, by removing some of the excessive 'lumpiness' (above all the 'oligarchs', regional bosses and special interests), prepared the ground for future democratic advance. Paradoxically, a regime that declared the end of transition was itself profoundly transitional.

From regime to governance, from stability to order

It is at this point that one of the starkest contradictions of Putin's rule creeps in. Rather than achieving the consolidation of the constitutional state, the priority was the consolidation of *regime* rule, not democracy. We defined the regime system as one in which an autonomous power centre becomes established in the interstices between the constitutional state and popular accountability. Under Putin the structure and operation of the regime system undoubtedly changed from under Yeltsin. There were major shifts in the balance of power between the components constituting the regime, above all between the presidency, factions of the state administration (for example, the security services) and societal inputs (above all, the end of direct access of oligarchs and other 'family' members to the corridors of power), and a more ordered and institutionalised system of governance was established. The presidency, indeed, allied with the constitutional resources of the state to secure greater autonomy from the regime that it nominally led. However, the constitutional state was used to strengthen the presidency and was unable to regain its own autonomy, where all parts of the regime (including the presidency) were equally subordinate to the rule of the law.

The full panoply of the Soviet repressive apparatus was not restored, but not enough was done to ensure the impartial operation of law and the solid defence of human and civil rights. Putin's Russia was not a more modern version of Brezhnev's Soviet Union, but neither was it a fully functioning liberal democracy. The tension between efficacy and democracy was not overcome. A gulf remained between the autonomy of the regime and its subordination to the constitutional principles that it espoused. The regime sought to strengthen the state, but the regime itself remained outside the constitutionality represented by the state. Improving the performance of the state simply strengthened the regime rather than reinforcing the rule of law and the constitutional state. Putin recognised that a state built on authoritarian foundations, as Russian history has repeatedly demonstrated, would be neither strong nor durable. His aim was to establish a system based on a self-sustaining order, but the inability of the regime to relax its grip on the management of democracy reintroduced the 'manual' system of stability.

The regime's espousal of universal citizenship came into contradiction with the restraints placed on the active exercise of this principle. The pedantic regulation of social life ultimately led to the suffocation of political activism. The concept of 'managed democracy' became less of a danger to be avoided than a programme to be implemented. The Putin regime was part of a much broader process of constitutive politics in post-communist states, where the regime becomes constitutive not only of its own preservation but of the foundations of the socio-political order in its entirety. Rather than operating as a delimited subsystem of governance reproducing itself within the norms of the system itself, the regime seeks to maintain itself independently. The degree to which it can reproduce itself in these conditions is unclear. The government merged into the regime, which itself at times is indistinguishable from the state. If for Carl Schmitt the tragedy of the Weimar Republic was that the political was swallowed up by the social, with social interests and movements able to exert direct and unmediated authority over the state, in Russia the political was in danger of swallowing the social. Schmitt in 1927 defined the political as the ability to choose between friend and foe, and to act accordingly, and Putin's regime represents the substantive reassertion of the political.

The constitution grants the presidency enormous powers, and under Yeltsin it emerged as a relatively independent political resource but over time was undermined by his physical debilitation and preference for personalised relations. Under Putin the presidency as an institution revived and became the core of a 'state gathering' project: the presidency became the key instrument of policy innovation and state development. The presidency remained relatively independent both from the normative and constitutional constraints governing the state (the political system); and relatively immune from oversight and accountability to social forces, above all those exercised by parliament. Under Putin the reconstitution of the state was a genuine attempt to enhance the rule of law and the constitution, and to that degree there was a shift from regime relations to governance. However, only when the regime is subordinate to the rule of law and itself at the mercy of the uncertainties of the democratic process can we say that the transition is over. As long as the administrative regime remains outside the political process and beyond the constraints of the constitutional state, the system remains based more on the maintenance of artificial stability than the reflection of a sustainable order.

The power of contradiction

In discussing contradictions, classic Marxism distinguishes between those that are solvable (non-antagonistic) and antinomies (antagonistic contradictions that cannot be resolved). There were plenty of contradictions of both sorts in Putin's leadership, but ultimately he was able for a time to finesse some of the most glaring antinomies while seeking to resolve some of the non-antagonistic contradictions. The contradictory nature of Putin's approach, paradoxically, was the source of much of his power. By adopting elements of both the reconstitution and reconcentration of the state, of neo-Soviet and post-Soviet identities, of continuity with the whole long history of Russian development while at the same time repudiating the negative pathologies of each of Russia's stages of historical evolution (above all, the imperial, the Soviet and the 'democratic'), Putin sought to achieve a historical reconciliation of the many threads of Russian identity and the many layers of Russian society. However, he left Russia still divided between those with power and marginalised political elites, a rising middle class and those still mired in poverty, and a Russia that had asserted itself in the world but had not been effectively integrated into the international system.

Normality or 'normalisation'?

Putin's presidency was polymorphic, capable of varying interpretations and driving simultaneously in different directions. It is for this reason that his leadership is capable of such dramatically divergent evaluations. His attempt to reconcile the various Soviet and Russian generations glossed over the substantial differences that they represented. For example, although Putin condemned the 'excessively politicised and bureaucratised' nature of the former Communist Youth League (Komsomol) and Young Pioneers, he insisted that 'there was a meaning in all of this. Along with these purely political ideas, people would receive many useful, general things – the new generation was raised in the spirit of love of the homeland, of their fatherland. There was a great deal of good in that system'.[11] While seeking to reconcile Russia's various pasts, Putin failed to open Russia to deeper introspection about the darker sides of its own past, and thus to greater openness in dialogue with its neighbours who shared elements of a common past.

Putin's reforms were imbued with numerous contradictions. Perhaps the most notable was the belief that the enhancement of the powers of the state would enable that same strengthened state to defend individual rights. Putin's reforms sought to remake the state; but they also represented yet another radical shift, so common in Russia, from a period of anarchy and ungovernability to the birth of a new Leviathan. Putin's reforms encouraged precisely the outcome that they were designed to avert, the erosion of democratic freedoms and the establishment of new forms of exclusive elite rule. Putin's presidency was increasingly condemned as 'a time of lost and wasted opportunities'.[12] Putin's administration delivered some substantive public goods, yet they were imbued with a statist managerialism that undermined the civic spirit and a competitive economy.

Putin repeatedly stressed his commitment to democracy, but Russia would do it in its own way. In his address to the Federal Assembly on 25 April 2005 he took issue with those who suggested that Russia was somehow not suited to democratic government, the rule of law and the basic values of civil society: 'I would like to bring those who think like that back to political reality ... Without liberty and democracy there can be no order, no stability and no sustainable economic policies'. Responding to Western criticism, however, Putin stressed that the 'special feature' of Russia's democracy was that it would be pursued in its own way and not at the price of law and order or social stability: 'Russia ... will decide for itself the pace, terms and conditions of moving towards democracy.'[13] Putin confirmed the arguments of those, like Claus Offe, who at the beginning of the post-communist transitions had argued that the establishment of capitalism and democracy in the region would be a directed and managed process.[14] Russia's democracy, in other words, would be designed to take into account Russia's special circumstances.

On a number of occasions Putin outlined what these were. First, the Soviet legacy according to Putin was a mixed one, and he would not repudiate the past in its entirety or allow full-scale decommunisation. This was reflected in dualistic political practices, where neo-Soviet features were balanced by post-Soviet elements. Second, Putin's view that the disintegration of the Soviet Union in 1991 rendered Russia a very fragile state runs as a red thread in his speeches. This was the central theme in his 2005 address to the Federal Assembly, acting as the counterpart of the 'sovereign democracy' theme. Putin described the break-up of the Soviet Union in 1991 as 'the biggest geopolitical catastrophe' of the twentieth century and a 'tragedy for the Russian people', and warned that the 'epidemic of collapse' was threatening Russia itself. He stressed, however, that the Soviet Union was a thing of the past, and the coherence of the Russian Federation depended not on retreating from democracy but on strengthening democratic institutions and principles throughout society. Third, the 1990s represented a threat to state autonomy, and Putin's presidency was in effect devoted to overcoming those elements of state capture that remained. In practice this meant curbing the pretensions of the nascent bourgeoisie (reduced to the threat of 'oligarchical revenge' in contemporary Russian parlance) and of regional leaders. The conclusion of all of this is clear: democracy in Russia has to create the conditions for its own existence. This is a giant bootstrapping operation of the sort described by Ernest Gellner in his discussion of the development of civil society in the post-communist world.[15]

State reconstitution under Putin was conducted in a non-ideological, technocratic, spirit under the banner of a 'common-sense' state patriotism and the depoliticisation of governance. The contradiction remained between

Putin's attempts to 'nativise' modern liberal democracy while at the same time repudiating 'Eurasianist' alternatives to Western capitalist democracy. Putin's rise can be seen as the triumph of a nativist strand of liberal patriotism. It was nativist because it sought to do what Dostoevsky had tried in the 1840s by developing the 'native soil' (*pochvennik*) idea; between backward-looking Slavophilism and impressionable Westernisers there lay a way of reconciling the imperatives of both. The greatest modern exponent of *pochvennichestvo* is Solzhenitsyn, and thus it is perhaps not surprising that Putin actively sought contact with him in the first period of his leadership. The very term 'liberal patriotism' may appear at first sight to be an oxymoron, but it has a long tradition in Russia. Stolypin, one of Putin's heroes, could be considered the greatest of its practitioners, seeking to modernise Russia while appealing to national pride, trying to achieve liberal reforms with an iron hand. In the realm of philosophy the idea was investigated and to a degree espoused by the likes of Semyon Frank and Peter Struve. The aim was to combine a liberal view of the political and ethical worth of the individual with a strong sense of the collective values represented by the community and its highest expression, the state. Many doubted whether such a combination is viable. The lesson of the national liberals in late nineteenth-century Germany appeared to show the dangers of such a synthesis. In the first years of the twentieth century they ended up by stressing rather more the 'national' than the 'liberal' side of their thinking.

This ambiguity is reflected in Putin's well-known statement, that we have cited before, that 'It will not happen soon, if it ever happens at all, that Russia will become a second edition of, say, the USA or Britain in which liberal values have deep historical traditions'. While some critics have taken this to mean that Russia will not become a liberal state, Putin is clearly saying the opposite: that Russia will become a liberal state, but in its own way. There appears to be a contradiction: has Russia given up exceptionalist *Sonderweg* aspirations or not? The old messianism has undoubtedly been jettisoned, of both the Slavophile populist and Marxist statist forms, together with Russian nationalist and neo-imperialist Eurasianism, but the basis of Putin's nativisation is both insubstantial and contradictory.

All 'third way' approaches suffer from a characteristic contradiction. The attempt to pursue a radical politics of the centre generates new forms of non-ideological extremism. While centrist politics assumes a politics based on consensus and the rational generation of policy, in practice a paradoxical *extremism of the centre* may emerge. The policies pursued are centrist, in that they are not sustained by intense class, national, religious or other ideological presumptions. However, their implementation and the fervour with which they are pursued undermines consensus: form comes into contradiction with content, and politics is 'depoliticised'. In Britain the third way by the time of New Labour's second term was marred by what some characterised as a fanatical commitment to 'modernisation' and a target-oriented mechanical managerialism designed to reshape the labour process in a narrow and alienating manner. In Russia the communists and others argued that Putin's radical modernising agenda failed to rebuild social solidarity, subordinating Russia to the power of the economic magnates and to foreign powers. The basic criticism is that Russia could not be rebuilt from the centre. Putin drew back from this extremism of the centre to pursue a more consensual centrism. Nevertheless, the combination of attempts to push through liberal modernising reforms while trying to avoid alienating significant political actors threatened either to lead to extremism (if the modernising agenda was pushed through vigorously) or stagnation (if it was not). If there was anything worse than extremism of the centre, it was stagnation of the centre.

Leadership and system

Putin was a child of the 'family' while at the same time an independent politician. There is a contradiction between Putin's reliance on liberals from St Petersburg while drawing on security personnel from the former KGB; a tension that is reflected in his own career path. A liberal security officer may, to paraphrase Leszek Kolakowski in his comments on liberal communism, be like warm ice, yet there are clear limits to the influence of the security establishment on policy formation in Putin's Russia. This is clearly a non-antagonistic contradiction. Putin may well have been a *chekist*, but *chekism* has not come to power with him. The contradictory nature of his past, however, is a significant power resource to Putin in developing his personnel policy and in appealing to mutually exclusive popular constituencies. Equally, the lack of an independent base meant that Putin was ready to work with some of the oligarchs, although reshaping the model of political economy to turn oligarchy into a bourgeoisie. It would be simplistic to see the model of corporatist capitalism that has emerged in Russia as a wholly negative phenomenon, since it has the potential to evolve towards a more transparent and internationally competitive business sector. The outlines of a modern corporate capitalism are emerging, with some of the oligarchs ready to ally with the reforming Kremlin.

The contradiction in personnel policy is reflected more broadly in policy: the tough language of state reassertion is balanced by a consistent commitment to a liberal economic policy and, more broadly, by looking for the support of the main constituency of liberalism in Russia, the intelligentsia and the middle class. When seeking class or group alliances the choices for Putin were limited, above all because of the absence of a substantive and legitimate property-based conservative middle class. The traditional conservative classes had long ago been swept away and the 'new Russians' who have emerged since the fall of communism are not yet a 'bourgeoisie' of the sort that Barrington Moore insisted were necessary for democracy to survive.[16] As for interests, Putin tried to ensure the broad support of the security apparatus and its personnel in all of their multifarious manifestations; of officialdom in all of its hydra-headed forms; of key segments in society like pensioners and peasants; and of big business, both organised and oligarch-ical. He avoided appealing directly to the working class out of fear that this could lead to demagogic populism. The *siloviki* have resolutely been excluded from influencing certain public policy spheres, above all in economic and informational matters (other than when directly connected to the Chechen war). In addition, although Putin is clearly a statist and patriot himself, he has to a remarkable extent been able to marginalise strident Russophilic nationalist statism. Their influence on the policy process is probably even less than it was under Yeltsin, while the ideology of statism or Russian great power thinking (the *derzhavniki*) has probably not been weaker in the last decade and a half. The only coherent policy-forming ideology today in Russia is pro-Western liberalism, however fragmented its political repre-sentation may be. Once again there is no antagonistic contradiction here, but the very existence of a contradiction is a source of power to Putin's regime.

Putin persecuted the oligarchs on a selective and partial, although not arbitrary, basis. With the others he struck a bargain: invest your ill-gotten gains in the manufacturing ('real') part of the Russian economy or else face the consequences. Putin thereby hoped to see filched assets return from offshore haunts and invested to revive the economy. Companies forged in the corrupt world of the epoch of *prikhvatizatsiya* ('grabbing') were to become good capitalists working with the state and developing transparent accounting standards, responsibility to shareholders (including minority ones) and leg-ally accountable directors. While Putin's policy is logical from a short-term perspective, this model of economic development effectively represents the state-sanctioned laundering of resources. In addition, there is much spec-ulation about how close this monopolistic system comes to earlier *chaebol* or *keiretsu* models. Can a healthy market economy can be achieved by increasing state regulation? The East Asian financial crises of 1997–8 were provoked in part by 'croney capitalism', and there is a danger that Russian *nomenklatura* capitalism could evolve into something equally unstable.

Putin's leadership style was characterised by an instinctive tendency to centralise when faced by a problem. While this may have provided some political and economic dividends in the early years of his leadership, this approach became stultifying and stifling by the time he entered the final period of his leadership. By 2005–6 Putinism had reached the limits of its potential, and while economic growth remained solid it was certainly far from spectacular. The country was simply too big and diverse to be micro-managed from Moscow, and a system that became increasingly dependent on central authority could not respond effectively to the diverse challenges that it faced. Already during Putin's leadership regional politics had become less predictable, despite the reforms intended to overcome segmented regionalism. Putin's successor would have to create conditions where spon-taneous initiatives in political and economic life could be given greater rein.

As the new agenda takes hold, Putin's stature will be reduced to that of his own predecessor Yeltsin. Like Yeltsin, Putin in historical perspectives will be seen as no less a transitional figure – not quite democracy's greatest friend, yet providing the conditions in which democracy and the market could thrive.[17]

Putin's leadership and beyond

The legitimacy of Putin's presidency was formally based on democratic and legal procedures, but his leadership also contained a charismatic element that transcended the legal-rational political order that was struggling to be born in post-communist Russia. As Weber noted, 'Charisma knows only inner determination and inner restraint. The holder of charisma seizes the task that is adequate for him and demands obedience and a following by virtue of his mission. His success determines whether he finds them. His charismatic claim breaks down if his mission is not recognized by those to whom he feels he has been sent'.[18] Putin's charisma, defined here as leadership qualities that had an appeal beyond the constraints of the formal authority endowed on him by the constitution, was intended to serve precisely the consolidation of constitutional authority. As so often in politics, the most effective route between intention and outcome is not always the shortest. Charismatic leadership is a powerful political resource, especially in a country such as Russia where the post-communist political terrain was bleak, with no long-established parties and few civic associations with the power, resources or willingness to build a dynamic, pluralistic, socially fair and democratic society. In this context there is inevitably a tension between preserving and transforming the system.

The concentrated nature of Russian politics and the weakness of checks and balances reinforced the consequences of Putin's personal choices. His power was certainly constrained by the inherited structure of power and elite relations, but his leadership consisted of far more than simply balancing the interests of Kremlin factions. Putin's mini-cult of the personality, although clearly offensive to many and retrograde in inhibiting the institutionalisation of authority and the maturing of civic democracy, was perhaps the price to pay for the presidency to retain its political autonomy. Putin was a pragmatic politician committed not only to the concentration of his own authority but also driven by a commitment to modernise Russia, with modernisation defined as the adoption of the norms prevalent in mature capitalist democracies, but with a Russian face. Although elements of both neo-Soviet and post-Soviet were in evidence throughout his rule, it is clear that Putin was the first genuine post-Soviet leader in Russian politics. Although Yeltsin may have become a democrat by necessity, his instincts remained steeped in Soviet practices. Putin was more of a democrat by conviction, but remained torn between neo- and post-Soviet impulses, imbuing his policies with contradictory qualities that added to the enigmatic and contradictory character of his rule. The approach was pragmatic, but in this case pragmatism did not mean that the end justified the means. Instead, in a manner reminiscent of Eduard Bernstein's insistence that the *movement* meant everything to him and the *final aim* of socialism nothing,[19] as a matter of principle Putin rejected revolutionary methods and sought to reunify ends and means. Pervasive regime interventionism, however, undermined this goal.

Is Putinism possible without Putin? Did a coherent and durable new political order emerge in the 2000s? Was the new system little more than the temporary consolidation of a regime based on the personality of the president, or a more permanent rearrangement of relations between the state, governing regime and society to create a new political order that would outlast Putin's presidency? Could the Putinite system survive the change of leadership in 2008? Putin's administration represented a new formulation of a Brezhnev-type stability system, where stability comes from outside the social order and is characterised by 'manual intervention' by the political regime. We have contrasted a stability system with the notion of an ordered system. In the latter there is a certain congruence and dynamic, if not organic, integration between the various level of society; whereas the stability achieved by mechanical means lacks effective institutions. The system established in the name of stability by Putin may ultimately be profoundly unstable. Neither the constitutional order nor the representative system in Putin's Russia became self-sustaining and self-reproducing systems, and instead the administrative regime managed political processes. The administrative system under Putin had undoubted successes to its credit, having presided over sustained economic growth and rising living standards, accompanied by a certain consolidation of society and foreign policy coherence. However, the fundamental problem for any stability system is its fundamental artificiality. The autonomy of the constitutional state was undermined by the prerogatives asserted by the administrative regime, while the spontaneous development of civil society, political parties and legislatures (together comprising the representative order) were stymied by those same prerogatives. The Putin system was not so much anti-constitution as paraconstitutional. The structural weaknesses of the constitutional state and representative systems were compensated by the overblown powers of the administrative regime. In Putin's hands this regime was able to devise reasonably effective policies that enjoyed popular support. Based on an ideology of liberal patriotism, a commitment to democratic values *à la Russe*, a mixed economy with state activism, and international integration while retaining autonomy and national sovereignty, Putin's leadership was indeed contradictory. While the consolidation of Putin's regime entailed one set of threats, the price of failure would have been no less dangerous. Putin's system could only be a temporary resolution of the contradictions that beset postcommunist Russian development.

Appendix

Russia at the turn of the millennium

by Vladimir Putin

29 December 1999

The contemporary world lives under the sign of two global events: the new millennium and the two-thousandth anniversary of Christianity. In my view the enormous interest in these two events represents something greater and deeper than just the tradition of celebrating significant dates.

New possibilities, new problems

It may or may not be a coincidence, but the onset of the new millennium coincides with a dramatic turn in global developments in the past 20–30 years. *I mean the rapid and profound changes in the life of humanity associated with the development of what we call the post-industrial society.* [Italics throughout in the original.] Its main features include:

- Changes in the economic structure of society, with the decreasing weight of material production and the growing share of secondary and tertiary sectors.
- The continuous renewal and rapid introduction of advanced technologies and the growing output of science-based commodities.
- The tempestuous development of information technologies and tele-communications.
- Priority attention to management and the modification of organisational and managerial systems in all spheres of social activity.
- And finally, human leadership. High levels of the education, professional training, entrepreneurial and social activity of the individual are becoming the main dynamic forces of progress today.

The development of a new type of society is a drawn-out enough process for attentive politicians, statesmen, scientists and all those who use their minds to observe *two elements of concern in this process.* The first is that changes bring not only new possibilities to improve life, but also new problems and dangers. These were first most clearly revealed in the ecological sphere, but other acute problems soon became apparent in all other spheres of social life. Even the most economically advanced states are not free from organised crime, growing cruelty and violence, alcoholism and drug addiction, and the weakening cohesion and educational role of the family, and the like.

The second alarming factor is that not all countries can take advantage of the benefits of modern economies and their associated standards of prosperity. The rapid progress of science, technology and advanced economy is underway in only a small number of states, populated by the so-called 'golden billion'. Quite a few other countries achieved much economic and social development in the outgoing century, but they were unable to enter the process of creating a post-industrial society. Most of them are still far from it, and there is much evidence to suggest that this gap will persist for quite some time yet. This is probably why humanity is looking into the future with both hope and trepidation at the turn of the new millennium.

The contemporary situation in Russia

It would be no exaggeration to say that this combination of hope and fear is particularly strong in Russia. There are few countries in the world that have faced so many trials as Russia in the twentieth century.

First, Russia is not among those states with the highest levels of economic and social development. And second, it is facing economic and social difficulties. Russia's GDP nearly halved in the 1990s, and its GNP [gross national product] is ten times smaller than that of the USA and five times smaller than that of China. After the 1998 crisis, per capita GDP dropped to roughly US$3,500, which is roughly five times smaller than the average level for G7 states.

The structure of the Russian economy has changed. The economy is now dominated by the energy sector, power engineering, and ferrous and non-ferrous metallurgy. These spheres account for some 15 per cent of GDP, 50 per cent of overall industrial output, and over 70 per cent of exports.

Labour productivity in the real economy is extremely low. In the raw materials and electricity sectors it has risen to comparable world levels, but in other fields it is 20–24 per cent of, for example, the US average. The technical and technological standards of manufactured commodities are largely dependent on the proportion of equipment that is less than five years old. This proportion fell from 29 per cent in 1990 to 4.5 per cent in 1998. Over 70 per cent of our machinery and equipment is over ten years old, which is more than double the figure in economically developed countries.

This is the result of consistently falling national investment, above all in the real economy. Foreign investors moreover are not rushing to contribute to the development of Russian industry. The overall volume of foreign direct investment in Russia amounts to barely 11.5 billion dollars. China has received as much as 43 billion dollars in foreign investment. Russia has been reducing allocations to research and development, while the 300 largest transnational companies invested 216 billion dollars in research and development in 1997, and some 240 billion dollars in 1998. Only 5 per cent of Russian enterprises are engaged in innovative production, and output of this type remains very low.

The lack of capital investment and insufficient attention to innovation resulted in a dramatic fall in the production of commodities that are competitive in world markets in terms of price–quality ratio. Foreign competitors have pushed Russia especially far back in the market for science-intensive civilian commodities. Russia accounts for less than 1 per cent of such commodities on the world market, while the USA provides 36 per cent and Japan 30 per cent.

The population's real income has been falling since the beginning of the reforms. The deepest fall was registered after the August 1998 crisis, and it will be impossible to restore the pre-crisis living standards this year. The overall monetary incomes of the population, calculated by the UN methods, comprise less than 10 per cent of the US figure. Health and average life expectancy, the indicators that determine the quality of life, have also deteriorated.

The current difficult economic and social situation in the country is the price that we have to pay for the economy we inherited from the Soviet Union. But then, what else could we have inherited? We had to introduce market mechanisms into a system based on completely different standards, with a gigantic and distorted structure. This was bound to affect the progress of the reforms.

We had to pay for the excessive focus of the Soviet economy on the development of the raw materials sector and defence industries, which negatively affected the development of consumer production and services. We are paying for the Soviet neglect of such key sectors as information science, electronics and communications. We are paying for the absence of competition between producers and industries, which inhibited scientific and technological progress and rendered the Russian economy non-competitive in world markets. This is the price to pay for the impediments and bans on initiative and entrepreneurship of companies and workers. Today we are reaping the bitter fruit, both material and intellectual, of past decades.

On the other hand, we could have avoided some of the problems in the renewal process. They are the result of our own mistakes, miscalculations and lack of experience. *And yet, we could not have avoided the main problems facing Russian society.* The road to the market and democracy was difficult for all states that entered it in the 1990s. They all broadly encountered the same problems, although to varying degrees.

Russia is completing the first, transition stage of economic and political reforms. Despite problems and mistakes, we have entered the main highway of human development. World experience convincingly shows that only this path offers the possibility of dynamic economic growth and higher living standards. There is no alternative.

The question for Russia today is what to do next. How can we make the new market mechanisms work to full capacity? How can we overcome the still deep ideological and political divisions in society? What strategic goals can consolidate Russian society? What place can Russia occupy in the international community in the twenty-first century? What economic, social and cultural frontiers do we want to attain in 10–15 years? What are our strong and weak points? And what material and spiritual resources do we have now?

These are the questions posed by life itself. Unless we find clear answers comprehensible to the people we will be unable to move forwards quickly to the goals that are worthy of our great country.

The lessons for Russia

Our future depends on the answers to these questions and the lessons we draw from our past and present. This is a long-term task for society as a whole, but some of these lessons are already clear.

1 For three-quarters of the twentieth century Russia was dominated by the attempt to implement communist doctrine. It would be a mistake not to recognise, and even more to deny, the unquestionable achievements of those times. But it would be an even bigger mistake not to realise the outrageous price our country and its people had to pay for that social experiment. What is more, it would be an even bigger mistake not to understand its historic futility. *Communism and Soviet power did not make Russia a prosperous country with a dynamically developing society and free people.* Communism vividly demonstrated its inability to promote sound self-development, dooming our country to persistently lagging behind economically advanced countries. However bitter it may now be to admit it, for nearly seven decades we were moving along a blind alley, far from the mainstream of civilisation.

2 *Russia has reached its limit for political and socio-economic upheavals, cataclysms and radical reforms.* Only fanatics or political forces that have absolutely no concern for Russia and are indifferent to its people can make calls for a new revolution. Be it under communist, national-patriotic or radical-liberal slogans, our country, our people cannot endure another new radical upheaval. The nation's patience and its ability to survive as well as its capacity to work creatively have reached their limits. Society will simply collapse economically, politically, psychologically and morally.

   Responsible socio-political forces should offer the country a strategy for Russia's revival and prosperity based on the positive experience that has been gained during the period of market and democratic reforms and implemented only by evolutionary, gradual and prudent methods. This strategy should be carried out on the basis of political stability and should not lead to the deterioration in the lives of any section or group of the Russian people. This indisputable condition arises from the present situation of our country.

3 The experience of the 1990s vividly demonstrates that our country's genuine renewal without excessive costs cannot be achieved by merely experimenting with abstract models and schemes taken from foreign textbooks. The mechanical copying of other nations' experience will not guarantee success, either.

Every country, Russia included, has to find its own path of renewal. We have so far not been very successful in this respect. Only in the past year or two have we started groping for our own road and our model of transformation. *Our future depends on combining the universal principles of the market economy and democracy with Russian realities.* Our scholars, analysts, experts, public servants at all levels and political and public organisations should work with this aim in mind.

A chance for a worthy future

Such are the main lessons of the outgoing century. They make it possible to outline the contours of a long-term strategy which will enable us, within a comparatively short time, to overcome the present protracted crisis and create conditions for the country's rapid and stable economic and social improvement. I stress the need for speed; we have no time to dawdle.

Let me quote the calculations of experts. It will take us approximately 15 years and annual GDP growth of 8 per cent to reach the per capita GDP level of present-day Portugal or Spain, which are not among the world's industrial leaders. If during the same 15 years we manage annually to increase our GDP by 10 per cent, we will then catch up with Britain or France.

Even if we suppose that these calculations are not quite accurate and our current economic backwardness is not that serious and we can overcome it faster, it will still require many years of work. That is why we should formulate our long-term strategy and start fulfilling it as soon as possible.

We have already taken the first step in this direction. In late December the Centre for Strategic Research, created on the initiative and with the active support of the government, began its work. This Centre will bring together the best minds of our country to draft recommendations and proposals for the government for both theoretical and applied projects. It will help devise the strategy and seek effective ways of implementing it. *I am convinced that ensuring the necessary growth dynamics is not only an economic problem. It is also a political and, in a certain sense, – and I am not afraid to use this word – an ideological problem.* To be more precise, it is an ideological, spiritual and moral problem. It seems to me that the latter is of particular importance in our current efforts to ensure the unity of Russian society.

(A) The Russian idea

The fruitful and creative work, which our country needs so badly, is impossible in a divided and internally atomised society, a society where the main social groups and political forces do not share basic values and fundamental ideological orientations.

Twice in the outgoing century Russia has found itself in such a state: after October 1917 and in the 1990s. In the first case, civil accord and social unity were achieved not so much by what was then called 'ideological-educational work' as by coercion. Those who disagreed with the ideology and policy of the regime were subjected to persecution and repression. That is why I think that the term 'state ideology', advocated by some politicians, publicists and scholars, is not quite appropriate. It creates certain associations with our recent Soviet past. Where there is a state ideology approved and supported by the state, there is practically no room for intellectual and spiritual freedom, ideological pluralism and freedom of the press. In other words, there is no political freedom.

I am against the restoration of an official state ideology in Russia in any guise. There should be no forced civil accord in a democratic Russia. Social accord can only be voluntary. That is why it is so important to achieve civic consensus on such basic issues as the aims, values and direction of development, which would be desirable for and attractive to the overwhelming majority of Russians. The absence of civil accord and unity is one of the reasons why our reforms are so slow and painful. Too much energy is spent on political squabbling instead of dealing with the concrete tasks of Russia's renewal. Nonetheless, some positive changes have appeared in this sphere in the past year and a half. Most Russians demonstrate greater wisdom and responsibility than many politicians. Russians want stability, confidence in the future and the ability to plan ahead for themselves and their children, not just for a month but for years and even decades. They want to work in peace, security and in a sound law-based order. They want to take advantage of the opportunities and prospects opened up by the diversity in the forms of ownership, free enterprise and market relations.

It is on this basis that our people have begun to understand and accept supranational universal values, which are above social, group or ethnic interests. Our people have accepted such values as freedom of expression, freedom to travel abroad and other fundamental political rights and human liberties. People value the fact that they can own property, engage in free enterprise, build up their own wealth, and so on and so forth.

Another foundation for the consolidation of Russian society is what can be called the primordial, traditional values of Russians. These values are clearly seen today.

Patriotism

This term is sometimes used ironically and even derogatively. However, for the majority of Russians it retains its original and positive meaning. Patriotism is a feeling of pride in one's country, its history and accomplishments. It is the striving to make one's country better, richer, stronger and happier. When these sentiments are free from the taint of nationalist conceit and imperial ambitions, there is nothing reprehensible or bigoted about them. Patriotism is the source of the courage, staunchness and strength of our people. If we lose patriotism and the national pride and dignity that are connected with it, we will lose ourselves as a people capable of great achievements.

The greatness of Russia (Derzhavnost)

Russia was and will remain a great power. It is preconditioned by the inseparable characteristics of its geopolitical, economic and cultural existence. They determined the mentality of Russians and the policy of the government throughout the history of Russia and they cannot but do so now. This Russian mentality however should incorporate new ideas. In today's world the might of a country is measured more by its ability to develop and use advanced technologies, a high level of popular wellbeing, the reliable protection of its security and the upholding of its national interests in the international arena than in its military strength.

Statism

It will not happen soon, if ever, that Russia will become the second edition of, say, the US or Britain in which liberal values have deep historic roots. Our state and its institutions and structures have always played an exceptionally important role in the life of the country and its people. For Russians a strong state is not an anomaly to be discarded. Quite the contrary, they see it as the source and guarantee of order, and the initiator and the main driving force of change.

Contemporary Russian society does not identify a strong and effective state with a totalitarian state. We have come to value the benefits of democracy, a law-based state, and personal and political freedom. At the same time, people are concerned by the obvious weakening of state power. The public wishes to see the appropriate restoration of the guiding and regulating role of the state, proceeding from the traditions and present state of the country.

Social solidarity

A striving for collective forms of social activity has always predominated over individualism. Paternalistic sentiments have struck deep roots in Russian society. The majority of Russians are used to depending more on the state and society for improvements in their conditions than on their own efforts, initiative and entrepreneurial abilities. It will take a long time for this habit to die out. We will not dwell on whether this is good or bad. The important thing is that such sentiments exist and, indeed, predominate.

That is why they cannot be ignored. They must be taken into consideration first and foremost in social policy.

I suppose that the new Russian idea will come about as a mixture or as an organic combination of universal general humanitarian values with the traditional Russian values that have stood the test of time, including the turbulent twentieth century. *This vitally important process must not be accelerated, discontinued and destroyed.* It is important to prevent the first shoots of civil accord from being crushed underfoot in the heat of political campaigns or elections. The results of the recent elections to the State Duma inspire great optimism in this respect. They reflect a turn in our society towards greater stability and civil consensus. The overwhelming majority of Russians rejected radicalism, extremism and revolutionary opposition. For probably the first time since the reforms began favourable conditions have been created for constructive co-operation between the executive and legislative branches of power.

Serious politicians, whose parties and movements are represented in the new State Duma, are advised to draw conclusions from this fact. I am sure that their sense of responsibility for the destiny of the nation will prevail and Russia's parties, organisations and movements and their leaders will not sacrifice Russia's common interests and prospects, requiring the consolidation of all healthy forces, to narrow partisan or opportunistic considerations.

(B) Strong state

We live in a time when even the most correct economic and social policies go awry during implementation because of the weakness of the state and managerial bodies. *The key to Russia's recovery and growth today lies in the state-political sphere. Russia needs strong state power and must have it.* I am not calling for totalitarianism. History proves all dictatorships, all authoritarian forms of government are transient. Only democratic systems are lasting. Whatever the shortcomings, humanity has not devised anything superior. *Strong state power in Russia is a democratic, law-based, workable federal state.*

I see the following aspects in its formation:

- a streamlined structure for bodies of state authority and governance; improved professionalism, discipline and responsibility of civil servants; intensification of the struggle against corruption
- a restructuring of state personnel policy to select the best people
- creating conditions that will foster the development in the country of a full-blooded civil society to balance and monitor the authorities
- a larger role for and greater authority of the judiciary
- improved federal relations, including budgetary and financial matters
- an active offensive on crime.

Amending the constitution does not seem to be an urgent, priority task. We have a good constitution. Its provisions concerning individual rights and freedoms are considered among the best constitutional arrangements of the kind in the world. Rather than draft a new basic law for the country the most serious task is to render the current constitution and the laws drafted on its basis the norms of the life of the state, society and each individual. A major problem is the constitutionality of adopted laws. Russia currently has over a thousand federal laws and several thousand laws of the republics, territories, regions and autonomous areas. Not all of them correspond to the above criterion. If the justice ministry, the prosecutor's office and the judiciary continue to be as slow in dealing with this matter as they are today, the mass of questionable or simply unconstitutional laws may become critical legally and politically. The constitutional security of the state, the federal centre's capabilities, the country's manageability and Russia's integrity would then be in jeopardy.

Another serious problem is inherent in government authority. International experience suggests that the main threat to human rights and freedoms, to democracy as such, arises from the executive authority. Of course, a legislature that makes bad laws also contributes, but the main threat emanates from executive authority. It organises the country's life, applies laws and can objectively quite substantively distort, although not always maliciously, these laws through executive orders. The global trend is towards stronger executive authority. Not surprisingly, society seeks to strengthen its control over the executive to preclude arbitrariness and the abuse of office. This is why I, personally, give priority attention to building partner relations between the executive authorities and civil society, to developing the institutions and structures of the latter, and to waging an active and merciless struggle against corruption.

(C) Efficient economy

I have already said that the reform years have generated many problems in the economy and social sphere. The situation is indeed complex, but, to put it mildly, it is too early to bury Russia as a great power. All troubles notwithstanding, we have preserved our intellectual potential and human resources. A number of research and development achievements and advanced technologies have not been wasted. We still have our natural resources. The country has a worthy future in store for it.

At the same time, we must learn the lessons of the 1990s and examine the experience of market transformations.

1 One of the main lessons is that throughout these years we were groping in the dark without a clear understanding of national objectives and advances that would ensure Russia's standing as a developed, prosperous and great country of the world. The lack of a long-range development strategy for the next 15–20 and more years has damaged the economy.

   The government firmly intends to structure its work on the basis of the principle of the unity of the strategy and tactics. Without it, we are doomed to patching up holes and operating in fire-fighting mode. Serious politics and big business are not conducted like that. *The country needs a long-term national strategy of development.* I have already said that the government has started devising it.

2   Another important lesson of the 1990s is the conclusion that Russia needs to form a coherent system of state regulation of the economy and social sphere. I do not mean to return to a system of planning and managing the economy by fiat, where the all-pervasive state regulated all aspects of an enterprise's work from top to bottom. I mean to make the Russian state an efficient co-ordinator of the country's economic and social forces that balances their interests, optimises the aims and parameters of social development and creates the conditions and mechanisms for their attainment.

   The above clearly goes beyond the standard formula that limits the state's role in the economy to devising rules of the game and ensuring their observance. With time, we are likely to evolve to this formula. But today's situation necessitates deeper state involvement in social and economic processes. While setting the parameters and mechanisms for state regulation we should be guided by the following principle: the state must act where and when it is needed; freedom must exist where and when it is required.

3   The third lesson is to adopt a reform strategy that is best suited to our circumstances. It should consist of the following elements.

   3.1   *To encourage dynamic economic growth*
   Primary here is the encouragement of investment. We have not yet resolved this problem. Investment in the real economy sector fell five-fold in the 1990s, including by 3.5 times in fixed assets. The material foundations of the Russian economy are being undermined. *We call for the pursuit of an investment policy that combines purely market mechanisms with state guidance.* At the same time, we will continue to create an investment climate attractive to foreign investors. Frankly speaking, without foreign investment our country's recovery will be long and hard. We do not have the time for slow growth. Consequently, we must do all in our power to attract foreign capital to the country.

   3.2   *To pursue an energetic industrial policy*
   The future of the country and the quality of the Russian economy in the twenty-first century will depend above all on progress in the high technology and science-intensive sectors. Ninety per cent of economic growth today depends on the introduction of new knowledge and technologies. *The government is prepared to pursue an economic policy of priority development of leading industries in the sphere of research and technological progress.* The requisite measures include:

   - Assisting the development of extra-budgetary internal demand for advanced technologies and science-intensive production, and supporting export-oriented high-tech production

- supporting non-raw materials industries working mostly to satisfy internal demand
- reinforcing the export possibilities of the fuel and energy and raw-materials complexes.
- We should use the mechanisms that have long been applied in the world to mobilise the funds necessary for pursuing this policy. The most important of them are target-oriented loan and tax instruments and the provision of privileges against state guarantees.

3.3 *To carry out a rational structural policy*

The government thinks that, as in other industrialised countries, there is a place in the Russian economy for financial–industrial groups, corporations, small and medium businesses. Any attempt to slow down the development of some, and artificially encourage the development of other, economic forms will only hinder the development of the economy. The government will create a structure that can ensure the optimal balance between all forms of economic activity.

Another major issue is the rational regulation of the natural monopolies. This is a key question, as monopolies largely determine the structure of production and consumer prices. They therefore influence both economic and financial processes, as well as people's incomes.

3.4 *To create an effective financial system*

This is a challenging task, which includes the following aspects:

- to improve the effectiveness of the budget as a major instrument of the state's economic policy
- to carry out a tax reform
- to put an end to non-payments, barter and other pseudo-monetary forms of settlement
- to maintain a low inflation rate and stability of the rouble
- to create civilised financial and stock markets, and to turn them into an instrument to accumulate investment resources
- to restructure the bank system.

3.5 *To combat the shadow economy and organised crime in the economic and financial-credit sphere*

All countries have shadow economies, but in industrialised countries their share of GDP does not exceed 15–20 per cent, while the figure for Russia is 40 per cent. To resolve this painful problem we should not just raise the effectiveness of the law-enforcement agencies but also strengthen licence, tax, hard currency and export controls.

3.6 *To integrate consistently the Russian economy into world economic structures*

If we do not do this we will not be able to rise to the high level of economic and social progress attained in the industrialised countries. The main directions of this work are:

- to ensure the state's active support of the foreign economic operations of Russian enterprises, companies and corporations. In particular, it is time to create a federal agency to support exports, which would guarantee the export contracts of Russian producers
- to combat resolutely discrimination against Russia in world commodity, services and investment markets, and to approve and apply national anti-dumping legislation
- to incorporate Russia into the international system of regulating foreign economic operation, above all the WTO.

3.7 *To pursue a modern agrarian policy*
The revival of Russia will be impossible without the revival of the countryside and agriculture. We need a farm policy that can organically combine measures of state assistance and state regulation with market reforms in the countryside and in land ownership relations.

4 We must recognise that virtually all changes and measures that entail a fall in the living conditions of the people are inadmissible in Russia. We have reached a point beyond which we must not go. *Poverty has reached an awesome scale in Russia.* In early 1998, the average weighted world per capita income amounted to some 5,000 dollars a year, but in Russia it was only 2,200 dollars. It dropped still lower after the August 1998 crisis. Since the beginning of reforms the share of wages in GDP has dropped from 50 per cent to 30 per cent.

This is the most acute social problem. The government is elaborating a new incomes policy designed to ensure stable growth in the real disposable incomes of the people. Despite these difficulties, the government is resolved to take new measures to support science, education, culture and health care. A country in which the people are not healthy physically and psychologically, are poorly educated and illiterate, will never rise to the peaks of world civilisation.

Russia is in the midst of one of the most difficult periods in its history. For the first time in the past 200–300 years, it is facing the real threat of slipping down to the second, and possibly even third, rank of world states. We are running out of time to avoid this. We must apply all the intellectual, physical and moral forces of the nation. We need co-ordinated creative work. Nobody will do it for us. Everything depends on us, and us alone, on our ability to recognise the scale of the threat, to unite and apply ourselves to lengthy and hard work.

This article first appeared on 29 December 1999 on the government of the Russian Federation's website (http://pravitelstvo.gov.ru/) and in *Nezavisimaya gazeta* and *Rossiiskaya gazeta*, 30 December 1999.

Notes

1 The path to power

1 Plato, *The Republic*, 'The Philosopher Ruler', Part Seven, Book Seven, translated by H. D. P. Lee (Harmondsworth, Penguin Books, 1955), p. 285.

2 In the late Soviet era 7 October was celebrated as Constitution Day and was a national holiday.

3 Oleg Blotskii, *Vladimir Putin: Istoriya zhizni*, Book 1 (Moscow, Mezhdunarodnye otnosheniya, 2002), p. 87.

4 Blotskii, *Vladimir Putin*, Book 1, p. 25.

5 A. A. Mukhin, *Kto est' mister Putin i kto s nim prishel? Dos'e na Prezidenta Rossii i ego spetssluzhby* (Moscow, Centre for Political Information, 2002), p. 9.

6 Yu. S. Bortsov, *Vladimir Putin* (Moscow and Rostov, Feniks, 2001), p. 28.

7 Blotskii, *Vladimir Putin*, Book 1, p. 211.

8 Blotskii, *Vladimir Putin*, Book 1, p. 25.

9 Bortsov, *Vladimir Putin*, p. 32.

10 Vera Gurevich, *Vospominaniya o budushchem prezidente* (Moscow, Mezhdunarodnye otnosheniya, 2001), p. 25.

11 Vladimir Putin, *First Person: An Astonishingly Frank Self-Portrait by Russia's President Vladimir Putin*, with Nataliya Gevorkyan, Natalya Timakova and Andrei Kolesnikov, translated by Catherine A. Fitzpatrick (London, Hutchinson, 2000), p. 12.

12 This period is described in detail by Blotskii, *Vladimir Putin*, Book 1, Chapters 6–8.

13 Blotskii, *Vladimir Putin*, Book 1, p. 68.

14 Gurevich, *Vospominaniya o budushchem prezidente*, p. 10.

15 Putin, *First Person*, p. 19.

16 Mukhin, *Kto est' mister Putin i kto s nim prishel?*, p. 19.

17 Vladimir Putin, *Ot pervogo litsa: Razgovory s Vladimirom Putinym*, with Nataliya Gevorkyan, Natal'ya Timakova and Andrei Kolesnikov (Moscow, Vagrius, 2000), pp. 20–1; Putin, *First Person*, p. 19.

18 Blotskii, *Vladimir Putin*, Book 1, p. 163.

19 Gurevich, *Vospominaniya o budushchem prezidente*, p. 31; Blotskii, *Vladimir Putin*, Book 1, pp. 110, 163.

20 Blotskii, *Vladimir Putin*, Book 1, p. 147.

21 *Komsomol'skaya pravda*, 12 January 2000.

22 Blotskii, *Vladimir Putin*, Book 1, p. 91.

23 In later years Putin was open about his admiration of Vysotsky and supported the initiative to make 2003 'the year of Vysotsky'.

24 *Rossiiskaya gazeta*, 16 February 2001.

25 Putin, *First Person*, p. 42.

26 Oleg Blotskii, *Vladimir Putin: doroga k vlasti*, Book 2 (Moscow, Mezhdunarodnye otnosheniya, 2002), p. 114.

27 For example, Gurevich, *Vospominaniya o budushchem prezidente*, p. 47.

28 Aleksandr Rar, *Vladimir Putin: 'Nemets' v Kremle*, (Moscow, Olma-Press, 2001), p. 28.

29 Mukhin, *Kto est' mister Putin i kto s nim prishel?*, p. 20.

30 See Yitzhak M. Brudny, *Reinventing Russia: Russian Nationalism and the Soviet State, 1953–1991* (Cambridge, MA, Harvard University Press, 1999).

31 Putin, *First Person*, p. 22.

32 Putin, *First Person*, p. 49.

33 *Kommersant-Daily*, 10 March 2000; Putin, *First Person*, p. 23.

34 See Roi Medvedev, *Neizvestnyi Andropov: Politicheskaya biografiya Yuriya Andropova* (Moscow, Prava Cheloveka, 1999), Chapter 4; Blotskii, *Vladimir Putin*, Book 1, pp. 173, 195–6, 283.

35 Gurevich, *Vospominaniya o budushchem prezidente*, p. 54.

36 Putin, *First Person*, p. 29.

37 Bortsov, *Vladimir Putin*, p. 59; Rar, *Vladimir Putin*, p. 34.

38 Mukhin, *Kto est' mister Putin i kto s nim prishel?*, p. 27.

39 Putin, *First Person*, p. 38.

40 Mukhin, *Kto est' mister Putin i kto s nim prishel?*, p. 12.

41 Bortsov, *Vladimir Putin*, p. 402.

42 Putin, *First Person*, pp. 41–2.

43 At that time only 4,783 out of the KGB's 296,591 staff were in the first department, Blotskii, *Vladimir Putin*, Book 2, p. 95.

44 Aleksandr Elisov, 'Prezident Putin v proshlom byl maoirom Platovym', *Moskovskii komsomolets*, 25 April 2003, p. 4; Blotskii, *Vladimir Putin*, Book 2, p. 175.

45 Putin, *First Person*, p. 77.

46 For details of Putin's time in Dresden, see Vladimir Usol'tsev, *Sosluzhivets: Neizvestnye stranitsy zhizni prezidenta* (Moscow, Eksmo, 2004).

47 Bortsov, *Vladimir Putin*, p. 96.

48 Blotskii, *Vladimir Putin*, Book 2, p. 229.

49 Mukhin, *Kto est' mister Putin i kto s nim prishel?*, p. 31.

50 Described in the book by Irene Pietsch, translated from German as Iren Pitch, *Pikantnaya druzhba: Moya podruga Lyudmila Putina, ee sem'ya i drugie tovarishchi* (Moscow, Zakharov, 2002).

51 Mukhin, *Kto est' mister Putin i kto s nim prishel?*, p. 32.

52 Putin, *First Person*, p. 76.

53 Bortsov, *Vladimir Putin*, p. 89.

54 Putin, *First Person*, p. 79.

55 Putin, *First Person*, p. 80.

56 Blotskii, *Vladimir Putin*, Book 2, p. 259.

57 Putin, *First Person*, p. 80.

58 Bortsov, *Vladimir Putin*, pp. 98, 100.

59 Blotskii, *Vladimir Putin*, Book 2, p. 273, 280–6.

60 Putin, *First Person*, p. 85.

61 Blotskii, *Vladimir Putin*, Book 2, p. 301; V. Lupan, *Russkii vyzov* (Moscow, Terra, 2001), p. 58.

62 Blotskii, *Vladimir Putin*, Book 2, pp. 290–1.

63 Putin, *Ot pervogo litsa*, p. 84.

64 Putin, *Ot pervogo litsa*, p. 85.

65 Full details are in Mukhin, *Kto est' mister Putin i kto s nim prishel?*, pp. 37–45.

66 For example, O. Lur'e, 'Kak V. Putin pytalsya spasti svoi gorod ot goloda', *Novaya gazeta*, 13–19 March 2000. The city council set up a committee headed

by Marina Sal'e to investigate the charges, but no evidence of Putin's complicity in wrongdoing was found.

67 'Putin's Shadowy Past', *Newsday*, 30 January 2000.
68 Lupan, *Russkii vyzov*, p. 66.
69 Putin, *First Person*, p. 113.
70 For details, see Evgenii Strigin, *Vladimir Putin: Vnedrenie v kreml'* (Moscow, Algoritm, 2006), pp. 234–47.
71 Shown on all TV channels; details reported in Bortsov, *Vladimir Putin*, p. 340.
72 For details of the St Petersburg elite, including those who followed Putin to Moscow, see Pavel Sheremet, *Piterskie tainy Vladimira Yakovleva* (Moscow, Partizan, 2005).
73 Sergei Bychkov and Aleksei Rukashnikov, 'V ch'ikh rukakh serdtse prezidenta?', *Moskovskii komsomolets*, 16 August 2000.
74 Once the thesis became available, Clifford Gaddy discovered that it draws generously, at least 16 pages of text and at least six diagrams, on a management text published in 1978 by two professors at the University of Pittsburgh, William R. King and David I. Cleland, *Strategic Planning and Policy*. David R Sands, 'Researchers Peg Putin as a Plagiarist over Thesis', *The Washington Times*, 25 March 2006. For a more detailed analysis, see the interview with Clifford Gaddy 'It all Boils down to Plagiarism', in *Washington Profile*, www.washprofile.org/en/node/4728, 31 March 2006. Perhaps as a sign of misgivings about the intellectual provenance of the work, Putin does not mention the thesis in his book of interviews, *In the First Person*, and is uncomfortable when asked about it. There was a long Soviet tradition, and one that continues today, of the academic works of politicians being ghostwritten by junior scholars. Members of the Russian political class retain their desire to prove their academic credentials.
75 The article and its context is analysed by Harley Balzer, 'The Putin Thesis and Russian Energy Policy', *Post-Soviet Affairs*, Vol. 21, No. 3, 2005, pp. 210–225.
76 Bortsov, *Vladimir Putin*, pp. 388–90.
77 V. V. Putin, 'Mineral'no syr'evye resursy v strategii razvitiya Rossiiskoi ekonomiki', *Zapiski Gornogo Instituta*, Vol. 144, 1999, pp. 3–9. There is a commentary and translation of the text in Harley Balzer, 'Vladimir Putin's Academic Writings and Russian Natural Resource Policy', *Problems of Post-Communism*, Vol. 53, No. 1, January–February 2006, pp. 48–54.
78 Bortsov, *Vladimir Putin*, p. 138.
79 Leonid Mlechin, *KGB predsedateli organov gosbezopasnosti: Rassekrechennye sud'by* (Moscow, Tsentrpoligraf, 2002), p. 836.
80 Putin, *First Person*, p. 129.
81 Bortsov, *Vladimir Putin*, pp. 140–1; Blotskii, *Vladimir Putin*, Book 2, p. 409.
82 Putin, *First Person*, p. 130.
83 Putin, *First Person*, p. 133.
84 Mlechin, *KGB predsedateli organov gosbezopasnosti*, p. 838.
85 Putin did not, however, reject his KGB past. For example, on the occasion of the eighty-fifth anniversary of Andropov's birth in December 1999, Putin, as prime minister, unveiled a plaque and placed a wreath to his memory and addressed the FSB Collegium with the following words: 'Let me report that the FSB staff sent to work in the government are satisfactorily fulfilling their duties', Mlechin, *KGB predsedateli organov gosbezopasnosti*, p. 816.
86 Mukhin, *Kto est' mister Putin i kto s nim prishel?*, p. 52.
87 In the spring of 1998 'three out of five Russians did not routinely receive the wages or pensions to which they were entitled', Richard Rose, 'Living in an Antimodern Society', *East European Constitutional Review*, Vol. 8, No. 1/2, Winter/Spring 1999, p. 71.

88 Samuel Charap, for example, stresses the biographical roots of Putin's foreign policy, 'The Petersburg Experience: Putin's Political Career and Russian Foreign Policy', *Problems of Post-Communism*, Vol. 51, No. 1, January–February 2004, pp. 55–62.

89 In the same way, as he moved up the career ladder he retained close links, as far as possible, with his earlier friends: Blotskii, *Vladimir Putin*, Book 2, pp. 344–5.

90 Putin participated in a book where the philosophy of judo, based on self-discipline, ceremony and the ability to turn your opponent's strength against him, is described: Vladimir Putin, Vasilii Shestakov and Aleksei Levitskii, *Uchimsya dzyudo s Vladirom Putinym* (Moscow, Olma-Press, 2002).

91 Mukhin, *Kto est' mister Putin i kto s nim prishel?*, p. 21.

92 Strobe Talbott, *The Russia Hand: A Memoir of Presidential Diplomacy* (New York, Random House, 2002), p. 335.

93 Talbott, *The Russia Hand*, pp. 335–6.

94 Talbott, *The Russia Hand*, pp. 336–7.

95 In a second meeting with Putin, Talbott describes how Putin effectively distanced himself from 'the Russian hawks' behind the sprint to the airport: 'Putin had managed simultaneously to position himself as a dove and to blame the U.S. for the awkward position in which the hawks had put government officials like himself', *The Russia Hand*, p. 344.

96 Bortsov, *Vladimir Putin*, p. 393.

97 For examples, see Yurii Drozdov and Vasilii Fartyshev, *Yurii Andropov i Vladimir Putin: na puti k vozrozhdeniyu* (Moscow, Olma-Press, 2001), p. 106; Bortsov, *Vladimir Putin*, p. 398.

98 Viktor Talanov, *Psikhologicheskii portret Vladimira Putina* (St Petersburg, B & K, 2000), p. 16.

99 R. F. Avramchenko, *Pokhoronit li Putin Rossiyu? Idei i kontsepsii preobrazovaniya Rossii* (Moscow, Editorial URSS, 2001), pp. 17, 24. Avramchenko had earlier sent the new president a draft plan to save Russia, *Put' Putina: do prezidenta ili reformatora? Novaya kontseptsiya razvitiya Rossii* (Moscow, self-published, 2000), and was most upset that Putin had not answered him personally.

100 Mukhin, *Kto est' mister Putin i kto s nim prishel?*, p. 24.

101 On a lighter note, the alternation between bald and hairy Russian and Soviet leaders has often been noted: Lenin's baldness gave way to a hairy Stalin, followed by a bald Khrushchev and a hairy Brezhnev, a bald Andropov and a hairy Chernenko, a bald Gorbachev and a hairy Yeltsin. Putin's receding hairline suggests a characteristically third-way approach to the question. Others, however, have suggested that the suffix -in may be more significant. Built up by the –ins (Len and Stal), the Soviet Union was brought down by the -evs and their ilk: Brezhn, Androp, Chernenk and Gorbach. To become a success, Vladimir Ilyich Ulyanov had to drop his -ev to become an -in. Boris Yeltsin demonstrated that to lead Russia you have to be a bisyllabic -in. In this context, Putin was a shoo-in. Letter from John Yates, Exeter, in *The Guardian*, 10 March 2000, p. 25.

102 Joseph A. Schumpeter, *Capitalism, Socialism and Democracy*, 5th edn (London, George, Allen & Unwin, 1976), p. 269.

103 Schumpeter, *Capitalism, Socialism and Democracy*, p. 272.

104 Every twist and turn is described by Leonid Mlechin, *Kreml' prezidenty Rossiyu: Strategiya vlasti ot B. N. El'tsina do V. V. Putina* (Moscow, Tsentrpoligraf, 2002).

105 Boris Yeltsin, *Midnight Diaries* (London, Weidenfeld & Nicolson, 2000), p. 29.

106 Yeltsin, *Midnight Diaries*, p. 103.

107 Mlechin, *KGB predsedateli organov gosbezopasnosti*, p. 843.

108 Yeltsin, *Midnight Diaries*, pp. 283–7.

109 Yeltsin, *Midnight Diaries*, p. 326.

110 Yeltsin, *Midnight Diaries*, p. 327.

111 Yeltsin, *Midnight Diaries*, p. 329.

112 Yeltsin, *Midnight Diaries*, p. 330.

113 Putin, *First Person*, p. 137.

114 Mlechin, *KGB predsedateli organov gosbezopasnosti*, p. 845.

115 Reported later in *Kommersant-Vlast'*, 28 March 2000, p. 16.

116 Putin, *First Person*, p. 204.

117 Putin's ability to deflect hostility and sense of humour was in evidence on this occasion. Both Yavlinsky and Zyuganov pretended that they had forgotten Putin's name, so in thanking deputies for their support he noted that he was especially grateful to 'Grigory Alekseevich Zyuganov' and 'Gennady Andreevich Yavlinsky', a mix of the two names, in Roi Medvedev, *Vremya Putina? Rossiya na rubezhe vekov* (Moscow, Prava Cheloveka, 2001), p. 165. The deputies fell about with laughter.

118 Vladimir Makarov had been responsible for personnel matters in the KGB and he took change of 'personnel policy' in the Presidential Administration, while Yeltsin's staff director was the FSB officer Vladimir Osipov. In addition to top-level appointments, a whole raft of secondary figures were brought in from the security agencies. For example, in the first two months of 1999 the career FSB officer Oleg Chernov became deputy secretary of the Security Council, the former KGB officer and SVR spokesman Yurii Kobaladze was appointed first deputy director of the Itar-Tass news agency, and the career SVR officer Boris Ivanov became deputy director of the presidential press service. There may well have been inter-service tensions at this time, with the former head of the SVR, Primakov, advancing his officers to counter the influence of the FSB, firmly in Yeltsin's hands in the form of the loyal Putin.

119 Eugene Huskey, *Presidential Power in Russia* (Armonk, NY, M. E. Sharpe, 1999), p. 96.

120 Medvedev, *Vremya Putina?*, p. 19.

121 Sergei Stepashin in *Nezavisimaya gazeta*, 14 January 2000. Lupan lists 26 atrocities committed in the region between September 1998 and October 1999, *Russkii vyzov*, pp. 117–20.

122 Peter Rutland, 'Putin's Path to Power', *Post-Soviet Affairs*, Vol. 16, No. 4, 2000, p. 323, fn. 24.

123 Amy Knight, 'The Enduring Legacy of the KGB in Russian Politics', *Problems of Post-Communism*, Vol. 47, No. 4, July/August 2000, p. 10.

124 The local police found sacks in the basement of a 13-storey apartment block, which apparently tested positive for hexogen, but Patrushev, Putin's close colleague at the head of the KGB, ordered the FSB to take the material and close the police investigation on the grounds that the operation had been no more than an exercise to test the alertness of the population, and that the sacks contained only sugar.

125 The explosive used was hexogen, which had allegedly been manufactured in a bomb-making factory in Chechnya. Among the many versions explaining the bombings is the one actively propagated by Berezovsky later, namely that the FSB either deliberately or by omission was responsible for the bombings. The 'Public Commission to Investigate the 1999 Explosions in Moscow and Volgodonsk and the Ryazan Exercises', chaired by State Duma deputy Sergei Kovalev, the former Russian human-rights commissioner, was an independent attempt to get to the bottom of these tragic events. The commission in effect took the place of what should have been a parliamentary commission, but the Duma had refused to set one up. A film sponsored by Berezovsky and compiled by Alexander Litvinenko called *Attack on Russia* was released in March 2002. It accused the government headed by Putin of being guilty of the crime, but the evidence was at best cir-

cumstantial. He was co-author of a later book, reissued after his death: Alexander Litvinenko and Yuri Feltshtinsky, *Blowing up Russia: The Soviet Plot to Bring back KGB Terror* (London, Gibson Square, 2007). The report on the atrocities issued by the Russian Federation Prosecutor General's office in April 2003 concluded that the 'foreign citizens Khattab and Amu Umar' were the organisers of the attacks with the involvement of Khakim Abayev, Denis Saitakov, the brothers Zaur and Timur Batchaev, Yusif Krymshamkhalov and Alam Dekkushiyev. Some of these had already been killed in the fighting in Chechnya, and the trials of Krymshamkhalov and Dekkushiyev were to follow. The jury remains out on who was responsible for the atrocities. An imaginative reconstruction of the apartment bombings, seen through the eyes of one family's experience, is presented in the film *Disbelief*, directed by Andrei Nekrasov and released in 2004.

126 See Pavel Baev, 'Chechnya and the Russian Military: A War too Far?', in Richard Sakwa (ed.), *Chechnya: From Past to Future* (London, Anthem Press; Sterling, VA, Stylus Publishers, 2005), pp. 117–30.

127 See Dale R. Herspring, *The Kremlin and the High Command: Presidential Impact on the Russian Military from Gorbachev to Putin* (Kansas, University Press of Kansas, 2006), Chapters 4–6.

128 Putin, *First Person*, p. 139.

129 Yeltsin, *Midnight Diaries*, p. 335.

130 Yeltsin, *Midnight Diaries*, p. 337.

131 Yeltsin, *Midnight Diaries*, p. 338.

132 Medvedev, *Vremya Putina?*, p. 23.

133 R. Kolchanov, 'Kremlevskii syurpriz', *Trud*, 5 January 2000; in Bortsov, *Vladimir Putin*, pp. 381–2.

134 Sergei Kovalev, 'Putin's War', *New York Review of Books*, 10 February 2000, p. 8.

135 Nikolai Petrov, 'Introduction: What Choice Faces Us?', in Michael McFaul, Nikolai Petrov and Andrei Ryabov (eds), *Rossiya nakanune dumskikh vyborov 1999 goda*, Moscow Carnegie Centre (Moscow, Gendal'f, 1999), p. 6.

136 Igor' Klyamkin and Liliya Shevtsova, *Vnesistemnyi rezhim Boris II: Nekotorye osobennosti politicheskogo razvitiya postsovetskoi Rossii* (Moscow, Moscow Carnegie Centre, 1999), p. 10.

137 Klyamkin and Shevtsova, *Vnesistemnyi rezhim Boris II*, p. 11.

138 Aleksandr Korzhakov, *Boris El'tsin: Ot rassveta do zakata* (Moscow, Interbuks, 1997).

139 Lilia Shevtsova, *Putin's Russia* (Washington, DC, Carnegie Endowment for International Peace, 2003), p. 46.

140 For details, see Richard Sakwa, 'Russia's "Permanent" (Uninterrupted) Elections of 1999–2000', *Journal of Communist Studies and Transition Politics*, Vol. 16, No. 3, September 2000, pp. 85–112.

141 *Itogi*, 23 December 1999, p. 7.

142 Yeltsin, *Midnight Diaries*, p. 4.

143 Putin recounts his own doubts in *First Person*, pp. 204–5: 'You know, Boris Nikolayevich, to be honest, I don't know if I'm ready for this or whether I want it, because it's a rather difficult fate', p. 204.

144 Yeltsin, *Midnight Diaries*, p. 6.

145 Yeltsin, *Midnight Diaries*, p. 7.

146 Yeltsin, *Midnight Diaries*, p. 14.

147 Bortsov, *Vladimir Putin*, p. 170. The text of the decree is in Dale R. Herspring (ed.), *Putin's Russia: Past Imperfect, Future Uncertain* (Oxford, Rowman & Littlefield, 2003), pp. 100–2.

148 A. Zinoviev in Lupan, *Russkii vyzov*, pp. 12–13.

149 Yulia Latynina, 'Weary Nation Lurks Behind Duma Results', *Moscow Times*, 22 December 1999, p. 8.

150 Quoted by John Thornhill, 'Paradoxes in the Wild East: After Six Years in Moscow', *Financial Times*, 8 July 2000.

151 Medvedev rightly insists that those who argue that 'Putin's authority was built on the Chechen campaign are mistaken', Medvedev, *Vremya Putina?*, p. 185.

152 In a survey of the most important events over the past decade, respondents in 2002 reacted most positively to Yeltsin's resignation (viewed positively by 86%), *Russian Political Weekly*, 18 March 2002.

153 Alexander Prokhanov in *Zavtra*, 29 February 2000, cited by Roi Medvedev, *Zagadka Putina* (Moscow, Prava cheloveka, 2000), p. 11; Medvedev, *Vremya Putina?*, p. 36.

154 Medvedev, *Zagadka Putina*, p. 18.

155 Medvedev, *Zagadka Putina*, p. 56.

156 ORT, *Vremya*, 5 March 2000.

157 This at least was the the view of Gleb Musikhin, 'Yavlinskii prav, no istina dorozhe', *Nezavisimaya gazeta*, 2 March 2000, p. 3.

158 Those who supported Putin in the election included Boris Nemtsov's Young Russia (*Rossiya Molodaya*), Sergei Kirienko's New Power (*Novaya Sila*) and Nikolai Brusnikin's New Generation (*Novoe Pokolenie*), together with a personal endorsement by Chubais.

159 RFE/RL, *Newsline*, 7 March 2000.

160 *Izvestiya*, 9 February 2000.

161 Vladimir Putin, 'Otkrytoe pis'mo Vladimira Putina k Rossiiskim izbiratelyam', *Izvestiya*, 25 February 2000, p. 5; www.putin2000.ru/07/05.html.

162 Published in Russian as Putin, *Ot pervogo litsa*, op. cit. fn. 16 for full reference; The book was published in English as Putin, *First Person*, op. cit. fn. 10. The '*Millennium Manifesto*' is published as an appendix, pp. 209–19.

163 Zh. Kas'yanenko, 'Saratovskaya nepreryvka. Konveier poddelok', *Sovetskaya Rossiya*, 18 March 2000.

164 A. Salii, 'Dagestanskaya tekhnologiya fal'sifikatsii. Zakon na koze ob"ekhali', *Sovetskaya Rossii*, 27 April 2000.

165 Yevgeniya Borisova, 'And the Winner Is?', *Moscow Times*, 9 September 2000; more details can be found at *The Moscow Times.Com Special Report/Election Fraud*; for associated material see www.moscowtimes.ru. A detailed analysis of the technology of fraud is provided by Vladimir Pribylovskii, 'Tsar'-to nenastoyashchii', in A. Verkhovskii, E. Mikhailovskaya and V. Pribylovskii, *Rossiya Putina: pristrastnyi vzglyad* (Moscow, Tsentr 'Panorama', 2003), pp. 146–58. Some interesting retrospective comments can be found by Matt Bivens in *The St Peterburg Times*, 23 September 2003.

166 For an unsuccessful attempt to explain the figures, see the Central Electoral Commission's comment 'O manipulatsiya mnimykh i deistvitel'nykh', www.fci.ru/expres_info/org.htm.

167 Aleksei Zudin, 'Soyuz pravykh sil', Moskovskii tsentr Karnegi, *Parlamentskie vybory 1999 goda v Rossii*, Byulleten' No. 2, December 1999, p. 18.

168 The point is made by Laura Belin, 'Commission Releases Final Results', RFE/RL, *Russian Election Report*, No. 5 (13), 7 April 2000.

169 Medvedev, *Vremya Putina?*, p. 69.

170 Nikolai Vavilov, '"Putin – absolyuten". Tak schitayut rossiyane, zhivushchie v stranakh SNG, i lidery gosudarstv Sodruzhestva', *Sodruzhestvo NG*, No. 3 (26), 29 March 2000, pp. 9, 12.

171 A study of 2000 respondents in Samara found that Putin 'was backed by 58 per cent of students and 20–25 year olds, compared to only 40 per cent of those over 55. He was also preferred by 50 per cent of women compared to 46.5 per cent of men. Sixty per cent of those whose living standard had improved over the past year backed Putin, compared to 40 per cent of those who said it had worsened'. The study also found that Putin drew his support from right across

the political spectrum. Three quarters of those who voted for Unity in the December Duma election backed Putin for president, as did 61 per cent of SPS supporters and 49 per cent of those who backed FatherlandAll Russia (OVR). Putin even beat Yavlinsky among Yabloko voters, by 37 to 36 per cent. More remarkable, 10 per cent of CPRF voters backed Putin. Putin was also the favourite of those who had abstained in the December 1999 poll, and of those who had voted 'against all': Jamestown Foundation, *Monitor*, 8 March 2000.

172 Henry E. Hale, 'Is Russian Nationalism on the Rise?', Program on New Approaches to Russian Security, Davis Center for Russian Studies, Harvard University, *Policy Memo Series*, No. 110, February 2000, p. 1.

173 For the tension between order and democracy in these elections, see Richard Rose and Neil Munro, *Elections without Order: Russia's Challenge to Vladimir Putin* (Cambridge, Cambridge University Press, 2002).

174 Data based on All-Russian Centre for the Study of Public Opinion (VTsIOM) polls, in Karaganov (ed.), *Strategiya dlya Rossii*, p. 28. See also Rose and Munro, *Elections without Order*.

175 Timothy J. Colton and Michael McFaul, *Are Russians Undemocratic?* (Carnegie Endowment for International Peace, Russian Domestics Politics Project, Russian and Eurasian Program, Working Paper No. 20, June 2001); republished in *Post-Soviet Affairs*, Vol. 18, No. 2, 2002, pp. 91–121; and a version called 'Putin and Democratization' in Herspring (ed.), *Putin's Russia*, Chapter 2, pp. 13–38.

176 See Yitzhak M. Brudny, 'In Pursuit of the Russian Presidency: Why and how Yeltsin Won the 1996 Presidential Election', *Communist and Post-Communist Studies*, Vol. 30, No. 3 (1997), p. 273.

177 Press conference televised at 1.30 a.m. on 27 March 2000. See also Laura Belin, How State Television Aided Putin's Campaign', RFE/RL, *Russian Election Report*, No. 5 (13), 7 April 2000.

178 Sergei Mitrokhin, 'Put', kotoryi my vybiraem', *Nezavisimaya gazeta*, 3 March 2000, p. 3.

179 The terms are used by Ian Traynor, 'Weary Nation Turns to Putin', *The Guardian*, 16 March 2000, p. 20.

180 Mlechin, *Kreml' prezidenty Rossii*, p. 611.

2 Ideas and choices

1 Itar-Tass, 28 February 2000.

2 For example, *Al'ternativa: Vybor puti. Perestroika upravleniya i gorizonty rynka* (Moscow, Mysl', 1990).

3 Yurii N. Afanas'ev (ed.), *Inogo ne dano* (Moscow, Progress, 1988).

4 Cited by Roi Medvedev, *Vladimir Putin – Deistvuyushchii Prezident* (Moscow, Vremya, 2002), p. 157. It was also the title of a hostile editorial in the *Wall Street Journal* soon after Putin was nominated acting president.

5 Mukhin took up the theme in his *Kto est' mister Putin i kto s nim prishel?* (*Who is Mr Putin, and who Came with Him?*). In Russian the word *zagadka* (a puzzle or a mystery) was often used, for example Roi Medvedev, *Zagadka Putina* (Moscow, Prava Cheloveka, 2000).

6 Alexander Zinoviev, 'Fenomen Putina', in his *Rasput'e*, (Moscow, Elefant, 2005), pp. 199–206.

7 Zinoviev in Lupan, *Russkii vyzov*, p. 5.

8 Interview with Alexander Solzhenitsyn, first published in *Der Spiegel*, by Fritjof Meyer, Jorg R. Mettke and Martin Derry, reprinted as 'Russia's Darkest Night of the Soul', *The Guardian*, 18 March 2000, p. 2.

9 'Mr Putin's Two Faces', *The Guardian*, 12 July 2000, p. 21.

10 *Nezavisimaya gazeta*, 2 November 2000.

11 Margarita Mommsen, 'The Sphinx in the Kremlin', *Internationale Politik: Translatlantic Edition*, Vol. 1, No. 3, 2000, pp. 21–2.

12 Vladimir Putin, 'Otkrytoe pis'mo Vladimira Putina k Rossiiskim izbiratelyam', *Izvestiya*, 25 February 2000, p. 5; www.putin2000.ru/07/05.html. Italics in original.

13 *Novaya gazeta*, No. 9, 9–11 February 2004, p. 8.

14 Aleksei Chadaev, *Putin: Ego ideologiya* (Moscow, Evropa, 2006). The work is based on an analysis of Putin's state of the nation speeches of 2004 and 2005, see below. The book's cover design features yellow, white and black, the colours of the Russian imperial flag, provoking much speculation about the author's neo-monarchical intent.

15 BBC Monitoring, 11 February 2006, in *JRL*, 2006/40/3.

16 Alexander Tsipko, 'Filosofiya ratsional'nogo optimizma', *Rossiiskaya gazeta*, 8 February 2006.

17 Harley Balzer, 'Vladimir Putin's Academic Writings and Russian Natural Resource Policy', *Problems of Post-Communism*, Vol. 53, No. 1, January–February 2006, pp. 48–54, with Putin's article 'Mineral Natural Resources in the Strategy for Development of the Russian Economy', at pp. 49–54.

18 Harley Balzer, 'The Putin Thesis and Russian Energy Policy', *Post-Soviet Affairs*, Vol. 21, No. 3, 2005, pp. 210–25.

19 Putin, 'Mineral Natural Resources in the Strategy for Development of the Russian Economy', p. 50.

20 'Stenogramma press-konferentsii dlya rossiiskikh i inostrannykh zhurnalistov', 31 January 2006, www.president.kremlin.ru/text/appears/2006/01/100848.shtml.

21 Matvei Maly, *Kak sdelat' Rossiyu normal'noi stranoi?* (St Petersburg, Dmitrii Bulanin, 2003), p. 7.

22 Ralf Dahrendorf, *Reflections on the Revolution in Europe* (London, Chatto & Windus, 1990), pp. 92–3.

23 Dahrendorf, *Reflections on the Revolution in Europe*, pp. 60, 85 and *passim*.

24 Joseph Schumpeter, *Capitalism, Socialism and Democracy*, 2nd edn (New York, Harper, 1947), p. 269.

25 G. O'Donnell, P. Schmitter, and L. Whitehead (eds), *Transitions from Authoritarian Rule*, Vol. 4, *Tentative Conclusions about Uncertain Democracies* (Baltimore, MD, Johns Hopkins University Press, 1986), p. 65.

26 S. I. Kaspe, 'Tsentr i vertikal': Politicheskaya priroda putinskogo prezidentstva', *Politiya*, No. 4 (22), Winter 2001–2, p. 5.

27 Clifford G. Gaddy and Barry W. Ickes, 'Russia's Virtual Economy', *Foreign Affairs*, Vol. 77, No. 5, September–October 1998, pp. 53–67.

28 Andrei Shleifer and Daniel Treisman, 'A Normal Country', *Foreign Affairs*, Vol. 83, No. 2, March–April 2004, pp. 20–39; see also Andrei Shleifer, *A Normal Country: Russia After Communism* (Cambridge, MA, Harvard University Press, 2005).

29 www.president.kremlin.ru/text/appears/2006/02/101129.shtml.

30 Aleksandr Tsipko, *Pochemu ya ne "demokrat" (Moscow, Algoritm, 2005)*.

31 Viktoriya Shokhina, 'Poety i gosudarstvo', *Nezavisimaya gazeta*, 20 December 2004, p. 2.

32 For the development of this argument, see Richard Sakwa, 'The Age of Paradox: The Anti-Revolutionary Revolutions of 1989–91', in Moira Donald and Tim Rees (eds), *Reinterpreting Revolution in Twentieth-Century Europe* (London, Macmillan, 2001), pp. 159–76.

33 Yeltsin, *Midnight Diaries*, p. 197.

34 In *First Person* (p. 21) Putin recounts an intriguing moment when one of his school teachers set the topic 'A revolution has a beginning, a revolution has no end'. Clearly this struck an echo in Putin's thinking, hence its appearance in his book.

35 RIA Novosti, 4 April 2001.

36 'Stenogramma "Pryamoi linii" Prezidenta Rossiiskoi Federatsii V. V. Putina', 24 December 2001, www.president.kremlin.ru/events/423.html.

37 Interview in a TV film made by Igor Shadkhan called 'Vladimir Putin: A Conversation in the Evening', BBC Monitoring; *JRL*, 2002/6483/6.

38 www.president.kremlin.ru/text/appears/2006/02/101129.shtml.

39 See Sheila Fitzpatrick, 'Postwar Soviet Society: The Return to Normalcy, 1945–1953', in Susan J. Linz (ed.), *The Impact of World War II on the Soviet Union* (Totowa, NJ, Rowman and Allanheld, 1985), pp. 129–56.

40 Andrei Kozyrev, 'Russia: A Chance for Survival', *Foreign Affairs*, Vol. 71, No. 2, Spring 1992, pp. 8–9.

41 Leszek Balcerowicz, *Common Fallacies in the Debate on the Economic Transition in Central and Eastern Europe* (London, European Bank for Reconstruction and Devolopment Working Paper 11, 1993).

42 For details about the October 1993 crisis and the institutional arrangements of the constitutional system introduced in December 1993, see Richard Sakwa, *Russian Politics and Society*, 3rd edn (London and New York, Routledge, 2002).

43 Peter Reddaway and Dmitri Glinski, *The Tragedy of Russia's Reforms: Market Bolshevism against Democracy* (Washington, DC, The United States Institute of Peace Press, 2001).

44 Vitalii Tret'yakov, *Russkaya politika i politiki v norme i v patologii* (Moscow, Ladomir, 2001), p. 771.

45 www.president.kremlin.ru/events/131.html.

46 *Moskovskii komsomolets*, 30 December 2000; *Monitor*, 2 January 2001.

47 The 'contradiction' between Russia and Western-generated models of development was symbolised by the shift of the capital from Russia's Muscovite heartland to St Petersburg as a 'window to the West'; and it perhaps was not accidental that a citizen of St Petersburg sought to resolve this contradiction.

48 Some of the most eloquent exponents of the alternativity thesis for Russia are the many works by Akhiezer. See, for example, A. S. Akhiezer, *Rosiiya: Kritika istoricheskogo opyta*, Vol. 1, *Ot proshlogo k budushchemu*, 2nd edn, reworked and extended (Novosibirsk, Sibirskii khronograf, 1997).

49 Guillermo O'Donnell, 'Delegative Democracy', *Journal of Democracy*, Vol. 5, No. 1 (January 1994), pp. 55–69.

50 Fareed Zakaria, 'The Rise of Illiberal Democracy', *Foreign Affairs*, Vol. 76, No. 6 (November/December 1997), pp. 22–43.

51 Larry Diamond, *Developing Democracy: Towards Consolidation* (Baltimore, MD, Johns Hopkins University Press, 1999).

52 Gordon M. Hahn, *Russia's Revolution from Above, 1985–2000: Reform, Transition, and Revolution in the Fall of the Soviet Communist Regime* (New Brunswick, NJ, Transaction Publishers, 2002), p. xii.

53 Hahn, *Russia's Revolution from Above*, p. 2.

54 Hahn, *Russia's Revolution from Above*, p. 9.

55 Samuel P. Huntington, *Political Order in Changing Societies* (New Haven, CT, Yale University Press, 1968).

56 V. V. Putin, *Razgovor s Rossiei: Stenogramma 'Pryamoi linii s Prezidentom Rossiiskoi Federatsii V. V. Putinym'*, 19 December 2002 (Moscow, Olma-Politizdat, 2003), p. 14.

57 Ralf Dahrendorf, *Society and Democracy in Germany* (London, Weidenfeld & Nicolson, 1968).

58 The document appeared on 29 December on the Russian Federation government website: www.gov.ru/ministry/isp-vlast47.html; also on www.pravitelstvo.gov.ru. Published in Russian in Vladimir Putin, 'Rossiya na rubezhe tysyacheletii', *Nezavisimaya gazeta*, 30 December 1999, p. 4. An English version can be found in Putin, *First Person*, pp. 209–19 and at the end of this book (to which the references refer).

59 Pechenev, *Vladimir Putin*, p. 45.
60 Putin, *First Person*, p 210; Sakwa, *Putin*, p. 322.
61 Putin, *First Person*, p 211; Sakwa, *Putin*, p. 323.
62 Putin, *First Person*, p 212; Sakwa, *Putin*, p. 324.
63 Putin, *First Person*, p 212; Sakwa, *Putin*, p. 324.
64 Putin, *First Person*, p 212; Sakwa, *Putin*, p. 325.
65 Putin, *First Person*, p 213; Sakwa, *Putin*, p. 326.
66 Putin, *First Person*, p 215; Sakwa, *Putin*, p. 327.
67 Putin, *First Person*, p 214; Sakwa, *Putin*, p. 327.
68 Putin, *First Person*, p 215; Sakwa, *Putin*, p. 328.
69 Full details about the Centre can be found in *Moskovskie novosti*, No. 6, 15–21 February 2000, p. 11.
70 Sergei Parkhomenko, 'Sostavitel's kontrakta', *Itogi*, 8 February 2000, pp. 21–4.
71 Lidiya Andrusenko, 'Oligarkhi sovetuyut', *Nezavisimaya gazeta*, 1 April 2000, p. 3.
72 www.kommersant.ru/Docs/reforma.htm, 'Reforming the Structure of the Presidential Administration', Gref Centre document, excerpts from Book No.2, 'Introduction'.
73 S. A. Karaganov (ed.), *Strategiya dlya Rossii: Povestka dnya dlya prezidenta-2000* (Moscow, Vagrius/SVOP, 2000), abstract.
74 Karaganov (ed.), *Strategiya dlya Rossii*, p. 6.
75 Karaganov (ed.), *Strategiya dlya Rossii*, p. 8.
76 Karaganov (ed.), *Strategiya dlya Rossii*, pp. 14–15.
77 Karaganov (ed.), *Strategiya dlya Rossii*, p. 17.
78 Karaganov (ed.), *Strategiya dlya Rossii*, p. 19.
79 Karaganov (ed.), *Strategiya dlya Rossii*, p. 21.
80 Karaganov (ed.), *Strategiya dlya Rossii*, p. 24.
81 Karaganov (ed.), *Strategiya dlya Rossii*, pp. 80–1.
82 Karaganov (ed.), *Strategiya dlya Rossii*, p. 96.
83 I. Ya. Bogdanov and A. P. Kalinin, *Korruptsiya v Rossii: Sotsial'no-ekonomicheskie i pravovye aspekty* (Moscow, Institute of Socio-Political research, RAS, 2001), p. 67.
84 One of the best analyses is A. A. Mukhin, *Rossiiskaya organizovannaya prestupnost' i vlast': Istoriya vzaimootnoshenii* (Moscow, Tsentr politicheskoi informatsii, 2003).
85 Pavel Khlebnikov, *Krestnyi otets Kremlya Boris Berezovskii ili Istoriya razgrableniya Rossii* (Moscow, Detektiv-Press, 2001), pp. 188–93.
86 Mukhin, *Rossiiskaya organizovannaya prestupnost' i vlast'*, p. 5.
87 Bogdanov and Kalinin, *Korruptsiya v Rossii*, p. 149.
88 Karaganov (ed.), *Strategiya dlya Rossii*, pp. 197–8.
89 Karaganov (ed.), *Strategiya dlya Rossii*, pp. 209–10.
90 Karaganov (ed.), *Strategiya dlya Rossii*, p. 211.
91 Karaganov (ed.), *Strategiya dlya Rossii*, p. 213.
92 *Vedemosti*, 15 May 2006.
93 'Vystuplenie pri predstavlenii ezhegodnogo Poslaniya Prezidenta Rossiiskoi Federatsii Federal'nomu Sobraniyu Rossiiskoi Federatsii', www.president.kremlin.ru/events/42.html.
94 RIA Novosti, 4 April 2001.
95 www.president.kremlin.ru/events/510/html.
96 'Ustalost' reform', *Izvestiya*, 24 April 2003, p. 1.
97 www.president.kremlin.ru/text/appears/2003/05/44623.shtml.
98 *Rossiiskaya gazeta*, 27 May 2004; www.kremlin.ru/eng/text/speeches/2004/05/262021_64906.shtml.
99 www.kremlin.ru/text/appears/2005/04/87049.shtml; *Rossiiskaya gazeta*, 25 April 2005; BBC Monitoring, in *JRL*, 9130/1.

100 www.president.kremlin.ru/text/appears/2006/05/105546.shtml.
101 www.president.kremlin.ru/text/appears/2007/04/125401.shtml.

3 Putin's path

1 George F. Kennan, 'America and the Russian Future', *Foreign Affairs*, Vol. 29, Issue 3, April 1951, pp. 351–70, at p. 355.
2 Cited by Bortsov, *Vladimir Putin*, pp. 19–20.
3 Medvedev, *Vremya Putina?*, p. 9.
4 Samuel P. Huntington, *The Third Wave: Democratization in the Late Twentieth Century* (Norman, University of Oklahoma Press, 1991), pp. 144ff.
5 See Peter Reddaway, 'Will Putin be Able to Consolidate Power?', *Post-Soviet Affairs*, Vol. 17, No. 1, 2001, pp. 23–44; see also his 'Is Putin's Power More Formal than Real?', *Post-Soviet Affairs*, Vol. 18, No. 1, 2002, pp. 31–40.
6 Hahn, *Russia's Revolution from Above*, pp. 520–1.
7 For a detailed analysis of the various groups, see Peter Rutland, 'Putin and the Oligarchs', in Herspring (ed.), *Putin's Russia*, Chapter 7, in particular pp. 138–9.
8 Igor Kharichev, 'Politseiskoe gosudarstvo grozit stat' nashim budushchim', *Nezavisimaya gazeta*, 8 February 2000.
9 *Financial Times*, 18 July 2000.
10 Yeltsin's daughter commented on Voloshin as follows: 'At work he is like some complex well-maintained machine that does not know tiredness. I sometimes don't know how he can stand it.' Mlechin, *KGB predsedateli organov gosbezopasnosti*, p. 844.
11 They bought large stakes from the London-based Trans-World Group (headed by Lev Chernoi) in the Krasnoyarsk (KrAZ) and Bratsk (BrAZ) aluminium plants and the Achinsk alumina enterprise. The head of the Anti-Monopoly Committee, Anatoly Yuzhanov, ruled that no anti-trust laws had been violated since none of the stakes sold were larger than 20% (ignoring the role of various front companies), a finding that suggested that Putin would not challenge the power of the oligarchs and that he would implement his plan for the creation of large vertically integrated companies.
12 To ensure that his consulting services remained necessary for Putin, Pavlovsky allegedly set about discrediting Gref's Centre for Strategic Studies, something that he did successfully, Mukhin, *Kto est' mister Putin i kto s nim prishel?*, pp. 62–3.
13 *Russian Regional Report*, Vol. 7, No. 20, 17 June 2002.
14 Elena Dikun, *Prism*, Vol. VI, Issue 6, Part 1, June 2000.
15 www.president.kremlin.ru/text/APPTemplAppearId16748.shtml.
16 *Segodnya*, 17 June 2000; *Monitor*, 19 June 2000.
17 *Moscow Times*, 22 June 2000.
18 V. I. Fartyshev, *Poslednii shans putina: Sud'ba Rossii v XXI veke* (Moscow, Veche, 2004), p. 383.
19 RIA Novosti, 20 December 2003.
20 *Komsomolskaya Pravda*, 26 January 2000; *Washington Times*, 7 February 2000.
21 Olga Kryshtanovkaya and Stephen White, 'Putin's Militocracy', *Post-Soviet Affairs*, Vol. 19, No. 4, October–December 2003, pp. 289–306, at p. 294.
22 Ol'ga Kryshtanovkaya and Stephen White, 'Inside the Putin Court: A Research Note', *Europe-Asia Studies*, Vol. 57, No. 7, November 2005, pp. 1065–75, at p. 1065.
23 Interview with Vladimir Kosarev and Yurii Gladkevich, *Profil*, No. 25, 2000.
24 Sharon Werning Rivera and David W. Rivera, 'The Russian Elite under Putin: Militocratic or Bourgeois?', *Post-Soviet Affairs*, Vol. 22, No. 2, 2006, pp. 125–44, at p. 136.
25 Rivera and Rivera, 'The Russian Elite under Putin', p. 126.

26 Bettina Renz, 'Putin's Militocracy? An Alternative Interpretation of *Siloviki* in Contemporary Russian Politics', *Europe-Asia Studies*, Vol. 58, No. 6, 2006, pp. 903–24.

27 Rivera and Rivera, 'The Russian Elite under Putin', p. 127.

28 Viktor Cherkesov, 'Moda na KGB?', *Komsomol'skaya Pravda*, 29 December 2004. The article is discussed by Victor Yasmann, 'The Burden of Maintaining the State has been Laid on our Shoulders', RFE/RL *Russian Political Weekly*, Vol. 5, No. 6, 10 February 2005.

29 25 October 2006 hot line with the people, www.president.kremlin.ru/text/appears/2006/10/112959.shtml.

30 www.president.kremlin.ru/text/appears/2006/05/105546.shtml.

31 Stephen Blank, 'Reading Putin's Military Tea Leaves', *Eurasia Daily Monitor*, Vol. 3, Issue 98, 19 May 2006.

32 Edwin Bacon and Bettina Renz with Julian Cooper, *Securitising Russia: The Domestic Politics of Putin* (Manchester, Manchester University Press, 2006).

33 Sophie Lambroschini, 'KGB Veterans Head Has High Hopes of Putin', *Newsline*, 30 June 2000. In 2006 Velichko's name figured in the 'planning of actions' documents against Paolo Guzzanti, the Italian senator heading the Mitrokhin commission investigating alleged KGB infiltration in Italy, and Mario Scaramella, who had seen Alexander Litvinenko on the day of his slow-motion assassination with polonium-210 on 1 November 2006 in London.

34 Vladimir Ryzhkov, *Novaya Gazeta*, No. 46, 22 June 2006.

35 Viktor Stepankov, *Leningradtsy v bor'be za Kreml'* (Moscow, Yauza, 2004) traces this in the Soviet period and beyond. Anthony D'Agostino, *Gorbachev's Revolution 1985–91* (Basingstoke, Macmillan, 1998), interprets Soviet politics through the prism of this tension.

36 Aleksei Mukhin, *Mikhail Kas'yanov: Moskovskii otvet 'piterskim'* (Moscow, Algoritm, 2005).

37 For full details of the Pitery, including biographies, see Boris Mazo, *Piterskie protiv Moskovskikh, ili kto est' kto v okruzhenii V. V. Putina* (Moscow, Eksmo Algoritm, 2003).

38 For a collection of the most significant writing about sovereign democracy, see Nikita Garadzha (ed.), *Suverenitet* (Moscow, Evropa, 2006).

39 Press conference with Sergei Markov at *Argumenty i fakty* press centre, 16 November 2005, in *JRL*, 9299/15.

40 In socio-occupational terms 21.9% of all Russian households considered themselves middle class; in terms of material position 21.2%; and in terms of self-identification 39.5%, Tatyana Maleva, *The Middle Class: Here and Now*, Carnegie Moscow Center, *Briefing Papers*, Vol. 4, Issue 12, December 2002. For an updated report by Maleva and her team, see *Nezavisimaya gazeta*, 24 January 2007, which reported that 54% of the middle class was made up by state-sector employees, and only 35% came from the private sector.

41 Milovan Djilas, *The New Class: An Analysis of the Communist System* (New York, Praeger, 1957).

42 Dmitrii Yur'ev, *Rezhim Putina: postdemokratiya* (Moscow, Evropa, 2005).

43 Thomas Graham, 'Novyi russkii rezhim', *Nezavisimaya gazeta*, 23 November 1995, p. 5.

44 See Kimitaka Matsuzato, 'Semipresidentialism in Ukraine: Institutionalist Centrism in Rampant Clan Politics', *Demokratizatsiya*, Vol. 13, No. 1, Winter 2005, pp. 45–58.

45 See, for example, Edward Schatz, *Modern Clan Politics: The Power of "Blood" in Kazakhstan and Beyond*, Jackson School Publications in International Studies (Seattle, University of Washington Press, 2004).

46 Jonathan Murphy, 'Illusory Transition? Elite Reconstitution in Kazakhstan, 1989–2002', *Europe-Asia Studies*, Vol. 58, No. 4, June 2006, pp. 523–54.

342 *Notes*

47 Andrei Ryabov interviewed by Avtandil Tsuladze, 'Putin Must Become the 'Father of the Nation' – to Maintain his Rating', *Segodnya*, 8 July 2000.
48 Andrew Wilson, *Virtual Politics: Faking Democracy in the Post-Soviet World* (New Haven, CT, Yale University Press, 2005).
49 See, for example, A. Tsuladze, *Bol'shaya manipulativnaya igra: Tekhnologii politicheskikh manipulyatsii v period vyborov 1999–2000* (Moscow, Algoritm, 2000).
50 Stephen White, 'Ten Years On: What do the Russians Think?', in Rick Fawn and Stephen White (eds), *Russia After Communism* (London, Frank Cass, 2002), p. 41.
51 White, 'Ten Years On', p. 42.
52 White, 'Ten Years On', p. 42.
53 Gleb Pavlovsky, 'Russia Can Be Easily Provoked into Revolution', *Kommersant-Vlast'*, No. 26, 4 July 2000.
54 Michael McFaul, *Generational Change in Russia*, PONARS Working Paper Series No. 21 (Washington, DC, CSIS, 2002).
55 Yury Chernega, 'Putin – nash teflonskii prezident', *Kommersant*, 7 July 2000.
56 www/riisnp.ru/contents.htm; *Russian Political Weekly*, 18 March 2002.
57 Richard Rose, *A Bottom Up Evaluation of Enlargement Countries: New Europe Barometer 1* (University of Strathclyde, Centre for the Study of Public Policy, Studies in Public Policy, 2002), No. 364, p. 8.
58 Rose, *A Bottom Up Evaluation of Enlargement Countries*, p. 13.
59 Rose, *A Bottom Up Evaluation of Enlargement Countries*, p. 24.
60 Public Opinion Foundation (FOM), http://english.fom.ru/reports/frames/ed030908.html.
61 *Argumenty i fakty*, No. 16, April 2003, p. 1.
62 http://english.fom.ru/reports/frames/ed031004.html.
63 http://english.fom.ru/reports/frames/ed030824.html.
64 www.levada.ru/press/2005122901.html.
65 D. N. Konovalenko (ed.), *Portret storonnika Putina: Nakanune 2008 goda* (Moscow, Evropa, 2005).
66 Konovalenko (ed.), *Portret storonnika Putina: Nakanune 2008 goda*, pp. 7–16.
67 *Izvestiya*, 27 October 2005, reporting on a survey of 35,000 people by FOM.
68 Konovalenko (ed.), *Portret storonnika Putina: Nakanune 2008 goda*, p. 17.
69 Konovalenko (ed.), *Portret storonnika Putina: Nakanune 2008 goda*, p. 27.
70 Stephen Whitefield, 'Putin's Popularity and its Implications for Democracy in Russia', in Alex Pravda (ed.), *Leading Russia: Putin in Perspective* (Oxford, Oxford University Press, 2005), pp. 139–60, quotation at p. 157.
71 Richard Rose, Neil Munro, and Stephen White, 'How Strong is Vladimir Putin's Support?', *Post-Soviet Affairs*, Vol. 16, No. 4, 2000, pp. 287–312.
72 Dmitri K. Simes, 'With Friends Like These, Putin Needs a Smarter Strategy', *Washington Post*, 16 July 2000.
73 http://english.fom.ru/reports/frames/ed030107.html.
74 Rose and Munro, *Elections without Order*, pp. 189–95.
75 The changes can be tracked on the basis of VTsIOM data, posted at www.russiavotes.org.
76 http://english.fom.ru/reports/frames/ed030921.html.
77 Nikolai Petrov notes 'the calculated way in which the political arena has been cleared of any real heroes other than the president himself', *Russia and Eurasia Review*, Vol. 2, Issue 8, 15 April 2003.
78 Elena Shestopal, 'Popular Perceptions of Vladimir Putin', paper presented to the British Association for Slavonic and East European Studies (BASEES) conference, Cambridge, 29–31 March 2003.
79 Robert Moore, *A Time to Die: The Kursk Disaster* (New York, Doubleday, 2002); Peter Truscott, *Kursk: Russia's Lost Pride* (London, Simon & Schuster, 2003).
80 Medvedev, *Vremya Putina?*, pp. 113–33 covers the tragedy in detail.

81 For a blow-by-blow account by one of the hostages, see Tat'yana Popova, *Nord-Ost glazami zalozhnitsy* (Moscow, Vagrius, 2002).

82 Viktor Stepankov, *Bitva za 'Nord-Ost'* (Moscow, Yauza/Eksmo, 2003), p. 59.

83 Alexander Cherkasov, 'Looking Back at Beslan', *Russian Analytical Digest*, No. 5, 2006, pp. 2–4.

84 *Nezavisimaya gazeta*, 6 September 2004, p. 2.

85 *Gazeta.ru*, 29 January 2003.

86 Figure cited by Andrei Ryabov interviewed by Avtandil Tsuladze, *Segodnya*, 8 July 2000.

87 Schumpeter, *Capitalism, Socialism and Democracy*, 5th edn, p. 270.

88 'The Rebirth of Right-Wing Charisma? The Cases of Jean-Marie Le Pen and Vladimir Zhirinovsky', *Totalitarian Movements and Political Religions*, Vol. 3, No. 3, Winter 2002, pp. 1–23.

89 Colin Lawson and Howard White, 'Images of Leadership in Ukraine and Russia: Preliminary Findings', paper presented to the BASEES conference, Cambridge, 6–8 April 2002.

90 He draws on the concept formulated by James MacGregor Burns in *Leadership* (New York, Harper & Row, 1978); Archie Brown, 'Introduction', in Archie Brown and Lilia Shevtsova (eds), *Gorbachev, Yeltsin, and Putin: Political Leadership in Russia's Transition* (Washington, DC, Carnegie Endowment for International Peace, 2001), pp. 6–8.

91 Sophie Lambroschini, 'Russia: Analysts Say Putin May Be Overreaching', *Newsline*, 11 July 2000.

92 *Monitor*, 19 July 2001.

93 For example, Aleksandr Ushakov, *Fenomenon Atatyurka: Turetskii pravitel', tvorets i diktator* (Moscow, Tsentropoligraf, 2002).

94 See, for example, Alexander Chubarov, *The Fragile Empire: A History of Imperial Russia* (London, Continuum, 1999). See also his *Russia's Bitter Path to Modernity: A History of the Soviet and Post-Soviet Eras* (London, Continuum, 2001).

95 See George W. Breslauer, *Gorbachev and Yeltsin as Leaders* (Cambridge, Cambridge University Press, 2002).

96 See Yevgenia Albats, 'Power Play: Two Evils Once Again on our Plate', *Moscow Times*, 22 June 2000.

97 Interview with Primakov, *Parlamentskaya gazeta*, 8 June 2000. Other cases are recounted in Medvedev, *Vremya Putina?*, p. 166.

98 Asked which political leaders he found most interesting, Putin answered De Gaulle and Erhard, *First Person*, p. 194. It may also be noted that Putin was only 47 years old on assuming the presidency; at that age De Gaulle was no more than a tank commander.

99 *Argumenty i fakty*, No. 12, 2000, p. 3.

100 V. A. Mironov, 'The December Prologue to the June Elections', *Prism*, No. 20, Part 2, December 1999.

101 Viktor Sheinis, 'Posle bitvy: Itogi parlamentskikh vyborov i novaya Gosudarstvennaya Duma', *Nezavisimaya gazeta*, 29 December 1999, p. 8.

102 Anthony Giddens, *The Third Way: The Renewal of Social Democracy* (Cambridge, Polity Press, 1998). See also Anthony Giddens, *The Third Way and its Critics* (Cambridge, Polity Press, 2000); Anthony Giddens (ed.), *The Global Third Way Debate* (Cambridge, Polity Press, 2001).

103 For a comparable discussion of radical centrism, see Michael Lind and Ted Halstead, *The Radical Center: The Future of American Politics* (New York, Doubleday, 2001). Note also the problems with the approach put forward by these two authors, trying to take the best from left and right and instead creating a mix of often incoherent and incompatible policies (quasi-centrism). It appears that in America, as much as in Russia, the attempt to generate a non-

ideological radical politics of the centre falls prey to anti-democratic techno-cratism (as under New Labour Britain).

104 Kaspe, 'Tsentr i vertikal', pp. 11–12.
105 Kenneth Jowitt, *New World Disorder: The Leninist Extinction* (Berkeley, University of California Press, 1992).
106 Huntington, *Political Order in Changing Societies*, op. cit.
107 Michael Mann, 'The Autonomous Power of the State: Its Origins, Mechanisms and Results', in John A. Hall (ed.), *States in History* (Oxford, Basil Blackwell, 1986), p. 112.
108 Alexander Yanov, 'Open Letter to Colleagues in the West'; *JRL*, 3410, 26 July 1999.

4 Parties, elections and the succession

1 Putin, *First Person*, p. 215.
2 V. A. Kolosov (ed.), *Mir glazami rossiyan: mify i vneshnyaya politika* (Moscow, Institut fonda 'Obshchestvennoe mnenie', 2003), p. 10.
3 See Stephen White, Richard Rose and Ian McAllister, *How Russia Votes* (Chatham, NJ, Chatham House Publishers, 1997).
4 Richard Rose, Neil Munro and Stephen White, 'Voting in a Floating Party System: the 1999 Duma Election', *Europe-Asia Studies*, Vol. 53, No. 3, May 2001, pp. 419–43.
5 Scott P. Mainwaring, *Rethinking Party Systems in the Third Wave of Transition: The Case of Brazil* (Stanford, Stanford University Press, 1999), p. 11.
6 Indem study cited by Alexander Domrin, 'The Sin of Party-Building in Russia', *Russia Watch*, No. 9, January 2003, p. 15.
7 *Value Change and the Survival of Democracy in Russia, 1995–2000* (Moscow, ROMIR, 2001).
8 Mukhin, *Kto est' mister Putin i kto s nim prishel?*, p. 4.
9 *Newsline*, 10 July 2000.
10 Federal'nyi zakon 'O politicheskikh partiyakh', proekt No. 43556–3 v tret'em chtenii.
11 Andrei Riskin, *Nezavisimaya gazeta*, 9 June 2006.
12 Vladislav Surkov, 'Suverenitet – eto politicheskii sinonim konkurentosposobnosti', *Moskovskie novosti*, No. 7, 3 March 2006.
13 Alexandra Samarina, *Nezavisimaya gazeta*, 27–28 October 2006. Amendments in 2005 to the 1999 Law on the Regions gave the party that won the most seats in regional PR elections the right to propose a candidate as governor.
14 Richard Rose, Neil Munro and Stephen White, 'Voting in a Floating Party System: the 1999 Duma Election', *Europe-Asia Studies*, Vol. 53, No. 3, May 2001, pp. 419–43.
15 For a full analysis, see Richard Sakwa, 'The 2003–2004 Russian Elections and Prospects for Democracy', *Europe-Asia Studies*, Vol. 57, No. 3, May 2005, pp. 369–98, from which this and the subsequent section draws.
16 *Vybory deputatov gosudarstvennoi dumy federal'nogo sobraniya Rossiiskoi Federatsii 2003: elektoral'naya statistika*, Central Electoral Commission (Moscow, Ves' Mir, 2004), p. 194.
17 Julie Corwin, RFE/RL *Russian Political Weekly*, Vol. 4, No. 1, 8 January 2004.
18 Kremlin.ru, 27 November 2003.
19 In his speech on 20 September Putin noted: 'I'd like to say that I don't get involved in party politics. For precisely that reason I try not to attend events like this one today. My presence here at your congress is an exception. I have done this deliberately, in gratitude to your members in the Duma for our work together over the past four years', BBC Monitoring, RTR Russia TV, Moscow, 1600 gmt, 20 September 2003, in *JRL*, 7331/18.

20 *Nezavisimaya gazeta*, 29 September 2003.
21 *Manifest vserossiikoi politicheskoi partii "Edinstvo i Otechestvo" – Edinaya Rossiya: Put' natsional'nogo uspekha* (Moscow, 2003).
22 *Vedemosti*, 8 December 2003.
23 Anatolii Chubais, 'Missiya Rossii v XXI veke', *Nezavisimaya gazeta*, 1 October 2003.
24 Itar-Tass, 20 September 2003.
25 For example, 'Russia: Before and after the Elections', 26 February 2004 at the Carnegie Endowment for International Peace, www.ceip.org/files/events.
26 Mikhail Khodorkovsky, 'Krizis liberalizma v Rossii', *Vedemosti*, 29 March 2004.
27 *Izbiratel'nyi blok 'Rodina' (Narodno-patrioticheskii Soyuz): Programmnye dokumenty*, mimeo (on CEC website).
28 *Russian Federation State Duma Elections 7 December 2003: Statement of Preliminary Findings and Conclusions*, www.osce.org. The Final Report was issued on 27 January 2004, www.osce.org/documents/odihr/2004/01/1947_en.pdf.
29 www.osce.org/news/show_news.php?id=3757.
30 *Nezavisimaya gazeta*, reproduced in WPS Monitoring Agency, www.wps.ru/e_index.htm, 3 December 2003; *JRL*, 7450/9.
31 Mikail Myagkov, Peter C. Ordeshook and Dimitry Shakin, 'Fraud or Fairytales: Russia and Ukraine's Electoral Experience', *Post-Soviet Affairs*, Vol. 21, No. 2, 2005, pp. 91–131.
32 *Kommersant-Vlast*, 15–21 December 2003, p. 34.
33 *Kommersant-Vlast*, 26 January–1 February 2004, p. 17.
34 *Nezavisimaya gazeta*, reproduced in WPS Monitoring Agency, www.wps.ru/e_index.htm, 28 January 2004; in *JRL*, 8037/23.
35 *Vedemosti*, 26 January 2004.
36 Full text at www.komitet2008.ru.
37 Yavlinsky pointed to the events in Sverdlovsk *oblast*, where Yabloko and other independent candidates were refused registration for the *oblast* Duma elections on 14 March 2004 because United Russia (and the governor, Eduard Rossel) feared competition. *Novaya gazeta*, No. 9, 9–11 February 2004, p. 6.
38 RFE/RL *(Un)Civil Societies*, Vol. 5, No. 1, 8 January 2004.
39 Alexei Titkov, *'Party Number Four' – Rodina: Whence and Why?* (Moscow, Panorama Centre, 2006), p. 18.
40 See Laura Belin, 'Glaz'ev Gambles and Loses', RFE/RL *Russian Political Weekly*, Vol. 4, No. 10, 17 March 2004.
41 Putin provided a broad analysis of the state of Russia when he came to power four years earlier, his achievements as president and his plans for the future, in a speech at Moscow State University on 12 February 2004, www.president.kremlin.ru/text/appears/2004/02/62215.shtml.
42 Lilia Shevtsova, 'Russia's Electoral Time Bomb', *Moscow Times*, 1 March 2004.
43 Turnout in Kabardino-Balkaria of 97.7% led the field, followed by Ingushetia at 96.2% and Mordovia with 94.5%, followed by Dagestan at 94.09% and Chechnya at 94%. At the other end of the spectrum Krasnoyarsk came bottom with only 51.09%, Irkutsk 52.4%, Ivanovo 53.34%, Novgorod 54.5% and Sakhalin 54.8%. Nowhere was turnout below 50%. *Vybory prezidenta Rossiiskoi Federatsii 2004:elektoral'naya statistika*, Central Electoral Commission (Moscow, Ves' Mir, 2004), pp. 104–5.
44 Putin won 98.18% per cent of the vote in Ingushetiya, 96.49% in Kabardino-Balkaria, while the lowest regions were Primorsk (59.37%), Orenburg (58.79%) and Belgorod at the bottom (54.82%), *Vybory prezidenta Rossiiskoi Federatsii 2004*, p. 116.
45 *Vremya novostei*, 15 March 2004, in *JRL*, 8118/3.
46 RIA Novosti 16 March 2004, in *JRL* 8121/1.
47 Anastasiya Kornya, 'Partiinyi feminizm Aleksandr Veshnyakova', *Nezavisimaya gazeta*, 1 September 2004, pp. 1, 2.

48 *Rossiiskaya gazeta*, 15 September 2004.
49 Kornya, 'Partiinyi feminizm Aleksandr Veshnyakova'.
50 *Itogi*, No. 12, March 2006.
51 Kornya, 'Partiinyi feminizm Aleksandr Veshnyakova'.
52 This was Alexander Veshnayakov's view, interviewed on Radio Mayak, 27 April 2005, in *JRL*, 9137/17.
53 Once again, Putin moved to deal with a problem that had long been tolerated elsewhere, notably in Italy. In that country's thirteenth parliament (1996–2001) 158 deputies had changed political allegiance, Tobias Jones, *The Dark Heart of Italy* (London, Faber and Faber, 2003), p. 188.
54 *Novaya gazeta*, No. 65, 6–9 September 2004.
55 *Rossiiskaya gazeta*, 23 November 2006; also 5 December 2006.
56 Gel'man, Vladimir, 'From "Feckless Pluralism" to "Dominant Power Politics"? The Transformation of Russia's Party System', *Democratization*, Vol. 13, No. 4, August 2006, p. 546.
57 *Nezavisimaya gazeta*, 27 October 2006.
58 Joel M. Ostrow, *Comparing Post-Soviet Legislatures: A Theory of Institutional Design and Political Conflict* (Columbus, Ohio State University Press, 2000). See also Joel M. Ostrow, 'Procedural Breakdown and Deadlock in the Russian State Duma: The Problems of an Unlinked Dual-Channel Institutional Design', *Europe-Asia Studies*, Vol. 50, No. 5 (1998), pp. 793–816; and Joel M. Ostrow, 'Conflict-Management in Russia's Federal Institutions', *Post-Soviet affairs*, Vol. 18, No. 1, 2002, pp. 49–70.
59 Thomas F. Remington, *The Russian Parliament: Institutional Evolution in a Transitional Regime* (New Haven, CT, Yale University Press, 2001). See also Thomas F. Remington, Steven S. Smith and Moshe Haspel, 'Decrees, Laws and Inter-Branch Relations in the Russian Federation', *Post-Soviet Affairs*, Vol. 14, No. 4, 1998, pp. 287–322.
60 Thomas F. Remington, 'Putin and the Duma', *Post-Soviet Affairs*, Vol. 17, No. 4, 2001, p. 288.
61 Federico Varese, *The Russian Mafia: Private Protection in a New Market Economy* (Oxford, Oxford University Press, 2001), p. 184.
62 For an examination of the question of measuring significance, and a discussion of the contradiction between the actual productivity of the Duma and its poor image, see Paul Chaisty and Petra Schleiter, 'Productive but Not Valued: The Russia State Duma, 1994–2001', *Europe-Asia Studies*, Vol. 54, No. 5, 2002, pp. 701–24.
63 Sergei Reshul'skii, 'Nizhnyaya palata prevratilas' v filial pravitel'stva', *Nezavisimaya gazeta*, 27 December 2001, p. 2.
64 *Novye izvestiya*, 27 January 2004.
65 Alexei Titkov, *'Party Number Four' – Rodina: Whence and Why?* (Moscow, Panorama Centre, 2006), p. 7.
66 Titkov, *'Party Number Four' – Rodina*, p. 64.
67 Chaisty and Schleiter, 'Productive but Not Valued', p. 715.
68 The Jamestown Foundation, *Monitor*, 19 July 2001.
69 Thomas Remington, 'Federal'noe Sobranie Rossiiskoi Federatsii (1994–2004)', *Sravnitel'noe konstitutsionnoe obozrenie*, No. 4 (53), 2005, pp. 40–52, at p. 45.
70 Henry E. Hale and Robert Orrtung, 'The Duma Districts: Key to Putin's Power', PONARS Policy Memo 290, September 2003.
71 Constitutional changes require not only a two-thirds majority in the Duma but also approval by three-quarters of the Federation Council and the endorsement of two-thirds of Russia's regional legislatures – as well as the signature of the president.
72 www.president.kremlin.ru/text/appears/2006/02/101129.shtml
73 www.president.kremlin.ru/text/appears/2003/05/44623.shtml

74 Andrei Kolesnikov, 'Vladimir Putin pozvolil sebe svobodu slov', *Kommersant*, 1 February 2006, p. 2.
75 Those in favour of the so-called 'project of the parliamentary majority' were allegedly the representatives of the 'family': Voloshin and his deputy Surkov, backed by the oligarch Khodorkovsky, who may well have had ambitions to take on the premiership himself. Pavel Ivanov, 'Putin's Sad Anniversary', *Asia Times*, 16 May 2003; *JRL*, 7184/7. At that time there was much speculation that after the end of his two terms as president allowed by the constitution, Putin would himself use the enhanced powers of the premiership to continue his leadership.
76 'Stenogramma press-konferentsii dlya rossiiskikh i inostrannykh zhurnalistov', 31 January 2006, www.president.kremlin.ru/text/appears/2006/01/100848.shtml.
77 www.president.kremlin.ru/text/appears/2006/02/101129.shtml.
78 A Levada Centre poll in May 2006 reported that 59% of respondents said that the constitution should be changed to allow Putin a third time, while 29% said no. The number supporting constitutional change to allow a third term had gone up since an equivalent poll in August 2005 found 41% approved, while 42% disapproved. The same poll in May 2006 found that 43% would be prepared to vote for any candidate nominated by Putin. Of all possible successors, Dmitry Medvedev led the field with 10.3% support, followed closely by Vladimir Zhirinovsky (7.3%), Sergei Ivanov (7.2%) and Gennady Zyuganov (6.8%). Dmitri Kamyshev and Viktor Khamraev, 'Nekonstitutsionnoe bol'shinstvo', *Kommersant*, 8 June 2006.
79 Vitalii Tret'yakov, *Nuzhen li nam Putin posle 2008 goda?* (Moscow, Rossiiskaya gazeta, 2005), pp. 146, 157.
80 For a full discussion of possible scenarios, see Boris Mazo, *Preemnik Putina, ili Kogo my budem vybirat' v 2008 godu* ((Moscow, Algoritm, 2005).
81 Press conference with Sergei Markov at *Argumenty i fakty* press centre, 16 November 2005, in *JRL* 9299/15.
82 *Kommersant*, 19 November 2005; quoted by Pavel Baev, 'Putin's Bureaucratic Response to Russia's Economic Misbalance', *Eurasia Daily Monitor*, Vol. 2, No. 217, 21 November 2005.
83 *Rossiiskie vesti*, No. 14, 13 April 2006.
84 Nick Paton Walsh, 'Putin Reshuffle Gives Clues to Choice of Heir', *The Guardian*, 15 November 2005, p. 23.
85 Nabi Abdullaev, 'Defense Minister Gets Boost in Kremlin Race', *Moscow Times*, 22 March 2006.
86 Yulia Latynina, 'What Really Happened to Medvedev', *Moscow Times*, 23 November 2005.
87 Dmitry Orlov, *Izvestiya*, 17 November 2005.
88 Anatoly Medetsky, 'Putin Reiterates He'll Pick Successor', *The Moscow Times*, 15 May 2006, p. 3. The comments were made on 13 May.
89 www.president.kremlin.ru/text/appears/2006/10/112959.shtml.

5 Regime, state and society

1 In Russian: 'V Rossii, kogda gosudarstvo krepnet, narod chakhnet'.
2 'Stenograficheskii otchet o vstreche s uchastnikami tret'ego zasedaniya Mezhdunarodnogo diskussionnogo kluba "Valdai"', 9 September 2006, www.president. kremlin.ru./text/appears/2006/09/111114.shtml.
3 François Mitterand, *Un coup d'état permanent* (Paris, Plon, 1964).
4 Thomas M. Nichols, *The Russian Presidency: Society and Politics in the Second Russian Republic* (Basingstoke, Macmillan, 2000), p. 2.
5 For the development of the Russian presidency, see Eugene Huskey, *Presidential Power in Russia* (Armonk, NY, M. E. Sharpe, 1999).

6 Igor Klyamkin and Liliya Shevtsova, *This Omnipotent and Impotent Government: The Evolution of the Political System in Post-Communist Russia* (Washington, DC, Carnegie Endowment for International Peace, 1999).

7 S. Holmes, 'Cultural Legacies or State Collapse? Probing the Post-Communist Dilemma', in M. Mandelbaum (ed.), *Post-Communism: Four Views* (New York, Council for Foreign Relations, 1996), p. 50.

8 Sakwa, *Russian Politics and Society*, 3rd edn, pp. 454–8; see also 'The Regime System in Russia', *Contemporary Politics*, Vol. 3, No. 1, 1997, pp. 7–25.

9 Speaking to a meeting of workers of the Soviet procuracy Gorbachev warned that there could be no return to the past, but equally ultra-radical positions were inadmissible, especially those that could lead to the disintegration of the country or the creation of parallel centres of power: 'there should be only one dictatorship for all – the dictatorship of law'. Mikhail Gorbachev, *Zhizn' i reformy*, Book 2 (Moscow, Novosti, 1995), p. 516.

10 Interfax, 31 January 2000.

11 *Izvestiya*, 14 July 2000.

12 Robert Dahl, *Polyarchy: Participation and Opposition* (New Haven, Yale University Press, 1971).

13 Together with the cabinet of ministers were security officials (the head of the FSB Nikolai Patrushev and the director of the SVR Sergei Lebedev), the director of the Central Bank Sergei Ignat'ev, the presidential envoys, the leaders of the presidential administration, the prosecutor-general Ustinov, the heads of various federal agencies in the regions, and all the regional governors were invited for the first time ever. Chechnya was represented by the newly elected president Alu Alkhanov and his predecessor, the acting president Sergei Abramov.

14 www.president.kremlin.ru/appears/2004/09/13/1514_type63374-type63378_76651.shtml.

15 'Obrashchenie Prezidenta Rossii Vladimira Putina', Kremlin, 4 September 2004; *Nezavisimaya gazeta*, 6 September 2004, p. 2.

16 Vladislav Surkov, 'Putin ukreplyaet gosudarstvo, a ne sebya', *Komsomol'skaya pravda*, 29 September 2004.

17 Thomas Graham, 'Tackling Tycoons: Revenge, or Rule of Law?', *Wall Street Journal*, 20 July 2000.

18 18 March 2000 interview on Radio Mayak, reported by Peter Reddaway, 'Will Putin be Able to Consolidate Power?', *Post-Soviet Affairs*, Vol. 17, No. 1, 2001, pp. 23–44, at p. 27, fn. 5.

19 See Andrei Kolesnikov, *Vladimir Putin: Ravnoudalenie oligarkhov* (Moscow, Eksmo, 2005).

20 7 February 2006, www.president.kremlin.ru/text/appears/2006/02/101129.shtml.

21 See Paul Klebnikov, *Godfather of the Kremlin: Boris Berezovsky and the Looting of Russia* (New York, Harcourt, 2000).

22 Cited in Dale R. Herspring and Jacob Kipp, 'Understanding the Elusive Mr. Putin', *Problems of Post-Communism*, Vol. 48, No. 5, September/October 2001, p. 9.

23 For his analysis of the anti-oligarch investigations and his dismissal, see Yurii Skuratov, *Variant drakona* (Moscow, Detektiv Press, 2000).

24 *The Guardian*, 18 July 2000, p. 12.

25 *Financial Times*, 18 July 2000.

26 *Segodnya*, 18 July 2000.

27 *The Guardian*, 18 July 2000, p. 12.

28 *Moscow Times*, 18 July 2000.

29 'Russia's President Bares his Teeth', *The Economist*, 15–21 July 2000.

30 *Kommersant*, 8 July 2000; *Newsline*, 10 July 2000.

31 *Business Week*, 24 July 2000; in *JRL*, 4402/7.

32 *Business Week*, 24 July 2000; in *JRL*, 4402/7.
33 *Izvestiya*, 18 July 2000.
34 The new media concern included ORT, TV6, *Kommersant, Nezavisimaya gazeta, Novye izvestiya, Ogonëk* and Nashe Radio, *Nezavisimaya gazeta*, 18 July 2000.
35 *Newsline*, 3 August 2000.
36 AFP, 24 January 2006, in *JRL*, 2006/22/30.
37 Amelia Gentleman, 'Putin Picks off Opponents who Matter Most', *The Guardian*, 14 July 2000, p. 20.
38 *Izvestiya*, 14 July 2000.
39 For an analysis of this, see A. A. Mukhin, *Novye pravila igry dlya bol'shogo biznesa, prodiktovannye logikoi pravleniya V. V. Putina* (Moscow, Tsentr politicheskoi informatsii, 2002).
40 Lilia Shevtsova, 'Whither Putin after the Yukos Affair?', *The Moscow Times*, 27 August 2003, p. 7.
41 Among those attending were Vagit Alekperov, head of Lukoil, at the time being investigated for alleged large-scale tax evasion; Vladimir Potanin, head of the Interros financial-industrial group, whom prosecutors accused of conspiring to defraud the state of $140 million in connection with the 1995 privatisation of Norilsk Nickel; Rem Vyakhirev, head of Gazprom, Russia's natural gas monopoly, whose offices were raided in connection with the criminal case against Media-Most chief Vladimir Gusinsky; Alfa Group co-founder Mikhail Fridman; Russian Aluminium co-founder Oleg Deripaska; Yevgeny Shvidler, the president of the Sibneft oil company; and United Energy Systems (UES) chief Anatoly Chubais, whose company, state auditors charged, may have been partially sold to foreigners in violation of Russian law. Leading absentees were Media-Most's Gusinsky; Berezovsky, the archetypal insider who at this time declared himself in 'constructive opposition' before later that year moving into 'unconstructive' opposition; Roman Abramovich, formally a State Duma deputy but the brains behind Sibneft and Oleg Deripaska's partner in Russian Aluminium; and Moscow banker Alexander Mamut, who was close to Abramovich and who remains a key Kremlin insider, *Monitor*, 27 July 2000. Although Berezovsky was not physically present, his interests were considered to be represented by Sibneft chief Yevgeny Shvidler and Deripaska, the head of Russian Aluminium, two companies partially owned by Berezovsky, Gregory Feifer, 'Oligarchs Hope for Agreement with Putin', *The St Petersburg Times*, 28 July 2000, p. 3.
42 Arkady Ostrovsky, 'Oligarchs to Seek Peace Deal with Putin', *Financial Times*, 24 July 2000.
43 The points were outlined by Nemtsov, in Arkady Ostrovsky, 'Oligarchs to Seek Peace Deal with Putin', *Financial Times*, 24 July 2000.
44 Reported in *El Mundo* and Russian agencies, in Jamestown Foundation, *Monitor*, 14 July 2000.
45 Vitaly Tretyakov, Editorial, *Nezavisimaya gazeta*, 22 June 2000.
46 Tretyakov, *Nezavisimaya gazeta*, 22 June 2000.
47 'Stenograficheskii otchet o press-konferentsii dlya rossiiskikh i inostranikh zhurnalistov' 20 June 2003, www.president.kremlin.ru/text/appears/2003/06/47449.shtml.
48 www.president.kremlin.ru/text/appears/2006/05/105546.shtml.
49 See Andrei Yakovlev, 'The Evolution of Business-State Interaction in Russia: From State Capture to Business Capture?', *Europe-Asia Studies*, Vol. 58, No. 7, November 2006, pp. 1033–56.
50 Putin, *First Person*, p. 197.
51 'Diktatura razrushit stranu', *Obshchaya gaezeta*, 13–20 May 2000.
52 'Vystuplenie', www.president.kremlin.ru/events/42.html.
53 *Izvestiya*, 14 July 2000.

54 Kiselev in the *Itogi* programme on NTV on 9 July 2000, who also asserted that when Putin referred to some of the media that 'carry out anti-state activity', he had above all NTV in mind.

55 Oksana Yablokovo, 'Newspapers Passing into Hands of Kremlin Allies', *Moscow Times*, 7 June 2006. Berezovsky sold his share to Badri Patarkatsishvili, his Georgian business partner, in February 2006 to try to insulate the paper from Kremlin pressure. It was rumoured later that year that Patarkatsishvili sold it on to Roman Abramovich's investment company Millhouse for $120 million (£65 million).

56 Dmitry Vinogradov, 'Russian Internet Remains an Island of Free Speech and Civil Society', *Russian Analytical Digest*, No. 9, 2006, pp. 12–16, at p. 12.

57 Robert Orttung, 'Kremlin Systematically Shrinks Scope of Russian Media', *Russian Analytical Digest*, No. 9, 2006, pp. 2–5, at p. 2.

58 www.rsf.org/article.php3?id_article=19388.

59 Wilson, *Virtual Politics*, has taken this demented view of politics in Russia at face value, and gives the various tropes and fantasies of the spin doctors' world a scholarly substantiation that provides an alarmingly perfect case of Western (and Ukrainian) 'orientalist' interpretation of Russian development.

60 Robert Sharlet, 'Putin and the Politics of Law in Russia', *Post-Soviet Affairs*, Vol. 17, No. 3, 2001, p. 196.

61 *Vedemosti*, 13 December 2006.

62 *Nezavisimaya gazeta*, 15 October 2006.

63 In Harry G. Broadman (ed.), *Unleashing Russia's Business Potential: Lessons from the Regions for Building Market Institutions* (Washington, DC, World Bank Discussion Paper No. 434, 2002).

64 Cf. Vadim Volkov, *Violent Entrepreneurs: The Use of Force in the Making of Russian Capitalism* (Ithaca, NY, Cornell University Press, 2002).

65 Maria Popova, 'Watchdogs or Attack Dogs? The Role of the Russian Courts and the Central Election Commission in the Resolution of Electoral Disputes', *Europe-Asia Studies*, Vol. 58, No. 3, May 2006, pp. 391–414, at p. 412.

66 Vladimir Pastukhov, 'Pravo pod administrativnym pressom v postsovetskoi Rossii', *Konstitutsionnnoe pravo: vostochnoevropeiskoe obozrenie*, No. 2 (39), pp. 105–12.

67 www.president.kremlin.ru/text/appears/2006/01/100848.shtml.

68 Pavel K. Baev, 'Ustinov's Firing Reveals Clan Maneuvering Inside Kremlin', *Eurasia Daily Monitoring*, Vol. 3, No. 108, 5 June 2006.

69 *Rossiiskaya gazeta*, 30 July 2006.

70 Comments on RTR Rossiya Television, Associated Press, 29 November 2006, reported by Charles Gurin, 'Gaidar's Apparent Poisoning Fuels Conspiracy Theories', *Eurasia Daily Monitor*, Vol. 3, Issue 222, 1 December 2006.

71 *Guardian*, 5 December 2005, p. 4.

72 *Newsline*, 12 July 2002.

73 *Moskovskie novosti*, 5 September 2002.

6 Bureaucracy, incorporation and opposition

1 Putin, *First Person*, p. 179.

2 Bortsov, *Vladimir Putin*, p. 236.

3 Robert J. Brym and V. Gimpelson, 'The Size, Composition and Dynamics of the Russian State Bureaucracy in the 1990s', *Slavic Review*, Vol. 63, No. 1, Spring 2004, pp. 90–113.

4 *Russia in Figures 2005* (Moscow, Rosstat, 2005), p. 46.

5 *Novaya gazeta*, No. 1, 12 January 2006.

6 A. E. Chirikova, 'Ispolnitel'naya vlast' v regionakh: pravila igry formal'nye in neformal'nye', *Obshchestvennye nauki i sovremennost'*, No. 3, 2004, pp. 71–80, at p. 73.

7 Karl W. Ryavec, *Russian Bureaucracy: Power and Pathology* (Lanham, MD, Rowman & Littlefield, 2003).

8 'Razgovor Goliafa s Leviafanom', *Nezavisimaya gazeta*, 11 July 2000.

9 www.president.kremlin.ru/text/appears/2006/05/105546.shtmlpresident.kremlin.ru/text/appears/2003/05/44623.shtml.

10 *Rossiiskaya gazeta*, 25 April 2005.

11 www.president.kremlin.ru/text/appears/2006/02/101129.shtml.

12 www.president.kremlin.ru/text/appears/2006/05/105546.shtml.

13 Eugene Huskey and Alexander Obolonsky, 'The Struggle to Reform Russia's Bureaucracy', *Problems of Post-Communism*, Vol. 50, No. 4, July/August 2003, pp. 22–33.

14 *Kommersant*, 14 April 2003.

15 *Novaya gazeta*, No. 1, 12 January 2006.

16 For a broader discussion, see Richard Sakwa, 'Russia: From a Corrupt System to a System with Corruption', in Robert Williams (ed.), *Party Finance and Political Corruption* (Basingstoke, Macmillan; New York, St Martin's Press, 2000), pp. 123–161.

17 Steven L. Solnick, *Stealing the Soviet State: Control and Collapse in Soviet Institutions* (Cambridge, MA, Harvard University Press, 1998).

18 www.transparency.org/policy_and_research/surveys_indices/cpi/2005. The 2006 Index placed Russia in 121st place, a slight improvement.

19 *Diagnostika rossiiskoi korruptsii: Sotsiologicheskii analiz*, www.indem.ru.

20 Natalya Alyakrinskaya, 'Inefficient Government Breeds Corruption', *Moscow News*, 11–17 January 2006.

21 Owen Matthews and Anna Nemsova, 'The New Feudalism', *Newsweek International*, 23 October 2006.

22 'Vo skol'ko raz uvelichilas' korruptsiya za 4 goda: rezul'taty novogo issledovaniya Fonda INDEM', www.indem.ru/russian.asp.

23 *Kommersant*, 31 October 2006.

24 Diana Schmidt, 'Fighting against Corruption, and Struggling for Status', *Russian Analytical Digest*, No. 11, 5 December 2006, pp. 2–5.

25 Nabi Abdullaev, 'Putin Scores Points in Anti-Graft Drive', *Moscow Times*, 23 June 2006.

26 *Rossiiskaya gazeta*, 7 November 2006.

27 Viktor Ivanov is chairman of the board at Aeroflot and heads the board of Almaz-Antei; Dmitry Medvedev is chair of the board of Gazprom; Vladislav Surkov is chair of the board at Transnefteprodukt; Igor Shuvalov is board member of Russian Railroads; Sergei Prikhodko is chairman of the board at TVEL (nuclear fuel producer); and the minister of finance Aleksei Kudrin is on the board of the Alrosa diamond monopoly and the country's second largest bank, Vneshtorgbank. There are numerous other instances.

28 Putin's meeting with Western academics and journalists, the Kremlin, 5 September 2005, personal notes.

29 These issues are explored in Sudipta Kaviraj and Sunil Khilnani (eds), *Civil Society: History and Possibilities* (Cambridge, Cambridge University Press, 2001).

30 See Alfred B. Evans Jr., Laura A. Henry and Lisa McIntosh Sundstrom (eds), *Russian Civil Society: A Critical Assessment* (Armonk, NY, M. E. Sharpe, 2005).

31 Lilia Shevtsova, *Elective Monarchy under Putin: Perspectives on the Evolution of the Political Regime and its Problems* (Moscow, Carnegie Center, 2001); available in Russian at http://pubs.carnegie.ru/briefings/2001/issue01–01.asp.

32 Anders Uhlin, *Post-Soviet Civil Society: Democratization in Russia and the Baltic States* (London, Routledge, 2006), p.26.

33 'O tselyakh i zadachakh Grazhdanskogo foruma', *Prezident*, No. 17 (226), 28 November–12 December 2001, p. 1.

34 Vladimir Putin, 'Grazhdanskoe obshchestvo nel'zya sozdat' po ukaske', *Prezident*, No. 17 (226), 28 November–12 December 2001, p. 1; *Grazhdanskii forum*, 22 November 2001, p. 2; www.civilforum.ru.
35 BBC Monitoring, 16 May 2003; *JRL*, 7186/1.
36 Dmitrii Polikanov, 'Konets demokratii?', *Vremya novostei*, 29 October 2004.
37 'Ob Obshchestvennoi Palate Rossiiskoi Federatii', http://document.kremlin.ru/index.asp.
38 The term is from Jeremy Bransten, 'Public Chamber Criticized as "Smokescreen"', RFE/RL *Russian Political Weekly*, Vol. 5, No. 13, 1 April 2005.
39 *Izvestiya*, 18 November 2005.
40 Nikolai Petrov, 'Where the State and Society Meet', *Moscow Times*, 18 January 2006.
41 The Russian Orthodox Church delegated Kliment, Metropolitan of Kaluga and Borovki, and Vladimir Korchagin, Bishop of Saratov. Russian Muslims were represented by the head of Russian muftis, Ravil Gainutdin, Jews by the chief rabbi Berl Lazar and Buddhists by their leader in Russia, Damba Ayusheev.
42 Anatoly Medetsky, 'Putin Gives Public Chamber a Warning', *Moscow Times*, 23 January 2006.
43 They included a charity commission, headed by billionaire Vladimir Potanin, a commission for supervision of law enforcement agencies, headed by lawyer Anatoly Kucherena. Roshal was made head of the health care commission, and the editor of *Moskovskii komsomolets*, Paevl Gusev (not the Kremlin's nominee for the post), was elected to head the commission for freedom of speech. Alexander Shokhin, president of the Russian Union of Industrialists and Entrepreneurs, was elected chair of the competitiveness, economic development and enterprise commission, Valery Tishkov, director of the Institute of Ethnology and Anthropology, headed the tolerance and freedom of religion commission, political scientist Vyacheslav Nikonov headed the international cooperation and diplomacy commission, and yet another political scientist, Andranik Migranyan, headed the globalism and national development strategy commission: Dmitrii Kamyshev, 'Kommissionnaya sbornaya', *Kommersant vlast'*, 30 January 2006, pp. 24–5.
44 'Obshchestvennaya palata reshila vnedrit'sya v Gosdumu', *Kommersant*, 2 February 2006, p. 2.
45 Medetsky, 'Putin Gives Public Chamber a Warning'.
46 Lawyer Genri Reznik, paediatrician Leonid Roshal, *Moskva* magazine editor Leonid Borodin and the head of the World Wildlife Fund's Moscow office Igor Chestin: Anatoly Medetsky, 'Four Seen as Critical Voices in Chamber', *Moscow Times*, 20 January 2006.
47 Voiced, for example, by Yury Dzhibladze, head of the Centre for the Development of Democracy and Human Rights, *Kommersant*, 23 January 2006.
48 Vitalii Naishul', Pochemu narod i vlast' govoryat na raznykh yazykakh', *argumenty i fakty*, No. 5, 2006, p. 7.
49 Nicolai Petro, *Crafting Democracy: How Novgorod has Coped with Rapid Social Change* (Ithaca, NY, Cornell University Press, 2004), pp. 46, 53.
50 www.oprf.ru, accessed 7 February 2006.
51 *Rossiiskaya gazeta*, 17 January 2006.
52 *Russian Regional Report*, Vol. 11, No. 9, 3 April 2006.
53 Bransten, 'Public Chamber Criticized as "Smokescreen"'.
54 Sarah L. Henderson, *Building Democracy in Contemporary Russia: Western Support for Grassroots Organizations* (Ithaca and London, Cornell University Press, 2003); and for a critical view, Janine R. Wedel, *Collision and Collusion: The Strange Case of Western Aid to Eastern Europe 1989–1998* (Basingstoke and London, Macmillan, 1998). For a general discussion, see Marina Ottaway and

Thomas Carothers (eds), *Funding Virtue: Civil Society Aid and Democracy Promotion* (Washington, DC, Carnegie Endowment for International Peace, 2000).

55 The strategy has also been reported to apply to Venezuela against Hugo Chávez. As Richard Gott puts it, 'The US-backed strategy is to use apparently neutral non-governmental organisations to tell the world that the elections are not free and fair, that press freedom is under threat, and that human rights are not respected. These allegations are then exaggerated and amplified in Washington': 'Democracy Under Threat', *The Guardian*, 6 December 2005, p. 20.

56 *Moscow Times*, 21 December 2005.

57 'O vnesenii izmenenii v nekotorye zakonodatel'nye akty Rossiiskoi Federatsii', *Rossiiskaya gazeta*, 17 January 2006.

58 Vladimir Gel'man, 'Political Opposition in Russia: A Dying Species?', *Post-Soviet Affairs*, Vol. 23, No. 3, 2005, pp. 226–46.

59 Roderic Lyne, Strobe Talbott and Koji Watanabe, *Engaging with Russia: The Next Phase*, a Report to The Trilateral Commission (Washington, Paris and Tokyo, The Trilateral Commission, 2006), p. 46.

60 Yelena Yakovleva, 'Gleb Pavlovsky on the Prospects for Civil Society in Russia', *Izvestiya*, 3 July 2002.

61 C. Seton-Watson, *Italy from Liberalism to Fascism* (London, Methuen, 1967), p. 51.

62 *Segodnya*, 29 December 2000.

63 Luke March, 'The Contemporary Russian Left after Communism: Into the Dustbin of History?', *The Journal of Communist Studies and Transition Politics*, Vol. 22, No. 4, December 2006, pp. 431–56.

64 Medvedev, *Vremya Putina?*, p. 89.

65 Grigory Yavlinsky, 'Going Backwards', *Journal of Democracy*, Vol. 12, No. 4, October 2001, pp. 79–86, at pp. 79, 80.

66 *Segodnya*, 6 July 2000.

67 Speech reported at the World Economic Forum Central and Eastern European Economic Summit in Salzburg, Austria: Paul Hofheinz, 'Putin's Critics Fear Russia's Resembles Pinochet's Chile', *Wall Street Journal*, 5 July 2000.

68 Grigory Yavlinsky, 'Un-Managing Democracy', *Russia Watch*, No. 9, January 2003, pp. 12–13.

69 Shevtsova, *Putin's Russia*, p. 51.

70 *Gazeta*, 2 July 2002; in *JRL*, 6325/8.

71 Polit.ru, 30 May 2002, in an interview with Mikhail Fishman; reported in *Monitor*, 31 May 2002.

72 *Nezavisimaya gazeta*, 28 January 2004.

73 'Demokraty posle bankrotstva', *Moskovskie novosti*, No. 47, 16–22 December 2003, p. 6.

74 www.indem.ru/GraKongr/RezoVibo.htm.

75 www.indem.ru/GraKongr/Pozd06GK.htm.

76 Boris Kagarlitsky, presenting his report 'Storm Warning: Corruption in Russia's Political Parties', *Rossiiskie vesti*, No. 13, 6 April 2006; in *JRL*, 2006/83/7.

77 Keston Institute, Oxford, *Keston News Service*, 3 July 2002.

78 Centre for Information and Analysis (SOVA), Annual Report, January 2006, http://xeno.sova-center.ru; reported and updated in Anna Zakatnova, 'Front liberalizma', *Rossiiskaya gazeta*, 15 May 2006, p. 2; AFP, 16 January 2007.

79 For details of the far-right scene, see Stephen Shenfield, *Russian Fascism: Traditions, Tendencies and Movements* (Armonk, NY, M. E. Sharpe, 2001).

80 Shenfield, *Russian Fascism*, p. 118.

81 'Chto budet s "Rodinoi"?', *Argumenty i fakty*, No. 5, February 2006, p. 13.

82 Polls conducted by the Levada Centre, reported in *Christian Science Monitor*, 23 January 2006.

83 *Christian Science Monitor*, 23 January 2006.

84 Speech at the extended collegium of the MVD, 17 February 2006, www.president. kremlin.ru/text/appears/2006/02/101824.shtml.
85 Eduard Limonov, *Takoi president nam ne nuzhen!* (Moscow, [no publisher indicated], 2005).
86 M. A. Fadeicheva, 'Ideologiya i diskursivnye praktiki "Nashizma" v sovremennoi Rossii', *Polis*, No. 4, 2006, pp. 53–60.
87 Vladislav Surkov, addressing students of the United Russia education centre on 7 February 2006, 'Suverenitet – eto politicheskii sinonim nashei konkurentosposobnosti', *Komsomol'skaya pravda*, 7 March 2006.
88 Sergei Markov, 'O prichinakh "oranzhevaya revolyutsiya" v Ukraine', in M. B. Pogrebinskii (ed.), '*Oranzheva revolyutsiya': Ukrainskaya versiya* (Moscow, Evropa, 2005), pp. 65–90.
89 *Vremya novostei*, No. 64, April 2003.

7 Putin's 'new federalism'

1 See Cameron Ross (ed.), *Regional Politics in Russia* (Manchester, Manchester University Press, 2002); and his *Federalism and Democratisation in Russia* (Manchester, Manchester University Press, 2002).
2 Kathryn Stoner-Weiss, 'Central Weakness and Provincial Autonomy: Observations on the Devolution Process in Russia', *Post-Soviet Affairs*, Vol. 15, No. 1, 1999, pp. 87–106.
3 For a useful discussion, see S. D. Valentei, *Federalizm: Rossiiskaya istoriya i Rossiiskaya real'nost'* (Moscow, Institute of the Economy, Centre for the Socio-Economic Problems of Federalism, RAS, 1998).
4 For a development of this argument, see Richard Sakwa, 'Russian Regionalism, Policy-Making and State Development', in Stefanie Harter and Gerald Easter (eds), *Shaping the Economic Space in Russia: Decision Making Processes, Institutions and Adjustment to Change in the El'tsin Era* (Aldershot, Ashgate, 2000), pp. 11–34.
5 Some of the arguments of this section are outlined in Richard Sakwa, 'Putin's New Federalism', *Russian Regional Report*, Vol. 5, No. 21, 31 May 2000, pp. 12–17.
6 Grigory Yavlinsky, 'The Last Phase of Agony', *Obshchaya gazeta*, 10–16 June 1999.
7 See Mikhail A. Alexseev, 'Introduction: Challenges to the Russian Federation', in Mikhail A. Alexseev (ed.), *Center-Periphery Conflict in Post-Soviet Russia: A Federation Imperiled* (Basingstoke, Macmillan, 1999), p. 1.
8 Leonid Smirnyagin, 'The Great Seven', *Russian Regional Report*, Vol. 5, No. 20, 24 May 2000.
9 Sophie Lambroschini, 'KGB Veterans Head Has High Hopes of Putin', *Newsline*, 30 June 2000.
10 Michael Burgess, *Comparative Federalism: Theory and Practice* (London, Routledge, 2006).
11 A theme explored by Kathryn Stoner-Weiss, *Local Heroes: The Political Economy of Russian Regional Governance* (Princeton, NJ, Princeton University Press, 1997).
12 James Hughes, 'Moscow's Bilateral Treaties Add to Confusion', *Transition*, 20 September 1996, p. 43.
13 *Izvestiya*, 4 November 1997; *Russian Regional Report*, Vol. 2, No. 38, 6 November 1997.
14 *Rossiiskaya gazeta*, 30 June 1999.
15 The issue is examined in A. Lavrov (ed.), *Federal'nyi byudzhet i regiony: Opyt analiza finansovykh potokov* (Moscow, Dialog-MGU, 1999). See also S. D. Valentei (ed.), *Ekonomicheskie problemy stanovleniya Rossiiskogo federalizma* (Moscow, Nauka, 1999).
16 *Russian Regional Report*, Vol. 4, No. 20, 27 May 1999.

17 For example, in Pskov, see Darrell Slider, 'Pskov Under the LDPR: Elections and Dysfunctional Federalism in One Region', *Europe-Asia Studies*, Vol. 51, No. 5, 1999, p. 764.

18 Daniel Treisman, 'The Politics of Intergovernmental Transfers in Post-Soviet Russia', *British Journal of Political Science*, Vol. 26, No. 3, July 1996, pp. 299–335. See also his 'Deciphering Russia's Federal Finance: Fiscal Appeasement in 1995 and 1996', *Europe-Asia Studies*, Vol. 50, No. 5, July 1998, pp. 893–906; Daniel Treisman, *After the Deluge: Regional Crises and Political Consolidation in Russia* (Ann Arbor, MI, University of Michigan Press, 1999).

19 Alistair McAuley, 'The Determinants of Russian Federal-Regional Fiscal Relations: Equity or Political Influence', *Europe-Asia Studies*, Vol. 49, No. 3, May 1997, pp. 431–44.

20 See Neil Robinson, 'The Global Economy, Reform and Crisis in Russia', *Review of International Political Economy*, Vol. 6, No. 4, Winter 1999, pp. 531–64.

21 'O koordinatsii mezhdunarodnykh i vnesheekonomicheskikh svyazei sub"ektov Rossiiskoi Federatsii', 4 January 1999, *Rossiiskay gazeta*, 16 January 1999.

22 For example, in the case of Gorno-Altai, discussed below, *Rossiiskaya gazeta*, 21 June 2000, pp. 5–6.

23 Peter Kirkow, *Russia's Provinces: Authoritarian Transformation versus Local Autonomy?* (Basingstoke, Macmillan, 1998), p. 125.

24 This is argued, for example, by Andreas Heinemann-Grüder, 'Asymmetry and Federal Integration in Russia', in Vladimir Tikhomirov (ed.), *Anatomy of the 1998 Russian Crisis* (University of Melbourne, Contemporary Europe Research Centre, 1999), Chapter 4, pp. 79–107.

25 The argument is developed in Richard Sakwa, 'The Republicanisation of Russia: Federalism and Democratization in Transition I', in Chris Pierson and Simon Tormey (eds), *Politics at the Edge*, The PSA Yearbook 1999 (Basingstoke, Macmillan, 1999), Chapter 16, pp. 215–26. See also the chapter by Cameron Ross in the same volume, Chapter 17, pp. 227–40.

26 Pechenev notes that as early as April–May 1994 a report commissioned by the head of the presidential administration, Sergei Filatov, had identified and condemned the divergences in constitutional norms between those expounded in the Russian Federation's constitution and the constitutions in republics such as Tatarstan, Bashkortostan, Tuva and Ingushetiya, *Vladimir Putin*, p. 56.

27 Darrell Slider, Vladimir Gimpel'son and Sergei Chugrov, 'Political Tendencies in Russia's Regions: Evidence from the 1993 Parliamentary Elections', *Slavic Review*, Vol. 53, No. 3, Fall 1994, pp. 711–32, at pp. 726, 730–1.

28 Putin, *First Person*, pp. 182–3.

29 Interview with *Welt am Sonntag*, June 2000, www.president.kremlin.ru/events/38.html.

30 'Vystuplenie na vstreche s liderami delovogo mira Italii', 6 June 2000, www.president.kremlin.ru/events/37.html.

31 For example in Tatarstan, as reported by Robert Orttung and Peter Reddaway, *Russian Regional Report*, Vol. 5, No. 25, 28 June 2000.

32 *Zvezda Povolzhia*, 20–26 January 2000, in Midkhat Faroukshin, 'Tatarstan Opposition Seeks Putin's Help', *Russian Regional Report*, Vol. 5, No. 4, 2 February 2000. A detailed description of how the electoral system was manipulated can be found in *Osobaya zona: Vybory v Tatarstane* (Ul'yanovsk, Kazan Branch of the International Human Rights Assembly, 2000).

33 www.president.kremlin.ru/events/34.html.

34 'Putin predupredil "politicheskikh tenevikov"', *Nezavisimaya gazeta*, 14 December 2000, p. 3.

35 *Rossiiskaya gazeta*, 16 May 2000.

36 *Rossiiskaya gazeta*, 17 July 1997.

37 Petr Akopov and Svetlana Babaeva, *Izvestiya*, 15 May 2000.
38 www.president.kremlin.ru/events/34.html.
39 *Newsline*, 18 May 2000.
40 Federal Law No. 113-F3 of 5 August 2000, 'O poryadke formirovaniya Soveta Federatsiya Federal'nogo Sobraniya Rossiiskoi Federatsii', *Rossiiskaya gazeta*, 5 August 2000.
41 'On Removing from Office the Regional Leaders of Legislative and Executive Bodies', *Izvestiya*, 20 July 2000; *Newsline*, 19 July 2000.
42 'Postanovlenie Konstitutsionnogo Suda Rossiiskoi Federatsii po delu o pro-verke konstitutsionnosti otdel'nykh polozhenii Konstitutsii Respubliki Altai i Federal'nogo zakona "Ob obshchikh printsipakh organizatsii zakonodatel'nykh (predstavitel'nykh) i ispolnitel'nykh organov gosudarstvennoi vlasti sub"ektov Rossiiskoi Federatsii', *Rossiiskaya gazeta*, 21 June 2000, pp. 5–6.
43 The ruling is discussed in *Russian Regional Report*, Vol. 5, No. 25, 28 June 2000.
44 *Rossiiskaya gazeta*, 13 May 2000.
45 *Russian Regional Report*, Vol. 5, No. 19, 17 May 2000.
46 See Robert Sharlet, 'Resistance to Putin's Campaign for Political and Legal Unification', in Robert Sharlet and Ferdinand Feldbrugge (eds), *Public Policy and Law in Russia: In Search of a Unified Legal and Political Space* (Leiden and Boston, Martinus Nijhoff Publishers, 2005), pp. 241–50.
47 www.kremlin.ru/text/appears/2006/03/103175.shtml.
48 The announcement was made after a meeting with Putin on 16 March 2000.
49 www.president.kremlin.ru/events/510/html.
50 The debate was one of the most heated seen in the Duma for years, and even United Russia split over the issue, but in the end the motion was carried by 306 votes for, 110 against and one abstention. Andrei Smirnov, 'Tatar Treaty Sug-gests Dissent inside Kremlin on Regional Policy', *Eurasia Daily Monitor*, Vol. 4, Issue 33, 15 February 2007.
51 Nikolai Petrov, 'The Budget Nomenklatura', *Moscow Times*, 31 October 2006.
52 *Izvestiya*, 20 July 2005.
53 'Ob obshchikh printsipakh organizatsii zokonodatel'nykh (predstavitel'nykh) i ispolnitel'nykh organov gosudarstvennoi vlasti sub'ektov Rossiiskoi Federatsii', *Rossiiskaya gazeta*, 19 October 1999, pp. 4–5.
54 *Russian Regional Report*, Vol. 8, No. 2, 3 February 2003. Julia Corwin reckons the Kremlin's success rate in gubernatorial elections as follows: 7 out of 44 in 2000, 7 out of 14 in 2001 and 10 out of 14 in 2002, *Russian Political Weekly*, Vol. 3, No. 1, January 2003.
55 Valery Kokov in Kabardino-Balkaria, Sherig-ool Oorzhak in Tyva, Magome-dali Magomedov in Dagestan and Kirsan Ilyumzhinov in Kalmykia.
56 The case was brought by an aggrieved citizen of Tyumen, Vladimir Grishke-vich, who argued that the appointment of the regional governor (Sergei Sobyanin) violated his constitutional right to participate in elections at all levels. His complaint was supported by SPS. The Court refused to consider two other provisions of the law: the president's right to dismiss a governor and the president's right to dissolve a regional legislature if it twice refused to support the proposed candidate. *Kommersant*, 22 December 2005.
57 Cf. Marie-Elisabeth Baudoin, 'Is the Constitutional Court the Last Bastion in Russia Against the Threat of Authoritarianism?', *Europe-Asia Studies*, Vol. 58, No. 5, July 2006, pp. 679–99.
58 In data published in December 2005, 66% were for the election of governors, 26% supported the new system, although 52% agreed that even an elected governor should take a vow of loyalty to the president; www.levada.ru/press/2005122901.html.
59 www.president.kremlin.ru/text/appears/2006/01/100848.shtml.

60 Nikolai Petrov, 'Undercutting the Senators', *Moscow Times*, 30 May 2006.
61 A. S. Avtonomov, A. A. Zakharov and Ye. M. Orlova, *Regional'nye parlamenty v sovremennoi Rossii*, Nauchnye doklady No. 118 (Moscow, MONF, 2000).
62 See Alexander Kynev, 'The Role of Political Parties in Russia's 2002 Regional Elections', *Russia and Eurasia Review*, Vol. 2, Issue 8, 15 April 2003.
63 For example, in Rostov, *Russian Regional Report*, 23 April 2003; Primorsk *krai*, *Russian Regional Report*, 7 May 2003.
64 See Derek S. Hutcheson, *Political Parties in the Russian Regions* (London, RoutledgeCurzon, 2003).
65 Ross, *Federalism and Democratisation in Russia*, p. 9.
66 Oleg Tsvetkov, 'Adygeya Leader Resigns, then Retracts Decision', *Russian Regional Report*, Vol. 11, No. 10, 14 April 2006.
67 Alexander Solzhenitsyn, *Rebuilding Russia* (London, Harvill, 1991), pp. 71–8.
68 For a discussion of these issues, see Galina Kurlyandskaya, *Budgetary Pluralism of Russian Authorities*, Open Society Institute, Local Government and Public Service Reform Initiative, Discussion Papers, No. 17, Budapest, 2001.
69 For details, see Tomila Lankina, *Governing the Locals: Local Self-Government and Ethnic Mobilization in Russia* (Lanham, MD, Rowman & Littlefield, 2004); Tomila Lankina, 'President Putin's Local Government Reforms', in Peter Reddaway and Robert W. Orrtung (eds), *The Dynamics of Russian Politics: Putin's Reform of Federal-Regional Relations*, Vol. 2 (Lanham, MD, Rowman & Littlefield, 2005).
70 Kozak denied that this would be an outcome of the changes, 'Reforma vlasti: kak podelit' na troikh?', *Argumenty i fakty*, No. 16, April 2003, p. 6.
71 www.president.kremlin.ru/text/appears/2006/02/101129.shtml.
72 Heinemann-Grüder, 'Asymmetry and Federal Integration in Russia', p. 80.
73 Aleksandr Belousov, 'Vertikal'', www.russ.ru/comments/103251448?mode=print.
74 ORT, 17 May 2000, 1700 GMT; www.president.kremlin.ru/events/34.html.
75 Interview with *Welt am Sontag*, June 2000, www.president.kremlin.ru/events/38.html.
76 *Moskovskii komsomolets*, 24 May 2000.
77 *Russian Regional Report*, Vol. 5, No. 29, 26 July 2000.
78 Cited by Sophie Lambroschini, 'Federation Coucil Aproves Putin-Led Reforms', *Newsline*, 27 July 2000.
79 Putin, *First Person*, p. 186.
80 *Russian Regional Report*, Vol. 5, No. 21, 31 May 2000.
81 *Moscow Times*, 24 May 2000.
82 Elena Chebankova, 'The Unintended Consequences of Gubernatorial Appointments in Russia, 2005–6', *The Journal of Communist Studies and Transition Politics*, Vol. 22, No. 4, December 2006, pp. 457–84, at p. 476.
83 Mikhail Kushtapin, 'Dolga ozhidano. I ne ozhidano', *Rossiiskaya gazeta*, 16 May 2000.

8 Reforging the nation

1 Address to Federal Assembly, 8 July 2000, www.president.kremlin.ru/events/42.html.
2 Charles Tilly, *Coercion, Capital, and European States* (Oxford, Blackwell, 1990).
3 For a recent analysis of the question, see Philip Bobbitt, *The Shield of Achilles* (London, Allen Lane, 2002).
4 Cf. Geoffrey Hosking, *Russia: People and Empire 1552–1917* (London, Harper Collins, 1997).
5 Mark Beissinger, *Nationalist Mobilization and the Collapse of the Soviet State* (Cambridge, Cambridge University Press, 2002).
6 Ernest Renan, What is a Nation?', in Homi K. Bhabha (ed.), *Nation and Narration* (London, Routledge, 1990), pp. 19, 11.

7 Putin, *First Person*, p. 213; Sakwa, *Putin*, p. 326.

8 Kolosov (ed.), *Mir glazami rossiyan*, p. 57.

9 Kolosov (ed.), *Mir glazami rossiyan*, p. 58.

10 'Yeltsin Call for "Unifying National Idea"', Itar-Tass, 12 July 1996. See Michael Urban, 'Remythologising the Russian State', *Europe-Asia Studies*, Vol. 50, No. 6, 1998, pp. 969–92.

11 Putin, *First Person*, p. 213; Sakwa, *Putin*, p. 326.

12 Interfax, 3 November 1999.

13 Itar-Tass, 22 December 1999.

14 Putin, *First Person*, p. 214; Sakwa, *Putin*, p. 326.

15 M. Steven Fish, 'Putin's Path', *Journal of Democracy*, Vol. 12, No. 4, October 2001, p. 73.

16 Vladimir Socor, 'Council of Europe Condemns Communism over Moscow's Opposition', *Eurasia Daily Monitor*, Vol. 3, No. 19, 27 January 2006.

17 Nanci Adler, 'The Future of the Soviet Past Remains Unpredictable: The Resurrection of Stalinist Symbols Amidst the Exhumation of Mass Graves', *Europe-Asia Studies*, Vol. 57, No. 8, December 2005, pp. 1093–119, at p. 1110.

18 'President: Russia not Psychologically Healthy', *The Baltic Times*, 19 June 2003; cited by Adler, 'The Future of the Soviet Past Remains Unpredictable', p. 1110.

19 Putin's defended his synthetic approach in *Komsomol'skaya pravda*, 6 December 2000.

20 The history of the flag, emblem and anthem are described in B. A. Anikin (ed.), *Natsional'naya ideya Rossii* (Moscow, State Management University, 2002), with the words of the new anthem on p. 44 – earlier versions pp. 45–7.

21 For many, the old Soviet anthem represented not wartime victories or Yury Gagarin's space flight, but the Gulag and repression. However, 'Putin decided that the Soviet hymn should be restored. And he got his way. That is a trait of his character', Mlechin, *Kreml' prezidenty Rossii*, p. 695.

22 Mlechin, for example, argues that because so many people would be upset by hauling Lenin's body out of the mausoleum, it was best to leave it there for the time being, *Kreml' prezidenty Rossii*, p. 695.

23 *Monitor*, 19 July 2001; *Moscow Times*, 19 July 2001.

24 *Izvestiya*, 1 February 2006.

25 Itar-Tass, 12 June 2006.

26 Putin, *Razgovor s Rossiei*, pp. 86–7.

27 A. I. Podberezkin and V. V. Makarov, *Strategiya dlya budushchego prezidenta Rossii: Russkii put'* (Moscow, RAU-Universitet, 2000).

28 Televised address by Boris Yeltsin, 13 September 1999.

29 Sven Gunnar Simonsen, 'Nationalism and the Russian Political Spectrum: Locating and Evaluating the Extremes', *Journal of Political Ideologies*, Vol. 6, No. 3, October 2001; in his *Pains of Partition: Nationalism, National Identity, and the Military in Post-Soviet Russia*, Department of Political Science, Faculty of Social Sciences, University of Oslo, 2001, p. 90.

30 Sven Gunnar Simonsen, 'Putin's Leadership Style: Ethnocentric Patriotism', *Security Dialogue*, Vol. 31, No. 3, 2000, pp. 377–80.

31 Vladimir Putin, 'Vystuplenie na torzhestvennom prieme v oznamenovanie 55-y godovshchinu pobedy v Velikoi Otechestvennoi voyne 1941–1945 godov', www.president.kremlin.ru/events/32.html.

32 Simonsen, 'Nationalism and the Russian Political Spectrum', p. 96.

33 Sergei Stankevich, 'Dlya chego perevozit chto-to iz Rossii v Rossiyu?', *Nezavisimaya gazeta*, 7 April 1992.

34 In December 1996 the Federation Council adopted a resolution moved by Luzhkov declaring Sevastopol a Russian city, see RFE/RL, *Daily Brief*, 6 December 1996.

35 Putin, *Razgovor s Rossiei*, 19 December 2002, p. 54.
36 *Komsomol'skaya pravda*, 11 February 2000.
37 'V Kreml' "cherez postel'" ne popadesh', *Argumenty i fakty*, No. 12, 2000, p. 9.
38 Putin, *Razgovor s Rossiei*, p. 52.
39 For an excellent analysis of Dostoevsky's relationship with the Slavophiles and other nativist traditions, see Sarah Hudsmith, *Dostoevsky and the Idea of Russianness: A New Perspective on Unity and Brotherhood* (London, Routledge-Curzon, 2003).
40 Konstantin Kazenin, 'Prezidentu prishlos' uchityvat' interesy vekh musul'-manskikh liderov', in *Chetyre goda s putinym* (Moscow, Vremya, 2004), p. 176.
41 Nicholas K. Gvosdev, 'The New Party Card: Orthodoxy and the Search for Post-Soviet Identity', *Problems of Post-Communism*, Vol. 47, No. 6, November–December 2000, pp. 29–38.
42 See Edwin Bacon, 'Church and State in Contemporary Russia: Conflicting Discourses', in Rick Fawn and Stephen White (eds), *Russia After Communism* (London, Frank Cass, 2002), pp. 97–116.
43 Blotskii, *Vladimir Putin*, Book 2, p. 21.
44 Mlechin, *Kreml' prezidenty Rossii*, p. 691.
45 Mlechin, *Kreml' prezidenty Rossii*, p. 692.
46 For the Patriarch's views, see Zoe Knox, 'Russian Orthodoxy, Russian Nationalism, and Patriarch Aleksii II', *Nationalities Papers*, Vol. 33, No. 4, December 2005, pp. 533–45.
47 Reuters, 9 June 2000.
48 This is the implication of Gvosdev's notion of 'the new party card', 'The New Party Card', op. cit.
49 Robert Jackson, 'Sovereignty in World Politics: A Glance at the Conceptual and Historical Landscape', *Political Studies*, Vol. XLVII, Special Issue 1999, *Sovereignty at the Millennium*, p. 434.
50 Viva Ona Bartkus, *The Dynamics of Secession* (Cambridge, Cambridge University Press, 1999), Chapter 8, '"Opportune Moments": a Reduction in the Costs of Secession', pp. 145–66.
51 UN Resolution 1244 recognised the 'sovereignty and territorial integrity of the Federal Republic of Yugoslavia', but from 2000 the international community began to envisage an independent Kosovo.
52 See Richard Sakwa, 'Chechnya: A Just War Fought Unjustly?', in Bruno Coppieters and Richard Sakwa (eds), *Contextualizing Secession: Normative Studies in Comparative Perspective* (Oxford, Oxford University Press, 2003), Chapter 8, pp. 156–86.
53 Metta Spencer (ed.), *Separatism: Democracy and Disintegration* (Lanham, MD, Rowman & Littlefield, 1998).
54 Moshe Gammer, *The Lone Wolf and the Bear: Three Centuries of Chechen Defiance of Russian Rule* (Pittsburgh, University of Pittsburgh Press, 2006) reflects this view.
55 For example, Robert K. Schaeffer, *Severed States: Dilemmas of Democracy in a Divided World* (Lanham, MD, Rowman & Littlefield, 1999).
56 Henry E. Hale, 'Is Russian Nationalism on the Rise?', Program on New Approaches to Russian Security (PONARS), Davis Center for Russian Studies, Harvard University, *Policy Memo Series*, No. 110, February 2000, p. 1.
57 There were popular protests in the first war and a degree of elite mobilisation to oppose it, and the financial and budgetary implications of both wars were far from negligible, but for most of the population the Chechen wars were perceived as being somehow 'foreign', even though they were fought precisely to ensure that Chechnya remained 'domestic'.
58 Anatol Lieven, *Chechnya: Tombstone of Russian Power* (New Haven and London, Yale University Press, 1998).

59 Dmitri Trenin and Aleksei Malashenko, with Anatol Lieven, *Russia's Restless Frontier: The Chechnya Factor in Post-Soviet Russia* (Washington DC, Carnegie Endowment for International Peace, 2004), p. 11.
60 Quoted by Rutland, 'Putin's Path to Power', p. 324.
61 Henry E. Hale and Rein Taagepera, 'Russia: Consolidation or Collapse?', *Europe-Asia Studies*, Vol. 54, No. 7, 2002, pp. 1101–125 analyse the degree to which Russia's disintegration really is a serious possibility.
62 Interview with Vladimir Putin by Mikhail Leont'ev, Vremya, ORT, 7 February 2000.
63 Putin, *First Person*, pp. 133–4.
64 Putin, *Ot pervogo litsa*, p. 135; *First Person*, pp. 141–2.
65 Putin, *Razgovor s Rossiei*, 19 December 2002, pp. 47–8.
66 *Monitor*, 1 February 2000.
67 Speech of 20 November 2000, *Newsline*, 21 November 2000. He was supported in his view by the Russian elite: a poll conducted by ROMIR-Gallup International in December 2000 found that the overwhelming majority, 92.1%, felt that Chechnya should remain part of the Russian Federation, reported in *JRL*, 4675/6.
68 'Zayavlenie Prezidenta Rossii', 24 September 2001, www.president.kremlin.ru/text/appears/2001/09/28639.shtml.
69 *Newsline*, 27 October 2000.
70 Otto Latsis, 'Ups and Downs of Political Will', *The Russia Journal*, 7–13 October 2000.
71 *Nezavisimaya gazeta*, 12 February 2000.
72 *Novaya gazeta*, 9–15 June 2003.
73 *Nezavisimaya gazeta*, 9 July 2002.
74 www.hro.org/war2006/02/26–1.php
75 *Moskovskie novosti*, No. 46, November 2000.
76 Latsis, 'Ups and Downs of Political Will'.
77 Zakhar Vinogradov, 'Vtoraya chechenskaya kampaniya: pobednyi god', *Nezavisimaya gazeta*, 6 October 2000, p. 4.
78 *Le Monde*, 12 April 2003; a report issued by Human Rights Watch on 7 April 2003 noted that the violation of humanitarian laws had not decreased, www.hrw.org/.
79 Plenty of evidence is adduced in the Jamestown Foundation's *Chechnya Weekly*, for example, 16 July 2002.
80 Interview by Said Bitsoev, *Novye Izvestia*, 19 July 2002; *Chechnya Weekly*, 24 July 2002.
81 Anna Politkovskaya, *A Dirty War: A Russian Reporter in Chechnya*, Introduction by Thomas de Waal, translated by John Crowfoot (London, The Harvill Press, 2001); Anna Politkovskaya, *A Small Corner of Hell*, translated by Alexander Burry and Tatiana Tulchinsky (Chicago, University of Chicago Press Pounds, 2003).
82 For a discussion of theories of secession, see Bruno Coppieters, 'Introduction', in Coppieters and Sakwa (eds), *Contextualizing Secession*.
83 According to VTsIOM, in December 2002 56% favoured negotiations with the separatists, while 36% supported continued military action, *Chechnya Weekly*, 22 January 2003.
84 www.levada.ru/press/2005122901.html. Accessed 5 January 2006.
85 Nikolai Petrov, 'Troshev Ouster and the Chechnya Policy', *Russia and Eurasia Review*, Vol. 2, No. 3, 4 February 2003.
86 For his own view of the conflict in Chechnya, see Gennadii Troshev, *Moya voina: Chechenskii dnevnik okopnogo generala* (Moscow, Vagrius, 2001).
87 In October 2002 Putin decreed that the military commandant in the republic would coordinate the work of the others, including the North Caucasus Military District, the Combined Federal Forces Group in the North Caucasus, the Regional

Operations Staff for Control of Counter-Terrorist Operations in the north Caucasus region, and the commander of the defence ministry forces in the republic.

88 www.president.kremlin.ru/text/appears/2006/01/100848.shtml.
89 *Chechnya Weekly*, 30 May 2001.
90 Cited by Paul Goble, 'On Equal Terms', *Newsline*, 14 March 2000.
91 *Nezavisimaya gazeta*, 23 July 2002; *Chechnya Weekly*, 29 July 2002.
92 VTsIOM poll, reported in *Chechnya Weekly*, 6 February 2003.
93 Putin, *Razgovor s Rossiei*, p. 41.
94 Primakov, *Rossiiskaya gazeta*, 10 September 2002.
95 Putin, *Razgovor s Rossiei*, p. 48.
96 BBC Monitoring, 16 May 2003; in *JRL*, 7186/1.
97 www.president.kremlin.ru/text/appears/2006/01/100848.shtml.
98 Posted on Kavkazcenter website on 9 January 2005, reported in 'Basaev Threatens to Cross the Volga', *Chechnya Weekly*, Vol. VII, Issue 2, 12 January 2005, and Andrei Smirnov, 'Russian Generals Warn of New Rebel Offensive in the North Caucasus', *Eurasia Daily Monitor*, Vol. 3, No. 8, 12 January 2006.
99 See Robert Bruce Ware, 'A Multitude of Evils: Mythology and Political Failure in Chechnya', in Richard Sakwa (ed.), *Chechnya: From Past to Future* (London, Anthem Press; Sterling, VA, Stylus Publishers, 2005), Chapter 5, pp. 79–116.
100 RFE/RL, *Russian Political Weekly*, Vol. 6, No. 6, 10 March 2006.
101 Chechenpress.org, 16 May 2005.
102 RFE/RL, *Russian Political Weekly*, Vol. 6, No. 6, 10 March 2006.
103 For the debate between Akhmed Zakaev, in favour of a traditional nationalist Chechen state-building agenda, and Movladi Udugov's call for the establishment of a global *khalifah* (caliphate), see www.kavkazcenter.com/eng, February 2006.
104 Jeronim Perovic, 'The North Caucasus: Taking Stock Two Years After Beslan', *Russian Analytical Digest*, No. 5, 2006, pp. 4–8, at pp. 5–6.
105 The question of why the extension of autonomy in some circumstances blunts the drive for secession while in others only whets the appetite of secessionist movements is at the core of Bartkus's conceptual model in her *The Dynamics of Secession*.

9 Russian capitalism

1 Konstantin Sonin, 'The Unbearable Lightness of Petrodollars', *Russia in Global Affairs*, Vol. 2, No. 3, pp. 94–100, at p. 100.
2 Joel S. Hellman, 'Winners Take All: The Politics of Partial Reform in Post-communist Transitions', *World Politics*, Vol. 50, 1998, pp. 203–34.
3 *Forbes*, 17 March 2003.
4 Vladimir Tikhomirov (ed.), *Anatomy of the 1998 Russian Crisis* (University of Melbourne, Contemporary Europe Research Centre, 1999)
5 Joseph Stiglitz, *Globalization and its Discontents* (London, Penguin Press, 2002), Chapter 5.
6 Larry Elliott, 'World Groups' Reputations Sinking', *The Russia Journal*, 20–6 March 2000, p. iv.
7 Vladimir Popov, 'Circumstances versus Policy Choices: Why Has the Economic Performance of the Soviet Success States Been So Poor?', in Michael McFaul and Kathryn Stoner-Weiss (eds), *After the Collapse of Communism: Comparative Lessons of Transition* (New York, Cambridge University Press, 2004), Chapter 3, pp. 86–129.
8 Stanley Fischer, 'Ten Years of Transition', *IMF Staff Papers*, Vol. 48, Special Issue, 2001, p. 7.
9 Stefan Hedlund, 'Will the Russian Economy Revive under Putin?', *Problems of Post-Communism*, March/April 2001, p. 59.

10 Philip Hanson, 'The Russian Economic Recovery: Do Four Years of Growth Tell us that the Fundamentals Have Changed?', *Europe-Asia Studies*, Vol. 55, No. 3, 2003, pp. 365–82.

11 For an evaluation, see William Tompson, 'Putin's Challenge: The Politics of Structural Reform in Russia', *Europe-Asia Studies*, Vol. 54, No. 6, September 2002, pp. 933–58.

12 *The Independent*, 23 August 2006.

13 Gérard Roland, 'The Russian Economy in the Year 2005', *Post-Soviet Affairs*, Vol. 22, No. 1, 2006, pp. 90–8, at p. 92.

14 Charles Wolf, 'A Mighty Country's Progress and Regress', www.rand.org/com mentary/010407PS.html.

15 Reported by Andrew E. Kramer, 'Russia Called Too Reliant on Petroleum', *New York Times*, 18 April 2006.

16 Elena Chinyaeva, 'The Russian Economy, Lost in the Dark', *Russia and Eurasia Review*, Vol. 2, No. 3, 4 February 2003.

17 Reported by finance minister Alexei Kudrin, *Rossiiskie vesti*, No. 40, 3 November 2006; Itar-Tass, 20 November 2006; with updated figures from deputy prime minister Alexander Zhukov, Interfax, 20 December 2006.

18 *Kommersant-Vlast'*, 8 May 2006, p. 10.

19 Interfax, 24 March 2006; Mosnews.com, 1 November 2006.

20 Vyacheslav Shironin, 'Not all Big Business', *Russia Profile*, Vol. 3, Issue 10, December 2006, pp. 13–15, at p. 13.

21 Carl Shreck, 'Russia Fall Further Behind Europe, US', *Moscow Times*, 13 November 2006.

22 Natalya Alyakrinskaya, 'Inefficient Government Breeds Corruption', *Moscow News*, 11–17 January 2006.

23 World Bank, *World Development Index 2005*, http://devdata.worldbank.org/ data-query/. See also *Growth, Poverty and Inequality: Eastern Europe and the Former Soviet Union* (Washington, DC, World Bank, 2005).

24 'Not a Sycophant', *Russia Profile*, Vol. 3, Issue 1, January–February 2006, pp. 15–18, at p. 17.

25 RIA Novosti, 8 February 2006.

26 *Forbes*, 27 March 2006.

27 Neil Buckley, 'From Shock Therapy to Consumer Cure: Russia's Middle Class Starts Spending', *Financial Times*, 31 October 2006.

28 *Russia in Figures 2005* (Moscow, Rosstat, 2005), p. 74.

29 Sergei Glaz'ev, *Vybor budushchego* (Moscow, Algoritm, 2005).

30 A. Zudin, 'Oligarkhiya kak politicheskaya problema rossiiskogo post-kommunizma', *Obshchestvennie nauki i sovremennost'*, No. 1, 1999, pp. 45–65.

31 *Moscow Times*, 23 August 2002.

32 See Peter Rutland (ed.), *Business and State in Contemporary Russia* (Boulder, CO, Westview, 2001).

33 A. A. Mukhin, *Biznes-elita i gosudarstvennaya vlast': Kto vladeet Rossiei na rubezhe vekov?* (Moscow, Tsentr politicheskoi informatsii, 2001).

34 *Russian Regional Report*, Vol. 7, No. 23, July 2002.

35 Ya. Sh. Pappe, *'oligarkhi': ekonomicheska khronika, 1992–2000*, 2nd edn (Moscow, Gosudarstvennyi universitet Vysshaya shkola ekonomiki, 2000).

36 A. Dynkin and A. Sokolov, 'Integrirovannye biznes-gruppy v rossiiskom ekonomike', *Voprosy ekonomiki*, No. 4, 2002, pp. 78–95.

37 Sergei Kolmakov, 'The Role of Financial Industrial Conglomerates in Russian Political Parties', *Russia Watch*, No. 9, January 2003, pp. 15–17.

38 Dynkin and Sokolov, 'Integrirovannye biznes-gruppy v rossiiskom ekonomike', p. 78.

39 Dynkin and Sokolov, 'Integrirovannye biznes-gruppy v rossiiskom ekonomike', p. 90.

40 World Bank, *From Transition to Development*, April 2004, www.worldbankorg.ru.

41 These issues are explored in the chapter by Stijn Claessens and Esen Ulgenerk in Harry G. Broadman (ed.), *Unleashing Russia's Business Potential: Lessons from the Regions for Building Market Institutions*, Discussion Paper No. 434 (Washington, DC, World Bank, 2002).

42 'Nefteglobalizatsiya', *Nezavisimaya gazeta*, 23 April 2003, pp. 1, 3.

43 *Moscow Times*, 23 April 2003, pp. 1–2.

44 Wolf, 'A Mighty Country's Progress and Regress'.

45 'Putin's Choice: A Survey of Russia', *The Economist*, 21 July 2001, p. 6.

46 Yulia Latynina, 'Forestry Industry: Ripe for Carving Up', *Moscow Times*, 17 July 2002.

47 Rusal commissioned a study by the Economist Intelligence Unit, published significantly under the title *The Russians are Coming: Understanding Emerging Multinationals* (Moscow, Rusal, 2006).

48 Anatolii Chubais, 'Missiya Rossii v XXI veke', *Nezavisimaya gazeta*, 1 October 2003; http://vip.lenta.ru/doc/2003/09/26/empire/_Printed.htm.

49 Andrei P. Tsygankov, 'If Not by Tanks, Then by Banks? The Role of Soft Power in Putin's Foreign Policy', *Europe-Asia Studies*, Vol. 58, No. 7, November 2006, pp. 1079–99.

50 For details of media holdings, for example, see Pappe, *'Oligarkhi'*, Tables 1 and 5.

51 Dynkin and Sokolov, 'Integrirovannye biznes-gruppy v rossiiskom ekonomike', p. 92.

52 Vladimir Mau, 'V ozhidanii promyshlennoi politiki', *Profil'*, 8 May 2006, p. 33.

53 Mukhin, *Biznes-elita i gosudarstvennaya vlast'*.

54 Bortsov, *Vladimir Putin*, p. 257.

55 Sergei Blagov, 'Illarionov Resignation Reduces Kremlin Debate on Economy, Energy Policy', *Eurasia Daily Monitor*, Vol. 3, Issue 5, 9 January 2006.

56 *Izvestiya*, 12 January 2006.

57 Interview in *Ekspert*, 4 April 2005, p. 75.

58 *Moscow Times*, 22 December 2005.

59 'Not a Sycophant', *Russia Profile*, Vol. 3, Issue 1, January–February 2006, pp. 15–18, at p. 15.

60 Blagov, 'Illarionov Resignation Reduces Kremlin Debate on Economy'.

61 *Moskovskii komsomolets*, 13 July 2002.

62 Andrei Piontovski, 'Russia's Misguided Democracy', *The Russian Journal*, 8–14 July 2000.

63 The phrase is from Aleksandr Buzgalin, '1999 Russian Presidential Elections: Just Begun or Already Over?', *Prism*, No. 20, Part 1, December 1999.

64 *Monitor*, 9 March 2000.

65 Putin, *Razgovor s Rossiei*, 19 December 2002, p. 84.

66 Mikhail Delyagin, 'Driving Russia to Oblivion', *The Russia Journal*, 15–21 July 2000.

67 *Izvestiya*, 10 April 2006.

68 Miriam Elder, 'US, Russia Sign 800-Page WTO Deal', *Moscow Times*, 20 November 2006.

69 This is made explicit by Pavel Felgenhauer, 'US Green Lights Russian WTO Membership, Seeks Agreement on Iran', *Eurasia Daily Monitor*, Vol. 3, Issue 212, 15 November 2006.

70 Louis Skyner (ed.), *Property, the Past and Present: Legal Reform and Political Culture in Contemporary Russia* (London, Routledge, forthcoming).

71 Mark Hertsgaard, 'Russia is an Eco-Disaster, and It Just Got Worse', *Washington Post*, 9 July 2000.

72 In 2005 Shell had signed a draft asset swap agreement with Gazprom whereby the latter planned to acquire a quarter of Sakhalin Energy in exchange for half of Zapolyarnoe, a large western Siberian gas field. A few days after the agree-

ment, Shell disclosed that Sakhalin's costs had doubled to $20bn, an announce-
ment that incensed the Russian government, since its share of revenues from the
project were indefinitely postponed. Carl Mortishead, 'Putin Signals End to
Overseas Ownership of Russian Energy', *The Times*, 12 December 2006.

73 Richard Wolin, *Heidegger's Children* (Princeton, NJ, Princeton University
Press, 2001), p. 195.

74 Medvedev, *Vremya Putina?*, p. 213.

10 Putin's new realism in foreign policy

1 Address to the Federal Assembly, 8 July 2000, www.president.kremlin.ru/
events/42.html.

2 Sergei Karaganov's, 'Rossiya – SShA: Obratno k mirnomu sosushchestvova-
niyu?', *Rossiiskaya gazeta*, 24 March 2006, p. 19.

3 For an overview of the issues, see Dmitry Trenin, *Integratsiya i identichnost':
Rossiya kak 'novyi zapad'* (Moscow, Evropa, 2006).

4 V. A. Kolosov (ed.), *Mir glazami rossiyan: Mify i vneshnyaya politika* (Moscow,
Institut fonda 'Obshchestvennoe mnenie', 2003), p. 11.

5 For the gulf between rhetoric and reality in the 1990s, see Sherman Garnett,
'Russia's Illusory Ambitions', *Foreign Affairs*, Vol. 72, No. 2, 1997, pp. 61–76.

6 Yevgeny Primakov, *A World Challenged: Fighting Terrorism in the Twenty-First
Century* (Washington, DC, Brookings Institution Press, 2004).

7 James M. Goldgeier and Michael McFaul, 'Russians as Joiners: Realist and Lib-
eral Conceptions of Postcommunist Europe', in Michael McFaul and Kathryn
Stoner-Weiss (eds), *After the Collapse of Communism: Comparative Lessons of
Transition* (New York, Cambridge University Press, 2004), Chapter 7, pp. 232–56.

8 Thomas Ambrosio, *Challenging America's Global Preeminence: Russia's Quest
for Multipolarity* (Ashgate, Aldershot, 2005).

9 Zimmerman, William, 'Slavophiles and Westernizers Redux: Contemporary
Russian Elite Perspectives', *Post-Soviet Affairs*, Vol. 21, No. 3, pp. 183–209.

10 Paradorn Rangsimaporn, 'Interpretations of Eurasianism: Justifying Russia's
Role in East Asia', *Europe-Asia Studies*, Vol. 58, No. 3, May 2006, pp. 371–89.

11 Zhan Parvulesko (Jean Parvulesco), *Putin i evraziiskaya imperiya*, translated
from French (St. Petersburg, Amfora, 2006).

12 Andrei P. Tsygankov, 'Vladimir Putin's Vision of Russia as a Normal Great
Power', *Post-Soviet Affairs*, Vol. 21, No. 2, 2005, pp. 132–58, at p. 133.

13 For an overview, see Alexander J. Motyl, Blair A. Ruble and Lilia Shevtsova
(eds), *Russia's Engagement with the West: Transformation and Integration in the
Twenty-First Century* (New York, M. E. Sharpe, 2003).

14 www.scrf.gov.ru/Documents.Decree/2002/24–1.html; *Nezavisimoe voennoe obozrenie*, 14 January 2000.

15 See Jakub M. Godzimirski, 'Russian National Security Concepts 1997 and
2000: A Comparative Analysis', *European Security*, Vol. 9, No. 4, Winter 2000,
pp. 73–91.

16 Vladislav Chernov in *Nezavisimaya gazeta*, 29 April 1993.

17 *Nezavisimaya gazeta*, 11 July 2000, pp. 1 and 6.

18 'The Foreign Policy Concept of the Russian Federation', www.mid.ru/mid/eng/
econcept.htm.

19 Russian Embassy London press release, 17 May 2002.

20 Dmitri Trenin, *The End of Eurasia: Russia on the Border Between Geopolitics
and Globalization* (Moscow, Carnegie Moscow Center, 2001).

21 Trenin, *Integratsiya i identichnost'*.

22 There is a large literature in Russia arguing that in fact Putin is pursuing a neo-
Eurasianist agenda. For example, Parvulesko describes the 'great imperial

eschatological project of Vladimir Putin': the destruction of the oligarchs and their socio-economic and political leadership, the return of the army to the centre of Russian life and strategy on a continental scale, and the militarisation of labour, education, culture and religion. The purpose of this project is for Russia 'to become a bridge from Europe to India, and through India to the whole of Asia', Parvulesko, *Putin i evraziiskaya imperiya*. Ill-informed Western commentators have taken this literature as a reflection of Putin's thinking.

23 For a discussion of the 'democratic peace' proposition – that democracies rarely if ever fight each other and that democracies in general are more peaceable than non-democracies – see Michael Brown, Sean Lynn-Jones and Steven Miller (eds), *Debating the Democratic Peace* (Cambridge, MA, MIT Press, 1996); and Michael W. Doyle, *Ways of War and Peace* (New York, W. W. Norton, 1997). For a critique of the democratic peace idea, Errol A. Henderson, *Democracy and War: The End of an Illusion?* (Boulder, CO, Lynne Rienner Publishers, 2002). Note also the argument that while democracies may not go to war with each other, democratising states are more prone to do so: Edward D. Mansfield and Jack Snyder, *Electing to Fight: Why Emerging Democracies Go to War* (Cambridge, MA, MIT Press, 2005).

24 For an early discussion of the idea of core and periphery, see Barry Buzan, 'New Patterns of Global Security in the Twenty-First Century', *International Affairs*, Vol. 67, No. 3, 1991, pp. 431–51. This model is developed by Goldgeier and McFaul, 'Russians as Joiners'.

25 Robert Cooper, *The Breaking of Nations: Order and Chaos in the Twenty-First Century* (London, Atlantic Books, 2003).

26 Robert Kagan, *Paradise and Power: America and Europe in the New World Order* (New York, Knopf, 2003), pp. 113–21.

27 John G. Ikenberry, *After Victory: Institutions, Strategic Restraint and the Rebuilding of Order after Major War* (Princeton, Princeton University Press, 2001).

28 John Williamson (ed.), *The Political Economy of Policy Reform* (Washington, DC, Institute for International Economics, 1994); Martin Wolf, *Why Globalization Works* (New Haven, Yale University Press, 2004).

29 The strategy of integration was outlined by Yeltsin's last foreign minister and Putin's first, Igor Ivanov, 'Russia, Europe at the Turn of the Century', *International Affairs* (Moscow), Vol. 46, No. 2, 2000, pp. 1–11.

30 Dov Lynch, 'Misperceptions and Divergences', in Dov Lynch (ed.), *What Russia Sees*, Chaillot Paper No. 74 (Paris, Institute for European Studies, January 2005), p. 9.

31 This is explored by Vladimir Baranovsky, 'Russia: Insider or Outsider?', *International Affairs* (Moscow), Vol. 46, No. 3, July 2000, pp. 443–59.

32 Joseph Nye, 'Hard and Soft Power in a Global Information Age', in Mark Leonard (ed.), *Re-Ordering the World* (London, The Foreign Policy Centre, 2002), pp. 2–10, at p. 5. For a more extended discussion of the various cultural and other ways in which 'soft power' is exercised by the United States, see Joseph S. Nye Jr., *Bound to Lead: The Changing Nature of American Power* (New York, Basic Books, 1990), Chapter 2.

33 Igor Ivanov, 'The New Russian Identity: Innovation and Continuity in Russian Foreign Policy', *The Washington Quarterly*, Vol. 24, No. 3, Summer 2001, p. 3.

34 See Igor Torbakov, 'Putin Urges Russian Diplomats to be more Active in the Post-Soviet States', The Jamestown Foundation, *Eurasia Daily Monitor*, 19 July 2004.

35 Bobo Lo, *Vladimir Putin and the Evolution of Russian Foreign Policy* (Blackwell, Royal Institute for International Affairs, 2003), Chapter 4.

36 www.president.kremlin.ru/text/appears.2001/01/28464.shtml.

37 Vladimir Putin, 'We Should Look for Partners Everywhere', *Diplomat*, September 2002; www.diplomat-cd.ru.

38 For an extended analysis, see Anatolii Utkin, *Bol'shaya vos'merka: tsena vkhozhdeniya* (Moscow, Algoritm, 2006).

39 Cited in Hannes Adomeit, 'Russia as a "Great Power" in World Affairs: Images and Reality', *International Affairs*, Vol. 71, No. 1, January 1995, p. 43.

40 Putin, *Ot pervogo litsa*, pp. 155–6.

41 'Putin Opens EU–Russia Summit', RFE/RL, *Newsline*, 29 May 2000.

42 *Newsline*, 12 July 2002.

43 Bobo Lo stresses the interplay between economisation and securitisation in Putin's foreign policy, 'The Securitization of Russian Foreign Policy under Putin', in Gabriel Gorodetsky (ed.), *Russia Between East and West: Russian Foreign Policy on the Threshold of the Twenty-First Century* (London, Frank Cass Publishers, 2003), Chapter 2, pp. 12–32.

44 See Richard Ullman, 'Redefining Security', *International Security*, Vol. 8, No. 1, Summer 1983; Barry Buzan, *People, States, Fear: An Agenda for International Security Studies in the Post-Cold War Era* (Hertfordshire, Harvester Wheatsheaf, 1991); Barry Buzan, Ole Waever and J. de Wilde, *Security: A New Framework for Analysis* (Boulder, CO and London, Lynne Rienner, 1998).

45 'New Priorities in Russian Foreign Policy', *Internationale Politik: Transatlantic Edition*, Vol. 1, No. 3, 2000, pp. 2, 3.

46 www.president.kremlin.ru/text/appears/2006/02/101129.shtml, 7 February 2006.

47 Igor S. Ivanov, *The New Russian Diplomacy* (Washington, DC, Brookings Institution Press, 2002), p. 95.

48 Itar-Tass, 9 October 2003.

49 Igor Bratchikov and Dmitrii Lyubinskii, 'Germany: the Mechanism of Strategic Partnership', *International Affairs*, Vol. 48, No. 3, 2002, pp. 149–56.

50 Stephen F. Cohen, *Failed Crusade: America and the Tragedy of Post-Communist Russia* (New York, W. W. Norton, 2000).

51 Lilia Shevtsova, *Putin's Russia* (Washington, DC, Carnegie Endowment for International Peace, 2003), p. 203.

52 'Zayavlenie Prezidenta Rossii', 24 September 2001, www.president.kremlin.ru/text/appears/2001/09/28639.shtml; Roi Medvedev, *Vladimir Putin – Deistvuyushchii Prezident* (Moscow, Vremya, 2002), p. 345.

53 G. G. Diligenskii, '"Zapad" i rossiiskoe obshchestvo', (Moscow, FOM, 2001), pp. 205–14; http://usa.fom.ru/razdel/mbi/382/936/3090.html.

54 Kolosov (ed.), *Mir glazami rossiyan*, p. 243.

55 *Gazeta*, 10–12 March 2006.

56 Yevgeny Primakov, *Mir posle 11 sentyabrya* (Moscow, Mysl', 2002).

57 Igor Ivanov, *Vneshnyaya politika rossii v epokhu globalizatsii* (Moscow, Olma-Press, 2002).

58 Published on the BBC's Russian-language service website, in *JRL*, 9293/14.

59 For example, Stephen Haseler, *Super-State: The New Europe and its Challenge to America* (London, I. B. Tauris, 2004).

60 On the long-standing concerns of the Europeans, see Evgenii Grigor'ev, "Bunt" evropeitsev: Politiki starogo kontinenta ne khotyat igrat' role' satellitov SShA', *Nezavisimaya gazeta*, 15 February 2002, p. 6.

61 Andrew Kuchins, Vyacheslav Nikonov and Dmitri Trenin, *U.S.–Russian Relations: The Case for An Upgrade* (Moscow, Moscow Carnegie Centre, 2005), p. 13.

62 Of this, $45.43 were for democracy programs, $51.43 million for economic and social reform, $5.60 million for humanitarian assistance, and $5.79 for cross-sectoral initiatives, US Department of State, Bureau of European and Eurasian Affairs, Fact Sheet, 15 September 2004, in *JRL*, 8370/25.

63 Mikhail Rykhtik argues that Putin welcomed a Republican victory because of shared concerns over WMD non-proliferation and the fight against terrorism, and the view that Bush would be less concerned about the 'democracy question'

in Russia than a Democratic president, *Why Did Russia Welcome a Republican Victory?* PONARS Policy Memo 330, November 2004.

64 James Richter, *"A Sense of His Soul": The Relations Between Presidents Putin and Bush*, PONARS Policy Memo 329, November 2004.

65 For a review of the reasons for support for Bush, see Igor Torbakov, 'Russia's Political Elites Want Bush Re-Elected', *Eurasia Daily Monitor*, 2 November 2004.

66 Kuchins *et al.*, *U.S.–Russian Relations*, p. 2.

67 Kuchins *et al.*, *U.S.–Russian Relations*, p. 2.

68 *Russia's Wrong Direction: What the United States Can and Should Do*, Independent Task Force Report No. 57, John Edwards and Jack Kemp (chairs), Stephen Sestanovich (project director), (New York, Council on Foreign Relations, 2006).

69 Vitalii Ivanov and Konstantin Simonov, 'Vernyi put' Rossii: chto khotyat sdelat' SShA?', *Nezavisimaya gazeta*, 28 April 2006, p. 10.

70 Press release of the Office of the Vice President, The White House, 4 May 2006.

71 Nikolai Zlobin, 'Limited Possibilities and Possible Limitations: Russia and the US – What's Next?', *Russia in Global Affairs*, Vol. 3, No. 1, January–March 2005.

72 Nikolai Zlobin, *Izvestiya*, 15 November 2004.

73 Dmitri Trenin, *Reading Russia Right*, Carnegie Endowment for International Peace, Policy Brief, Special Edition 42, October 2005, p. 8.

74 William Zimmerman, *The Russian People and Foreign Policy: Russian Elite and Mass Perspectives, 1993–2000* (Princeton, NJ, Princeton University Press, 2002), p. 92.

75 Anatol Lieven, 'Why are we Trying to Reheat the Cold War', *Los Angeles Times*, 19 March 2006.

76 Viatcheslav Morozov, *The Forced Choice Between Russia and the West: The Geopolitics of Alienation*, PONARS Policy Memo 327, November 2004.

77 *Nezavisimaya gazeta*, 17 November 2004.

78 'Wider Europe – Neighbourhood: Proposed New Framework for Relations with the EU's Eastern and Southern Neighbours', March 2003 Communication of the Commission to the Council.

79 Quoted in *Budapest Analyses*, No. 39, 23 March 2004.

80 Yuri Lotman, 'Rol' dual'nykh modelei v dinamike russkoi kul'tury', in *Istoriya i tipologiya russkoi kul'tury* (St Petersburg, Iskusstvo–SPB, 2002), pp. 89–90.

81 Viatcheslav Morozov, *Inside/Outside: Europe and the Boundaries of Russian Political Community*, PONARS Working Paper, October 2004.

82 'Intervyu V. Putina Devidu Frostu', *Kommersant'*, No. 39, 7 March 2000, p. 2; Alexander Golts, 'Putin Could Aim for Europe Alliance', *The Russia Journal*, 20–26 March 2000, p. 8.

83 Margot Light, Stephen White and John Löwenhardt, 'A Wider Europe: the View from Moscow and Kyiv', *International Affairs*, Vol. 76, No. 1, January 2000, pp. 77–88.

84 Oleg Varfolomeyev, 'Is Ukraine Ready to Join NATO?', *Russia and Eurasia Review*, Vol. 1, Issue 4, 16 July 2002.

85 M. L. Titarenko (ed.), *Kitai na puti modernizatsii i reform: 1949–1999* (Moscow, Vostochnaya Literatura, 1999).

86 See Sherman Garnett, *Rapprochement or Rivalry: Russia–China Relations in a Changing Asia* (Washington, DC, Carnegie Endowment for International Peace, 2000).

87 See, for example, Andrei Komarov, 'Rossiya i kitai kritikuyut gumanitarnoe vmeshatel'stvo', *Nezavisimaya gazeta*, 16 March 2000, p. 6. The interview reported here was with Oleg Mironov, the Russian human rights commissioner,

on a visit to China where he shared Russian experience with the post of commissioner. He noted that China had signed up to no fewer than 17 international
conventions and protocols on human rights.

88 Jeanne L. Wilson, *Strategic Partners: Russian-Chinese Relations in the Post-
Soviet Era* (Armonk, NY, M. E. Sharpe, 2004).

89 *Monitor*, 14 March 2000.

90 Wilson, *Strategic Partners*, p. 100.

91 Richard Weitz, 'The Sino–Russian Arms Dilemma', *China Brief*, Vol. 6, Issue
22, 8 November 2006, pp. 9–12.

92 Keir A. Lieber and Daryl G. Press, 'The Rise of U.S. Nuclear Primacy', *Foreign
Affairs*, Vol. 85, No. 2, March/April 2006, pp. 42–54.

93 Hsiu-Ling Wu and Chien-Hsun Chen, 'The Prospects for Regional Economic
Integration Between China and the Five Central Asian Countries', *Europe-Asia
Studies*, Vol. 56, No. 7, November 2004, pp. 1059–80.

94 Trenin, *The End of Eurasia*.

95 MacFarlane, 'NATO in Russia's Relations with the West', p. 284.

96 Kolosov (ed.), *Mir glazami rossiyan*, pp. 266–7.

97 *Rossiiskaya gazeta*, 20 April 2002.

98 www.president.kremlin.ru/text/appears/2006/02/101129.shtml.

99 Armenia, Kazakhstan, Kyrgyzstan, Tajikistan and Uzbekistan in 1992 and
Azerbaijan, Belarus and Georgia in 1993–94.

100 Roy Allison, Stephen White and Margot Light, 'Belarus between East and
West', *The Journal of Communist Studies and Transition Politics*, Vol. 21, No. 4,
December 2005, pp. 487–511, at p. 494.

101 As Putin put it, 'Indeed, you know that as far as all post-Soviet space is concerned, I am concerned above all about attempts to resolve legal issues by illegal
means. That is the most dangerous thing. It is most dangerous to think up a
system of permanent revolutions – now the Rose Revolution, or the Blue Revolution. You should get used to living according to the law, rather than according
to political expediency defined elsewhere for some or other nation – that is what
worries me most. Certain rules and procedures should mature within society. Of
course, we should pay attention to, support and help democracies but, if we
embark on the road of permanent revolutions, nothing good will come from this
for these countries, and for these peoples. We will plunge all the post-Soviet space
into a series of never-ending conflicts, which will have extremely serious consequences.' Vladimir Putin, 'This Year Was Not an Easy One', *International
Affairs* (Moscow), Vol. 51, No. 1, January 2005, pp 3–5, at p. 2.

102 Kolosov (ed.), *Mir glazami rossiyan*, p. 159.

103 David Marples, 'The Isolation of Europe's Last Dictator', *Russia and Eurasia
Review*, 17 December 2002.

104 *Newsline*, 14 June 2002.

105 Andrei Lobatch, 'Peculiarities of the Integration Process Between Belarus and
the Russian Federation: Economic and Political Aspects', in Kimitaka Matsuzato (ed.), *Emerging Meso-Areas in the Former Socialist Countries: Histories
Revised or Improvised?* (Sapporo, Slavic Research Center, Hokkaido University,
2005), pp. 155–76, at p. 172.

11 Conclusion: the power of contradiction

1 Address to the Federal Assembly, 16 May 2003, www.president.kremlin.ru/text/
appears/2003/05/44623.shtml.

2 http://bd.english.fom.ru/report/map/projects.

3 Cf. Glinski's comment three years earlier: 'For the overwhelming majority of
Russians ... the costs of transition to normalcy still clearly outweigh the

benefits ... ', Dmitri Glinksi, 'Waiting for a Democratic Left', PONARS Policy Memo No. 257, October 2002, p. 51.

4 Gleb Pavlovsky, 'Russia Can be Easily Provoked into Revolution', *Kommersant-Vlast'*, No. 26, 2000.

5 The point is made by Alexander Zinoviev, *Nezavisimaya gazeta*, 15 November 2000, p. 5.

6 Interview with Sergei Kovalev by Thomas Lubeck, in VI ICCEES World Congress News, 1 August 2000, p. 4.

7 For an early account of Putin as an unmitigated centraliser, see Julie A. Corwin, 'The New Centralizer', *Newsline*, 21 June 2000. She notes his typical tactics: 'unleashing federal bureaucrats, via a reorganised or somehow empowered federal organ, and letting loose law enforcement officials and making a few high level arrests – or at the very least, threatening to'.

8 Elena Tregubova, *Baiki kremlevskogo diggera* (Moscow, Ad Marginem, 2003), p. 147.

9 Egor Gaidar, *Gibel' imperii: uroki dlya sovremmennoi Rossii* (Moscow, Rosspen, 2006).

10 Juan J. Linz and Alfred Stepan, 'Toward Consolidated Democracies', *Journal of Democracy*, Vol. 7 (April 1996), p. 17.

11 Putin, *Razgovor s Rossiei*, p. 56.

12 Vladimir Pribylovsky, head of the Panorama Information-Research Centre, May 2003; in *JRL*, 7193/13.

13 www.kremlin.ru/text/appears/2005/04/87049.shtml; *Rossiiskaya gazeta*, 25 April 2005.

14 Claus Offe, 'Capitalism by Democratic Design: Democratic Theory Facing the Triple Transition in East Central Europe', *Social Research*, Vol. 58, No. 4, Winter 1991, pp. 865–902; also in Claus Offe, *Varieties of Transition: The East European and East German Experience* (Cambridge, Polity Press, 1996), pp. 29–49.

15 Ernest Gellner, *Conditions of Liberty: Civil Society and its Rivals* (New York, Viking, 1994).

16 As he put it, 'No bourgeois, no democracy'. Barrington Moore, Jr, *Social Origins of Dictatorship and Democracy: Lord and Peasant in the Making of the Modern World* (Harmondsworth, Peregrine, 1967), p. 418.

17 Cf. Aron's comments on Yeltsin, Leon Aron, *Boris Yeltsin: A Revolutionary Life* (London, HarperCollins, 2000), p. 734.

18 *Max Weber on Charisma and Institution Building*, Selected Papers, edited and with an introduction by S. N. Eisenstadt (Chicago and London, University of Chicago Press, 1968), p. 20.

19 Eduard Bernstein, *Evolutionary Socialism: The Classic Statement of Democratic Socialism* (New York, Shocken Books, 1961).

Select bibliography

Autobiography and speeches

Ezhegodnye poslaniya Prezidenta RF Federal'nomu sobraniyu, 1994–2005gg. (Novosibirsk, Sibirskoe universitetskoe izdatel'stvo, 2006).

Putin, Vladimir, *First Person: An Astonishingly Frank Self-Portrait by Russia's President Vladimir Putin*, with Nataliya Gevorkyan, Natalya Timakova, and Andrei Kolesnikov, translated by Catherine A. Fitzpatrick (London, Hutchinson, 2000).

Putin, Vladimir, *Ot pervogo litsa: Razgovory s Vladimirom Putinym*, with Nataliya Gevorkyan, Natal'ya Timakova and Andrei Kolesnikov (Moscow, Vagrius, 2000).

Putin, Vladimir, *Razgovor s Rossiei: Stenogramma "Pryamoi linii s Prezidentom Rossiiskoi Federatsii V. V. Putinym'*, 19 December 2002 (Moscow, Olma-Politizdat, 2003).

Biography

Blotskii, Oleg, *Vladimir Putin: istoriya zhizni*, Book 1 (Moscow, Mezhdunarodnye otnosheniya, 2002).

Blotskii, Oleg, *Vladimir Putin: doroga k vlasti*, Book 2 (Moscow, Mezhdunarodnye otnosheniya, 2002).

Bortsov, Yu. S., *Vladimir Putin* (Moscow and Rostov, Feniks, 2001).

Chadaev, Aleksei, *Putin: ego ideologiya* (Moscow, Evropa, 2006).

Charap, Samuel, 'The Petersburg Experience: Putin's Political Career and Russian Foreign Policy', *Problems of Post-Communism*, Vol. 51, No. 1 (January–February 2004), pp. 55–62.

Drozdov, Yurii and Vasilii Fartyshev, *Yurii Andropov i Vladimir Putin: na puti k vozrozhdeniyu* (Moscow, Olma-Press, 2001).

Gurevich, Vera, *Vospominaniya o budushchem prezidente* (Moscow, Mezhdunarodnye otnosheniya, 2001).

Gurevich, Vera, *Vladimir Putin: Roditeli. Druz'ya. Uchitelya*, 2nd edn (expanded) (St Petersburg, Izdatel'stvo Yuridichekogo instituta, 2004).

Medvedev, Roi, *Zagadka Putina* (Moscow, Prava cheloveka, 2000).

Medvedev, Roi, *Vremya Putina? Rossiya na rubezhe vekov* (Moscow, Prava Cheloveka, 2001).

Medvedev, Roi, *Vladimir Putin – Deistvuyushchii Prezident* (Moscow, Vremya, 2002).

Medvedev, Roi, *Vladimir Putin: Chetyre goda v Kremle* (Moscow, Vremya, 2004).

Mukhin, A. A., *Kto est' mister Putin i kto s nim prishel? Dos'e na Prezidenta Rossii i ego spetssluzhby* (Moscow, Centre for Political Information, 2002).

Mukhin, A. A., *Piterskoe okruzhenie prezidenta* (Moscow, Centre for Political Information, 2003).

Mukhin, A. A. and P. A. Kozlov, *"Semeinye" tainy ili neofitsial'nyi lobbizm v Rossii* (Moscow, Centre for Political Information, 2003).

Pitch, Iren, *Pikantnaya druzhba: moya podruga Lyudmila Putina, ee sem'ya i drugie tovarishchi* (Moscow, Zakharov, 2002); from the German, Irene Pietsch, *Heikle Freundschaften* (Vienna, Molden Verlag, 2001).

Rar, Aleksandr, *Vladimir Putin: 'Nemets' v Kremle*, translated from the German by I. Rozanov (Moscow, Olma-Press, 2001); Alexander Rahr, *Wladimir Putin: Der 'Deutsche' im Kreml*, 2nd edn (Munich, Universitas Publishing House, 2000).

Seiffert, Wolfgang, *Wladimir W. Putin: Wiedergeburt einer Weltmacht?* (Munich, Langen Müller, 2000).

Shevtsova, Lilia, 'Power and Leadership in Putin's Russia', in Andrew Kuchins (ed.), *Russia after the Fall* (Washington, DC, Carnegie Endowment for International Peace, 2002).

Strigin, Evgenii, *Vladimir Putin: Vnedrenie v kreml'* (Moscow, Algoritm, 2006).

Talanov, Viktor, *Psikhologicheskii portret Vladimira Putina* (St Petersburg, B & K, 2000).

Usol'tsev, Vladimir, *Sosluzhivets: Neizvestnye stranitsy zhizni prezidenta* (Moscow, Eksmo, 2004).

General analysis

Allison, Graham, 'Deepening Russian Democracy: Progress and Pitfalls in Putin's Government', *Harvard International Review*, Vol. 24, No. 2, 2002.

Avramchenko, R. F., *Put' Putina: Do prezidenta ili reformatora? Novaya kontseptsiya razvitiya Rossii* (Moscow, self-published, 2000).

Avramchenko, R. F., *Pokhoronit li Putin Rossiyu? Ideii i kontsepsii preobrazovaniya Rossii* (Moscow, Editorial URSS, 2001).

Baev, Pavel, 'The Evolution of Putin's Regime: Inner Circles and Outer Walls', *Problems of Post-Communism*, Vol. 51, No. 6, November/December 2004, pp. 3–13.

Balzer, Harley, 'Managed Pluralism: Vladimir Putin's Emerging Regime', *Post-Soviet Affairs*, Vol. 19, No. 3, 2003, pp. 189–227.

Balzer, Harley, 'The Putin Thesis and Russian Energy Policy', *Post-Soviet Affairs*, Vol. 21, No. 3, 2005, pp. 210–225.

Balzer, Harley, 'Vladimir Putin's Academic Writings and Russian Natural Resource Policy', *Problems of Post-Communism*, Vol. 53, No. 1, January–February 2006, pp. 48–54.

Barnes, A., 'Russia's New Business Groups and State Power', *Post-Soviet Affairs*, Vol. 19, No. 2, 2003, pp. 154–86.

Belkovskii, Stanislav and V. Golyshev, *Biznes Vladimira Putina* (Ekaterinburg, Ul'tra. Kul'tura, 2006).

Black, J. L., *Vladimir Putin and the New World Order: Looking East, Looking West?* (Lanham, MD, Rowman & Littlefield, 2003).

Brown, Archie, 'From Democratization to "Guided Democracy"', *Journal of Democracy*, Vol. 12, No. 4, October 2001, pp. 35–41.

Brown, Archie and Lilia Shevtsova (eds), *Gorbachev, Yeltsin, and Putin: Political Leadership in Russia's Transition* (Washington, DC, Carnegie Endowment for International Peace, 2001).

Chetyre goda s Putinym (Moscow, Vremya, 2004).

Colton, Timothy J. and Michael McFaul, *Are Russians Undemocratic?* (Carnegie Endowment for International Peace, Russian Domestics Politics Project, Russian and Eurasian Program, Working Paper No. 20, June 2001); republished in *Post-Soviet Affairs*, Vol. 18, No. 2, 2002, pp. 91–121.

Fartyshev, V. I., *Poslednii shans putina: Sud'ba Rossii v XXI veke* (Moscow, Veche, 2004).

Fedorov, Valerii and A. M. Tsuladze, *Epokha Putina* (Moscow, Eksmo, 2003).

Fish, M. Steven, 'Putin's Path', *Journal of Democracy*, Vol. 12, No. 4, October 2001, pp. 71–8.

Frye, Timothy, 'Markets, Democracy and New Private Business in Russia', *Post-Soviet Affairs*, Vol. 19, No. 1, 2003, pp. 24–45.

Garadzha, Nikita (ed.), *Suverenitet* (Moscow, Evropa, 2006).

Gel'man, Vladimir, 'From "Feckless Pluralism" to "Dominant Power Politics"? The Transformation of Russia's Party System', *Democratization*, Vol. 13, No. 4, August 2006, pp. 545–61.

Glaz'ev, Sergei, *Vybor budushchego* (Moscow, Algoritm, 2005).

Goldman, Marshall, 'Putin and the Oligarchs', *Foreign Affairs*, Vol. 83, No. 6 (November-December 2004), pp. 33–44.

Gorodetsky, Gabriel (ed.), *Russia Between East and West: Russian Foreign Policy on the Threshold of the Twenty-First Century* (London, Frank Cass Publishers, 2003).

Graham, Thomas, *Russia's Decline and Uncertain Recovery* (Washington, DC, Carnegie Endowment for International Peace, 2002).

Hanson, Stephen E., 'Can Putin Rebuild the Russian State', *Security Dialogue*, Vol. 32, No. 2, 2001, pp. 263–72.

Hashim, S. Mohsin, 'Putin's *Etatization* Project and Limits to Democratic Reforms in Russia', *Communist and Post-Communist Studies*, Vol. 38, 2005, pp. 25–48.

Hedlund, Stefan, 'Will the Russian Economy Revive under Putin?', *Problems of Post-Communism*, Vol. 48, No. 2, March/April 2001, pp. 54–62.

Herspring, Dale R. and Jacob Kipp, 'Understanding the Elusive Mr. Putin', *Problems of Post-Communism*, Vol. 48, No. 5, September/October 2001, pp. 3–17.

Herspring, Dale R. (ed.), *Putin's Russia: Past Imperfect, Future Uncertain*, 3rd edn (Lanham, MD, Rowman & Littlefield, 2006).

Hoffman, David E., *The Oligarchs: Wealth and Power in the New Russia* (New York, Public Affairs, 2002).

Hyde, Matthew, 'Putin's Federal Reforms and their Implications for Presidential Power in Russia', *Europe-Asia Studies*, Vol. 53, No. 5, 2001, pp. 719–43.

Ivanov, Vitalii, *Putin i regiony: Tsentralizatsiya rossii* (Moscow, Evropa, 2006).

Jack, Andrew, *Inside Putin's Russia* (London, Granta, 2004).

Karaganov, S. A. *et al.*, *Strategiya dlya Rossii:Ppovestka dnya dlya prezidenta – 2000* (Moscow, Vagrius, 2000).

Kaspe, S. I., 'Tsentr i vertikal': Politicheskaya priroda putinskogo prezidentstva', *Politiya*, No. 4 (22), Winter 2001–2, pp. 5–24.

Klebnikov, Paul, *Godfather of the Kremlin: Boris Berezovsky and the Looting of Russia* (New York, Harcourt Brace, 2000); translated into Russian as Pavel Khlebnikov, *Krestnyi otets Kremlya Boris Berezovskii ili Istoriya razgrableniya Rossii* (Moscow, Detektiv-Press, 2001).

Knight, Amy, 'The Enduring Legacy of the KGB in Russian Politics', *Problems of Post-Communism*, Vol. 47, No. 4, July/August 2000, pp. 3–15.

Knight, Amy and B. A. Ruble, 'The Two Worlds of Vladimir Putin', *The Wilson Quarterly*, Vol. 24, No. 2, 2000.

Kokoshin, A. A., *Real'nyi suverenitet v sovremennoi miropoliticheskoi sisteme* (Moscow, URSS, 2006).

Kolesnikov, Andrei, *Vladimir Putin: Elitnoe podrazdelenie* (Moscow, Eksmo, 2005).

Kolesnikov, Andrei, *Vladimir Putin: Ravnoudalenie oligarkhov* (Moscow, Eksmo, 2005).

Kolosov, V. A. (ed.), *Mir glazami rossiyan: Mify i vneshnyaya politika* (Moscow, Institut fonda 'Obshchestvennoe mnenie', 2003).

Konovalenko, D. N. (ed.), *Portret storonnika Putina: Nakanune 2008 goda* (Moscow, Evropa, 2005).

Korolev, Yurii, *Za kremlevskoi stenoi* (Moscow, Novyi Vek, 2003).

Kovalev, Sergei, 'Putin's War', *New York Review of Books*, Vol. 47, No. 2, 10 February 2000, pp. 6–8.

Kryshtanovskaya, Olga, *Anatomiya Rossiiskoi elity* (Moscow, Zakharov, 2005).

Kryshtanovkaya, Olga and Stephen White, 'Putin's Militocracy', *Post-Soviet Affairs*, Vol. 19, No. 4, October–December 2003, pp. 289–306.

Kryshtanovkaya, Olga and Stephen White, 'Inside the Putin Court: A Research Note', *Europe-Asia Studies*, Vol. 57, No. 7, November 2005, pp. 1065–75.

Kuchins, Andrew, *Russia after the Fall* (Washington, DC, Carnegie Endowment for International Peace, 2002).

Limonov, Eduard, *Takoi president nam ne nuzhen!* (Moscow, [no publisher indicated], 2005).

Lo, Bobo, *Vladimir Putin and the Evolution of Russian Foreign Policy* (Oxford, Blackwell Publishing and the Royal Institute of International Affairs, 2003).

Lukin, Alexander, 'Putin's Regime: Restoration or Revolution?', *Problems of Post-Communism*, Vol. 48, No. 4, July/August 2000, pp. 38–48.

Lupan, V., *Russkii vyzov*, translated and with an introduction by A. Zinoviev (Moscow, Terra, 2001); Victor Loupan, *Le défi Russe* (Paris, Editions des Syrtes, 2001).

Lyne, Roderic, Strobe Talbott and Koji Watanabe, *Engaging with Russia: The Next Phase*, a report to The Trilateral Commission (Washington, Paris, Tokyo, The Trilateral Commission, 2006).

McFaul, Michael, 'Putin in Power', *Current History*, No. 99, October 2000, pp. 307–14.

Maly, Matvei, *Kak sdelat' Rossiyu normal'noi stranoi?* (St Petersburg, Dmitrii Bulanin, 2003).

Matsuzato, Kimitaka (ed.), *Fenomen Vladimira Putina i Rossiiskie regiony:Ppobeda neozhidannaya ili zakonomernaya?*, Slavic-Eurasian Studies, Vol. 1, Centre for Slavic Studies, Hokkaido University (Moscow, Materik, 2004).

Mazo, Boris, *Piterskie protiv Moskovskikh, ili kto est' kto v okruzhenii V. V. Putina* (Moscow, Eksmo Algoritm, 2003).

Mazo, Boris, *Preemnik Putina, ili Kogo my budem vybirat' v 2008 godu* (Moscow, Algoritm, 2005).

Mendelson, Sarah E., 'The Putin Path: Civil Liberties and Human Rights in Retreat', *Problems of Post-Communism*, Vol. 47, No. 5, September/October 2000, pp. 3–12.

Mlechin, Leonid, *Kreml' prezidenty Rossii: Strategiya vlasti ot B. N. El'tsina do V. V. Putina* (Moscow, Tsentrpoligraf, 2002).

Mlechin, Leonid, *KGB predsedateli organov gosbezopasnosti: Rassekrechennye sud'by* (Moscow, Tsentrpoligraf, 2002).

Moore, Robert, *A Time to Die: The Kursk Disaster* (New York, Doubleday, 2002).

Mukhin, A. A., *Novye pravila igry dlya bol'shogo biznesa, prodiktovannye logikoi pravleniya V. V. Putina* (Moscow, Tsentr politicheskoi informatsii, 2002).

Mukhin, A. A., *Rossiiskaya organizovannaya prestupnost' i vlast': Istoriya vzaimootnoshenii* (Moscow, Tsentr politicheskoi informatsii, 2003).

Mukhin, A. A., *'Osobaya papka' Vladimira Putina: Itogi pervogo prezidentskogo sroka I otnosheniya s krupnymi sobstvennikami* (Moscow, Tsentr politicheskoi informatsii, 2004).

Mukhin, A. A., *Mikhail Kas'yanov: Moskovskii otvet 'piterskim'* (Moscow, Algoritm, 2005).

Parvulesko, Zhan (Jean Parvulesco), *Putin i evraziiskaya imperiya*, transl. from French (St. Petersburg, Amfora, 2006).

Pechenov, Vadim, *Vladimir Putin – poslednii shans Rossii?* (Moscow, Infra-M, 2001).

Politkovskaya, Anna, *A Dirty War: A Russian Reporter in Chechnya*, Introduction by Thomas de Waal, translated by John Crowfoot (London, The Harvill Press, 2001).

Politkovskaya, Anna, *A Small Corner of Hell*, translated by Alexander Burry and Tatiana Tulchinsky (Chicago, IL, University of Chicago Press Pounds, 2003).

Politkovskaya, Anna, *Putin's Russia* (London, Harvill, 2004).

Politkovskaya, Anna, *Putin's Russia: Life in a Failing Democracy* (New York, Metropolitan, 2006).

Popova, Tat'yana, *Nord-Ost glazami zalozhnitsy* (Moscow, Vagrius, 2002).

Portret storonnika putina nakanune 2008 goda (Moscow, Evropa, 2005).

Reddaway, Peter, 'Will Putin Be Able to Consolidate Power?', *Post-Soviet Affairs*, Vol. 17, No. 1, 2001, pp. 23–44.

Reddaway, Peter, 'Is Putin's Power More Formal than Real?', *Post-Soviet Affairs*, Vol. 18, No. 1, 2002, pp. 31–40.

Reddaway, Peter and Robert W. Orrtung (eds), *The Dynamics of Russian Politics: Putin's Reform of Federal–Regional Relations*, Vol. 1 (Lanham, MD, Rowman & Littlefield, 2003).

Reitschuster, Boris, *Wladimir Putin* (Berlin, Rowohlt, 2004).

Remington, Thomas F., 'Putin and the Duma', *Post-Soviet Affairs*, Vol. 17, No. 4, 2001, pp. 285–308.

Renz, Bettina, 'Putin's Militocracy? An Alternative Interpretation of *Siloviki* in Contemporary Russian Politics', *Europe-Asia Studies*, Vol. 58, No. 6, September 2006, pp. 903–24.

Rivera, Sharon Werning and David W. Rivera, 'The Russian Elite under Putin: Militocratic or Bourgeois?', *Post-Soviet Affairs*, Vol. 22, No. 2, April–June 2006, pp. 125–44.

Rose, Richard, Neil Munro, and Stephen White, 'How Strong is Vladimir Putin's Support?', *Post-Soviet Affairs*, Vol. 16, No. 4, 2000, pp. 287–312.

Rose, Richard and Neil Munro, *Elections without Order: Russia's Challenge to Vladimir Putin* (Cambridge, Cambridge University Press, 2002).

Rose, Richard, Neil Munro and William Mishler, 'Resigned Acceptance of an Incomplete Democracy: Russia's Political Equilibrium', *Post-Soviet Affairs*, Vol. 20, No. 3, July–September 2004, pp. 195–218.

Rutland, Peter, 'Putin's Path to Power', *Post-Soviet Affairs*, Vol. 16, No. 4, 2000, pp. 313–54.

Sakwa, Richard, *Russian Politics and Society*, 3rd edn (London and New York, Routledge, 2002).

Sharlet, Robert, 'Putin and the Politics of Law in Russia', *Post-Soviet Affairs*, Vol. 17, No. 3, 2001, pp. 195–234.

Sheremet, Pavel, *Piterskie tainy Vladimira Yakovleva* (Moscow, Partizan, 2005).

Shestopal, E. B., *Obrazy vlasti v post-sovetskoi Rossii* (Moscow, Aleteia, 2004).

Shevtsova, Lilia, *Putin's Russia* (Washington, DC, Carnegie Endowment for International Peace, 2003).

Shevtsova, Lilia, *Putin's Legacy: How the Russian Elite is Coping with Russia's Challenges* (Washington, DC, Carnegie Endowment for International Peace, 2006).

Shleifer, Andrei and Daniel Treisman, 'A Normal Country', *Foreign Affairs*, Vol. 83, No. 2, March/April 2004.

Shlapentokh, Vladimir, 'Putin's First Year in Office: The New Regime's Uniqueness in Russian History', *Communist and Post-Communist Studies*, Vol. 34, No. 4, December 2001, pp. 371–99.

Shlapentokh, Vladimir, 'Hobbes and Locke at Odds in Putin's Russia', *Europe-Asia Studies*, Vol. 55, No. 7, November 2003, pp. 981–1008.

Simonsen, Sven Gunnar, 'Putin's Leadership Style: Ethnocentric Patriotism', *Security Dialogue*, Vol. 31, No. 3, 2000, pp. 377–80.

Stepankov, Viktor, *Bitva za "Nord-Ost" (Moscow, Yauza/Eksmo, 2003)*.

Stepankov, Viktor, *Leningradtsy v bor'be za Kreml'* (Moscow, Yauza, 2004).

Talbott, Strobe, *The Russia Hand: A Memoir of Presidential Diplomacy* (New York, Random House, 2002).

Telen', Lyudmila, *Pokolenie putina: Portrety-intervyu* (Moscow, Vagrius, 2004).

Tikhomirov, Vladimir (ed.), *Russia After Yeltsin* (Aldershot, Ashgate, 2001).

Tompson, William, 'Putin's Challenge: The Politics of Structural Reform in Russia', *Europe-Asia Studies*, Vol. 54, No. 6, September 2002, pp. 933–58.

Tregubova, Elena, *Baiki kremlevskogo diggera* (Moscow, Ad Marginem, 2003).

Trenin, Dmitry, *Integratsiya i identichnost': Rossiya kak 'novyi zapad'* (Moscow, Evropa, 2006).

Tret'yakov, Vitalii, *Nuzhen li nam Putin posle 2008 goda? Sbornik statei* (Moscow, Rossiiskaya gazeta, 2005).

Troshev, Gennadii, *Moya voina: Chechenskii dnevnik okopnogo generala* (Moscow, Vagrius, 2001).

Truscott, Peter, *Kursk: Russia's Lost Pride* (London, Simon & Schuster, 2003).

Truscott, Peter, *Putin's Progress* (London, Simon and Schuster, 2004).

Tsygankov, Andrei P., 'Vladimir Putin's Vision of Russia as a Normal Great Power', *Post-Soviet Affairs*, Vol. 21, No. 2, 2005, pp. 132–58.

Tyukov, N. *Vlastnye vertikali: Pravitel'stvo, administratsyiya prezidenta, sovet bezopasnosti i federal'nye okruga*, 2nd edn (Moscow, SPIK-Tsentr, 2001).

Utkin, Anatolii, *Bol'shaya vos'merka: Tsena vkhozhdeniya* (Moscow, Algoritm, 2006).

Yur'ev, Dmitrii, *Rezhim Putina: Postdemokratiya* (Moscow, Evropa, 2005).

Verkhovskii, A., E. Mikhailovskaya and V. Pribylovskii, *Rossiya Putina: Pristrastnyi vzglyad* (Moscow, Tsentr 'Panorama', 2003).

Index

9/11 (United States) 61, 99, 142, 143,
  230, 280, 281, 289, 291, 294,
Abkhazia 224, 230, 273, 274, 295, 296
Abramovich, Roman 20, 28, 72, 147,
  148, 248, 258
Administrative Violations Code 156
advokatura 156
Adygeya 202, 204, 207
Aeroflot 144, 145
Afghanistan 35, 229, 261, 280, 281, 289
Agency of Regional Political Studies
  (ARPI) 85
Akaev, Askar 173, 295, 297
AKS Sistema 251
Aksenenko, Nikolai 74
Albats, Yevgeniya 73
Alekseeva, Ludmila 173, 180
Aleksii II, Patriarch 225, 226, 227
Aliev, Mukhu 204, 239
Alkhanov, Alu 236, 237
All Russia (*Vsya Rossiya*) political
  block 24, 102
All-Russia Civic Congress 180
Altai Republic and Altai Krai 207
alternative civilian service (ACS) 160
Andijan 297
Andropov, Yury 7, 8, 14, 40, 74, 78, 93,
  257
arbitration courts 156
arbitrazh courts 155, 157
Armenia 230, 294, 296
Aslakhanov, Aslambek 232
August putsch (1991) 221, 222
Aushev, Ruslan 203, 211
authoritarianism 30, 39, 40, 50, 63, 74,
  75, 78, 88, 91, 97, 130, 138, 141, 158,
  161, 180, 204, 279, 290, 300, 306,
  309, 324; conservative 97; liberal 97;
  Putin's 41, 60, 63, 87, 92, 93, 97, 145,

  161, 195, 207, 300, 301, 305; regional
  186, 187, 192, 194, 203, 212, 297
Avisma 258
Avtovaz 144, 146, 252, 258, 261
Ayatskov, Dmitry 200
Azerbaijan 230, 294

Babakov, Alexander 107, 125, 182
Babitsky, Andrei 150, 151
Baburin, Sergei 125
Baikal, Lake 263
Balcerowicz, Leszek 48
Baraev, Movsar 89
Barkashov, Alexander 182
Basaev, Shamil 21, 89, 229, 234, 237,
  killed 238
Bashkortostan 115, 188, 190, 199, 200,
  201, 204, 205, 229
Belarus oil pipeline crisis 298
Belarus 72, 73, 91, 92, 93, 129, 173–74,
  293, 296, 297–98
Bellona (group) 159, 263
Bem, Horst 9
Berdyaev, Nikolai 39
Berezovsky, Boris 20, 58, 71, 72, 92,
  105, 114, 116, 144, 152,153, 249;
  attitudes towards Putin and Duma
  145–46, 148, 174; and Litvinenko 159
Berlin Wall 1, 9
Beslan events 63, 89, 117, 118, 141,
  142–43, 153, 157, 164, 169, 233, 236,
  237, 239, 278, 279, 297
Black Sea Fleet 224
Blavatnik,Leonard 248
Blotsky 4, 5
Blowing up Russia 159
Bolsheviks 39
bombing campaign, 1996 21, 223
Border Guard Service 78

Bordyuzha, Nicolai 14, 18
Borodin, Pavel 13, 26, 72, 151
BP 251
Brezhnev, Leonid 5, 47, 50, 51, 301, 308, 316
Brezhnev doctrine 297
Brown, Archie 91
Burbulis, Gennady 274
bureaucracy, growth of, Russia 163, 164
bureaucratisation 163
Bush, George W. 273, 279–80

capitalism, Russian 98, Chapter 9, 303, 311; bureaucratic capitalism 143, 179, 179, 180; corporate 313; crony capitalism 314; democratic 52, 300; Russian transition to 15, 45, 179, 242; models of 249ff, 262; nomenklatura capitalism 71, 72, 315; oligarchs and 44, 143, 147, 150, 164, 255–59, 265, 305; predatory capitalism 264; Putin and 40, 42, 95, 265; Yeltsin and 38, 52
Carnegie Moscow Centre 72
Caucasus, north 89–90, 164, 184, 201, 202, 227–28, 230, 12, 234, 237, 238, 239
Central Bank (Russia) 243, 247
Central Electoral Commission (CEC) 29, 104, 109, 118, 121
Centre for Strategic Studies 31, 52, 56
Chadaev, Aleksei 41
chaebol 259
Chaika, Yury 158
Chechen-Ingush Republic 207
Chechenisation 235ff
Chechnya 30, 33, 80, 88, 89, 149, 150, 156, 159, 161, 166, 172, 189, 200, 201, 202, 239, 227ff, 263, 271. 281, 290, 304; Chechenisation 201, 233, 235–37, 238, *see also* Dagestan; comparison to My Lai incident 231; and independence 187, 188, 229, 238, 273, 296, 290; Putin and 33, 34, 35, 62, 92, 143, 179, 223ff, 228–30, 232–33, 235, 236, 290, 314; Ella Pamfilova and 160
Chechen War 20–22, 27, 34, 27–28, 76, 87, 88, 151, 203, 223, 228, 230 passim, 237, 274, 277, 276, 277, 314
Cheka 74
chekisty 74, 76, 313
Chemezov, Sergei 258
Cheney, Dick 64

Cherkesov, Victor 14, 75, 76
Chernobyl 263
Chernomyrdin, Viktor 11, 16, 18, 118
China 160, 183, 240, 251, 265, 290–92, 293, 298, 303, 318; border arrangements with Russian regions 191; economy of, compared to Russian 53, 77, 78, 245, 268, 318; oil Yukos pipeline to 147; relations with Russia 272, 278, 291–92
chinovniks 163
Chizhova, Tamara 3
Christian Democratic Union 105
Chubais, Anatoly 11, 33, 113, 115, 246
Chuev, Alexander 105
Chuvashia 211
Civic Forum 167ff
Civil Liberties Foundation 146
civil society 167
clan system and political structure 81–82
Clark, Wesley 17
Clinton, Bill 279
Cold War, second 5, 40; post-Cold War world 57, 267, 272ff, 274, 290
Collective Security Treaty Organisation (CSTO) 295, 296
Committee 2008 115, 180
Common Economic Space 296–97
Common Foreign and Security Policy 288
Commonwealth of Independent States (CIS) 83, 230, 271, 273, 274, 279, 294, 296, 298
Communist Party of the Russian Federation (CPRF) 23–24, 54, 106, 116, 118–19, 124, 125, 126, 129, 135, 178, 181, 183, 205, 219, 223
Congress of Russian Communities (KRO) 113
Congress of the Chechen Peoples 235
constitution, Russian 134, 155, 187, 192, 194, 195, 203, 222, 274–75, 301
Constitutional Court 121, 155, 156, 158, 192, 193, 198, 204; interpretation of state sovereignty 198–99, 212
constrained great powerism (*derzhavnost'*) 278
Conventional Forces in Europe (CFE) Treaty 67, 294–95
corruption 12, 14, 23, 27, 29, 57, 58–59, 68, 69, 103, 145, 149, 138, 151, 155, 158, 162ff, 164, 165–67, 178, 180–81, 188, 198, 228, 233, 238, 257, 243–44,

262, 274, 285, alleged 198, Yeltsin
and 26, 34, 38, 39, 84; Putin,
attitudes towards 23, 38, 44, 60, 63,
64, 87, 96, 98, 139–40, 147, 165, 247,
301; charges against Putin 11;
various Russian politicians 13
Corruption Perceptions Index 165
Council for Foreign and Defence Policy
(CFDP) 57
Council of Europe 157, 277;
Parliamentary Assembly of the
Council of Europe (PACE) 159, 218
Council of Legislators 199
Council on National Projects 131
CPRF 111, 114
CPSU 2, 11
Crimea 34, 224
Criminal Procedure Code (UPK) 123,
155–56, 157
Crisis of Russian Liberalism, The,
(Khodorkovsky) 113
Czechoslovakia, invasion of (1968) 6, 7,
49, 50

Dagestan 21, 32, 89, 115, 150, 188, 192,
204, 228, 229, 230, 233, 238
Dahrendorf, Ralf 43, 52
Danilov, Valentin 160
Danilov-Danilyan, Viktor 263
Davos economic forum 37
Day of National Unity 221
De Gaulle, Charles 52, 90, 127, 136, 277
democracy 40–41, 44, 49–50, 52;
categories of 50, Russian 50, 81,
83–84, 95–98, 134, 135, 178, 195,
269, 307; Putin and 300, statist 79ff, 95
Democratic Choice 107
Deng Xiaoping 290
Depretis, Agostino 177–78
Deripaska, Oleg 147, 148
dictatorship of the law (Putin term) 40,
138–39, 141, 195
Dignity and Honour (veterans'
association) 78
Djilas, Milovan 81
Doha Round 261
Dorenko, Sergei 151
Dubrovka theatre siege 88–89, 115,
152, 235
Dugin, Alexander 185
Duma 33, 59, 86, 101, 104, 105, 123,
125ff, 148, 157, 159, 160, 179, 191,
197, 198, 203, 210, 219, 224; elections
to 110–11, 119–21; 1999, elections

23, 25, 26, 32, 95, 101, 124, 216, 223;
2003 elections 62, 103, 110, 111–15,
116, 117, 119, 125, 135; 2004
electoral reform 117–23, 124; 2005
Council of the Duma 124; imperative
mandate 125; and Kyoto 263;
pluralism in 134; and Public
Chamber 169–70, 171; and Putin 19,
96, 200
Durkheim, Emile 41
Dyachenko, Tatyana 20, 72
Dzerzhinsky, Feliks 74
Dzhabrailov, Umar 30

East Siberian-Pacific Ocean (ESPO)
pipeline 263–64, 281
Eatwell, Roger 91
Ekho Moskvy radio station 152
elections, Russia Chapter 4; abolition
of minimum turnout 122; fraud in
114–15; presidential 2004 116–17
Elections, Russian, 1999 23, reform
117ff
Electoral law, Russian 109–10, 114, 119
elites, continuity of in Russia 50
Energy Charter Treaty 304
Eurasia and Eurasianism 185, 216, 218,
224, 227, 236. 254, 267, 269, 270,
272, 273, 277, 279, 288, 290,293
passim, 312
Eurasia Party 185
Eurasian Economic Community
(EAEC/EvrAsEs or EurAsEc) 182,
295, 296
Euro-Asian Alliance of Youth 182
European Convention on Human
Rights 41
European Court of Human Rights 127
European Neighbourhood Policy
(ENP) 273
European Security and Defence Policy
288
European Union 83, 113, 243, 245, 263,
279; Russian relations with EU 61,
112, 246, 247, 261, 272, 273, 274,
276, 277, 285–89, 291, 293; Russian
and EU economies compared 268;
Single European Act (1986) 297
Evdokimov, Mikhail 184

FAPSI 78
Fatherland (*Otechestvo*) movement 24,
30, 102
Fatherland party 80

Fatherland-All Russia 106
Federal Anti-Narcotics Service (FSKN) 76
Federal Assembly 59, 62, 64, 75, 92, 103, 123; Putin speeches to 150, 151–52, 163, 164, 168, 173
Federal Border Service 18
federal districts 196
Federal Registration Service (FRS) 105, 106, 174
federalism, new, Russian 192ff, fiscal 201
federalism, purposes of 212–13
Federation Council 104, 107, 123, 125, 158, 172, 197, 198, 303
Federation of Independent Trade Unions of Russia 257
Fedorov, Boris 223–24
Fedorov, Nikolai 211
Financial Action Task Force (FATF) 246
financial industrial conglomerate FIC 250, 254, 255, 256, 257
financial-industrial group (FIG) 250
First Department (of KGB) (*Pervoe glavnoe upravlenie, PGU*) 8
First Person (Putin) 194, 211
Foreign Agents Registration Act (US) 174
foreign direct investment (FDI) 53
Foreign Intelligence Service (SVR) 10, 14
Foreign Policy Concept (Russia) 271, 272
Forward, Russia! 223
Foundation for Effective Politics 28
Fradkov, Mikhail 117, 131, 133, 158, 248
Fridman, Mikhail 148, 170, 251, 252, 253, 170, 251
FSB (Federal Security Service) 1, 14, 19, 21, 74, 75, 78, 149, 157, 159, 160, 189, 203, 263, in Chechnya 232, *see also* Putin

Gaidar, Yegor 24–25, 159, 304
Gavrin, Alexander 73, 263
Gazprom and Gazprom-Media 130, 131, 136, 144, 151, 152, 153, 246, 253, 258, 259
Gazprominvestholding 153
Gel'man, Vladimir 176
Georgia 153, 230, 274, 277, 294, 295
German Democratic Republic (GDR) 1, 9–10, 40, 258

Germany 53, 158, 206, 217, 218, 265, 277, 278, 282, 297, 298, 312
Giddens, Anthony 97, 98
glasnost' 217
Glaz'ev, Sergei 113, 116, 178, 248
GONGO 168
Gorbachev, Mikhail 5, 6, 37, 38, 50, 57, 71, 75, 129, 139, 217, 218, 219, 262, 268; 281, 3012, 302; contrasted to Putin 47, 270; and East Germany 9, 10; and law course 7, 15; period of office 270, 302; *see also* perestroika
Gorno-Altai, sovereignty declaration 198–99
Gorodnicheva, Yulia 170
gosudarstvenniki 223
government bonds, Russian 241
Govorukhin, Stanislav 29
great power nationalism (*derzhavnost'*) 41, 279, 314
Gref, German 31, 52, 56, 79, 131, 153, 246, 260
GRINGO 168, 175
Grishankov, Mikhail 165
Group of Eight (G8) 54, 57, 64, 180, 262, 276
Grozny 21, 22, 89, 231, 233, 237
GRU (Military Intelligence) 237
Gryzlov, Boris 133
GUAM 294–95
Gurevich, Vera 3, 4
Gusinsky, Vladimir 16, 20, 144, 146, 148, 149, 151
Gutseriev, Khamzad 203

Hahn, Gordon 50
Hashimoto, Ryutaro 293
Haviv Abd al-Rahman (Khattab) 21, 227
Honecker, Erich 9
human rights 159–60
Huntington, Samuel 51, 71
Husak, Gustav 50
hydroelectric scheme, Irkutsk 261

Illarionov, Andrei 56, 247, 248, 228
Ilyukhin, Victor 201
Ilyumzhinov, Kirsan 192
IMF 241, 242
Indem Foundation 165, 180
Independence Day, becoming Russia Day 221
Infrastructure Investment Fund 131

Ingushetia 89, 203
interior ministry (MVD) 78, 149, 183, 188, 232, 237, 238
Interros 146
Ivanov, Alexander 153
Ivanov, Ivan 272, 274, 277–78
Ivanov, Sergei 14, 75, 79, 131–32, 133, 153
Ivashov, Leonid 76
Izvestiya 146, 153

Jackson, Mike 17
Japan 56, 107, 137, 157, 217, 245, 251, 256, 293, 303, 319
John Paul II, Pope 225
Jordan, Boris 152
Jowitt, Kenneth 97
judicial system reform 126
Judicial system, Russia 155ff
Judiciary, independence of 199–200
jury trials 156
Just Russia (JR, *Spravedlivaya Rossiya*) 102, 119, 122–23, 125, 134, 182, 205

Kabardino-Balkaria 202
Kadyrov, Akhmad 231, 232, 235, 237
Kadyrov, Ramzan 201, 235
Kaliningrad 7, 113, 172, 189, 191, 192, 287, 288
Kalugin, Oleg 151
Kalyuzhny, Viktor 20, 73
Kandaurov, Alexei 114
Karachaevo-Cherkessia 144
Karaganov, Sergei 57–59
Karelia 191, 221
Karimov, Islam 23, 130, 297
Karpov, Anatoly 170
Kasparov, Gari 115, 176, 180
Kasyanov, Mikhail 57, 72–73, 74, 79, 105, 117, 124, 248, 260
Katyrin, Sergei 171
Kavkaz Centre 238
Kazakhstan 67, 81, 166, 183, 292, 293, 296, 297
Kerensky, Alexander 7, 15
KGB (Committee for State Security) 1, 5, 6, 7, 38, 74, 77, 78, 188, 258; office in Germany 9–10; Putin and 8, 73, 219, 301; *see also* Vladimir Putin, FSB
Khakamada, Irina 115
Khanty-Mansiisk 191
Kharitonov, Nikolai 116
Khasavyurt Accord 20, 229, 230, 234

Khasbulatov, Ruslan 234
Khattab see Haviv Abd al-Rahman
Khinstein, Alexander 150, 151
Khloponin, Alexander 133, 202
Khodorkovsky, Mikhail 60, 74, 113, 114, 115, 127, 146–47, 152, 173, 175, 253, 304
Khrushchev, Nikita 6, 47, 222
Kirienko, Sergei 71, 112, 165, 241
Kiselev, Yevgeny 115, 151, 152
Klebanov, Ilya 88
Klebnikov, Paul 154
Kola peninsula 263
Kolakowski, Leszek 313
Kolosov, Vladimir 215–16
Kommersant-daily 151
kompromat 73
Komsomol 4, 7
Kondopoga incident 221
Korzhakov, Alexander 24
Kosovo war 191, 291
Kosovo 16, 224, 227, 272, 273, 280, 289, 290, 295–96
Kovalev, Sergei 301
Kozak, Dmitry 73, 78–79, 133, 155, 164, 202; Kozak reforms 157–58, 208, 238
Kozlov, Andrei 251
Kozma, Petr 72
Kozyrev, Andrei 48, 275
Kremlin, Moscow (metonym) 13, 20, 26, 27, 30, 75, 127, 147, 149, 152, 170, 255; Chechen strategy 231, 235; and control of TV 153–54; and oligarchs 313; and opposition 176, 182
Krupskaya, Nadezhda 2, 3
Kuchma, Leonid 273, 297
Kudrin, Alexei 11, 13, 79, 131
Kurile Islands 293
Kursk submarine 88
Kvashnin, General Anatoly 76
Kyoto Protocol 261, 263
Kyrgyzstan 173, 228, 292, 295, 296

Labour Code 264
Laden, Osama bin 230
Land Code 179, 264
Latynina, Yulia 27, 212
Lavrov, Sergei 159
Law on Political Parties (2001) 14
Law on Regions 190
Lebed, Alexander 18, 20–21, 30
Lebedev, Platon 147

Lebedev, Vyacheslav 199–200
Legitimism 45ff
Lenin, Vladimir 2, 7, 15, 93, 97, 212,
    221, 222, 229; possible reburial of
    220; symbolism of 220; Leninist
    legacy 97
Leningrad (now St Petersburg, *which
    also see*) 1, 2–3, 8, 10, 54, 74, 75, 76
Leningrad State University (LGU) 7, 8,
    10
Levada, Yuri 115
Liberal Democratic Party of Russia
    (LDPR) 29, 108, 118, 126, 183
Liberal Russia (party) 92, 105, 146
liberals, economic 79
Limanski, Georgy 123
Limonov, Eduard 183
Litvinenko, Alexander 158–59
Logovaz 144
Lubyanka 40, 78, 175, 226–27
Lukashenko, Alexander 91, 130, 173–74,
    290, 297–98
Lukin, Vladimir 161, 224
Lukoil 144, 146, 250, 252, 254 255, 258,
    263
Luzhkov, Yury 20, 24, 28, 30, 34, 74,
    80, 93, 101, 102, 151, 201, 224, 251

Magomedov, Magomedali 239
Main Control Directorate (GKU),
    Kremlin 13
Mainwaring, Scott 103
Makhashev, Kazbek 234
Malashenko, Igor 151
Maly, Matvei 41
Malyshkin, Oleg 117
Mamut, Alexander 72
MANGO 168
Markov, Sergei 80, 97, 168
Marxism 310
Maskhadov, Aslan 21, 229, 231, 234,
    237; death 238, 239
Maslyukov, Yury 71
Matvienko, Valentina 80, 91
Mau, Vladimir 56
Mayak nuclear plant 263
Media-Most 144, 146, 149
Medvedev, Dmitry 79, 130, 131, 132,
    133, 156, 258
Memorial (group) 159, 218
Menatep 147
Merzoev, Gazen 170
middle class 80–81
Military Doctrine (Russia) 271

military, Russian 76–78
military, spending on 77
Millennium Manifesto (Putin, 1999) 31,
    45, 46, 52, 55, 59, 96, 140, 215, 216,
    228; text of 317ff
Milošević, Slobodan 173, 214, 274
Milyukov, Paul 176
Ministry of International Trade and
    Industry (MITI), Japan 56
Ministry of Natural Resources 262
Mironov, Oleg 160–61
Mironov, Sergei 79, 107–8, 133, 198,
    201–2
Mitrokhin, Sergei 35
Mitvol, Oleg 264
Modrow, Hans 10
Moldova 214, 235, 274, 287, 294, 295
Moltenskoi, Colonel General Vladimir
    232
Mommsen 40
Moscow (metonym) 10, 11, 38, 54, 158,
    163, 170, 184, 187, 190, 202, 230, 297
Moscow Bar Association 157
Moscow city 192
Moscow consensus 242
Moscow Helsinki Group 159, 173, 180
Moskalenko, Karina 88–89
Moskovsky komsomolets 151
Movement Against Illegal Immigration
    (DPNI) 181, 221
Mukhin 15
Muravlenko, Sergei 114
Muslim Central Spirtual Board, Ufa
    191
MVD 149, 183

Nagorno-Karabakh 230, 294
Nalchik 238
Napoleon Bonaparte 70
Nashi movement 173, 183
National Bolshevik Party 186
National Democratic Union 105
national identity, Russian 223ff
National Security Concept 271
nationalism 95, 224
Nato 67, 76, 272, 274, 279, 288;
    enlargement 67, 76, 271, 281, 289–90
    294, 296; Russia and 272, 273, 277,
    284
Nazdratenko, Yevgeny 17, 192, 198,
    203
Nemtsov, Boris 11, 113, 115, 148, 178–80
neo-Sovietism 39, 315
Nevzlin, Leonid 115, 147

New Economic Policy 249
Nezavisimaya gazeta 153
NGO 63, 106, 166, 167–68, 170, 171, 173ff
Nikitin, Alexander 150, 159, 263
nomenklatura 70, 71, 72, 84, 140, 315
Norilsk Nickel 144, 148
normalcy/normalisation 42–45, 47ff, 69, 83, 310ff
North Ossetia 89
NTV station 20, 148, 149, 151, 152, 153, 154
Nurgaliev, Rashid 237

Obshchaya gazeta 151
OECD 246
oligarchs 11, 16, 20, 24, 72, 143–50, 153, 241, 304, 313; under Yeltsin 249; Putin and 249, 261, 314; Putin's campaign against 143 passim, list 252–53
On Counteracting Extremist Activity (Putin law) 171
one-party system 180
Open Letter by Vladimir Putin to the Russian Voters 31
Open Russia Foundation 173
opposition, Russia 24, 27, 35, 93, 107, 112, 115, 116, 121, 124ff, Chapter 6, 194; communist 24, 33, 118, 211, 255, 306, 324; Putin and 63, 85, 146, 149, 178, 180, 183, 324
Orange Revolution (Ukraine) 121, 131, 146, 173, 273, 277, 295
Ordnungspolitik 51
Organisation for Security and Co-operation in Europe (OSCE) 112, 114, 118, 119, 234, 271, 277, 294–95
Organisation of Entrepreneurs' Organisations of Russia (Ob'edineinie predprinimatel'skikh organizatsii Rossi, OPORA) 257
organised crime 58–59
ORT (became Channel One) 144, 146, 153
Our House is Russia (Nash Dom – Rossiya, NDR), party 11, 25, 103, 106, 118

Pacific Fleet 160
Pamfilova, Ella 160
parade of sovereignties 205
Parfyenov, Leonid 152
Paris Club 243

Parkhomenko, Sergei 115
Parliamentary realignment 123ff
Party of Life 107, 108, 122
Party of Pensioners 114
Pasko, Grigorii 160
Patarkatsishvili, Badar 153
Patrushev, Nikolai 14, 75, 133
Pavlovsky, Gleb 28, 70, 72, 73, 80, 154, 168, 176–77, 225, 300
Pel'she, Arvid 13
People's Patriotic Union 125
People's Will party 125
perestroika 6, 125, 180, 181, 215, 216, 214
Petrov, Nikolai 23
Pichugin, Alexei 147
Pioneers 4
Pitery 78–79, 137, *see also* St Petersburg
pluriculturalism 215
Podberezkin, Alexei 30, 223
Poland 48
political extremism, law against 122
Politkovskaya, Anna 89, 154. 159
pollution 263
Poltavchenko, Georgy 133
poryadok 51
post-Soviet period, Russia 38, 39–40, 113, 129, 164, 262, 293ff, 310, 315
Potanin, Vladimir 146, 147, 170, 251
presidential election, 2000 28
Presidential Human Rights Commissioner 160
prikhvatizatsiya ('grabbing') 314
Primakov 24, 28, 30, 34, 71, 93, 101, 127, 151, 152, 270, 275, 276, 278, 290, 294
privatisation 44
Prusak, Mikhail 107
Public Anti-Corruption Council (OSA)
Public Chamber 45, 168, 169ff; Duma and 171; Putin and 171; regional chambers 172
Public Russian Televison (ORT) 20, 151
Pugachev, Sergei 79, 227
Pugacheva, Alla 170
Putilin, Vladimir 132
Putin elite 71–72
Putin, Vladimir: 37ff, 216; early life 1, 2ff; birth 2; family history 2, childhood and youth 3–5; early political awareness 5; acquires car 6; influenced by 1970s 6; influence of spy thrillers on 6; decision to become

lawyer 7; breaking off first engagement 7; academic career 7, 8, 12; marriage 7; doctoral dissertation 10, 15, 41, 253–54; in East Germany 1, 9–10, 40, 258; return to Russia 10; appointed head of Inotdel 10; in Leningrad City Soviet 10–11; enters central government 12ff; rise to power 299; coming to power 242, 299; CP membership 103; election and 85–86, 115–17, 193, 212, 268; as prime minister 14, 15, 17, 18ff; becoming President 1, 20, 24, 25–26, 28ff; and 2000 election 28ff; achievements 265–66, 301ff; and administrative paternalism 51; as anti-revolutionary 46ff; and Asia 290ff; attitudes towards 85–86, 151; authoritarianism of 41, 60, 63, 87, 92, 93, 97, 145, 161, 195, 207, 300, 301, 305; and balance of power within Russia 209–10; Beslan 89,117, 118, 278; and bilateral treaties 200; and biographers 17; and business-state relations 255ff, 262, 265–66; and bureaucracy 163ff, 260; changes in federal arrangements initiated 196ff; character 15–16, 18; and charisma 40, 315; and Chechen crisis 21, 22, 34, 89, 92, 223, 227ff, 233–39, 296; and China 290, 291; concept of 'dictatorship of the law' 40, 138–39, 217, 195; and concept of state 216ff; as consolidator 70–71, 308; constitutional conservatism 138; 'constitutional coup' 141–43; contradictions within regime 310; and corruption 165, 166, 243; critics of 115; on defence 68; and democratic statists 79–80; and democracy 42, 152, 308ff, 312; dismissal of Ustinov 158; dualism of 39–40, 42, 300; Dubrovka theatre siege 88–89; and Duma 112–13, 117–18; 123ff, 150, 152; and economy 58ff, 68, Chapter 7; and economic liberals 79; and economic development 243ff; economic policy 201, 259ff, Chapter 9, 275ff, 303–4; and electoral system 122, 135; election 2003 103; election 2004 115–17, 197; encouraging SMEs 246; environmentalism 262ff; and ESPO 264; and Eurasianism 269, 293;

Europeanism 276, 277, 278, 282; and European Union 285ff; family 31, federalism Chapter 5; Federal Assembly address 2005 45; federal relations reform 207ff; fishing as a hobby 9; and Foreign Intelligence Service (SVR) 10; foreign policy Chapter 10, 304; foreign policy pragmatism 270ff; and freedom of speech 150ff; and FSB 14–15, 16, 189, 263; and future political development 55ff; and G8 58, government of 178, 270–71, 300; gradualism 207; ideology 40–41, 95, 216, 249, 268–70, 301–2, 316; investigative activities 13; and judicial reform 155, 194, 195; and judiciary, 194; and KGB; joining 7, 8, 35–36, 219; in KGB 5, 8, 73,301; leaving KGB 11; and Kursk disaster 88; labour reform 264–65; languages 8, 9; Law on Regions 190; and leadership 90ff, 313ff; legacy 315ff; legal reform 155–59; and legitimism 297; as legitimist 294, 297; martial arts 4; membership of political parties 103; and media 151–55; and middle class 80–81; *Millennium Manifesto* 52–55: see separate entry; and military 76–78, Napoleon comparison 70; nationalism 223; and national identity 214, 215, 216, 223ff; and Nato 289ff; neo-Sovietism 220, 299, NGOs 173–75; and normalcy 42–43. 46, 47–48, 49ff, 304–5, 310; and oligarchs 44, 143–50, 256, 308, 314; opposition to 175ff, and OSCE 277; and other states of CIS 224–25, 230, 273, 277, 279, 285, 294, 295, 296–97, 298; and party system 103, 126ff, 206; and the past 217ff; as patriot 40, 223, 224–25; and the people 83ff; Pitery 78–79, 137, policies Chapter 3, 112ff, 300ff; political economy 166–67; political ideology 39ff, 208–9, 299ff; political independence 18, 22, 71; and political opposition 175ff; political reform 104, 106, 109, Chapter 5; political views 299; as President 17, 19, 42, 70ff, 305; and Primakov 94; pro-business policies 249; problems faced as president 267; providing political normality 42ff; Public

Chamber establishment 169–73; rebalancing centre-regional powers and authority 209ff, 308ff; reconstruction of the state 161, 162; reducing national debt 245; and reform 39 ff, Chapter 4, 103, 187ff, 240, 305–6; reform of regional organisation 196ff, 208,233; regime compared to The Risorgimento 177–78; and regional groupings 80, 205ff; and regionalism 192, 193, 194, 195ff, 203, 204, 205, 206ff; relations with USA 279ff; and relationship between state and economy 241; relegitimisation of state power 45–46; religion of 3, 7, 226–27; and revolution 46–47; rhetorical phraseology 16–17; on Russian economic development 41–42, 52–53, Chapter 9; and 'St Petersburg mafia' 17, 73; securitisation of foreign policy 277; sense of humour 17; and siloviki 74–76, 158; and Anatoly Sobchak 1, 7, 10, 11, 12, 14, 19, 40; and soft power 274; speeches by 203; on the state 44, 309; and state construction 139–40, 219, 303; and state treaties 190; statism 138, State of the nation speeches 59ff; 2000 59–60, 103, 138, 139, 143, 152, 194–95; 2001 60–61; 2002 61; 2003 61–62; 2004 62–63; 2005 63–64; 2006 64–67; 2007 67–68; and state-sponsored economy 250; strategic planning 12–13; strengthening the state 186, 300, 307; style of leadership 93; successor 107, 129–33, 197, 29; and symbolism 219ff, 239; 'third way' 95ff; and Ukraine 273; on various political parties 112, 113; view of Russia 162, 224; views of 40, 41–42, 44, 45, 54, 66, 168–69; views on 37ff, 112–13; as Westerniser 45, 224, 278–79; and WTO 260–61, 276; and Yeltsin 17, 18ff, 38–39, 70–71, 72–75, 85, 92–93, 98, 194, 220, 244, 248, 295, 300ff; *see also* Chechnya, 'dictatorship of the law', *First Person*, FSB, KGB, *Millennium Manifesto*, Russia, Boris Yeltsin
Putin, Katerina (daughter) 8
Putin, Maria (daughter) 8
Putin, Spiridon Ivanovich (grandfather) 2

Putin, Vladimir Spiridonovich (father) 2, 3
Putin, Maria Ivanova (mother) 2, 3
Putin's bloc 71, 81–84, 85
Putinite system 108, 180, 199, 300, 303, 314, 316

racially motivated crime 181–82, 183
Radaev, Salman 21
Rakhimov, Murtaza 204
Rebirth of Russia (party) 124
Red Banner (Krasnoznammenyi) Institute, Balashikh (now Foreign Intelligence Academy) 8–9
regional governors 202–3
Regional party and electoral systems 205
Regionalism: fragmented 187; segmented 189ff, 211, 213; regional developments Chapter 7, 309
religion and the Russian state 225ff
Remchukov, Konstantin 152
Reporters Without Borders 154
Revolution 53, 55
Reznik, Genri 156–57, 170
Rhineland model of capitalism 95
Robertson, Lord George (head of Nato) 76
Rodina 102, 103, 107, 108, 111, 113–14, 116, 125, 126, 182, 183, 221
Rogozin, Dmitry 113, 116, 180, 182, 221
Rosagropromstroi 114
rose revolution (Georgia) 173
Roshal, Leonid 137
Rosneft 249, 253, 258, 259
Rosoboronexport 258
Rosprirodnadzor agency 264
Rossel, Eduard 80
RUIE (Russian Union of Industrialists and Entrepreneurs) 304
Rule of law, and rule by law 40
Rushailo, Vladimir 20
Russia at the Turn of the Millennium (Putin) *see Millennium Manifesto*
Russia Today channel 154
Russia/Russian Federation 14, 17, 23, 24, 37, 38, 39, 41, 62, 64ff, 95, 112, 142, 153, 180, 190, 227, 229, 239, in Asia 290ff; authoritarianism 30, 39, 40, 50, 63, 74, 75, 78, 88, 91, 97, 130, 138, 146, 158, 161, 180, 195, 204, 279, 300, 306, 309, 324; budget 190; bureaucracy 163, 165, 166, 175; business elite in 146ff; capitalism 180,

314, Chapter 9; CFE treaty 67; charters with other FSU republics 189ff, 277; civil society 167ff; and coalition against terror 280, 289; commodity boom 243; concept of state 42; constitution 26, 27, 35, 178–79, 194, 195, 198, 199, 227, 274; corruption 58, 165–66; Council of Europe 157, 174; democracy in 27, 49–50, 51–52, 55, 57, 58, 62, 63, 80, 81, 83–84, 87, 92, 95ff, 104, 113, 127, 135, 138, 149, 151, 158, 161, 176, 178, 179, 180, 184, 185, 192, 220, 234, 307, 310–11; demographics in 65–66, 78, 248; development of 41–43, 99; economy of 60, 61, 62, 67, 68, 96, Chapter 9, 259, 268, 303, 314; elections in 10, 19, 27ff, 205ff; electoral system 109ff, 118, 122; and European Court of Human Rights 127; relations with EU 61, 112, 246, 247, 261, 272, 273, 274, 276, 277, 285–89, 291, 293; failure of democratic system 113, 114, 180, 190; federalism 193ff, 205, Chapter 7; foreign debt 243, 245; foreign investment in 64; foreign policy 16, 57, 58, 67–68, 191, 217, 268ff, 296, 300; future of 54, 57, 60, 64, 138, 139, 144, 150, 171, 179, 312; as G8 member 58, 64; as Great Power 62, 267, 275; historical perception in 46–47, 49, 52, 55, 56, 58, 83, 98, 310; human rights 159–61; imperialism 113, 214. 216, 217, 225, 228, 231, 239, 242, 270; in 90s 19, 43, 46, 48, 57, 71, 73, 270; in 21st century 24, 37, 47, 53, 55, 191, 196; imperial past 217–18; international perceptions of 63, 154; and Iran 283; judicial system and reform 155ff, 199ff; legislature 123; links with China 290–93; as market economy 246ff; media 152, 154; military-industrial complex 132; modernisation 264ff, 268; Moscow-St Petersburg rivalry 78–79; and Nato 76; nature of 225; national anthem 220; national identity 85, 215ff, 223ff, 226, 269, 272, 280, 294, 299, 310; national imagery 214ff; natural resources 264; and need for capitalism 42; NGOs in 173ff, 19; oil revenue 65; opposition in 159, 180, 182, 184; parliament 125, 196; party system in Chapter 4, 149, 205ff; development 101–2, 108, 118, 127; emergence of parties 102ff; patriotism 86; political accountability 138; politics in 39, 75–76, 75–76, 83ff, 90, 91, 126, 128, 134, 135, 136, 143, 145, 256, 259; political structure 148, 167, 189ff, 270, 305; polity 35, 43, 68, 123, 143, 184, 307; pollution in 263; post-Communist 6, 33, 48, 50, 54, 68, 74, 85, 90, 91, 136, 138, 142, 152, 188, 205, 217; poverty in 62, 63, 117, 240, 243, 247, 267, 310; Presidency 115ff, 122, 123, 128, 129ff, 133, 137,143, 186, 195; presidential succession 129ff; prison population 156; public sphere in 57; regime politics in 137ff, 285; regional legislatures 106–7, 120, 191, 202ff, 303; regionalism 132, 139, 187ff, 194,202, Chapter 7, 303; religion in 225–27; renaming of cities 222; and revolution 42, 46–47, 48, 49, 50,53–54, 81, 82, 162; role of state 96; and Russian Orthodox Church 226; Russian state structure 80, 129, 193ff, 199, 239; security services in 74ff, 159; shadow economy in 58–59; Soviet legacy 217–19, 221–22; state 140, 141, 142, 143, 169, 182–83, 189, 197; state building Chapter 8; subdivisions 196ff, 202ff; subregional sovereignty 190, 193, 195, 198–99; symbolism 219ff; territorial integrity 131; 'third way' in 95ff; transition from Soviet Union 25, 33, 37, 64, 74, 162, 189, 214, 221–22, 223, 224, 305, 311, 314, 315, 316; and WTO 66, 112, 260; TV 153–54, violence in 89; *see also* Beslan, Chechnya, constitution, Duma, dictatorship of the law, Federal Assembly, *First Person*, Gorbachev, oligarchs, Putin, Soviet Union, Yeltsin, various former Soviet States by name

Russia's Choice (*Vybor Rossii*, party), afterwards Russia's Democratic Choice 25, 95

Russia-Belarus Union 72, 73, 151, 297–98

Russian Aluminium 147

Russian Association of Lawyers 156

Russian Communist Worker's Party 105

Russian defence industry 249–50
Russian flag 219, 220
Russian industry, privatisation of 250
Russian March 221
Russian national anthem 219–20
Russian National Party 182
Russian National Unity Party 182
Russian Orthodox Church 175, 225ff
Russian Railroads 133
Russian revolution 219
Russia-Nato Founding Act 289
Russkii dom (*Russia House*) 227
Rutskoi, Alexander 110
Ryabov, Andrei 72, 90
Rybkin, Ivan 116
Ryzhkov, Vladimir 78, 176, 180

Saakashvili, Mikheil 173
Sadulaev, Abdul-Kalim 237
Sakhalin-2 energy project 253, 264
Samara 122, 192
samizdat 5
Saratov, Georgy 121, 166
Sarkharov, Andrei 40
Satarov, Georgi 165, 180
Savostyanov, Yevegeny 30
Sberbank 251
sblizhenie 274
Schroeder, Gerhard 278
Schumpeter, Joseph 17, 43, 90
Sechin, Igor 132, 201
Security Council (Russian) 75
Seleznev, Gennady 114, 12r
semibankirshchina 249
semidesyatnik 6, 47
Semnadsat' mgnovenii vesny (*Seventeen Moments of Spring*) 6
Sergeev, Igor 22
Sevastopol 224
Shaimiev, Mintimir 24, 80, 195, 200
Shakhnazarov, Karen 170
Shakhrai, Sergei 189
Shakirov, Raf
Shanghai Co-operation Organisation (SCO) 292–93
Shanghai Five 292
Shchekochikhin, Yuri 159
Shcherbinsky, Oleg 184
Shchit i mech (*Sword and Shield*: film) 6
Sheinis, Victor 96
Shell 253, 264
Shenderovich, Viktor 115
Shestopal, Elena 40–41, 88
Shevchenko, Yury 8, 117

Shkrebnëva, Lyudmila (Putin's wife) 7–8, 226
Shleifer, Andrei 43
Shoigu, Sergei 24, 78
Shpigun, Gennady 21
Sibneft 144, 145, 147, 253, 258
Sidanko 251
siloviki 72, 74–76, 107, 132, 133, 137, 158, 201, 219
Simonyan, Margarita 154
single-mandate districts (SMD) 118
Skuratov, Yuri 29, 145
Slavneft 259
Slavophilism 99, 226, 269, 270, 312
sliyanie 274
small and medium-sized enterprises (SMEs) 246
Smirnov, Igor 295
Smolensk 199
Smolensky, Alexander 145
Sobchak, Anatoly 1, 7, 10, 11–12, 14, 15, 19, 79
Sobyanin, Sergei 130, 132, 133
Solzhenitsyn, Alexander 38, 53, 207
Sonderweg 278
Sootechestvennik 294
Sorokina, Svetlana 152
Soskovets, Oleg 250
South Ossetia 224, 230, 273, 295
Soviet Northern Fleet 263
Soviet Union 1, 39, 62, 65, 139, 218, 221–22, 224, 229, 274 293, 304; transition to Russia 163, 210, 225, 227, 239, 301, 305, 311; 1991 declarations of independence 187–88, 305; economy of 240, 253; regional institutions 189
Spiritual Heritage (Dukhovnoe nasledie) movement 223
St Petersburg (sometime Leningrad, *which also see*) 1, 10, 24, 38, 54, 64, 74, 76, 80, 103, 155, 158, 170, 180, 187, 201, 206, 243
St Petersburg Mining Institute 12, 41
Stalin, Josef 6, 58, 143, 217, 222, symbolism of 220
Stalingrad 222
Stankevich, Sergei 224
State Committee for Environmental Protection 262
State Committee on Forestry 263
State Council 45, 197–98, 202, 209
State Narcotics Service 78
state, nature of Russian 162ff

Statist and statism 42, 50, 55, 90, 96, 193, 211, 216, 233, 242, 248, 305. 311, 312, 314, 323; democratic statist 72, 79–80, 133, 137; liberal statist 37, 86, 95, 223, 224; patriotic 216; and pluralism 40; Putin as 76, 81, 138, 139, 140, 143, 193, 223, 224, 314; pluralistic 140, 193; statist economy 257; types of 140
Stiglitz, Joseph 241
Stolypin, Peter 60
Stpashin 32
Strategic Partnership Treaty (EU-Russia) 287
Strategy for Russia (Putin) 59
Supreme Court 159, 160, 234, 263
Surgutneftegaz 145
Surkov, Vladislav 41, 72, 79, 106, 108, 132, 143, 183
Suslov, Mikhail 79
Sutyagin, Igor 160
Svanidze, Nikolai 170
Svyazinvest privatisation scandal 148
Sychev, Andrei 171
syroviki 79
Syvazinvest 258

Tajikistan 281, 296
Talbott, Strobe 16, 17
Tarkhov, Viktor 122
Tatarstan 24, 80, 112, 115, 117, 183, 187, 189, 190, 191, 194, 195, 201, 222, 224, 229
Tax Code 201
Tikhon, Father/archimandrite 12, 226
Titov, Konstantin 29, 32, 116
Tkachev, Alexander 133
TNK 251, 253
trade unions, Russian 264–65
Transdneister 273, 274, 277, 295
Transneft 191, 263
Transparency International 165
Trasformismo 176ff
treaties within Russian Federation 189
treaty process, within Russian Federation 200
Trenin, Dimitry 293
Treisman, Daniel 43
Trepashkin, Mikhail 160
Tret'yakov, Vitaly 49, 149
Trilateral Commission 176
Troshev, General Gennady 93, 233
Tsaritsyn 222
Tsipko, Alexander 41

Tsuladze, Avtandil 90
Tula 190
Tuleev, Aman 133
Tulip revolution (Kyrgyzstan) 173, 297
Turkey 273
TV stations, state control of 153–54
Tyulkin, Viktor 105
Tyumen Oil Company 148

Udmurtia 192
Udugov, Movladi 238
Ukraine 34, 121, 128, 131, 146, 217, 224, 273, 277, 279, 280, 292, 293, 294, 295, 297
Umarov, Dokku 238
Umazheva, Malika 231
Unified Energy Systems 136
Union of Right Forces (*Souyz pravykh sil*, SPS) 24, 25, 30, 32, 33, 95, 111, 112–13, 115, 148, 176, 179, 180
United Energy Systems (UES) 246, 258
United Nations Development Programme Annual Human Development Index 245
United Nations 268
United Russia (*Edinaya Rosiya*), party 80, 86, 92, 102, 103, 106–7, 108, 111, 112, 114, 118 passim, 133, 185, 205, 206, 235, 258
United States 65, 174, 183, 192, 246, 261, 267, 268, 271, 272, 273, 274, 276, 279ff, 284, 290, 291, 293; foreign policy 283; policy 47; and Russia compared 53, 55, 60, 77, 136, 156, 157, 212, 312; terrorist attacks in, and terrorism 277, 230, 180
Unity (*Edinstv*) 24, 80, 102, 106, 123, 145
Usmanov, Alisher 153
Ustinov, Vladimir 73, 89, 158
Uzbekistan 23, 130, 228, 292, 296

Velichko, Valentin 78
Velikhov, Yevgeny 171
Verkhovna Rada (Ukraine) 121, 128
Veshnyakov, Alexander 118, 119, 122
Victory day 221
Vidmanov, Viktor 114
Vike-Freiberga 219
Vneshtorgbank 258
Volgograd 222
Voloshin, Alexander 18, 72, 74
vory v zakone 157
vremenshchiki 220

war against terrorism 22
Washington consensus 242
Weber, Max 91, 137
West, the 38, 10, 42, 43, 45, 53, 63, 69, 76, 77, 83, 84, 97, 98, 99, 104, 113, 142, 151, 156, 215, 217, 218, 226, 230,238, 253, 254, 255, 267, 268, 269, 273, 276, 277, 278, 281, 282, 283, 288, 290, 291, 292, 298, 300, 302, 303, 304; leaders of 68
Western Group of Forces (East Germany) 10
Western viewpoint 15, 17; democracy 6; Russian relations with 16, 22, 23, 37, 39, 40, 55, 138, 171, 173, 175, 183, 262, 269, 270, 271, 272, 274, 275, 277, 278, 279, 280, 286, 293, 294, 295, 305, 311, 314; technology 9
Williamson, John 242
Wolf, Marcus 9
World Bank 241, 243, 246, 264
World Trade Organisation (WTO) 66, 112, 260–61, 263, 276, 296
World War II/Great Fatherland War 47, 221

Xenophobia 183
Xinxiang 290

Yabloko 95, 111, 112, 113, 118, 161, 176, 178, 180, 224
Yakovlev, Vladimir 12, 24, 80, 91, 94, 133, 179
Yakutia 188, 200
Yamadaev, Sulim 237
Yandarbiev, Zelimkhan 159
Yanov, Alexander 99
Yanukovich, Victor 63, 273, 297
Yasin, Yevgeny 56
Yastrzhembsky, Sergei 234
Yavlinsky, Grigory 29, 32–33, 113, 115, 117, 178, 179

Yegorov, Nikolai 13
Yekaterinburg summit 278
Yeltsin, Boris 1, 6, 10, 13, 16, 18, 38, 45, 46, 50, 56, 57, 70, 71, 80, 85, 118, 128, 137, 145, 149, 173, 179, 188, 211, 214, 215, 216, 217, 223, 224, 240, 271, 279, 315; corruption in Yeltsin period 165, 305; and FSU treaties 189; Yeltsin period 84, 97, 99, 112, 140, 143, 144 181, 195, 200, 201, 211, 219, 219, 262, 270, 273; new constitution 48; and constitutional reform 222, 309; and oligarchs 249; political agenda 37, 48–49, 302; political shock therapy 48; and Putin 17, 18ff, 33, 38–39, 96, 220; and regional governors 202; resignation 25ff, 52, 259; post Yeltsin era 17, 300, 305; legacy 130, 144, 149, 187, 249ff, 315; views on 300–301; Yeltsin team/ family and Yeltsinites 71, 72–75, 95, 117, 136–37, 144, 158, 301; Yeltsinism 241
Yuditskaya, Mina Moiseevna 4
Yuganskneftegaz 258
Yugoslavia 16, 17, 214, 227
Yukos oil company 41, 44, 60, 62, 67, 73, 79, 114, 131, 147, 149, 150, 157, 173, 183, 191, 251, 253, 258, 259
Yumashev, Valentin 72
Yushchenko, Victor 62, 159, 273, 281, 297

zachistki 232
Zakaev, Akhmed 234
Zhirinovsky, Vladimir 29, 108, 117, 126
Zhukov, Alexander 132
Zinoviev, Alexander 27, 38
Zyazikov, Murat 203
Zyuganov, Gennady 28, 29, 32–33, 34, 35, 54, 70, 116, 117, 188, 223, 225